D1504033

Pro SQL Server 2005 Database Design and Optimization

Louis Davidson
with Kevin Kline and Kurt Windisch

Apress®

Pro SQL Server 2005 Database Design and Optimization

Copyright © 2006 by Louis Davidson, Kevin Kline, and Kurt Windisch

All rights reserved. No part of this work may be reproduced or transmitted in any form or by any means, electronic or mechanical, including photocopying, recording, or by any information storage or retrieval system, without the prior written permission of the copyright owner and the publisher.

ISBN-13 (pbk): 981-1-59059-529-9

ISBN-10 (pbk): 1-59059-529-7

Printed and bound in the United States of America 9 8 7 6 5 4 3 2

Trademarked names may appear in this book. Rather than use a trademark symbol with every occurrence of a trademarked name, we use the names only in an editorial fashion and to the benefit of the trademark owner, with no intention of infringement of the trademark.

Lead Editor: Matthew Moodie
Technical Reviewers: Dejan Sarka, Andrew Watt
Editorial Board: Steve Anglin, Ewan Buckingham, Gary Cornell, Jason Gilmore, Jonathan Gennick, Jonathan Hassell, James Huddleston, Chris Mills, Matthew Moodie, Dominic Shakeshaft, Jim Sumser, Keir Thomas, Matt Wade
Project Manager: Elizabeth Seymour
Copy Edit Manager: Nicole LeClerc
Copy Editors: Susannah Pfalzer, Nicole LeClerc
Assistant Production Director: Kari Brooks-Copony
Production Editor: Laura Esterman
Compositor: Lynn L'Heureux
Proofreader: Lori Bring
Indexer: Valerie Perry
Cover Designer: Kurt Krames
Manufacturing Director: Tom Debolski

Distributed to the book trade worldwide by Springer-Verlag New York, Inc., 233 Spring Street, 6th Floor, New York, NY 10013. Phone 1-800-SPRINGER, fax 201-348-4505, e-mail orders-ny@springer-sbm.com, or visit http://www.springeronline.com.

For information on translations, please contact Apress directly at 2560 Ninth Street, Suite 219, Berkeley, CA 94710. Phone 510-549-5930, fax 510-549-5939, e-mail info@apress.com, or visit http://www.apress.com.

The information in this book is distributed on an "as is" basis, without warranty. Although every precaution has been taken in the preparation of this work, neither the author(s) nor Apress shall have any liability to any person or entity with respect to any loss or damage caused or alleged to be caused directly or indirectly by the information contained in this work.

The source code for this book is available to readers at http://www.apress.com in the Source Code section.

To my wife Val and daughter Chrissy for putting up with me again spending two months of Sundays stuck behind a laptop. Their love and support mean the world to me.

—Louis Davidson

Contents at a Glance

Contents

Foreword

If you're standing in a bookstore trying to decide whether or not to buy this book, let me help you out—go ahead and get it! If you're looking for a book like this, then you need *this* book, not the next one on the shelf. Keep reading and I'll tell you why.

Database design is an important thing. Project success or failure can hinge on solid design. If done poorly, it's one of the most crippling things you can do during the lifetime of a project, and one of the most expensive to repair. Implementation of the design is also important, and it's also easy to mess this up.

Many books cover design, and many others cover implementation. Finding complete coverage of both topics in a single tome allows you to get a consistent, logical view from beginning to end. Although I've read both the SQL 2000 version and the SQL 2005 version of this book, I wanted to see what others have said about the SQL 2000 version. Readers have given Louis a 4.5 (out of 5). I agree. This is a fine book.

The book and Louis are similar in many ways. His friendly, easy-to-understand writing style reflects Louis himself. He holds the coveted MVP award (Most Valuable Professional) for SQL Server from Microsoft in recognition of his expertise and SQL community support. Louis blogs regularly and is a valuable speaker and Special Interest Group (SIG) leader for the Professional Association for SQL Server (PASS). Studying with this book feels like getting advice and mentoring from a trusted friend.

Louis credits a few special mentors with his early training—people who wanted to do things right. In the same way, his book can help you learn how to do things right. You'll get practical advice and ideas that, combined with your good work, can lead to successful projects.

Do not fear—you can do this! Many books on this subject are difficult to read, littered with relational formulas. You will understand what Louis has to say, and you'll get a quick kick-start on best practices. I encourage you to read the book slowly and carefully, however. Engage your brain. Think about the alternatives that Louis presents, understand them, and apply them to your own environment.

I like Louis Davidson. I like this book. You will too!

Wayne Snyder
Managing consultant, Mariner (http://www.mariner-usa.com)
PASS Board of Directors (http://www.sqlpass.org)

About the Authors

LOUIS DAVIDSON has been in the IT industry for more than 14 years as a corporate database developer and architect. The majority of his experience has been with Microsoft SQL Server, in every version that has been released since 4.21a. Louis is a senior data architect for Compass Technology, supporting the Christian Broadcasting Network and NorthStar Studios in Nashville, Tennessee.

Louis has a bachelor's degree in computer science from the University of Tennessee at Chattanooga, with a minor in mathematics. He has been a volunteer with the Professional Association for SQL Server (PASS) for more than 5 years. In October 2004, Louis was awarded the Most Valuable Professional (MVP) award for SQL Server by Microsoft, an honor he is proud to have been given. In his "free" time, Louis can often be found writing for his blog http://spaces.msn.com/drsql, or on the Microsoft SQL Server newsgroups and forums.

KURT WINDISCH is a senior technical specialist with Levi, Ray & Shoup, Inc., a global provider of technology solutions with headquarters in Springfield, Illinois. He has more than 15 years of experience in IT, and is a DBA and technical architect for the internal IT department at LRS. He spent 5 years serving on the board of directors for PASS, has written for several SQL Server magazines, and has presented at conferences internationally on the topic of database programming with SQL Server.

KEVIN KLINE is the technical strategy manager for SQL Server solutions at Quest Software, a leading provider of award-winning tools for database management and application monitoring on the SQL Server platform. Kevin is the president of the international Professional Association for SQL Server (PASS). He has been a Microsoft SQL Server MVP since 2004. Kevin is the lead author of *SQL in a Nutshell: A Desktop Quick Reference* (O'Reilly Media Inc., 2004) and *Transact-SQL Programming* (O'Reilly Media, Inc., 1999). Kevin writes the monthly SQL Server Drilldown column for *Database Trends & Applications*, blogs at http://www.sqlmag.com, and is a resident expert at SearchSQLServer.com. Kevin is a top-rated speaker, appearing at international conferences such as Microsoft TechEd, DevTeach, PASS, Microsoft IT Forum, and SQL Connections. When he's not pulling his hair out over work, he loves to spend time with his four kids and in his flower and vegetable gardens.

About the Technical Reviewers

DEJAN SARKA, SQL Server MVP, Solid Quality Learning Mentor, is a trainer and consultant working for many CTECs and development companies in Slovenia and other countries. Besides training, he continuously works on OLTP, OLAP, and data mining projects, especially at the design stage. He is a regular speaker at some of the most important international conferences, such as TechEd, PASS, and the MCT conference. He's also indispensable at regional Microsoft TechNet meetings; at the NT Conference, the hugest Microsoft conference in Central and Eastern Europe; and some other events. He's the founder of the Slovenian SQL Server Users Group. As a guest author, he contributed to two books—*Inside Microsoft SQL Server 2005: T-SQL Querying* (Microsoft Press, 2006) and *Inside Microsoft SQL Server 2005: T-SQL Programming* (Microsoft Press, 2006)—both written by main author Itzik Ben-Gan. Dejan Sarka also developed two courses for Solid Quality Learning: Data Modeling Essentials and Data Mining with SQL Server 2005.

ANDREW WATT is a Microsoft Most Valuable Professional (MVP) for SQL Server. He is an experienced author and independent consultant specializing in Microsoft technologies.

Acknowledgments

Thanks go to:

My savior *Jesus Christ*, without whom I wouldn't have had the strength to complete the task of writing this book.

My daughter *Chrissy Davidson* for taking the cover picture.

My best friend in the world who got me started with computers back in college when I still wanted to be a mathematician.

My mentors *Mike Farmer, Chip Broecker*, and *Don Plaster* for the leading they gave me over the years.

Gary Cornell for giving me a chance to write the book that I wanted to write.

Ben Miller and *Frank Castora* for doing a beta read of the book.

My managers (chronologically speaking) *Chuck Hawkins* and *Julie Porter* for their understanding and patience with me when my eyes were droopy after a late night of writing, along with all my friends at Compass Technology (http://www.compass.net).

Wayne Snyder for writing the awesome foreword.

Kevin Kline and *Kurt Windisch* for taking up the slack with topics I didn't want to (couldn't) tackle.

The fantastic editing staff I've had, without whom the writing would sometimes appear to come from an illiterate baboon. Most of these are included on the copyright page, but I want to say a specific thanks to *Tony Davis* (who left the company just before the end) for making this book great, despite my frequently rambling writing style.

Raul Garcia, who works on the Microsoft SQL Server Engine team, for information about using EXECUTE AS and certificate-based security.

James Manning for the advice on READ COMMITTED SNAPSHOT.

Jan Shanahan for putting up with my annoying questions over the past two years.

All the MVPs that I've worked with over the past year and a half. Never a better group of folks have I found. *Steven Dybing* and now *Ben Miller* have been great to work with. I want to list a few others individually for things they've specifically done to help me out: *Dejan Sarka* and *Andrew Watt* for reviewing this book with incredible vigor, and not letting me slide on even small points; *Steve Kass* for giving me the code for demonstrating what's wrong with the money datatypes, as well as giving cool solutions to problems in newsgroups that made me think; *Erland Somarskog* for helping me to understand a bit more about how error handling works, and many other topics (not to mention his great website, http://www.sommarskog.se/); *Adam Machanic* for helping me with many topics on my blog and in newsgroups; *Aaron Bertrand* for his great website http://www.aspfaq.com and the shoe memories; *Kalen Delaney* for all she has done for me and the community; *Dr. Greg Low* for putting me on his http://www.sqldownunder.com podcast; *Kim Tripp* for the wonderful paper on SNAPSHOT isolation levels. I also want to thank *Tony Bain, Hillary Cotter, Mike Epprecht, Geoff Hiten, Tom Moreau, Andrew Kelly, Tony Rogerson, Linchi Shea, Paul Nielson, Hugo Kornelis, Tibor Karaszi, Greg Linwood, Dr. Tom Moreau, Dan Guzman, Jacco Schalkwijk, Anith Sen, Jasper Smith,*

Ron Talmage, and *Kent Tegels*, because all of you have specifically helped me out over the past year in the newsgroups, teaching me new things to make my book far better.

To the academics out there who have permeated my mind with database theory, such as *E. F. Codd*, *C. J. Date*, *Fabian Pascal*, and *Joe Celko*; my professors at the University of Tennessee at Chattanooga; et al. I wouldn't know half as much without you.

Even with this large number of folks I have mentioned here, I am afraid I may have missed someone. If so, thank you!

Louis Davidson

First off, I want to thank Louis for asking me to help contribute to such a practical book on SQL Server 2005. He's very knowledgeable and great to work with, and his commitment is something I admire. I'd also like to thank SQL Server guru Gert Drapers, whose insight into the SQLCLR and its uses provided lots of ideas to explore with the new technology. Thanks to all my friends in the PASS organization—past and present members of the board of directors, members of the Microsoft SQL Server Development and Product Services and Support teams, PASS volunteers, and PASS members with whom I've had the privilege of meeting and building lasting friendships. Their wisdom and friendship is something I value.

Thanks especially to my son Ron, and three daughters Lauren, Alicia, and Courtney, who consistently remind me of what's really important. Finally, thanks to my wife, Sue, who had to endure many nights and weekends listening to me complain about code not working. She allows me my computer time but also reminds me there's more to life than fast-running queries.

Kurt Windisch

Introduction

I am not young enough to know everything.

—Oscar Wilde

There was a time when I felt I knew everything about SQL and database design. That time was just before I wrote my first book, *Professional SQL Server 2000 Database Design*.[1] Even now, my percentage of all knowledge is dwindling, while at the same time the amount of stuff that I know grows every day. I realize now that books could be written on what I don't know about SQL Server, and this keeps getting truer and truer as the years pass. On the bright side, this has more to do with the reality that SQL Server just keeps growing and adding more complex and cool features than one person could master. It turns out that a book can be written on what I *do* know about SQL Server, and you hold in your very hands the third generation of that book (or you could be looking at an electronic copy, but the image of a person staring at an electronic device isn't nearly as poetic, even if I do prefer a book I can read on my Pocket PC over one I'd have to lug around).

If you have had any contact with the previous versions of the book (either the Apress model from 2003, or the one with my mug shot adorning the front cover from 2001, from another publisher), you may well wonder if it's worth your time and hard-earned money for this book. If you never saw these books, you might be figuring you've done well enough so far without it. "Do I really need this book?" Face it, asking me is like asking a vacuum-cleaner salesperson if your old vacuum cleaner needs to be replaced. I am not the most reliable person to ask. If I had my way, this book would be used by everybody for everything. Beyond requiring every programmer in every discipline to own one copy for home and one for office, children would read it in tenth grade English as one of the classics of American (technical) literature. I would even suggest that Oprah feature it as her book of the month, and for having read this far in the introduction you would be required to purchase ten copies right now and give them to ten people you know, promising them bad luck if they failed in the task. Then I could afford to send my daughter to Northwestern, or maybe buy a rocket ship (either of which would be quite nice).

To illustrate the theme of each chapter, I've picked quotes from some great folks to start each chapter (even a Dilbert cartoon), but I wanted to highlight one of my favorite quotes:

A man with one watch knows what time it is; a man with two watches is never quite sure.[2]

—Lee Segall

---

1. Luckily, that unbounded enthusiasm got me started. If I hadn't thought I knew everything, I don't know if I could have ever started on that first book.

2. I should also be clear that Mr. Segall wasn't talking about anything technology related. The first part of the quote is: "It is possible to own too much . . ." As a gadget fanatic, I have to disagree with this part, but it makes a good point about stuff that tells you the "same things."

Have you ever been in a room with two clocks, and the time didn't match? My wife's alarm clock is always set ten minutes fast, and occasionally when I'm groggily looking around to see if it's time to get up, I look at the wrong clock and end up awake and out of bed far too early. Because of mismatched data, I made a poor decision and ended up out of bed before eight o'clock. (I know that all you morning people think I'm nuts, but every one of you who constantly replace alarm clocks because the snooze buttons are worn out understand exactly where I'm coming from.)

One of the themes that you'll find repeated throughout the book is that if you only have one version of a data value, there's no question which one is the most correct. Of course, your data is only as right as the person who entered it. The old adage of garbage in, garbage out still applies. My wife's clock is intentionally set ten minutes off, after all. Removing my clock wouldn't make it right, but I'd eventually get used to the fact that I don't want to get up before ten after eight on her clock, instead of eight. The process of eliminating redundancy is known as normalization, and is covered in its own large chapter (Chapter 4).

Once normalized, databases are straightforward to work with, because everything is in its logical place, much like a well-organized cupboard. When you need paprika, it's easier to go to the paprika slot in the spice rack than it is to have to look for it "wherever it was put," but many systems are organized just this way. Even if every item has an assigned place, what value is it if it's too hard to find? Imagine if a phone book wasn't sorted at all. What if the dictionary was organized by placing a word where it would fit in the text? With proper organization, it will be almost instinctive where to go to get the data you need, even if you have to write a join or two. I mean, isn't that fun after all?

A common misconception that I hope to alleviate with this book is the difference between denormalization and a poorly designed database. Too often the term *denormalized* is used as a nice word to cover up for a poor design. The key is that a denormalized database was, at some time in its lifespan, normalized. Carefully applied denormalizations are sometimes useful for performance. Not much time is spent on denormalizing in the book, simply because it's the process of undoing the process of normalization. (Reading Chapter 4 in reverse will do the trick nicely. OK, maybe it takes a bit more than that.)

You might also be surprised to find out that database design is quite a straightforward task, and not as difficult as it may sound. Doing it right is going to take more up-front time at the beginning of a project than just slapping together the data storage as you go along, but it pays off throughout the full lifecycle of a project. This brings me to one of the most challenging things about doing database design right: it takes more time than not doing it (this is a battle that can frequently be had in project planning meetings). Because there's nothing visual to excite the client, database design is one of the phases of a project that often gets squeezed to make things seem to go faster. Even the least challenging or uninteresting user interface is still miles more interesting to the average customer than the most beautiful data model. Programming the UI takes center stage, even though the data is generally why a system gets funded and finally created. It's not that your colleagues won't notice the difference between a cruddy data model and one that's a "thing of beauty." They certainly will, but the amount of time required to decide the right way to store data correctly can be overlooked when programmers need to "code." I wish I had an answer for that problem, because I could sell a million books with just that answer. This book will assist you with some techniques and processes that will help you through the process of designing databases, in a way that's clear enough for novices and helpful to even the most seasoned professional.

This process of designing and architecturing the storage of a data is a different role to those of database setup and administration. For example, in the role of data architect, I seldom create users, perform backups, or set up replication or clustering. Little is mentioned of these tasks, which are considered more as administration and the role of the DBA. It isn't uncommon to wear both these hats (in fact, when you work in a smaller organization, you may find that you wear so many hats your neck tends to hurt), but your designs will generally be far better thought out if you can divorce your mind from the more implementation-bound roles that make you wonder how hard it will be to use the data. For the most part, database design looks harder than it is.

Note To be safe, I have to make one thing clear: if you've done any programming, you'll undoubtedly disagree with some of the opinions and ideas in this book. I fully accept that this book is hardly the gospel of St. Louis of Yukon. My ideas and opinions have grown from more than 14 years of working with and learning about databases, supplemented with knowledge from many disparate people, books, college classes, and seminars. I thank many of these in the Acknowledgements, but there have been hundreds more whose names I've forgotten, although I've had some tidbit of knowledge imprinted on my brain from them. The design methodology presented in this book is a conglomeration of these ideas. I hope it proves a useful learning tool, and that through reading this book and other people's works, plus a healthy dose of trying out your own ideas, you'll develop a methodology that will suit you, and will make you a successful database designer.

The book is comprised of the following chapters:

Chapter 1: Introduction to Database Concepts
A basic overview of essential terms and concepts.

Chapter 2: Data Modeling
Introduction to the main tool of the data architect: the model. In this chapter, I introduce one modeling language (IDEF1X) in detail, as it's the modeling language that's used throughout the book to present database designs. I then introduce a few other common modeling languages, for those of you who have need to use these types of models for preference or corporate requirements.

Chapter 3: Conceptual Data Modeling
In conceptual modeling, the goal is to discuss the process of taking a customer's set of requirements, and put the tables, columns, relationships, and business rules into a data model format where possible.

Chapter 4: The Normalization Process
The next step in the process is normalization. The goal of normalization is to take the set of tables, columns, relationships, and business rules and format them in such a way that every value is stored in one place, and that every table represents a single "thing." Normalization can feel unnatural the first few times you do it, because instead of worrying about how you'll use the data, you must think of the data and how the structure will affect the quality of the data. However, once mastered, it will feel wrong not to store data in a normalized manner.

Chapter 5: Implementing the Base Table Structures
This is the first point in the database design process in which we fire up SQL Server and start building scripts to build database objects. In this chapter, I cover building tables— including choosing the datatype for columns—as well as relationships. Part of this discussion notes how the implemented structures might differ from the model that we arrived at in the normalization process.

Chapter 6: Protecting the Integrity of Your Data
Beyond the way data is arranged in tables and columns, there can be other business rules that need to be enforced. The front line of defense for enforcing data integrity conditions in SQL Server is CHECK constraints and triggers, as users cannot innocently avoid them. I also discuss the various other ways that data protection can be enforced using stored procedures and client code.

Chapter 7: Securing Access to the Data
Security is high in most every programmer's mind these days, or it should be. In this chapter, I cover some strategies to use to implement data security in your system, such as employing views, triggers, encryption, and even using Profiler.

Chapter 8: Table Structures and Indexing
In this chapter, I show the basics of how data is structured in SQL Server, as well as some strategies for indexing data for better performance.

Chapter 9: Coding for Concurrency
As part of the code that's written, some consideration needs to be taken when you have to share resources. In this chapter, I describe several strategies for how to implement concurrency in your data access and modification code.

Chapter 10: Code-Level Architectural Decisions
In this chapter (the latter half of which is written by Kurt Windisch), many of the concepts and concerns of writing code that accesses SQL Server are covered. I cover *ad hoc* SQL versus stored procedures (including all the perils and challenges of both, such as plan parameterization, performance, effort, optional parameters, SQL injection, and so on), as well as discuss whether T-SQL or CLR objects are best, including samples of the different types of objects that can be coded using the CLR.

Chapter 11: Database Interoperability
Finally, in this chapter written by Kevin Kline, the challenges of building databases that not only have to run on SQL Server, but other database server platforms, are discussed.

Finally, please don't hesitate to give me feedback on the book anytime. (Well, as long it has nothing to do about where you feel this book should be stuck.) I'll try to improve any sections that people find lacking and publish them to my blog (http://spaces.msn.com/members/drsql) under the tag DesignBook. I'll be putting more information there as it comes available pertaining to new ideas, goof-ups I find, or additional materials that I choose to publish.

■ ■ ■

CHAPTER 1

Introduction to Database Concepts

There are no variations except for those who know a norm, and no subtleties for those who have not grasped the obvious.

—C. S. Lewis, *An Experiment in Criticism*

The question often arises as to why a person needs to know the theory and fundamentals of database design, since sometimes they are often considered useless by many programmers and frankly boring by most anyone else. While there might be some truth in that statement, would you build a bridge designed by an engineer who did not understand physics? Or would you get on a plane designed by someone who didn't understand the fundamentals of flight? Sounds quite absurd, right? So why expect your clients to come to you to get a database designed if you don't understand the core concepts that underpin effective database design?

The first half of this book is devoted to the different, distinct phases of relational database design and how to carry out each phase effectively, so you are able to arrive at a final design that can fulfill the business requirements and ensure the integrity of the data in your database. However, before starting this design process in earnest, we need to explore a few core relational database concepts. Therefore, this chapter discusses at the following topic areas:

- *Database design phases*: The next section provides an overview of the four major phases of relational database design: *conceptual*, *logical*, *implementation*, and *physical*. For time and budget reasons, it is often tempting to skip the earlier database design phases and move straight to the implementation phase. I explain why skipping any or all of these phases can lead to an incomplete and/or incorrect design, as well as one that does not support high-performance querying and reporting.

- *Relational data structures*: I'll provide concise descriptions of some of the fundamental database objects, including the database itself, as well as tables, columns, and keys. These objects are likely familiar to most, but there are some common misunderstandings in their usage that can make the difference between a mediocre design and a high-class, professional design. In particular, misunderstanding the vital role of keys in the database can lead to severe data integrity issues, and to the mistaken belief that such keys and constraints can be effectively implemented outside the database. (They can't.)

- *Relationships*: I'll briefly survey the different types of binary and nonbinary relationships that can exist between relational tables.

- *SQL*: I'll examine the need for a single, standard, set-based language for interrogating relational databases.

- *Dependencies*: I'll discuss the concepts of dependencies between values and how they shape the process of designing databases later in the book.

As a side effect of this discussion, we will reach agreement on the meaning of some of the important terms and concepts that will be used throughout the book when discussing and describing relational databases. Some of these terms are misunderstood and misused by a large number (if not a majority) of people. If we are not in agreement on their meaning from the beginning, then eventually you are going to wonder what the heck I am talking about. As such, it is important that we get on the same page when it comes to concepts and the basic theories that are fundamental to proper database design.

Database Design Phases

Too often when programmers sit down to build a system that requires data storage, their knee-jerk reaction is to start thinking in terms of how to fulfill an immediate need. Little regard is given to the future needs of the data, and even less to the impact the design will have on future business needs, reporting requirements and, most crucial of all, the integrity of the data.

The problem with this mind-set is that obvious things are missed and, late in the project, the programmers have to go back and tweak (and re-tweak) the model. Too often, too much time is spent deciding how to build a system as quickly (and cheaply!) as possible, and too little time is spent considering the desired outcome. Clearly the goal of any organization is to work efficiently, but it is still important to get things as right as possible the first time.

A thorough database design process will undergo four distinct phases, as follows:

- *Conceptual*: This is the "sketch" of the database that you will get from initial requirement gathering and customer information. During this phase, you attempt to identify what the user wants. You try to find out as much as possible about the business process for which you are building this data model, its scope and, most important, the business rules that will govern the use of the data. You then capture this information in a conceptual data model consisting of a set of "high-level" entities and the interactions between them.

- *Logical*: The logical phase is a refinement of the work done in the conceptual phase, transforming the loosely structured conceptual design into a full-fledged relational database design that will be the foundation for the physical design. During this stage, you fully define the required set of entities, the relationships between them, the attributes of each entity, and the domains of these attributes (i.e., the sort of data the attribute holds and the range of valid values).

- *Implementation*: In this phase, you adapt the logical model for implementation in the host relational database management system (RDBMS; in our case, SQL Server).

- *Physical*: In this phase, you create the model where data is mapped to physical disk structures.

The first half of this book is concerned with the conceptual and logical design phases, and I make only a few references to SQL Server. Generally speaking, the logical model of any relational database will be the same, be it for SQL Server, Oracle, Informix, DB2, or MySQL.

Conceptual

The conceptual design phase is essentially a process of analysis and discovery, the goal being to define the organizational and user data requirements of the system. Two of the core activities that make up this stage are as follows:

- Discovering and documenting a set of conceptual entities and the basic relationships between them

- Discovering and documenting the business rules that define how the data can and will be used, and also the scope of the system that you are designing

Your conceptual data model should capture, at a high level, the fundamental "sets" of data that are required to support the business processes and users' needs. Entity discovery is at the heart of this process. *Entities* are generally nouns (people, places, and things) that are fundamental to the business processes being modeled. Consider a basic business statement such as the following:

People place **orders** in order to buy **products**.

Immediately, you can identify three conceptual entities (in bold type) and begin to understand how they interact.

Note An entity is *not* a table. Sometimes an entity will map to a table in the physical model, but often it won't. Some conceptual entities will be too abstract to ever be implemented.

During this conceptual phase, you need to do the requisite planning and analysis so that the requirements of the business and its customers are met. The conceptual design should focus steadfastly on the broader view of the system, and it may not even vaguely correspond to the final, implemented system. However, it is a vital step in the process and provides a great communication tool for participants in the design process.

The second essential element of the conceptual phase is the discovery of *business rules*. These are the rules that govern the operation of your system, certainly as they pertain to the process of creating a database and the data to be stored in the database. Often, no particular tool is used to document these rules. It is usually sufficient that business rules are presented as a kind of checklist of things that a system must or must not do, for example:

- Users in group X must be able to change their own information.

- Each company must have a ship-to address and optionally a bill-to address if its billing address is different.

- A product code must be ten characters in length and be in the format XXX-XXX-XXXX.

From these statements, the boundaries of the final implemented system can be determined. These business rules may encompass many different elements of business activity. They can range from very specific data-integrity rules (e.g., an order date has to be the current date), to system processing rules (e.g., report X must run daily at 12:00 am), to a rule that defines part of the security strategy (e.g., only this category of users should be able to access these tables). Expanding on that final point, a security plan ought to be built during this phase and used to implement database security in the implementation phase. Too often, security measures are applied (or not) as an afterthought.

■**Note** It is beyond the scope of this book to include a full discussion of business rule discovery, outside of what is needed to shape and then implement integrity checks in the data structures. However, business rule discovery is a very important process that has a fundamental impact on the database design. For a fuller treatment of this topic, I suggest reading *Beginning Relational Data Modeling, Second Edition* by Sharon Allen and Evan Terry (Apress, 2005).

During this process, you will encounter certain rules that "have to" be enforced and others that are conditionally supported. For example, consider the following two statements:

- Applicants must be 18 years of age or older.

- Applicants should be between 18 and 32 years of age, but we can accept people of any age.

The first rule can easily be implemented in the database. If an applicant enters an age of 17 years or younger, the RDBMS can reject the application and send back a message to that effect.

However, the second is rule is not quite so easy to implement. In this case, you would probably require some sort of workflow process to route the request to a manager for approval. T-SQL code is not interactive, and this rule would most certainly be enforced outside of the database, probably in the user interface (UI).

■**Note** Ideally, the requirements at this point would be perfect and would contain all business rules, processes, and so forth needed to implement a system. The conceptual model would contain in some form every element needed in the final database system. However, we do not live in a perfect world. Users generally don't know what they want until they see it. Business analysts miss things, either because they jump to conclusions or don't fully understand the system. Hence, some of the activities described as part of building a conceptual model can spill over to the logical modeling phase.

Logical

The logical phase is a refinement of the work done in the conceptual phase. The output from this phase will be a complete blueprint for the design of the relational database. Note that during this stage you should still think in terms of entities and their attributes, rather than physical tables and columns. No consideration should be given at this stage to the exact details of "how" the system will be implemented. As previously stated, a good logical design could be built on any RDMBS. Core activities during this stage include the following:

- Drilling down into the conceptual model to identify the full set of entities that define the system.

- Defining the attribute set for each entity. For example, an `Order` entity may have attributes such as `Order Date`, `Order Amount`, `Customer Name`, and so on.

- Identifying attributes (or a group of attributes) that are candidate keys (i.e., could uniquely identify an instance of an entity). This includes primary keys, foreign keys, surrogate keys, and so on (all described in Chapter 5).

- Defining relationships and cardinalities.

- Identifying an appropriate domain (which will become datatypes) for each attribute and its nullability.

- Applying normalization rules.

While the conceptual model was meant to give the involved parties a communication tool to discuss the data requirements, the logical phase is about applying proper design techniques. The logical modeling phase defines a blueprint for the database system, which can be handed off to someone else with no knowledge of the system to implement.

Note Before we begin to build this model, I need to introduce a complete data modeling language. In our case, we will be using the IDEF1X modeling methodology, described in Chapter 2.

Implementation

During the implementation phase, you fit the logical design to the tool that is being used (again, in our case, SQL Server). This involves choosing storage types, building tables, applying constraints, writing triggers, and so on, to implement the logical model in the most efficient manner. This is where platform-specific knowledge of SQL Server, T-SQL, and other technologies becomes essential.

Occasionally this phase will entail some reorganization of the designed objects to make them easier to implement or to circumvent some limitation of the RDBMS. In general, I can state that for most designs there is seldom any reason to stray too far from the logical model, though the need to balance user load and hardware considerations can make for some tough design decisions. Ultimately, though, one of the primary goals is that no data that has been specified or integrity constraints that have been identified in the conceptual and logical phases will be lost. Data can (and will) be added, often to handle the process of writing programs to use the data. The key is to not take data away.

It is at this point in the project that code will be applied to handle the business rules that were identified during the conceptual part of the design. This includes the security for the system. We will work through the implementation phase of the project in Chapters 5, 6, 7, 9, and 10.

Physical

The goal of the physical phase is to optimize data access—for example, by implementing effective data distribution on the physical disk storage, or by judicious use of indexes. While the purpose of the RDBMS is to largely isolate us from the physical aspects of data retrieval and storage, it is important to understand how SQL Server physically implements the data storage in order to optimize database access code.

During this stage, the goal is to optimize performance, but to not change the logical design in any way to achieve that aim. This is an embodiment of Codd's rule 11, which states the following:

> *An RDBMS has distribution independence. Distribution independence implies that users should not have to be aware of whether a database is distributed.*

■**Note** Codd's rules are discussed in detail in Appendix A.

It may be that it is necessary to distribute data across different files, or even different servers, but as long as the published logical names do not change, users will still access the data as columns in rows in tables in a database.

■**Note** In many modeling tools, the physical phase denotes the point where the logical model is actually generated in the database. This was called the "implementation phase" because the physical model is also used to discuss how the data is physically laid out onto the hardware.

Our discussion of the physical model will be limited. I will start out by looking at entities and attributes during conceptual and logical modeling. In implementation modeling, I will switch gears to deal with tables, rows, and columns. The physical modeling of records and fields will be dealt with only briefly (in Chapter 8). If you want a deeper understanding of the physical implementation, check out *Inside Microsoft SQL Server 2005: The Storage Engine* by Kalen Delaney (Microsoft Press, 2006).

Relational Data Structures

This section introduces the following core relational database structures and concepts:

- Database and schema

- Tables, rows, and columns

- The Information Principle

- Keys

- Missing values (nulls)

You are no doubt familiar with some of these concepts, but you may find there are quite a few points presented here that you haven't thought about—for example, the fact that a table is made up of unique rows or that a column must only represent a single value. These subtle points make the difference between having a database of data that the client relies on without hesitation and having one in which the data is constantly challenged.

Database and Schema

A database is simply is a structured collection of facts or data. It need not be in electronic form; it could be a card catalogue at a library, your checkbook, a SQL Server database, an Excel spreadsheet, or even just a simple text file. Typically, when a database is in an electronic form, it is arranged for ease and speed of search and retrieval.

In SQL Server, the database is the highest-level container that you will use to group all of the objects and code that serve a common purpose. At the next level down is the *schema*. You use schemas to group together objects in the database with common themes or even common owners. All objects on the database server can be accessed by knowing the database they reside in and the schema:

```
databaseName.schemaName.objectName
```

Schemas will play a large part of our design, not only to segregate objects of like types, but also because segregation into schemas allows us to control access to the data and restrict permissions, if necessary, to only certain subsets of the implemented database.

■**Note** Once the database is actually implemented, it becomes the primary container used to hold, back up, and subsequently restore data when necessary.

Tables, Rows, and Columns

The object central to all of our design and code is the *table*. In our designs, a table will be used to represent *something*, either real or imaginary. A table can be used to represent people, places, things, or ideas (i.e., nouns, generally speaking), about which information needs to be stored.

The word "table" is a very implementation-oriented term, for which Dictionary.com (http://www.dictionary.com) has the following definition:

> *11. An orderly arrangement of data, especially one in which the data are arranged in columns and rows in an essentially rectangular form.*

During the conceptual and logical modeling phases, the process will be to identify the entities that define the system. Each entity is described by a unique set of attributes. An entity is often implemented as a table (but remember, there is not necessarily a direct relationship between the two), with the attributes defining the *columns* of that table. Each *instance* of an entity can be thought of as analogous to a *row* in the table.

A basic example of a table that most people are familiar with is a Microsoft Excel spreadsheet, such as that shown in Figure 1-1.

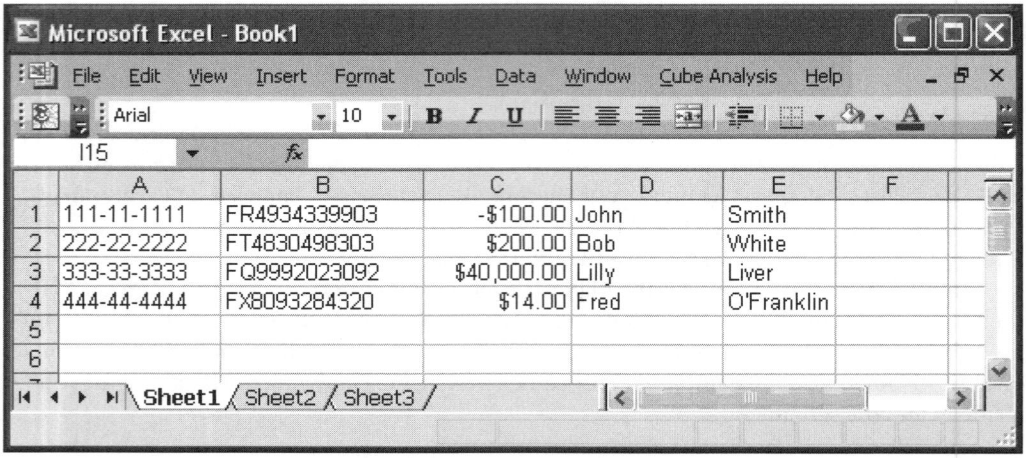

Figure 1-1. *Excel table*

In Figure 1-1, the rows are numbered 1–6 and the columns are lettered A–F. The spreadsheet itself is the Accounts table. Every column represents an attribute of an account (i.e., a single piece of information about the account); in this case, you have a Social Security number, an account number, an account balance, and the first and last names of the account holder attributes. Each row of the spreadsheet represents one specific account. So, for example, row 1 might be read as follows: "John Smith, holder of account FR4934339903, with SSN 111-11-1111, has a balance of –$100."[1]

Tables, rows, and columns at this level are pretty simple, but there is more to the story. In the world of relational databases, these terms have been slightly refined, and the different meanings can get quite confusing. While these terms (i.e., table, column, and row) are commonly used, in relational databases the terms have been refined and have more specific meanings. Let's look at the different terms and how they are presented from the following perspectives:

- Mathematical

- Logical/conceptual

- Implementation

- Physical

Table 1-1 lists all of the different names that tables are given from the various viewpoints.

---

1. No offense if there is actually a John Smith with SSN 111-11-1111 who is broke—I just made this up!

Table 1-1. *Table Term Breakdown*

Viewpoint	Name	Definition
Mathematical	Relation	This term is seldom used by nonacademics, but some literature uses this term exclusively to mean what most programmers think of as a table. It is made up of rows and scalar-valued columns, with no duplicate rows. There is absolutely no ordering implied in the structure of the table, either rows or columns.
		Relational databases take their name from this term, because they represent related information; the name does not come from the fact that tables can be related. (Relationships are covered later in this chapter.)
Logical/ conceptual	Entity	An entity can be loosely represented by a table with columns and rows. By "loosely," I mean that you may have untablelike columns in the entity as you work to refine the model. An entity is not as strict as a table, and it is often thought of as important. For example, if you are modeling a human resources application, an employee photo would be an attribute of the Employees entity. If you are modeling an application for analyzing pictures, the photo would become an entity. In the implementation model, they may both become their own table.
		During the logical modeling phase, many entities will be identified, some of which will actually become tables, and some of which will become several tables. The formation of the implementation tables is based on a process known as *normalization*, which I'll cover extensively in Chapter 4.
Implementation	Recordset	A *recordset* is a table that has been made physical for a use, such as sending results to a client. Recordsets do have order, in that usually (based on implementation) the columns and the rows can be accessed by position and rows by their location in the table of data. (Although it's questionable if they should be accessed in this way.) Seldom will you deal with recordsets in the context of database design.
		A "set" in mathematical terms has no ordering, so technically a recordset is not a set, per se. I didn't come up with the name, but it's common terminology.
Implementation	Table	The term "table" is exactly the same as a relation. It is a particularly horrible name, as the structure that this list of terms is in is a "table." These tables, much like the Excel tables, *had* order. It cannot be reiterated enough that tables have *no* order (the section "The Information Principle" later in this chapter will clarify this concept further). *This one naming issue causes more problems for new SQL programmers than any other.*
Physical	File	In many database systems (like Microsoft FoxPro), each operating file represents a table (sometimes a table is referred to as a database, but that is just way too confusing). Multiple files make up the database.

Table 1-2 lists all of the different names that columns are given from the various viewpoints. One thing I should state before moving on is that a column denotes a single value in all cases.

Table 1-2. *Column Term Breakdown*

Viewpoint	Name	Definition
Logical/ conceptual	Attribute	The term "attribute" is very common in the programming world. It basically specifies some information about an object. In early logical modeling, this term can be applied to almost anything, and it may actually represent other entities. Just as with entities, normalization will change the shape of the attribute to a specific format.
Implementation	Column	A column is a single value within a row. It may only contain scalar or fixed vector values. Another common term for what a column may store is *atomic values*, basically indicating that the values are in their lowest form and will not be divided for use in the database system. The position of a column within a table must be unimportant. All access to a column will be by name, not position.
Physical	Field	The term "field" has a couple of meanings. One meaning is the intersection of a row and a column, as in a spreadsheet (this might also be called a cell). The other meaning is more related to early database technology: a field was the physical location in a record (we'll look at this in more detail in Table 1-3). There are no set requirements that a field store only scalar values, merely that it is accessible by a programming language.

Finally, Table 1-3 describes the different ways to refer to a row.

Table 1-3. *Row Term Breakdown*

Viewpoint	Name	Definition
Mathematical	Tuple (pronounced "tupple," not "toople")	This is a finite set of related named scalar values. By "named," I mean that each of the scalar values is known by a name (e.g., Name: Fred; Occupation: Gravel Worker). "Tuple" is a term seldom used except in academic circles, but you should know it, just in case you encounter it when you are surfing the Web looking for database information.[2]

Ultimately, "tuple" is a better term than "row," since a row gives the impression of something physical, and it is essential to not think this way when working in SQL Server with data. |
Logical/ conceptual	Instance	Basically this would be one of whatever was being represented by the entity.
Implementation	Row	This is essentially the same as a tuple, though the term "row" implies it is part of something (in this case, a row in a table). Each column represents one piece of data of the thing that the row has been modeled to represent.
Physical	Record	A record is considered to be a location in a physical file. Each record is made up of fields, which all have physical locations.

---

2. Not to mention the fact that this knowledge will make you more attractive to the opposite sex. Well, not really, but maybe at the PASS conference!

If this is the first time you've seen the terms listed in Tables 1-1 through 1-3, I expect that at this point you're banging your head against something solid, trying to figure out why such a great variety of terms are used to represent pretty much the same things. Many a newsgroup flame-war has erupted over the difference between a "field" and a "column," for example. Nine out of ten times, the people fighting are arguing over semantics, but too often the person who is using a term incorrectly actually does not understand the underlying principles.

The Information Principle

The first of Codd's rules for an RDBMS states simply

> *All information in a relational database is represented explicitly at the logical level in exactly one way—by values in tables.*

This rule is known as the *Information Principle* (or *Information Rule*). It means that there is only one way to associate data in a relational database, and that is by comparing values in columns. For example, the only way of knowing that employee A works for department B is by comparing the values in the relevant columns. There should be no backdoor way of finding this out (e.g., by accessing the data directly on disk).

This leads smoothly to Codd's second rule, known as the *Guaranteed Access Rule*:

> *Each and every datum (atomic value) in a relational database is guaranteed to be logically accessible by resorting to a table name, primary key value, and column name.*

The second thing that the Information Principle implies is that there is *no* order on tables in the database. Just because rows are retrieved from a table and seem to be in a given order, there is no contract between us and SQL Server to return rows in any given order, unless a given order is specified in a retrieval operation. Hence it is not necessary to access the row by its position in the table.

The concept of order can be a big sticking point for many programmers. The confusion is made worse by the fact that data is always viewed in an arraylike format. For example, consider a table T with columns X and Y:

```
SELECT  X, Y
FROM    T
```

This returns the following:

X	Y
1	A
2	B
3	C

It is easy to assume that this data is in this fixed order in the table. A more "accurate" (but admittedly not easier) way to picture data storage is as a group of values floating about somewhere in space, as shown in Figure 1-2.

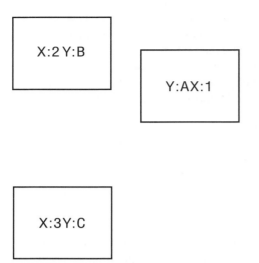

Figure 1-2. *Logical view of table data*

As such, how the rows are output is a function of the commands you use to retrieve them. So the following view of the data is equivalent to the previous table shown:

```
X       Y
---     ---
2       B
1       A
3       C
```

It is, of course, the same set of data—it's just ordered differently. Any database server has the right to return data in a different order if it is more convenient for it to do so. If you desire a guaranteed order, you must use an ORDER BY clause:

```
SELECT  X, Y
FROM    T
ORDER   BY X DESC
```

Which now returns the data in the order specified:

```
X       Y
---     ---
3       C
2       B
1       A
```

Keep in mind that while the output of a SELECT statement has order, since the tables being selected from do *not* have order, a particular order cannot be assumed unless the order is forced by using an ORDER BY clause. Assuming the ordering of the result of a SELECT statement is one of the common mistakes made when dealing with SQL Server. Not to beat a dead horse, but this a very important point.

Domains

The *domain* of a column is the set of valid values that the column is intended to store. For example, consider a column that is intended to store an employee's date of birth. The following list covers the types of data and a few boundaries that need to be considered.

- The value must be a calendar date with no time value.

- The value must be a date prior to the current date. (Otherwise, the person will not have been born yet.)

- The value of the date value should evaluate such that the person is at least 16 or 18 years old, since we couldn't legally (and likely wouldn't want to!) hire a 10-year-old, for example.

- The value of the date value should probably evaluate to less than 70 years ago, since rarely will an employee (especially a new employee) be that age.

- The value must be less than 120 years ago, since we certainly won't have a new employee that old. Any value outside these bounds would clearly be in error.

Together, these points could be taken to define the domain of the DateOfBirth column. In Chapter 6, I'll cover how you might implement this domain, but in the logical phase of the design, you just need to document the domain.

A great practice (not just a best practice!) is to have *named domains* to associate common attributes. For example, in this case there could be an employeeBirthDate domain. Every time the employee birth date is needed, it will be associated with this named domain.

Domains do not have to be so specific, though. For example, you might have the following named domains:

- positiveInteger: Values 0 and higher

- date: Any valid date value

- emailAddress: A string value that must be formatted as a valid e-mail address

- 30CharacterString: A string of characters that can be no longer than 30 characters

Keep in mind that if you actually define the domain of a string to any positive integer, the maximum is theoretically infinity. Today's hardware boundaries allow some pretty far out maximum values (e.g., 2,147,483,647 for a regular integer). It is rare that a user will have to enter a value approaching 2 billion, but if you do not constrain the data within your domains, then reports and programs will need to be able handle such large data. In this case, the domain documentation will play a key role in the testing phase of system implementation.

Note Domains and columns need not contain only single scalar values. As long as the values are accessible only through predefined operations, you can have fixed vector values, such as a point in a plane (e.g., longitude and latitude). The ability to represent these values in SQL Server data is actually new to SQL Server 2005 and will be discussed in Chapter 5.

Metadata

Codd's fourth rule states the following:

> *The database description is represented at the logical level in the same way as ordinary data, so that authorized users can apply the same relational language to its interrogation as they apply to regular data.*

This means that you should be able to interrogate the system metadata using the same language you use to interrogate the user data (i.e., SQL).

According to relational theory, a relation is made up of two parts:

- *Heading*: The set of column name/datatype name pairs that define the columns of the table. This serves as a layer between the definitions that the SQL programmer sees and the actual implementation that the RDBMS programmer used to implement the database server architecture.

- *Body*: The rows that make up the table.

In SQL Server—and most databases—it is common to consider the catalog as a collective description of the tables and other structures in the database. SQL Server exposes the heading information in a couple of ways:

- In a set of views known as the *information schema*. It is best to use this as the primary means of viewing the properties of the objects in our database as far as is possible. It consists of a standard set of views used to view the system metadata and should exist on all database servers of any brand.

- In the SQL Server–specific *catalog* (or *system*) *views*. These views give us information about the implementation of our objects and many more physical properties of our system.

Keys

In relational theory, a relation is not allowed to have duplicate tuples. In all RDBMS products, however, there is no limitation that says that there must not be duplicate rows; this is largely a practical limitation. For example, if you need to import data from a text file, then if uniqueness was enforced strictly in a RDBMS, you would have to do the cleansing of duplicate data in the text file. It is much easier to import the data and do the cleansing inside the database. Also, SQL Server does not have to be used in a proper relational manner, and some people don't mind having duplicate rows. However, in general, not defining keys and therefore allowing duplicate rows is very poor practice, as I will discuss in the next section.

Purpose of Keys

Every table should have at least one *candidate key*—an attribute (or combination of attributes) that can uniquely and unambiguously identify each instance of an entity (or, in the implementation model, each row in the table). In order to enforce this, candidate keys must not allow duplicate values.

Consider the following table, T, with columns X and Y:

```
X      Y
---    ---
1      1
2      1
```

If the design allowed the following INSERT operation:

```
INSERT T (X,Y)
VALUES (1,1)
```

then there would be two identical rows in the table. This would be problematic for a couple of reasons:

- It would be impossible to distinguish between these rows, meaning that there would be no logical method of accessing a single row. This makes it tricky to use, change, or delete an individual row.

- If more than one row has the same attributes, it describes the same object, so if you try to change one of the rows, then the other row should also change, and this becomes a messy situation.

Remember that rows in a table are unordered. Hence, without keys, there would be no way to tell which of the rows with value (1,1) in the preceding table were which.

If you had defined a key on column X, then the previous INSERT would fail, as would any other insert a value of 1 for the X column, such as VALUES (1,3). Alternatively, if you create a key based on both columns X and Y (known as a *composite key*), the (1,3) insert would be allowed, but the (1,1) insert would still be forbidden.

■**Note** In a practical sense, no two rows can really be exactly the same, because there are hidden attributes in the implementation details that prevent this situation from occurring (such as a row number or the exact location in the physical storage medium). However, this sort of physical thinking has no place in relational database design.

In summary, a key defines the uniqueness of rows over a column or set of columns. A table may have as many keys as is required to maintain the uniqueness of its columns. The name "candidate key" might seem odd for this item, but it is so named because it may be used in a couple of ways, either as a primary key or as an alternate key.

Primary and Alternate Keys

A *primary key* (PK) is used as the primary identifier for an entity. It is used to uniquely identify every instance of that entity. It may be that you have more than one key that can perform this role, in which case, after the primary key is chosen, each remaining candidate key would be denoted as an *alternate key* (AK).

Note Alternate keys are implemented as unique constraints.

For example, in the United States, you wouldn't want two employees with the same Social Security number (this would likely kick off a quick investigation with your friendly neighborhood IRS agent). Every employee probably also has a unique, company-supplied identification number. One of these could be chosen as a PK (most likely the employee number), and the other would then be denoted as the AK.

The choice of primary key is largely a matter of convenience and what is easiest to use. I'll discuss primary keys further later in this chapter in the context of relationships. The important thing to remember is that when you have values that should exist only once in the database, you need to protect against duplicates.

Choosing Keys

While keys may be made up of any number of columns, it is best to try to limit as much as possible the number of columns in a key. For example, you may have a Book table with the columns Publisher_Name, Publisher_City, ISBN_Number, and Book_Name. From these attributes, the following three keys might be defined:

- Publisher_Name, Book_Name: A publisher will likely publish more than one book. Also, it is safe to assume that book names are not unique across all books. However, it is probably true that the same publisher will not publish two books with the same title (at least, I assume that this is true!).

- ISBN_Number: The ISBN number is the unique identification number assigned to a book when it is published.

- Publisher_City, ISBN_Number: Because ISBN_Number is unique, it follows that Publisher_City and ISBN_Number combined is also unique.

The choice of (Publisher_Name, Book_Name) as a composite candidate key seems valid, but the (Publisher_City, ISBN_Number) key requires more thought. The implication of this key is that in every city, ISBN_Number can be used again, a conclusion that is obviously not appropriate. This is a very common problem with composite keys, which are often not thought out properly. In this case, you might choose ISBN_Number as the PK and (Publisher_Name, Book_Name) as the AK.

■Note It is important to not confuse unique indexes with keys. There may be valid performance-based reasons to implement the `Publisher_City, ISBN_Number` index in your SQL Server database. However, this would not be identified as a key of a table. In Chapter 6, I'll discuss implementing keys, and in Chapter 8, I'll cover implementing indexes for data access enhancement.

Having established what keys are, let's next discuss the two main types of keys: natural keys (including smart keys) and surrogate keys.

Natural Keys

Wikipedia (`http://www.wikipedia.com`) defines the term *natural key* as "a candidate key that has a logical relationship to the attributes within that row." In other words, it is a "real" attribute of an entity that can also be used to uniquely identify each instance of an entity. From our previous examples, all of our candidate keys so far—employee number, Social Security number (SSN), ISBN, and the (`Publisher_Name, Book_Name`) composite key—have been examples of natural keys.

Some common examples of good natural keys are as follows:

- *For people*: These could be SSNs (in the United States), driver's license numbers, or other assigned IDs (e.g., customer numbers or employee numbers).

- *For transactional documents (e.g., invoices, bills, and computer-generated notices)*: These usually have some sort of number assigned when they are printed.

- *For products for sale*: These could be product numbers (product names are likely not unique).

- *For companies that clients deal with*: These are commonly assigned a customer/client number for tracking.

- *For buildings*: This is usually the complete address, including the postal code.

- *For mail*: These could be the addressee's name and address, and the date the item was sent.

There are many more examples, but by now you should understand what I mean by a natural key. Identifying unique natural keys in the data will be one of the very first steps to perform as the design of the database gets rolling.

Be careful when choosing a natural key. Ideally, you are looking for something that is stable, that you can control, and that is definitely going to allow you to uniquely identify every row in your database. Although I identified the SSN as a potential natural key, you should bear in mind that the government owns SSNs, not you. If the government decides to change its format at some point, this could break your design.

Given that three-part names are common in the United States, it is rare that you'll have two people working in the same company or attending the same school who have the same name. However, "rare" or even "extremely rare" does not implement well. If you happen to hire two people called Sir Lester James Fredingston III, then the second of them probably isn't going to take kindly to being called "Les" for short, just so your database system isn't compromised.

One notable profession where names must be unique is acting. No two actors who have their union cards can have the same name. Some change their names from Archibald Leach to something more pleasant like Cary Grant, but in some cases the person wants to keep his or her name, so in the actors database they add a *uniquifier* to the name to make it unique.

A uniquifier might be some meaningless value added to a column or set of columns to give us a unique key. For example, four people are listed on The Internet Movie Database site (http://www.imdb.com) with the name Gary Grant (not Cary, but Gary). Each has a different number associated with his name to make him a unique Gary Grant.[3]

■**Tip** I tend to think of names in most systems as a kind of semiunique natural key. This isn't good enough for identifying a single row, but it's great for a human to find a value. The phone book is a good example of this. Say you need to find Ray Janakowski in the phone book. There might be more than one person with this name, so it might be a "good enough" way to look up a person's phone number. This semiuniqueness is a very interesting attribute of a table and should be documented for later use, but only in rare cases would you use the semiunique values and make a key from them using a uniquifier.

Smart Keys

A commonly occurring type of natural key in computer systems is a *smart* or *intelligent key*. Some identifiers will have additional information embedded in them, often as an easy way to build a unique value for identifying some real-world thing. In most cases, the smart key can be disassembled into its parts. In some cases, however, the data will probably not jump out at you. Take the following example of a product serial number: XJV102329392000123.

- *X*: Type of product (tube television)

- *JV*: Subtype of product (32" console)

- *102*: Lot that the product was produced in (the 102nd batch produced)

- *293*: Day of year

- *9*: Last digit of year

- *2*: Color

- *000123*: Order of production

Smart keys serve a great purpose, in that the technician who received the product can decipher the value and see that in fact this product was built in a lot that has defective whatchamajiggers, and he needs to replace it. During the logical design phase it is imperative to find all of the bits of information that make them up.

Smart keys, while useful in some cases, present us with smaller problems that will occur over time. For example, it is possible to run out of unique values, or some part of the key (e.g., the product type or subtype) may change. It is imperative that you be very careful and plan ahead if you make use of smart keys to represent multiple pieces of information.

---

3. Of course, none has hit it big yet, but when one of them does, look out!

■**Note** Smart keys are useful tools to communicate a lot of information to the user in a small package. However, all of the bits of information that make up the smart key need to be identified, documented, and implemented in a straightforward manner. Optimum SQL code expects the data to all be stored in individual columns and, as such, it is of great importance that you needn't ever base computing decisions on decoding the value. I will talk more about the subject of choosing keys in Chapter 5.

Surrogate Keys

Surrogate keys (sometimes described as *artificial keys*) are kind of the opposite of natural keys. The word "surrogate" means "something that substitutes for," and in this case, a surrogate key substitutes for a natural key. Sometimes there may not be a natural key that you feel is stable or reliable enough to use, in which case you may decide to use a surrogate key.

A surrogate key can uniquely identify each instance of an entity, but it has no actual meaning with regard to that entity. Surrogate keys are usually maintained by the system. Common methods for creating surrogate key values are using a monotonically increasing number (e.g., an Identity column), some form of hash function, or even a globally unique identifier (GUID), which is a very long identifier that is unique on all machines in the world.

The concept of a surrogate key can be troubling to purists. Since the surrogate key does not describe the row at all, can it really be an attribute of the row? Nevertheless, an exceptionally nice aspect of a surrogate key is that the value of the key should never change. This, coupled with the fact that surrogate keys are always a single column, makes several aspects of implementation far easier.

The only reason for the existence of the surrogate key is to identify a row. The main reason for an artificial key is to provide a key that an end user never has to view and never has to interact with; it serves simply as a kind of pointer and nothing else. Think of it like your driver's license number, an ID number that is given to you when you begin to drive. It may have no other meaning than a number that helps a police officer look up who you are when you've been testing to see just how fast you can go in sixth gear (although in the UK it is a scrambled version of the date of birth). The surrogate key should always have some element that is just randomly chosen, and it should never be based on data that can change. If your driver's license number was a smart key and decoded to include your hair color, the driver's license number might change daily. No, this value is only good for looking you up in a database.

■**Note** In some ways, surrogate keys should probably not even be mentioned in the logical design section of this book, but it is important to know of their existence, since they will undoubtedly still crop up in some logical designs.

Just as the driver's license number probably has no meaning to the police officer other than a means to quickly call up and check your records, the surrogate is used to make working with the data programmatically easier. Since the source of the value for the surrogate key does not have any correspondence to something a user might care about, once a value has been associated with a row, there is not ever a reason to change the value. This is an exceptionally nice aspect of surrogate keys. The fact that the value of the key does not change, coupled with the fact that it is always a single column, makes several aspects of implementation far easier. This will be made clearer later in the book when choosing a primary key.

Thinking back to the driver's license analogy, if the driver's license card has just a single value (the surrogate key) on it, how would Officer Sloudoun determine if you were actually the person identified? He couldn't, so there are other attributes listed, such as name, birth date, and usually your picture, which is an excellent unique key for a human to deal with (except possibly for identical twins, of course). In this very same way, a table ought to have other keys defined as well, or it is not a proper table.

Consider the earlier example of a product identifier consisting of seven parts:

- *X*: Type of product (tube television)

- *JV*: Subtype of product (32" console)

- *102*: Lot that the product was produced in (the 102nd batch produced)

- *293*: Day of year

- *9*: Last digit of year

- *2*: Color

- *000123*: Order of production

A natural key would be made up of these seven parts. There is also a product serial number, which is the concatenation of the values such as XJV102329392000123 to identify the row. Say we also have a surrogate key on the table that has a value of 3384038483. If the only key defined on the rows is the surrogate, the following situation might occur:

```
SurrogateKey  ProductSerialNumber
------------  -------------------
10            XJV102329392000123
3384038483    XJV102329392000123
3384434222    ZJV104329382043534
```

The first two rows are not duplicates, but since the surrogate key values have no real meaning, in essence these are duplicate rows, since the user could not effectively tell them apart.

This sort of problem is common, because most people using surrogate keys do not understand that only having a surrogate key opens them up to having rows with duplicate data in the columns where the data has some logical relationship to each other. A user looking at the preceding table would have no clue which row actually represented the product he or she was after, or if both rows did. (You are now at least one step ahead of the user!)

Note When doing logical design, I tend to model each table with a surrogate key, since during the design process I may not yet know what the final keys will in fact turn out to be. This approach will become obvious throughout the book, especially in the case study presented throughout much of the book.

Missing Values (NULLs)

If you look up the definition of a "loaded subject" in a computer dictionary, you will likely find the word NULL. In the database, there must exist some way to say that the value of a given column is not known. In many cases, when a person wishes to denote that a spreadsheet value isn't known or is missing, an "invalid" value will be used. For decades, programmers have used ancient dates in a column to indicate that a certain value does not matter, or they use a negative value where it does not make sense in the context of a column, or they simply use a text string of 'UNKNOWN' or 'N/A'. These approaches are fine, but special coding is required to deal with these values, for example:

```
IF (value<>'UNKNOWN') THEN …
```

This is OK if it needs to be done only once. The problem, of course, is that this special coding is needed *every time* a new type of column is added. Instead, it is easier to use a value of NULL, which in mathematics means an empty set or a set with no value. Going back to Codd's rules, rule 3 states the following:

> NULL *values (distinct from empty character string or a string of blank characters or zero) are supported in the RDBMS for representing missing information in a systematic way, independent of data type.*

There are a couple of properties of NULL that you need to consider:

- Any value concatenated with NULL is NULL. NULL can represent any valid value, so if an unknown value is concatenated with a known value, the result is still an unknown value.

- All math operations with NULL will return NULL, for the very same reason that any value concatenated with NULL returns NULL.

- Logical comparisons can get tricky when NULL is introduced.

Let's expand this last point somewhat. When NULL is introduced into Boolean math, the truth tables get more complex. When evaluating a condition, there are three possible outcomes: TRUE, FALSE, or UNKNOWN. Only if the search condition evaluates to TRUE will a row appear in the results. If one of your conditions is "if NULL=1", you might be tempted to assume that the answer to this is FALSE, when in fact it is UNKNOWN. Remember that I said that NULL values represent missing values—"missing" implies that a value *may* exist.

This is most interesting because of queries such as the following:

```
select case when 1=NULL or NOT(1=NULL) then 'True' else 'NotTrue' end
```

Many people would expect NOT(1=NULL) to evaluate to TRUE, but in fact 1=NULL is UNKNOWN, so NOT (1=NULL) is also UNKNOWN.

Table 1-4 shows the truth table for the NOT operator.

Table 1-4. *NOT Truth Table*

Operand1	NOT(Operand1)
TRUE	FALSE
UNKNOWN	UNKNOWN
FALSE	TRUE

Table 1-5 shows the truth tables for the AND and OR operators.

Table 1-5. *AND and OR Boolean Truth Table*

Operand1	Operand2	AND	OR
TRUE	TRUE	TRUE	TRUE
TRUE	FALSE	FALSE	TRUE
TRUE	UNKNOWN	UNKNOWN	TRUE
FALSE	FALSE	FALSE	FALSE
FALSE	UNKNOWN	FALSE	UNKNOWN

I just want to point out that NULLs exist and are a part of the basic foundation of relational databases; I don't intend to go too awfully far into how to program with them. Just be aware that NULLs can be tricky if you aren't aware of how they affect comparisons and Boolean expressions (e.g., when used in WHERE clauses).

Relationships

Relationships are what make the tables we've created useful; they provide a way to link tables together. Without the concept of a relationship, it would be necessary to simply put all data into a single table, which would be a very bad idea (as will be made very clear in Chapter 4 when we cover normalization).

In the sections that follow, I'll discuss foreign keys and how they relate to relationships, as well as the various types of relationships you can create in a database.

Foreign Keys

The first thing to discuss concerning relationships is the concept of a *foreign key*. In the previous section, I discussed the concept of a primary key, which is used to uniquely identify a row in a table. A foreign key doesn't uniquely identify a row in the table it is in; it is actually a column or combination of columns whose value(s) match the key of another table. The existence of a foreign key in a table represents the implementation of a relationship between the tables.

For an example of a relationship between two tables, consider the relationship between a Parent table, which stores the SSNs and names of parents, and a Child table, which does the same for the children, as shown in Figure 1-3.

Parent

SSN	Parent Name
111-11-1111	John Smith
222-22-2222	Fred Jones
333-33-3333	Bob Who

Child

Parent SSN	Child Name
111-11-1111	Tad
222-22-2222	Barney
222-22-2222	Joe
333-33-3333	Cindy Lou

Figure 1-3. *Sample Parent and Child tables*

In the Child table, the Parent SSN is the foreign key. It is used in a Child row to associate the child with the parent. From these tables, it can be seen that Tad's dad is John, and the parent of Cindy Lou is Bob Who.

The fact that I used parents and children as an example was not happenstance. Not only is it an example that everyone can understand, but also it introduces two common terms that are central to the implementation of relationships. The table containing the primary key is known as the *parent* table, and the table that receives the primary key and uses it as the foreign key is the *child* table. These terms will be used quite often throughout the book.

In formal terms, I refer to the SSN key *migrating* from the parent to the child to establish the relationship.

■**Note** For a little history, I should mention that the Integrity Independence Rule (Codd's rule 12) requires that for all nonoptional foreign key values in the database, there must be a matching primary key value in the related table.

Types of Relationships

Relationships need not be of the form of one table's primary key being referenced by another table via a foreign key. This is the way it will be represented in the database implementation, because foreign keys are limited to specifying one table in the key (and you can also only join one table at a time in the FROM clause of SQL statements), but real-world relationships are often more complex than that and will span more than two tables.

In this section, we'll discuss the *logical* relationship types, and we'll cover how to implement thee relationships later. These relationships can be divided at this point into two basic types:

- Binary relationships

- Nonbinary relationships

The distinction between the two types lies in the number of tables involved in the relationship. A *binary relationship* involves two tables (in some cases, only one table is involved, as a table may be related to itself; logically speaking, one table is related to a copy of itself). A *nonbinary relationship* involves more than two tables. This may seem like a small distinction, but it really is not. Tables in relational databases are limited to binary relationships, while there is no such restriction in the real world.

When you design databases, you must keep this distinction in mind and learn to recognize each of the possible relationships. When I introduce data modeling in Chapter 2, you'll learn how to represent each of these graphically in a data model.

Binary Relationships

As previously mentioned, a binary relationship is between two tables. Most of the relationships dealt with on a regular basis will fit into this category.

The number of child rows that may participate in each side of the relationship is known as the *cardinality*. Different cardinalities of binary relationships will be introduced in this section:

- One-to-N relationships

- Many-to-many relationships

Each of these relationship types has specific uses and specific associated challenges.

One-to-N Relationships

One-to-N relationships are the class of relationships whereby one table migrates its primary key to another table as a foreign key. As discussed earlier, this is a commonly referred to as a parent/child relationship and only concerns itself with the relationship between the two tables. A child may have only one parent, but a parent may have many children.

I should note that for each relationship type there exists the possibility of an *optional relationship*. Generally, for each row on the "one" side of the relationship (the parent), it is common to not require that a child row exists. If you consider the earlier Parent/Child tables, this means that a child may exist without a parent. If the relationship between parent and child were optional, it would be OK to have a child named Larry who did not have a parent, as shown in Figure 1-4.

The missing value is denoted in the table as NULL, so the row for Larry would be stored as (NULL, Larry). Optional relationships are covered in Chapter 2.

The one-to-N relationship has several subcategories. The way in which you deal with these relationships depends on their cardinality. The relationship subtypes are as follows:

- One-to-many

- One-to-exactly-N

- One-to-one

- Recursive

Parent

SSN	Parent Name
111-11-1111	John Smith
222-22-2222	Fred Jones
333-33-3333	Bob Who

Child

Parent SSN	Child Name
111-11-1111	Tad
222-22-2222	Barney
222-22-2222	Joe
333-33-3333	Cindy Lou
	Larry

Figure 1-4. *Sample table including a parentless child*

One-to-Many Relationship

The one-to-many relationship is the most common and the most important relationship type. For each parent row, there may exist unlimited child records. An example one-to-many relationship might be State to Address, as illustrated in Figure 1-5. Obviously, there are many addresses for a single state, although an address can be in only one state.

State Id Number	State
1	Amabala
2	Aksala
3	Sasnakra

State Id No.	Address	No. of bedrooms	No. of bathrooms
1	402 Database Drive	1	1
1	1222 Administrator Avenue	2	1
2	23 Login Lane	2	1
2	246 Cardinality Close	1	1
2	893 Server Street	3	2
3	107 Query Quay	2	1
3	293 Primary Key Place	4	2

Figure 1-5. *One-to-many example*

Quite often, a one-to-many relationship will be of the "has" (or "has-a") variety. For example, a parent has a child. A team has players. A class has students. This category generally indicates ownership by the parent of the child.

One-to-Exactly-N Relationship

This is a lesser-used relationship type, but it does crop up now and again. For example, a rule might be made that a user may have only two e-mail addresses. Figure 1-6 shows how one-to-two relationship cardinality might be used to implement the User to Email relationship.

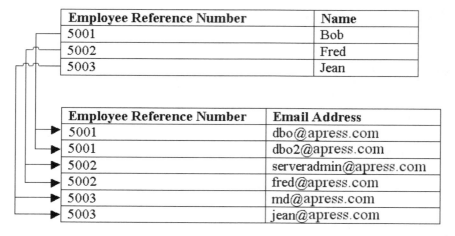

Employee Reference Number	Name
5001	Bob
5002	Fred
5003	Jean

Employee Reference Number	Email Address
5001	dbo@apress.com
5001	dbo2@apress.com
5002	serveradmin@apress.com
5002	fred@apress.com
5003	md@apress.com
5003	jean@apress.com

Figure 1-6. *Example of a one-to-two relationship*

One-to-One Relationship

A one-to-one relationship is merely a specialized version of the one-to-exactly-N relationship type. It indicates that for any given parent, there may exist only a single instance of the child. An example of this type of relationship might be House to Address, as illustrated in Figure 1-7.

■**Note** Discussion of why all of this data might not be located in the same table will be deferred until Chapter 4. It might or it might not, depending on the rest of the design. Suffice it to say that there are often cases where one row in a table will be related to only a single row in another.

A one-to-one relationship may be a simple "has-a" relationship like this example (i.e., a house has a location), or it may be what is referred to as an "is-a" relationship. "Is-a" relationships are used to let one entity extend another. For example, say there exists a person entity and an employee entity. Employees are all people (in most companies), thus they need the same attributes as employees, so I will use a one-to-one relationship: employee is a person. This is referred to as *subtyping*, and I cover it further in Chapter 2.

House Id	House Type
1001	1
1002	2
1003	1
1004	3
1005	4

House Id	Address
1001	21212 Database Drive
1002	444 Administration Avenue
1003	181 SQL Street
1004	12 Primary Key Place
1005	200 Business Rules Boulevard

Figure 1-7. *Example of a one-to-one relationship*

Recursive Relationship

In a recursive relationship, the parent and the child are in the same table. This kind of relationship is used to implement a tree using SQL constructs. If you implement a recursive relationship of cardinality one-to-two, you can implement a treelike data structure.

The classic example of the recursive relationship is a bill of materials. Take something as simple as a ceiling fan. In and of itself, a ceiling fan can be considered a part for sale by a manufacturer, and each of its components, which also have part numbers, are a part that makes up the whole. Some of these components are also made up of parts. In this example, the ceiling fan could be regarded as made up recursively of each of its parts, and in turn each part is made up of all of its constituent parts.

```
Part Number        Description           Used In Part Number
-----------        -----------           -----------
1                  Ceiling Fan
2                  White Fan Blade Kit    1
3                  Light Assembly         1
4                  Light Globe            3
```

The preceding table is small subset of the parts that make up a ceiling fan. Each of the parts 2, 3, and 4 are all parts of a ceiling fan. You have a blade and a light assembly (among other things). Then part number 4, the globe that protects the light, is part of the light assembly. (OK, let's stop this example before this turns into a Time-Life home improvement book!)

Many-to-Many Relationships

The final type of binary relationship is the many-to-many relationship. Instead of there being a single parent and one or more children, there would be more than one parent with more than one child. For example, a child has (biologically, at least) more than one parent: a mother and a father. This mother and father may have more than one child.

Another common example of a many-to-many relationship is a car dealer. Pick nearly any single model of car, and you'll see that it is sold by many different car dealers. Then take one car dealer. It in turn sells many different car models.

The many-to-many relationship is impossible to implement using just two tables, so the demonstration of such tables is not easy to do at this point. In Chapter 2, I'll present more examples and discuss how to implement the many-to-many relationship.

Nonbinary Relationships

Nonbinary relationships involve more than two tables in the relationship. Nonbinary relationships can be very troublesome to deal with, and they are far more common than you might expect, for example:

> A **Room** is used for an **Activity** in a given **Time Period**.

> **Publishers** sell **Books** through **Bookstores**.

Each of these will begin with three entities and one associative relationship that relates all tables together:

Room (room_number)

Activity (activity_name)

Time_Period (time_period_name)

Room_Activity_TimePeriod (room number, activity_name, time_period_name)

From there, it may or may not be possible to break these entities down further into a series of binary relationships between the three tables (i.e., a ternary relationship). In many cases, what looks to be a ternary relationship is actually discovered to be a couple of binary relationships. This is part of the normalization process that will be covered in the "Advanced Normalization" section of Chapter 4.

Data Access Language (SQL)

One of the more important aspects of relational theory is that there must be a high-level language through which all data access takes place. Codd's rule 5 states the following:

> *A relational system may support several languages and various modes of terminal use (for example, the fill-in-blanks mode). However, there must be at least one language whose statements are expressible, by some well-defined syntax, as character strings, and whose ability to support all of the following is comprehensible: data definition, view definition, data manipulation (interactive and by program), integrity constraints, and transaction boundaries (begin, commit, and rollback).*

This language has been standardized over the years in SQL. Throughout this book, I will use most of the capabilities listed in rule 5 in some way, shape, or form:

- *Data and view definition*: Chapters 5 and 6

- *Data manipulation*: Chapter 10

- *Integrity constraints*: Chapter 6

- *Transaction boundaries*: Chapter 9

■**Note** SQL that is used to define objects is commonly referred to as *Data Definition Language* (DDL), and SQL that is used to manipulate data is known as *Data Manipulation Language* (DML). In this book, I assume that you have used SQL before, so you know that most everything done is handled by four statements: SELECT, INSERT, UPDATE, and DELETE.

SQL is a relational language, in that you work on relations or *sets* of data at a time, rather than on one row at a time. This is a very important concept. Codd's rule 7 states the following:

The capability of handling a base relation or a derived relation as a single operand applies not only to the retrieval of data but also to the insertion, update, and deletion of data

What is amazingly cool about SQL as a language is that one statement represents hundreds and thousands of lines of actual code. Most of this code executes in the physical realm, accessing data on disk drives, moving that data into registers, and performing operations in the CPU.

An overarching goal of efficient SQL usage is to do as much work on data in our tables using set-based operations. SQL tables are built to effectively work on lots of data at one time. Where a normal language might be optimized for running many single statements over and over, SQL is optimized for running one statement that does many things.

Finally, the last point I'll mention relates to Codd's rule 12, called the *Nonsubversion Rule*. It states the following:

If an RDBMS has a low-level (single-record-at-a-time) language, that low-level language cannot be used to subvert or bypass the integrity rules or constraints expressed in the higher-level (multiple-records-at-a-time) relational language.

While rule 5 (mentioned earlier) states that a language must exist that operates within a certain set of parameters and boundaries, supporting several types of constructs and objects, it does not preclude other languages from existing. Rule 12 does state that all languages that act on the data must follow the rules that are defined on the data.

Understanding Dependencies

Beyond basic database terms, I want to introduce a few mathematic concepts now before they become interesting later on. They center on the concept of *dependencies*.

The structure of a database is based on the ability to determine one value from another value. For example, take a person. If you can identify the person, you can also determine other information about the person (such as hair color, eye color, height, or weight). These values may change over time, but at any given time, they will be the same. So at any given instant, there can be only one answer to the question "What is the person's weight?"

I'll discuss three different concepts related to this in the sections that follow: functional dependency, determinant, and multivalued dependency. Each of these is based on the idea that one value depends on the value of another.

Functional Dependency

Functional dependency is one of those terms that sounds more complicated than it is. It is actually a very simple concept. Consider the case where you execute a function on one value (let's call it Value1) and the output of this function is *always* the exact same value (Value2). Then Value2 is functionally dependent on Value1.

For example if fn(1) = 2, then getting the value 2 is functionally dependent on value 1 for function fn. Note that it does not go both ways: fn(-1) = 2 is a legitimate functional dependency as well (the function might simply be to return 2 for every value!).

In a table, consider the functional dependency of nonkey columns to key columns. For example, consider the following table T with a key of column X:

```
X     Y
---   ---
1     1
2     2
3     2
```

You can think of column Y as functionally dependent on the value in X, or fn(x) = y. Clearly, Y may be the same for different values of X, but not the other way around. This is a pretty simple yet important concept that needs to be understood. As you will see quite clearly in Chapter 4, poorly understood functional dependencies are at the heart of many database problems, for example:

```
X     Y     Z
---   ---   ---
1     1     1
2     2     4
3     2     4
```

In this example, fn(x) = y, but as far as it appears in this small subset of data, f(y) = z. A complete third of the process of normalization is concerned with what this will cause. Consider that f(y) = z, and you want to modify the z value to 5 for the second row:

```
X     Y     Z
---   ---   ---
1     1     1
2     2     5
3     2     4
```

Now there is a problem with our stated dependency of $f(y) = z$ because $f(2) = 5$ AND 4. A really interesting example of this is the date of birth attribute and an age attribute. The date a person is born determines his or her current age, yet a person's age does not determine his or her birth date (it does indicate a range of values, but not the value itself).

Determinant

An additional term that is related to functional dependency is *determinant*, which can be defined as "any attribute or combination of attributes on which any other attribute or combination of attributes is functionally dependent." So in our previous example, X would be considered the determinant. Two examples of this come to mind:

- Consider a mathematical function like 2 * X. For every value of X, a particular value will be produced. For 2 you will get 4; for 4 you will get 8. Any time you put the value of 2 in the function, you will always return a 4, so 2 functionally determines 4 for function (2 * X). In this case, 2 is the determinant.

- In a more database-oriented example, consider the serial number of a product. From the serial number, additional information can be derived, such as the model number and other specific, fixed characteristics of the product. In this case, the serial number functionally determines the specific, fixed characteristics and, as such, the serial number is the determinant in this case.

If this situation seems familiar, as you looked at in the previous section, it is because any key of a table will functionally determine the other attributes of the table, and each key will be a determinant, since it functionally determines the attributes of the table. If you have two keys, such as the primary key and alternate key of the table, each will be a determinant of the other.

■**Note** If this seems confusing, bear with me; it will all make more sense in Chapter 4.

Multivalued Dependency

A less intuitive concept to understand is that of the multivalued dependency. In the previous section, I discussed functional dependency in a single-valued case. It is less intuitive because while normal functional dependency is very mathlike

$X + 1 = Y$

If X = 1, Y must equal 2.

the multivalued dependency is not quite as straightforward.

As an illustration of a multivalued dependency, let's consider the fact that this book was written by a single primary author (more or less, though I had help from Kurt and Kevin). If you consider the author function on this book, you would have a single value every time. However, if there existed a technical editor function, it would return many values, as several technical editors reviewed this book. Hence, technical editor is multidependent on book.

You will come across the concept of functional dependency again in Chapter 4 when I discuss normalization.

Summary

In this chapter I've introduced some of the basics of database objects and some aspects of theory. It's very important that you're clear on all of the concepts discussed in this chapter, since from now on, I'll assume you understand them.

I introduced relational data structures and defined what a database is. Then I covered what tables, rows, and columns are. From there, I discussed the Information Principle (which defines that data is accessible *only* in tables, and that tables have no order), defined keys, and introduced NULLs and relationships. I also presented a basic introduction to the impetus for how SQL works.

Next, I discussed the mathematical concept of dependencies, which basically is concerned with noticing when the existence of a certain value requires the existence of another value. This information will be used again in Chapter 4 as we reorganize our tables for optimal storage.

Finally, I went over a road map for the different phases our database design will go through. This road map will, in fact, be the process that will be used throughout the rest of the book. The road map phases are as follows:

- *Conceptual*: Identify what the user needs.

- *Logical*: Design the database only in terms of what the user needs in a manner that is conducive to straightforward implementation.

- *Implementation*: Design and implement the database in terms of the tools used (in the case of this book, SQL Server 2005).

- *Physical*: Design and lay out the data on physical hard disks based on usage patterns and what works best for SQL Server.

In the next few chapters, as we start to formulate a conceptual and then a logical design, I will primarily refer to entities and their attributes. After we have logically designed our tables in the logical design phase, I'll shift gears to the implementation phase and speak of tables, rows, and columns. Here is where the really exciting part comes, as the database construction starts and our database starts to become real. Then all that is left is to load our data into a well-formed, well-protected relational database system, and set our users loose!

It all starts with the material presented here, though: understanding what a table is, what a row is, and so on. As a last reminder, tables have no order. None.

CHAPTER 2

■ ■ ■

Data Modeling

A picture is worth a thousand words.

—Royal Baking Powder advertisement[1]

It's sad that the preceding quote came from a commercial advertisement for a cooking product, but it really did. Regardless of the source of the saying, though, I'm sure you can think of a number of instances in which it holds true. For example, consider a painting of any reasonable merit. With a little imagination, you can travel off into a dreamworld. And I know that when I see a picture of a new gadget, I start thinking of a thousand reasons why I must have it.

In this chapter, I will introduce the concept of *data modeling*, in which a "picture" will be produced that shows the objects involved in the database design and how they interrelate. But whereas the goal of a painting, for example, is to inspire, the purpose of the picture that will be produced throughout this chapter is to communicate a specific meaning.

In the next section, I'll provide some basic information about data modeling and introduce the modeling tool I prefer for data modeling: IDEF1X. I'll then cover how to use the IDEF1X methodology to model and document the following:

- Entities

- Attributes

- Relationships

- Descriptive information

Next, I'll introduce several other alternative modeling methodology styles, including Information Engineering and the Chen methodology. I'll also devote some time to a discussion of the diagramming capabilities built into SQL Server Management Studio.

Introduction to Data Modeling

Data modeling is a concept at the foundation of database design. In order to start designing databases, you need to be able to effectively communicate the design as well as make it easier to visualize. Most of the objects introduced in Chapter 1 have graphical representations that

---

1. Not Confucius!

make it easy to get an overview of a vast amount of database structure and metadata in a very small amount of space.

One common misconception about the data model is that it is solely about the graphical display. In fact, the model itself can exist without the graphical parts; it can consist of just textual information. Almost everything in the data model can be read in a manner that makes grammatical sense. The graphical nature is simply there to fulfill the baking powder prophecy—that a picture is worth a thousand words. It is a bit of a stretch, because as you will see, the data model will have lots of words on it!

■**Note** There are many types of models or diagrams: process models, data flow diagrams, data models, sequence diagrams, and others. For the purpose of database design, however, I will focus only on data models.

Several popular modeling languages are available to use, and each is generally just as good as the others at the job of communicating a database design. When choosing my data modeling methodology, I looked for one that was easy to read and could display and store everything required to implement very complex systems. The modeling language I use is Integration Definition for Information Modeling (IDEF1X).

IDEF1X is based on Federal Information Processing Standards Publication 184, published September 21, 1993. To be fair, the other major methodology, Information Engineering, is pretty much just as good, but I like the way IDEF1X works, and it is based on a publicly available standard. IDEF1X was originally developed by the U.S. Air Force in 1985 to meet the following requirements:

- Support the development of data models.

- Be a language that is both easy to learn and robust.

- Be teachable.

- Be well tested and proven.

- Be suitable for automation.

■**Note** At the time of this writing, the full specification for IDEF1X is available at http://www.itl.nist.gov/ fipspubs/idef1x.doc. The exact URL of this specification is subject to change, but you can likely locate it by searching the http://www.itl.nist.gov site for "IDEF1X".

While the selection of a data modeling methodology may be a personal choice, economics, company standards, or features usually influence tool choice. IDEF1X is implemented in many of the popular design tools, such as the following, which are just a few of the products available that claim to support IDEF1X (note that the URLs listed here were correct at the time of publication, but are subject to change in the future):

- AllFusion ERwin Data Modeler: http://www3.ca.com/Solutions/Product.asp?ID=260

- CASE Studio: http://www.casestudio.com/enu/default.aspx

- ER/Studio: http://www.embarcadero.com/products/erstudio34

- Visible Analyst DB Engineer: http://www.visible.com/Products/Analyst/vadbengineer.htm

- Visio Enterprise Edition: http://www.microsoft.com/office/visio

Let's next move on to practice modeling and documenting, starting with entities.

Entities

In the IDEF1X standard, *entities* (which, as discussed previously, are synonymous with tables) are modeled as rectangular boxes, as they are in most data modeling methodologies. Two types of entities can be modeled: *identifier-independent* and *identifier-dependent*, usually referred to as *independent* and *dependent*, respectively.

The difference between a dependent entity and an independent entity has to do with how the primary key of the entity is structured. The independent entity is so named because it has no primary key dependencies on any other entity or, to put it in other words, there are no foreign key columns from other entities in the primary key.

Chapter 1 introduced the term "foreign key," and the IDEF1X specification introduces an additional term: *migrated*. The term "migrated" can be misleading, as the definition of *migrate* is "to move." The primary key of one entity is not actually moving; rather, in this context the term refers to the primary key of one entity being copied as an attribute in a different entity, thus establishing a relationship between the two entities.

If the primary key of one entity is migrated into the primary key of another, it is considered dependent on the other entity, because one entity is dependent on the existence of the other to have meaning. If the attributes are migrated to the nonprimary key attributes, they are "independent" of any other entities. All attributes that are not migrated as foreign keys from other entities are referred to as *owned*, as they have their origins in the current entity.

For example, consider an invoice that has one or more line items. The primary key of the invoice entity might be invoiceNumber. So, if the invoice has two line items, a reasonable choice for the primary key would be invoiceNumber and then lineNumber. Since the primary key contains invoiceNumber, it would be dependent upon the invoice entity. If you had an invoiceStatus entity, and it was related to invoice, it would be independent, as an invoice's existence is not really predicated on the existence of a status (even if a value for the invoiceStatus to invoice relationship *is* required).

An independent entity is drawn with square corners, as follows:

Independent

The dependent entity is the converse of the independent entity, as it will have the primary key of one or more entities migrated into its primary key. It is called "dependent" because its identifier depends on the existence of another entity. It is drawn with rounded-off corners, as follows:

■**Note** The concept of dependent and independent entities lead us to a bit of a chicken and egg paradox. The dependent entity is dependent on a certain type of relationship. However, the introduction of entity creation can't wait until after the relationships are determined, since the relationships couldn't exist without entities. If this is the first time you've looked at data models, this chapter may require a reread to get the full picture, as the concept of independent and dependent objects are linked to relationships.

Entity Naming

One of the most important aspects of designing or implementing any system is how objects, variables, and so forth are named. If you have ever had to go back and work on code that you wrote months ago, you understand what I mean. For example, @x might seem like an OK variable name when you first write some code, and it certainly saves a lot of keystrokes versus typing @holdEmployeeNameForCleaning, but the latter is much easier to understand after a period of time has passed (for me, this period of time is approximately ten minutes, but your mileage may vary).

Naming database objects is no different, and actually, it is possibly more important to name database objects clearly than it is for other programming objects, as quite often your end users will get used to these names: the names given to entities will be translated into table names that will be used by programmers and users alike. The conceptual and logical model will be considered your primary schematic of the data in the database and should be a living document that you change before changing any implemented structures.

Most discussions on how objects should be named can get heated because there are several different "camps," each with different ideas about how to name objects. The central issue is plural or singular. Both ways have merit, but one way has to be chosen. I choose to follow the IDEF1X standard, which says to use singular names. The name itself refers to an instance of what is being modeled, but some folks believe that the table name should name the set of rows. Is either way more correct? Not really—just pick one and stick with it. The most important thing is to be consistent and not let your style go all higgledy-piggledy as you go along. Even a bad set of naming standards is better than no standards at all.

In this book, I will follow these basic guidelines for naming entities:

- *Entity names should never be plural.* The primary reason for this is that the name should refer to an instance of the object being modeled rather than the collection. It is uncomfortable to say that you have an "automobiles row," for example—you have an "automobile row." If you had two of these, you would have two automobile rows.

- *The name given should directly correspond to the essence of what the entity is modeling.* For instance, if you are modeling a person, name the entity `Person`. If you are modeling an automobile, call it `Automobile`. Naming is not always this cut and dried, but it is wise to keep names simple and to the point. If you need to be more specific, that is fine, too. Just keep it succinct (unlike this explanation!).

Entity names frequently need to be made up of several words. During logical modeling, it is acceptable to include spaces, underscores, and other characters when multiple words are necessary in the name, but it is not required. For example, an entity that stores a person's addresses might be named `Person Address`, `Person_Address` or, using the style I have recently become accustomed to and the one I'll use in this book, `PersonAddress`. This type of naming is known as *Pascal case* or *mixed case*. (When you don't capitalize the first letter, but capitalize the first letter of the second word, this style is known as *camelCase*.) Just as in the plural/singular argument, I'm not going to come out and say which is "correct," just that I'm going to follow a certain guideline to keep everything uniform.

Regardless of any style choices you make, no abbreviations should be used in the logical naming of entities. Every word should be fully spelled out, as abbreviations lower the value of the names as documentation and commonly cause confusion. Abbreviations may be necessary in the implemented model due to some naming standard that is forced upon you, and that will be your problem. If you do decide to use abbreviations in your names of any type, make sure that you have a standard in place to ensure the names use the same abbreviation every time. One of the primary reasons to avoid abbreviations is so you don't have `Description`, `Descry`, `Desc`, `Descrip`, and `Descriptn` all used for the same attribute. We'll delve into naming items in the implementation model further in Chapter 5.

A word of warning: You also don't want to go too far in the other direction with long, descriptive sentence names for an entity, such as `leftHandedMittensLostByKittensOnSaturdayAfternoons` (unless the entity will be quite different from `leftHandedMittensLostByKittensOnSundayMornings`), as this name will be painful to use in the logical and implementation models, and prove cumbersome if you need many different tables to represent multiple things that are just categorizations of the same item. A better entity and name might be simply `mitten`. Much of what is encoded in that name will likely be attributes of mittens: `mitten status`, `mitten hand`, `mitten used by`, and so forth. However, the whole question of what is an attribute or column actually falls more under the heading of normalization, which I'll discuss in detail in Chapter 4.

It is often the case that novice database designers elect to use a form of *Hungarian notation* and include prefixes and or suffixes in names—for example, `tblEmployee` or `tblCustomer`. The prefix is not needed and is considered a really bad practice. Using Hungarian notation is a good idea when writing functional code (like in Visual Basic or C#), since objects don't always have a very strict contextual meaning that can be seen immediately upon usage, especially if you are implementing one interface with many different types of objects. With database objects, however, it is rare that there is a question as to what each object is when it is used. It is very easy to query the system catalog to determine what the object is if it is not readily available. Not to go too far into implementation right now, but you can use the `sys.objects` catalog view to see the type of any object. For example, this query will list all of the different object types in the catalog:

```
SELECT  distinct type_desc
FROM    sys.objects
```

Here's the result:

```
type_desc
-------------------------------------------
CHECK_CONSTRAINT
DEFAULT_CONSTRAINT
FOREIGN_KEY_CONSTRAINT
INTERNAL_TABLE
PRIMARY_KEY_CONSTRAINT
SERVICE_QUEUE
SQL_SCALAR_FUNCTION
SQL_STORED_PROCEDURE
SQL_TABLE_VALUED_FUNCTION
SQL_TRIGGER
SYNONYM
SYSTEM_TABLE
USER_TABLE
VIEW
```

We will use sys.objects more in Chapter 5 and beyond to view properties of objects that we create.

Attributes

All attributes in the entity must be uniquely named within it. They are represented by a list of names inside of the entity rectangle:

AttributeExample

```
Attribute1
Attribute2
```

■**Note** The preceding image shows a technically invalid entity, as there is no primary key defined (as required by IDEF1X). I'll cover the notation for keys in the following section.

At this point, you would simply enter all of the attributes that have been defined in the discovery phase. In practice, it is likely that you would have combined the process of discovering entities and attributes with the initial modeling phase. It will all depend on how well the tools you use work. Most data modeling tools cater for building models fast and storing a wealth of information to document their entities and attributes.

In the early stages of logical modeling, there can be quite a large difference between an attribute and what will be implemented as a column. As I will demonstrate in Chapter 4, the attributes will be transformed a great deal during the normalization process. For example, the attributes of an `Employee` entity may start out as follows:

Employee

| EmployeeNumber |
| FirstName |
| LastName |
| Address |
| PhoneNumber |

However, during the normalization process, tables like this will often be broken down into many attributes (e.g., `address` might be broken into `number`, `street name`, `city`, `state`, `zip code`, etc.) and possibly many different entities.

■**Note** Attribute naming is one place where I tend to deviate from IDEF1X standard. The standard is that names are unique within a model. This tends to produce names that include the table name followed by the attribute name, which can result in unwieldy, long names.

Just as with entity names, there is no need to include Hungarian prefixes or suffixes in the attribute names now or in implementation names. The type of the attribute can be retrieved from the system catalog if there is any question about it.

Primary Key

As noted in the previous section, an IDEF1X entity must have a primary key. This is convenient for us, as in Chapter 1 an entity was defined such that each instance must be unique. The primary key may be a single attribute, or it may be a composite of multiple attributes. A value is required for every attribute in the key (logically speaking, no nulls are allowed in the primary key).

The primary key is denoted by placing attributes above a horizontal line through the entity rectangle. Note that no additional notation is required to indicate that the value is the primary key.

PrimaryKeyExample

PrimaryKey
Attribute1 Attribute2

For example, consider the `Employee` entity from the previous section. The `EmployeeNumber` attribute is going to be unique, so this would be an acceptable primary key:

Employee

EmployeeNumber
FirstName LastName Address PhoneNumber

In the early logical modeling phase, I generally do not like to spend time choosing the final primary key attribute(s). The main reason for this is to avoid worrying too much about what the key is going to be. I tend to add a meaningless primary key to migrate to other entities to help me see when there is any ownership. In the current example, `employeeNumber` clearly refers to an employee, but not every entity will be so clear. For example, consider an entity that models a product manufactured by a company. The company may identify the product by the type, style, size, and series:

Product

Type Style Size Series
ProductName

The name may be a good key, and more than likely there is also a product code. Which is the best key—or which is even truly a key—may not become apparent until much later in the process. There are many ways to implement a good key, and the best way may not be instantly recognizable.

Instead of choosing a primary key during this part of the process, I add a surrogate value to the entity for identification purposes. I then model all candidate keys (or unique identifiers) as alternate keys. The result is that it is very clear in the logical model what entities are in an ownership role to other entities, since the key that is migrated contains the name of the modeled entity. I would model this entity as follows:

Product

ProductId
Type Style Size Series Name

■**Note** Using surrogate keys is certainly not a requirement in logical modeling; it is a personal preference that I have found a useful documentation method to keep models clean, and it corresponds to my method of implementation later. Not only is using a natural key as the primary key in the logical modeling phase reasonable, but also many architects find it preferable. Either method is perfectly acceptable.

Alternate Keys

As defined in Chapter 1, an *alternate key* is a set of one or more attributes whose uniqueness needs to be guaranteed over all of the instances of the entity. Alternate keys do not have a specific location like primary keys, and they are not migrated for any relationship. They are identified on the model in a very simple manner:

AlternateKeyExample

PrimaryKey
AlternateKey1 (AK1) AlternateKey2Attribute1 (AK2) AlternateKey2Attribute2 (AK2)

In this example, there are two alternate key *groups*: group AK1, which has one attribute as a member, and group AK2, which has two attributes. Thinking back to the product example, the two keys would then be modeled as follows:

Product

ProductId
Type (AK1) Style (AK1) Size (AK1) Series (AK1) Name (AK2)

One extension that ERwin adds to this notation is shown here:

AlternateKeyExample

PrimaryKey
AlternateKey1 (AK1.1) AlternateKey2Attribute1 (AK2.1) AlternateKey2Attribute2 (AK2.2)

A position number notation is tacked onto the name of the key (AK1 and AK2) to denote the position of the attribute in the key. In the logical model, technically the order of attributes in the key should not be considered and certainly should not be displayed. It really does not matter which attribute comes first in the key; all that really matters is that you make sure there are unique values across multiple attributes. When a key is implemented, the order of columns *will* become interesting for performance reasons, as SQL Server implements uniqueness with an index, but uniqueness will be served no matter what the order of the columns of the key is.

Foreign Keys

As I've alluded to, foreign keys are also referred to as migrated attributes. They are primary keys from one entity that serve as a reference to an instance in another entity. They are again a result of relationships (which we'll look at later in the chapter). They are indicated much like alternate keys by adding the letters "FK" after the foreign key:

```
ForeignKeyExample
 PrimaryKey
 ForeignKey (FK)
```

For example, consider an entity that is modeling a music album:

```
Album
 AlbumId
 Name (AK1)
 ArtistId (FK)(AK1)
 PublisherId (FK)(AK1)
 CatalogNumber (AK2)
```

The artistId and publisherId represent migrated foreign keys from the artist entity and the publisher entity. We'll revisit this example in the "Relationships" section later in the chapter.

One tricky thing about this example is that the diagram doesn't show what entity the key is migrated from. This can tend to make things a little messy, depending on how you choose your primary keys. This lack of clarity about what table a foreign key migrates from is a limitation of most modeling methodologies, as it would be unnecessarily confusing if the name of entity where the key came from was displayed, for a couple of reasons:

- There is no limit (nor should there be) on how far a key will migrate from its original owner entity (the entity where the key value was not a migrated foreign key reference).

- It is not unreasonable that the same attribute might migrate from two separate entities, especially early in the logical design process.

One of the reasons for the primary key scheme I will employ in logical models is to add a key named <entityName>Id as the identifier for entities. The name of the entity is easily identifiable, it lets us easily know where the original source of the attribute is, and we can see the attribute migrated from entity to entity.

Domains

The term "domain" is regrettably used in two very similar contexts in the database world. In Chapter 1, a domain referred to a set of valid values for an attribute. In IDEF1X, you can define named, reusable specifications known as domains, for example:

- `String`: A character string

- `SocialSecurityNumber`: A character value with a format of ###-##-####

- `PositiveInteger`: An integer value with an implied domain of 0 to `max(integer value)`

- `Truth`: A five-character value with a domain of (`'FALSE'`,`'TRUE'`)

Domains in the specification not only allow us to define the valid values that can be stored in an attribute, but also provide a form of inheritance in the datatype definitions. *Subclasses* can then be defined of the domains that inherit the settings from the base domain. It is a good practice to build domains for any attributes that get used regularly, as well as domains that are base templates for infrequently used attributes. For example, you might have a character type domain where you specify a basic length, like 60. Then you may specify common domains like *name* and *description* to use in many entities. For these, you should choose a reasonable length for the values, plus you should require that the data cannot be an empty string.

Regardless of whether or not you are using a tool, it is useful to define common domains that you use for specific types of things (kind of like applying a common pattern to solve a common problem). For example, a person's first name might be a domain. The reason that this is so cool is that you don't have to think "Hmm, how long to make a person's name?" more than once. After you make a decision, you just use what you have used before.

In logical modeling, you'll likely want to keep a few bits of information, such as the general type of the attribute: character, numeric, logical, or even binary data. It's also important to document in some form the legal values for an attribute that is classified as being of the domain type. This is generally done using some pseudocode or in textual manner, either in your modeling tool or even in a spreadsheet.

It is extremely important to keep these domains as implementation-independent datatype descriptions. For example, you might specify a domain of `GloballyUniqueIdentifier`, a value that will be unique no matter where it is generated. In SQL Server, a unique identifier could be used (GUID value) to implement this domain. In another operating system (created by a company other than Microsoft) where there is not exactly the same mechanism, it might be implemented differently; the point is that it is a value that is statistically guaranteed to be unique every time the value is generated.

When you start implementation modeling, you will use the same domains to assign the implementation properties. This is the real value in using domains. By creating reusable template attributes that will also be used when you start creating columns, you'll spend less effort and time building simple entities, which make up the bulk of your work. Doing so also provides a way for you to enforce companywide standards, by reusing the same domains on all corporate models (predicated, of course, on you being diligent with your data model over time!).

Later on, implementation details such as datatype, constraints, and so forth will be chosen, just to name a few of the more basic properties that may be inherited. Since it is very likely that you will have fewer domains than implemented attributes, the double benefit of speedy and consistent model assembly is achieved. However, it is not reasonable or even useful to employ the inheritance mechanisms when building tables by hand. Implementation of domains is way too much trouble to do without a tool.

As an example of a domain hierarchy, consider this set of character string domains:

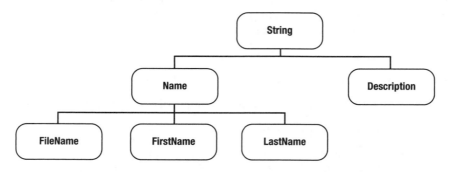

Here, String is the base domain from which you can then inherit Name and Description. FileName, FirstName, and LastName are inherited from Name. During logical modeling, this might seem like a lot of work for nothing, because most of these domains will share some basic details, such as not allowing NULLs or blank data. However, FileName may be optional, whereas LastName might be mandatory. It is important to set up domains for as many distinct attribute types as possible, in case rules or datatypes are discovered that are common to any domains that already exist.

Domains are a nice feature of IDEF1X. They provide an easy method of building standard attribute types, reducing both the length of time required for repeating common attribute types and the number of errors that occur in doing so. Specific tools implement domains with the ability to define and inherit more properties throughout the domain chain to make creating databases easier. During logical modeling, domains can optionally be shown to the right of the attribute name in the entity:

DomainExample

| AttributeName: DomainName |
| AttributeName2: DomainName2 |

So if I have an entity that holds domain values for describing a type of person, I might model it as follows:

Person

| PersonId: SurrogateKey |
| Description: Description
FirstName: PersonFirstName
LastName: PersonLastName |

To model this example, I defined four domains:

- `SurrogateKey`: The surrogate key value. (Implementation is not implied by building a domain, so later this can be implemented in any manner.) I could also choose to use a natural key.

- `Description`: The same type of domain as the name domain, except to hold a description (can be 60 characters maximum).

- `PersonFirstName`: A person's first name (30 characters maximum).

- `PersonLastName`: A person's last name (50 characters maximum).

The choice of the length of name is an interesting one. I searched on Google for "person first name varchar" and found lots of different possibilities: 10, 35, unlimited, 25, 20, 15—all on the first page of the search! Just as you should use a consistent naming standard, you should use standard lengths every time like data is represented, so when you hit implementation the likelihood that two columns storing like data will have different definitions is minimized.

Naming

Attribute naming is a bit more interesting than entity naming. I stated earlier that my preference is to use singular, not plural, entity names. The same issues that apply in entity naming are technically true for attribute naming (and no one disagrees with this!). However, until the logical model is completed, the model may still have attribute names that are plural. Leaving a name plural can be a good reminder that you expect multiple values. For example, consider a `Person` entity with a `Children` attribute identified. The `Person` entity would identify a single person, and the `Children` attribute would identify sons and daughters of that person.

The naming standard I follow is very simple:

- Generally, it is not necessary to repeat the entity name in the attribute name, though it is common to do so with a surrogate key, since it is specific for that table. The entity name is implied by the attribute's inclusion in the entity.

- The chosen attribute name should reflect precisely what is contained in the attribute and how it relates to the entity.

- As with entities, no abbreviations are to be used in attribute names. Every word should be spelled out in its entirety. If for some reason an abbreviation must be used (e.g., due to naming standard currently in use), then a method should be put into place to make sure the abbreviation is used consistently, as discussed earlier in the chapter. For example, if your organization has a ZRF "thing" that is commonly used and referred to in general conversation as a ZRF, you might use this abbreviation. In general, however, I recommend avoiding abbreviations in all naming unless the client is insistent.

- The name should contain absolutely no information other than that necessary to explain the meaning of the attribute. This means no Hungarian notation of the type of data it represents (e.g., `LastNameString`) or prefix notation to tell you that it is in fact an attribute.

■Note Attribute names in the finalized logical and implementation models will not be plural, but we'll work this out in Chapter 4 when normalizing the model. At this point it is not a big deal at all.

Consistency is the key to proper naming, so if you or your organization does not have a standard naming policy, it's worthwhile to develop one. My naming philosophy is to keep it simple and readable, and to avoid all but universally standard corporate abbreviations. This standard will be followed from logical modeling into the implementation phase. Whatever your standard is, establishing a pattern of naming will make your models easy to follow, both for yourself and for your programmers and users. Any standard is better than no standard.

Relationships

Up to this point, the constructs we have looked at have been pretty much the same across all data modeling methodologies. Entities are always signified by rectangles, and attributes are quite often words within the rectangles. In IDEF1X, every relationship is denoted by a line drawn between two entities, with a solid circle at one end of that line.

This is where things start to get confusing when it comes to the other methodologies, as each approaches relationships a bit differently. I favor IDEF1X for the way it represents relationships. To make the concept of relationships clear, I need to go back to the terms "parent" and "child." Consider the following definitions from the IDEF1X specification's glossary:[2]

- Entity, Child: The entity in a specific connection relationship whose instances can be related to zero or one instance of the other entity (parent entity)

- Entity, Parent: An entity in a specific connection relationship whose instances can be related to a number of instances of another entity (child entity)

- Relationship: An association between two entities or between instances of the same entity

In the following image, the primary key of the parent is migrated to the child. This is how to denote a foreign key on a model.

There are several different types of relationships that we'll examine in this section:

- *Identifying*, where the primary key of one table is migrated to the primary key of another. The child will be a dependent entity.

- *Nonidentifying*, where the primary key of one table is migrated to the nonprimary key attributes of another. The child will be an independent entity as long as no identifying relationships exist.

---

2. These are remarkably lucid definitions to have been taken straight from a government specification!

- *Optional identifying*, when the nonidentifying relationship does not require a child value.

- *Recursive*, when a table is related to itself.

- *Subtype* or *categorization*, which is a one-to-one relationship used to let one entity extend another.

- *Many-to-many*, where an instance of an entity can be related to many in another, and in turn many instances of the second entity can be related to multiples in the other.

We'll also cover the *cardinality* of the relationship (how many of the parent relate to how many of the child), *role names* (changing the name of a key in a relationship), and *verb phrases* (the name of the relationship).

Relationships are a key topic in database design, but not a completely simple one. A lot of information is related using a few dots and lines.

■**Tip** All of the relationships (except the last one) discussed in this section are of the one-to-many variety, which encompasses *one-to-zero, one, many,* or perhaps *exactly-n* relationships. Technically, it is more accurately *one-to-(from M to N)*, as this enables specification of the *many* in very precise (or very loose) terms as the situation dictates. However, the more standard term is "one-to-many," and I will not try to make an already confusing term more so.

Identifying Relationship

The *identifying relationship* indicates that the migrated primary key attribute is migrated to the primary key of the child. It is drawn as follows:

In the following example, you can see that the `ParentId` attribute is a foreign key in the `Child` entity, from the `Parent` entity.

The child entity in the relationship is drawn as a rounded-off rectangle, which as you learned earlier in this chapter means it is a dependent entity. It is called an identifying relationship because it will need to have to have a parent instance in order to be able to identify a child instance record. The essence (defined as "the intrinsic or indispensable properties that serve to characterize or identify something") of the child instance is defined by the existence of a parent.

Another way to look at this is that generally the child in an identifying relationship is a part of the parent. Without the existence of the parent, the child would make no sense.

A common example is an invoice and the line items being charged to the customer on the invoice:

Without the existence of the invoice, the line items would have no reason to exist. It can also be said that the line items are identified as being part of the parent.

Nonidentifying Relationship

The *nonidentifying relationship* indicates that the primary key attribute is not migrated to the primary key of the child. It is denoted by a dashed line between the entities:

Nonidentifying relationships are used more frequently than identifying relationships. Whereas the identifying relationship indicated that the child was an essential part of the parent entity, the nonidentifying relationship indicates that the child represents an attribute of the parent.

Taking again the example of an invoice, consider the vendor of the products that have been sold and documented as such in the line items. The product vendor does not define the existence of a line item, because with or without knowing the vendor, the line item still makes sense.

The difference between identifying and nonidentifying relationships can be tricky. If the parent entity defines the need for the existence of the child (as stated in the previous section), then use an identifying relationship. If, on the other hand, the relationship defines one of the child's attributes, then use a nonidentifying relationship.

Consider the following examples:

- *Identifying*: You have an entity that stores a contact and an entity that stores the contact's telephone number. The Contact defines the phone number, and without the contact, there would be no need for the ContactPhoneNumber.

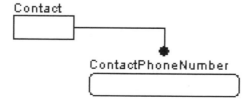

- *Nonidentifying*: Consider the entities that were defined for the identifying relationship, along with an additional entity called ContactPhoneNumberType. This entity is related to the ContactPhoneNumber entity, but in a nonidentifying way, and defines a set of possible phone number types (Voice, Fax, etc.) that a ContactPhoneNumber might be. The type of phone number does not identify the phone number; it simply classifies it.

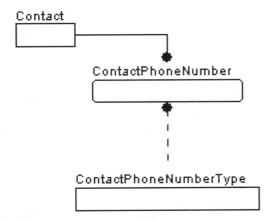

The ContactPhoneNumberType entity is commonly known as a *domain entity* or *domain table*, or sometimes as a *lookup table*. Rather than having a fixed domain for an attribute, an entity is designed that allows programmatic changes to the domain with no recoding of constraints or client code. As an added bonus, you can add columns to define, describe, and extend the domain values to implement business rules. It also allows the client user to build lists for users to choose values with very little programming.

Optional Identifying Relationship

While every nonidentifying relationship defines the domain of an attribute of the child table, sometimes when the row is created it's not necessary that the values are selected. For example, consider a database where you model houses, like for a neighborhood. Every house would have a color, a style, and so forth. However, not every house would have an alarm company, a mortgage holder, and so on. The relationship between the alarm company and bank would be optional in this case, while the color and style relationships would be mandatory.

■**Note** Here I assume you would need a table for color and style. Whether or not this is required is something that will be discussed in the next couple of chapters. (Hint: You usually will.)

The difference in the implemented table will be whether or not the child table's foreign key will allow nulls. If a value is required, then it is considered *mandatory*. If a value of the migrated key can be null, then it is considered *optional*.

The optional case is signified by an open diamond at the opposite end of the dashed line from the black circle, as shown here:

In the mandatory case, the relationship is drawn as before, without the diamond. Note that an optional relationship may have a cardinality of zero, while a mandatory relationship must have a cardinality of one or greater. (The concept of cardinality will be discussed further in the next section.)

So why would you make a relationship optional? Consider once again the nonidentifying relationship between the invoice line item and the product vendor. The vendor in this case may be required or not required as the business rules dictate. If it is not required, you should make the relationship optional.

■**Note** You might be wondering why there is not an optional identifying relationship. This is due to the fact that you may not have any optional attributes in a primary key, which is true in relational theory and for SQL Server 2005.

For a one-to-many, optional relationship, consider the following:

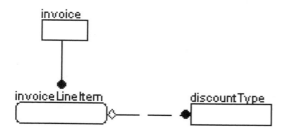

The invoiceLineItem entity is where items are placed onto an invoice to receive payment. The user may sometimes apply a standard discount amount to the line item. The relationship then from the invoiceLineItem to the discountType entity is an optional one, as no discount may have been applied to the line item.

For most optional relationships like this, there is another possible solution, which can be modeled as required, and in the implementation a row can be added to the discountType table that indicates "none."

An example of a mandatory relationship could be genre to movie in a movie rental shop's database:

The relationship is genre <classifies> movie, where the genre entity represents the one and movie represents the many in the one-to-many relationship. Every movie being rented must have a genre, so that it can be organized in the inventory and then placed on the appropriate rental shelf.

Cardinality

The cardinality of the relationship denotes the number of child instances that can be inserted for each parent of that relationship. The following table shows the six possible cardinalities that relationships can take on (see Figures 2-1 through 2-6). The cardinality indicators are applicable to either mandatory or optional relationships.

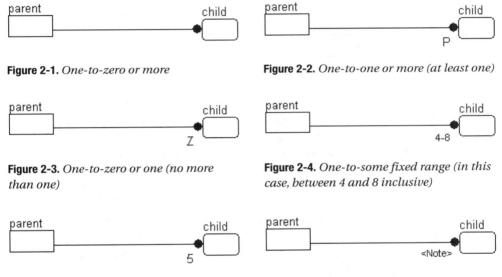

Figure 2-1. *One-to-zero or more*

Figure 2-2. *One-to-one or more (at least one)*

Figure 2-3. *One-to-zero or one (no more than one)*

Figure 2-4. *One-to-some fixed range (in this case, between 4 and 8 inclusive)*

Figure 2-5. *One-to-exactly N (in this case, 5, meaning each parent must have five children)*

Figure 2-6. *Specialized note describing the cardinality*

For example, a possible use for the one to one-or-more might be to represent the relationship between a guardian and a student in a school database:

This is a good example of a zero-or-one to one-or-more relationship, and a fairly complex one at that. It says that for a guardian record to exist, a student must exist, but a student record need not have a guardian for us to wish to store the guardian's data. Note that I did not limit the number of guardians in the example, since it is not clear at this point if there is a limit.

Next, let's consider the case of a club that has members with certain positions that they should or could fill, as shown in Figures 2-7 through 2-9.

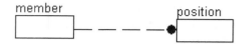

Figure 2-7. *Example A*

Figure 2-8. *Example B*

Figure 2-9. *Example C*

Figure 2-7 shows that a member can take as many positions as there are possible. Figure 2-8 shows that a member can serve in no position or one position, but no more. Finally, Figure 2-9 shows that a member can serve in zero, one, or two positions. They all look about the same, but the Z or 0–2 is important in signifying the cardinality.

■**Note** I considered including examples of each of these cardinality types, but in most cases they were too difficult or too silly.

Role Names

A *role name* is an alternative name you can give an attribute when it is used as a foreign key. The purpose of a role name is to clarify the usage of a migrated key, either because the parent entity is very generic and a more specific name is needed or because the same entity has multiple relationships. As attribute names must be unique, it is often necessary to assign different names for the child foreign key references. Consider this example:

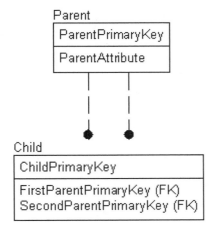

In this diagram, there are two relationships from the Parent entity to the Child entity, and the migrated attributes have been named as FirstParentPrimaryKey and SecondParentPrimaryKey.

In diagrams, you can indicate the original name of the migrated attribute after the role name, separated by a period (.), as follows:

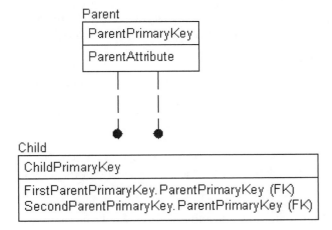

As an example, say you have a User entity, and you want to store the name or ID of the user who created a DatabaseObject entity. It would then end up as follows:

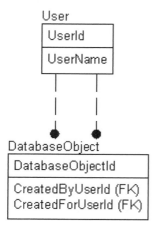

Note that there are two relationships to the DatabaseObject entity from the User entity. It is not clear from the diagram which foreign key goes to which relationship.

Other Types of One-to-N Relationships

There are a few other, less important relationship types that are not employed nearly as much as the previously mentioned ones. However, it's extremely important that you understand them, as they are a bit tricky and provide advanced solutions to problems that are not easily solved.

- *Recursive*: Used to model hierarchies in data

- *Subtypes*: Used to model a limited type of inheritance that allows specific types of entities to be built to extend general entities

Recursive

One of the more difficult—but most important—relationships to implement is the *recursive relationship*, also known as a *self-join, hierarchical, self-referencing,* or *self-relationship.* This is modeled by drawing a nonidentifying relationship not to a different entity, but to the same entity. The migrated key of the relationship is given a role name. (I generally use a naming convention of adding "parent" to the front of the attribute name, but this is not a necessity.)

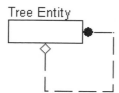

The recursive relationship is useful for creating tree structures, as in the following organizational chart:

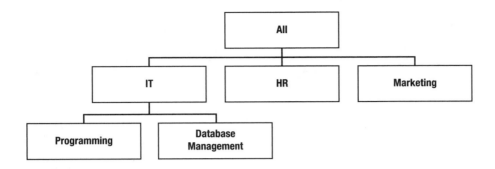

To explain this concept fully, I will show the data that would be stored to implement this hierarchy:

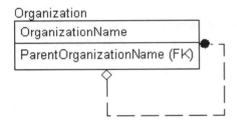

Here is the sample data for this table:

organizationName	parentOrganizationName
All	
IT	All
HR	All
Marketing	All
Programming	IT
Database Management	IT

The organizational chart can now be traversed by starting at `All` and getting the children to `ALL`, for example: `IT`. Then you get the children of those values, like for `IT` one of the values is `Programming`.

As a final example, consider the case of a `Person` entity. If you wanted to associate a person with a single other person as the first person's spouse, you might design the following:

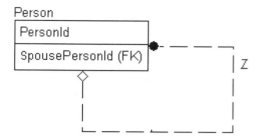

Notice that this is a one-to-zero or one relationship, since (in most places) a person may have no more than a single spouse, but need not have one. If you require one person to be related as a child to two parents, an associative entity is required to link two people together.

■**Note** As an aside, a tree where each instance can have only one parent (but unlimited children) is called a *binary tree*. If you model the relationship as a many-to-many using an associative entity, allowing an instance to have more than one parent, this implements a *graph*.

Subtypes

Subtypes (also referred to as *categorization relationships*) are another special type of one-to-zero or -one relationship used to indicate whether one entity is a specific type of a generic entity. Note also that there are no black dots at either end of the lines; the specific entities are drawn with rounded corners, signifying that they are indeed dependent on the generic entity.

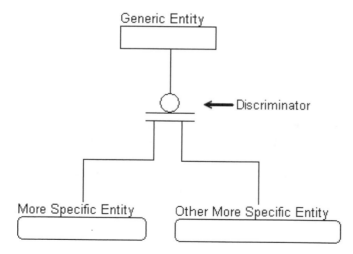

There are three distinct parts of the subtype relationship:

- *Generic entity*: This entity contains all of the attributes common to all of the subtyped entities.

- *Discriminator*: This attribute acts as a switch to determine the entity where the additional, more specific information is stored.

- *Specific entity*: This is the place where the specific information is stored, based on the discriminator.

For example, let's look at a video library. If you wanted to store information about each of the videos that you owned, regardless of format, you might build a categorization relationship like the following:

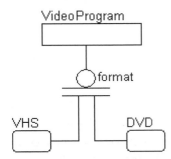

In this manner, you might represent each video's price, title, actors, length, and possibly description of the content in the Video entity, and then, based on format, which is the discriminator, you might store the information that is specific to VHS or DVD in its own separate entity (e.g., special features and menus for DVDs, long or slow play for VHS tapes, etc.).

Tip The types of relationships in this example are what I referred to earlier as "is-a" relationships: a VHS is a video, and a DVD is also a video.

There are two distinct category types: *complete* and *incomplete*. The complete set of categories is modeled with a double line on the discriminator, and the incomplete set is modeled with a single line (see Figure 2-10).

Figure 2-10. *Complete (left) and incomplete (right) sets of categories*

The primary difference between the complete and incomplete categories is that in the complete categorization relationship, each generic instance must have one specific instance, whereas in the incomplete case this is not necessarily true. An instance of the generic entity can be associated with an instance of only one of the category entities in the cluster, and each instance of a category entity is associated with exactly one instance of the generic entity. In other words, overlapping subentities are not allowed.

For example, you might have a complete set of categories like this:

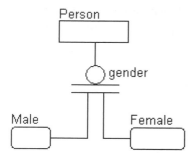

This relationship is read as follows: "A Person *must* be either Male or Female." This is certainly a complete category. This is not to say that you know the gender of every person in every instance of all entities. Rather, it simply means that if the instance has been categorized, any person must fall in one of the two buckets (male or female).

However, consider the following incomplete set of categories:

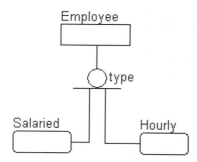

This is an incomplete subtype, because employees are either salaried or hourly, but there may be other categories, such as contract workers. You may not need to store any additional information about them, though, so there is no need to implement the specific entity. This relationship is read as follows: "An Employee can be either Salaried or Hourly or other."

Many-to-Many Relationship

The many-to-many relationship is also known as the *nonspecific relationship*, which is actually a better name, but far less well known. It is common to have many-to-many relationships in the data model. In fact, the closer you get to your final database model, the more you'll find that quite a few of your relationships will be of the many-to-many type.

These relationships are modeled by a line with a solid black dot at either end:

There is one real problem with modeling a many-to-many relationship: it is often necessary to have more information about the relationship than that simply many EntityX instances
are connected to many EntityY instances. So the relationship is usually modeled as follows:

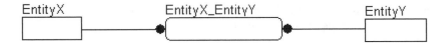

Here, the intermediate EntityX_EntityY entity is known as an *associative entity* or *resolution
entity*. In modeling, I will often stick with the former representation when I haven't identified any
extended attributes to describe the relationship and the latter representation when I need to add
additional information to the model.

▪**Tip** I should also note that you can't implement a many-to-many relationship in the relationship model
without using a table for the resolution. This is because there is no way to migrate keys both ways. You will
notice when you use a many-to-many relationship that no key is migrated from either table, so there would
be no data to substantiate the relationship. In the database, you are required to implement all many-to-many
relationships using a resolution entity.

To clarify the concept, let's look at the following example:

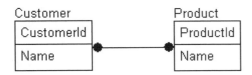

Here I have set up a relationship where many customers are related to many products.
This is a common situation, as in most cases companies don't create specific products for
specific customers; rather, any customer can purchase any of the company's products. At
this point in the modeling, it is reasonable to use the many-to-many representation. Note
that I am generalizing the customer-to-product relationship. It is not uncommon to have a
company build specific products for only one customer to purchase.

Consider, however, the case where the Customer need only be related to a Product for a
certain period of time. To implement this, you can use the following representation:

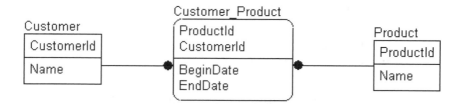

In fact, almost all of the many-to-many relationships tend to require some additional information like this to make them complete. It is not uncommon to have no many-to-many relationships modeled with the black circle on both ends of a model, so you will need to look for entities modeled like this to be able to discern them.

Verb Phrases (Relationship Names)

Relationships are given names, called *verb phrases*, to make the relationship between a parent and child entity a readable sentence and to incorporate the entity names and the relationship cardinality. The name is usually expressed from parent to child, but it can be expressed in the other direction, or even in both directions. The verb phrase is located on the model somewhere close to the line that forms the relationship:

The relationship should be named such that it fits into the following general structure for reading the entire relationship:

parent cardinality – parent entity name – relationship name – child cardinality – child entity name

For example, the following relationship

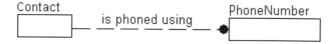

would be read as

One contact is phoned using zero, one, or more phoneNumber(s).

Of course, the sentence may or may not make perfect grammatical sense, as this one brings up the question of how a contact is phoned using zero phone numbers. If presenting this phrase to a nontechnical person, it would make more sense to read it as follows:

One contact can have either no phone number or one or more phoneNumbers.

The modeling language does not take linguistics into consideration when building this specification, but from a technical standpoint, it does not matter that the contact is phoned using zero phone numbers, since it follows that they have no phone number.

Being able to read the relationship helps you to notice obvious problems. For instance, consider the following relationship

It looks fine at first glance, but when read like this

One contactType classifies zero or one contact.

it doesn't make logical sense. It means to categorize all of the contacts it would be required to have a unique ContactType row for each Contact. Not reasonable at all. This would be properly modeled as follows:

which now reads

One contactType classifies zero or more contacts.

Note that the type of relationship, whether it is identifying, nonidentifying, optional, or mandatory, makes no difference when reading the relationship.

You can also include a verb phrase that reads from child to parent. For a one-to-many relationship, this would be of the following format:

One child record (relationship) exactly one parent record.

In the case of the first example, you could have added an additional verb phrase:

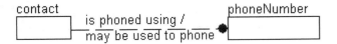

The parent-to-child relationship name again is

One contact is phoned using zero, one, or more phoneNumber(s).

You can then name the relationship from child to parent. Note that when naming in this direction, you are in the context of zero or one phone number to one and only one contact.

Zero or one phoneNumber(s) may be used to phone exactly one contact.

Since this is going from many to one, it is assumed that the parent in the relationship will have one related value, and since you are reading in the context of the existence of the child, you can also assume that there is zero or one child record to consider in the sentence.

For the many-to-many relationship, the scheme is pretty much the same. As both entities are parents in this kind of relationship, you read the verb phrase written above the line from left to right and from right to left for the verb phrase written below it.

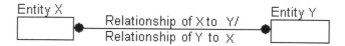

■**Tip** Getting people to take the time to define verb phrases can be troublesome, because they are not actually used in the implementation of the database. However, they make for great documentation, giving the reader a good idea of why the relationship exists and what it means.

Descriptive Information

We have drawn entities, assigned attributes and domains to them, and set up relationships between them, but this is not quite the end of the road yet. I have discussed naming entities, attributes, and the relationships, but even with well-formed names, there will still likely be confusion as to what exactly an attribute is used for.

We also need to add comments to the pictures in the model. When sharing the model, comments will let the eventual reader—and even yourself—know what you originally had in mind. Remember that not everyone who views the models will be on the same technical level: some will be nonrelational programmers, or indeed users or (nontechnical) product managers who have no modeling experience.

Descriptive information need not be in any special format. It simply needs to be detailed, up to date, and capable of answering as many questions as can be anticipated. Each bit of descriptive information should be stored in a manner that makes it easy for users to quickly connect it to the part of the model where it was used, and it should be stored either in a document or as metadata in a modeling tool.

You should start creating this descriptive text by asking questions such as the following:

- What is the object supposed to represent?

- How will the object be used?

- Who might use the object?

- What are the future plans for the object?

- What constraints are not specifically implied by the model?

The scope of the descriptions should not extend past the object or entities that are affected. For example, the entity description should refer only to the entity, and not any related entities, relationships, or even attributes unless necessary. An attribute definition should only speak to the single attribute and where its values might come from.

Maintaining good descriptive information is equivalent to putting decent comments in code. As the eventual database that you are modeling is usually the central part of any computer system, comments at this level are more important than any others. For example, say the following two entities have been modeled:

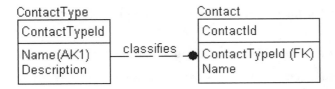

The very basic set of descriptive information in Tables 2-1 and 2-2 could be stored to describe the attributes created.

Table 2-1. *Entities*

Contact	Persons That Can Be Contacted to Do Business With
Attributes	**Description**
ContactId	Surrogate key
ContactTypeId	Primary key pointer to a contactType
Name	The full name of a contact

ContactType	Domain of Different Contact Types
Attributes	**Description**
ContactTypeId	Surrogate key
Name	The name that the contact type will be uniquely known as
Description	The description of exactly how the contact should be used as

Table 2-2. *Relationships*

Parent Entity Name	Phrase	Child Entity Name	Definition
ContactType	Classifies	Contact	Contact type classification. Was required by specifications.

Alternative Modeling Methodologies

In this section, I will briefly describe a few of the other modeling methodologies that you will likely run into frequently when designing databases for SQL Server 2005. You will see a lot of similarities among them—for example, most every methodology uses a rectangle to represent a table, and a line to indicate a relationship. You will also see some big differences among them, such as how the cardinality and direction of a relationship is indicated. Where IDEF1X uses a filled circle on the child end and an optional diamond on the other, one of the most popular methodologies uses multiple lines on one end and several dashes to indicate the same things.

All of the examples in this book will be done in IDEF1X, but knowing about the other methodologies may be helpful when you are surfing around the Internet, looking for sample diagrams to help you design the database you are working on. I will briefly discuss the following:

- *Information Engineering (IE)*: The other main methodology, commonly referred to as the *crow's feet* method

- *Chen Entity Relationship Model (ERD)*: The methodology used mostly in academic texts

- *Management Studio database diagrams*: The database object viewer that can be used to view the database as a diagram right in Management Studio

Information Engineering

The *Information Engineering* (IE) methodology is well known and widely used. It does a very good job of displaying the necessary information.

Tables in this method are basically the same as in IDEF1X, and they are denoted as rectangles. According to the IE standard, attributes are not shown on the model, but most models show them the same as in IDEF1X—as a list, although the primary key denoted by underlining the attributes, rather than the position in the table. (I have seen other ways of denoting the primary key, as well as alternate/foreign keys, but they are all very clear.) Where things get very different using IE is when dealing with relationships.

Just like in IDEF1X, IE has a set of symbols that have to be understood to indicate the cardinality and ownership of the data in the relationships. By varying the basic symbols at the end of the line, you can arrive at all of the various possibilities for relationships. Table 2-3 shows the different symbols that can be employed to build relationship representations.

Table 2-3. *Information Engineering Symbols*

Symbol	Relationship Type	Description
——<	Many	The entity on the end with the crow's foot denotes that there can be greater than one value related to the other entity.
——◇——	Optional	This symbol indicates that there does not have to be a related instance on this end of the relationship for one to exist on the other. This relationship has been described as zero-or-more as opposed to one-or-more.
——|——	Identifying	The key of the entity on the other end of the relationship is migrated to this entity.
- - - - -	Nonrequired	A set of dashed lines on one end of the relationship line indicates that the migrated key may be null.

Figures 2-11 through 2-14 show some examples of relationships in IE.

Figure 2-11. *One-to-many nonidentifying mandatory relationship*

Figure 2-12. *One-to-many identifying mandatory relationship*

Figure 2-13. *One-to-one identifying optional relationship*

Figure 2-14. *Many-to-many relationship*

I have never felt that this notation was as clean as IDEF1X, but it does a very good job and is likely to be used in some of the documents that you will come across in your work as a data architect. IE is also not always fully implemented in tools; however, the circle and the crow's feet are generally implemented properly.

■Tip You can find more details about the Information Engineering methodology in the book *Information Engineering, Books 1, 2, and 3* by James Martin (Prentice Hall, 1990).

Chen ERD

The Chen Entity Relationship Model (ERD) methodology is quite a bit different from IDEF1X, but it's pretty self-explanatory. You will seldom see this methodology anywhere other than in academic texts, but since quite a few of these types of diagrams are on the Internet, it's good to understand the basics of the methodology. Here's a very simple Chen ERD diagram:

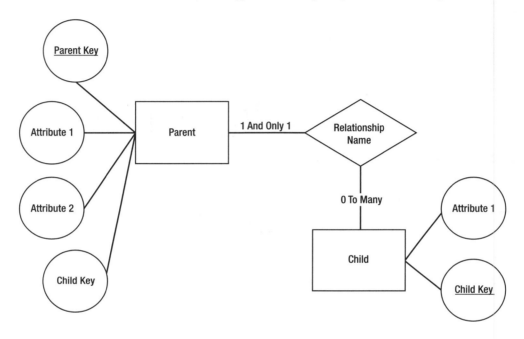

Each entity is again a rectangle; however, the attributes are not shown in the entity but are instead attached to the entity in circles. The primary key either is not denoted or, in some variations, is underlined. The relationship is denoted by a rhombus, or diamond shape.

The cardinality for a relationship is denoted in text. In the example, it is *1 and Only 1 Parent rows <relationship name> 0 to Many Child rows.*

The primary reason for including the Chen ERD format is for contrast. Several other modeling methodologies—for example, Object Role Modeling (ORM) and Bachman—implement attributes in this style, where they are not displayed in the rectangle.

While I understand the logic behind this approach (entities and attributes are separate things), I have found that models I have seen using the format with attributes attached to the entity like this seemed overly cluttered, even for very small diagrams. The methodology does, however, do an admirable job with the logical model and does not overrely on an arcane symbology to describe cardinality.

■**Note** You can find further details on the Chen ERD methodology in the paper "The Entity Relationship Model - Toward a Unified View of Data" by Peter Chen (http://www.cobase.cs.ucla.edu/pub/dblp/html/db/journals/tods/Chen76.html).

■**Note** While I am not saying that such a tool does not exist, I personally have not seen the Chen ERD methodology implemented in a mainstream database design tool other than some versions of Microsoft Visio. Many of the diagrams you will find on the Internet will be in this style, however, so it is interesting to understand at least the basics of the Chen ERD methodology.

Management Studio Database Diagrams

The database diagramming capability built into SQL Server 2005 is not really a good modeling tool, in my opinion. It can be a useful tool to view the structure of an existing database (a picture really *is* worth a thousand words!), but because it works directly against the implemented tables, it is not overly useful for design but only for the final implementation. You could do this design on an empty database, but it is seriously too clunky of a tool for design.

The following is an example of a one-to-many relationship in Management Studio:

The primary keys are identified by the little key in an attribute. The relationship is denoted by the line between the entities, with the one end having a key and the many end having an infinity sign.

You can display the entities in several formats by just showing the names of the entities or by showing all of the attributes with datatypes, for example:

Child *		
Column Name	Data Type	Allow Nulls
🔑 ChildId	int	☐
Attribute1	varchar(50)	☐
ParentId	int	☐
		☐

While the database diagram tool does have its place, it isn't a full-featured data modeling tool and shouldn't be used as such if you can avoid it. I am including coverage of the SQL Server modeling methodology here because it's included in SQL Server and in some situations it's the best tool you may have access to. It does give access to all implementation-specific features of SQL Server, including the ability to annotate your tables and columns with descriptive information. Unfortunately, if you decide to implement a relationship in a trigger, it will not know that the trigger exists. (I cover triggers in Chapter 6, so if you have no idea what a trigger is right now, don't worry.)

In most cases, the SQL Server tool isn't the optimal way to see actual relationship information that is designed into the database, but it does offer a serviceable look at the database structure when needed.

Note In the Business Intelligence tools for SQL Server 2005, there is also another tool that resembles a data model in the Data Source view. It is used to build a view of a set of tables, views, and (not implemented) queries for building reports from. It is pretty much self-explanatory as a tool, but it uses an arrow on the parent end of the relation line to indicate where a primary key came from. This tool is not pertinent to the task of building or changing a database, but I felt I should at least mention it briefly, as it does look very much like a data modeling tool.

Best Practices

The following are some basic best practices that can be very useful to follow when doing data modeling:

- *Entity names*: There are two ways you can go with these: plural or singular. I feel that names should be singular (meaning that the name of the table describes a single instance, or row, of the entity, much like an OO object name describes the instance of an object, not a group of them), but many other highly regarded data architects and authors feel that the table name refers to the set of rows and should be plural. Whichever way you decide to go, it's most important that you are consistent. Anyone reading your model shouldn't have to guess why some entity names are plural and others aren't.

- *Attribute names*: It's generally not necessary to repeat the entity name in the attribute name, except for the primary key. The entity name is implied by the attribute's inclusion in the entity. The chosen attribute name should reflect precisely what is contained in the attribute and how it relates to the entity. And as with entities, no abbreviations are to be used in the logical naming of attributes; every word should be spelled out in its entirety. If any abbreviation is to be used, due to some naming standard currently in place, for example, then a method should be put into place to make sure the abbreviation is used consistently, as discussed earlier in the chapter.

- *Relationships*: Name relationships with verb phrases, which make the relationship between a parent and child entity a readable sentence. The sentence expresses the relationship using the entity names and the relationship cardinality. The relationship sentence is a very powerful tool for communicating the purpose of the relationships with nontechnical members of the project team (e.g., customer representatives).

- *Domains*: Define domains for your attributes, implementing type inheritance wherever possible to take advantage of domains that are similar. Using domains gives you a set of standard templates to use when building databases that ensures consistency across your database and, if used extensively, all of your databases.

- *Objects*: Define every object so it is clear what you had in mind when you created a given object. This is a tremendously valuable practice to get into, as it will pay off later when questions are asked about the objects, and it will serve as documentation to provide to other programmers and/or users.

Summary

In this chapter I presented the basic process of graphically documenting the objects that were introduced in the first chapter. I focused heavily on the IDEF1X modeling methodology, taking a detailed look at the symbology that will be used through database designs. The base set of symbols outlined here will enable us to fully model logical databases (and later physical databases) in great detail.

The primary tool of a database designer is the data model. It's such a great tool because it can show the details not only of single tables at a time, but the relationships between several entities at a time. Of course it is not the only way to document a database; each of the following is useful, but not nearly as useful as a full-featured data model:

- Often a product that features a database as the central focus will include a document that lists all tables, datatypes, and relationships.

- Every good DBA has a script of the database saved somewhere for re-creating the database.

- SQL Server's metadata includes ways to add properties to the database to describe the objects.

I also briefly outlined the other types of model methodologies, such as Information Engineering, Chen ERD, and Microsoft Management Studio.

Now that we've considered the symbology required to model the database, I'll use data models throughout the book to describe the entities in the conceptual model (Chapter 3), the logical model (Chapter 4), and throughout the implementation presented in the rest of the book.

Conceptual Data Modeling

DILBERT: © Scott Adams/Dist. by United Feature Syndicate, Inc.

Ah, Mr. Adams, I wish you weren't so darn accurate sometimes. Too often database design projects have roots that make this cartoon seem tame in comparison. Trade magazines might be great tools to the discerning mind, but in the hands of a high-level manager, all the buzz words affect them just like whiteboard markers affect programmers: they make them euphoric to do "something." (It's a good thing whiteboard markers are nontoxic!)

When tasked to design a database system, you have to be mindful that users often aren't technologists. When tasked to implement a new system and the requirements need to be gathered, relying on users to know what they want, and how to implement it, is almost always complete folly. On the flip side, keep in mind that you're building a system to solve a business problem for the user (as well as the people who sign the checks), not for yourself, so you must consider what the user wants as well. There's an old saying that you shouldn't build users a Cadillac when all they want is a Volkswagen (though when this saying was coined, a VW wasn't quite as expensive as it is today). Even worse, though, is when you make your users a Cadillac when what they wanted was a dump truck. These two things are similar in that they're both vehicles, but they have very different uses.

This chapter is entitled "Conceptual Data Modeling" because the goal is to get the concepts for the final product down in a document, not the final model. We're still early in the process. In this book, my focus is on the database designer, but you also might have to gather requirements other than just those that are data related. This can be a hard task because of the (seemingly) conflicting needs of the database designer (data integrity) and the UI designer (useful interface that is easy to use), but they aren't conflicting needs in the end. No matter what, the most important need is to give users a useful interface that manipulates their data and maintains data integrity.

Understanding the Requirements

Without the designer having a solid understanding of the requirements, the system will be based on guesses. It isn't necessary to gather every requirement about every area of a large system initially; the system can be broken down into portions, often called *subject areas*. The size of the subject area is based upon the needs of the team and methodology used. For example, the Scrum methodology breaks down everything into 30-day units for design, coding, and testing. If that were your team's methodology, the subject area might be small. Just as common would be to break the design up into subject areas that are function oriented. For example, reasonable subject areas might be an accounts-payable module in an accounting system, or a user-management module for a website.

For gathering requirements, there are many tools and methodologies for documenting processes, business rules, and database structures. The Unified Modeling Language (UML) is one possible choice; the Microsoft Solutions Framework (which employs UML) another. There are also several model types in the IDEF family of methods; I'll employ the Entity-Relationship (E-R) modeling method IDEF1X to model databases. I won't be covering any of the actual modeling tools, but will rather be using a manual Spreadsheet method, which is by far the most common method of documenting requirements—even in medium-sized organizations where spending money on documentation tools can be harder than teaching your pet fish to play "fetch."

Regardless of the tools used to document the requirements, the needs for the database design process are the same. Specifications need to be acquired for the following:

- Entities and relationships

- Attributes and domains

- Business rules that can be enforced in the database

- Processes that require the use of the database

Without these specifications, you'll either have to go back to the client and ask a bunch of questions, or start making guesses. Although guessing wrong a few times is a good education in how not to do things, it's certainly no way to work efficiently (unless you guess right 99.9 percent of the time).

As a major part of this process, you'll produce a graphical model of the database. As stated in the previous chapter, I'll be using IDEF1X-based diagrams. In a real situation, it isn't uncommon to have the conceptual model done using Microsoft Visio but the logical model completed with a tool that's strictly used for data modeling, such as CA ERwin or Embarcadero ER/Studio. A general-purpose tool such as Visio is generally not as costly, and gives the analyst far greater leeway to build many different types of diagrams. Visio does have data modeling capabilities, but they're nowhere near as rich as with the data modeling-specific tools. Data modeling tools can be expensive to purchase for larger numbers of the staff, but they give you lots of great functionality that's useful for database design, and more importantly, implementation (code generation is the most important reason).

A word of caution when gathering requirements: common structures and solutions to problems will immediately come to mind and you might want to start coding right away. From experience, you might already have some idea of how to structure tables, and how to format the tables. Soon you stop listening to the client drone on about something to which you should be paying attention, and start hacking away. During the early parts of a project, figuring out the "what" and "why" comes first, then you can work on the "how." Once you know the details of what needs to be built, the process to get it built will be reasonably natural.

In this chapter, I'll get the project started by going through the following steps to determine what the database system will do:

- *Documenting the process*: I'll briefly introduce the types of concerns you'll have throughout the project process in terms of documenting requirements.

- *Looking for requirements*: Here I'll talk about the places to find information, and some techniques for mining this information.

- *Identifying objects*: You'll go through the documentation and build the conceptual model, and identify tables, relationships, and columns as they exist in the requirements.

- *Identifying business rules and processes*: You'll look for the rules that form the boundaries for our system usage, as well as common processes that need to be designed for.

- *Follow-up*: This section will cover the final steps in the conceptual design process, which center largely around communicating with the user to make sure that you don't just start building like crazy.

For those readers who are new to database design, you should initially follow the principles outlined in this chapter unaltered to ensure the best result for your project. Take care that I said "new to database design," not new to creating and manipulating tables in SQL Server. Although these two things are interrelated (I'll spend more than a third of this book looking at creating and manipulating tables in SQL Server), they can be quite different.

The process taken in this book will probably seem a bit rigid, and this is a valid argument. Must the process be so strict? Of course not, and most accomplished database designers are likely to acquire "shortcuts" that make sense, and that move quickly from requirements to logical model to implemented database. However, the results achieved are always far better the more methodically I take these preliminary steps prior to firing up SQL Server Management Studio and "building stuff." In my experience, the more time I spend on design, the less time I spend trying to go back and change my ideas to match the desires of the client.

■**Tip** Throughout the process of design and implementation, you'll no doubt find changes to the original requirements. Make sure to continue to update your documentation, because the best documentation in the world is useless if it's out of date.

Documenting the Process

Before going too deeply into gathering requirements or building a conceptual model, it's important to say a bit about documentation and communications with clients. If you've ever traveled to a place where no one speaks the same language as you, you know the feeling of being isolated based solely on communication. Everything everyone says sounds weird to you, and no matter how often you ask where the bathroom is, all you get is this blank look back. It has nothing to do with intelligence; it's because you aren't speaking the same language.

Information technology professionals and our clients tend to have these sorts of conversations, because frequently we technology types don't speak the same language as our clients. Clients tend to think in the language of their industry, and we tend to think in terms of computer solutions.

During this process of analysis, you should adopt one habit early on: document as much of the information that you acquire as reasonably possible. It's horrible to think about, but you might get hit by a bus tomorrow, and every bit of information in your head will be rendered useless while you recover. Less morbidly, if a project team member decides to take a month off, someone else will have to take over his or her work (it could be you!). So you should document, document, document, and do it during a meeting or immediately after it, or you risk forgetting vital details. It's imperative that you don't try to keep everything in your head, because even people with the best memory tend to forget the details of a project (especially if they're hit by that bus I talked about earlier).

The following are a few helpful tips as you begin to take notes on users' needs:

- Try to maintain a set of documents that will share system design and specification information. Important documents to consider include design-meeting notes, documents describing verbal change requests, and sign-offs on all specifications, such as functional, technical, testing, and so on.

- Beyond formal documentation, it's important to keep the members of your design team up to date and fully informed. Develop and maintain a common repository for all the information and keep it up to date.

- Note anywhere you add information that the users haven't approved.

- Set the project's scope early on and keep it in mind at all times. This will prevent the project from getting too big or diverse to be achievable within a reasonable period of time and be within the budget. (Hashing out changes that affect the budget early in the process will avoid future animosity!)

Once you document something, there's a crucial step: make sure the client agrees with your version of the documentation. As you go through the entire database design process, the client will no doubt change his mind on entities, data points, business rules, user interface, colors—just about anything that he can—and you have to prepare yourself for this. Whatever the client wants or needs is what you have to endeavor to accomplish. The client is in ultimate control of the project, and you have to be flexible enough to run with any proposed changes, whether minor or major (though they do need to be realistic).

Clients change their minds, and sometimes it seems to be a daily occurrence. Most frequently, they want more and more features. The common term for this is *scope creep*. The best way to avoid conflict is to make sure that you get your client's approval at regular stages throughout the design process. This is sometimes known as the principle of CYA, which I think has something to do with covering all your bases, though the letters probably have a more sinister meaning.

In addition to talking to the client, it's important to acquire as many notes, printouts, screen shots, CD-ROMs loaded with spreadsheets, database backups, Word documents, e-mails, handwritten notes, and so on that exist for any current solution to the problem. This data will be useful in the process of discovering data elements, screens, reports, and so on that you'll need to design into your applications. Often you'll find information in the client's artifacts that's invaluable when putting together the data model.

Requirements Gathering

One of the primary jobs of the design team is to specify a scope (mission statement or mission objectives) that describes what's supposed to be accomplished. The design team will likely consult this document during the design and implementation, and upon completion (and in many cases the scope changes at least a few times during the course of a project). However, if the project's objectives and aims aren't decided to some reasonable level early in the process, and nothing is written down, there's a strong chance that there will be conflicts between your design team and your clients as your ideas and theirs diverge, particularly when the invoices start to roll in. Vagueness or indecision might cause unnecessary discussions, fights, or even lawsuits later on in the process. So, make sure your clients understand what you're going to do for them, and use language that will be clearly understood, but that's specific enough to describe what you learn in the information-gathering process. This kind of process is beyond the scope of this book; I'll assume that it has been done by the business analysts.

Throughout the process of discovery, *artifacts* will be gathered and produced that will be used throughout the process of implementation as reference materials. Artifacts are any kind of physical documents that will be important to the design; for example, interview notes, e-mails, sample documents, and so on. In this section, I'll discuss the following types of artifacts or activities in some detail:

- Client interviews
- Prototypes and existing systems
- Various other types of documentation

By no means is this an exhaustive list of where to find and acquire documentation; in fact, far from it. The goal is simply to get your mind clicking and thinking of information to try to get the client to give you so your job will be easier.

Client Interviews

It's often the case that the person designing the data storage (commonly referred as the *data architect*) will never meet the user, let alone be involved in formal interviews. The project manager, business analyst, and system architect might provide all the required information. Other projects might only involve a data architect, or a single person wearing more hats than then the entire 4th Army on maneuvers. I've done it both ways: I've been in the early design sessions, and I've worked from documentation. The better the people you work with, the more pleasant the latter is. In this section, I'll talk quickly about the basics of client interviews, because on most any project you'll end up doing some amount of interviewing the client.

Client interviews are commonly where the project gets started. It's where the free, unstructured flow of information starts. However, it's also where the communication gap starts. Many clients generally think visually—in terms of forms, web pages, and simple user interfaces in particular. As the data architect, your job is to balance the customers' perceived need with their real need: a properly structured database that sits nicely behind a user interface. Changing a form around to include a new text box, label, or whatever, is a relatively simple task, giving the user the false impression that creating a database application is an easy process. If you want proof, make the foolish mistake of showing a user a near-finished prototype application with hard-coded values. The clients might be impressed that you've put together something so quickly and expect you to be nearly done. Rarely will they understand that what exists under the hood—namely the database and the middle-tier business objects— is where all main work takes place.

■Tip While visual elements are great places to find a clue to what data a user will want, as you go along in the process you'll want to be careful not to center your design around a particular interface. The structure of the data needs to be dictated on what the data means, not how it will be presented. Presentation is more of a interface design task, not a database design one. You can present the data in many different ways using SQL.

Brainstorming sessions can also yield great results for gathering a lot of information at once, as long as the group doesn't grow too large. The key here is to make sure that someone is facilitating the meeting and preventing the "alpha" person from beating up on the others and giving only his or her own opinions. Treat information from every person interviewed as important, as each person will likely have different viewpoints. Sometimes the best information comes not from the executive, but from the person who does the work. Don't assume that the first person speaks for the rest, even if they're all working on the same project or if this individual is the manager (or even president or owner of a major corporation, though a great amount of tact is required sometimes to walk that tightrope).

In many cases, when the dominant person cannot be controlled, or the mousey person cannot be prodded into getting involved, one-on-one sessions allow clients to speak their mind, without untimely interruptions from colleagues. Be mindful of the fact that the loudest and boldest people might not have the best ideas and the quiet person who sits at the back and says nothing might have the key to the entire project. Make sure to at least consider everybody's opinions.

The more that's written down and filed away, rather than just committed to memory, the more information will be available later after 20 long, sleepless weeks, so the clients can verify the information by reviewing it. This means that not only can you improve relations with your clients, but you also enhance your chances of identifying the data that they'll want to see again, as well as provide the design team with the information required to design the final product.

This part of the book is written with the most humility, because I've made many mistakes in this part of the design process. The client interview is one of the most difficult parts of the process that I've encountered. It might not seem a suitable topic for experienced analysts, but even the best of us need to be reminded that jumping the gun, bullying the clients, telling them what they want before they tell you, and even failing to manage the user's expectations can lead to the ruin of even a well-developed system. If you have a shaky foundation, the final product will likely be shaky as well.

Questions to Be Answered

The following are some questions that are important to the database design aspects of a system's development. Again, this isn't an exhaustive list, but it's certainly enough to get you started.

What Data Is Needed?

If the data architect is part of the design session (other than the one-person team), some data is clearly needed for the system. Most users, at a high level, know what data they want to see out of the system. For example, if they're in accounting, they want to see dollars and cents summarized by such-and-such a group.

How Will the Data Be Used?

Knowing what your client is planning to use the data in the system for is an important piece of information indeed. Not only will you understand the process, but you can also begin to get a good picture of the type of data that needs to be stored.

For example, imagine you're asked to create a database of contacts for a dental office. You might want to know the following:

- Will the contact names be used just to make phone calls, like a quick phone book?

- Will the client be sending e-mail or posting to the members of the contact lists? Should the names be subdivided into groups for this purpose?

- Will the client be using the names to solicit a response from the mail, such as appointment reminders?

- Is it important to have family members documented? Do they want to send cards to the person on important dates?

What Rules Govern the Use of the Data?

Taking our previous example of contacts, you might discover the following:

- Every contact must have a valid e-mail address.

- Every contact must have a valid street address.

- The client checks every e-mail address using a mail routine, and the contact isn't a valid contact until this routine has been successfully executed.

- Contacts must be subdivided by the type of issues they have.

It's important not to infer too many rules from documentation. At least be sure and confirm them with the client before assuming them to be true. Something might seem obvious to you, but could be wrong (business rules are far too often made to be broken). Although you might guess, at least write things down in your documentation in a form that the client can access.

Case in point: what is a "valid" e-mail address? Well, it's the e-mail address that accurately goes with the contact. Sure, but how on earth do you validate that? Fact is, you don't. Usually this means that something like the e-mail address is valid, in that it has an ampersand character between other characters, and a dot (.) between one or more alphanumeric values (such as %@%.%, plus all characters between A and Z, or 0 and 9), but the value is completely up to interpretation.

If you're too strict, your final product might be unacceptable because you've placed a rule on the data that the client doesn't want, or you've missed a rule that the client truly needs. I made this mistake once, which torpedoed a system for a long time. Rules that *seemed* like they were always to be enforced were easy for their users to override, based on their client's desires. Unfortunately, our program didn't make it easy for the user to override these rules, so teeth were gnashed and sleep was lost fixing the problem (even worse, it was a fixed-bid contract, and it cut into our possible bonus).

Some rules might have another problem: the client wants the rule, but it isn't possible or practical to implement it. For example, the client might request that all registered visitors of the client's website have to insert a valid mobile phone number, but is it certain that visitors would provide this data? And what is a valid mobile number? How can you validate that—by format alone, or does it have to be checked? What if users provide a land line instead?

Who Will Use the Data?

The answer to the question of who will use the data might indicate other people who might need to be interviewed, and will likely be of importance when you come to define the security for the system.

What Do You Want to See on Reports?

Reports are often one of the most frequently forgotten parts of the design process. Many novice developers leave implementing them until the last minute (a mistake I've made more than once over the years). However, users are probably more interested in the reports that are generated from the data than anything else you do. Reports are used as the basis of vital decision making and can make or break a company.

Looking back at the contact example, what name does the client want to see on the reports?

- First name, last name

- First name, middle name, last name

- Last name, first name

- Nickname

It's important to try to nail such issues down early, no matter how small or silly they seem to you. They're important to the client, who you should always remember is paying the bill.

From a database design standpoint, the content of the reports is extremely important, as it might help to discover data requirements that aren't otherwise thought of. Avoid being concerned with the physical design of the reports yet, as it might lead to the temptation of coding and away from modeling.

■Tip Don't overlook existing reports. They're the most important part of any system, and you'll often discover that clients have important data in reports that they never even think about when they're expressing needs. One of my company's clients is rebuilding its database systems, and it has hundreds of reports currently in production.

Where Is the Data Now?

It would be nice once in a while to have the opportunity to create a totally new database with absolutely no pre-existing data. This would make life so easy. Unfortunately, this is almost never the case, except possibly when building a product to be sold to end users in a turn-key fashion (then the pre-existing data is their problem, or yours if you purchase their system). Most of the time you have to consider converting existing data that's important to the end users.

Every organization is different. Some have data in one location, while others have it scattered in many locations. Rarely, if ever, is the data already in well-structured databases that you can easily access. If that were the case, why would the client come to you at all? Clients typically have data in the following sundry locations:

- *Mainframe or legacy servers*: Millions of lines of active COBOL still run many corporations.

- *Spreadsheets*: Spreadsheets are wonderful tools to view, slice, and dice data, but are inappropriate places to maintain complex databases. Most users know how to use a spreadsheet as a database but, unfortunately, are not so experienced in ensuring the integrity of their data.

- *Desktop databases such as Microsoft Access*: Desktop databases are great tools and are easy to deploy and use. However, this often means that these databases are constructed and maintained by nontechnical personnel and are poorly designed, potentially causing many problems when the databases have to be enlarged or modified.

- *Filing cabinets*: Many companies still have few or no computers and maintain vast stockpiles of paper documents. Your project might simply be to replace a filing cabinet with a computer-based system, or to supply a simple database that logs the physical locations of the existing paper documents.

Data that you need to include in the SQL Server database you're designing will come from these and other weird and wonderful sources that you discover from the client. Truth is commonly stranger than fiction. Of course, spreadsheets and filing cabinets don't enforce data integrity (and often desktop database and mainframe applications don't do a perfect job either), so this can be a clue to be prepared for dirty data that will have to be cleaned up before storage in your nice new database.

Will the Data Need to Be Integrated with Other Systems?

Once you have a good idea of where the client's important data is located, you can begin to determine how the data in your new SQL Server solution will interact with the data that will stay in its original format. This might include building intricate gateway connections to mainframes, linked server connections to other SQL Servers or Oracle boxes, or even linking to spreadsheets. You can't make too many assumptions about this topic at this point in your design. Just knowing the architecture you'll need to deal with can be helpful later in the process.

How Much Is This Data Worth?

It's also important to place value judgments on data. In some cases, data will have great value in the monetary sense. For example, in the dental office example that will be presented later in this chapter, the value lies in the record of what has been done to the patient, and how much has been billed to the patient and his or her insurance company. Without this documentation, it might take hours and days to dig this data out, and eventually get paid for the work done. This data has a specific monetary value, because the quicker the payment is received, the more interest is drawn, meaning more profits. If the client shifts the turnover of payments from one month to one week due to streamlining the process, this might be worth quite a bit more money.

On the other hand, just because existing data is available doesn't necessarily mean that it should be included in the new database. The client needs to be informed of all the data that's available, and should be provided with a cost estimate of transferring it into the new database. The cost of transferring legacy data can be high, and the client should be offered the opportunity to make decisions that might conserve funds for more important purposes.

Existing Systems and Prototypes

If you're writing a new version of a current database system, then access to the existing system can be both a blessing and a curse. Obviously, the more information you can gather about how any previous system and its data was previously structured, the better. All the screens, data models, object models, user documents, and so on are important to the design process.

However, unless you're simply making revisions to an existing system, often the old database system is only reasonable as a reference point for completeness, not as an initial blueprint. On most occasions, the existing system you'll be replacing will have many problems that need to be fixed, not emulated. If it has no problems, why are you replacing an existing system?

Prototypes from the early design process might also exist. Prototypes can be useful tools to communicate how to solve a real-world problem using a computer, or when you're trying to reengineer how a current process is managed. Their role is to be a "proof of concept"—an opportunity to flesh out with the design team and the end users the critical elements of the project on which success or failure will depend.

The real problem with prototypes is that the database they're built upon is rarely worth anything. So, by the time database design starts, you might be directed to take a prototype database that has been hastily developed and "make it work" or, worse yet, "polish the database up." Indeed, you might inherit an unstructured, unorganized prototype, and your task will be to turn it into a production database.

Bear in mind that you should only consider prototypes as interactive pictures to get the customer to sign a contract with your company. Sometimes you might be hired to implement the prototype (or the failed try at a production system that's now being called a prototype) that another consultant was hired to create (or worse yet, an employee that still works there and has a chip on his shoulder the size of a large African elephant). It's better to start from scratch, developing the final application using structured and supported design and coding standards. As a data architect, you must work as hard as possible to use prototype code *only* as a working model—a piece of documentation that you use to enhance your own design. Prototypes help you to be sure you're not going to miss out on any critical pieces of information that the users need—such as a name field, a search operation, or even a button (which might imply a data element)—but they may not tell you anything about the eventual database design at all.

Other Types of Documentation

Apart from interviews and existing systems, you can look to other sources to find data rules and other pieces of information relevant to the design project. Often the project manager will obtain these documents.

Request for Quote or Request for Proposal

Two of the primary documents are as follows:

- *Request for Quote (RFQ)*: A document with a fairly mature specification, which an organization sends out to firms to determine how much something would cost

- *Request for Proposal (RFP)*: For less mature ideas that an organization wishes to expand on using free consulting services

A copy of an RFP or an RFQ needs to be added to the pile of information that you'll need later on in the process. Although these documents generally consist of sketchy information about the problem and the desired solution, you can use them to confirm the original reason for wanting the database system and for getting a firmer handle on what types of data are to be stored within it.

No matter what, if you can get a copy of these documents, you'll be able to see the client's thought pattern and why the client wants a system developed.

Contracts or Client Work Orders

Getting copies of the contract can seem like a fairly radical approach to gathering design information, depending on the type of organization you're with. Frankly, in a corporate structure, you'll likely have to fight through layers of management to make them understand why you need to see the contract at all. Contracts can be inherently difficult to read due to the language they're written in. However, be diligent in filtering out the legalese, and you'll uncover a basic set of requirements for the database system—requirements that you must fulfill exactly or you might not get paid.

What makes the contract so attractive is simple. It is, generally speaking, the target you'll be shooting at. No matter what the client says, or what the existing system was, if the contract specifies that you deliver some sort of water craft, and you deliver a motorcycle because the lower-level clients change their minds without changing the contract, your project could still be deemed a failure (figuratively speaking of course, since who doesn't like motorcycles?).

Level of Service Agreement

One important section of contracts that's important to the design process is the required level of service. This might specify the number of pages per minute, the number of rows in the database, and so on. All this needs to be measured, stored, tested for, and so on. When it comes to the optimization phase, knowing the level of service can be of great value. You may also find some data that needs to be stored to validate that a service level is being met.

Don't Forget About Audits

When you build a system, you must consider whether the system is likely to be audited in the future, and by whom. Government, ISO 9000 clients, and other clients that are monitored by standards organizations are likely to have strict audit requirements. Other clients also have financial audit processes. These audit plans might contain valuable information that can be used in the design process.

Reports, Forms, and Spreadsheets

A large percentage of computer systems are built around the filling out of forms—government forms, company forms, all kinds of forms. You can guarantee that all this data is going to be scattered around the company, and it's imperative to find it *all*. It's virtually certain that these sources will contain data that you'll need for your project, so make sure that the client gives you all such items.

It's kind of ironic that I only spend such a small amount of text on this topic, because it will take up a good amount of your time. There are so many forms—new forms, old forms, proposed forms, and so on. Dealing with forms is a simple thing, but depending on the size of the user community, and the number of reports and screens in an application, it can be a long process indeed. Every distinct physical piece of output that you can find that the existing system produced will be useful.

One system I'm working on has well over 800 distinct reports (hopefully by the time this book is published I will refer to it as the "successful project"). It was a terrible mess to catalog all the reports, and thankfully the job of several of my colleagues. It was a tedious process, but essential. The information retrieved from those reports helps to run the business.

Identifying Objects and Processes

The process of discovery is theoretically complete at this point. Someone has interviewed all the relevant clients, documented the outcome, and gathered artifacts ranging from previous system documentation, to sketches of what the new system might look like, to prototypes, to whatever is available. Now the fun part starts: sifting through all the documentation and looking for database entities and attributes. In the rest of this chapter I'll introduce the following processes:

- *Identifying entities*: Looking for all the "things" that need to be modeled in the database.

- *Identifying relationships between entities*: Relationships between entities are what make entities useful. Here the goal is to look for natural relationships between high-level entities.

- *Identifying attributes and domains*: Looking for the individual data points that describe the entities.

- *Identifying business rules*: Looking for the boundaries that are applied to the data in the system that go beyond the domains of a single attribute.

- *Identifying fundamental processes*: Looking for different processes (code and programs) that the client tends to execute that are fundamental to its business.

■Note I'm going to approach this process in a linear manner, identifying all entities first, all attributes next, and so on. In a real situation, you'll likely look for all at the same time.

Identifying these items is the most difficult part of the process, because as technical people, our deep-down desire is to "build stuff." I know I didn't start writing SQL code with a mind to read loads of mind-numbing documentation. But if you tear off and start designing structures and writing code, you'll likely find out that you missed something that gave you deep insight into the client's structures, and that you might have to restructure your solution. When you waste time doing that once, you don't want to repeat the process.

Throughout the rest of the chapter, the following example piece of documentation will be used as the basis of our examples. In a real system, this might be just a single piece of documentation that has been gathered. (It always amazes me how much useful information you can get from a few paragraphs.)

The client manages a couple dental offices. One is called the Chelsea Office, the other the Downtown Office. The client needs the system to manage its patients and appointments, alerting the patients when their appointments occur, either by e-mail or phone, and then assisting in the selection of new appointments. The client wants to be able to keep up with the records of all the patients' appointments without having to maintain lots of files. The dentists might spend time at each of the offices throughout the week.

For each appointment, the client needs to have everything documented that went on, and then invoice the patient's insurance, if he or she has insurance (otherwise the patient pays). Invoices should be sent within one week after the appointment. Each patient should be able to be associated with other patients in a family for insurance and appointment purposes. We will need to have an address, phone number (home, mobile, and/or office), and optionally an e-mail address associated with each family, and possibly each patient if the client desires. Currently the client uses a patient number in its computer system that corresponds to a particular folder that has the patient's records.

The system needs to track and manage several dentists, and quite a few dental hygienists who the client needs to allocate to each appointment as well. The client also wants to keep up with its supplies, such as sample toothpastes, toothbrushes, and floss, as well as dental supplies. It has had problems in the past keeping up with when it's about to run out of supplies, and wants this system to take care of this for both locations. For the dental supplies, we need to track usage by employee, and especially any changes made in the database to patient records.

Through each of the following sections, our goal will be to acquire all the pieces of information that need to be stored in our new database system. Sounds simple enough, eh? Well, although it's much easier than it might seem, it takes time and effort (two things every programmer has in abundance, right?).

Identifying Entities

Entities are the most straightforward objects to identify while you're scanning through documentation. Entities generally represent people, places, objects, ideas, or things referred to grammatically as nouns. For example, our dental office includes the following:

- *Person*: A patient, a doctor, hygienist, and so on

- *Place*: Dental office, patient's home, the hospital

- *Object*: A dental tool, stickers for the kids, toothpaste

- *Idea*: A document, insurance, a group (such as a security group for an application), the list of services provided, and so on

There's clearly overlap in several of the categories (for example, a building is a "place" or an "object"). It isn't critical to identify that an entity is a person, place, object, or idea. However, if it fits nicely within a specific group, it can help to assign some attributes, such as a name for a person or an address for the location of a building.

Things will be classified as people, places, and objects, and this will help to define some basic information needed later when defining attributes. Also, this will help to ensure that all the documentation necessary is located to describe each entity.

Tip How an entity is implemented in a table might be different from the initial entities you specify. It's better not to worry about this at this stage in the design process—you should try hard not to get too wrapped up in the eventual database implementation. This sounds simple enough, but can be the hardest thing to do. When building the initial design, you want the document to come initially from what the user wants. Then you'll fit what the user wants into a common mold later if possible. However, at this point, a change in the design is a mouse click away, because all you're doing is specifying the foundation; hopefully the rest of the house hasn't been built yet.

Let's look at each of these types of entities and see what kinds of things can be discovered from the documentation sample in each of the aforementioned entity types.

People

Nearly every database needs to store information about people. Most databases have at least some notion of users (generally thought of as people, though not always). As far as real people are concerned, a database might need to store information about many different types of people. For instance, a school's database might have a `student` entity, a `teacher` entity, and an `administrator` entity.

In our example, four people entities can be found—patients, dentists, hygienists, and employees:

*. . . the system to manage its **patients** . . .*

Also

*. . . manage several **dentists**, and quite a few dental **hygienists** . . .*

Patients are clearly people, as are hygienists and dentists (yes, even the evil ones are people). Because they're people, specific attributes can be inferred (such as that they have names, for example).
Also

*. . . we need to track usage by **employee** . . .*

Dentists and hygienists have already been mentioned. It's clear that they'll be employees as well. For now, document that there are four new entities: patients, hygienists, dentists, and employees. Our model starts out as shown in Figure 3-1.

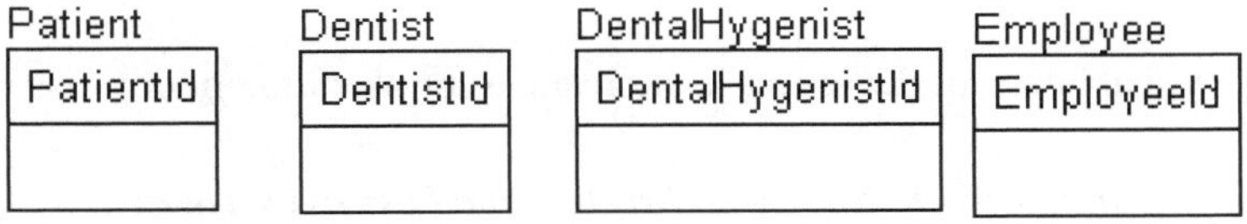

Patient   Dentist   DentalHygenist   Employee
| PatientId | | DentistId | | DentalHygenistId | | EmployeeId |

Figure 3-1. *Four new entities*

■**Tip** Note that I have started with giving each entity a surrogate key. This serves as the placeholder while I do the modeling, particularly to make it more clear when I start relating tables to one another. This isn't a required practice at all, but a shorthand I use to show ownership of the relationship in the conceptual and logical model.

Places

Users will want to store information in many different types of places. One obvious place entity is in our sample set of notes:

*. . . manages a couple dental **offices** . . .*

From the fact that these are places, later we'll be able to infer that there's address information about the office, and probably phone numbers, staffing concerns, and so on. It also gives us an idea that the two offices aren't located too close to each other, so there might be business rules about having appointments at different offices, or even preventing the situation in which a dentist might be scheduled at two places at one time. "Inferring" is just slightly informed guessing, so verify all inferences with the client.

I add the Office entity to the model, as shown in Figure 3-2.

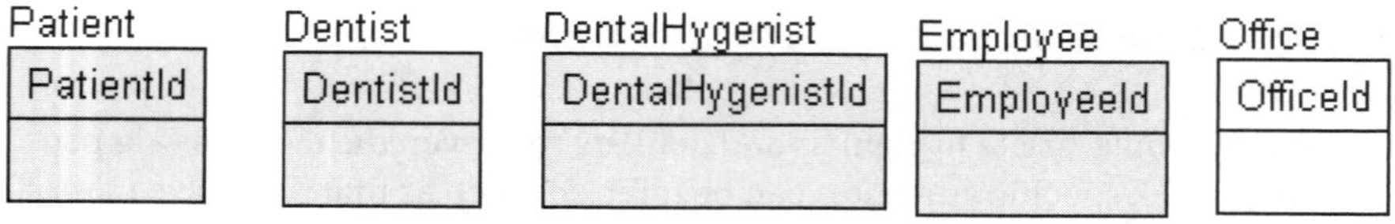

Figure 3-2. *Added Office as an entity*

■**Note** In the models, things that haven't changed from the previous step in the process are colored in gray, while new things aren't colored at all.

Objects

Objects refer primarily to physical items. In our example, there are a couple different objects:

> . . . *with its* **supplies**, *such as sample toothpastes, toothbrushes, and floss, as well as* **dental supplies** . . .

Supplies, such as sample toothpastes, toothbrushes, and floss, as well as dental supplies, are all things that the client needs to run its business. Obviously most of the supplies will be simple, and the client won't need to store a large amount of descriptive information about them. For example, it's possible to come up with a pretty intense list of things you might know about something as simple as a tube of toothpaste:

- *Tube size*: Perhaps the length of the tube, or amount in grams

- *Brand*: Colgate, Crest, or some off brand

- *Format*: Metal tube, pump, and so on

- *Flavor*: Mint, bubble gum (uck), cinnamon

- *Manufacturer information*: Batch number, expiration date, and so on

This could go on and on, but it's unlikely that the users will have business need for this information, because they probably just have a box of whatever they have and give it out to all their patients. This process of design is one abstraction, as is the process to abstract their real working environment down to something manageable by only modeling things that are of actual business interest. To do this, apply "selective ignorance" to the process and ignore the different attributes of things that have no business interest.

Only one entity is necessary—Supply—but document that "Examples given were sample items, such as toothpaste or toothbrushes, plus there was mention of dental supplies. These supplies are the ones that the dentist and hygienists use to perform their job."

So I add the Supply entity to the model, as shown in Figure 3-3.

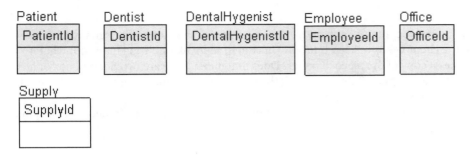

Figure 3-3. *Added the Supply entity*

Ideas

No law requires that entities should be real objects or even exist physically. At this stage of discovery, you need to consider information on objects that the user wants to store that don't fit the already established "people," "places," and "objects" categories, and which might or might not be physical objects.

For example, consider the following:

> *. . . and then invoice the patient's **insurance**, if he or she has insurance (otherwise the **patient pays**) . . .*

Insurance is an obvious important entity, but another looks like a verb, rather than a noun. The phrase "patient pays" tends to infer that there might be some form of payment entity to deal with.

■**Tip** Not all entities will be adorned with a sign flashing "Hey buddy, I am an entity!" A lot of the time, you'll have to read into what has been documented and sniff it out like a pig on a truffle.

The model now looks like Figure 3-4.

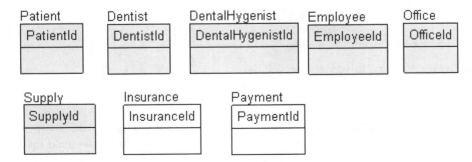

Figure 3-4. *Added the Insurance and Payment entities*

Documents

For many, the term "documents" normally refers to tangible pieces of paper containing information that the client needs to keep track of. This might seem like splitting hairs, but what if someone makes a copy of the piece of paper? Does that mean there are two documents, or are they both the same document? Usually it isn't the case, but sometimes people do need to track physical pieces of paper.

On the other hand, most of the time, even though it's a piece of paper, it merely represents something intangible:

> . . . and then invoice the patient's insurance, if he or she has insurance (otherwise the patient pays) . . .

Invoices are pieces of paper (or e-mails) that are sent to a customer after the services have been rendered. However, no mention was made as to how invoices are delivered. They could be e-mailed or postal mailed—it isn't clear—nor would it be prudent for the database design to force it to be done either way unless this is a specific business rule. At this point, just identify the entities and move along; again, it usually isn't worth it to spend too much time guessing how the data will be used. This is something you should interview the client for.

> . . . appointments, **alerting** the patients when their appointments occur, either by e-mail or phone . . .

This type of document almost certainly isn't delivered by paper, but by an e-mail message or phone call. The e-mail is also used as part of another entity, an Alert. The alert can either be an e-mail or phone alert.

Next we add the Invoice and Alert entities to the model, as shown in Figure 3-5.

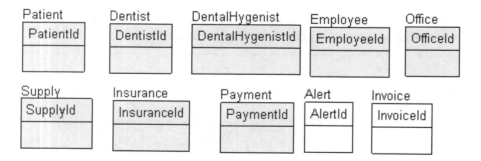

Figure 3-5. *Added the Alert and Invoice entities*

Groups

Another idea-type entity is a group of things, or more technically, a grouping of entities. For example, you might have a club that has members, or certain types of products that make up a grouping that seems more than just a simple attribute. In our sample we have one such entity:

*Each patient should be able to be associated with other patients in a **family** for insurance and appointment purposes.*

Although a person's family is an attribute of the person, it's more than that. So we add a `Family` entity, as shown in Figure 3-6.

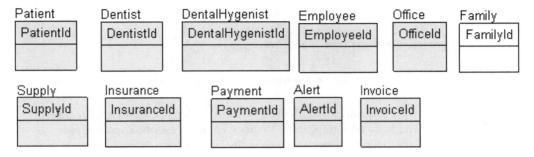

Figure 3-6. *Added the Family entity*

Other Entities

The following sections outline some additional common objects that are perhaps not as obvious as the ones that have been presented. They don't always fit a simple categorization, but they're pretty straightforward.

Audit Trails

Audit trails, generally speaking, are used to track changes to the database. You might know that the RDBMS uses a log to track changes, but this is off limits to the average user. So in cases where the user wants to keep up with who does what, entities need to be modeled to represent these logs. They would be analogous to a sign in/out sheet, or a library card (remember those?) with which users check books out and back in, or just a list of things that went on in any order.

Consider the following example:

For the dental supplies, we need to track usage by employee, and especially any changes made in the database to the patient records.

In this case, the client clearly is keen to keep up with the kinds of materials that are being used by each of its employees. Perhaps a guess can be made that the user needs to be documented when dental supplies are taken (the difference between dental supplies and nondental supplies will certainly have to be discussed in due time). Also, it isn't necessary at this time that the needed logging be done totally on a computer, or even by using a computer at all.

A second example of an audit trail is as follows:

*For the dental supplies, we need to track usage by employee, **and especially any changes made in the database to the patient records**.*

A typical entity that you need to define is the audit trail or a log of database activity, and this entity is especially important when the data is sensitive. An audit trail isn't a normal type of entity, in that it stores no user data, and as such, should generally be deferred to the implementation design stage. The only kinds of entities to be concerned with at this point are those that users wish to store in directly. As such, you shouldn't deal with these types of statements at this stage, but leave them until the implementation phase.

Events

Event entities generally represent verbs or actions:

> For each **appointment**, the client needs to have everything documented that went on . . .

An appointment is an event, in that it's used to record information about when patients comes to the office and have something done to them. For most events, appointments included, it's important to have a schedule of when the event is (or was) and where the event will occur. It's also not uncommon to want to have data that documents an event's occurrence (what was done, how many people attended, and so on). Hence, many event entities will be tightly related to some form of document entity. In our example, appointments are more than likely scheduled for the future, and when the appointment occurs, a record of what was done is made, so the dentist can get paid.

There are all sorts of events to look for beyond the obvious examples, such as meter readings, weather readings, equipment measurements, and so on. Note that an event isn't necessarily so grand a thing that it has to have people attend it. It's just something that happens at a given point in time—an occurrence.

Records and Journals

The last of the entity types to examine at this stage is a record or journal of activities. Note that I mean "record" in a nondatabase sort of way. A record could be any kind of activity that a user might previously have recorded on paper. In our example, the user wants to keep a record of each visit:

> The client wants to be able to keep up with the **records of all the patients'** appointments without having to maintain lots of files.

This kind of thing is one of the main advantages of building database systems: eliminating paper files, and making data more accessible. How many times must I tell the doctor what medicines I'm taking, all because her files are insane clutters used to cover her billing process, rather than being a useful document of my history? Covering one's self by doing due diligence is fine, but by leveraging the RDBMS, the information our computer systems are constantly gathering comes alive, and trends can be seen instantly in ways it would take hours to see on paper.

This is another entity type that's similar to an audit log, but would potentially contain more information, such as notes about a contact, rather than just a record that a contact had taken place.

The model after the changes looks like Figure 3-7.

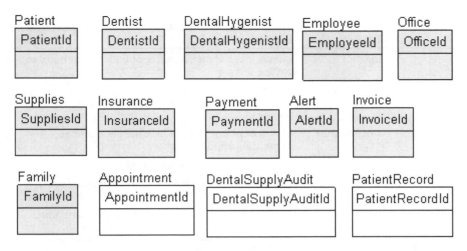

Figure 3-7. *Added the Appointment, DentalSupplyAudit, and PatientRecord entities*

Entity Recap

So far we've discovered the following list of preliminary entities. It makes a pretty weak model, but this will change in the next section as we begin adding attributes.

Before progressing any further, stop, define, and document the entities, as shown in Table 3-1.

Table 3-1. *Entity Listing*

Entity	Type	Description
Patient	People	The people that are the customers of the dental office. Services are performed, supplies are used, and patients are billed for them.
Family	Idea	A group of patients grouped together for convenience.
Dentist	People	People who do the most important work at the dental office. Several dentists are working for the client's practice.
Hygienists	People	People who do the basic work for the dentist. There are quite a few more hygienists than dentists. *(Note: Check with client to see if there are guidelines for the number of hygienists per dentist. Might be needed for setting appointments.)*
Employee	People	Any person who works at the dental office. Dentists and hygienists are clearly a type of employee.
Office	Places	Locations where the dentists do their business. They have multiple offices to deal with and schedule patients for.
Supplies	Objects	Examples given were sample items, such as toothpaste or toothbrushes, plus there was mention of dental supplies. These supplies are the ones that the dentist and hygienists use to perform their job.
Insurance	Idea	Used by patients to pay for the dental services–rendered work.

continued

Table 3-1. *Continued*

Entity	Type	Description
Payment	Idea	Money taken from insurance or patients (or both) to pay for services.
Invoice	Document	A document sent to the patient or insurance company explaining how much money is required to pay for services.
Alert	Document	E-mail or phone call made to tell patient of an impending appointment.
Dental Supply Audit	Audit Trail	Used to track the usage of dental supplies.
Appointment	Event	The event of a patient coming in and having some dental work done.
Patient Record	Record	All the pertinent information about a patient, much like a patient's chart in any doctor's office.

Implementation modeling note: Log any changes to sensitive/important data.

The descriptions are based on the facts that have been derived from the preliminary documentation. Note that the list of entities that have been specified are directly represented in the customer's documentation.

Relationships Between Entities

Next I'll present relationships between entities. Here the idea is to find how each of the entities will work with one another to solve the client's needs. I'll start first with the one-to-N type of relationships, then the many-to-many. It's also important to consider elementary relationships that aren't directly mentioned in your requirements, but be careful not to make too many inferences at this point in the process.

One-to-N Relationships

In each of the one-to-N (commonly one-to-one or one-to-many) relationships, the table that is the "one" table in the relationship is considered the parent, and the "N" is the child or children.

The one-to-N relationship is frequently used in implementation, but is uncommonly encountered during early database design. The reason for this is that most of the natural relationships that users tell you about turn out to be many-to-many relationships.

I'll classify some of our relationships as has-a or is-a, but not all will fit in this mold. I'll present examples of each type in the next couple sections.

The "Has-A" Relationship

The main special type of relationship is the "has-a" relationship. It's so named because the parent table in the relationship has one or more of the child entities employed as attributes of the parent. In fact, the "has-a" relationship is the way you implement an attribute that often occurs more than once.

In our example paragraph, consider the following:

> *. . . then invoice the **patient's insurance**, if he or she has insurance . . .*

In this case, the relationship is between the Patient entity and the Insurance entity. It's an optional relationship, because it says "if he or she has insurance." Add the following relationship to the model, as shown in Figure 3-8.

Figure 3-8. *Added the relationship between the Patient and Insurance entities*

Another example of a "has-a" relationship is found in the following example:

*Each **patient** should be able to be associated with other patients in a **family** for insurance and appointment purposes.*

In this case, we identify that a family has patients. Although this sounds odd, it makes perfect sense in the context of a medical office. Instead of maintaining ten different insurance records for families of ten, the client wishes to have a single one where it makes sense. So, it can be inferred that

Each patient should be able to be associated with other patients in a family for insurance and appointment purposes.

Family is covered by insurance is also a possible relationship in Figure 3-9. It has already been specified that patients have insurance. This isn't unlikely, because even if a person's family has insurance, one of the members might have an alternative insurance plan. It also doesn't contradict our earlier notion that patients have insurance, although it does give them two different paths to identify the insurance. This isn't necessarily a problem, but when two insurance policies exist, you might have to decide which one takes precedence. Again, this is something to discuss with the client, and probably not something to start making up.

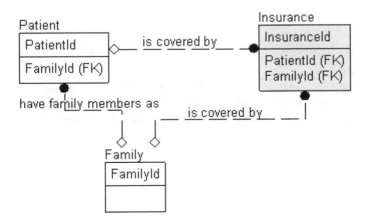

Figure 3-9. *Relationships added between the Patient, Insurance, and Family entities*

Here's another example of a has-a relationship, shown in Figure 3-10:

> ... **dental offices** ... *The client needs the system to manage its patients and* **appointments** ...

In this case, make a note that each dental office will have appointments. Clearly an appointment can only be for a single dental office, so this is a has-a relationship. One of the attributes of an event type of entity is a location. It's unclear at this point whether or not a patient only comes to one of the offices, or if the patient can float between offices. This will be a question for the clients when you go back to get clarification on your design.

Now add the relationship shown in Figure 3-10.

Figure 3-10. *Relationship added between the Office and Appointment entities*

The "Is-A" Relationship

The idea behind an "is-a" relationship is that the child entity in the relationship extends the parent. For example, cars, trucks, RVs, and so on are all types of vehicles, so a car *is a* vehicle. The cardinality of this relationship is always one-to-one, as the child entity simply contains more specific information that qualifies this extended relationship. The reason for having this sort of relationship is conceptual. There would be some information that's common to each of the child entities (stored as attributes of the parent entity), but other information that's specific to each child entity (stored as attributes of the child entity).

In our example, the following snippets exist:

> ... *manage several* **dentists**, *and quite a few* **dental hygienists** *who the client* ...

and

> ... *track usage by employee, and especially* ...

From these statements, you can see there are three entities, and there's a relationship between them. A dentist is an employee, as is a dental hygienist. There are possibly other employees for whom the system needs to track supply usage as well. Figure 3-11 represents this relationship.

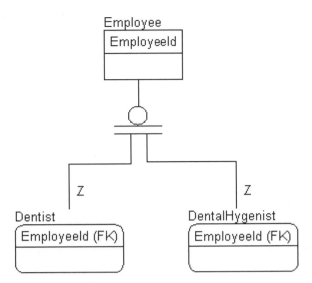

Figure 3-11. *Identified subtyped relationship between the Employee, Dentist, and DentalHygenist entities*

■**Note** Because the subtype manifests itself as a one-to-one identifying relationship (remember from Chapter 2, the Z on the relationship line indicates a one-to-one relationship), separate surrogate keys for the `Dentist` and `DentalHygienist` entities aren't needed.

Many-to-Many Relationships

Many-to-many relationships are far more prevalent than you might think. In fact, as you refine the model, a great number of relationships may end up being many-to-many relationships as the real relationship between entities is realized. However, early in the design process, only a few many-to-many relationships might be recognized. In our example, one is obvious:

> *The dentists might spend time at each of the offices throughout the week.*

In this case, multiple dentists can work at more than one dental office. A one-to-many relationship won't suffice; it's wrong to state that one dentist can work at many dental offices, because this implies that each dental office has only one dentist. The opposite, that one office can support many dentists, implies dentists only work at one office. Hence, this is a many-to-many relationship (see Figure 3-12).

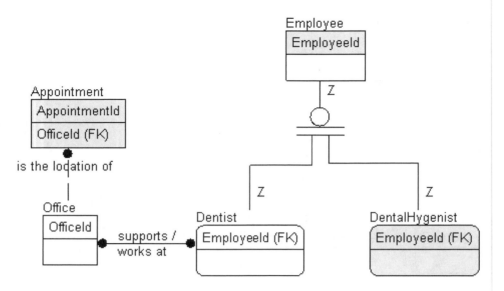

Figure 3-12. *Added a many-to-many relationship between Dentist and Office*

An additional many-to-many relationship that can be identified is:

. . . dental supplies, we need to track usage by employee . . .

This quote says that multiple employees can use different types of supplies, and for every dental supply, multiple types of employees can use them. However, it's possible that controls might be required to manage the types of dental supplies that each employee might use, especially if some of the supplies are regulated in some way (such as narcotics).

The relationship shown in Figure 3-13 is added.

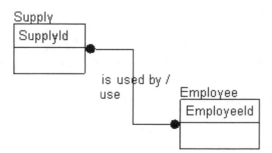

Figure 3-13. *Added a many-to-many relationship between the Supply and Employee entities*

I'm also going to remove the DentalSupplyAudit entity, because it's clear from this diagram that this entity is a report (in a real situation you'd ask the client to make sure, but in this case I'm the client, and I agree).

Listing Relationships

Figure 3-14 shows the model so far.

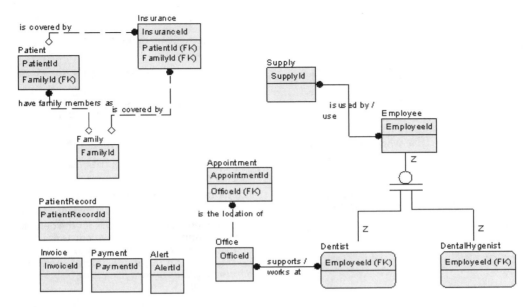

Figure 3-14. *The model so far*

There are other relationships in the text that I won't cover explicitly, but I've documented them in the descriptions in Table 3-2, which is followed by the model with relationships identified, and the definitions of the relationships in our documentation (note that the relationship is documented at the parent only).

Table 3-2. *Initial Relationship Documentation*

Entity	Type	Description
Patient	People	The persons that are the customers of the dental office. Services are performed, supplies are used, and they are billed for them.
	Is covered by Insurance	Identifies when the patient has personal insurance.
	Is reminded by Alerts	Alerts are sent to patients to remind them of their appointments.
	Is scheduled via Appointments	Appointments need to have one patient.
	Is billed with Invoices	Patients are charged for appointments via an invoice.
	Makes Payment	Patients make payments for invoices they receive.
	Has activity listed in PatientRecord	Activities that happen in the doctor's office.

continued

Table 3-2. *Continued*

Entity	Type	Description
Family	Idea	A group of patients grouped together for convenience.
	Has family members as Patients	A family is made up of multiple patients.
	Is covered by Insurance	Identifies when there's coverage for the entire family.
Dentist	People	Persons who do the most important work at the dental office. There are several dentists working for the client's practice.
	Works at many Offices	Dentists can work at many offices.
	Is an Employee	Dentists have some of the attributes of all employees.
	Do work during Appointments	Appointments might require the services of one dentist.
Hygienists	People	Persons who do the basic work for the dentist. There are quite a few more hygienists than dentists. *(Note: Check with client to see if there are guidelines for the number of hygienists per dentist. Might be needed for setting appointments.)*
	Is an Employee	Hygienists have some of the attributes of all employees.
	Have Appointments	All Appointments need to have at least one hygienist.
Employee	People	Any person who works at the dental office. Dentists and hygienists are clearly a type of employee.
	Use Supplies	Employees use supplies for various reasons.
Office	Places	Locations where the dentists do their business. They have multiple offices to deal with and schedule patients for.
	Is the location of Appointments	Appointments are made for a single office.
Supplies	Objects	Examples given were sample items, such as toothpaste or toothbrushes, plus there was mention of dental supplies. These supplies are the ones that the dentist and hygienists use to perform their job.
	Are used by many Employees	Employees use supplies for various reasons.
Insurance	Idea	Used by patients to pay for the dental services rendered.
Payment	Idea	Money taken from insurance or patients (or both) to pay for services.
Invoice	Document	A document sent to the patient or insurance company explaining how much money is required to pay for services.

Table 3-2. *Continued*

Entity	Type	Description
	Has Payments	Payments are usually made to cover costs of the invoice (some payments are for other reasons).
Alert	Document	E-mail or phone call made to tell patient of an impending appointment.
Appointment	Event	The event of a patient coming in and having some dental work done.
PatientRecord	Record	All the pertinent information about a patient, much like a patient's chart in any doctor's office.

Figure 3-15 shows how the model has progressed.

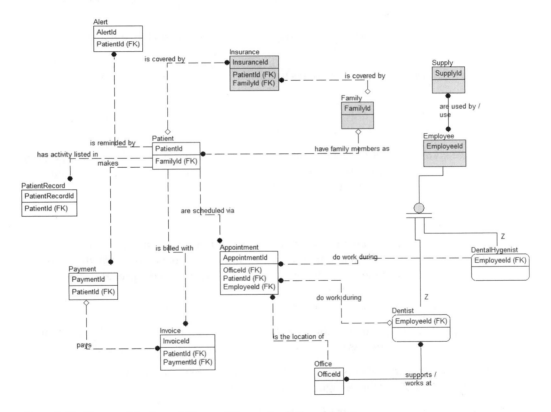

Figure 3-15. *The model after adding entities and relationships*

Identifying Attributes and Domains

Next, the goal is to look for items that identify, make up, and describe the entity you're trying to represent, or—to put this into more computing-like terms—the properties of an entity. For example, if the entity is a person, attributes might include driver's license number, Social

Security number, hair color, eye color, weight, spouse, children, mailing address, and e-mail address. Each of these things serves to represent the entity in part.

Identifying which attributes to associate with an entity requires a similar approach to identifying the entities themselves. You can frequently find attributes by noting adjectives that are used to describe an entity you have previously found. Some attributes will simply be discovered because of the type of entity they are (person, place, and so on).

Domain information for an attribute is generally discovered at the same time as the attributes, so at this point you should identify domains whenever you can conveniently locate them.

Following is a list of some of the common types of attributes to look for during the process of identifying attributes and their domains:

- *Identifiers*: Any information used to identify a single instance of an entity. This is loosely analogous to a key, though identifiers won't always make proper keys.

- *Descriptive information*: Information used to describe something about the entity, such as color, amounts, and so on.

- *Locators*: Identify how to locate what the entity is modeling, such as a mailing address, or on a smaller scale, a position on a computer screen.

- *Related information*: Data that relates to the entity, such as websites, family members, automobiles, and so on.

- *Values*: Things that quantify something about the entity, such as monetary amounts, counts, dates, and so on.

As was true during our entity search, these aren't the only places to look for attributes, but they're a good place to start. The most important thing for now is that you'll look for values that make it more clear *what* the entity is modeling.

Identifiers

The reason to start looking for attributes with identifiers is that they're the most important. Every entity needs to have at least one identifying attribute or set of attributes. Without attributes, there's no way that different objects can be identified later on in the process. These identifiers are keys, as defined in Chapter 1.

For example, here are some common examples of good identifiers:

- *For people*: Social Security numbers (in the USA), full names (not always a perfect identifier), or other IDs (such as customer numbers, employee numbers, and so on)

- *For transactional documents (invoices, bills, computer-generated notices)*: These usually have some sort of number assigned for tracking purposes

- *For books*: The ISBN numbers (titles aren't unique)

- *For products for sale*: Product numbers for a particular manufacturer (product names aren't unique)

- *For companies that clients deal with*: These are commonly assigned a customer/client number for tracking

- *For buildings*: The complete address including ZIP/postal code

- *For mail*: The addressee's name and address, and the date it was sent

There are many more examples, but by now you should understand what identifiers mean. Thinking back to the relational model stuff back in Chapter 1, each instance of an entity must be unique. Identifying unique natural keys in the data is the first step in implementing a design.

Make certain that what you think of as a unique item is actually unique. Look at people's names. To us they're almost unique, but there are hundreds of Louis Davidsons in the United States, and that isn't a common name. Thousands, if not millions, of John Smiths are out there!

In our example, the first such example of an identifier is found in this phrase:

*The client manages a couple dental offices. One is **called** the **Chelsea Office**, the other the **Downtown Office**.*

Usually when something is given a name such as this, it's a good attribute to identify the entity, in our case Name for Office. This makes it a likely candidate for a key because it's unlikely that the client has two offices that it refers to as its "Downtown Office," as that would be confusing. So I add the following attribute to the Office entity in the model (shown in Figure 3-16). I'll create a generic domain for these types of generic names, for which I generally choose 60 characters as a reasonable length. This isn't a replacement for validation, as the client might have specific size requirements for attributes, though most of the time the client doesn't have a clear idea at design time.

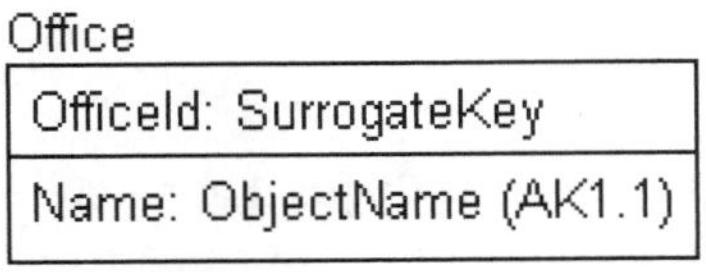

Office

| OfficeId: SurrogateKey |
| Name: ObjectName (AK1.1) |

Figure 3-16. *Added the Name attribute to the Office entity*

Another identifier is found here:

Currently the client uses a patient number in its computer system that corresponds to a particular folder that has the patient's records.

Hence, the system needs a patient number attribute for the Patient entity. Again, this is one of those places where querying the client for the specifications of the patient number is a good idea. For this reason, I'll create a specific domain for patient number that can be tweaked if needed. The client is using eight-character–long patient numbers from the existing system, on further discussion with the client (see Figure 3-17).

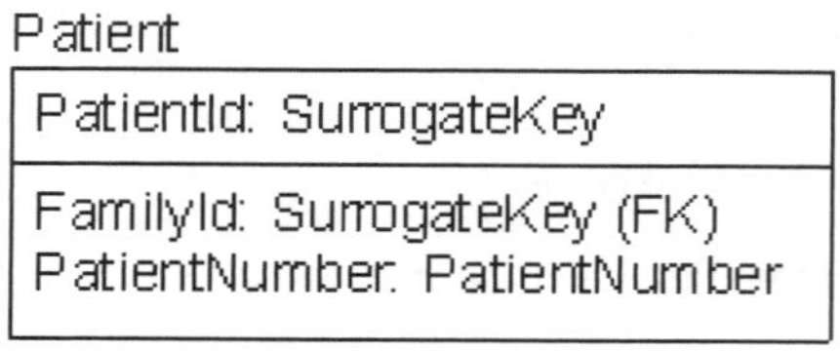

Patient

PatientId: SurrogateKey
FamilyId: SurrogateKey (FK) PatientNumber: PatientNumber

Figure 3-17. *Added the PatientNumber attribute to the Patient entity*

■**Note** I used the name `PatientNumber` in this entity, even though it repeated the name of the table. I did this because it's a common term to the client. Just like the term `PurchaseOrderNumber` is common, or `DriversLicenseNumber`, its meaning sticks out to the client. No matter what your naming standards, it's generally best to make sure that terms that are common to the client appear as the client normally uses them.

For the most part, it's usually easy to discover an entity's identifier, and this is especially true for the kinds of naturally occurring entities that you find in user-based specifications. Most everything that exists naturally has some sort of way to differentiate itself, although differentiation can become harder when you start to dig deeper. (It's easy to differentiate between toothpaste and floss, but how to differentiate between two different tubes of toothpaste? And do you really care? It's clear that no one cares which tube of toothpaste is given to little Johnny, but this knowledge might be more important when it comes to the narcotics that might be distributed. More discussion with the client would be necessary, but my point is that differentiation isn't always simple.)

Descriptive Information

Descriptive information is usually easy to find. Adjectives used to describe things that have been previously identified as entities are common, and will usually point directly to an attribute. In our example, different types of supplies are identified, namely sample and dental:

> . . . *their supplies, such as **sample** toothpastes, toothbrushes, and floss, as well as **dental** supplies.*

Another thing you can identify is the possible domain of an attribute. In this case, the attribute is "Type Of Supply," and the domain seems to be "Sample" and "Dental." Hence I create a specific special domain: SupplyType (see Figure 3-18).

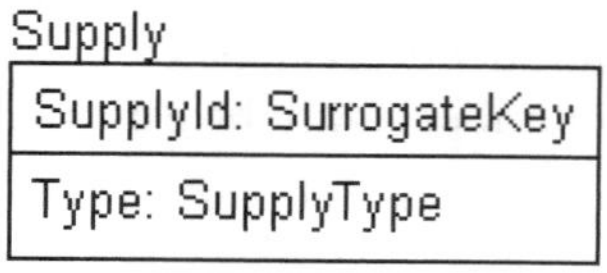

Supply

SupplyId: SurrogateKey
Type: SupplyType

Figure 3-18. *Added the Type attribute to the Supply entity*

Locators

The concept of a locator is not unlike the concept of a key, except that instead of talking about locating something within the electronic boundaries of our database, the locator finds the geographic location or position of something.

For example, the following are examples of locators:

- *Mailing address*: Every address leads us to some physical location on earth, such as a mailbox at a house, or even a post office box in a building.

- *Geographical references*: Things such as longitude and latitude, or even textual directions on how to get to some place.

- *Phone numbers*: Although you can't always pinpoint a physical location using the phone number, you can use it to locate a person.

- *E-mail addresses*: As with phone numbers, you can use these to locate and contact a person.

- *Coordinates of any type*: These might be a location on a shelf, pixels on a computer screen, an office number, and so on.

Anything that's a place is bound to have one or more of these attributes, as a nonmoving target can always be physically located with an address or geographic coordinates. Figure 3-19 shows an example of a implied locator, which I'm implying from the following bit of text from our sample document:

. . . manages a couple dental offices . . .

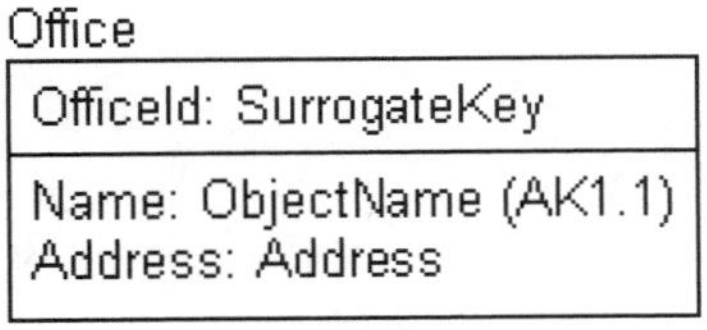

Office

| OfficeId: SurrogateKey |
| Name: ObjectName (AK1.1)
Address: Address |

Figure 3-19. *Added an Address attribute to the Office entity*

Because an office is a place, it must have an address where it's located. Hence, the dental Office entity will also have an attribute for the specific location information about the different offices. Each office can only have one address that identifies its location, so the address is a specific locator. Also important is that the domain for this address be a physical address, not a post office box.

However, places aren't the only things you can locate. People are locatable as well. In this loose definition, a person's location can be a temporary location or a contact that can be made with the locator, such as addresses, phone numbers, or even something like GPS coordinates, which might change quite rapidly. In this next example, there are three typical locators:

*. . . have an **address**, **phone number** (home, mobile, and/or office), and optionally an **e-mail address** associated with each family, and possibly patient if the client desires . . .*

Most customers, in this case the dental victims—er, patients—have phone numbers, addresses, and e-mail address attributes. The dental office uses these to locate and communicate with the patient for many different reasons; for example, billing, making and canceling appointments, and so on. Note also that many families don't live together, because of college, divorce, and so on, but you might still have to associate them for insurance and billing purposes. From these factors you get these sets of attributes on families and patients; see Figure 3-20.

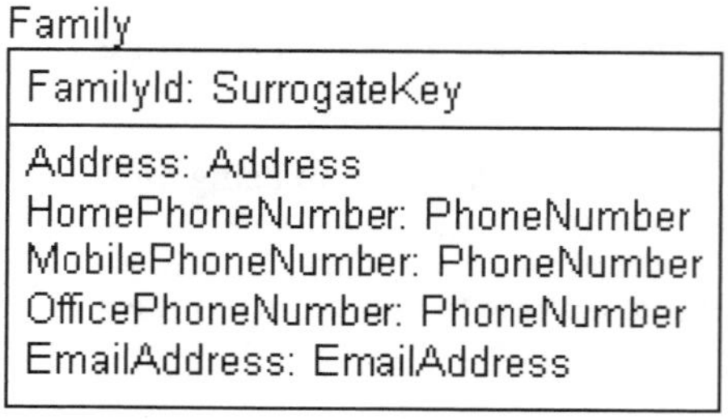

Family

FamilyId: SurrogateKey
Address: Address HomePhoneNumber: PhoneNumber MobilePhoneNumber: PhoneNumber OfficePhoneNumber: PhoneNumber EmailAddress: EmailAddress

Figure 3-20. *Added location-specific attributes to the Family entity*

The same is found for the patients, as shown in Figure 3-21.

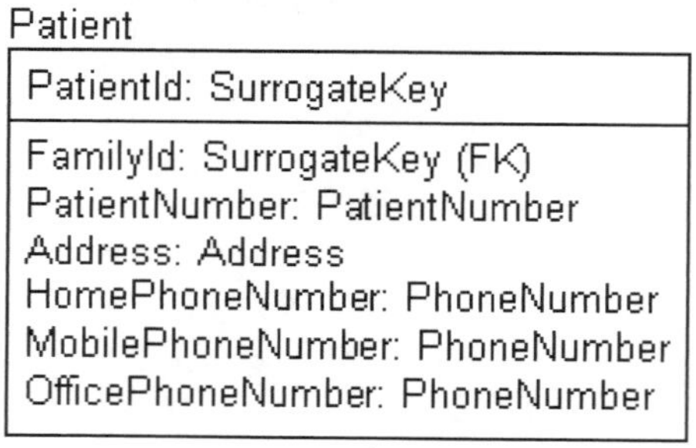

Patient

PatientId: SurrogateKey
FamilyId: SurrogateKey (FK) PatientNumber: PatientNumber Address: Address HomePhoneNumber: PhoneNumber MobilePhoneNumber: PhoneNumber OfficePhoneNumber: PhoneNumber

Figure 3-21. *Added location-specific attributes to the Patient entity*

This is a good place to mention one of the major differences between a column and an attribute. An attribute doesn't have any specific requirement for its shape. It might be a scalar value, it might be a vector, and it might be a table in and of itself. A column in your implemented database needs to fit a certain mold of being a scalar or fixed vector and nothing else. In conceptual modeling, the goal is documentation. The normalization process shapes all our attributes into the proper shape for implementation in our relational database.

It's enough in conceptual modeling to realize that when users see the word "address" in the context of this example, they think of a generic address used to locate a physical location. In this manner, you can avoid any discussion of how the address is implemented, not to mention all the different address formats that might need to be dealt with when the address attribute is implemented later in the book.

Related Data

In some cases (though not in our example), we'll need related information as attributes for our entities. Some examples of this might be as follows:

- *Additional materials*: Anywhere that you have an entity that describes a book or some other type of media (think http://www.amazon.com), you'll likely want to list additional resources that the user can also look up.

- *Websites, FTP sites, or other assorted web resources*: You'll often need to identify the website of an entity, or the URL of a resource that's identified by the entity; such information would be defined as attributes.

Savvy readers will realize that in some cases, related data often turns out to need more tables and more relationships. I'll leave this area untouched for now, because Chapter 4, on normalization, goes through this process in detail.

Values

Numbers are some of the most powerful attributes, because often math is performed with them. If you get a text value wrong, such as the color of a person's eyes, that isn't a great problem. However, get the number of dependents wrong for a person, and his or her taxes will be messed up. Or get your wife's weight wrong on a form, and she might just beat you with some sort of cooking device (sad indeed).

Values are generally numeric, such as the following examples:

- *Monetary amounts*: Financial transactions, invoice line items, and so on

- *Quantities*: Weights, number of products sold, counts of items (number of pills in a prescription bottle), number of items on an invoice line item, number of calls made on a phone, and so on

- *Other*: Wattage for light bulbs, size of a TV screen, RPM rating of a hard disk, maximum speed on tires, and so on

Numbers are used all around as attributes, and are generally important. They're also likely candidates to have domains chosen for them to make sure that their values are reasonable. If you were writing a package to capture tax information about a person, you would almost certainly want a domain to state that the count of dependents must be greater than or equal to zero. You might also want to set a likely maximum value, such as 30. It might not be a hard and fast rule, but it would be a sanity check, because most people don't have 30 dependents (well, most sane people). Domains don't have to be hard and fast rules at this point (only the hard and fast rules will likely become database constraints, but they have to be implemented somewhere).

In our example paragraphs, there's one such attribute:

*The client manages a **couple** dental offices.*

The question here is what attribute this would be. In this case, it turns out it won't be a numeric value, but instead some information about the cardinality of the dental Office entity.

Relationship Attributes

Every relationship that's identified might imply bits of data to support it. For example, consider a common relationship such as Customer pays Invoice. Simple enough; this implies a relationship between the Customer entity and the Invoice entity. But the relationship implies that an invoice needs to be paid, hence (if you didn't know what an invoice was already) it's now known that an invoice has some form of amount attribute.

As an example in our database, in the relationship Employees use supplies for various reasons, the "for various reasons" part may lead us to the related-information type of attribute. What this tells us is that the relationship isn't a one-to-many relationship between Person and Supplies, but it is a many-to-many relationship between them. However, it does imply that an additional entity may later be needed to document this fact, since it's desired to identify more information about the relationship.

■**Tip** Don't fret too hard that you might miss something essential early in the conceptual design. Often the same entity, attribute, or relationship will crop up in multiple places.

A List of Entities, Attributes, and Domains

Figure 3-22 shows the conceptual graphical model as it stands now.

The following table shows the entities, along with descriptions and column domains. The attributes of an entity are indented within the Entity/Attribute column (I've removed the relationships found in the previous document for clarity). Note I've taken the list a bit further to include all the entities I've found in the paragraphs, and will add the attributes to the model after the list is complete.

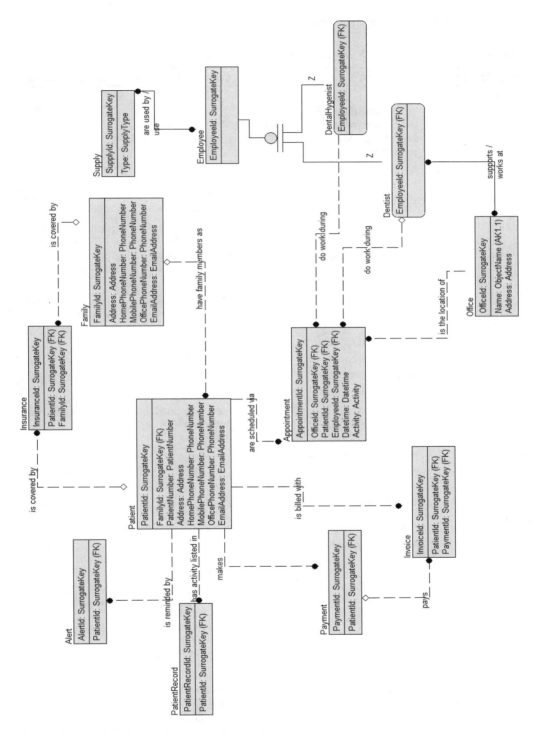

Figure 3-22. *Graphical model of the patient system*

Table 3-3 lists the descriptive metadata.

Table 3-3. *Final Model for the Dental Office Example*

Entity/Attribute	Description	Column Description	Column Domain
Patient	The persons that are the customers of the dental office. Services are performed, supplies are used, and they are billed for them.		
PatientNumber		Used to identify a patient's records, in the computer and on the chart	Unknown, generated by current computer system
HomePhoneNumber		Phone number to call patient at home	Any valid phone number
MobilePhoneNumber		Phone number to call patient away from home	Any valid phone number
OfficePhoneNumber		Phone number to call patient during work hours *(Note: Do we need to know work hours for the patient?)*	Any valid phone number
Address		Postal address of the family	Any valid address
EmailAddress		Electronic mail address of the family	Any valid e-mail address
Family	Groups of persons who are associated, likely for insurance purposes.		
HomePhoneNumber		Phone number to call patient at home	Any valid phone number
MobilePhoneNumber		Phone number to call patient away from home	Any valid phone number
OfficePhoneNumber		Phone number to call patient during work hours *(Note: Do we need to know work hours for the patient?)*	Any valid phone number
Address		Postal address of the family	Any valid address
EmailAddress		Electronic mail address of the family	Any valid e-mail address

Table 3-3. *Continued*

Entity/Attribute	Description	Column Description	Column Domain
	FamilyMembers	Patients that make up a family unit	Any patients *(Note: Can patient only be a member of one family?)*
Dentist	Persons who do the most important work at the dental office. There are several dentists working for the client's practice.		
Hygienists	Persons who do the basic work for the dentist. There are quite a few more hygienists than dentists. *(Note: Check with client to see if there are guidelines for the number of hygienists per dentist. Might be needed for setting appointments.)*		
Employee	Any person who works at the dental office. Dentists and hygienists are clearly a type of employee.		
Office	Locations where the dentists do their business. They have multiple offices to deal with and schedule patients for.		
	Address	Physical address where the building is located	Address that is not a PO box
	Name	The name used to refer to a given office	Unique
Supply	Examples given were sample items, such as toothpaste or toothbrushes, plus there was mention of dental supplies. These supplies are the ones that the dentist and hygienists use to perform their job.		
	Type	Classifies supplies into different types	"Sample" or "Dental" identified
Insurance	Used by patients to pay for the dental services rendered work.		
Payment	Money taken from insurance or patients (or both) to pay for services.		
Invoice	A document sent to the patient or insurance company explaining how much money is required to pay for services.		

continued

Table 3-3. *Continued*

Entity/Attribute	Description	Column Description	Column Domain
	SentTo	To whom the invoice was sent	"Insurance" or "Patient"
Alert	E-mail or phone call made to tell patient of an impending appointment.		
	Type	How the alert is to be sent	"E-mail," "Home Phone," "Mobile Phone," or "Office Phone"
	SendTo	The patient that the alert is sent to	Any patient
Appointment	The event of a patient coming in and having some dental work done.		
	DateTime	The point in time when the appointment will start, or started	Valid date
	Activity	Identifies the different procedures and examinations that a patient has had during an appointment	

Implementation modeling note: Log any changes to sensitive or important data. The relationship between employees and supplies will likely need additional information to document the purpose for the usage.

Note Consider the use of the term "any valid." The scope of these statements needs to be reduced to a reasonable form. (In other words, what does "valid" mean? Having valid dates means that there might be invalid dates. This in turn could mean the "November 31st" kind of invalid, or that it isn't valid to schedule an appointment during the year 1000 BC. Common sense can take us a long way, but computers seriously lack common sense without human intervention.)

Many databases that store phone numbers and addresses cannot cope with all the different formats used in all regions of the world, mainly because it is no simple task. What will be handled must be programmed into the software.

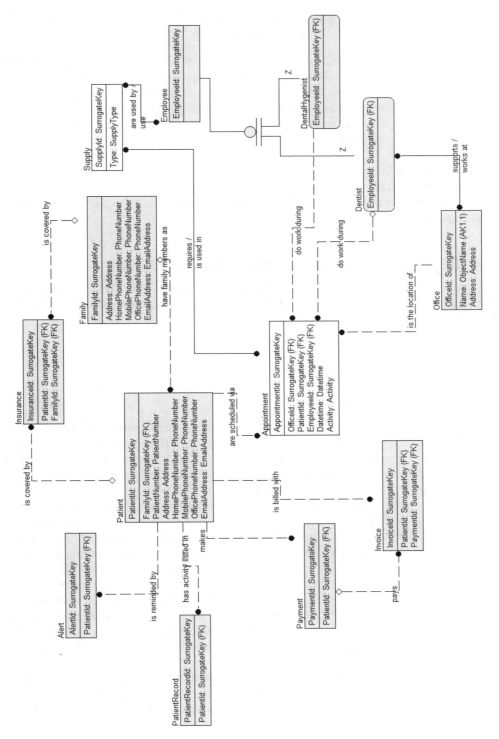

Figure 3-23. *Model with all entities, attributes, and relationships*

Note that I added another many-to-many relationship between Appointment and Supply to document that supplies are used during appointments. Figure 3-23 shows the final graphical model.

At this point, the entities and attributes have been defined. Note that nothing has been added to the design that wasn't explicitly stated in the requirement artifacts. When doing this kind of activity in a "real" setting, all the steps of finding entities, relationships, attributes would be handled at one time. In this chapter, I've performed the steps in a deliberate, step-by-step process only to focus on one at a time to make the process more clear. If this had been a real design session, whenever I found something to add to the model, I would have added it immediately.

It might also be interesting to note that the document is now several pages long—all from analyzing three small paragraphs of text. When you do this in a real project, the resulting document will be much larger, and there will likely be quite a bit of redundancy in much of the documentation.

Identifying Business Rules and Processes

In this section, the process moves from defining the structural parts of the conceptual database design to the parts that cause us to define some of the constraints and usage of the data. I'll introduce the following concepts:

- Identifying business rules

- Identifying fundamental processes

Identifying Business Rules

Business rules can be defined as statements that govern and shape business behavior. Depending upon an organization's methodology, these rules can be in the form of bulleted lists, simple text diagrams, or other formats. A business rule's existence doesn't imply the ability to implement it in the database at this point in the process. The goal is to get down all data-oriented rules for use later in the process.

When defining business rules, there might be some duplication of rules and attribute domains, but this isn't a real problem at this point. Get as many rules as possible documented, as missing business rules will hurt you more than missing attributes, relationships, or even tables. You'll frequently find new tables and attributes when you're implementing the system, usually out of necessity, but finding new business rules at a late stage can wreck the entire design, forcing an expensive rethink or an ill-advised "kludge" to shoehorn them in.

Recognizing business rules isn't generally a difficult process, but it is time consuming and fairly tedious. Unlike entities, attributes, and relationships, there's no straightforward, specific clue for identifying all the business rules. However, my general practice when I have to look for business rules is to read documents line by line, looking for sentences including language such as "once . . . occurs," ". . . have to . . . ," ". . . must . . . ," ". . . will . . . ," and so on. However, documents don't always include every business rule. You might look through a hundred or a thousand invoices and not see a single instance where a client is credited money, but this doesn't mean that it never happens. In many cases, you have to mine business rules from two places:

- *Old code*: It's the exception, not the rule, that an existing system will have great documentation. Even the ones that start out with wonderful system documentation tend to have their documentation grow worse and worse as time grows shorter and client desires grow. It isn't uncommon to run into poorly written spaghetti code that needs to be analyzed.

- *Client experience*: Using human memory for documentation can be as hard as asking teenagers what they did the night before. Claims of forgetting, or simply making up stuff that they think you want to hear, is just part of human nature. I've already touched on how difficult it is to get requirements from users, but when you get into rules, this difficulty grows by at least an order of magnitude because most humans don't think in details, and a good portion of the business-rules hunt is about minute details.

Getting business rules from either of these sources is rarely on the top of the list of things to do on a Saturday night or even on a Monday morning. If you're lucky, you'll be blessed by a business analyst who will take care of this process, but in a lot of cases the business analyst won't have the programming experience to ferret out subtle business rules from code, and a programmer will have to handle this task. That's not to mention that it's hard to get to the minute details until you understand the system.

In our "snippet of notes from the meeting" example, a few business rules need to be defined. For example, I've already discussed the need for a customer number attribute, but was unable to specify a domain for the customer number. Take the following sentence:

For each appointment, the client needs to have everything documented that went on . . .

You can derive a business rule such as this:

For every appointment, it is required to document every action on the patient's chart so it can be charged.

Note that this rule brings up the likelihood that there exists yet another attribute of a patient's chart—Activity—and another attribute of the activity—ActivityPrices. This relationship between Patient, PatientRecord, Activity, and ActivityPrices gives you this feeling that it might be wrong. It *is* wrong, very wrong. Normalization corrects this sort of dependency (see, I promised in the last chapter that it would come up again). It's logical that there exists an entity for activities with attributes of name and price, and relates them back to the PatientRecord entity that has already been created. Either way is acceptable during conceptual modeling, as long as it makes sense to the readers of the documents. I'll go ahead and add an Activity entity with a name and a price for this requirement.

Another sentence in our example suggests a further possible business rule:

The dentists might spend time at each of the offices throughout the week.

Obviously a doctor cannot be in two different locations at one time. Hence the following rule:

Doctors must not be scheduled for appointments at two locations at a time.

Another rule that's probably needed is one that pertains to the length of time between appointments for doctors:

The length of time between appointments for dentists at different offices can be no shorter than X.

Not every business rule will manifest itself within the database, even some that specifically deal with a process that manages data. For example, consider this rule:

Invoices should be sent within one week after the appointment.

This is great and everything, but what if it takes a week and a day, or even two weeks? Can the invoice no longer be sent to the patient? Should there be database code to chastise the person if someone was sick and it took a few hours longer than a week? No; although this seems much like a rule that could be implemented in the database, it isn't. This rule will be given to the persons doing system documentation and UI design for use when designing the rest of the system. The other persons working on the design of the overall system will often provide us with additional entities and attributes.

The specifics of some types of rules will be dealt with later in Chapters 5 and 6, as you implement tables and integrity constraints.

Identifying Fundamental Processes

A process is a coherent sequence of steps undertaken by a program that uses the data that has been identified to do something. It might be a computer-based process, such as "process daily receipts," where some form of report is created, or possibly a deposit is created to send to the bank. It could be something manual, such as "creating new patient," which details that first the patient fills out a set of forms, then the receptionist asks many of the same questions, and finally the nurse and doctor ask the same questions again once arriving in the room. Then some of this information is keyed into the computer after the patient leaves, so the dental office can send a bill.[1]

As a reasonable manual-process example, consider the process of getting a driver's license (at least here in Tennessee):

1. Fill in learner's permit forms
2. Obtain learner's permit
3. Practice
4. Fill in license forms
5. Pass eye exam
6. Pass driving exam
7. Have picture taken
8. Receive license

Processes might or might not have each step well enumerated during the conceptual or even logical phases, and many times a lot of processes are fleshed out during the implementation phase. I should mention that most processes have some amount of *process rules* associated with them (which are business rules that govern the process, much like those that govern data values). For example, you must complete each of those steps (taking tests, practicing driving, and so on) before you get your license. Note that some business rules are also lurking about in here, because some steps in a process might be done in any order (the eye exam could be before the driving

---

1. I don't know if they document that process, but doctors do seem to ask the same questions over and over.

exam and the process would remain acceptable), and others must be done in order (as originally noted, if you received the license without passing the exams, that would be kind of stupid).

In general, I would include the data-type rules in the database design, but would probably avoid most of the process rules, because often a process rule can be either overridden or can change.

In the license process, not only do you have the explicit order that some tasks must be performed, but there are other rules, such as that you must be 15 to get a learner's permit, you must be 16 to get the license, you must pass the exam, practice must be with a licensed driver, and so on. If you were the business analyst helping to design a driver's-license project, you would have to document this process at some point.

Identifying processes (and the rules that govern them) is relevant to the task of data modeling. Many procedures in database systems require manipulation of data, and processes are critical in these tasks. Each process usually translates into one or more queries or stored procedures, which might require more data than has been specified.

In our example, there are a few examples of such processes:

The client needs the system to manage its patients and appointments . . .

This implies that the client needs to be able to make appointments, as well as manage the patients—presumably the information about them. Making appointments is one of the most central things our system will do. This is certainly a process that you would want to go back to the client and understand.

. . . and then invoice the patient's insurance, if he or she has insurance (otherwise the patient pays).

I've discussed invoices already, but the process of creating an invoice might require additional attributes to identify that an invoice has been sent electronically or printed (possibly reprinted). Document control is an important part of many processes when helping an organization that's trying to modernize a paper system. Note that sending an invoice might seem like a pretty inane event—press a button on a screen and paper pops out of the printer.

All this requires is selecting some data from a table, so what's the big deal? However, when a document is printed, we might have to record the fact that the document was printed, who printed it, and what the use of the document is. We might also need to indicate that the documents are printed during a process that includes closing out and totaling the items on an invoice. The most important point here is that you shouldn't make any major assumptions.

Here are other processes that have been listed:

- *Track and manage dentists and hygienists*: From the sentence, "The system needs to track and manage several dentists, and quite a few dental hygienists who the client needs to allocate to each appointment as well."

- *Track supplies*: From "The client has had problems in the past keeping up with when it's about to run out of supplies, and wants this system to take care of this for both locations. For the dental supplies, we need to track usage by employee, and especially any changes made in the database to the patient records."

- *Alert patient*: From "alerting the patients when their appointments occur, either by e-mail or phone . . ."

Each of these processes identifies a unit of work that you must deal with during the implementation phase of the database design procedure.

Finishing the Conceptual Model

In this section, I'll briefly cover the steps involved in completing the task of establishing a working set of documentation. There's no way that we have a complete understanding of the documentation needs now, nor have we yet discovered all the entities, attributes, relationships, business rules, and processes that the final system will require. However, the better the job you do is a good predictor of how easy the rest of the process of designing and implementing the final system will be.

On the other hand, be careful, because there's a sweet spot when it comes to the amount of design needed. After a certain point, you could keep designing and make little—if any—progress. This is commonly known as *analysis paralysis*. Finding this sweet spot requires experience. Most of the time too little design occurs, usually because of a deadline that was set without any understanding of the realities of building a system. On the other hand, without strong management, I've found that I easily get myself into analysis paralysis (hey, the book focuses on design for a reason; to me it's the most fun part of the project).

The final steps of this discovery phase remain (the initial discovery phase anyhow, because you'll have to go back occasionally to this process to fill in gaps that were missed the first time). There are a few more things to do, if possible, before starting to write code:

- Identify obvious additional data needs.

- Review the progress of the project with the client.

- Repeat the process until satisfied, *and* the client is happy and signs off on what has been designed.

These steps are part of any system design, not just the data-driven parts.

Identifying Obvious Additional Data Needs

Up until this point, I've been reasonably careful not to broaden the information that was included from the discovery phase. The purpose has been to achieve a baseline to our documentation, staying faithful to the piles of documentation that were originally gathered. Mixing in our new thoughts prior to agreeing on what was in the previous documentation can be confusing to the client, as well as to us. However, at this point in the design, you need to change direction and begin to add the attributes that come naturally. Usually there's a fairly large set of obvious attributes and, to a lesser extent, business rules that haven't been specified by any of the users or initial analysis. Make sure that any assumed entities, attributes, relationships, and so on, stand out from what you have gotten from the documentation.

For the things that have been identified so far, go through and specify additional attributes that will likely be needed. For example, take the Patient entity, as shown in Table 3-4.

Table 3-4. *Completed Patient Entity*

Entity	Description	Domain
Patient	The persons that are the customers of the dentist office. Services are performed, supplies are used, and they are billed for them.	
Attributes		
PatientNumber	Used to identify a patient's records, in the computer and on the chart.	Unknown; generated by current computer system
Insurance	Identifies the patient's insurance carrier.	Unknown *(Note: Check for common formats used by insurance carriers, perhaps?)*
Relationships		
Has Alerts	Alerts are sent to patients to remind them of their appointments.	
Has Appointments	Appointments need to have one patient.	
Has Invoices	Patients are charged for appointments via an invoice.	
Makes Payment	Patients make payments for invoices they receive.	

The following additional attributes would be desirable:

- *Name*: The contact's full name is probably the most important attribute of all.

- *Birth date*: If the person's birthday is known, a card might be sent on that date. This is probably also a necessity for insurance purposes.

You could certainly add more attributes for the Patient entity, but this set should make the point clearly enough. There might also be additional tables, business rules, and so on, to recommend to the client. In this phase of the design, document them and add them to your lists.

One of the main things to do is to identify when you make any large changes to the customer's model. In this example, the client might not want to keep up with the birthdates of its patients (though as noted, it's probably an insurance requirement that wasn't initially thought of).

The process of adding new stuff to the client's model based on common knowledge is essential to the process, and will turn out to be a large part of the process. Rarely will the analyst think of everything. The normalization process will highlight the issues with the conceptual model, as you'll see in Chapter 4.

Review with the Client

Once you've finished putting together this first-draft document, it's time to meet with the client. Show the client where you've gotten to in your design, and have the client review every bit of this document. Make sure the client understands the solution that you're beginning to devise for it.

It's also worthwhile to devise some form of sign-off document, which the client signs before you move forward in the process. In some cases, your signoff documents could well be legally binding documents, and will certainly be important should the project go south later for one reason or another. Obviously, the hope is that this doesn't happen, but projects fail for many reasons, a good number of them not related to the project itself. It's always best if everyone is on the same page, and this is the place to do that.

Repeat Until the Customer Agrees with Your List of Objects

It isn't likely that you'll get everything right in this phase of the project. The most important thing is to get as much correct as you can, and get the customer to agree with this. Of course, it's unlikely that the client will immediately agree with everything you say, even if you're the greatest data architect in the world. It usually takes several attempts to get the list of objects right, and every iteration will move you and the client closer to your goal.

I don't want to make you think that repeating these items only pertains to this part of the project. There will be many times later in the project that you might have to revisit this part of the design and find something you missed, or something that the client forgot to share with you. As you get through more and more iterations of the design, it becomes increasingly important to make sure that you have your client sign off at regular times; you can point to these documents when the client changes his or her mind later on.

If you don't get agreement, often in writing or in a public forum, such as a meeting with enough witnesses, you can get hurt. This is especially true when you don't do an adequate job of handling the review and documentation process and there's no good documentation to back up your claim versus the clients. I've worked on consulting projects where the project was well designed, and agreed upon, but documentation of what was agreed upon wasn't made too well (a lot of handshaking at a higher level, to "save" money). As time went by, and many thousands of dollars were spent, the client reviewed the agreement document and it became obvious that we didn't agree on much at all. Needless to say, it worked out about as well as hydrogen-filled dirigibles.

Note I've been kind of hard on clients in this chapter, making them out to be conniving folks who will cheat you at the drop of a hat. This is seldom the case, but it only takes one. The truth is that almost every client will appreciate you keeping him or her in the loop and getting approval for the design at reasonable intervals.

Best Practices

The following list of some best practices can be useful to follow when doing conceptual modeling:

- *Be diligent*: Look through everything to make sure that what's being said makes sense. Be certain to understand as many of the business rules that bound the system as possible before moving on to the next step. Mistakes made early in the process can mushroom later in the process.

- *Document*: The point of this chapter has been just that. Document every entity, attribute, relationship, business rule, and process identified (and anything else you discover, even if it won't fit neatly into one of these buckets). The format of the documentation isn't important, only that the information is there and that it's understandable by all parties involved.

- *Communicate*: Constant communication with clients is essential to keep the design on track. The danger is that if you start to get the wrong idea of what the client needs, every decision past that point might be wrong. Get as much face time with the client as possible.

Note This mantra of "review with client, review with client, review with client" is probably starting to get a bit old at this point. This is one of the last times I'll mention it, but it's so important that I hope it has sunk in.

Summary

In this chapter, I've presented the process of discovering the entities that will eventually make up the dental-office database solution. We've weeded through all the documentation that had been gathered during the information-gathering phase, doing our best not to add our own contributions to the solution until we processed all the initial documentation, so as not to add our personal ideas to the solution. This is no small task; in our initial example, we had only three paragraphs to work with, yet we ended up with a few pages of documentation from it.

First I introduced some of the basics of documentation and requirements gathering. This is the most important part of the process, because it's the foundation of everything that follows. If the foundation is solid, the rest of the process has a chance. If the foundation is shoddy, the rest of the system that gets built will likely be the same. The purpose of this process is to acquire as much information about what the client wants out of its system. As a data architect, this might be something that's delivered to you, or at least most of it. Either way, the goal is to understand the user's needs.

Once you have as much documentation as possible from the users, the real work begins. Through all this documentation, the goal is to discover as many of the following as possible:

- Entities and relationships

- Attributes and domains

- Business rules that can be enforced in the database

- Processes that require the use of the database

From this, a conceptual data model will emerge that has many of the characteristics that will exist in our actual implemented database. In the upcoming chapters, the database will certainly change, but it will share many of the same characteristics.

CHAPTER 4

■■■

The Normalization Process

Everything should be made as simple as possible, but not simpler.

—Albert Einstein

Mr. Einstein describes in one sentence probably the most important lesson one can learn in life, and it's the central topic in normalization as well. In essence, database normalization is a set of "rules" or levels that, when applied to our relational data as part of the logical modeling phase, helps eliminate data redundancy and protects data integrity by breaking down entities into simpler forms. More entities can seem more complex to work with, but at the base level, each entity is easier to deal with.

These "rules" are formally known as *Normal Forms*. There are several Normal Forms, but I'll focus on the primary six. I'll start with First Normal Form (1NF), which eliminates data redundancy (such as a name being stored in two separate places), and continue through to Fifth Normal Form (5NF), which deals with the decomposition of ternary relationships. (One of the Normal Forms I'll present isn't numbered; it's named for the people who devised it.) Each level of normalization indicates an increasing degree of adherence to the recognized standards of database design. As you increase the *degree of normalization* of your data, you'll naturally tend to create an increasing number of tables of decreasing width (fewer columns).

In this chapter, I'll start out by addressing two fundamental questions:

- *Why normalize*: I'll take a detailed look at the numerous reasons why you should normalize your data. The bottom line is that you should normalize to increase the efficiency of, and protect the integrity of, your relational data.

- *How far to normalize*: This is always a contentious issue. Normalization tends to optimize your database for efficient storage and updates, rather than querying. It dramatically reduces the propensity for introducing update anomalies (different records displaying different values for the same piece of data), but it increases the complexity of your queries, as you might be forced to collect data from many different tables.

I'll then walk through each of the Normal Forms in turn, explaining with clear examples the requirements of each one, the programming anomalies they help you avoid, and the tell-tale signs that your relational data is flouting that particular Normal Form. I'll then wrap up with an overview of some normalization best practices.

Why Normalize?

Before discussing the mechanics of the normalization process, I'll discuss some of the reasons why to normalize. In the following sections, I'll discuss reasons that might not be obvious, even after finishing the sections on how to normalize, such as the following:

- Eliminating data that's duplicated, increasing the chance it won't match when you need it

- Avoiding unnecessary coding needed to keep duplicated data in sync

- Keeping tables thin, increasing the number of values that will fit on a page

- Maximizing the use of clustered indexes, allowing for more optimum data access and joins

- Lowering the number of indexes per table, because indexes are costly to maintain

Many of these topics are implementation issues, or even pertain more to physical modeling (how data is laid out on disk). Since this is a professional book, I'm assuming that you have some knowledge of such things. If not, don't worry about it; later chapters of the book will cover these issues.

Eliminating Duplicated Data

Any piece of data that occurs more than once in the database is an error waiting to happen. No doubt you've all been beaten by this once or twice in your life: your name is stored in multiple places, then one version gets modified and the other doesn't, and suddenly you have more than one name where before there was just one.

The problem with storing redundant data will be obvious to anyone who has moved to a new address. Every government authority requires citizens to change our address information individually on tax forms, driver's licenses, auto registrations, and so on, rather than making one change centrally. Getting this information updated for a simple move can be a complicated process.

Avoiding Unnecessary Coding

Extra programming in triggers, stored procedures, or even in the business logic tier can be required to handle poorly structured data, and in turn impairs performance significantly. Extra coding also increases the chance of introducing new bugs into a labyrinth of code required to maintain redundant data.

Keeping Tables Thin

When I refer to a thinner table, the idea is that a relatively small number of columns are in the table. Thinner tables mean more data fits on a given page in the database, therefore allowing the database server to retrieve more rows for a table in a single read than would otherwise be possible. This all means that there will be more tables in the system when you're finished normalizing. However, there's a common-sense cut-off point (for example, there should be few cases where a table has only a single column).

Maximizing Clustered Indexes

Clustered indexes order a table natively in SQL Server. Clustered indexes are special indexes in which the physical storage of the data matches the order of the indexed data, which allows for better performance of queries using that index. Typically, you use them to order a table in a convenient manner to enhance performance. Each table might have only a single clustered index. The more clustered indexes in the database, the less sorting needs to be performed, and the more likely it is that queries can use the MERGE JOIN—a special type of fast join technique that requires sorted data. Sorting is a costly operation that you should avoid if possible. Chapter 8 will cover clustered indexes, and indexes in general, in great detail.

The concept of clustered indexes applies to normalization in that that you'll have more tables when you normalize. The increased numbers of clustered indexes increase the likelihood that joins between tables can use merge joins, which are the fastest types of joins.

Lowering the Number of Indexes Per Table

The fewer indexes per table, the fewer the number of *pages* that can be moved around on a modification or insertion into the table. By pages, I'm referring to pages of memory. In SQL Server, data and indexes are broken up and stored on 8K pages (Chapter 8 covers this in more detail). Of course, SQL Server usually cannot keep the whole database in RAM at any one time. It keeps a "snapshot" of what's being looked at. To keep the illusion of having the whole database in memory, SQL Server moves the pages in and out of a high-speed fast-access storage space when they're required, but this space can only contain a limited number of pages at any one time. Therefore, SQL Server moves the pages in and out of the space on the principle that the most frequently accessed remain in. The operation of moving pages in and out of memory is costly in terms of performance, and especially painful if clients are twiddling their thumbs waiting for an operation to complete. So, to keep performance as high as possible, the goal is to minimize physical page transfers. Normalization helps to keep indexing to a minimum by keeping tables thin and specific, rather than having lots of columns to deal with.

How Far to Normalize

As I noted in the introduction to this chapter, database normalization can be a polarizing topic for the database architect, especially when dealing with other developers. If you have no idea what normalization is, ignore this section for now, but most every person who has any knowledge of databases has heard about the Normal Forms, and disagreements (a.k.a. knockdown, drag-out fights) often arise between database architects and client developers over how to store data. They're hard to resolve, mainly because there's never a single indisputably "correct" design. Furthermore, normalization appears to be a complex process, and certainly, it takes a lot of time and planning initially to build applications on top of *properly structured* tables. However, in my opinion, you simply cannot afford not to put some time and effort into your data design, and to normalize your data correctly as far as necessary. There's no magic number or completely ideal process to follow.

I mention a magic number because it's commonly thought that Third Normal Form is that magic level, but truly, this is rarely the case. Even without you knowing it, most databases turn out to be in Fourth Normal Form, and even Fifth. Having basic knowledge of what these Normal Forms are makes it easier to look out for the pitfalls that they do cover (they're not just something that super mathematician database geeks came up with to make themselves look cool to the ladies).

The original sin of most every new database designer is to fall (to some level or another) for the false logic that the fewer tables the data is stored in, the less code is required, and the fewer user interfaces are needed. If there's less code, then the solution will be much faster to develop than if there are only 20 tables, right? Although this thinking is easy to grasp on a certain level, it's completely wrong on many far more important levels. Relationships between the different data elements have to be understood and dealt with, and this is what normalization is all about.

The truth is that normalization isn't that complex a subject, and with a little effort you can achieve an efficient, durable design that you won't find yourself needing to chop and change, and that won't be subject to data-integrity issues. I'm not saying that once the design has been implemented, it can't or won't need to be changed. Expansions and changes in business practices are common. However, it's easier to add new information and new entities to a well-normalized database.

The punch line of the process for me is this: "Every entity in a database should represent one single thing." When you're modeling entities, the ultimate desire is that each table represents a thing, at the lowest appropriate level of abstraction. For example, if you're designing a database to store sales information about Diet Coke, it's generally unnecessary to have an entity to represent the individual atoms in the liquid unless the goal is to build a database for a research scientist who's breaking down all the atoms of Diet Coke. It takes experience designing databases to know what the user wants, so you can provide the proper level of normalization for any situation. However, the Third Normal Form will rarely meet the need.

The Process of Normalization

The process of normalization is simple enough: take complex entities and make simpler entities from them. The process continues until every table in the database represents one thing. This will become more apparent throughout the chapter, as I work through the different Normal Forms.

In 1970, in his now-famous paper, "A Relational Model of Data for Large Shared Data Banks," E. F. Codd presented the world with the First Normal Form, based on the shape of the data, and the Second and Third Normal Forms, based on functional dependencies in the data. Codd and R. Boyce further refined these as the Boyce-Codd Normal Form (BCNF). Finally, the Fourth and Fifth deal with multivalued and join dependencies in the data. I'll break down normalization into three categories of steps:

- Entity and attribute shape

- Relationships between attributes

- Multivalued and join dependencies in entities

Note that every step should be performed, and preferably in order, as each Normal Form is built upon the precept that the lower forms have been done.

Entity and Attribute Shape: First Normal Form

The First Normal Form is centered around making sure that entities and attributes are shaped correctly. The requirements largely mirror the requirements for a relation in relational theories. For an entity to be in First Normal Form, it must have the following characteristics:

- All attributes must be atomic; that is, only a single value represented in a single attribute in a single instance of an entity.

- All instances of an entity must contain the same number of values.

- All instances of an entity must be different.

First Normal Form violations manifest themselves in the implemented model with messy data-handling situations, usually because of having to decode multiple values stored where a single one should be.

All Attributes Must Be Atomic

In computer science terms, *atomic* means that the value cannot (or should not) be broken down into smaller parts.[1] If you want to get technical, most any value can be broken down into smaller parts. For the database definition, consider "atomic" to refer to a value that needn't be broken down any further for use in the relational database. The reasons for this should make more sense after reading this entire section.

The goal of this part of the First Normal Form is that each attribute should only represent one value, not multiple values. This means there should be no arrays, no delimited data, and no other types of multivalued attributes that you could dream up represented by a single attribute. For example, consider the value 1, 2, 3, 6, 7. This likely represents five separate values. It might not be, but for darn sure it needs to be looked at. Datatypes can contain more than one value, as long as

- There are always the same number of values

- The values are rarely, if ever, dealt with individually

For example, consider geographic location. Two values are always used to locate something on Earth, these being the longitude and the latitude. Most of the time, either of these, considered individually, has some (if incomplete) meaning, but taken together, they pinpoint an exact position on the Earth. Implementing as a complex type can give us some ease of implementing data-protection schemes, and can make using the types in formulas easier. I'll present an example of implementing complex types in the next chapter, in the section on user-defined datatypes.

When it comes to First Normal Form, the test of reasonability is left up to the designer, but generally speaking, the goal is that any data you ever need to deal with as a single value is modeled as its own attribute, so it's stored in a column of its own (for example, as a search argument, or a join criterion).

---

1. Atoms of course can be broken down, but the Greeks didn't realize that when they created the word atomos, from which the term atomic is derived.

As an example of taking First Normal Form to the full extreme, consider a text document with ten paragraphs. This might easily be categorized as another attribute with ten different values, but there's little reason to do this, as you'll be unlikely to deal with a paragraph as a single value in the SQL database language.

As further examples, consider some of the common violations of this rule of the First Normal Form:

- E-mail addresses
- Names
- Telephone numbers
- Mailing addresses

Each of these gives us a slightly different kind of issue with atomicity that needs to be considered when designing attributes.

E-Mail Addresses

In an e-mail message, the e-mail address is typically stored in a format such as the following:

```
name1@domain1.com;name2@domain2.com;name3@domain3.com
```

This format is fine for the FROM: line of an e-mail, because that's the format in which the e-mail database (not generally relational in nature) uses it. However, if you need to store the values in a relational database, this is a clear violation of First Normal Form, as it represents more than one e-mail address in a single email attribute. Each e-mail address should be represented individually in a separate row.

It's arguable whether or not any given e-mail address is in First Normal Form as well. name1@domain1.com contains two or three obvious parts. The e-mail address is made up of the following:

- *AccountName*: name1
- *Domain*: domain1.com

Whether this is desirable will usually come down to whether you intend to access the individual parts separately in your code. For example, if all you'll ever do is send e-mail, then a single column is perfectly acceptable. On the other hand, if you need to consider what domains you have e-mail addresses stored for, then it's a completely different matter.

Finally, the domain is made up of two parts: domain1 and com. These values are rarely stored in separate columns, but they could be. The decision is simple: if it's necessary to rely on a "substring" operation to access parts of the data in an attribute, then it isn't in First Normal Form.

Names

Consider the name "John Q Public." The first name, middle initial, and last name are in a single attribute. Break the name into three parts into FirstName, MiddleInitial (or MiddleName, which is probably preferable), and LastName. This is usually the reasonable limit chosen, because a person's name in the USA is generally considered to have three parts. In some situations, this might not be enough, and the number of parts might not be known until the user enters the data. Knowing the data requirements is important in these kinds of situations.

Telephone Numbers

American telephone numbers are of the form "1-423-555-1212," plus some possible extension number. From our previous examples, you can see that several attributes are probably in that telephone number. Additionally, there's frequently the need to store more than just American telephone numbers in a database. The decision on how to handle this situation might be based on how often the users store international phone numbers, as it would be a hard task to build a table or set of entities to handle every situation.

So, for an American-style telephone number, you can represent the address with five different attributes for each of the following parts, "C-AAA-EEE-NNNN-XXXX":

- *(C) Country code*: Dialed for numbers that aren't within the area code, and signals to the phone that you're dialing a nonlocal number

- *(AAA) Area code*: Indicates a calling area located within a state

- *(EEE) Exchange*: Indicates a set of numbers within an area code

- *(NNNN) Number:* Number used to make individual phone numbers unique

- *(XXXX) Extension*: Number that must be dialed after connecting using the previous numbers

One of the coding examples later in this section will cover the sorts of issues that come up when storing phone numbers.

Mailing Addresses

It should be clear by now that an address has many attributes—certainly for street address, city, state, and postal code (from here on I'll ignore the internationalization factor and focus on American-style addresses, for brevity). However, you can break street addresses down, in most cases, into number, street name, suite number, apartment number, post-office box, and so on. Addresses can be a complex issue. Take the following example:

> 1818 Whoknows Lane
> Box 12A
> Somewhere, SM 21234-2123

The common solution to the Address entity might appear as shown in Figure 4-1.

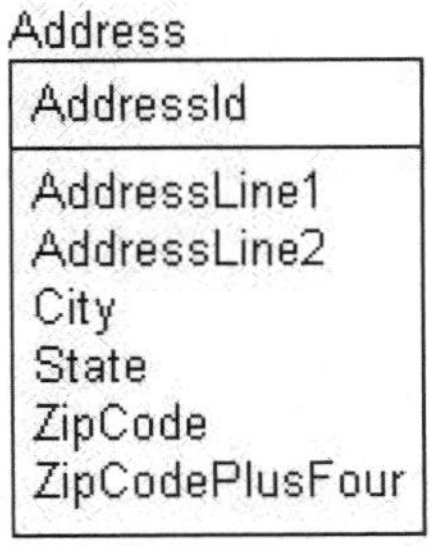

Figure 4-1. *The Address entity*

It's simple, to the point, and gets the job done. But this Address entity is far from perfect. Consider the parts of the AddressLine1 attribute: 1818, Whoknows, and Lane. If you're doing serious mailing in your system, these values will be dealt with as three separate values (to format the address perfectly so mailing can be computerized). The same is true of the AddressLine2 value: Box 12a. This can be split up and re-formed, as shown in Figure 4-2.

Address
AddressId
StreetName StreetNumber StreetType City State ZipCode ZipCodePlusFour

Figure 4-2. *A refinement of the Address entity*

Fine, but what of the following address?

PO Box 12394
Somewhere Else, EL 32342

Well, it needs parts of the address used before—the City, State, ZipCode, and ZipCodePlusFour— but not others—the StreetNumber, StreetName, and StreetType. However, it does have a new attribute: PoBoxNumber. I'll use a subtype and add a type for a post office box–style address, as shown in Figure 4-3.

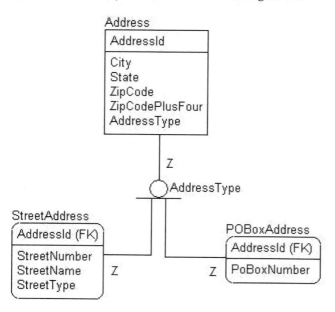

Figure 4-3. *Adding a subtype to the design*

There are a few other common address types, such as the rural route type. Obviously, the model could get far too messy to deal with if it exhaustively modeled even most of the possible cases (rural routes, office buildings, apartments, and so on). The resulting model would end up being a great deal of work that the user interface developer would simply use to have you committed to "Uncle Joe's House of Pancakes and Sanitarium" for being a loony. The truth is, if you're building a database from which you send thousands and thousands of pieces of mail, creating such an exhaustive model may not be a bad idea at all. Users will hate it if you give them ten choices for address type, but using a little bit of programming prowess, you can allow the user to look primarily at the following:

> 1818 Whoknows Lane
> Somewhere, SM 21234-2123

while storing this data in the following style:

```
ColumnName      Value
------------    -----------
StreetNumber    1818
StreetName      Whoknows
StreetType      Lane
City            Somewhere
State           SM
ZipCode         21234
ZipPlus4        2123
```

Again, the user interface shouldn't mimic the database structure in most cases, or the user will hate you. Addresses especially can turn out to be a difficult area when you try to go past the good old standard of attributes such as addressLine1, addressLine2, and addressLine3, or a single attribute to hold the whole street line, including carriage returns and line fees. You might not end up gaining much. Use this rule of thumb: "Break values down only as far as you will deal with the parts individually."

■Tip Every nation has its own idiosyncrasies when it comes to addresses. Things are compounded when it comes to dealing with addresses in multiple countries at the same time. However, the process and problems are the same. Break down parts of an address until you reach the point where you'll never need to deal with the pieces and parts separately (or at least the point where the cost to implement the solution outweighs the cost to deal with the pieces and parts).

All Instances in an Entity Must Contain the Same Number of Values

This part of the First Normal Form says that every instance has the same number of attributes. There are two interpretations of this:

- Entities have a fixed number of attributes (and tables have a fixed number of columns).

- Entities should be designed such that every attribute has a fixed number of values associated with it.

The first interpretation is simple. You cannot have a table with one instance, such as {Name, Address, HairColor} and another such as {Name, Address, PhoneNumber, EyeColor}. This kind of implementation was common with record-based implementations, but isn't possible with a relational database table.

The second is a more open interpretation. As an example, if you're building an entity that stores a person's name, then if one row has one name, all rows must only have one name. If they might have two, all instances must have precisely two (not one sometimes, and certainly never three). If they may have a different number, it's inconvenient to deal with using SQL commands, which is the main reason a database is being built in an RDBMS! You must take some care with the concept of unknown values (NULLs) as well. The values aren't required, but there should always be the same number (even if the value isn't immediately known).

You can find an example of a violation of this rule of the First Normal Form in entities that have several attributes with the same base name suffixed (or prefixed) with a number, such as Payment1, Payment2, and so on, as shown in Figure 4-4.

Customer

Customerld
Name (AK1) <<other attributes>> Payment1 Payment2

Figure 4-4. *Violating First Normal Form with a variable number of attributes*

Usually, this is an attempt to allow multiple values for a single attribute in an entity. In the rare cases where there's always precisely the same number of values, then there's technically no violation of First Normal Form. In this case, you could state a business rule that "each entity has exactly two payments." Even in such cases, allowing multiple values still isn't generally a good design decision. That's because users can change their minds frequently as to how many payments there are; for example, if the person only paid a half payment, or some craziness that people always seem to do. To overcome all this, you should create a child entity to hold the values in the malformed entity, as shown in Figure 4-5.

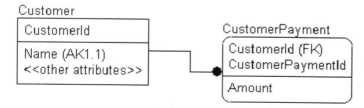

Figure 4-5. *A child entity holds the offending values*

This form also allows us to have virtually unlimited cardinality, whereas the previous solution had a finite (and small) number of possible configurations. One of the issues to deal with is that the child instances you create require sequencing information to get the rows properly organized for usage. You can use cardinality rules as described in the previous chapter to constrain the number of possible values. If need be, it's easy enough to choke things back, because our model states that we only need a maximum of two children, and a minimum of one child. Cardinality provides the mechanism for describing this.

■**Caution** Another common concern is the use of attributes such as UserDefined1, UserDefined2,..., UserDefinedN. This practice is heinous for many reasons, one of them related to proper application of the First Normal Form. However, using such attributes is also directly against the essence of Codd's rule 4: Dynamic On-Line Catalog Based on the Relational Model. It states that the database description is represented at the logical level in the same way as ordinary data, so that authorized users can apply the same relational language to its interrogation that they apply to regular data.

Putting data into the database into more-or-less nameless attributes requires extra knowledge about the system beyond what's included in the system catalogs.

All Occurrences of an Entity Type in an Entity Must Be Different

This part of the First Normal Form requires that every entity have a key defined (primary or unique). Take care, however, because as discussed in Chapter 1, adding a single artificial key to an entity might technically make the entity comply with the letter of the rule, but it certainly won't comply with the purpose. The purpose is that no two instances represent the same thing. Because an artificial key has no meaning by definition, it won't fix the problem.

Another minor issue can involve rows that use a date and time value to differentiate between rows. If the date and time value is part of the row's identification, such as a calendar entry or a row that's recording some event, this is not only acceptable, but ideal. On the other hand, simply tossing on a date and time value to force uniqueness is no better than just adding a random number or GUID on the row.

The key of the row should have some meaning, if at all possible. It isn't reasonable 100 percent of the time to have a completely meaningful key, but it is nearly always the case. Here's an example: a key might not be found that could be an entity that represents a single physical item in a situation where you cannot tell the physical items apart. An example is a small can of corn (or any vegetable, really). Two cans cannot be told apart, so you might assign a value that has no meaning as part of the key, along with the things that differentiate the can from other similar objects, such as large cans of corn, or small cans of spinach. You might also consider just keeping a count of the objects in a single row, depending on your needs (which will be dictated by your requirements).

Programming Anomalies Avoided by First Normal Form

Violations of the First Normal Form are often awkward if users frequently access the columns affected. The following examples will identify some of the situations we can avoid by putting our entities in the First Normal Form.

Note that for these programming anomalies, I'll switch over into using tables, rather than entities. This is because the issues will eventually be manifested in our implemented table structures. Using tables also gives you some detail as to *why* this process is useful in tables, and isn't just academic hooha.[2]

Modifying Lists in a Single Value

SQL isn't set up to handle nonatomic values in a straightforward or consistent way. Consider our previous example of the e-mail addresses attribute. Suppose that the following table named Person exists with the following schema:

```
CREATE TABLE Person
(
    PersonId int NOT NULL PRIMARY KEY,
    Name varchar(100) NOT NULL,
    EmailAddress varchar(1000) NOT NULL
)
```

If users are allowed to have more than one e-mail address, our email attribute might look like this: davidsons@d.com;ldavidson@email.com. Also consider that many users in the database might use the davidsons@d.com e-mail address (for example, if it were the family shared e-mail account). Consider the situation if one of the addresses changed, changing the e-mail address for all uses of davidsons@d.com to davidsons@domain.com. You could try to execute code such as the following for every person who uses this e-mail address:

```
UPDATE dbo.person
SET    EmailAddress = replace(EmailAddresses,'davidsons@d.com',
       'davidsons@domain.com')
WHERE  ';' + emailAddress + ';' like '%;davidsons@d.com;%'
```

This code might not seem like that much trouble, but what about the case where there is also the e-mail address thedavidsons@d.com? This code invalidly replaces that value as well. How to deal with this? The proper solution would be to have another table to hold each e-mail address in its own row, as shown in Figure 4-6. Now these rows can be related to the Person entity.

You can take this one step further and note that each e-mail address includes two values before and after an @. The first value is the e-mail name, the second the domain, as shown in Figure 4-7.

---

2. No, hooha isn't a real word, but I felt that a different word might be a bit strong for a show such as ours that's on during family time.

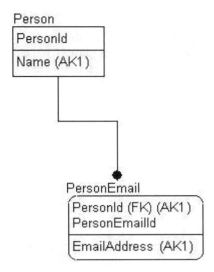

Figure 4-6. *A separate entity holds the e-mail details*

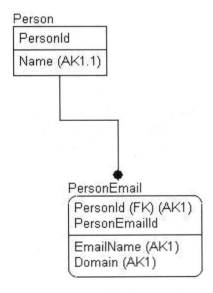

Figure 4-7. *We've split the e-mail address into the Name and the Domain*

Frankly, you can legitimately go either way (and you can even break out domain type if it makes sense). Because the e-mail name and the domain are rarely, if ever, dealt with as separate things, there's little reason to do this unless you analyze the places where you get or send e-mail. This is in contrast to phone numbers, where you'll often find it behooves you to keep the parts separate, as the next section will demonstrate.

Modifying Multipart Values

The programming logic required to change part of the multipart value can be confusing. For example, take the case of telephone area codes. In the USA, people have more phones, pagers, cell phones, and so on than the creators of the area code system ever thought of, so they frequently change or introduce new area codes.

I could start to model the phone number as shown in Figure 4-8.

PhoneNumber

PhoneNumber

Figure 4-8. *Modeling the phone number*

The code to modify existing area codes to a new area code is pretty messy, and certainly not the best performer. Usually, when an area code splits, it's for only certain exchanges. Assuming a format of C-AAA-EEE-NNNN where C equals country code, AAA equals area code, EEE equals exchange, and NNNN equals the phone number, then the code looks like this:

```
UPDATE dbo.PhoneNumber
SET PhoneNumber = substring(PhoneNumber,1,2) + '423' + substring(PhoneNumber,6,9)
WHERE substring(PhoneNumber,3,3) = '615'
    AND substring(PhoneNumber,7,3) IN ('232','323',...,'989') --area codes generally
                                                              --change for certain
                                                              --exchanges
```

This code requires perfect formatting of the phone number data to work, and unless the formatting is forced upon the users, this is unlikely to be the case. If all values are stored in single atomic containers, as shown in Figure 4-9, updating the area code would take a single, easy-to-follow, one-line SQL statement.

PhoneNumber

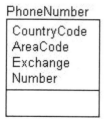

CountryCode
AreaCode
Exchange
Number

Figure 4-9. *Splitting the phone number into atomic attributes*

Here's an example of the SQL:

```
UPDATE dbo.PhoneNumber
SET    AreaCode = '423'
WHERE  CountryCode = '1'
  AND  AreaCode = '615'
  AND  Exchange IN ('232','323',...,'989')
```

Again, this is one of those case-by-case decisions. Using three separate values is easier for these reasons, and as a result will be the better performer in most all cases. One value (with forced formatting) has merit and will work. You might even use a complex type to implement this value. Sometimes I use a single column with a check constraint to make sure that all the dashes are in there. Due to programmer pressure, I usually then add computed columns to the resulting table to view the data in its parts.

Dealing with a Variable Number of Facts in an Attribute

The main issue that arises when an attribute allows a variable numbers of facts is dealing with the different situations that come up when you need to work with one of the values instead of the other. A possible solution might be a basic structured table, such as Figure 4-10 shows.

Account

AccountNumber
<<other attributes>> Payment1 Payment2

Figure 4-10. *A simple representation of a bank account*

The first payment would go in the Payment1 column, but when the second payment is made, it would go in the Payment2 column. To do this, you'd have to do something such as the following:

```
UPDATE dbo.account
SET Payment1 = case WHEN Payment1 IS NULL THEN 1000.00 ELSE Payment1 END,
    Payment2 = case WHEN Payment1 IS NOT NULL AND Payment2 IS NULL THEN
    1000.00 ELSE Payment2 END
WHERE accountId = 1
```

What then about Payment3, or even Payment4? Of course, it's unlikely that this kludgey code would be using SQL to deal with values such as this, but even if this logic is done on the client side by giving multiple blocks for payments, or if it's predetermined which of the payments needs to be made, this code is going to be problematic to deal with.

The alternative is to have an entity structured as shown in Figure 4-11.

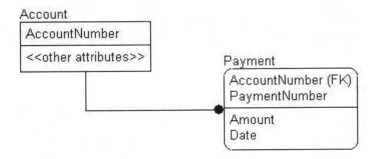

Figure 4-11. *The payments are now in a separate entity*

Then, adding payments would be as simple as adding a new row to the Payment table:

```
INSERT dbo.Payment (AccountNumber, PaymentNumber, Amount, Date)
VALUES ('000002324', $300.00, '20000612')
INSERT dbo.Payment (AccountNumber, PaymentNumber, Amount, Date)
VALUES ('000002324', $100.00, '20000712')
```

You could calculate the payment number from previous payments, which is far easier to deal with using set-based SQL statements.

Not only is it easier to insert a new payment, but it clears up a host of problems, such as the following:

- *Deleting a payment*: Much like the update that had to determine what payment slot to fit the payment into, deleting anything other than the last payment requires shifting. For example, if you delete the payment in Payment1, then Payment2 needs to be shifted to Payment1, Payment3 to Payment2, and so on.

- *Updating a payment*: Say Payment1 equals 10 and Payment2 equals 10. Which one should you modify if you have to modify one of them? Does it matter?

- *Lack of information about a value*: When was the payment made? Why was the payment changed? Because the "event" of the payment has additional interesting information, the Payment table offers a more natural place to record it.

Clues That Existing Data Is Not in First Normal Form

Next we'll take a look at some ways to recognize whether data in a given database is already likely to be in First Normal Form or not. Each of these clues isn't by any means a perfect test. Generally speaking, they're clues that you can look for in your data structures for places to dig deeper. Normalization is a fluid set of rules that are largely based on the content and purpose of your data.

The following sections describe some data characteristics that suggest that the data isn't in First Normal Form.

Predominantly Alphabetic Data That Contains Nonalphabetic Characters

Nonalphabetic characters include commas, brackets, parentheses, pipe characters, and so on. These act as warning signs that the data is likely a multivalued attribute. However, be careful not to go too far. For instance, if you're designing a solution to hold a block of text, you've probably normalized too much if you have a word entity, a sentence entity, and a paragraph entity (if you had been considering it, give yourself three points for thinking ahead, but don't go there). This clue is more aligned to entities that have structured, delimited lists.

Attribute Names with Numbers at the End

As noted, an obvious example would be finding entities with Child1, Child2, and similar attributes, or my favorite, UserDefined1, UserDefined2, and so on. These kinds of entities are usually messy to deal with and should be considered for a new, related table. They don't have to be wrong; for example, your entity might need exactly two values to always exist. In that case, it's perfectly allowable to have the numbered columns, but be careful that what's thought of as "always" is actually always. Too often, "exceptions" cause this solution to fail. "A person always has two forms of identification noted in fields ID1 and ID2, *except when . . .*" In this case, *always* doesn't mean always.

These kinds of attributes are a common holdover from the days of flat file databases. Multi-table data access was costly, so developers put many fields in a single file structure. Doing this in a relational database system is a waste of the power of the relational programming language.

Coordinate1, Coordinate2 might be acceptable in cases that always require two coordinates to find a point in a two-dimensional space, never any more, or never any less (though XCoordinate and YCoordinate might be better attribute names). Also, when you have attributes such as these, which have no meaning without the other, you can design them as a complex datatype. For example, consider the attributes XCoordinate and YCoordinate. As mentioned previously, it would be perfectly acceptable to implement these attributes as a single complex datatype—call it a point—with two values, X and Y. Because these two values are part of the same attribute—the location of something—it can be reasonable to have them as a complex type, though not required.

Relationships Between Attributes

The next set of Normal Forms to look at is concerned with the relationships between attributes in an entity, and most importantly, the key in that entity. These Normal Forms deal with minimizing functional dependencies between the attributes. As discussed in Chapter 1, being functionally dependent implies that when running a function on one value (call it Value1), if the output of this function is *always* the same value (call it Value2), then Value2 is functionally dependent on Value1.

For example, consider the following situation. There are two values: Product Type and Serial Number. Because a product's Serial Numbers usually imply a particular Product Type, they're functionally dependent. If you change the Product Type but fail to reflect this in the Serial Number, then your Serial Number and Product Type will no longer match, and the values will no longer be of any value. Because the two values are functionally dependent on each other, then they both must be modified at the same time.

I'll introduce the Second Normal Form, Third Normal Form, and Boyce-Codd Normal Form (BCNF) in the upcoming sections. Each of these forms can be introduced by the following sentence:

> *Non-key attributes must provide a detail about the key, the whole key, and nothing but the key.*

This means that non-key attributes have to further describe the key of the entity, and not describe any other attributes. I'll cover the following Normal Forms:

- *Second Normal Form*: Relationships between non-key attributes and part of the primary key

- *Third Normal Form*: Relationships between non-key attributes

- *BCNF*: Relationships between non-key attributes and any key

This will become clearer as I introduce each of the different Normal Forms throughout this section.

Second Normal Form

Second Normal Form deals with the relationships and functional dependencies between non-key attributes. An entity complying with Second Normal Form has to have the following characteristics:

- The entity must be in First Normal Form.

- Each attribute must be a fact describing the entire key.

■**Note** Second Normal Form is technically only relevant when a composite key (a key composed of two or more columns) exists in the entity.

The Entity Must Be in First Normal Form

It's important that the entity be in First Normal Form; it's essential to go through each step of the normalization process to eliminate problems in data. It might be impossible to locate Second Normal Form problems if there are still First Normal Form problems. Otherwise, some of the problems identified that you're trying to fix by using this rule might show up in any misshapen attributes not dealt with in the previous rule.

Each Non-Key Attribute Must Describe the Entire Key

Each non-key attribute must depict the entity described by *all* attributes in the key, and not simply parts. If this isn't true, and any of the non-key attributes are functionally dependent on a subset of the attributes in the key, then there will be data modification anomalies. For example, consider the structure in Figure 4-12.

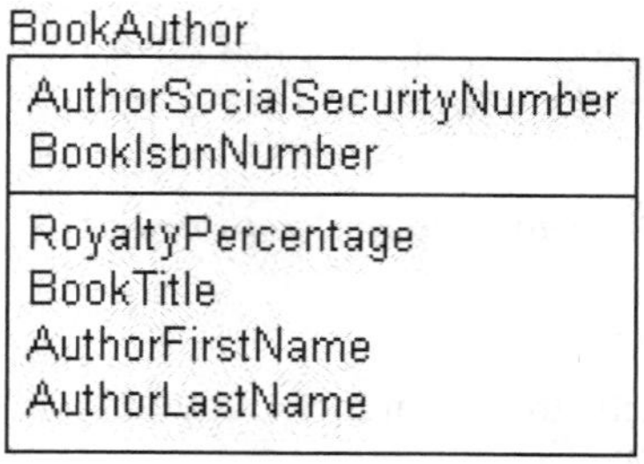

```
BookAuthor
┌─────────────────────────────────┐
│ AuthorSocialSecurityNumber      │
│ BookIsbnNumber                  │
├─────────────────────────────────┤
│ RoyaltyPercentage               │
│ BookTitle                       │
│ AuthorFirstName                 │
│ AuthorLastName                  │
└─────────────────────────────────┘
```

Figure 4-12. *An entity that contains information about a book's author*

The BookIsbnNumber attribute uniquely identifies the book, and AuthorSocialSecurityNumber uniquely identifies the author. Hence, these two columns create one key that uniquely identifies an author for a book. The problem is with the other attributes. The RoyaltyPercentage attribute defines the royalty that the author is receiving for the book, so this refers to the entire key. The BookTitle describes the book, but doesn't describe the author at all. The same goes for the AuthorFirstName and AuthorLastName attributes. They describe the author, but not the book.

This is a prime example of a troublesome functional dependency that at first glance might not just pop out at you. For every distinct value in the BookIsbnNumber column, there must exist the same book title and author information, because it's the same book. But for every BookIsbnNumber, it isn't true that the same RoyaltyPercentage value will exist—this is dependent on *both* the author and the book, not one or the other. That's because when books are cowritten, the split might be based on many factors: celebrity, how much of the book each author produced, and so on.

Hence, there are problems, so I'll create three separate entities for this data, as shown in Figure 4-13.

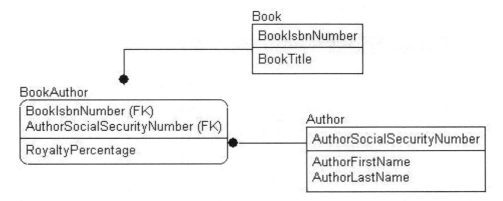

Figure 4-13. *The details are now in three separate entities*

After splitting the entities, the RoyaltyPercentage attribute is still a fact describing the author writing the book, the BookTitle is now an attribute describing the entity defined by the BookIsbnNumber, and the author's name attributes are attributes of the Author entity, identified by the AuthorSocialSecurityNumber.

Note that the Book to BookAuthor relationship is an identifying type of relationship. Second Normal Form violations are often remodeled as identifying relationships in which the primary key of the new entity is migrated to the entity where the original problem occurred. Our previous illustration demonstrates this concept well. In the corrected example, the functional dependencies are isolated such that attributes that are functionally dependent on another attribute are functionally dependent on the key.

Because there are no columns that aren't functionally dependent on a part of the key, (that is, all columns are dependent on the entire key of the table), these entities are in Second Normal Form.

Programming Problems Avoided by Second Normal Form

All the programming issues that arise with the Second Normal Form (as well as the upcoming Third and Boyce-Codd Normal Forms) deal with functional dependencies. The programming issue is simple. Consider the data you're modeling, and how it would be affected if it were implemented, then execute the following statement:

```
UPDATE dbo.BookAuthor
SET    BookTitle = 'Database Design'
WHERE  BookIsbnNumber = '1234567890'
```

Here, you're updating an attribute that clearly represents a singular thing (in this case a book's title). If your update query in which you intend to change what seems like a single thing (such as a book) might modify more than one row, there's a problem with the structure of the design.

The crux of the problem is that many programmers don't have their database-design thinking caps on when they're churning out applications, so you end up with tables created with client screens such as the one shown in Figure 4-14.

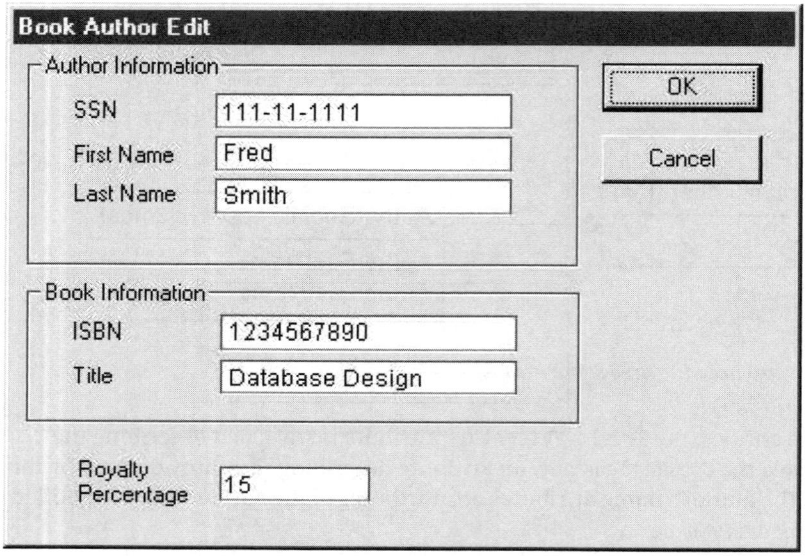

Figure 4-14. *A possible graphical front-end to our example*

This design of this screen looks reasonable, doesn't it? If this was in a prototype, I doubt anyone, including myself, would even notice the data issues (well, perhaps if I took the time to read it over I'd notice, but it's rare that a DBA pays attention when the UI programmer is presenting a design).

You need to consider the cases where it's obvious that an entity models more than a single noun. In each of the issues identified, this is the problem. The BookAuthor entity isn't only the author of the book, but rather it's the book, the author, and their relationship to each other that presents the problem.

■**Tip** There was nothing *sinfully* wrong with the screen in Figure 4-14. If the design calls for this sort of data to be entered, and the client wants this, fine. However, this is clearly a UI design issue, and not a question of database structure. Don't let user interface dictate the database structure.

The problem is that you commonly need to deal with these independent things not in terms of their relationship, but individually (Books or Authors rather than BookAuthors). It turns out that with the attributes in the same entity, it's impossible to do this in a reasonable way. For example, to delete the Author but leave the Book, you could nullify each of the Author's attribute values. To be honest, this will work if you only ever have one author for a book, but with one example of a multi-author book, the design fails. The even bigger issue is, what if one author writes more than one book? The same author's information would have to be duplicated amongst all the books.

It's even more complicated when you start to insert or delete the data for one of the independent entities that are muddled in the BookAuthor table. You cannot delete only a book, and keep the author around. And what if the author had written two different books, and they both are "deleted" and the book attributes nullified? Then two rows exist with the same author information and no book. In essence, a duplicated row would then exist. You could write functional routines to take care of such things, but a relational database, and in particular normalization, is set up to handle this situation by making every "thing" its own table. If you recall Figure 4-13, deleting a book wouldn't affect the author, but it would require that the relationship between the book and the author be severed. Going the other way, deleting an author doesn't mean the book doesn't exist.

Tip Business rules will dictate how to handle such situations as the book-to-author relationship. If you delete a book, it probably doesn't make sense to delete the author, but if you delete an author, does it make sense to keep the book around without knowledge of the author? Probably not. Understanding needs and desires of this kind will help when implementing relationships in the next chapter.

As an aside, consider also what happens if this screen is used to change the title of a multi-author book in a database that has BookAuthor tables such as that shown in the first diagram in the previous section, "Each Non-Key Attribute Must Describe the Entire Key." If the book has two authors, this book would need two BookAuthor rows. Now a user opens the editing screen and changes the title, as shown back in Figure 4-14. When he saves the change, it only alters the BookAuthor row for Fred Smith, not the one for his coauthor. The two BookAuthor rows, originally for the same book, now show different titles.

This problem was rectified by applying the Second Normal Form, as shown in the second diagram in that section. In this form, the Book table connects to two BookAuthor tables. Changing the title in this editor screen changes the BookTitle value for this single Book table. The two BookAuthor tables are only linked to the Book table by the BookIsbnNumber attribute, so the database still shows both authors as having coauthored the same book. Everything remains in sync.

Tip The issue of multiple authors for a book is also related to Fourth Normal Form. The reason why will become clearer later in the chapter when covering that Normal Form (I will explain!).

Clues That an Entity Is Not in Second Normal Form

The clues for detecting whether entities are in the Second Normal Form aren't as straightforward as the clues for the First Normal Form. In some cases, detection can take some careful thought, and some thorough examination of your structures:

- Repeating key attribute name prefixes, indicating that the values are probably describing some additional entity

- Data in repeating groups, showing signs of functional dependencies between attributes

- Composite keys without a foreign key, which might be a sign that you have key values that identify multiple things in the key, rather than a single thing

Repeating Key Attribute Prefixes

The situation of repeating key attribute prefixes is one of the dead giveaways. Let's revisit our previous example, as shown in Figure 4-15.

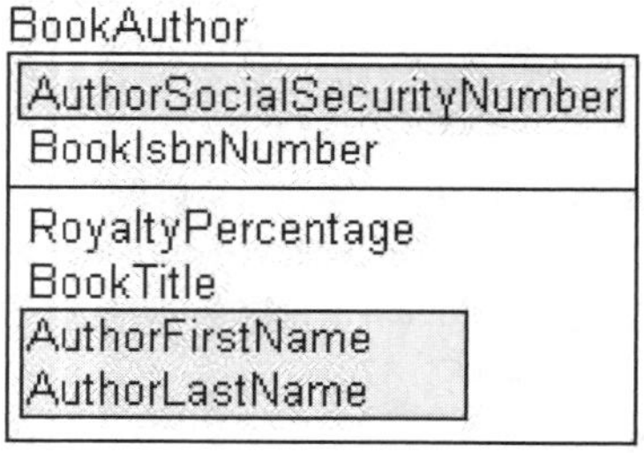

BookAuthor

| AuthorSocialSecurityNumber |
| BookIsbnNumber |

| RoyaltyPercentage |
| BookTitle |
| AuthorFirstName |
| AuthorLastName |

Figure 4-15. *The Author entity*

Here we have AuthorFirstName and AuthorLastName, which are functionally dependent on AuthorSocialSecurityNumber. We also have BookTitle and BookIsbnNumber, with the same situation.

Having such an obvious prefix on attributes such as Author% or Book% is awfully convenient, but it isn't always the case. However, this prefix is a rather common tip-off, especially when designing new systems.

Repeating Groups of Data

More difficult to recognize are the repeating groups of data. Imagine executing multiple SELECT statements on a table, each time retrieving all rows (if possible), ordered by each of the important columns. If there's a functionally dependent attribute on one of the attributes—anywhere one of the values is equal to X—we'll see the dependent attribute, Y.

Take a look at some example entries:

AuthorSocialSecurityNumber	BookIsbnNumber	RoyaltyPercentage
111-11-1111	1111111111	2
222-22-2222	2222222222	3
333-33-3333	3333333333	3

BookTitle	AuthorFirstName	AuthorSecondName
Instant Tiddlywinks	Vervain	Delaware
Beginning Ludo	Vervain	Delaware
Instant Tiddlywinks	Gordon	Gibbon

BookTitle is, of course, dependent on BookIsbnNumber, so any time we see an ISBN number that equals 1111111111, we can be sure that the book title is *Instant Tiddlywinks*. If it isn't, then there's something wrong in the database (which is why we wouldn't leave the entity modeled in this manner).

Composite Keys Without a Foreign Key

If there's more than one attribute in the key that isn't migrated from another table as a foreign key, consider the relationship between this attribute and the non-key attributes. There's a chance that it may be violating the Second Normal Form.

In our previous example of a key that was made up of the book ISBN number and author identification, consideration of the non-key attributes clearly gave us two keys that don't represent the same thing: in this case a book and an author.

Second Normal Form violations aren't always so cut and dried. Consider the example earlier of a phone number, in which each of the pieces of the phone number made up the key. Because the three parts made up one thing (in this case a phone number), each part of the key might not relate on its own to the other possible attributes of the phone number, such as the local calling rate or type of phone number (for example, if it was a mobile number, land line, and so on). On the other hand, if a description of the area code was required, putting this attribute in the phone number table would be a violation, since this description wouldn't describe the whole phone number key.

For every table, carefully consider what the composite key values are made up of. In the case of the phone number, the different parts of the phone number come together to identify a logically singular thing: a phone number.

Existing Code That Maintains the Problem Data

Scouring any existing database code is one good way of discovering problems, based on the lifespan of the system we're analyzing. Many times a programmer will simply write code to make sure the Second Normal Form violation isn't harmful to the data, rather than remodeling it into a proper structure (though often it won't even be noticed). At one time in the history of databases, this might have been the only way to handle this situation for performance reasons; however, now that technology has more than caught up with the relational theory, this is far less the case.

■**Caution** I'm not trying to make the case that theory has changed a bit due to technology. Relational theory has been pretty much stable throughout the years, with few of the concepts changing in the past decade. Ten years ago, we had quite a few problems making a normalized system operational in the hardware and operating-system constraints we had to deal with (my first experience with a SQL Server machine had 16MB of RAM and 200MB of disk space), so corners were cut in our models for "performance" reasons.

Using modern server hardware, there's usually no need to begin to cut normalization corners for performance. It's best to resolve these issues with SQL joins instead of spaghetti code to maintain denormalized data. Of course, at this point in the design process, it's best not even to consider the topics of implementation, performance, or any subject where we are not simply working towards proper logical storage of data. This might not be 100 percent true when working with a mobile database, but this sort of exception is pretty rare.

Third Normal Form

An entity that's in Third Normal Form has the following characteristics:

- The entity must be in Second Normal Form

- An entity is in violation of Third Normal Form if a non-key attribute is a fact about another non-key attribute

The Third Normal Form differs from the Second Normal Form in that it deals with the relationship of non-key data to non-key data. The problems are the same, and many of the symptoms are the same, but it can be harder to locate the general kinds of violations that this form tends to deal with. The main difference is that data in one attribute, instead of being dependent on the key, is dependent on data in another non-key attribute. The requirements for the Third Normal Form are as follows.

The Entity Must Be in Second Normal Form

Once again, it's important that the entity be in Second Normal Form. It might be hard to locate Third Normal Form problems if Second Normal Form problems still remain.

Non-Key Attributes Cannot Describe Other Non-Key Attributes

If any of the attributes are functionally dependent on an attribute other than the key, then we're again going to have data-modification anomalies. Because we're in Second Normal Form already, we've proven that all our attributes are reliant on the whole key, but we haven't looked at the relationship of the attributes to one another.

In the example shown in Figure 4-16, we take our Book entity and extend it to include the publisher and the city where the publisher is located.

Title defines the title for the book defined by the BookIsbnNumber, and Price indicates the price of the book. The case can clearly be made that PublisherName describes the book's publisher, but the PublisherCity doesn't make sense in this context, as it doesn't directly describe the book. It could be possible that the book was published in a given place, but this is unlikely to be the case, as publishing a book is a process that can cover a vast geography these days.

Figure 4-16. *The extended Book entity with publisher information added*

To correct this situation, we need to create a different entity to identify the publisher information, as shown in Figure 4-17.

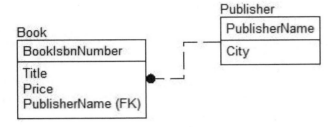

Figure 4-17. *We now place the publisher information in a separate entity*

Now the Publisher entity has only data concerning the publisher, and the Book entity has book information. An interesting offshoot of this is that now, if we want to add information to our schema concerning the publisher—for instance, contact information or an address—it's obvious where we add that information. Now we have our City attribute identifying the publisher, not the book. Once we get into physical modeling, we'll discuss the merits of having the PublisherName attribute as the primary key, but this is a reasonable key.

Note that the resolution of this problem was to create a *nonidentifying* relationship: Publisher publishes Book. Because the malevolent attributes weren't in the key to begin with, they don't go there now.

■**Tip** Third Normal Form can be summed up as follows:

All attributes must be a fact describing the key, the whole key, and nothing but the key.

If it sounds familiar, it should. This little saying is the backbone for the whole group of Normal Forms concerned with the relationship between the key and non-key attributes.

Programming Problems Avoided by the Third Normal Form

Although the methods of violating the Third Normal Form are close to the violations of the Second Normal Form, there are a few interesting differences. As we aren't dealing with key values, every attribute's relationship to every non-key attribute needs to be considered, and so does every combination of attributes. In the book example, we structured the entity as shown in Figure 4-16.

You should consider every attribute against every other attribute. If entities are of reasonable size, then the process of weeding out Third Normal Form problems won't be too lengthy. (Ten to twenty attributes in an entity is probably as many as seems reasonable to have without violating some normalization rule; though this doesn't always hold, it's a good rule of thumb.) In our example, doing a "perfect" job of comparing each attribute against each of the other attributes, we need to check each attribute against the other three attributes. As there are four attributes, we need to consider the $N * (N - 1)$ or $(4 * 3) = 12$ (ignoring the fact that we'll check some values more than once) different permutations of attribute relations to be safe. In our example entity we must check the following:

- `Title` against `Price`, `PublisherName`, and `PublisherCity`

- `Price` against `Title`, `PublisherName`, and `PublisherCity`

- `PublisherName` against `Price`, `Title`, and `PublisherCity`

- `PublisherCity` against `Price`, `Title`, and `PublisherName`

From this we notice that, when we check `PublisherName` against the other three attributes, it becomes clear that `PublisherCity` is functionally dependent on `PublisherName`, hence a Third Normal Form violation.

After designing quite a few entities, common attributes will jump out as problems, and only a few attributes will have to be considered in routine normalization checks. Note that our example has tailored names to make it seem simple, but in reality, if you aren't starting from scratch, names can be far more cryptic. Take our example entity, and put it in terms that might exist in a client's legacy database, as shown in Figure 4-18.

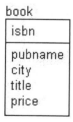

book

isbn
pubname city title price

Figure 4-18. *A legacy book entity*

These names are certainly less cryptic than those that exist in some legacy database entities; however, they're already ambiguous enough to cause problems. The `city` attribute seems almost fine here, unless we carefully consider that most books don't have a `city` attribute, but publishers might. The following example code shows what happens if we want to change the `city` attribute and keep it in sync.

■**Tip** Your first step in working with legacy systems ought to be to toss them in a data model and give them logical names that make it clear what each column is used for.

If we were in the logical design phase we should have named things better, but we won't always be normalizing for design's sake. We might simply be normalizing a table to try to eliminate some problem areas. In this case, we have to be careful.

Take, for example, the situation where we have the table as built previously:

```
CREATE TABLE book
(
    isbn varchar(20) NOT NULL,
    pubname varchar(60) NOT NULL,
    city varchar(30) NOT NULL,
    title varchar(60) NOT NULL
    price money NOT NULL
)
```

This has the Third Normal Form violations that we've identified. Consider the situation in which we want to update the city column for ISBN 3232380237, from a value of Virginia Beach to a value of Nashville. We first would update the single row:

```
UPDATE dbo.book
SET city = 'Nashville'
WHERE isbn = '23232380237'
```

But because we had the functional dependency of the pubname to city relationship, we now have to update all the books that have the same publisher name to the new value as well:

```
UPDATE dbo.book
SET city = 'Nashville'
WHERE city = 'Virginia Beach'
    AND pubname = 'Phantom Publishing' --publisher name
```

Although this is the proper way to ensure that the batch code updates the city properly, as well as the book, in most cases this code will be buried in the application, not tied together with a transaction—much less one in a batch. It's also easy to forget these types of relationships within the row when writing new processes that are required, as the system changes over time.

Make any errors in one UPDATE statement, and data can be compromised (clearly something we're trying to avoid by spending all this time working on our structures). For existing SQL Server applications that are being redesigned, employ the SQL Server Profiler to check what SQL the application is sending to SQL Server.

Even more troublesome than errors in the UPDATE statement is the fact that you can't represent a publisher without identifying a book. Of course, because the ISBN number of the book is the primary key, nothing stops the user from creating a phony ISBN number, and because giving the book phony column values to get a new publisher in. Again, this is more work, because do you eliminate the phony ISBN number when you add a book? It's horribly troublesome to keep all this in sync.

The point here is that you could write code to keep the table in sync, but it's a mess to maintain; the database is hard to modify; and it won't be faster, even if some folks will try to make you feel that denormalization performs better. Perhaps a join might be eliminated, but if the data isn't read only, you'll pay the cost in modifications. If you want denormalized views of your data, consider indexed views, which are automaintaining.

Clues That Entities Are Not in Third Normal Form

The clues for Third Normal Form are similar to those for Second Normal Form, as they try to solve the same sort of problem—making sure that all non-key attributes refer to the key of the entity:

- Multiple attributes with the same prefix, much like Second Normal Form, only this time not in the key

- Repeating groups of data

- Summary data that refers to data in a different entity altogether

Multiple Attributes with the Same Prefix

Let's revisit our previous example, as shown in Figure 4-19.

Figure 4-19. *A revised Book entity*

It's obvious that PublisherName and PublisherCity are multiple attributes with the same prefix. In some cases, the prefix and context used might not be so obvious, such as PubName, PblishCity, or even LocationPub—all *excellent* reasons to establish a decent naming standard.

Repeating Groups of Data

Repeating groups of data have much the same application as for the Second Normal Form, but we need to consider more permutations of comparisons, because each attribute should be compared against the other non-key attributes.

Summary Data

One of the common violations of the Third Normal Form that might not seem obvious is *summary data*. This is where attributes are added to the parent entity that refer to the child rows and summarize them. Summary data has been one of the most frequently necessary evils that we've had to deal with throughout the history of the relational database. There might be cases where calculated data needs to be stored in a table in violation of Third Normal Form, but in logical modeling there's *absolutely* no place for it. Not only is summary data not functionally dependent on non-key attributes, it's dependent on nonentity attributes. This causes all sorts of confusion, as I'll demonstrate. Summary data should be reserved either for physical design or the data warehousing steps.

Take the example of an auto dealer, as shown in Figure 4-20. The dealer has an entity listing all the automobiles it sells, and it has an entity recording each automobile sale.

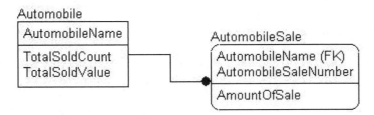

Figure 4-20. *The auto dealer has two entities*

Summary data generally has no part in logical modeling, because the sales data is available in another entity. Instead of accepting that the total number of vehicles sold and their value is available, the designer has decided to add attributes in the parent entity that refer to the child rows and summarize them.

Is this required during the implementation? Unlikely, but possible, depending on performance needs. However, it's common that the complexity of the implemented system has most likely increased by an order of magnitude, as we'll have to have triggers on the AutomobileSale entity that calculate these values for any change in the AutomobileSale entity. If this is a highly active database with frequent instances added to the AutomobileSale entity, this tends to slow the database down considerably. On the other hand, if it's an often inactive database, then there will be few instances in the child entity, so the performance gains made by quickly being able to find the numbers of vehicles sold and their value will be small anyway.

The key is that in logical modeling, including summary data on the model isn't required, because the data modeled in the total attributes exists in the Sales entity. Data that we identify in our logical models should be modeled to exist in only one place, and any values that could be calculated from other values shouldn't be represented on the model. This aids in keeping the integrity of the design of the data at its highest level possible.

■**Tip** One way of dealing with summary data is to use a view. An automobile view might summarize the automobile sales. In many cases, you can index the view and the data is automatically maintained for you. The summarized data is easier to maintain using the indexed view, though it can have negative performance repercussions on modifications, but positive ones on reads. Only testing your actual situation will tell, but this is not the implementation part of the book! I'll discuss indexes in some detail in Chapter 8.

Overnormalizing

The goal of normalization is to store only one piece of data in one place. However, you could reduce multiple values down to being stored in a single place, when more than one value is required. Overnormalizing is not to be confused with denormalizing. "Overnormalizing" is normalizing without considering all the consequences. Sometimes in the normalization process, we can lose important information. A common example of this is an invoice line item and the price that's being charged. Consider the model shown in Figure 4-21.

In particular, look at the `InvoiceLineItem.ProductCost` attribute. The product has a cost associated with it already, so do we need the product cost repeated for the `InvoiceLineItem`? At the time of the invoice being printed, we can get the cost from the product, and bam, we're done—right?

Will the price *always* be the same? And if not, what of the invoice information? We could no longer see the price that the customer was charged, losing some information in the process. When normalizing (and doing *any* logical data modeling), we must focus on making sure that we deal with things that are always true. In this case, what happens if the cost of the product changes? Do we need to come up with an elaborate history of product costs and how to relate them to invoices during periods of time? Perhaps, but what if the manager that day says "Aw, give it to 'em for half off." Then even storing what the value was on a given day won't cover the price that the user paid. So in this case, it's better to have the data as it existed when the sale was made in the row with the sale (and you might want to keep up a table of values as the price changes as well). A way to make this decision is to consider whether updating one value necessitates that you update another.

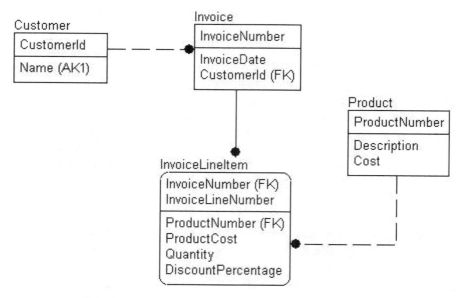

Figure 4-21. *An overnormalized design*

You might also have noticed an absence of a total value for the `LineItem`. This value can be calculated by `ProductCost * Quantity * ( 1 - DiscountPercentage )`, and shouldn't vary from that. Hence, adding a total value would violate Third Normal Form because the total would be functionally dependent on the ProductCost, Quantity, and DiscountPercentage.

The most important thing to remember here is always to consider the side effects of normalizing your tables, especially in consideration of the business rules. They can dictate whether a given attribute is functionally dependent on another attribute, based on usage and modifyability rules.

Boyce-Codd Normal Form

The *Boyce-Codd Normal Form* (BCNF) is named after Ray Boyce, one of the creators of SQL, and Edgar Codd, who I introduced in the first chapter as the father of relational databases. It's a better-constructed replacement for both the Second and Third Normal Forms, that takes the meaning of the Second and Third Normal Forms and restates it in a more general way. Note that, to be in BCNF, there's no mention of Second Normal Form or Third Normal Form. The BCNF encompasses them both, and is defined as follows:

- The entity is in First Normal Form; we won't rediscuss this one further.

- All attributes are fully dependent on a key.

- An entity is in BCNF if every determinant is a key.

Let's look at the last two rules individually.

All Attributes Are Fully Dependent on a Key

We can rephrase this like so: "All attributes must be a fact about *a* key and nothing but *a* key." This is a slight but important deviation from our previous rules for Second Normal Form and Third Normal Form. In this case, we don't specify *the entire* key or just *the* key—now it is *a* key. How does this differ? Well, it does and it doesn't. It expands the meaning of Second Normal Form and Third Normal Form to deal with the typical situation in which we have more than one key. As mentioned before, a key can be *any* candidate key, whether the primary key or an alternate key.

■**Caution** Depending on the choice of primary key, this can be a great distinction. There's a massive movement towards using meaningless surrogate keys (of which I am a big fan). If you don't deal with the case of more than one key, it's easy to forget that the important keys are the natural keys of the entity, and normalization should take them into consideration. Too often when answering newsgroup posts, the problem of poor key choices for a table has to be solved before solving the problem at hand.

The attribute must be fully dependent on a key. Keys are defined as the unique identifier for an instance of the entity, regardless of whether we use a natural key or otherwise. Using the key, you're able to find the row within the set that makes up the entity. The entity is the logical representation of a single object, either real or imaginary. Think of the key in terms of being the entity's ID badge, Social Security number (SSN), or user name. It's the way we tell it apart from other entities.

For example, let's take a person who works for a company and model that person. First we choose our key; let's say SSN, as shown in Figure 4-22.

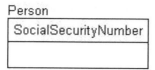

Person

SocialSecurityNumber

Figure 4-22. *Our Person entity has its SSN as the key*

Then we start adding the other attributes we know about our employees—their name, hair color, eye color, the badge number they're given, their driver's license number, and so on. Now we have the entity shown in Figure 4-23.

Person

SocialSecurityNumber
FirstName LastName Height Weight BadgeNumber EyeColor DriversLicenseNumber HairColor ShoeSize

Figure 4-23. *An enlarged Person entity*

Careful study of the entity shows that it's in Third Normal Form, because each of the attributes further describes the entity. The FirstName, Height, BadgeNumber, and others all refer to the entity. The same might be said for the SocialSecurityNumber. It has been chosen as the key, primarily because it was the first thing we came upon. In logical modeling, the choice of which attribute is a primary key isn't all that meaningful, and we can change the primary key at any time. (Chapter 5 will discuss the various choices of primary keys for a table.)

As I mentioned in the previous chapter as I built a sample conceptual data model, in practice I'll use a value that's simply the name of the table with "Id" appended to it for the primary key in the logical modeling phase. For example, in a previous example, we had Person and PersonEmail entities. For the key of the PersonEmail, the key was PersonId and EmailAddress. In a typical design, I choose to model this situation as shown in Figure 4-24.

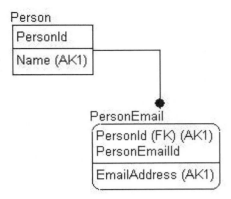

Figure 4-24. *Modeling a person's personal e-mail address*

In this book, I'll for the most part do examples of each style of modeling keys, sometimes using surrogates, sometimes using natural keys. In the case study, I'll use surrogate keys exclusively.

An Entity Is in Boyce-Codd Normal Form If Every Determinant Is a Key

The second part of the quest for BCNF is to make sure that every determinant is a key, or a unique identifier for the entity. I've adapted our definition of a determinant from Chapter 1 to include the following:

> *Any attribute or combination of attributes on which any other attribute or combination of attributes is functionally dependent.*

Based on our study of the Second and Third Normal Forms, we can see that this is nearly the same as the definition of a key. Because all attributes that aren't keys must be functionally dependent on a key, the definition of a determinant is close to the same as the definition of a key.

The BCNF simply extends the previous Normal Forms by saying that an entity might have many keys, and all attributes must be dependent on one of these keys. It's simplified a bit by noting that every key must uniquely identify the entity, and every non-key attribute must describe the entity.

One interesting thing that should be noted is that each key is a determinant for all other keys. This is because, in every place where one key value is seen, we can replace it with the other key value without losing the meaning of the entity. This is not to say that an alternate key cannot change values—not at all. The driver's license number is a good key, but if the Department of Motor Vehicles issues all new numbers, it's still a key, and it will still identify and describe the entity. If the value of any candidate key changes, this is perfectly acceptable.

With this definition in mind, consider the example entity shown in Figure 4-23 again.

Person

SocialSecurityNumber
FirstName
LastName
Height
Weight
BadgeNumber
EyeColor
DriversLicenseNumber
HairColor
ShoeSize

What we're looking for now are attributes or groups of attributes that are dependent on the key, and also that are unique to each instance of this entity.

FirstName isn't unique by itself, and it wouldn't be good to assume that FirstName and LastName are unique. (It all depends on the size of the target set as to whether or not the user would be willing to accept this. At least we would need to include middle initial and title, but still this isn't a good key.) Height describes the person, but isn't unique. The same is true for Weight. BadgeNumber should be unique, so we'll make it a key. (Note that we don't have BadgeIssuedDate, as that would refer to the badge and doesn't help the BCNF example. However, if we did have a badge-issue date, we could easily have a Badge entity with a BadgeNumber primary key that's migrated to this table.)

The DriversLicenseNumber attribute is probably unique, but consider variations across localities. Two governments might have similar numbering schemes that might cause duplication. Taken with DriversLicenseState (which I'll add), this will be a key. HairColor and ShoeSize describe the person, but neither could be considered unique. Even taking the person's Height, Weight, EyeColor, HairColor, and ShoeSize together, you can't guarantee uniqueness between two random people. So now we model the entity as shown in Figure 4-25.

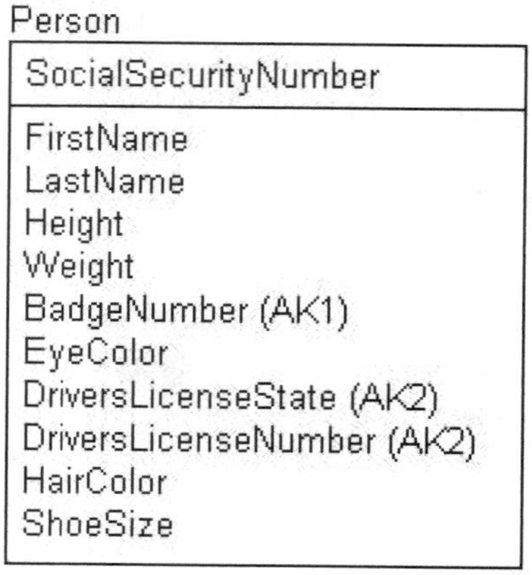

Person

SocialSecurityNumber
FirstName
LastName
Height
Weight
BadgeNumber (AK1)
EyeColor
DriversLicenseState (AK2)
DriversLicenseNumber (AK2)
HairColor
ShoeSize

Figure 4-25. *The license and badge number attributes are used as keys*

We now have three keys for this object. When we do the modeling for the implementation, we'll choose the proper key from the keys we have defined, or use an artificial key. As discussed in Chapter 1, an artificial key is simply a value that's used as a pointer to an object, much like BadgeNumber is a pointer that a company uses to identify an employee, or like the government using SSNs to identify individuals in the USA. (The SSN is a smart key, as some digits identify where the number was issued, and it has an artificial element, probably a simple sequence number.)

It's also worth considering that an SSN isn't always a good key either. Even dealing only with people in the USA, plenty of people don't have an SSN. And if we want to accommodate people from outside the USA, then the SSN will never work. It depends on the situation, as there are many circumstances where the user is required to have an SSN, and some where an SSN or green card is required to identify the user as a valid resident of the USA. The situation always dictates the eventual solution, and this choice needs to be made during design to decide on the appropriate path.

Clues and Programming Anomalies

The clues for determining that an entity is in BCNF are the same as for Second Normal Form and Third Normal Form. The programming anomalies cured by the BCNF are the same too.

Once all the determinants are modeled during this phase of the design, implementing the determinants as unique keys will be far more likely of an occurrence. This prevents users from entering nonunique values in the columns that need to have unique values in them.

This completes our overview of the first four Normal Forms. I should probably state here that a great deal of people feel that this is "far" enough to take normalization. This is usually true, but only because there aren't often problems in data models that the Fourth and Fifth Normal Forms cover. I suggest you don't ignore the next section, thinking that knowing the first three Normal Forms is good enough. At the least this section will put the idea in the back of your mind of what situation you might be getting into if your tables are of a certain type. What's that type? Sorry, you'll have to read on . . .

Multivalued Dependencies in Entities

In this section, we'll look closely at the next level of normalization. It's just as important as the first three, though it isn't commonly used because of perceived drawbacks in terms of both the time taken to implement the normalization, and the cost in performance of the resulting database.

In the previous sections, we dealt with the structure of attributes, and the relationship between non-key attributes and keys. The next couple Normal Forms deal again with the relationship among the non-key attributes, but now we're dealing with the cardinality of the relationship and the kinds of problems that can arise.

Third Normal Form is generally considered the pinnacle of proper database design, but as I'll discuss in the following section, some serious problems might still remain in our logical design. To be more specific, the Normal Forms that this section will cover deal with the case of multivalued dependencies between attributes. When we have keys that have three parts or more, the relationship between these attributes can cause us some serious problems. For our purposes, we'll look at the Fourth Normal Form in some detail, and then introduce two others simply in light format.

Fourth Normal Form

Our rules of normalization so far have resolved redundancies among columns in an entity, but haven't resolved problems that arise from entities having composite primary keys while still possessing redundant data between rows. Normalizing entities to Fourth Normal Form addresses such problems. In a simple case, moving to Fourth Normal Form takes care of issues such as the modeling of an attribute that appears as if it's a single value but is actually multiple values. The second type of problem is more elusive, as it deals with ternary relationships.

Briefly, consider the case of an entity of students in a class (note that multiple classes present a different problem). We need to store the teacher of each student, so we put teachers and students in the ClassAssignment entity as shown in Figure 4-26.

ClassAssignment

| Class |
| Teacher |
| Student |

Figure 4-26. *A class assignment entity*

However, it turns out that this entity is unsatisfactory, because now if we want to change the teacher for a class, we have to consider all the students for the class, which isn't optimal. That's not to mention that we need to deal with the difficulties trying to delete or insert a class, teacher, or student without affecting the existence of all three. The key here is that for a class there are multiple students, a student can be in multiple classes and have multiple teachers, and so on. So these one-to-many relationships are enclosed in this relationship that needs to be dealt with properly.

This is a large part of what the Fourth Normal Form is all about. We have to break up this ternary relationship into more useful forms. To do this, we note that the relationship centers on the Class attribute, because a Class has one or more Teachers, and indeed one or more Students. Figure 4-27 shows our modified design.

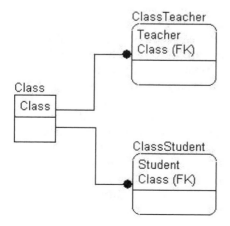

Figure 4-27. *The modified class model*

This example illustrates that the following conditions must be met for an entity to be in Fourth Normal Form:

- *The entity must be in BCNF*: This condition ensures that all keys will be appropriately defined, and all values in an entity will be properly dependent on its key.

- *There must not be more than one* multivalued dependency *(MVD) between an attribute and the key of the entity*: No more than one attribute can store multiple values that relate to a key in any entity, otherwise there will be data duplication. In addition, we should ensure that we don't repeat single-valued attributes for every multivalued one.

We'll look at a few examples to help make these ideas clearer. Let's first look at the three main forms that Fourth Normal Form violations take:

- Ternary relationships

- Lurking multivalued attributes

- Status and other attributes for which we need to know the previous values

Fourth Normal Form, in my opinion, is critical to understand. The methods are easy enough to follow. There are some important misconceptions about the Normal Forms past the Third being meaningless, and they're wrong. I feel that once you normalize to the Fourth level, you won't even consider ignoring what it stands for.

Ternary Relationships

We briefly looked at ternary relationships back in Chapter 1. Often in real life, relationships won't manifest themselves in simple binary-type relationships, and the ternary or greater relationships are common. Any place where we see three (or more) identifying or mandatory nonidentifying relationships in an entities key, we're likely to have trouble (consider also the case in which keys aren't perfectly chosen).

Take, as an example, a situation where we've designed a set of entities to support a conference planner, storing information concerning the session, presenter, and room where a session is to be given.

Let's also assume the following set of open business rules is to be enforced:

- More than one presenter may be listed to give a presentation

- A presentation may span more than one room

Figure 4-28 models the relationship **presenter-*presents*-session-*in*-room**.

Each of these entities is a BCNF entity; however, the relationship between the three is troublesome because of the three-column key, especially with all attributes being migrated from other entities. There might be nothing wrong with this at all, but any case in which this situation occurs bears some investigation to make sure that no multivalued dependencies will cause eventual problems in our data.

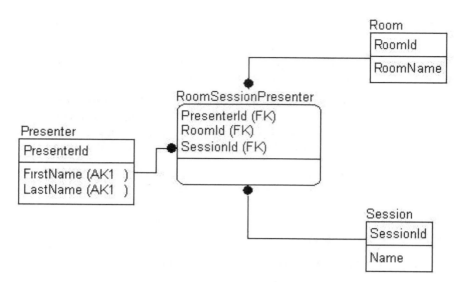

Figure 4-28. *The presenter-presents-session-in-room relationship*

Consider the case that each of the sessions is going on at the same time. The table would require a session time, which would complicate matters. At this point, we're dealing with the case of one session time for all sessions. Let's look at a set of sample data (we've joined Room, Presenter, and Session to look at the natural keys):

Session	Presenter	Room
101	Davidson	River Room
202	Davidson	Stream Room
202	Hazel	Stream Room
404	Hawkins	Brook Room
404	Hawkins	Stream Room

In the first row, there's no problem, as we have one row for session 101, which has one presenter, Davidson, and one room, the River Room. A problem becomes apparent in the next two rows, as one session 202 has two different presenters, and yet a single room. This forces us to repeat data unnecessarily in the Room attribute, because we now have stored in two places that session 202 is in the Stream Room. If the session moves, we have to change it in two places, and if we forget this property, and update the room based on a value that we aren't currently displaying (for example, through the use of an artificial key), then we end up with the following values:

Session	Presenter	Room
202	Davidson	Stream Room
202	Hazel	"Changed to Room"

In this example, we have duplicated data in the Session and Room attributes, and the 404 session duplicates Session and Presenter data. The real problem with our scenario comes when adding to or changing our data. If we need to update the Session number that Davidson is giving with Hazel in the Stream Room, then two rows will require changes. Equally, if a Room assignment changes, then several rows will have to be changed.

When we implement entities in this fashion, we might not even see all the rows filled in as fully as this. Next, we see a set of rows that are functionally equivalent to the set in the previous entity:

```
Session   Presenter    Room
-------   ---------    -----------
101       Davidson     <null>
101       <null>       River Room
202       Davidson     <null>
202       <null>       Stream Room
202       Hazel        <null>
404       <null>       Brook Room
404       Hawkins      <null>
404       <null>       Stream Room
```

In this example, we have nulls for some rooms, and some presenters. We have eliminated the duplicated data, but now all we have is some pretty strange-looking data with nulls everywhere. Furthermore, we aren't able to use nulls clearly to stand for the situation where we don't yet know the presenter for a session. We're storing an equivalent set of data to that in the previous example, but the data in this form is difficult to work with.

To develop a solution to this problem, let's first make the Presenter entity primary, as shown in Figure 4-29.

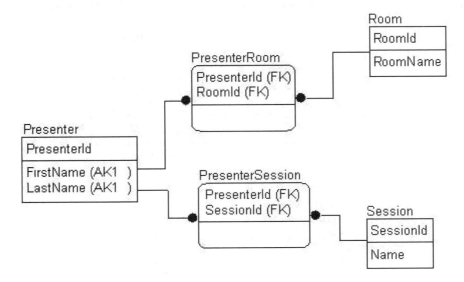

Figure 4-29. *The Presenter entity is primary*

Then we take the data in the RoomSessionPresenter entity and break it into the entities in Figure 4-30.

Presenter
Davidson
Hazel
Hawkins

Presenter	Room
Davidson	River Room
Davidson	Stream Room
Hazel	Stream Room
Hawkins	Stream Room
Hawkins	Brook Room

Presenter	Session
Davidson	101
Davidson	202
Hazel	404
Hawkins	404

Figure 4-30. *Data rearranged in a Presenter-centric way*

This is obviously not a proper solution, because we would never be able to determine what room a session is located in, unless a presenter had been assigned. Also, Davidson is doing a session in the River Room as well as the Stream Room, and there's no link back to the session that's being given in the room. When we decompose any relationship and we lose meaning to the data, the decomposition is referred to as a *lossy decomposition*. This is one such case, so isn't a reasonable solution to our problem.

Next we try centering on the room where the sessions are held, as shown in Figure 4-31.

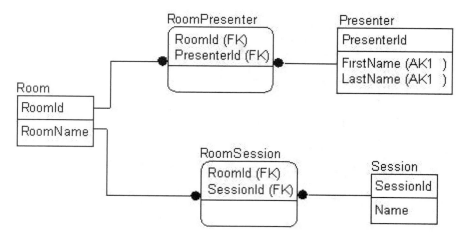

Figure 4-31. *The Room entity is now primary*

Taking the data and fitting into the entities once again, see Figure 4-32.

Room
River Room
Brook Room
Stream Room

Room	Presenter
River Room	Davidson
Stream Room	Davidson
Stream Room	Hazel
Stream Room	Hawkins
Brook Room	Hawkins

Room	Session
River Room	101
Stream Room	202
Brook Room	202
Stream Room	404

Figure 4-32. *Data rearranged in a Room-centric way*

Again, this is a lossy decomposition because we're unable to determine, for example, exactly who's presenting the 202 presentation. It's in the Stream Room; and Davidson, Hazel, and Hawkins are all presenting in the Stream Room; but they're not all presenting the 202 session. So once again we need to consider another design. This time we center our design on the sessions to be held, as shown in Figure 4-33.

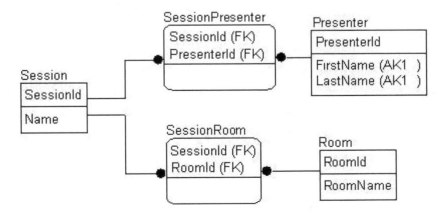

Figure 4-33. *The Session entity is now primary*

Look at the data in Figure 4-34.

Session
101
202
404

Session	Room
101	River Room
202	Stream Room
404	Brook Room
404	Stream Room

Session	Presenter
101	Davidson
202	Davidson
202	Hazel
404	Hawkins

Figure 4-34. *Data rearranged in a Session-centric way*

We have finally hit upon a solution to the problem. From this data, we're able to determine precisely who is presenting what and where, and we'll have no problem adding or removing presenters, or even changing rooms. For example, take session 404. We have the data in the following sets of results in the sessionRoom and sessionPresenter entities for this session:

```
Session   Room
--------  -------------
404       Brook Room
404       Stream Room


Session   Presenter
--------  -------------
404       Hawkins
```

To add a presenter named Evans to the slate, we simply add another row:

```
Session   Presenter
-------   -------------
404       Hawkins
404       Evans
```

This is now a proper decomposition, and won't have the problems we outlined in our original entity. Now that we've set the session separately from the presenter, the nulls are no longer required in the foreign key values, because if we want to show that a room hasn't been chosen, we don't create a sessionRoom instance. The same is true if we haven't yet chosen a presenter. More importantly, we can now set multiple rooms for a session without confusion, and we certainly cannot duplicate a value between the Session and the Room.

If we need to have additional data that extends the concept of SessionPresenter, for example to denote alternate presenter (or indeed primary and secondary presenter), we now have a clean and logical place to store this information. Note that if we had tried to store that information in the original entity, it would have violated BCNF because the AlternatePresenter attribute would only be referring to the Session and Presenter, and not the Room.

The key to this process is to look for relationships between the attributes. In this case, there was a relationship between the session and who was presenting, as well as the session and where it was being given. On the other hand, there was no direct relationship between the presenter and where the session was located.

Lurking Multivalued Attributes

We consider some attributes to be *lurking* because they don't always stand out as problems at first glance. To illustrate this idea, let's consider the design model shown in Figure 4-35.

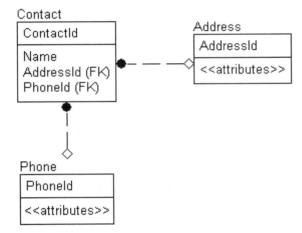

Figure 4-35. *A design that includes lurking multivalued attributes*

A problem arises here when we consider the Contact entity, because we have three attributes: the contact's name (assume that this name is in First Normal Form), the phone number, and address. The name is fine, as every contact has a single name by which we'll refer to them, but these days, many people have more than one address and phone number. We therefore have multivalued attributes that require further normalization to resolve them. To allow for such multiple addresses and phone numbers, we might modify our design as shown in Figure 4-36.

Although having multiple phone numbers isn't a First Normal Form violation (because they're all different types of phone numbers, rather than multiples of the same type), we do have a further problem. Because we have simply added the type of attribute to the name of the attribute (for example, HomeAddressId, FaxPhoneId), we'll have further multivalue attribute problems if, for example, the user has two fax phones, or indeed two mobile phones. Furthermore, we're in the less-than-ideal situation of needing multiple nullable values for each of the attributes when the attribute doesn't exist. This is a messy representation of the relationship. For example, if the client requires a spouse's office phone number attribute for a contact, we'll have to change the model, in all probability leading us to rewriting the application code.

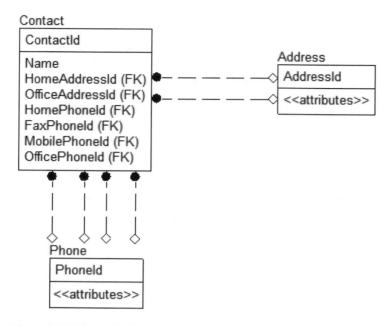

Figure 4-36. *The model now allows multiple addresses and phone numbers*

Let's further modify the design, so as to have separate `Contact` and `ContactInformation` entities, as shown in Figure 4-37.

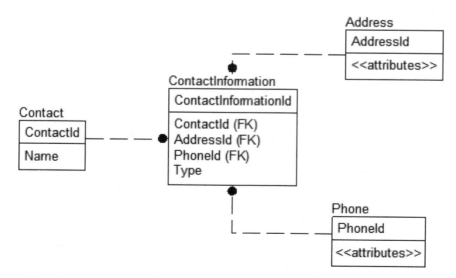

Figure 4-37. *Separate Contact and ContactInformation entities*

The `Type` attribute denotes the type of contact information that we're storing in an instance, so we can now have a `ContactInformation` instance with a `Type` of 'Home', and attach an address and phone number to it. This now allows us to add as many phone numbers and addresses as a user requires. However, because address and phone are held in the same table, we end up with null values where a contact has different numbers of home addresses and phone numbers.

At this stage, we need to decide how we want to proceed. We might want a phone number to be linked with an address (for example, linking a home address with a home phone number). In our case, we'll split the ContactInformation entity into ContactAddress and ContactPhone (though this isn't the only possible solution to the problem), as shown in Figure 4-38.

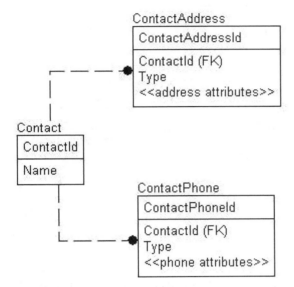

Figure 4-38. *ContactAddress and ContactPhone entities now represent the contact information*

This modification has eliminated the remaining multivalued dependencies, because we can now have many addresses and many phone numbers independently of one another, and are able to define as many types as desired without needing to modify our entity structures. However, we can take one further step, by modeling the phone number and address as different entities in the logical model, and adding domain entities for the Type column. In this way, we can prevent users from typing "Home," "Homer," "Hume," and so on, when they mean "home." Modeling the phone number and address as different entities also gives us a user-configurable constraint so we can add additional types without having to change the model. We'll add a Description attribute to the domain entities, allowing us to describe the actual purpose of the type. This allows for situations such as where we have an address type of "Away" that's standard for a given organization, but confusing to first-time users. We could then assign a description such as "Address for contact when traveling on extended sales trips." Figure 4-39 shows our final model.

Note that I've made the additional attributes of Address and PhoneNumber alternate keys, to avoid duplicating an address every time it's used in the system. This way, if we have five contacts that have the same address for their office, we only have to change one item. This might or might not be desirable in the final implementation, as it can increase complexity, and might or might not be worth it from a business perspective.

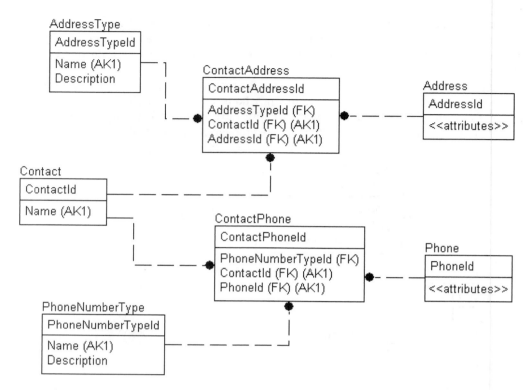

Figure 4-39. *The final model*

You'll tend to catch many of these types of issues during the First, Second, Third, or Boyce-Codd Normal Form checks. For example, think back to Payment1, Payment2, and so on from First Normal Form. If the field had just read Payment, would it have been as noticeable? Maybe not. This is especially true if you're strict with your search for entities and realize that a payment is an independent thing from a customer.

■**Note** This is one of the reasons why Fourth Normal Form is the most important Normal Form. It forces you to look deeper at the relationship between non-key and key attributes.

Attribute History

We might also encounter problems with our design model in a situation where we need to store status-type information for an instance of some entity. For example, in Figure 4-40, we've built two entities that store the header of an order, as well as a domain entity for the order status.

The problem here is that the order status changes (and hence the value of the OrderStatusTypeId attribute) based both on the values of the other date attributes, and other external factors. For example, when the order is taken from the customer, the TakenDate attribute would be filled in with a date. The order then might be in 'Pending' status. After the customer's payment method has been verified, we'd then modify the VerifiedDate attribute with the date verified, and set the status to 'InProcess'. 'InProcess' could mean more than one thing, such as "sent to shipping" or "bill sent."

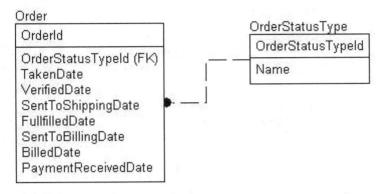

Figure 4-40. *A model of an Order entity*

Here, we're concerned with the OrderStatusTypeId attribute on the Order entity. It contains the current status for the Order instance. How do you answer questions about when an order got sent to the shipping department, or when the order-verification department verified the order? The modeler of the data has added several attributes in the Order entity to store these bits of information, but what if it failed verification once? Do we care? And is the FulfilledDate the date when the order was either fully shipped or canceled, or strictly when it was fully shipped? Do we need to add another attribute for CanceledDate?

To solve these problems, we'll have to change our model to allow the storing of multiple values for each of the attributes we've created, as shown in Figure 4-41.

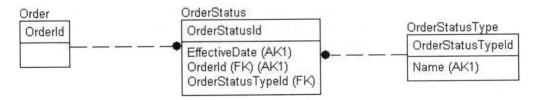

Figure 4-41. *We can now store multiple values for each attribute*

Now whenever the order status changes, all we have to do is add an instance to the OrderStatus entity. Whatever instance has the latest EffectiveDate value is the current status. We could also implement our model to allow more than one status value at a time. For instance, not all statuses are fulfilled in a sequential fashion. In an Order type entity, for instance, you might send the invoice to be verified, then once it's verified, send it to be processed by shipping and billing at the same time. With the new structure that we've created, when our order fails to be shipped, we can record that it failed to ship. We can also record that the client has paid. Note that, in this case, we only want to model the status of the overall order, and not the status of any items on the order.

Modeling and implementing this type of Fourth Normal Form solution sometimes requires a state diagram to determine in what order a status is achieved. For example, Figure 4-42 can be used to describe the process of an order being taken, from the time it was ordered to the time it was closed out. (We won't consider canceling or modifying an order, or indeed backorders in this example. The solution to that problem would be much the same, however.)

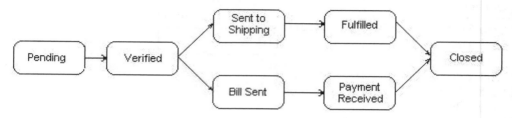

Figure 4-42. *The ordering process*

We can model this kind of simple state diagram fairly easily with one additional entity (the From relationship is optional), as shown in Figure 4-43.

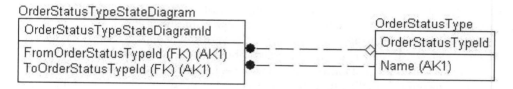

Figure 4-43. *Modeling the state diagram*

■**Note** This is a type of recursive relationship, with the recursive structure split out in the OrderStatusType table. If a child can only have one parent, then it's a tree (and you can use a one-table recursive relationship for that). If you can have more than one parent (as is the case for the closed value), it is considered a graph.

Consider that we had our seven states in the OrderStatusType entity:

```
OrderStatusTypeId      Name
-----------------      ---------
1                      Pending
2                      Verified
3                      Shipping
4                      Bill Sent
5                      Fulfilled
6                      Paid
7                      Closed
```

To define our state diagram, we'd need the following instances for the `OrderStatusType`➥ `StateDiagram` entity (leaving off the key this time, and including `Name` for clarity):

fromOrderStatusTypeId	Name	toOrderStatusTypeId	Name
1	Pending	2	Verified
2	Verified	3	Shipping
2	Verified	4	Bill Sent
3	Shipping	5	Fulfilled
4	Bill Sent	6	Paid
5	Fulfilled	7	Closed
6	Paid	7	Closed

In this manner, we can see whether or not we're in a particular state, what state we were previously in, and what state we can be in next. This state diagram also allows us to define the flow of our business rules in data, rather than hard-coding a bunch of fixed values.

In this case, our status might go through several values, and in fact might have multiple statuses at any given time. You would have to document business rules outlining exactly how the process works in a given situation. In reality, the exception processing requires the most amount of time, with up to 80 percent of coding time generally spent on the exceptions to the rule.

Tip Data warehousing technologies have eliminated much of the need for most historical information being stored in an OLTP-type system. The data warehouse takes a snapshot of the data at a given point of time and saves history in a useful manner for reporting. In practice, it's best to keep only as much history in the OLTP system as you need to support day-to-day operations. History is better kept in the dimensional model used in data warehousing.

Fifth Normal Form

Not every ternary relationship can be broken down into two entities related to a third. The aim of the Fifth Normal Form is to ensure that any ternary relationships that still exist in a Fourth Normal Form entity that can be decomposed into entities are decomposed. This eliminates problems with update anomalies due to multivalued dependencies, much like in Fourth Normal Form, only these are more tricky to find.

The idea is that ternary relationships are safer to deal with if you break all ternary relationships down into binary relationships. We saw in Fourth Normal Form that some ternary relationships could be broken down into two binary relationships without losing information. When the breakdown into two binary relationships became a lossy one, it was declared that the relationship was in Fourth Normal Form.

At this point, Fifth Normal Form would suggest that it's best to break down any existing ternary relationship into three binary relationships. In some cases, you cannot break a ternary relationship down. For example, consider the case of the following `Teacher`, `Student`, and `Class` data:

Teacher	Student	Class
Bob	Louis	Normalization
Bob	Fred	T-SQL
Larry	Fred	Normalization

Break this down into three sets of data, TeacherStudent, TeacherClass, and StudentClass, respectively:

Teacher	Student
Bob	Louis
Bob	Bob
Larry	Fred

Teacher	Class
Bob	Normalization
Bob	T-SQL
Larry	Normalization

Student	Class
Louis	Normalization
Fred	T-SQL
Fred	Normalization

Now, the problem is that we can erroneously infer invalid data from looking at each set of data separately:

- Bob at one time taught Fred.

- Bob taught Normalization.

- Fred took a class on Normalization.

Hence, from this path through the data, Bob must have been Fred's teacher on Normalization. Wrong answer! Larry did that. So the StudentTeacherClass tables were in Fifth Normal Form already, because we needed all three pieces of information together to state a condition. One thing of note here is that the business rules play a part in our ability to break this table down further. If only one teacher could teach the Normalization class, we wouldn't have had any problems with this entity. This is a large part of what makes Fifth Normal Form elusive and difficult to test for.

What can be gleaned from Fifth Normal Form, and indeed all the Normal Forms, is that when you feel you can break down a table into smaller parts with different natural keys, it's likely better to do so. If you can join the parts together to represent the data in the original, less-broken-down form, your database will likely be better for it. Obviously, if you can't reconstruct the table from the joins, then leave it as it is.

Denormalization

Denormalization is used primarily to improve performance in cases where overnormalized structures are causing overhead to the query processor, and in turn other processes in SQL Server, or to tone down some complexity to make things easier to implement. As I've tried to highlight in this chapter, although it can be argued that denormalizing to Third Normal Form might simplify queries by reducing the number of joins needed, this risks introducing data anomalies. Any additional code written to deal with these anomalies needs to be duplicated in every application that uses the database, thereby increasing the likelihood of human error. The judgment call that needs to be made in this situation is whether a slightly slower (but 100 percent accurate) application is preferable to a faster application of lower accuracy.

It's this book's contention that during logical modeling, we should never step back from our normalized structures to performance-tune our applications proactively. As this book is centered around OLTP database structures, the most important part of our design is to make certain that our logical model represents all the entities and attributes that the resulting data-base will hold. During, and most importantly, *after* the process of *physical* modeling, there might well be valid reasons to denormalize the structures, either to improve performance or reduce implementation complexity, but neither of these pertain to the *logical* model. We'll always have fewer problems if we implement physically what is true logically. I always advo-cate waiting until the physical modeling phase to implement solutions, or at least until we find a compelling reason to do so (such as if some part of our system is failing), before we denormalize.

Best Practices

The following are a few guiding principles that I use when normalizing a database. If you understand the fundamentals of why to normalize, these five points pretty much cover the entire process:

- *Follow the rules of normalization as closely as possible*: The chapter summary summa-rizes these rules. These rules are optimized for use with relational database management systems, such as SQL Server. Keep in mind that SQL Server now has, and will continue to add, tools to help with normalized and denormalized structures, because the goal of SQL Server is to be all things to all people. The principles of normalization are 30-plus years old, and are still valid today.

- *All attributes must describe the essence of what's being modeled in the entity*: Be certain to know what that essence is. For example, when modeling a person, only things that describe or identify a person should be included.

- *At least one key must uniquely identify and describe the essence of what the entity is modeling*: Uniqueness alone isn't a sufficient criterion for being an entities-only key. It isn't wrong to have a uniqueness-only key, but it shouldn't be the only key.

- *Choice of primary key isn't necessarily important at this point*: Keep in mind that the primary key is changeable at any time. We have taken a stance that only a surrogate or placeholder key is sufficient for now. This isn't a required practice, it's just a convenience that must not supplant choice of a proper key. We'll choose all sorts of primary keys in the text for examples.

- *Normalize as far as possible during the logical phase*: There's little to lose by designing complex structures in the logical phase of the project; it's trivial to make changes at this stage of the process. The well-normalized structures, even if not implemented as such, will provide solid documentation on the actual "story" of the data.

Summary

In this chapter, I've presented the criteria for normalizing our databases so they'll work properly with relational database management systems. At this stage, it's pertinent to summarize quickly the nature of the main Normal Forms we've outlined in this and the preceding chapter, in Table 4-1.

Table 4-1. *Normal Form Recap*

Form	Rules
First Normal Form	All attributes must be atomic; one value per attribute. All instances of an entity must contain the same number of values. All instances of an entity must be different from one another.
Second Normal Form	The entity must be in First Normal Form. All attributes must be a fact about the entire key and not a subset of the key.
Third Normal Form	The entity must be in Second Normal Form. An entity is in Third Normal Form if every non-key attribute is a fact about a key attribute. All attributes must be a fact about the key, and nothing but the key.
BCNF	All attributes are fully dependent on a key; all attributes must be a fact about a key, and nothing but a key. An entity is in BCNF if every determinant is a key.
Fourth Normal Form	The entity must be in BCNF. There must not be more than one multivalued dependency represented in the entity.
Fifth Normal Form	The entity must be in Fourth Normal Form. All relationships are broken down to binary relationships when the decomposition is lossless.

So is it always necessary to go through the steps one at a time? Not exactly. Once you have done this a few times, you'll usually realize that what you're modeling is not quite right, and you'll work through the list of three things I mentioned originally:

- *Check attribute shape*: One attribute, one value.

- *Validate the relationships between attributes*: Attributes are either a key, or describe something about the entity identified by the key.

- *Scrutinize multivalued dependencies*: Only one per entity. Make sure relationships between three values or tables are correct. Reduce all relationships to binary relationships if possible.

Taking this one step further, the goal is simple. Make sure that

All entities are relations and represent only a single thing!

By making entities identify a *single* person, place, thing, or idea, we reduce all the modification anomalies on the data we have stored. In this way, any time we change an attribute of an entity, we're simply changing the description of that single entity, and cannot effect an incidental change in the data.

Bonus Example

In this chapter, I felt that an extra example to fortify the material would be helpful to you to take in the material. Here, we'll work with a small example to tie all the material together. For this chapter, we'll take a check and normalize it. We won't work with an entire check register, but the attributes of the single entity one might arrive at that is the check.

So, I've dummied up the sample document shown in Figure 4-44 (some of the handwriting is my wife's, but most everything else has been "rearranged" to protect the innocent, as well as me).

Note that for variety the names in this section are created using underscore characters between words, instead of Pascal cased.

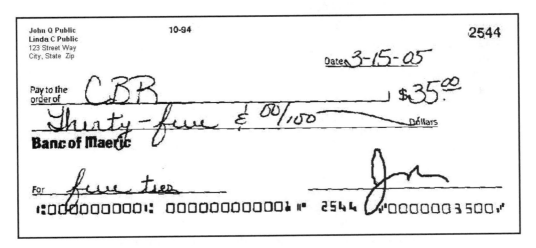

Figure 4-44. *Our sample document*

Now, let's create one entity that has all the attributes that we find on the check. First, we go through and identify all the fields on the check, as identified in Figure 4-45.

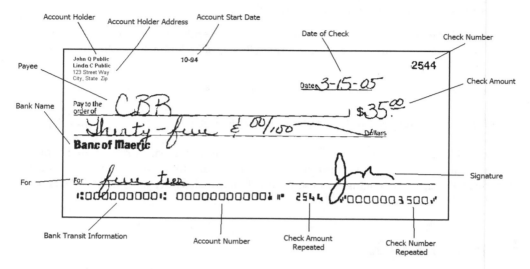

Figure 4-45. *The fields that make up the check*

Then, we take these fields and add them as attributes on a single check entity in a new data model, as shown in Figure 4-46.

check

check_id
check_number
date
account_holders
account_holders_address
payee
account_start_date
amount
bank_name
for
signed_by
bank_transit
account_number

Figure 4-46. *The data model of the check entity*

First we start with checking these attributes against the First Normal Form:

- All attributes must be atomic, one value per attribute.

- All instances of an entity must contain the same number of values.

- All instances of an entity must be different.

Any violations? There are three:

- *account_holders*: Because we can have one or more persons on the account, we ought to make this its own table. (I might have used attributes `account_holder1`, `account_holder2` for the two names, but the effect would have been the same.)

- *account_holders_address*: In the `account_holder` entity, I'll break this down into the parts of an address.

- *bank_transit*: I didn't originally realize it, but this value is made up of several values (information taken from the Magtek website: `http://www.magtek.com/support/knowledge_base/faq/check_reading.asp`). The transit field is routing number (four digits), bank number (four digits), and check digit.

I set the check number attribute to be unique, so all instances of the check entity will be unique (you probably realize that check numbers are only unique for a given account, but with the blinders on we pretend we don't know this yet).

We add an `account_holder` table, and break down the transit field to two columns (leaving off the check digit, because we won't be using this value outside of this system).

From the information we have, I don't currently know how to make the `account_holder` unique, because people's names are hardly unique. So, I inquire with the client, and it uses its customer's `tax_identification_number` and `tax_identification_number_type`. This is either the `social_security_number`, or a number that the person can use to keep his or her SSN private (see Figure 4-47).

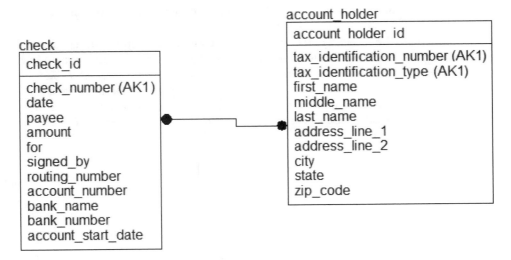

Figure 4-47. *The account_holder entity has been added to the model*

Next, we look for Boyce-Codd violations, as they encompass Second and Third Normal Forms. As a refresher, in BCNF

- All attributes are fully dependent on a key; all attributes must be a fact about a key, and nothing but a key.

- An entity is in BCNF if every determinant is a key.

We determined that the key of the entity is the check_number. None of the other attributes will work as a key. So we examine the other attributes of the check entity for violations:

- *date*: The check was produced on a date, so this is fine.

- *payee*: The check does have a payee, so this is fine.

- *account_start_date*: This is the date the account was started, not directly associated with the check. So we add an account entity to the model. We also rearrange the account_holder entity such that it's associated with the account. We look also for any other account-related attributes; in this case account_number, account_start_date, bank_name, and bank_number. I'll set the key to be the account_number and the bank information.

- *bank_name and bank_number*: These attributes describe a bank, so we create a bank entity. Both the number and the name are acceptable keys.

- *amount*: Checks have amounts, so this attribute is fine.

- *for*: The individual check is for a certain purpose, so this is fine.

- *signed_by*: Because the only person who can sign a check is an account holder, we add a relationship to the account_holder table.

- *routing_number*: This attribute pertains to the particular account, so I move it to the account.

The changes from our examination of the check entity are shown in the model in Figure 4-48.

Next we move on to the account_holder entity. The account holder represents a person who has an account, so we change the relationship from being to the check entity to the account entity. We then add an associative entity named account_holder_association. The relationship from account_holder to check for the signed_by relationship is also changed to the account_holder_association entity because we only want to record that account holders sign checks (I don't mind if other people use my deposit slips, but not my checks!). These changes are reflected in Figure 4-49.

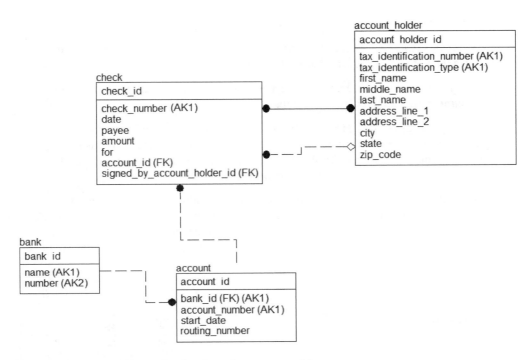

Figure 4-48. *The model now has bank and account entities*

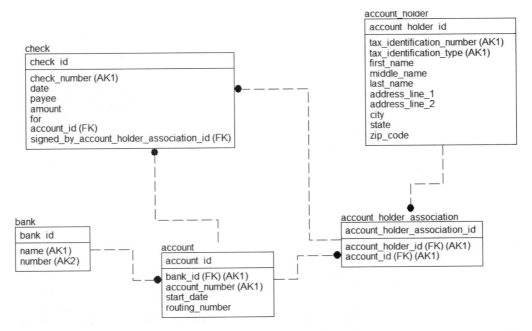

Figure 4-49. *Cleaning up the relationship between account_holder and check/account*

We'll look at the next attributes in groups:

- *tax_identification_number*, *tax_identification_type*: These values refer to the person who is the account_holder, and as such, belong here.

- *first_name*, *middle_name*, *last_name*: Just as with the identification number attributes, the name of the person certainly belongs here.

- *address_line_1*, *address_line_2*, *city*, *state*, *zip_code*: A case could be made that every person on an account might have a unique address, and it would be a correct one. However, we're only modeling a simple check, not a general banking system. The address information for the check goes in the account entity.

Finally, I look around the model again (and again) to validate that the choices I've made still stand. One additional thing I'll go ahead and do is change the unique key for the check to check_number and account_id. Now we're technically set up to record checks from multiple checking accounts. These changes are reflected in the final diagram of our example, shown in Figure 4-50.

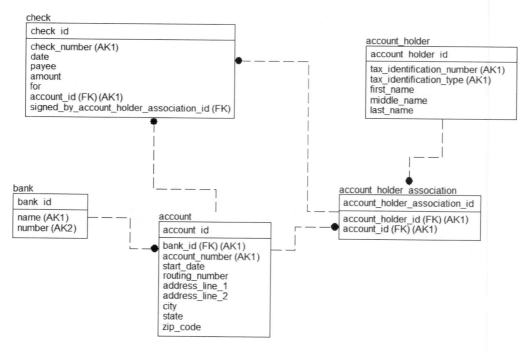

Figure 4-50. *Final model for the example*

The only obvious multivalued dependencies for this model revolve around addresses. Is there really only one address per account? (Doubtful.) I already mentioned that address information could be attached to an account_holder. Certainly the account_holder_association table could have an address to tell the account holder's information based on the association. The bank has addresses for paying bills to, for corresponding with about problems, and a physical address for branches (branches could be another entity).

Needless to say, in a more complete model attributes would be required for phone numbers, overdrafts, deposits, and so on. This example was simply to normalize the fields that we found on a check. We could easily get carried away and end up with a complete model of a banking system, but it's time to get on with the process of implementation in Chapter 5.

The Story of the Book So Far

This is the "middle" of the process of designing a database, so I want to take a page here and recap the process we have covered:

- You've spent time gathering information, doing your best to be thorough without going *Apocalypse Now* on your client. You know what the client wants, and it knows that you know what it wants. And you know that . . .

- Then you looked for tables, columns, attributes, business rules, and so on, in this information and drew a picture, creating a model that gives an overview of the structures in a graphical manner.[3]

- Finally, these tables were broken down such that every table relayed a single meaning. One noun equals one table, pretty much. I'll bet if it's your first time normalizing, but not your first time working with SQL, you don't like this process of normalization right now. I don't blame you; it's a startling change of mind. Just keep reading; it will make sense (all those little tables look troublesome the first few times!). Then read it again, and then do the process over again a few times.

If you're reading this book in one sitting (I hope you aren't doing it in the bookstore without buying it), be aware that we're about to switch gears and I don't want you to hurt yourself. We're turning away from the theory and we're going to start working with SQL Server 2005 objects in reality. It's probably what you thought you were getting when you first started the book. Well, it's here. We're heading off to such statements as CREATE and ALTER TABLE, CREATE TRIGGER, CREATE PROCEDURE, and many others. If you aren't excited by this, then you just aren't doing something right.

If you haven't done so, go ahead and get access to a SQL Server, such as the free SQL Server Express from Microsoft. Or download a trial copy from http://www.microsoft.com/sql/. Everything done in this book will work on all versions of SQL Server other than the Mobile Edition.

You will also need the AdventureWorks database installed for some of the examples. The version that ships with SQL Server will work fine, or if your server does not have Adventure-Works loaded, you can get it from http://www.microsoft.com/downloads and search for AdventureWorks. Current of this book being published, there is a case sensitive and case insensitve version. I assume that you are using the case insensitive version. You may have issues with the examples otherwise.

---

3. The phrase "create a model" always makes me think about a Frankenstein Cosmetics–sponsored beauty pageant.

■■■

CHAPTER 5

Implementing the Base Table Structures

Every man's work, whether it be literature or music or pictures or architecture or anything else, is always a portrait of himself.

—Samuel Butler (1612–1680), English satirical poet. *The Way of All Flesh*, Ch. 14.

In the logical design part of this book (the first four chapters), I discussed in quite some detail the process of defining the structure of the data the user needs to store. In this chapter, I'll take a logical model, convert it into a blueprint for the database implementation, and then create database objects from the model. In other words, work through the process of converting a logical database model into an implementation model, and in the process implement tables, keys, and relationships that comprise a relational database.

As has been stated several times already in this book, there's never a single "correct" design to a corresponding set of data storage and processing needs. In the same way, each person tasked with designing a relational database will take a subtly (or even dramatically) different approach to the design process. The final design will always be, to some extent, a reflection of the person who designed it. I present here the steps that I follow when transforming a logical design into an implementation design. This approach is based on many years of experience, and hopefully will guide you effectively through the process. Of course, it isn't the only possible approach, but the steps you take in your own designs will be somewhat close to these, if not in the same order (most of the time the steps are done in a nonlinear fashion).

The Design Process

Our logical model was database agnostic. The logical design process is unaffected by whether you ultimately wish to implement the design on Microsoft SQL Server, Microsoft Access, Oracle, Sybase, or any relational database management system (even MySQL). However, during this stage, in terms of the naming conventions that are defined, the datatypes chosen, and so on, the design is geared specifically for implementation on SQL Server 2005.

■Note For this and subsequent chapters, I'm going to assume that you have SQL Server 2005 installed on your machine. For the purposes of this book, I recommend you use the Developer Edition, which is available for a small cost from `http://www.microsoft.com/sql/howtobuy`. Another possibility is SQL Server Express Edition, which is free, but doesn't come with the full complement of features that the Developer Edition has. I won't make required use of any of the extended features, but if you're learning SQL Server you'll probably want to have the full feature set. You can acquire the Express Edition at `http://www.microsoft.com/sql/`.

The process I'll take in this chapter is as follows:

- *Review the logical design*: I'll take one last chance to make zero-cost (at least low-cost) changes to the model.

- *Transform the logical model into an implementation model*: I'll look at some of the different design situations that are in (or not in) the logical model that are needed, or that make implementing the database in SQL Server unnecessarily difficult.

- *Implement the design*: I'll take the design and build tables in SQL Server.

I'll work on a new example in this chapter, rather than continue with the example of the previous chapter. The reasons for this are twofold. First, it will introduce as many different design scenarios as possible in as simple a model as possible, and second, it will allow a higher degree of modularity. If you're specifically interested only in this logical-to-physical phase, I won't expect you to have read the previous chapter first to follow through this one.

The main example in this chapter is based around a movie-rental store database. Figure 5-1 shows the logical database design for this application, on which I'll base the physical design. You can find larger, PDF printable versions of all large diagrams for this chapter in the Source Code area of the Apress website (`http://www.apress.com`).

For the most part, it should, by this time in the book, be easy enough for you to read the data model, but I should point out a few things. Most important are the entities `Movie`, `MovieRentalPackage`, and `MovieRentalInventoryItem` (see Figure 5-2).

Figure 5-1. *Full logical model of movie rental store database*

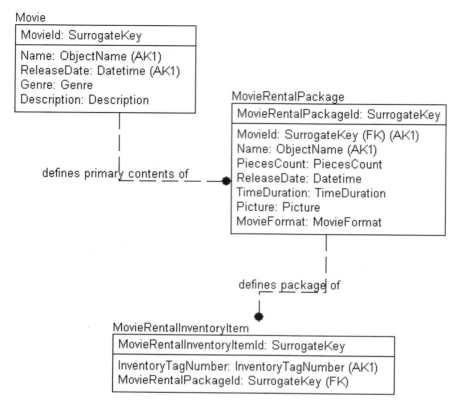

Figure 5-2. *Primary example tables*

The Movie table represents a general movie, regardless of how it's packaged. For example, take *The Good, The Bad, and the Ugly*. Several versions of this movie have been released in the United States (where our hypothetical movie store is located), but they're all basically the same film. The Movie table is used to record the fact that this movie *may* be available for rent at this store in *some* format. The MovieRentalPackage table documents the packaging of the movie, such as Special Edition, Extended Edition, and so on. It also notes in what format the movie is packaged: DVD or videotape (there could be a case for having another level of normalization for movie edition or packaging). The MovieRentalInventoryItem is the actual item that's for rent. Each item for rent gets its own number or bar code that's affixed to the box so the movies can be tracked. These items are what will be tracked as the customer rents movies.

I occasionally diverge from this example to demonstrate specific physical design strategies and choices that cannot easily be illustrated within this model. However, the preceding design will largely drive the narrative of this chapter.

■**Note** All diagrams from now on will include the ordering part of the AK symbol to denote unique keys. This isn't, strictly speaking, a standard notation, but it's quite useful for seeing which columns will come first whenever we start to build the key or index. Usually the ordering should be from the most unique column to the least unique. For example, consider an `invoiceLineItem` table's keys. If you had `InvoiceNumber` and `LineNumber`, the `InvoiceNumber` would be the logical choice for the first column in the index because it's unique for each invoice's items. However, each Invoice will have a line number 1, so this wouldn't be a great first column of the index. So the `InvoiceNumber` column would be AK-labeled 1.1, and the `LineNumber` column would be AK 1.2. I cover indexing in more detail in Chapter 8.

Reviewing the Logical Design

This review stage is a crucial juncture. Once you start implementing SQL Server objects, it's going to be much harder to change things. (Each change can have a ripple effect, causing other objects to change, hence causing middle-tier and UI design to change, which makes the programming team far less happy than does waiting another afternoon for a final review.) Reviewing the logical design one more time with the users is certainly the prudent thing to do. Despite best efforts and asking the most insightful questions possible during the discovery phase, you'll often find that something is suddenly "remembered" that requires you to make small (or maybe not so small) amendments to your design. The only thing that can be predicted with 100 percent accuracy is that nothing can be predicted with 100 percent accuracy (except that). Try to describe the design in terms that the user will understand. Although 95 percent of all humans will give you that dog-staring-at-a-stop-sign look if you use the word "cardinality" in a description, those same people will have no problem with the concept of a person having between one and three active accounts (or whatever the case may be).

Finally, review your design with the DBAs and developers—they might well have alterations to suggest that will help the design best support the applications that must use it. These suggestions may affect how you approach the next section, "Transforming the Design." There might be architectural concerns as well, depending on the tools being used by the implementation teams.

Just as building engineers take an architect's blueprint and examine it to see what materials are needed and whether everything is realistic, I'll take the logical model and tweak out those parts that might be unfeasible or too difficult to implement. Certain parts of an architect's original vision might have to be changed to fit what's realistic, based on factors that weren't known when the blueprint was first conceived, such as ground type, hills, material costs, and so on. We, too, are going to have to go through the process of translating things from raw concept to implementation.

Transforming the Design

Hardware and software advances, coupled with data warehousing methodologies, potentially allow us to implement our database almost exactly as it was logically designed. However, care must still be taken when designing the physical database, as you should never try to implement something that's entirely too difficult to use in practice.

Caution It can be too tempting to give in to the cries of the programmer who feels the tables are too "complex" to work with. Data integrity is almost always the most important thing for any corporate application. As with anything, there can be balance, especially when talking about more hobbyist-type applications. The big trick is to know the difference, and not every interface programmer will feel the same way.

In this section, I'll cover the following topics to transform the logical design into the implementation design from which to build the database:

- *Naming concerns*: In this section, I'll mention naming concerns for tables and columns.

- *Dealing with subtypes*: You can implement subtypes in multiple tables or single tables. I'll look at why this might be done.

- *Choosing primary keys*: Throughout the earlier bits of the book, you've made several types of primary key choices. In this section, you'll make a final choice.

- *Domains or tables*: In this section, I'll discuss the differences between using a domain table, or a column with a constraint for some types of values.

- *Domain implementation*: In this section, the domains that have been specified will be extended to cover datatype and nullability.

- *Adding operational columns*: In this section, you'll add columns that have no specific data value to the logical model, but that are useful for the users to know things about the modification of the data.

- *Setting up schemas*: In SQL Server 2005, you can set up groups of tables as schemas that provide groupings of tables for usage, as well as security.

- *Reviewing the "final" implementation model*: One more review before getting down to the business of producing DDL.

Naming Concerns

The target database for our model is SQL Server 2005, so our table and column naming conventions must adhere to the rules imposed by this database, and generally be consistent and logical. In this section, I'll briefly look at some of the different concerns when naming tables and columns.

Table Naming

Object names in SQL Server are stored in a system datatype of `sysname`. The `sysname` datatype is defined as a 128-character (or less, of course) string using double-byte Unicode characters. SQL Server's rules for the names of objects consist of two distinct naming methods:

- *Regular identifiers*: The preferred method, with the following rules.

  - The first character must be a letter as defined by Unicode Standard 3.2 (generally speaking, Roman letters A to Z, upper and lower case, though this also includes other letters from other languages), or the underscore character (_). You can find the Unicode Standard at `http://www.unicode.org`.

  - Subsequent characters can be Unicode letters, numbers, the "at" sign (@), or the dollar sign ($).

  - The name must not be a SQL Server reserved word. There's a large list of reserved words in SQL Server 2005 Books Online (look in the "Reserved Keywords" section). Some of the keywords won't cause an error, but it's better to avoid all keywords if possible.

  - The name cannot contain spaces.

- *Delimited identifiers*: These should either have square brackets or double quotes around the name (though double quotes are only allowed when the `SET QUOTED_IDENTIFIER` option is set to on). By placing delimiters around an object's name, you can use *any* string as the name. For example, [`Table Name`] or [`3232 fjfa*&(&^(`] would both be legal (but really annoying) names. Delimited names are generally a bad idea when creating new tables, and should be avoided if possible, as they make coding more difficult. However, they can be necessary for interacting with data tables in other environments.

■Note If you need to put a "]" character in the name, you have to include]], just like when you need to include a single quote within a string.

Although the rules for creating an object name are pretty straightforward, the more important question is, "What kind of names should be chosen?" The answer is predictable: "Whatever you feel is best, as long as others can read it." This might sound like a cop-out, but there are more naming standards than there are data architects out there (some of us regularly argue with ourselves as to what is right!).

The standard I generally go with is the standard that was used in the logical model, that being Pascal-cased names. With space for 128 characters, there's little reason to do much abbreviating.

■Caution Because most companies have existing systems, it's a must to know the shop standard for naming tables so that it matches existing systems, and so that new developers on your project will be more likely to understand your database and get up to speed more quickly.

As an example, let's name the object that will be used in the sample model to store individual items for rental. The following list shows several different ways to build the name of this object:

- `movie_rental_inventory_item`: Use underscores to separate values. Most programmers aren't big friends of underscores, as they're cumbersome to program until you get used to them.

- `[movie rental inventory item]` *or* `"movie rental inventory item"`: Delimited by brackets or quotes. Not favored by most programmers, as it's impossible to use this name when building variables in code, and it's easy to make mistakes with them. Using double quotes as delimiters (which is the ANSI standard) can be troublesome because most languages use double quotes to denote strings (SQL uses single quotes). On the other hand, the brackets [and] don't denote strings, though they aren't standard and are a Microsoft-only convention. Many programming languages, such as C# and Visual Basic, use double quotes as string delimiters, so using double quotes in identifiers can cause confusion and break applications.

- `MovieRentalInventoryItemtelevisionScheduleItem` *or* `movieRentalInventoryItem`: Pascal or camel case (respectively), using mixed case to delimit between words. I'll use this style in the examples, as it's the style that I like. (It's my book. You can choose whatever style you want!)

- `mvRentlInvItem` *or* `mvrent_item` *or* `[mv rnt itm]` *(something along these lines)*: Abbreviated forms. These are problematic because you must be careful always to abbreviate the same word in the same way in all your databases. You must maintain a dictionary of abbreviations, or you'll get multiple abbreviations for the same word; for example, "description" as "desc," "descr," "descrip," and/or "description."

Choosing names for objects is ultimately a personal choice, but should never be made arbitrarily, and should be based on existing corporate standards, existing software, and legibility.

Column Naming

The naming rules for columns are the same as for tables as far as SQL Server is concerned. As for how to choose a name for a column—again, it's one of those tasks for the individual architect, based on the same sorts of criteria as before (shop standards, best usage, and so on). This book follows this set of guidelines:

- Other than the primary key, my feeling is that the table name should rarely be included in the column name. For example, in an entity named Person, it isn't necessary to have columns called PersonName or PersonSocialSecurityNumber. No column should be prefixed with the table name other than with two exceptions:

  - A surrogate key such as PersonId. This reduces the need for rolenaming (modifying names of attributes to adjust meaning, especially used in cases where multiple migrated foreign keys exist).

  - Columns that are naturally named with the entity name in them, such as PersonNumber, or something that's common in the language of the client.

- The name should be as descriptive as possible. Use few abbreviations in names. There are a couple notable exceptions:

  - *Complex names*: Much like in table names, if you have a name that contains multiple parts, such as "Conglomerated Television Rating Scale," you might want to implement a name such as `ConTvRatScale`, even though it might take some training before your users become familiar with its meaning.

  - *Recognized abbreviations*: As an example, if we were writing a purchasing system and we needed a column for a purchase-order table, we could name the object `PO`, because this is widely understood. Often users will desire this, even if some abbreviations don't seem that obvious. For example, I always use "id" instead of "identifier," because it's a common abbreviation that's known to most people.

Note that I didn't mention a Hungarian-style notation to denote the type of the column. I've never been a big fan of this style. If you aren't familiar with Hungarian notation, it means prefixing the names of columns and variables with an indicator of the datatype and possible usage. For example, you might have a variable called `vc100_columnName`, to indicate a `varchar(100)` datatype. Or you might have a Boolean or bit column named `bIsCar` or `bCarFlag`.

In my opinion, such prefixes are overkill, because it's easy to tell the type from other documentation you can get from SQL Server or other methods. Our usage indicators typically go at the end of the name, and are only needed when it would be difficult to understand what the value means without the indicator. Consider also what happens if you want to change the type of a column from `varchar(100)` to `varchar(200)` because the data is of a different size than was estimated. Then the user interface must change, the ETL to the data warehouse has to change, and all scripts and procedures have to change, even if there's no other reason to change. Otherwise the change could be trivial, possibly only needing to expand the size of a few variables (and in some languages, this wouldn't be required).

Another particularly heinous practice is to include something in the name to indicate that a column is a column, such as `colFirstName` or `colCity`. Please don't do this. It's clear by the context that the column is a column. It can only be used as a column. This practice, just like the other Hungarian-style notations, makes perfect sense in a functional programming language where the type of object isn't clear just from context, but this practice is never needed with SQL tables.

By keeping the exact type out of the names, you avoid clouding the implementation details with the entity identity. One of the beauties of using relational databases is that an abstraction layer hides the implementation details. To expose them via column naming is to set in concrete what changing requirements might make obsolete (for example, extending the size of a variable to accommodate a future business need).

■**Note** I'm going to use the same naming conventions for the implementation model as I did for the logical model: Pascal-cased names with a few abbreviations ("id" for "identifier" is the main one that I use). I'll also use a Hungarian-style notation for objects other than tables and columns, such as constraints, and for coded objects, such as procedures. Tables and columns are commonly used directly by users. They write queries and build reports directly using database object names, and shouldn't need to change the displayed name of every column and table. On the other hand, using a Hungarian-style notation for constraints and procedures can avoid clashes with the table and column names.

Dealing with Subtypes

Dealing with categories and subtypes is a key element in determining how logical entities transform into tables. A category is a group of entities that can be divided into a number of different *types* of the whole data set. Each group has a supertype and one or more subtypes, and all members of the supertype are included in one or more of the subtypes.

For example, there might exist a person category, consisting of a person subtype, and subtypes that extend the meaning of "person"—for example, employee, teacher, customer, and so on. Subtypes are particularly significant in logical design, but don't be too quick to rush to a particular implementation, as there are also good reasons to keep them intact in our physical design too. I'll now present examples of cases where you *will* and *will not* want to transform the subtyped entities directly into tables.

One of the primary tests I use to decide whether or not to "roll" up the subtype into one table is how similar the subtypes are. If they share many characteristics, but just have some small differences, roll them up. If there are major differences, it's generally best to leave them as different tables.

Example 1: Rolling up Subtypes

Consider from our model the MovieRentalPackage entity that represents the different configurations for rent. DVDs and videotapes have several different characteristics that customers will be interested in when they're choosing which package they want to rent. So the logical model specifies two subtypes, VideoTape and Dvd, based on the discriminator MovieFormat, which can have values 'VideoTape' or 'Dvd' (see Figure 5-3).

The format is interesting from an informational standpoint because DVDs have many more features than videos, the most important of which are region encoding and the sound format. There's a special DvdSoundFormat entity for DVDs as a many-to-many relationship, because DVDs support multiple sound formats on the same discs. For the VideoTape type, there are only columns for hi-fi and stereo sound.

A few things about this implementation are interesting:

- To create a new media rental, you have to create rows in at least two tables (MovieRentalPackage and VideoTape or Dvd, and another in DvdSoundFormat for a DVD). This isn't a tremendous problem, but can require some special handling.

- To see a list of all the items available for rental, including their sound properties, you have to write a moderately complex query that joins MovieRentalPackage with VideoTape, and union this with another query between MovieRentalPackage and Dvd, which might be too slow or simply too cumbersome to deal with.

These are common issues with subtypes. You have to decide how valuable it is to keep a given set of tables implemented as a subtype. When considering what to do with a subtype relationship, one of the most important tasks is to determine how much each of the subtyped entities have in common, and how many of their attributes they have in common.

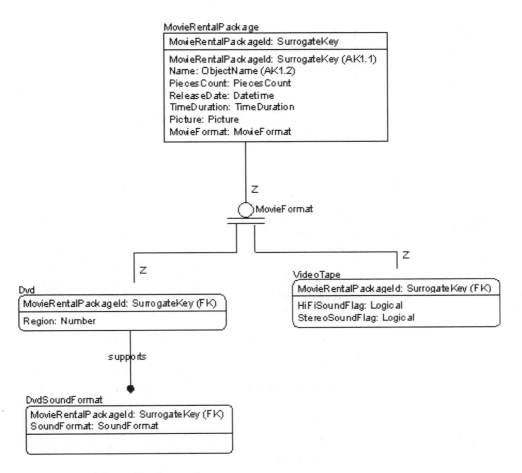

Figure 5-3. *MovieRentalPackage subtype*

A simple survey of the attributes of the subtyped tables in this example shows that they have much in common. In most cases, it's simply a matter of cardinality. Take the DVD: RegionEncoding is specific to this medium, but some videos have different versions, and technically every video product has an aspect ratio (the ratio of the height and width of the picture) that will be of interest to any enthusiast. Although it's true that you can specify the sound properties of a videotape using two simple checkboxes, you can use the same method of specifying the sound as you do for a DVD. You'd then have to enforce a limit on the cardinality of SoundFormat on a video, while Dvd might have up to eight different sound formats documented in the MovieRentalPackageSoundFormat table.

Redraw the subtype relationship as shown in Figure 5-4.

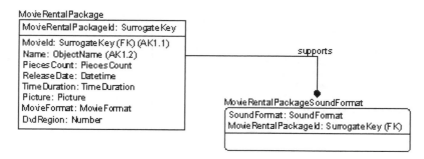

Figure 5-4. *Rolled up subtyped table*

The last point that has to be made is that, because the structure has changed and you're storing multiple types of information in the same entity, you must be careful not to allow improper data to be entered into the table. For example, when MediaFormat is 'VideoTape', the DvdRegion value doesn't apply, and must be set to NULL. It's also true that some of the formats that will be used won't be applicable to 'VideoTape', but would apply to 'Dvd'. In this way, the structures becomes less and less self documenting, requiring more code to keep everything straight, and requiring constraints and triggers, because the values in one table are based on the values in another.

Rolling up (or combining) the subtype into a single table can seem to make implementation easier and more straightforward. The problem is that you're offloading the work of keeping things straight to triggers, rather than relying on the structure of the tables to dictate what values make sense. This in turn increases modification time and costs down the road.

█Caution Note also that NULL means something different than previously. Here, NULL means the inapplicability of a value, rather than a value that isn't known.

Example 2: Leaving As Separate Tables

As a second example, let's look at a case where it doesn't make sense to roll up the subtype. You generally have subtypes that shouldn't be rolled up when you have two (or more) objects that share a common ancestor, but, once subtyped, the subtypes of the items have little or no relationship to one another. Look at Figure 5-5.

There's a Person table that has a name and other attributes, including some that are implemented as additional tables with relationships to the Person table (in our simplistic model, only address information has been included). In the example, employees and customers are both people, but the similarities in how the data is treated end there. So, in this case, it's best to leave the subtype as it is.

The only concern here is that, when someone wants to deal with the data, he or she has to touch multiple tables. Is this a problem? Not really, mostly because it's rare that you'd deal with the Customer table and MovieRental table in the same query. Needing to touch multiple tables in a query does make working with these tables more trouble than if they were in one single table.

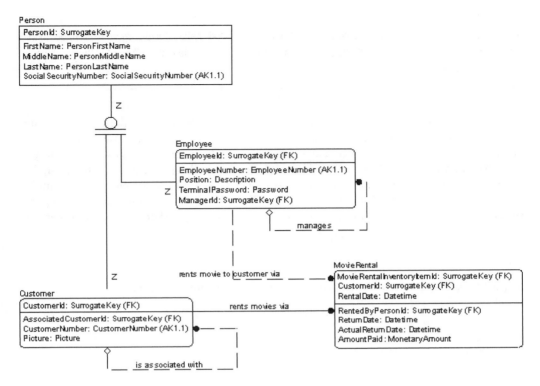

Figure 5-5. *Person subtype*

■**Tip** A third alternative that I'll only mention here in passing is to have an `Employee` table and a `Customer` table that aren't implemented as subtypes. This can also be a valid way to deal with subtypes, but it does cause some things to be more difficult to implement, because now the same person has to have his or her information entered twice, which can cause confusion. This also makes the requirement inferred by the subtype (that a person cannot be a customer and an employee at the same time) difficult to implement.

Determining when to roll up a table is one of those things that comes with time and experience. In most cases, the logical nature of the data is best preserved by implementing subtypes exactly how they're logically modeled as follows:

- Consider rolling up when the subtyped tables are similar in characteristics to the parent table, especially when most columns will frequently be seen in a list together.

- Leave as subtypes when the data in the subtypes shares the common underpinnings, but isn't logically related to the rest of the data in additional ways.

■**Note** As you'll see later, in many cases, the primary features that make subtypes more reasonable to use revolve around creating views that make, for example, the Employee table look as if it contains the values for Person as well.

Another thing I should mention is that in the current configuration, a person can be both a customer and an employee, since we did not implement a discriminator. This might or might not be a reasonable choice to make, depending on the business rules of the company. In some companies, this might not be a logical choice, but in this particular situation, if an employee wants to rent a video, there might be a special process to go through that pertains only to employees (which this model isn't going to model, or, if you want to implement a person as only an employee or customer, you would add a column like PersonType to the Person table).

Trees

Chapter 2 discussed tree structures. The tree structure in Figure 5-6 exists in our sample model.

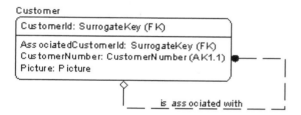

Figure 5-6. *Customer table example of a tree structure*

In this tree structure, the root nodes of each tree are the people who are the primary customers. The leaf nodes are customers that are on the same account. The main thing to understand about tree structures is that some people like to separate the structure from the data itself, and in many cases this can certainly make for a more descriptive structure. For example, in our Customer entity, the tree structure could be changed to the structure in Figure 5-7.

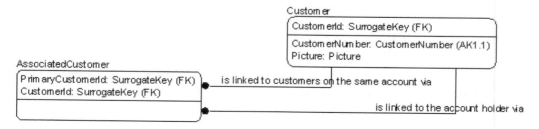

Figure 5-7. *Alternative modeling of a tree structure*

Unless there's a need for a row to have multiple parents, I usually just stick to the recursive relationship. It's easier to implement and just as valid. (I'll revert the `Customer` table back to the original form it was in.)

Other methods that exist tend to include metadata about the tree in data, rather than just relying on the data in the tree. Metadata includes information such as the level in the tree, siblings, and so on. I won't delve deeper to cover these, but Joe Celko has a method called the Nested Sets, and has written an entire book on the subject: *Joe Celko's Trees and Hierarchies in SQL for Smarties* (Morgan Kaufmann, 2004). There are also tons of resources on the Web giving various methods for implementing trees using various metadata formats. Most any way you wish to implement trees will be fine, as long as it's equivalent in data to the logical model.

Choosing Primary Keys

As discussed in the logical modeling chapters, defining keys is one of the most important tasks in database design. In this section, I won't look at why keys are defined, but rather how to implement them in the implementation model. I've already discussed two different types of unique keys:

- *Primary*: Contains the primary access to a row in the table

- *Alternate*: Contains alternate access to a row in the table; also protects any unique conditions that need to exist amongst one or more columns in the table

Primary and alternate keys are hybrid objects—logically constrained, but physically implemented as an index. Constraints declare that some factor must be true for an object. For keys, this is declaring that the values in the table must be unique.

Declarative key constraints are also implemented as indexes. A basic understanding of how indexes work will give us a base level to determine what kinds of indexes to use. If you don't understand how SQL Server stores data and implements indexes in SQL Server 2005, read Chapter 8 on indexes. The most important thing to do is to make sure that constraints are applied on all the keys defined in the logical design phase.

Choosing a primary key for implementation is one of the most important choices made concerning the implementation. This value will be migrated to other tables as a pointer to a particular value. Choosing a primary key style is also one of the most argued-about topics on the newsgroups. In this book, I'm going to be reasonably agnostic about the whole thing, and I'll present several methods for choosing the implemented primary key (after reading the entire book, you'll no doubt know my personal style).

Presumably, during the logical phase you've identified all the different ways the user uniquely identified rows. Hence, there should be several choices for the primary key:

- Use an existing column or columns defined by the logical phase.

- Create a simple column that identifies the row, possibly by defining a function on data in the table

- Use a surrogate key, such as an integer column with the `IDENTITY` property, or use a hash function, or even a GUID.

Each of these choices has pros and cons. I'll look at them in the following sections.

Using Existing Columns

In many cases, a table will have an obvious, easy-to-use primary key. This is especially true when talking about independent entities. For example, take an entity such as a product. It would have a productNumber defined. A person usually has some sort of identifier, either government issued or company issued (my company has an employeeNumber that I have to put on all documents for computer use).

The primary keys for dependent entities then generally take the primary key of the independent entity, add one or more attributes, and presto: primary key.

For example, I have a Ford SVT Focus, made by the Ford Motor Company, so to identify this particular model I might have a row in the Manufacturer table for Ford Motor Company (as opposed to GM or something). Then I'd have an automobileMake row with a key of manufacturerName = 'Ford Motor Company' and makeName = 'Ford' (instead of Lincoln, Mercury, Jaguar, and so on), style = 'SVT', and so on for the other values. This gets messy to deal with, because the key of the automobileModelStyle table would be used in many places to describe which products are being shipped to which dealership. Note that this isn't about the size in terms of the performance of the key, just the number of values that make up the key. Performance will be better the smaller the key, as well, but this is true not only of the number of columns, but this also depends on the size of the values.

Note that the complexity in a real system such as this would be compounded by the realization that you have to be concerned with model year, possibly body style, different prebuilt packages, and so on.

Using a Single Column for the Primary Key

A common thing to do is to use only a single column for the primary key, regardless of the size of the other keys. In this case, you'd specify that every table will have a single primary key and implement alternate keys in your tables, as shown in Figure 5-8.

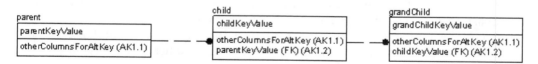

Figure 5-8. *Single-column key example*

Note that all the relationships at this point are nonidentifying, and that they're all required. For all intents and purposes, they have the same requirements as if they were the primary key. This method has some advantages:

- *Every table has a single-column primary key:* It's much easier to develop applications that use this key, because every table will have a key that follows the same pattern.

- *The primary key index will be small and will have only one column:* Thus, operations that use the index to access a row in the table will be faster. Most update and delete operations will likely modify the data by accessing the data based on primary keys that will use this index.

- *Joins between tables will be easier to implement:* That's because all migrated keys will be a single field.

There can be disadvantages to this method, such as always having to join to a table to find out what the value of the primary key means, not to mention that you'll need other joins to access data. Because the goals of our OLTP system are to keep keys small, speed up modifications, and ensure data consistency, this strategy is not only acceptable, but favorable.

Another issue is that some parts of the self-documenting nature of relationships are obviated because using only single-column keys eliminates all identifying relationships.

Let's look at two methods of implementing these keys, either by deriving the key from some other data, or using a meaningless surrogate value.

Deriving a Key

By deriving a key, I'm referring to using some value from the data to use as the key, either in a stripped-down version or exactly as it is. For example, take the tables in Figure 5-9 from the model we're working with.

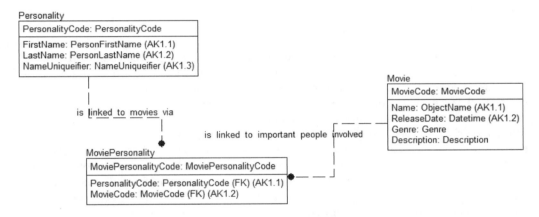

Figure 5-9. *Personality, Movie, and MoviePersonality tables*

If there was an actor `'John Smith (II)'` (II is the uniqueifier, because there have been other people named John Smith who were in the actor's union) who worked in the movie *Blazing Adders*, you might have the following three key values:

- `PersonalityCode: 'john-smith-ii'`

- `MovieCode: 'blazing-adders'`

- `MoviePersonalityCode: 'john-smith-ii--blazing-adders'`

The first two seem reasonably natural, but the third is pretty clunky. You could use some other derivation, or you could use parts of the words, or let the users come up with something whenever they create the row.

This sort of key strategy is seen quite often in the real world, for things such as model numbers of products, serial numbers, automotive VIN numbers, license numbers, and so on. Part of the key might not have any actual meaning or, like in an `employeeId`, it might be that the hiring department is part of the number. Social Security numbers (SSNs) have some information embedded in them, such as the state where they were issued. The key value need not be understandable to its user.

One thing is for sure: it should be memorable if a user will use it directly. The values should either be broken up into memorable chunks, or the values should just be short enough. For example, SSNs are in the format XXX-XX-XXXX, so users can remember them. People can generally remember about six to eight values; certainly they're forced to reuse them often enough.

In many cases, it's also a good idea to have these values be verifiable using an algorithm, especially if the values are all numbers. For example, you could use a check digit. Say you've defined a key to be AANNNNC, where A equals any letter from A to Z (excluding O), N equals a numeric digit, and C is a check digit. You might calculate the value by taking the sum of digits together (for letters taking the position of the letters in the alphabet), except for the last digit. This last (check) digit is calculated from the one's-place sum of the other digits (so if it was 59, the check digit would be 9.) For example, say the base key is 'AA1111':

```
A = 1, A = 1, so 1 + 1 + (1 + 1 + 1 + 1 ) = 6
```

'AA11116' would be the key value. 'AA11115' would be an invalid value. Say the base value was QC1343:

```
Q = 17, C = 3, so 17 + 3 + (1 + 3 + 4 + 3) = 31
```

'QC13431' would be the key value. This is a good key strategy, if you can come up with random values, such that you don't have collisions when you generate keys. This strategy also serves as a deterrent to guessing the value. Credit card numbers have this property, as not every 16-digit value could be used as a valid account number.

Sometimes a natural key cannot be 100 percent derived from data. For example, say you wanted to represent each can of food in a model for a grocery store. For the DVDs this is easy: slap a sticker on each box. Although we could do this for cans of food, there's little reason to do so. We might have hundreds of cans of corn, and who cares which is which. One solution is to have a single row that identifies the natural key of a can of corn (manufacturer, type of food, size of can, UPC barcode, and so on), and add a surrogate key. Then, when a customer purchases ten cans of corn, ten randomly chosen rows are tagged as being purchased.

The alternative would be to identify the same natural key but then have a single row with an accumulator column stating how many cans of corn are available, incrementing and decrementing it every time stock is accumulated or sold. Which method is right? It depends. In a data warehouse, it's important to have every row in a fact table have the same granularity (referred to as the grain). Hence, having a row for every item sold would be helpful. It would also make it easier to categorize sales. On the other hand, just having one row that gets modified all the time will take up much less space, and you can build the same kinds of rows for your data warehouse by getting information out of your sales tables. I don't think either idea is right or wrong, but they're certainly different.

Using Only a Meaningless Surrogate Key

Another popular way to define a primary key is to keep the meaningless surrogate key that I've modeled previously, such as using a column with the IDENTITY property, which automatically generates a unique value. In this case, you rarely let the user have access to the value of the key, but use it primarily for programming.

It's exactly what was done for most of the entities in the logical models worked on in previous chapters: simply employing the surrogate key while we didn't know what the actual value for the primary key would be. This method has one nice property:

You never have to worry about what to do when the primary key value changes.

Once the key is generated for a row, it never changes, even if all the data changes. This is an especially nice property when you need to do analysis over time. No matter what any of the other values in the table have been changed to, as long as the surrogate key value represents the same thing, you can still relate it to its usage in previous times. Consider the case of a row that identifies a company. If the company is named Bob's Car Parts and it's located in Topeka, Kansas, but then it hits it big, moves to Detroit, and changes the company name to Car Parts Amalgamated, only one row is touched: the row where the name is located. Just change the name, and it's done. Keys may change, but not primary keys.

Over time, in a data warehouse this company would be the same company, and the name change would be reflected, as would the company's location, and any other information that changed. This allows some neat historical queries to be done. Using surrogate keys makes the ETL to load this data far easier.

Using a surrogate key value doesn't in any way prevent you from creating additional single part keys, like we did in the previous section. In fact, for most tables, having a small code value is likely going to be a desired thing. Many clients hate long values, as they involve "too much typing." For example, say you have a value such as "Fred's Car Mart." You might want to have a code of "FREDS" for them as the shorthand value for their name. Some people are even so programmed by their experiences with ancient database systems that had arcane codes that they desire codes such as "XC10" to refer to "Fred's Car Mart."

In the demo model, all the keys are already set to a surrogate key, except the many-to-many resolution tables. So we change all these to single-part keys and add alternate keys for the previous primary keys (see Figure 5-10).

MovieRental

MovieRentalInventoryItemId: SurrogateKey (FK) CustomerId: SurrogateKey (FK) RentalDate: Datetime
RentedByEmployeeId: SurrogateKey (FK) ReturnDate: Datetime ActualReturnDate: Datetime AmountPaid: MonetaryAmount

Figure 5-10. *MovieRental table with composite primary key*

This becomes the table in Figure 5-11.

Notice too that the table is no longer modeled with rounded corners, because the primary key no longer is modeled with any migrated keys in the primary key.

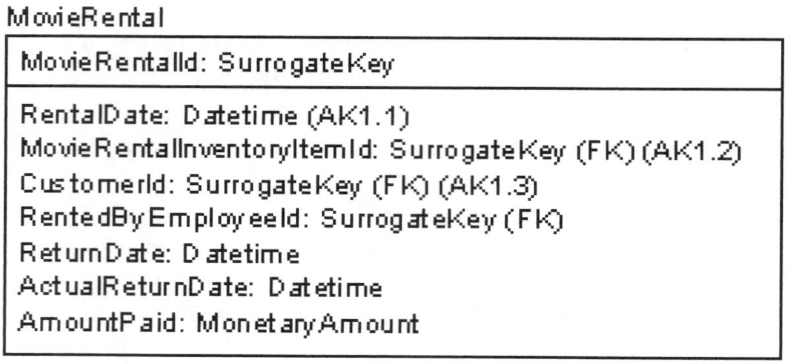

MovieRental

MovieRentalId: SurrogateKey
RentalDate: Datetime (AK1.1)
MovieRentalInventoryItemId: SurrogateKey (FK) (AK1.2)
CustomerId: SurrogateKey (FK) (AK1.3)
RentedByEmployeeId: SurrogateKey (FK)
ReturnDate: Datetime
ActualReturnDate: Datetime
AmountPaid: MonetaryAmount

Figure 5-11. *MovieRental table with single-column surrogate primary key*

Having a common style for every table is valuable, to have a common pattern for programming with the tables as well. Because every table has a single-column key that isn't updatable, and is the same datatype, it's possible to exploit this in code, making code generation a far more straightforward process. Note once more that nothing should be lost when you use surrogate keys, as a surrogate of this style replaces an existing natural key.

By implementing tables using this pattern, I'm covered in two ways: I always have a single primary key value, but I always have a key that cannot be modified, which eases the difficulty for loading a warehouse.

■**Caution** A primary key that's meaningless in the logical model shouldn't be your only defined key. One of the ultimate mistakes made by people using such keys is to ignore the fact that two rows whose only difference is a system-generated value are not different. That's because from the user's perspective, all the data that users will value is exactly the same. At this point, it becomes more or less impossible to tell one row from another.

No matter the choice of human-accessible key, surrogate keys are the style of key that I use for all tables in databases I create, for every table.

Updating the Physical Model

For each of the tables that don't already have a single-value surrogate key, I'll go through and change the table to include the surrogate key (see Figure 5-12), and then make the previous primary key an alternate key (*very important*).

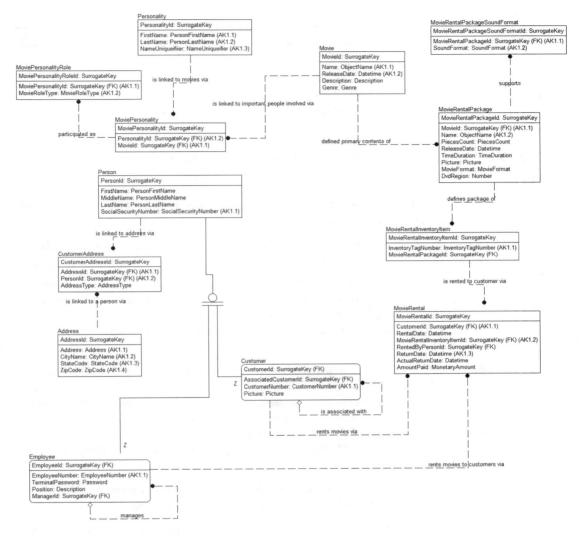

Figure 5-12. *Full model with all single-column surrogate keys and subtype modifications*

Domain Specification

In logical modeling, the concept of domains involves specifying templates for datatypes and column types that are used over and over again. In physical modeling, domains are the same, but with additional properties added for physical needs.

For example, in the logical modeling phase, domains are defined for such columns as name and description, which occur regularly across a database. The reason for defining domains might not have been completely obvious at the time of logical design, but it becomes clear during physical modeling. For example, for the ObjectName domain that's used often in the MovieRental model, you might specify the contents of Table 5-1.

Table 5-1. *Sample Domain*

Property	Setting
Name	ObjectName
Nullability	NOT NULL
Datatype	varchar(100)
CHECK constraint	LEN(RTRIM(Name)) > 0 –– may not be blank
DEFAULT	n/a

I'll defer the CHECK *constraint and* DEFAULT *bits to the next chapter, where I discuss data protection using these objects.*

Several tables will have a name column, and you'll use this template to build every one of them. This serves at least two purposes:

- *Consistency*: Define every name column in precisely the same manner; there will never be any question about how to treat the column.

- *Ease of implementation*: If the tool you use to model and implement databases supports the creation of domain and template columns, you can simply use the template to build columns and you won't have to set the values over and over. If the tool supports property inheritance, when you change a property in the definition, the values change everywhere.

Domains aren't a requirement of logical or physical database design, nor does SQL Server use them precisely, but they enable easy and consistent design and are a great idea. Of course, consistent modeling is always a good idea regardless of whether or not you use a tool to do the work for you. As mentioned when we started out with domains, if you're doing modeling without a tool that supports it, you'd probably give this process a miss.

In the next two subsections, I'll discuss a couple topics concerning how to implement domains:

- *Column or table*: You need to decide whether a value should simply be entered into a column, or whether to implement a new table to manage the values.

- *Choosing the datatype*: SQL Server gives us a wide range of datatypes to work with, and I'll discuss some of the issues concerning making the right choice.

NULLS

As discussed in logical modeling, values for an attribute, now being translated to a physical column, may be optional or mandatory. Whether or not a column value is mandatory or optional is translated in the physical model as nullability. Before discussing how to implement NULLs, it's necessary to briefly discuss what "NULL" means. Although it can be inferred that a column defined as NULL means that the data is optional, this is an incomplete definition. A NULL value should be read as "unknown value." If you need to specify explicitly that a value doesn't apply, it's best to implement a value that explicitly states this. In this case, "optionality" means it's optional to specify the value.

Column or Table?

Although many domains have almost unlimited possible values, often a domain will specify a fixed set of values that a column might have. For example, in the demonstration table Movie, a column Genre has a domain of Genre (see Figure 5-13).

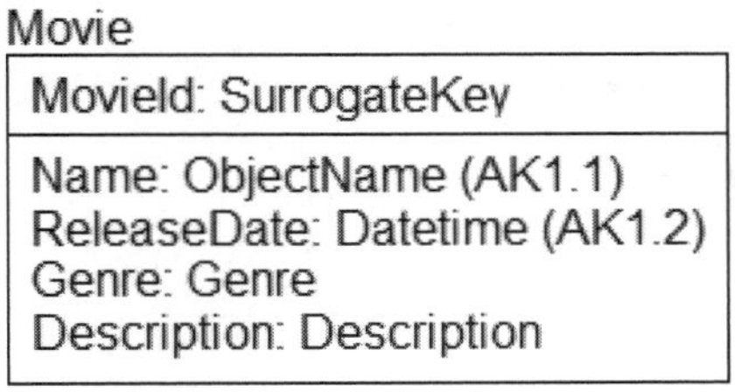

Movie

Movield: SurrogateKey
Name: ObjectName (AK1.1) ReleaseDate: Datetime (AK1.2) Genre: Genre Description: Description

Figure 5-13. *Movie table with domains modeled as columns*

You could specify this domain, as in Table 5-2.

Table 5-2. *Genre Domain*

Property	Setting
Name	Genre
Nullability	NOT NULL
Datatype	varchar(16)
CHECK constraint	IN ('Comedy', 'Drama', 'Family', 'Special Interest')
DEFAULT	n/a

This is certainly an acceptable way to implement this domain, and in turn, the column. There are a couple concerns with this form:

- Unless you have one of each of the values specified in the CHECK constraint, it isn't easy to know what the possible values are without either foreknowledge of the system, or looking in the metadata. If you're doing rental activity reports by Genre, it won't be easy to find out what Genres had no activity.

- Often, a value such as this could easily have additional information associated with it. For example, this domain might have information about where the shelves are located. When a customer asks that familiar question, "Where is the comedy section?" the information is on the computer.

- This form can be quite limiting. What if the manager of the store decides that customers don't want to rent "Comedy" movies anymore, so he tries "Humor" (hey, this isn't a marketing book). To do this would require a programming change, while if the value was in a table, it would be a simple data change.

So, I nearly always include tables for all domains, again using a surrogate key for the actual primary key, for the same reasons mentioned previously. In fact, it's probably even more important to do this for domain tables because on a small scale (one rental store) the manager might change requirements and need new values. I'll change the Movie table to the format shown in Figure 5-14.

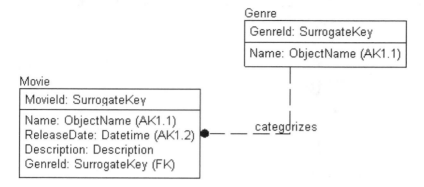

Figure 5-14. *Movie entity with Genre broken out as a domain table*

Choosing the Datatype

Choosing proper datatypes to match the domain chosen during logical modeling is an important task. One datatype might be more efficient than another of a similar type. For example, you can store integer data in an integer datatype, a numeric datatype, or even a floating point datatype, but these datatypes are certainly not alike in implementation or performance.

It's important to choose the best possible datatype when building the column. The following list contains the intrinsic datatypes and a brief explanation of each of them:

- *Precise numeric data*: Stores numeric data with no possible loss of precision.

  - bit: Stores either 1, 0, or NULL; frequently used for "Boolean"-like columns (1 = True, 0 = False, NULL = Unknown). (Up to 8 bit columns can fit in 1 byte.)

  - tinyint: Non-negative values between 0 and 255 (1 byte).

  - smallint: Integers between -32,768 and 32,767 (2 bytes).

  - int: Integers between 2,147,483,648 to 2,147,483,647 (-2^{31} to $2^{31} - 1$). (4 bytes.)

  - bigint: Integers between 9,223,372,036,854,775,808 to 9,223,372,036,854,775,807 (that is, -2^{63} to $2^{63} - 1$). (8 bytes.)

  - *Decimal (numeric is a synonym)*: All numbers between $-10^{38} - 1$ through $10^{38} - 1$ (between 5 and 17 bytes, depending on precision).

- *Approximate numeric data*: Stores approximations of numbers, typically for scientific usage. Gives a large range of values with a high amount of precision, but might lose precision of very large or very small numbers.

  - *Float (N)*: Values in the range from -1.79E + 308 through to 1.79E + 308 (storage varies from 4 bytes for N between 1 and 24, and 8 for N between 25 and 53).

  - *Real*: Values in the range from -3.40E + 38 through to 3.40E + 38. real is a synonym for a float(24) datatype (4 bytes).

- *Date and time*: Stores date values, including time of day.

  - `smalldatetime`: Dates from January 1, 1900, through to June 6, 2079, with accuracy to 1 minute (4 bytes).

  - `datetime`: Dates from January 1, 1753, to December 31, 9999, with accuracy to 3.33 milliseconds (8 bytes).

- *Binary data*: Strings of bits; for example, files or images. Storage for these datatypes is based on the size of the data stored.

  - `binary(N)`: Fixed-length binary data up to 8,000 bytes long.

  - `varbinary(N)`: Variable-length binary data up to 8,000 bytes long.

  - `varbinary(max)`: Variable-length binary data up to $(2 \wedge 31) - 1$ bytes (2GB) long. All the typical functionality of the `varbinary` columns is allowed on these types.

- *Character (or string) data*:

  - `char(N)`: Fixed-length character data up to 8,000 characters long.

  - `varchar(N)`: Variable-length character data up to 8,000 characters long.

  - `varchar(max)`: Variable-length character data up to $(2 \wedge 31) - 1$ bytes (2GB) long. All the typical functionality of the `varchar` columns is allowed on these types (I'll discuss this one after presenting the datatypes).

  - `nchar`, `nvarchar`, `nvarchar(max)`: Unicode equivalents of `char`, `varchar`, and `varchar(max)`.

- *Other datatypes*:

  - `sql_variant`: Stores any datatype. It's generally a bad idea to use this datatype, but it is handy in cases where you don't know the datatype of a value before storing. Best practice would be to describe the type in your own metadata when using this type.

  - `rowversion` *(`timestamp` is a synonym)*: Used for optimistic locking to version-stamp a row. It changes on every modification. The name of this type was `timestamp` in all SQL Server versions before 2000, but in the ANSI SQL standards, the `timestamp` type is equivalent to the `datetime` datatype. I'll discuss the `rowversion` datatype in detail in Chapter 9.

  - `uniqueidentifier`: Stores a GUID value.

  - `XML`: Allows you to store an XML document in a column. The `XML` type gives you a rich set of functionality when dealing with structured data that cannot be easily managed using typical relational tables. You shouldn't use the `XML` type as a crutch to violate the First Normal Form by storing multiple values in a single column.

Several datatypes weren't listed because they're soon to be deprecated. Their use was common in previous versions of SQL Server, but they're being replaced by types that are far easier to use:

- `image`: Replace with `varbinary(max)`

- `text` *or* `ntext`: Replace with `varchar(max)` and `nvarchar(max)`

Although there weren't that many changes to datatypes in SQL Server 2005 (these two changes and the XML type were the only ones), this change is big; in fact, really big. In the past, when you needed to store a value that might be greater than 8,000 characters (or 4,000 of Unicode data), you had to use a datatype that was awful to deal with. You couldn't even put the value into a variable unless it was a parameter of a procedure (and you still couldn't do anything with it other than using it in a DML statement). Once, I built a solution that required storing text into variables, and had to go out into the OS to accomplish what will now be a simple task in a T-SQL stored procedure.

varchar(max) and the other (max) types behave much like their smaller counterparts. You can use all the typical string functions, and you can use them after triggers (this functionality isn't available for the image, text, or ntext types). There are slight differences between the (max) types and the conventional <= 8,000 byte datatypes, in that you can do chunked updates using the .WRITE clause in the UPDATE statement.

Appendix B covers this topic in more detail; I'll discuss datatypes in greater detail there, and discuss the situations and give examples of where datatypes are best used.

Tip The most important thing when choosing a datatype is to be careful to pick the one that best matches what you're trying to store.

For example, say you want to store a person's name and date of birth. You could choose to store the name in a varchar(max) column, and the date of birth in a sql_variant column. In all cases these choices would work well enough, but they wouldn't be *good* choices. The name should be in something such as a varchar(30) column, and the date of birth in a smalldatetime column. Notice that I used a variable size type for the name. This is because you don't know the length, and not all names are the same size. Because most names aren't nearly 30 bytes, this will save space in our database.

In reality, seldom would anyone make such poor choices of datatype as putting a date value in a varchar(max) column. Most choices are reasonably easy. However, it's important keep in mind that the datatype is the first level of domain enforcement. A business rule states the following:

The name must be greater than or equal to 5 characters and less than or equal to 30 characters.

You can enforce this at the database level by declaring the field as a varchar(30). This field won't allow a 31-character or longer value to be entered. It isn't possible to enforce the rule of greater than or equal to 5 characters using only a datatype. I'll discuss more about how to enforce these types of rules in the next chapter, on integrity enforcement.

Monetary Values

You might have noticed in the section on datatypes that the following items were omitted:

- money: 922,337,203,685,477.5808 through 922,337,203,685,477.5807 (8 bytes)

- smallmoney: Money values from -214,748.3648 through +214,748.3647 (4 bytes)

In general, the money datatype sounds like a cool idea, but it has some confusing consequences from using it. In Appendix B, I spend a bit more time covering these consequences, but there are two problems:

- There are definite issues with roundoff because intermediate results are calculated using only four decimal places.

- Money data output includes formatting, including a monetary sign (such as $ or £).

- Inserting **$100** and **£100** results in the same value being represented in the variable or column.

Hence, it's generally accepted that it's best to store monetary data in decimal datatypes. This also gives you the ability to assign the types as are reasonable for the situation. For example, take the MovieRental table, as shown in Figure 5-15.

```
MovieRental
┌─────────────────────────────────────────┐
│ MovieRentalId: SurrogateKey              │
├─────────────────────────────────────────┤
│ RentalDatetime: Datetime                 │
│ MovieRentalInventoryItemId: SurrogateKey │
│ CustomerId: SurrogateKey                 │
│ RentedByEmployeeId: SurrogateKey         │
│ ReturnDate: Datetime                     │
│ ActualReturnDate: Datetime               │
│ AmountPaid: MonetaryAmount               │
└─────────────────────────────────────────┘
```

Figure 5-15. *MovieRental table with domains listed*

For the AmountPaid column, I'll use a decimal (4,2) datatype, because a single rental will never cost more than $99.99, or business will be pitiful for sure (see Figure 5-16).

```
MovieRental
┌─────────────────────────────────────────┐
│ MovieRentalId: int                       │
├─────────────────────────────────────────┤
│ RentalDatetime: smalldatetime            │
│ MovieRentalInventoryItemId: int          │
│ CustomerId: int                          │
│ RentedByEmployeeId: int                  │
│ ReturnDate: smalldatetime                │
│ ActualReturnDate: smalldatetime          │
│ AmountPaid: decimal(4,2)                 │
└─────────────────────────────────────────┘
```

Figure 5-16. *MovieRental table with datatype chosen for money amount*

Boolean/Logical Values

Booleans are another of the hotly debated choices that are made for SQL Server data. There's no Boolean type in SQL, so a suitable datatype needs to be chosen. There are two common choices:

- There's the bit datatype -1 = True, 0 = False. This is by far the most common datatype because it works directly with programming languages such as VB.NET with no translation. The checkbox and option controls can directly connect to these values, even though VB uses -1 to indicate True.

- You could use a char(1) value as well, with a domain of 'Y', 'N', 'T', 'F', or other values. This is the easiest for ad-hoc users who don't want to think about what 0 or 1 mean, but it's generally the most difficult from a programming standpoint. Sometimes a char(3) is even better to go with 'yes' and 'no'.

To demonstrate this, I'll add a flag to the Customer table that tells whether people can rent movies meant for young people only, or if they can rent anything the store sells (see Figure 5-17).

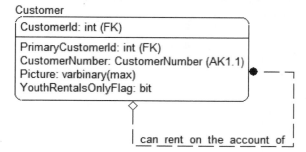

Figure 5-17. *Customer table with flag column for youth rentals*

Flag columns are only to be used when you have a single yes or no condition. If you have multiple flag columns, there's sometimes a problem with the design. For example, requirements might state that the user could choose the types of ratings the customer could rent. The table shown in Figure 5-18 would be a bad idea.

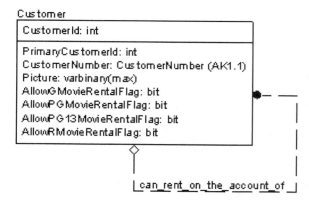

Figure 5-18. *Customer table with multiple columns for different levels of rentals*

If you notice this pattern in your tables, rebuild them as shown in Figure 5-19.

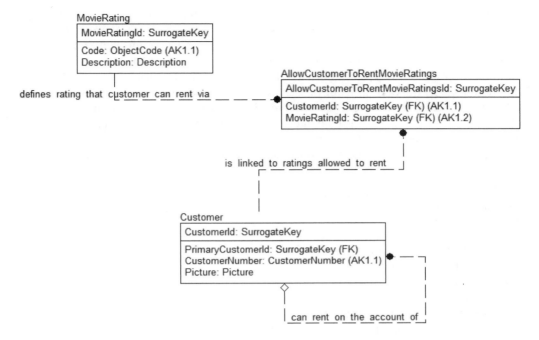

Figure 5-19. *Customer table with dynamic modifiable levels*

Another resolution would be to add an Ordering column to the MovieRating table, and a MaximumMovieRating column to the Customer table. There are many ways to skin the cat (which has my cat terrified) in a reasonable way, without resorting to multiple flag columns that have similar meanings. The key is that all columns shouldn't have any relation to one another, as stated in Third Normal Form. If multiple columns share a common meaning, then this meaning may be able to stand on its own, just as in this case movie ratings are a thing in and of themselves that deserve a modeled table of their own.

To the actual model, I'll add the MovieRating table and relate it to the Movie table. It has a column AllowYouthRentalFlag to enable enforcement of the YouthRentalFlag.

Date Values

Because there are no datatypes that store *only* date, or *only* time, adding date values is a common issue that needs to be dealt with. It's typical practice simply to use the smalldatetime datatype when you need only the date, or only the time for a column. It's a bother to have the additional information in the column. However, because SQL Server has a relatively rich set of date manipulation functions, it usually isn't worth the effort to use another type, either that's built in the Common Language Runtime (CLR), or that's simply a column to hold a number of units from an offset. (In Appendix B, I demonstrate a technique for doing this with a user-defined function.)

For example, the date might be stored as the number of days since January 1, 1800. Calculating what day this represents would be simple and straightforward. Alternatively, if you needed a datatype with a finer granularity than the three milliseconds that the datetime datatype gives you, you could use the offset of milliseconds from midnight.

In either case, however, you couldn't use all the date manipulation facilities of SQL Server without translating the value into one of datetime datatypes, where you'd lose the value of the additional precision. Alternatively, you could rewrite all the functionality that's part of SQL Server date handling, but this is problematic and costly. Hence, for the most part I choose simply to use the datetime datatypes in 99 percent of the cases.

In the sample model, several dates are in the MovieRental table (see Figure 5-20).

MovieRental

MovieRentalId: int
RentalDatetime: smalldatetime (AK1.1) MovieRentalInventoryItemId: int (AK1.2) CustomerId: int (AK1.3) RentedByEmployeeId: int ReturnDate: smalldatetime ActualReturnDate: smalldatetime AmountPaid: decimal(4,2)

Figure 5-20. *Setting date datatypes on the MovieRental table*

For all these date-valued columns, I've used a smalldatetime datatype because there's no need for old dates, nor precision lower than a minute necessary. ("This movie was rented at 12:30:23.007 o'clock"? A bit much.) If it's critical that only date values get stored in the database, a trigger could be written that can be used to strip off any time data that might get inserted. I'll cover triggers in detail in the next chapter.

Images

In the model, the client had a Picture attribute on the Customer entity. How best to deal with and store images in a database is an oft-discussed topic. The question is whether to put the actual binary values in the database, or simply to store a path to the images.

Generally speaking, though the change from the image type in pre-2005 versions of SQL Server to varbinary(max) certainly improves storing binary values, the Windows file system is still the best place to store images. The tools to deal with files from a user interface standpoint are usually so much easier to deal with that it's worth it to go this direction. For example, you can generally build a web page by simply formatting the output as follows:

```
'<img src = "' + <path> + '">'
```

If this data were stored in the database, it would have to be materialized onto disk as a file first, and then used in the page, which is pretty slow.

There are a few considerations that make it more favorable to store the graphic data in the SQL Server versus the file system:

- *Transactional integrity*: It's far easier to guarantee that the image is stored and remains stored. If the file is in the file system, it could be deleted without the knowledge of the database system.

- *Security*: If the image's integrity is important to the business process (such as the picture on a security badge that's displayed to a security guard when a badge is swiped), then it's worth it to pay the extra price for storing the data in the database, where it's much harder to make a change. That's because it's difficult indeed to store an image using Management Studio.

In the sample model, there are two examples of images, with two different needs. First, there's the Picture column on the MovieRentalItem table.

Because this is just the picture of a movie, I'm going to choose to store a path to the data. This data will be used to present electronic browsing of the store's stock on an in-store kiosk, as well as on a web page for the customer to rent online and pick up at the store. So, I'll change the column from a domain of Picture to UncFileName, which will be a varchar(200) to allow for the filename as well as the UNC file path (see Figure 5-21).

MovieRentalPackage

MovieRentalPackageId: int
MovieId: int (AK1.1) Name: varchar(20) (AK1.2) PiecesCount: tinyint ReleaseDate: datetime TimeDuration: TimeDuration Picture: varchar(200) MovieFormatId: int DvdRegion: tinyint

Figure 5-21. *MovieRentalPackage table with Picture datatype set as a path to a file*

Choosing a length for a filename can be tricky. Two hundred is very long for most cases, but it's a fine generic size. Of course, even if the column is defined as varchar(8000), the actual data space used is determined by the data, not the maximum size, so better safe than sorry.

An alternative example is found in the Customer table (see Figure 5-22). To fight fraud, this particular movie rental chain decided to start taking customer pictures and comparing them whenever customers rented an item. This data is far more important from a security standpoint, and has privacy implications. For this, I'll use a varbinary(max). Speed isn't a big deal, because only one image needs to be fetched at a time, and performance will be adequate as long as the image displays before the rental transaction is completed. Don't get me wrong, the varbinary(max) types aren't that slow, but performance would be acceptable for these purposes even if they were.

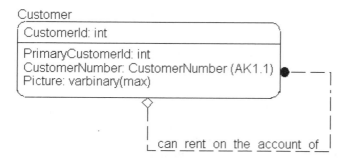

Figure 5-22. *Customer table with picture stored as data in the table*

Complex Datatypes

As discussed in the previous chapters, it's acceptable to have complex datatypes in a normalized database. Complex types should follow the same rules as any other datatypes, in that you must always have the same number of values (no arrays) and such.

In SQL Server 2005, it's finally possible to create these types, but for the most part you should only use them in the cases where it makes compelling reason to do so. There are a few different possible scenarios where you could reasonably use user-defined types (UDTs) to extend the SQL Server type system with additional scalar types or different ranges of data of existing datatypes. Some examples include specialized datetime types for different countries, currency of various countries, a time- or date-only datatype, and unsigned integers. Here are some other potential uses of UDTs:

- Datatypes where you need specialized formatting, checks, or operations. For example, a coordinate, IP address, or SSN.

- Complex types that are provided by an owner of a particular format, such as a media format that could be used to interpret a varbinary(max) value as a movie, or an audio clip. This type would have to be loaded on the client to get any value from the datatype.

- Complex types for a specialized application that has complex needs, when you're sure your application will be the only user.

Although the possibilities are virtually unlimited, I would suggest that CLR UDTs only be considered for specialized circumstances that make the database design more robust and easy to work with. CLR UDTs are a nice addition to the DBA's and developer's toolkit, but they should be reserved for those times when adding a new scalar datatype solves a business problem.

Later in the chapter, I'll demonstrate creating an American Social Security domain, though I'm not sure I'd go through the trouble in a real system.

Updating the Model

For each of the domains that have been set up in the model, go through and assign datatypes. For example, take the Person table in Figure 5-23.

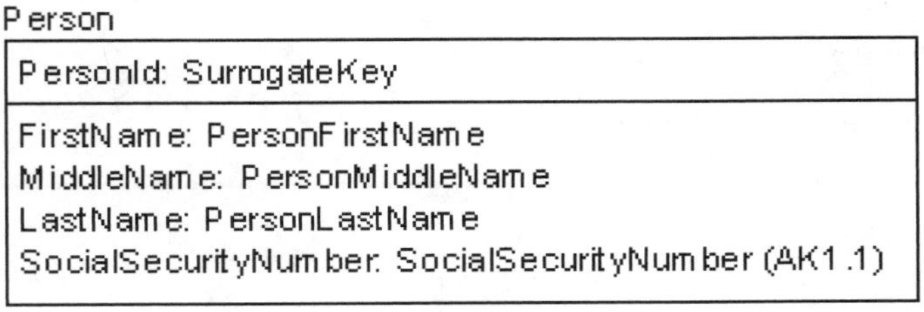

```
Person
┌─────────────────────────────────────────────────────┐
│ PersonId: SurrogateKey                                │
├─────────────────────────────────────────────────────┤
│ FirstName: PersonFirstName                            │
│ MiddleName: PersonMiddleName                          │
│ LastName: PersonLastName                              │
│ SocialSecurityNumber: SocialSecurityNumber (AK1.1)    │
└─────────────────────────────────────────────────────┘
```

Figure 5-23. *Choosing datatypes for the Person table*

- SurrogateKey: I generally use an integer for this. For larger databases, it can be useful to be specific and use one of the smaller datatypes for some of the surrogate key values, because most tables won't need the ability to have approximately four billion different values.

- PersonFirstName, PersonMiddleName, PersonLastName: All varchar(30). PersonMiddleName allows NULLs, but the others don't.

- SocialSecurityNumber: This is a CLR datatype, so this domain is left as SocialSecurityNumber datatype.

This table now looks like Figure 5-24.

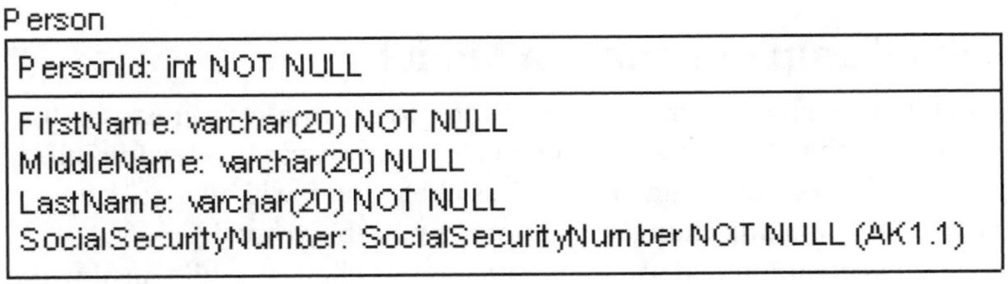

```
Person
┌─────────────────────────────────────────────────────┐
│ PersonId: int NOT NULL                                │
├─────────────────────────────────────────────────────┤
│ FirstName: varchar(20) NOT NULL                       │
│ MiddleName: varchar(20) NULL                          │
│ LastName: varchar(20) NOT NULL                        │
│ SocialSecurityNumber: SocialSecurityNumber NOT NULL (AK1.1) │
└─────────────────────────────────────────────────────┘
```

Figure 5-24. *Datatypes chosen for the Person table*

I'll then set up each of the other domains as SQL Server types. The entire model will be displayed in the next few pages, once schemas have been added.

Setting up Schemas

In SQL Server 2005, you can use an additional level of organization to segregate the tables in a database. Between database and table name, instead of owner, you can specify a schema. Schemas are great to segregate objects within a database for clarity of use.

For example, in the AdventureWorks sample database that ships with SQL Server 2005, five schemas are present: HumanResources, Person, Production, Purchasing, and Sales. Use the following query:

```
SELECT  table_name
FROM    information_schema.tables
WHERE   table_schema = 'Purchasing'
```

You can see the tables that make up the schema:

```
table_name
--------------------
ProductVendor
Vendor
PurchaseOrderDetail
VendorAddress
vVendor
VendorContact
PurchaseOrderHeader
ShipMethod
```

All of them are centered around purchasing. What makes schemas so nice is that you can deal with permissions on a schema level, rather than on an object-by-object level. Chapter 7 will discuss using schemas for security in more detail.

I'll segregate the MovieRental database model into three schemas: Inventory, People, and Rentals. The model in the next section will reflect this.

Reviewing the "Final" Implementation Model

OK, nothing is "final" and I'll make changes later in this chapter to the model to illustrate this point (I just thought of new stuff that illustrated another point, but it serves this twofold purpose). The better the job that has been done already, the less likely that it will be required to make big changes, but admittedly making changes is almost impossible to avoid.

The model in Figure 5-25 is the model I'll use for the rest of this chapter, while turning the model into implemented tables and columns.

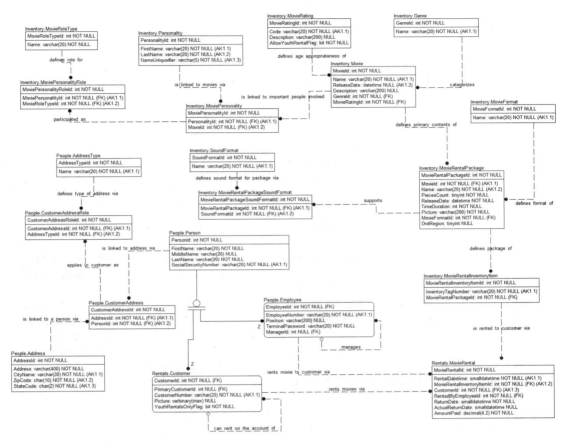

Figure 5-25. *Final MovieRental model database*

Property Tables

A technique that doesn't fit well into this example, but one that I would be remiss if I completely ignored, is property tables. These are also known by a few different names, such as Entity, Attribute, Value (EAV) Schema, Loose Schema, or Open Schema. The idea is that for some cases, it won't be possible to know all the attributes at design time. The examples where this makes sense are usually uncommon, but it's a good technique to have if needed.

If you have the identifier for some object, you can then define properties at runtime, and then associate values with them. For example, say you were building a program to gather properties about objects where the types of attributes aren't known. The last time I used this type of construct was to gather the properties on networking equipment. Each router, modem, and so on, on a network has various properties (and hundreds or thousands of them at that). The model for this is as shown in Figure 5-26.

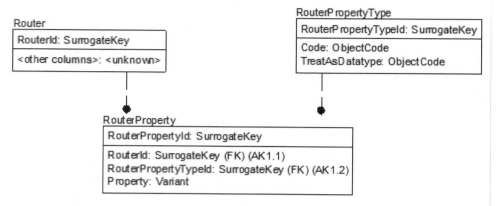

Figure 5-26. *Property schema for storing router properties with unknown attributes*

The Router table contained the information that identified and described a router. Any type of property that was identified was given a code and a datatype (which the client would use to determine how to display and validate the value).

Finally the value is placed in the Property column, which is a variant (datatype sql_variant) type. Now any value, of any type of data, could be stored for any property that the user defines. Using these values in queries isn't a simple task at all, and as such you should avoid loose schemas like this unless absolutely necessary. Check out the SQL Server 2005 PIVOT syntax in a SELECT statement for a clever way to change these properties into columns.

One of the big reasons I didn't feature property tables in the model is it's generally poor database design to build tables such as this. Putting metadata into relational tables is considered poor practice. The big problem is that all too often when this is done, a user is trying to implement all domain tables in one table (see Figure 5-27).

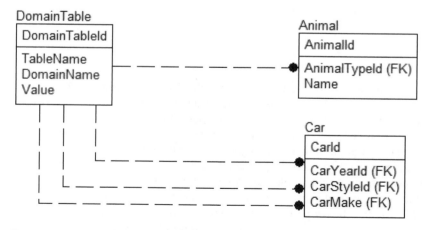

Figure 5-27. *One-size-fits-all domain table*

This is a bad idea indeed, because it's hard to index properly, and just plain difficult to work with. Going back to the logical design, every table should represent one and only one thing. When you see a column in a table by itself, there should be no question as to what it means, yet in this design, you have to query more metadata to find out the context of the value and then what it means. Perhaps the worst part of this design is that the values aren't extensible. What if you want to add a description on the domain value? It can't be done without changing the domain structure for multiple tables.

Some tools that implement an "object oriented" view of a design tend to use this frequently, because it's easy to implement tables such as this and use a cached object. One table means one set of methods instead of hundreds of different methods for hundreds of different objects—er, tables. (The fact that it stinks when you go to use it in the database for queries is of little consequence, because generally systems like this don't intend for you to go into the database and do queries, except through special interfaces that take care of this situation for you.)

Implementing the Design

This is the mechanical part of the chapter, in that all that's left is to implement tables. The blueprints have been drawn up and now I can grab a hammer and start driving nails.

Just like in the rest of the book, I'm going to do this work manually, as it will help you to understand what the tool is building for you. It's also a good exercise for any database architect or DBA to review the SQL Server syntax; just don't do this on a database with 90 tables unless you have a few months where you're trying to look busy. The same tools that could be used to do the logical modeling usually can be used to create the tables and at least some of the associated code.

No matter how you do the work, you need to make sure that you save the scripts you use to create objects in some manner in the file system, because they're invaluable tools for the DBA to apply changes to production, test, development, QA, or whatever environments have been set up to allow developers, users, and DBAs to coexist throughout the process. Many DBAs do all their work using scripts and never use a database design/generation tool.

Development databases are characterized as containing data that has no active business value. Developers should be able to modify or destroy any of the sample data (not structures) when developing code to access a database.

Before starting to build anything else, you'll need a database. I'm going to create this database using all default values, and my installation is totally generic on my laptop. I use the Developer Edition, and I used all the default settings when installing. I hate to state the completely obvious, but you'll need to do this with an account that has rights to create a database, especially if you're doing this on a shared server, such as your company dev server. Feel free to name your database anything you want, as what the database is named won't be important to the process.

The steps I'll take along the way are as follows:

- *Basic table creation*: Building the base objects with columns

- *Adding uniqueness constraints*: Using primary and unique constraints to enforce uniqueness between rows in the table

- *Building default constraints*: Assisting users in choosing proper values when it isn't obvious

- *Adding relationships*: Defining how tables relate to one another

- *Considering large value datatypes*: One of the interesting choices to make is how to use large value datatypes—the (max) types—and what the implications are

- *Collations*: How the collation of data can affect how it's used, and how to use COLLATE to change the collation as needed temporarily

- *Computed columns*: How to use computed columns to avoid single table denormalizations

- *Complex datatypes*: How the CLR types and datatype aliases can be used

- *Documentation*: Including documentation directly in the SQL Server objects

The following statement creates a small database in your default directory, which if you took all defaults (as I did on my laptop) is "C:\Program Files\Microsoft SQL Server\MSSQL.1\ MSSQL\DATA\". If you want to be more fancy with your database or file location, more power to you. We need little in the way of size for this database.

```
CREATE DATABASE MovieRental
```

The database is owned by the user who created the database, as you can see from the following query:

```
SELECT  name, suser_sname(sid) as [login]
FROM    sys.sysusers
WHERE   name = 'dbo'
```

This query returns the following result:

name	login
dbo	MYDOMAIN\LBDAVI

Basic Table Creation

Tables are the central objects you'll deal with. Looking at the full syntax for the CREATE TABLE statement, you'll see that there are many different optional parameters. Throughout this chapter, and part of the next, I'll look at table-creation statements and how best to choose what to do with each variation.

```
CREATE TABLE [<database>.][<schema>.]<tablename>
    [ ON { partition_scheme_name ( partition_column_name )
        | filegroup
        | " DEFAULT " } ]
    [ { TEXTIMAGE_ON { filegroup | " DEFAULT " } ]
(
    <column specification>
)
```

I'll demonstrate the column specifications in a later section.

The first required clause is straightforward:

```
CREATE TABLE [<database>.][<schema>.]<tablename>
```

I'll expand upon the items between the angle brackets (< and >). Anything in square brackets ([and]) is optional.

- <database>: It's seldom necessary to specify the database in the CREATE TABLE statements. If not specified, this defaults to the current database where the statement is being executed. Specifying the database means that the script will only be executable in a single database, which precludes us from using the script unchanged to build alternate databases on the same server, should the need arise.

- <schema>: This is the schema to which the table will belong.

- <tablename>: This is the name of the table. I'll briefly discuss how to name tables in the next section.

■**Tip** If the first character of the table name is a single # symbol, the table is a temporary table. If the first two characters of the table name are ##, it's a global temporary table. Temporary tables are not so much a part of database design as a mechanism to hold intermediate results in complex queries.

The combination of schema and tablename must be unique in a database.

■**Note** In versions of SQL Server prior to 2005, the second part of the name was the owner, and almost every best-practice guide would suggest that all tables were owned by the dbo (database user).

Also note that the word *schema* has two usages. One means a container of objects within a database, and the other simply refers to the tables within the schema. I'll try to be clear as to which meaning I'm using.

I should briefly mention a couple settings that may be interesting for the CREATE TABLE syntax:

```
[ ON { partition_scheme_name ( partition_column_name )
    | filegroup
    | " DEFAULT " } ]
```

These settings allow you to place the table on a specific filegroup, or partition the data across multiple files or filegroups using partitions. The following setting lets you place the text and image overflow data on a given filegroup:

```
[ { TEXTIMAGE_ON { filegroup | " DEFAULT " } ]
```

Briefly, filegroups let you split your databases up into different files to speed access to them by allowing for parallel I/O operations. I'll discuss filegroups and partitioning in more detail in Chapter 8 when discussing how the data tables are stored physically on disk.

Limits

Before going any further, here are a few of the limits to work with when building tables in SQL Server. Five limits are important to us when building a table:

- *Number of tables*: There's a maximum of two billion tables in a database.

- *Number of columns*: The maximum number of columns in a table is 1,024. If the database is properly normalized, this is way (way!) beyond reasonable requirements.

- *Number of bytes per index entry*: The limit on this is 16 columns and 900 bytes, and for good reason. A page is roughly 8,060 bytes, so if an index was much larger than 900, it would become ineffective.

- *Number of indexes*: The limit is 1 clustered and 249 nonclustered. It could be possible to get close to this limit in read only (for example, data warehousing systems), but never in an OLTP database. Having 250 indexes on a table in an OLTP system would reduce performance drastically because of the frequent modifications that are likely to be made to the data. I'll discuss clustered and nonclustered indexes in Chapter 8.

- *Number of bytes per row*: The maximum number of bytes in a row is 8,060 (this is the number of usable bytes on a page, after overhead). Unlike the number of columns, the maximum number of bytes isn't quite as hard to reach. This is because you can have columns that store 8,000 characters.

  - When you have `varchar`, `nvarchar`, `varbinary`, or `sql_variant` columns in your table, SQL Server 2005 now allows you to break this barrier and store more than 8,060 bytes on a single row. However, this would generally not be a good thing to do, as the row would take up multiple pages, requiring more and more I/O to read or modify.

Schema

Back in the first main section of the book, schemas were set up for each of the tables in the implemented databases. In SQL Server 2005, the owner has been changed to the more proper schema. A *schema* is a namespace: a container where database objects are contained, within a database. By ANSI-92 standards, the schema objects are all owned by a single owner. However, unlike in earlier versions of SQL Server, because the schema isn't tightly tied to a user, you can drop the user without changing the exposed name of the object. Changing owners of the schema changes owners of the table.

In SQL Server 2000 and earlier, the table was owned by a user; in SQL Server 2005 a schema is owned by a user, and tables are contained in a schema. Just as in 2000, the generally suggested best practice was that all tables were owned by the `dbo` user. In 2005, this is done by having the schema owned by the `dbo`.

Not just tables are bound to a given schema; just about every object is schema bound. You can access objects using the following naming method:

```
[<databaseName>.][<schemaName>.]objectName
```

The `<databaseName>` defaults to the current database. The `<schemaName>` defaults to the user's default schema.

Schemas are of great use to segregate objects within a database for clarity of use. If you look at the AdventureWorks database, you'll see that instead of all the tables still being "owned" by dbo, they're now members of various schemas. For example, using the new sys.schemas system view, you can list the schemas in the database:

```
SELECT name,
       USER_NAME(principal_id) as principal
FROM   sys.schemas
```

Cutting out all the system schemas (run the query for yourself!), the AdventureWorks database has the following schemas:

name	schemaName	principal
HumanResources	HumanResources	dbo
Person	Person	dbo
Production	Production	dbo
Purchasing	Purchasing	dbo
Sales	Sales	dbo

For example, now let's look at the different tables owned by the Purchasing schema:

```
SELECT  table_name
FROM    information_schema.tables
WHERE   table_schema = 'Purchasing'
```

You see the following tables:

table_name
ProductVendor
Vendor
PurchaseOrderDetail
VendorAddress
vVendor
VendorContact
PurchaseOrderHeader
ShipMethod

When you access an object using a single part name, in editions of SQL Server before 2005, it always defaulted to dbo. In 2005, you can specify a default schema, other than the dbo schema (which mimics earlier versions for easier backward compatibility). Then when you execute SELECT columnName FROM tableName, instead of defaulting to dbo.tablename, it would use the defaultSchemaName.tablename.

This is done using the following code:

```
CREATE USER <schemaUser>
       FOR LOGIN <schemaUser>
       WITH DEFAULT SCHEMA = schemaname
```

There's also an ALTER USER command that allows the changing of default schema for existing users. What makes schemas so nice is that you can deal with permissions on a schema level, rather than on an object-by-object level. Schemas also give you a logical grouping of objects when you view them within a list, such as in Management Studio.

I'm not going to go any further into the security aspects of using schemas at this point in the book, but I'll just mention that they're a good idea. Throughout the book, I'll always name the schema that a table is in when doing examples. Schemas will be a part of any system I design in this book, simply because it's going to be a best practice to do so going further. On a brief trip back to the land of reality, I would expect that beginning to use schemas in production systems will be a slow process, because it hasn't been the normal method in years past. Chapter 7 will discuss using schemas for security in more detail.

For all the tables in the MovieRental database, we'll create the following three schemas. We'll do this and all operations while logged in as the user who created the database:

```
CREATE SCHEMA Inventory --tables pertaining to the videos to be rented
GO
CREATE SCHEMA People --tables pertaining to people (nonspecific)
GO
CREATE SCHEMA Rentals --tables pertaining to rentals to customers
GO
```

Note that CREATE SCHEMA must be the first statement in the batch. We'll also create another schema for tables that are for demonstration of some concept that isn't a part of the MovieRental "experience":

```
CREATE SCHEMA Alt
GO
```

Columns and Base Datatypes

The lines with the arrows are the ones used to define a column:

```
      CREATE TABLE [<database>.][<schema>.]<tablename>
      (
➤         <columnName> <datatype> [<NULL specification>]
                                        [IDENTITY [(seed,increment)]]
          -- or
➤         <columnName> AS <computed definition>
      )
```

The <columnName> placeholder is where you specify the name of the column. There are two types of columns:

- *Implemented*: This is an ordinary column, in which physical storage is allocated and data is stored for the value.

- *Computed (or virtual)*: These columns are made up by a calculation derived from any of the physical columns in the table.

Most of the columns in any database will be implemented columns, but computed columns have some pretty cool uses, so don't think they're of no use just because they aren't talked about much. You can avoid plenty of denormalization code by using computed columns. (I'll demonstrate them later in this chapter.)

Nullability

In the column-create phrase, simply change the <NULL specification> in our physical model to NULL to allow NULLs, or NOT NULL not to allow NULLs:

<columnName> <data type> [<NULL specification>]

For example:

```
CREATE TABLE Alt.NullTest
(
    NullColumn varchar(10) NULL,
    NotNullColumn varchar(10) NOT NULL
)
```

There's nothing particularly surprising there. Leaving off the NULL specification altogether, the SQL Server default is used. To determine the current default property for a database, execute the following statement:

```
SELECT    name, is_ansi_null_default_on
FROM      sys.databases
```

This has the following results:

name	is_ansi_null_default_on
MovieRental	0

To set the default for the database, you can use ALTER DATABASE. The syntax to change the setting is as follows:

```
ALTER DATABASE MovieRental
    SET ANSI_NULL_DEFAULT OFF
```

Tip I would recommend having this setting always OFF, so that if you forget to set it explicitly, you won't be stuck with nullable columns that quickly fill up with NULL data you'll have to clean up.

To set the default for a session, use the following command:

```
SET ANSI_NULL_DFLT_ON OFF
```

Or use ON if you want the default to be NULL.

> *Yes, it is confusing to be setting an option to* OFF.

Here's an example:

```
--turn off default NULLs
SET ANSI_NULL_DFLT_ON OFF

--create test table
CREATE TABLE Alt.testNULL
(
    id    int
)

--check the values
EXEC sp_help 'Alt.testNULL'
```

This code returns the following:

Column_name	[...]	Nullable
Id	...	no

■**Note** Considerable stuff has been removed from the sp_help output here for space reasons. sp_help returns information about the tables, columns, and constraints.

Let's take one of the tables from the model and demonstrate the syntax (see Figure 5-28). Create the table using the following DDL:

```
CREATE TABLE Inventory.Movie
(
        MovieId              int NOT NULL,
        Name                 varchar(20) NOT NULL,
        ReleaseDate          datetime NULL,
        Description          varchar(200) NULL,
        GenreId              int NOT NULL,
        MovieRatingId        int NOT NULL
)
```

This builds the table, though this isn't "good enough," because nothing prevents the user from creating duplicate rows. In the next section, you'll implement the surrogate key (in this case MovieId), followed by key constraints to prevent duplication.

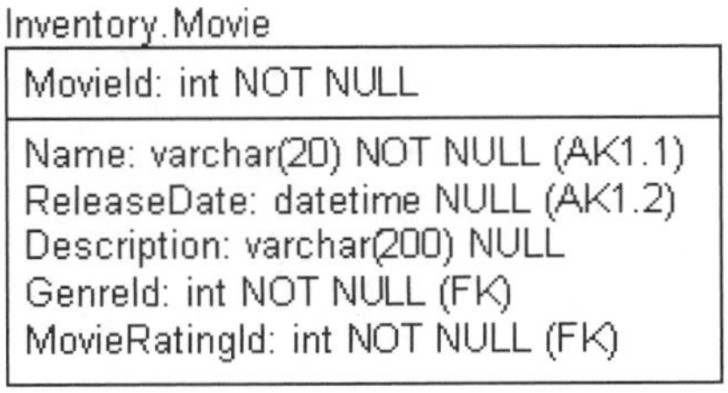

```
Inventory.Movie
┌─────────────────────────────────────────────┐
│ MovieId: int NOT NULL                         │
├─────────────────────────────────────────────┤
│ Name: varchar(20) NOT NULL (AK1.1)            │
│ ReleaseDate: datetime NULL (AK1.2)            │
│ Description: varchar(200) NULL                │
│ GenreId: int NOT NULL (FK)                    │
│ MovieRatingId: int NOT NULL (FK)              │
└─────────────────────────────────────────────┘
```

Figure 5-28. *Inventory.Movie table to be created*

Surrogate Keys

Finally, before building any actual tables, there's one more thing to discuss. In the first section of this chapter, I discussed how to implement a surrogate key. In this section, I'll present the method that I typically use. I break down surrogate key values into two types that I use:

- Manually managed:

  - Letting the client choose the surrogate value. This could mean using GUIDs or some hash function to create a value. I won't cover this topic any more than to say that it's up to the client to build such values and include them in the INSERT statements when creating new rows.

  - Manually created by the DBA during load (for read-only tables).

- Automatically generated using the IDENTITY property. For tables where data is created by users, the IDENTITY property is employed.

Manually Managed (Read-Only Tables)

A couple good examples of tables where there's no need to allow users access to create new rows manually are the Genre and MovieRating tables (values from these two tables are a part of the next example as well). The way these values are used, adding a new value would require changes to the code of the system, and probably changes in the physical realm of the rental store. Hence, instead of building tables that require code to manage, as well as user interfaces, we simply choose a permanent value for each type. It gives you control over the values in the key (which you won't have nearly as much of when using the IDENTITY property), and allows usage of the surrogate key directly in code if desired (likely as a constant construct in the host language). It also allows a user interface to cache values from this table (or even implement them as constants), with confidence that they won't change without the knowledge of the programmer who is using them (see Figure 5-29).

```
Inventory.MovieRating                               Inventory.Genre
┌─────────────────────────────────────┐            ┌──────────────────────────────────────┐
│ MovieRatingId: int NOT NULL           │            │ GenreId: int NOT NULL                  │
├─────────────────────────────────────┤            ├──────────────────────────────────────┤
│ Code: varchar(20) NOT NULL (AK1.1)    │            │ Name: varchar(20) NOT NULL (AK1.1)     │
│ Description: varchar(200) NULL        │            └──────────────────────────────────────┘
│ AllowYouthRentalFlag: bit NOT NULL    │
└─────────────────────────────────────┘
```

Figure 5-29. *Manually managed domain tables*

Create these tables and load some data:

```
CREATE TABLE Inventory.MovieRating (
        MovieRatingId       int NOT NULL,
        Code                varchar(20) NOT NULL,
        Description         varchar(200) NULL,
        AllowYouthRentalFlag bit NOT NULL
)
```

Then load data into the table, manually creating the key values:

```
INSERT INTO Inventory.MovieRating
            (MovieRatingId, Code, Description, AllowYouthRentalFlag)
VALUES (0, 'UR','Unrated',1)
INSERT INTO Inventory.MovieRating
            (MovieRatingId, Code, Description, AllowYouthRentalFlag)
VALUES (1, 'G','General Audiences',1)
INSERT INTO Inventory.MovieRating
            (MovieRatingId, Code, Description, AllowYouthRentalFlag)
VALUES (2, 'PG','Parental Guidance',1)
INSERT INTO Inventory.MovieRating
        (MovieRatingId, Code, Description, AllowYouthRentalFlag)
VALUES (3, 'PG-13','Parental Guidance for Children Under 13',1)
INSERT INTO Inventory.MovieRating
            (MovieRatingId, Code, Description, AllowYouthRentalFlag)
VALUES (4, 'R','Restricted, No Children Under 17 without Parent',0)
```

A common shorthand I often use in place of NULL values to indicate no value (rather than unknown value) is to have a row with a 0 as a surrogate key that explicitly states this value. Then load the Genre table:

```
CREATE TABLE Inventory.Genre (
        GenreId             int NOT NULL,
        Name                varchar(20) NOT NULL
)
GO
INSERT INTO Inventory.Genre (GenreId, Name)
VALUES (1,'Comedy')
INSERT INTO Inventory.Genre (GenreId, Name)
VALUES (2,'Drama')
INSERT INTO Inventory.Genre (GenreId, Name)
VALUES (3,'Thriller')
INSERT INTO Inventory.Genre (GenreId, Name)
VALUES (4,'Documentary')
```

I don't include a 0 value here because there isn't a case where the Genre of a movie doesn't exist. I didn't allow NULLs for the Genre in the Movie table because in this sort of database, the genre of a movie will have been chosen so the movie can be sorted on shelves.

Note that it's generally expected that once you manually create a value, the meaning of this value will never change. For example, if you had a row (1, STOP), it would be fine to change it to (1, HALT), but not to (1, GO). This consistency allows you to cache values with little concern for how long (does it matter if one user chooses STOP and the other HALT?). Also, the key you choose will be excellent for ETL to a data warehouse.

Generation Using the IDENTITY Property

Most of the time, tables are created to allow users to create new rows. Implementing a surrogate key on these tables is commonly done using (what are commonly referred to as) IDENTITY columns. For any of the precise numeric datatypes (the numeric type, and any of the integer types other than bit), there's an option to create an automatically incrementing column whose value is guaranteed to be unique for the table it's in. The column that implements this IDENTITY column must also be defined as NOT NULL. From our initial section on columns, I had this for the column specification:

```
<columnName> <data type> [<NULL specification>] IDENTITY [(seed,increment)]
```

The seed portion specifies the number that the column values will start with, and the increment is how much the next value will increase. For example, take the Movie table created earlier, this time implementing the IDENTITY-based surrogate key:

```
DROP TABLE Inventory.Movie
GO
CREATE TABLE Inventory.Movie
(
        MovieId             int NOT NULL IDENTITY(1,2),
        Name                varchar(20) NOT NULL,
        ReleaseDate         datetime NULL,
        Description         varchar(200) NULL,
        GenreId             int NOT NULL,
        MovieRatingId       int NOT NULL
)
```

In this CREATE TABLE statement, I've added the IDENTITY property for the MovieId column. The seed of 1 indicates that the values will start at 1, and the increment says that the second value will be 2 greater, in this case 3, the next 5, and so on.

The following script inserts three new rows into the Movie table:

```
INSERT INTO Inventory.Movie (Name, ReleaseDate,
                            Description, GenreId, MovieRatingId)
SELECT 'The Maltese Falcon','19411003',
       'A private detective finds himself surrounded by strange people ' +
       'looking for a statue filled with jewels',2,0
       --Genre and Ratings values create as literal values because the Genre and
       --Ratings tables are built with explicit values

INSERT INTO Inventory.Movie (Name, ReleaseDate,
                            Description, GenreId, MovieRatingId)
SELECT 'Arsenic and Old Lace','19440923',
       'A man learns a disturbing secret about his aunt's methods ' +
       'for treating gentleman callers',1,0
```

Now view the new values with the following code:

```
SELECT  MovieId, Name, ReleaseDate
FROM    Inventory.Movie
```

This produces the following results:

MovieId	Name	ReleaseDate
1	The Maltese Falcon	1941-10-03 00:00:00.000
3	Arsenic and Old Lace	1944-09-23 00:00:00.000

The IDENTITY property is useful for creating a surrogate primary key that's small and fast. The int datatype requires only four bytes and is good, because most tables will have fewer than two billion rows (you should hope so, unless you have incredible hardware!). I'll discuss primary keys in some detail later in this chapter.

Note that IDENTITY values are apt to have holes in the sequence. If an error occurs when creating a new row, the IDENTITY value that was going to be used will be lost. (This is one of the things that allows them to be good performers when you have heavy concurrency needs. Because IDENTITY values aren't affected by transactions, other connections don't have to wait until another's transaction completes).

If a row gets deleted, the deleted value won't be reused. Hence, you shouldn't use IDENTITY columns if you cannot accept this constraint on the values in your table. The value of a column with the IDENTITY property cannot be updated. You can insert your own value by using SET IDENTITY_INSERT <tablename> ON, but for the most part you should only use this when starting a table using values from another table. Lastly, you cannot alter a column to turn on the IDENTITY property, but you can add an IDENTITY column to an existing table.

Keep in mind the fact (I hope I've said this enough) that the surrogate key should not be the only key on the table, or that the only uniqueness is a more-or-less random value! For example, executing the INSERT again now for the *Arsenic and Old Lace* row would end up with the following:

MovieId	Name	ReleaseDate
1	The Maltese Falcon	1941-10-03 00:00:00.000
3	Arsenic and Old Lace	1944-09-23 00:00:00.000
5	Arsenic and Old Lace	1944-09-23 00:00:00.000

There could be two movies with the same name, but never (based on the database we've designed) released on the same day.

Uniqueness Keys

As I've mentioned several times, it's important that every table have at least one constraint that prevents duplicate rows from being created. In this section, I'll highlight the syntax of creating the following:

- Primary key constraints

- Alternate (UNIQUE) key constraints

Both types of constraints are built using unique indexes to enforce the uniqueness. It's conceivable that you could use unique indexes instead of constraints, but using a constraint is the favored method of implementing an alternate key and enforcing uniqueness.

Constraints are intended to semantically represent and enforce constraints on data, and indexes (which are covered in detail in Chapter 8) are intended to speed access to data. In actuality, it doesn't matter how the uniqueness is implemented, but it is necessary to have either unique indexes or unique constraints in place. In some cases, other RDBMSes don't always use indexes to enforce uniqueness by default. They can use hash tables that are only good to see if the values exist, but not to look up values. By and large, when you need to enforce uniqueness it's also the case that the user is searching for values in the table.

Primary Keys

The syntax of the primary key declaration is straightforward:

[CONSTRAINT constraintname] PRIMARY KEY [CLUSTERED | NONCLUSTERED]

I'll talk more about the index options in Chapter 8. Note that the constraint name is optional. I'll name primary key constraints using a name such as PK<tablename>. For a single column implemented with a clustered index (the default), you can specify it when creating the table, such as the domain table in Figure 5-30. 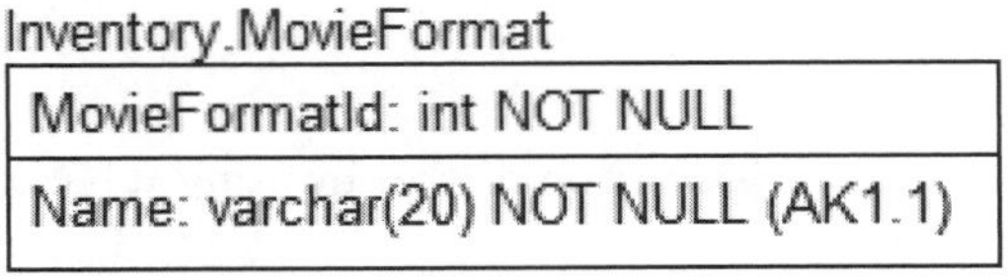

Inventory.MovieFormat

MovieFormatId: int NOT NULL
Name: varchar(20) NOT NULL (AK1.1)

Figure 5-30. *Primary key generation sample table*

```
CREATE TABLE Inventory.MovieFormat (
    MovieFormatId       int NOT NULL
        CONSTRAINT PKMovieFormat PRIMARY KEY CLUSTERED,
    Name                varchar(20) NOT NULL
)
```

Then you load the data:

```
INSERT INTO Inventory.MovieFormat(MovieFormatId, Name)
VALUES (1,'Video Tape')
INSERT INTO Inventory.MovieFormat(MovieFormatId, Name)
VALUES (1,'DVD')
```

Crud, I accidentally tried to create duplicate values:

```
Msg 2627, Level 14, State 1, Line 3
Violation of PRIMARY KEY constraint 'PKMovieFormat'. Cannot insert duplicate key in
object 'Inventory.MovieFormat'.
The statement has been terminated.
```

Then you can fix the data and resubmit:

```
INSERT INTO Inventory.MovieFormat(MovieFormatId, Name)
VALUES (2,'DVD')
```

■**Tip** The primary key and other constraints of the table will be members of the table's schema, so you don't need to name your constraints for uniqueness over all objects, just those in the schema.

If you're using natural keys for your primary keys, when dealing with multiple column keys you need to specify the column names:

```
CREATE TABLE Alt.Product
(
    Manufacturer varchar(30) NOT NULL,
    ModelNumber varchar(30) NOT NULL,
    CONSTRAINT PKProduct PRIMARY KEY NONCLUSTERED (Manufacturer, ModelNumber)
)
DROP TABLE Alt.Product
```

You can also add a PRIMARY KEY constraint to a table with no primary key by using ALTER TABLE, which I'll do to all the other tables already created:

```
ALTER TABLE Inventory.MovieRating
    ADD CONSTRAINT PKMovieRating PRIMARY KEY CLUSTERED (MovieRatingId)

ALTER TABLE Inventory.Genre
    ADD CONSTRAINT PKGenre PRIMARY KEY CLUSTERED (GenreId)

ALTER TABLE Inventory.Movie
    ADD CONSTRAINT PKMovie PRIMARY KEY CLUSTERED (MovieId)
```

Note that you might not have any NULL columns in a primary key, even though you might have NULL columns in a unique index. The reason for this is simple. The primary key is the row identifier, and a NULL provides no form of record identification.

Chapter 8 addresses the choice of clustered or nonclustered indexes on the primary key, but typically when using an integer-based primary key column, the primary key is set as the clustered index for performance reasons.

■Tip Although the CONSTRAINT <constraintName> part of any constraint declaration isn't required, it's a good idea always to name constraint declarations using some name. Otherwise, SQL Server will assign a name for you, and it will be ugly. For example, create the following object in tempdb:

```
CREATE TABLE Test (TestId int PRIMARY KEY)
```

Look at the object name with this query:

```
SELECT constraint_name
FROM   information_schema.table_constraints
WHERE  table_schema = 'Inventory'
  and  table_name = 'test'
```

You see the name chosen is something like PK__Test__09DE7BCC.

Alternate Keys

Alternate key creation is an important task of implementation modeling. Enforcement of these keys is just as important. When implementing alternate keys, it's best to use a UNIQUE constraint. These are pretty much the same thing as primary key constraints, and can even be used as the target of a relationship (relationships are covered later in the chapter).

The syntax for their creation is as follows:

[CONSTRAINT constraintname] UNIQUE [CLUSTERED | <u>NONCLUSTERED</u>]

For example, take the Personality table from the MovieRental model (see Figure 5-31).

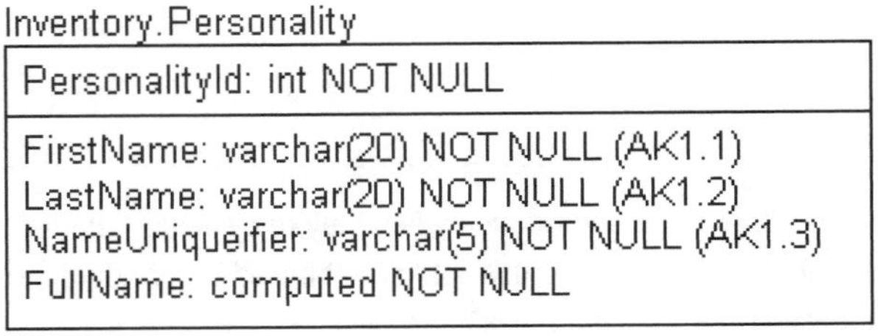

Inventory.Personality

PersonalityId: int NOT NULL
FirstName: varchar(20) NOT NULL (AK1.1) LastName: varchar(20) NOT NULL (AK1.2) NameUniqueifier: varchar(5) NOT NULL (AK1.3) FullName: computed NOT NULL

Figure 5-31. *Alternate key generation sample table*

You can create this table using the following code:

```
CREATE TABLE Inventory.Personality
(
        PersonalityId       int NOT NULL IDENTITY(1,1)
            CONSTRAINT PKPersonality PRIMARY KEY,
        FirstName           varchar(20) NOT NULL,
        LastName            varchar(20) NOT NULL,
        NameUniqueifier     varchar(5) NOT NULL,
            CONSTRAINT AKPersonality_PersonalityName UNIQUE NONCLUSTERED
                (FirstName, LastName, NameUniqueifier)
)
```

Alternately, you can add the constraint to existing tables using ALTER TABLE. For example, these tables were already created with primary keys:

```
ALTER TABLE Inventory.Genre
  ADD CONSTRAINT AKGenre_Name UNIQUE NONCLUSTERED (Name)

ALTER TABLE Inventory.MovieRating
  ADD CONSTRAINT AKMovieRating_Code UNIQUE NONCLUSTERED (Code)

ALTER TABLE Inventory.Movie
  ADD CONSTRAINT AKMovie_NameAndDate UNIQUE NONCLUSTERED (Name, ReleaseDate)
```

Viewing the Constraints

You can see information about the indexes and constraints using the information and sys schema views:

- information_schema.table_constraints

- information_schema.key_column_usage

- sys.indexes

▪Tip Always use the information_schema views for system information when they're available. There are a plethora of sys schema objects. However, they can be messy to use, and aren't based on standards, so they're apt to change in future versions of SQL Server, just as these views are replacing the system tables from previous versions of SQL Server.

For example, use this code to see the constraints that we've created in the MovieRental database we've been building throughout this chapter:

```
SELECT CONSTRAINT_SCHEMA, TABLE_NAME, CONSTRAINT_NAME, CONSTRAINT_TYPE
FROM   INFORMATION_SCHEMA.table_constraints
ORDER  BY CONSTRAINT_SCHEMA, TABLE_NAME
```

This returns the following results:

CONSTRAINT_SCHEMA	TABLE_NAME	CONSTRAINT_NAME	CONSTRAINT_TYPE
Inventory	Genre	PKGenre	PRIMARY KEY
Inventory	Genre	AKGenre_Name	UNIQUE
Inventory	Movie	PKMovie	PRIMARY KEY
Inventory	Movie	AKMovie_NameAndDate	UNIQUE
Inventory	MovieFormat	PKMovieFormat	PRIMARY KEY
Inventory	MovieRating	PKMovieRating	PRIMARY KEY
Inventory	MovieRating	AKMovieRating_Code	UNIQUE
Inventory	Personality	PKPersonality	PRIMARY KEY
Inventory	Personality	AKPersonality_Personality	UNIQUE

Other Indexes

I need to mention briefly that although constraints are built with indexes (and need upkeep like indexes), you shouldn't think of them in the same way as indexes. Indexes have a primary responsibility for increasing performance. Any indexes that are added in addition to those used to enforce uniqueness should be taken care of when dealing with performance tuning.

This is an important distinction that ought to be understood. Indexes make accessing data in a certain way faster, but they also have overhead. Every time a change affects any of the columns that are indexed, the index must be modified. On a single change, the time is probably pretty small, but the more active the system, the more this will affect performance.

In an OLTP system, it's usually a bad practice to do performance "guessing"—adding indexes before a need is shown—versus performance "tuning," where you respond to *known* performance problems. Only at that time is it reasonable to decide how a performance "tune" will affect the rest of the database. I'll discuss more about non-constraint–based indexes in Chapter 8.

Default Constraints

If a user doesn't know what value to enter into a table, the value can be omitted, and the default constraint sets it to a valid predetermined value. This helps, in that you help users avoid having to make up illogical, inappropriate values if they don't know what they want to put in a column, yet they need to create a row.

For example, consider that an experienced SQL Server user must enter a value into a column called boogleFlag, which is a bit column (boogleFlag was chosen because it has just as much meaning to you as some of the columns that make sense have for other users). Not knowing what boogleFlag represents, but forced to create a new row, the user might choose to enter a 1 (hopefully *boogle* isn't shorthand for blowing up the world!). Using default values gives the users an example of a likely value for the column. There's no question that setting default values for columns is convenient for the user.

The command to add a default follows this structure:

```
ALTER TABLE <tableName>
   ADD [ CONSTRAINT <DefaultName> ]
   DEFAULT <constantExpression>
   FOR <columnName>
```

I'll use a simple naming standard for constraints:

```
Dflt<tableName>_<columnName>
```

The `<constantExpression>` is a scalar expression that can be either a literal value, a `NULL`, or a function. You'll look at several different scenarios for constant expressions in the following section. You'll look at two styles of defaults:

- *Literals*: A single value that will always be the same value.

- *Rich expressions*: These use functions to set a default value based on a situation.

Literal Defaults

A literal is a simple single value in the same datatype that requires no translation by SQL Server. For example, Table 5-3 has sample defaults for a few datatypes.

Table 5-3. *Sample Default Values*

Datatype	Possible Default Value
Int	1
varchar(10)	'Value'
binary(2)	0x0000
datetime	'12/31/2000'

As an example in our sample database, I'll set the default in the `YouthRentalsOnlyFlag` column in the `Customer` table to 0. (First, I need to create the `Person` table and the `Customer` table.) I include the relationship between the tables as well (relationships are discussed in more detail later); see Figure 5-32.

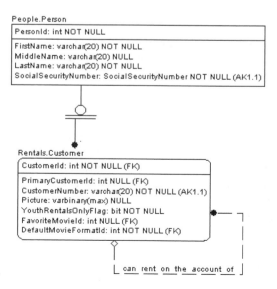

Figure 5-32. *Subtype implementation*

You can create the tables using the following DDL:

```
CREATE TABLE People.Person (
      PersonId              int NOT NULL IDENTITY(1,1)
         CONSTRAINT PKPerson PRIMARY KEY,
      FirstName             varchar(20) NOT NULL,
      MiddleName            varchar(20) NULL,
      LastName              varchar(20) NOT NULL,
      SocialSecurityNumber char(11) --will be redefined using CLR later
         CONSTRAINT AKPerson_SSN UNIQUE
)

CREATE TABLE Rentals.Customer (
      CustomerId            int NOT NULL
         CONSTRAINT PKCustomer PRIMARY KEY,
      CustomerNumber        char(10)
         CONSTRAINT AKCustomer_CustomerNumber UNIQUE,
      PrimaryCustomerId    int NULL,
      Picture              varbinary(max) NULL,
      YouthRentalsOnlyFlag bit NOT NULL
         CONSTRAINT People_Person$can_be_a$Rentals_Customer
             FOREIGN KEY (CustomerId)
                       REFERENCES People.Person  (PersonId)
                       ON DELETE CASCADE  --cascade delete on SubType
                       ON UPDATE NO ACTION,
         CONSTRAINT  Rentals_Customer$can_rent_on_the_account_of$Rentals_Customer
             FOREIGN KEY (PrimaryCustomerId)
                       REFERENCES Rentals.Customer  (CustomerId)
                       ON DELETE NO ACTION
                       ON UPDATE NO ACTION
)
```

Now, I add a column to store the default movie format for the customer (again with relationship information).

Finally, the part that is of interest for this section follows:

```
ALTER TABLE Rentals.Customer
   ADD CONSTRAINT DfltCustomer_YouthRentalsOnlyFlag DEFAULT (0)
       FOR YouthRentalsOnlyFlag
```

Now, when a customer is created without specifying this column, 0 is set:

```
INSERT INTO People.Person(FirstName, MiddleName, LastName, SocialSecurityNumber)
VALUES ('Larry','','Quince','111-11-1111')
--skipping several of the columns that are either nullable or have defaults
INSERT INTO Rentals.Customer(CustomerId, CustomerNumber)
SELECT Person.PersonId, '1111111111'
FROM   People.Person
WHERE  SocialSecurityNumber = '111-11-1111'
```

Then view the data:

```
SELECT CustomerNumber, YouthRentalsOnlyFlag
FROM   Rentals.Customer
```

The data returns the following result:

CustomerNumber	YouthRentalsOnlyFlag
1111111111	0

As another example, consider a table to store URLs. (I could have forced this into the example schema, but it didn't fit. It's a pretty good example for using defaults, however.)

```
--Using the Alt schema for alternative examples
CREATE TABLE Alt.url
(
        scheme          varchar(10) NOT NULL, --http, ftp
        computerName    varchar(50) NOT NULL, --www, or whatever
        domainName varchar(50) NOT NULL, --base domain name (microsoft, amazon, etc.)
        siteType varchar(5) NOT NULL, --net, com, org
        filePath varchar(255) NOT NULL,
        fileName varchar(20) NOT NULL,
        parameter varchar(255) NOT NULL,
        PRIMARY KEY (scheme, computerName, domainName, siteType,
                              filePath, fileName, parameter)
)
```

Entering data into this particular table would be a pain, especially by hand. For example, say you wanted to enter http://www.microsoft.com:

```
INSERT INTO alt.url (scheme, computerName, domainName, siteType,
                          filePath, filename, parameter)
VALUES ('http','www','microsoft','com','','','')

SELECT    scheme + '://' + computerName +
                  case when len(rtrim(computerName)) > 0 then '.' else '' end +
                  domainName + '.'
          + siteType
          + case when len(filePath) > 0 then '/' else '' end + filePath
          + case when len(fileName) > 0 then '/' else '' end + fileName
          + parameter as display
FROM alt.url
```

This code returns the following result:

```
display
---------------------------
http://www.microsoft.com
```

Most of these parts are common, so it isn't unreasonable to default all the common parts of the table. For example, most URLs entered start with http, most then have www, and are com-type sites. Execute the following:

```
ALTER TABLE Alt.url
    ADD CONSTRAINT dfltUrl_scheme
    DEFAULT ('http') FOR scheme

ALTER TABLE alt.url
    ADD CONSTRAINT dfltUrl_computerName
    DEFAULT ('www') FOR computerName

ALTER TABLE alt.url
    ADD CONSTRAINT dfltUrl_siteType
    DEFAULT ('com') FOR siteType

ALTER TABLE alt.url
    ADD CONSTRAINT dfltUrl_filePath
    DEFAULT ('') FOR filePath

ALTER TABLE alt.url
    ADD CONSTRAINT dfltUrl_fileName
    DEFAULT ('') FOR fileName

ALTER TABLE alt.url
    ADD CONSTRAINT dfltUrl_parameter
    DEFAULT ('') FOR parameter
```

Now, to insert a simple URL, such as http://www.usatoday.com, simply enter the following code:

```
INSERT INTO alt.url (domainName)
VALUES ('usatoday')
```

Running the SELECT again, you'll see that you now have two rows:

```
display
---------------------------
http://www.microsoft.com
http://www.usatoday.com
```

Defaults are useful for systems in which a lot of hand coding is required. If you want to see the defaults for a given table, you can check the INFORMATION_SCHEMA.columns table:

```
SELECT cast(column_name as varchaR(20)) as column_name, column_default
FROM   information_schema.columns
WHERE  table_schema = 'Alt'
  AND  table_name  = 'url'
```

In this case it returns the following:

```
column_name          column_default
-------------------- ----------------
scheme               ('http')
computerName         ('www')
domainName           NULL
siteType             ('com')
filePath             ('')
fileName             ('')
parameter            ('')
```

Rich Expressions

An alternative to hard-coding a default value is to use an expression to return the default value. This expression can include any scalar function (system or user defined). You may not reference any other column in the table, or have any SELECT statements, even if they return scalars (though you can include statements in a user-defined function). A common example is a physical-only column that tells you when the row was created. For example, take the MovieRental table in Figure 5-33.

Rentals.MovieRental

MovieRentalId: int NOT NULL
RentalDatetime: smalldatetime NOT NULL (AK1.1) MovieRentalInventoryItemId: int NOT NULL (FK) (AK1.2) CustomerId: int NOT NULL (FK) (AK1.3) RentedByEmployeeId: int NOT NULL (FK) ReturnDate: smalldatetime NOT NULL ActualReturnDate: smalldatetime NULL AmountPaid: decimal(4,2) NOT NULL

Figure 5-33. *Rentals.MovieRental table for applying a complex default statement*

```
CREATE TABLE Rentals.MovieRental (
       MovieRentalId          int NOT NULL IDENTITY(1,1)
            CONSTRAINT PKMovieRental PRIMARY KEY,
       ReturnDate             smalldatetime NOT NULL,
       ActualReturnDate       smalldatetime NULL,
       MovieRentalInventoryItemId int NOT NULL,
       CustomerId             int NOT NULL,
       RentalDatetime         smalldatetime NOT NULL,
       RentedByEmployeeId     int NOT NULL,
       AmountPaid             decimal(4,2) NOT NULL,
       CONSTRAINT AKMovieRental UNIQUE (RentalDatetime,
            MovieRentalInventoryItemId, CustomerId)
)
```

A default could make sense in two columns: the `RentalDatetime` and the `ReturnDate`. For the `RentalDatetime`, the default is just the date and time that the row is created. For the `ReturnDate`, build a constraint that sets it to 10:00 pm on the fourth day after the rental occurs:

```
ALTER TABLE Rentals.MovieRental
    ADD CONSTRAINT DfltMovieRental_RentalDatetime
        DEFAULT (GETDATE()) FOR RentalDatetime

ALTER TABLE Rentals.MovieRental
    ADD CONSTRAINT DfltMovieRental_ReturnDate
        --Default to 10:00 on the fourth day
        DEFAULT (DATEADD(Day,4,CONVERT(varchar(8),getdate(),112) + ' 22:00'))
            FOR ReturnDate
```

Then create a row (leaving all the other columns as 0, because they aren't germane to the example):

```
INSERT  Rentals.MovieRental (MovieRentalInventoryItemId, CustomerId,
        RentedByEmployeeId, AmountPaid)
VALUES (0,0,0,0.00)
```

Then look at the data in the defaulted columns:

```
SELECT  RentalDatetime, ReturnDate
FROM    Rentals.MovieRental
```

You can see the resulting values:

```
RentalDatetime          ReturnDate
----------------------  -----------------------
2005-10-28 13:20:00     2005-11-01 22:00:00
```

Although there are some uses for using functions (including user-defined functions) in default statements, this is quite often not the best idea. In the `MovieRental` database, an example could be created to use a user-defined function to access some data to decide how long to set the rental date for. However, usually business rules that surround this sort of operation are more complex than are allowed for using a default at all.

For scalar expressions, or simple system functions, functions often make sense, such as in our example. However, more complex defaults that use other data are usually done using a trigger, or more commonly using the client objects. I cover triggers in detail in the next chapter.

Relationships (Foreign Keys)

I've covered relationships in some length already, so I'll try to avoid saying too much more about why to use them. In this section, I'll simply discuss how to implement relationships. It's common to add constraints using the ALTER TABLE statement, but you can also do this using the CREATE TABLE statement. However, because tables are frequently created all at once, it's usually more likely that the ALTER TABLE command will be used, because parent tables needn't be created before dependent child tables in scripts.

The foreign key is just a unique key of another table migrated to the child table that represents the entity that it comes from. Almost all the time, the unique key will be the primary key of the table. There are several issues to consider and work through when creating relationships:

- Validating data being entered into a column against the values in a foreign key

- Cascading operations

- Relationships that span different databases or servers

The syntax of the statement for adding foreign key constraints is pretty simple:

```
[CONSTRAINT <constraintName>]
FOREIGN KEY REFERENCES <referenceTable> (<referenceColumns>)
[ON DELETE <NO ACTION | CASCADE | SET NULL | SET DEFAULT> ]
[ON UPDATE <NO ACTION | CASCADE | SET NULL | SET DEFAULT> ]
```

Where

- `<referenceTable>` is the parent table in the relationship.

- `<referenceColumns>` is a comma-delimited list of columns in the child table in the same order as the columns in the primary key of the parent table.

- `ON DELETE` or `ON UPDATE` clauses specify what to do in case of an invalid value. Each of these cases is covered in detail later in this section. For this section, I'll use the `NO ACTION` option, which causes "no action" to take place and an error to be raised.

You might need to implement an optional relationship (where the migrated key is nullable), such as the one in Figure 5-34.

Figure 5-34. *Optional parent-to-child relationship requires NULL on the migrated key*

The `child.parentId` column needs to allow NULLs. This is all you need to do, as SQL Server knows that when the referencing key allows a NULL, the relationship value is optional. You don't have to have a NULL primary key value for the relationship because, as discussed, it's impossible to have a NULL attribute in a primary key.

Let's go back to the tables that have been central to the examples so far (see Figure 5-35).

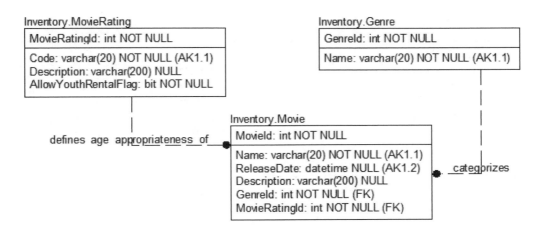

Figure 5-35. *Tables for implementing relationships*

Now create the relationships between these tables as follows:

```
ALTER TABLE Inventory.Movie
      ADD CONSTRAINT
          Inventory_MovieRating$defines_age_appropriateness_of$Inventory_Movie
            FOREIGN KEY (MovieRatingId)
                            REFERENCES Inventory.MovieRating  (MovieRatingId)
                            ON DELETE NO ACTION
                            ON UPDATE NO ACTION
ALTER TABLE Inventory.Movie
      ADD CONSTRAINT Inventory_Genre$categorizes$Inventory_Movie
            FOREIGN KEY (GenreId)
                            REFERENCES Inventory.Genre (GenreId)
                            ON DELETE NO ACTION
                            ON UPDATE NO ACTION
```

It's as simple as this to protect the parent-child relationships that have been set up in the design. I'll present examples of relationships and cascading deletes, as well as a brief discussion of cross-database relationships, shortly. Let's try to create a Movie without a valid Genre:

```
INSERT INTO Inventory.Movie (Name, ReleaseDate,
                                Description, GenreId, MovieRatingId)
SELECT 'Stripes','19810626',
        'A loser joins the Army, though the Army is not really '+
        'ready for him',-1,-1
```

This causes the following error:

```
Msg 547, Level 16, State 0, Line 2
The INSERT statement conflicted with the FOREIGN KEY constraint
"Inventory_MovieRating$defines_age_appropriateness_of$Inventory_Movie". The
conflict occurred in database "MovieRental", table "Inventory.MovieRating",
column 'MovieRatingId'.
```

In this query, look up the correct values:

```
INSERT INTO Inventory.Movie (Name, ReleaseDate,
                            Description, GenreId, MovieRatingId)
SELECT 'Stripes','19810626',
       'A loser joins the Army, though the Army is not really '+
       'ready for him',MovieRating.MovieRatingId, Genre.GenreId
FROM   Inventory.MovieRating as MovieRating
       CROSS JOIN Inventory.Genre as Genre
WHERE  MovieRating.Code = 'R'
  AND  Genre.Name = 'Comedy'
```

There's one tricky bit about using this sort of code to get surrogate values for the new row. If either of the values turned out to not exist, then no rows would be returned, and no error would be raised. Checking @@rowcount after the statement would tell you if a row was created.

When naming foreign key constraints, I use the following convention:

```
<parentTableSchema>_<parentTable>$<verbPhrase>$<childTableSchema>_<childTable>
```

This makes any system messages that pertain to the constraints easier to trace. Any naming convention will suffice. I realize that sometimes these names seem almost comically long and a little bizarre. However, they work great in action, and will generally keep you from automatically coming up with duplicate names. Frankly, as long as you don't let SQL Server generate a name for you, whatever naming convention you decide on is perfectly fine. Just make sure that it makes sense to the other people who need to be able to figure it out.

Because the relationship is defined using NO ACTION, see what happens if you now try to delete the row from the Genre table for comedy:

```
DELETE FROM Inventory.Genre
WHERE  Name = 'Comedy'
```

The following error is raised:

```
Msg 547, Level 16, State 0, Line 2
The DELETE statement conflicted with the REFERENCE constraint
"Inventory_Genre$categorizes$Inventory_Movie". The conflict occurred in
database "MovieRental", table "Inventory.Movie", column 'GenreId'.
```

To delete this row, all rows in the child table (Inventory.Movie) that used the GenreId value that corresponds to 'Comedy' would need to be deleted. The next section covers ways around this.

Automated Relationship Options

In the previous example, the database prevented us from deleting the parent row if a child row existed with a reference to the parent. This is the desired action in most cases, but there are cases where the data in the child table is so integrated with the data of the parent table that, when the parent table is changed or deleted, SQL Server would always seek to modify or delete the child record without any further interaction with the user.

In this section, I'll talk more about the two clauses that were glossed over when the FOREIGN KEY constraint was first introduced—ON DELETE and ON UPDATE:

```
ALTER TABLE <tablename>
   ADD [CONSTRAINT <constraintName>]
   FOREIGN KEY REFERENCES <referenceTable> (<referenceColumns>)
   [ON DELETE <NO ACTION | CASCADE | SET NULL | SET DEFAULT> ]
   [ON UPDATE <NO ACTION | CASCADE | SET NULL | SET DEFAULT> ]
```

The default (as underlined) is the action demonstrated earlier. If the action violates referential integrity by deleting a child row, or changing a key value to something other than a value that matches a child row, just fail the operation. There are three other options, the latter two being new to SQL Server 2005:

- CASCADE: ON DELETE, delete child rows; ON UPDATE, change child rows.

- SET NULL: ON DELETE or UPDATE of key values, set child row values to NULL.

- SET DEFAULT: ON DELETE or UPDATE, set child values to a default value.

In each of the following sections, I'll introduce the cascading types in pairs, on the UPDATE and DELETE operations together. In reality, you can apply them in any combination (UPDATE CASCADE, DELETE SET NULL, and so on).

CASCADE

When a child table exists only as part of the parent table, it's often desired to delete all the rows in the child as part of the delete of the parent. The litmus test I use is to consider whether the child is either of the following:

- *A part of the parent, such as an Invoice and an Invoice Line Item*: In this case, it usually makes sense to clean up the items on the invoice automatically because they only exist to be a part of the invoice. Many-to-many resolution tables are often places where cascading makes sense.

- *Just related, like a Customer and an Invoice*: Deleting a customer shouldn't automatically, with no warning, delete all the invoices in the system. This kind of thing likely needs a user interface to warn the user and delete the child rows. For this, leave the constraint set to ON DELETE NO ACTION.

For example, consider the Personality and Movie tables' relationships to the MoviePersonality table (see Figure 5-36).

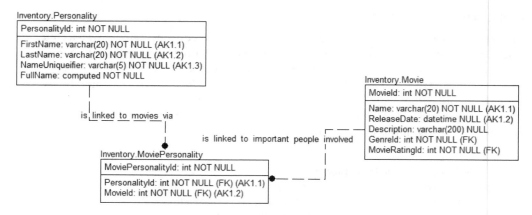

Figure 5-36. *Sample tables for implementing cascading relationships*

We haven't created the MoviePersonality table yet, so let's create it:

```
CREATE TABLE Inventory.MoviePersonality (
      MoviePersonalityId   int NOT NULL IDENTITY (1,1)
      CONSTRAINT PKMoviePersonality PRIMARY KEY,
      MovieId              int NOT NULL,
      PersonalityId        int NOT NULL,
      CONSTRAINT AKMoviePersonality_MoviePersonality
         UNIQUE (PersonalityId,MovieId)
)
```

Next, create the relationships to the Movie and Personality tables, in both cases setting the ON DELETE CASCADE option. If a Movie is deleted, go ahead and delete the connection between the movie and the People in it, and vice versa:

```
ALTER TABLE Inventory.MoviePersonality
      ADD CONSTRAINT
         Inventory_Personality$is_linked_to_movies_via$Inventory_MoviePersonality
            FOREIGN KEY (MovieId)
                     REFERENCES Inventory.Movie  (MovieId)
                     ON DELETE CASCADE
                     ON UPDATE NO ACTION

ALTER TABLE Inventory.MoviePersonality
      ADD CONSTRAINT
         Inventory_Movie$is_linked_to_important_people_via$Inventory_MoviePersonality
            FOREIGN KEY (PersonalityId)
                     REFERENCES Inventory.Personality  (PersonalityId)
                     ON DELETE CASCADE
                     ON UPDATE NO ACTION
```

UPDATE is left at NO ACTION because there's no need to update a surrogate primary key. Now, because we haven't yet added personalities, we'll add a couple:

```
INSERT INTO Inventory.Personality (FirstName, LastName, NameUniqueifier)
VALUES ('Cary','Grant','')
INSERT INTO Inventory.Personality (FirstName, LastName, NameUniqueifier)
VALUES ('Humphrey','Bogart','')
```

Then, load some data into the MoviePersonality table:

```
INSERT INTO Inventory.MoviePersonality (MovieId, PersonalityId)
SELECT  Movie.MovieId, Personality.PersonalityId
FROM    Inventory.Movie as Movie
           CROSS JOIN Inventory.Personality as Personality
WHERE   Movie.Name = 'The Maltese Falcon'
  AND   Personality.FirstName = 'Humphrey'
  AND   Personality.LastName = 'Bogart'
  AND   Personality.NameUniqueifier = ''
UNION ALL
SELECT  Movie.MovieId, Personality.PersonalityId
FROM    Inventory.Movie as Movie
           CROSS JOIN Inventory.Personality as Personality
WHERE   Movie.Name = 'Arsenic and Old Lace'
  AND   Personality.FirstName = 'Cary'
  AND   Personality.LastName = 'Grant'
  AND   Personality.NameUniqueifier = ''
```

Then use the following code to see the data in the tables:

```
SELECT Movie.Name as Movie,
       Personality.FirstName + ' '+ Personality.LastName as Personality
FROM   Inventory.MoviePersonality as MoviePersonality
          LEFT OUTER JOIN Inventory.Personality as Personality
              On MoviePersonality.PersonalityId = Personality.PersonalityId
          LEFT OUTER JOIN Inventory.Movie as Movie
              ON Movie.MovieId = MoviePersonality.MovieId
```

This code returns the following results:

```
Movie                    Personality
-------------------      ----------------------------------------
The Maltese Falcon       Humphrey Bogart
Arsenic and Old Lace     Cary Grant
```

See what happens if you delete a row from the Movie table:

```
DELETE FROM Inventory.Movie
WHERE  Name = 'Arsenic and Old Lace'
```

Re-executing the SELECT statement from earlier, this only returns one row:

Movie	Personality
The Maltese Falcon	Humphrey Bogart

If you're using editable keys, you can use the UPDATE CASCADE option to cascade changes from the primary key values to the child table. As an example, I'll build an alternate couple of tables, much like the tables already created (again using the Alt schema for tables that aren't a part of our actual solution):

```
CREATE TABLE Alt.Movie
(
    MovieCode    varchar(20)
        CONSTRAINT PKMovie PRIMARY KEY,
    MovieName    varchar(200)
)
CREATE TABLE Alt.MovieRentalPackage
(
    MovieRentalPackageCode varchar(25)
        CONSTRAINT PKMovieRentalPackage PRIMARY KEY,
    MovieCode    varchar(20)
        CONSTRAINT Alt_Movie$is_rented_as$Alt_MovieRentalPackage
                FOREIGN KEY References Alt.Movie(MovieCode)
                ON DELETE CASCADE
                ON UPDATE CASCADE
)
```

Now, insert one of the movies with a user-defined key:

```
INSERT INTO Alt.Movie (MovieCode, MovieName)
VALUES ('ArseOldLace','Arsenic and Old Lace')
INSERT INTO Alt.MovieRentalPackage (MovieRentalPackageCode, MovieCode)
VALUES ('ArsenicOldLaceDVD','ArseOldLace')
```

Then, once you realize that the key you've chosen sounds kind of weird, you update the primary key of the Movie row:

```
UPDATE Alt.Movie
SET    MovieCode = 'ArsenicOldLace'
WHERE  MovieCode = 'ArseOldLace'
```

Then, check the rows in the tables:

```
SELECT *
FROM   Alt.Movie
SELECT *
FROM   Alt.MovieRentalPackage
```

The following rows are in the table:

MovieCode	MovieName
ArsenicOldLace	Arsenic and Old Lace

MovieRentalPackageCode	MovieCode
ArsenicOldLaceDVD	ArsenicOldLace

SET NULL

The SET NULL functionality on a constraint is new to SQL Server 2005, but it isn't new to the relational database. Prior to 2005, SET NULL relationship types were implemented using triggers. The idea is that instead of deleting child rows, you simply set the foreign key value to NULL, in essence invalidating the value. For example, say in our Person table we have the person's default media format (this is a video-store customer, perhaps).

To use the SET NULL relationship type, the relationship must be defined as optional and the migrated foreign key columns set to allow NULLs. To demonstrate this, add a relationship between the Movie table and the Customer table.

Now, let's add the new column to support the user's favorite movie choice (see Figure 5-37).

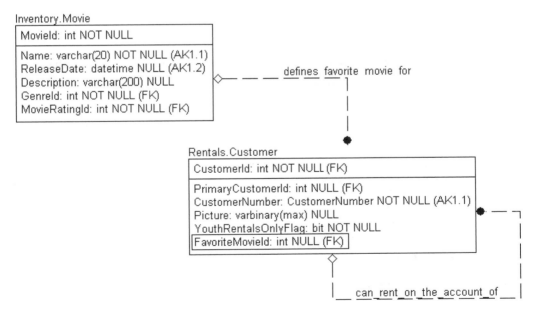

Figure 5-37. *Added FavoriteMovie relationship to Rentals.Customer*

```
ALTER TABLE Rentals.Customer
    ADD FavoriteMovieId INT NULL --allow nulls or SET NULL will be invalid

--Next define the foreign key constraint with SET NULL:
ALTER TABLE Rentals.Customer
    ADD FOREIGN KEY (FavoriteMovieId)
                    REFERENCES Inventory.Movie  (MovieId)
                    ON DELETE SET NULL
                    ON UPDATE NO ACTION
```

Now, create a new customer:

```
INSERT INTO People.Person(FirstName, MiddleName, LastName, SocialSecurityNumber)
VALUES ('Jerry','J','Smork','222-22-2222')

INSERT INTO Rentals.Customer(CustomerId, CustomerNumber,
                            PrimaryCustomerId, Picture, YouthRentalsOnlyFlag,
                            FavoriteMovieId)
SELECT Person.PersonId, '2222222222',NULL, NULL, 0, NULL
FROM   People.Person
WHERE  SocialSecurityNumber = '222-22-2222'
```

This person does the search for his favorite movie, *Stripes*:

```
SELECT MovieId, ReleaseDate
FROM   Inventory.Movie
WHERE   Name  = 'Stripes'
```

The list is returned with the release date, which is part of the natural key of the table:

MovieId	ReleaseDate
7	1981-06-26 00:00:00.000

Now set the FavoriteMovieId for this customer to 7 (your value for this might be different for the key, because this is an identity key):

```
UPDATE  Rentals.Customer
SET     FavoriteMovieId = 7
WHERE   CustomerNumber = '2222222222'
```

Then view the data:

```
Select  Customer.CustomerNumber, Movie.Name AS FavoriteMovie
FROM    Rentals.Customer AS Customer
          LEFT OUTER JOIN Inventory.Movie AS Movie
            ON Movie.MovieId = Customer.FavoriteMovieId
WHERE   Customer.CustomerNumber = '2222222222'
```

This returns the following result:

```
CustomerNumber        FavoriteMovie
--------------------  --------------------
2222222222            Stripes
```

Say the movie gets deleted:

```
DELETE  Inventory.Movie
WHERE   Name = 'Stripes'
  AND   ReleaseDate = '19810626'
```

You can run the SELECT again to show that the favorite movie is now NULL:

```
CustomerNumber        FavoriteMovie
--------------------  --------------------
2222222222            NULL
```

■ **Note** I won't demonstrate the UPDATE SET NULL capability, as it's of limited use. Any change to the value of the key in the parent causes the value in the child table to change to NULL. This would be used whenever the change to the key means that the row means something different than it did before, not just a tweak to the value of the key. I'd suggest you handle this in a nonautomatic way using T-SQL code.

SET DEFAULT

The example for SET DEFAULT is quite similar to SET NULL. However, in this case you don't want the value to become unknown; you also need to set it to a common value to use as a default value. Because it isn't necessary to define the column as NOT NULL, this can be better than SET NULL. A common usage could be to have a domain value of 'None', 'Not Applicable', and so on to tell the user that the value is known, and it's just nothing.

For the example, I'm going to use the default example previously created using the Customer table. I created a default such that a new customer who didn't choose a default movie format was initially set to 'Dvd'. In this example, consider that a new format is added (see Figure 5-38). (I won't be adding a new subtype table for this type, because I'll be deleting the format quickly just for this example.)

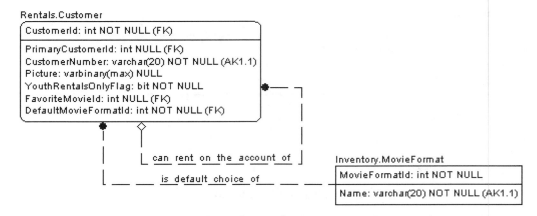

Figure 5-38. *Adding a relationship to allow Customers their default MovieFormat*

First create the new format:

```
INSERT INTO Inventory.MovieFormat(MovieFormatId, Name)
VALUES (3, 'Playstation Portable')
```

Next, add the new column and constraint:

```
ALTER TABLE Rentals.Customer
   ADD DefaultMovieFormatId INT NOT NULL
         CONSTRAINT DfltCustomer_DefaultMovieFormatId
               DEFAULT (2) --DVD (Can hard code because surrogate key
                            --hand created)
```

Add the referential integrity (RI) constraint:

```
ALTER TABLE Rentals.Customer
 ADD FOREIGN KEY (DefaultMovieFormatId)
         REFERENCES Inventory.MovieFormat  (MovieFormatId)
             ON DELETE SET DEFAULT
             ON UPDATE NO ACTION
```

Using the customer that was previously created, set the DefaultMovieFormat to 3 (PlaystationPortable):

```
UPDATE Rentals.Customer
SET    DefaultMovieFormatId = 3
WHERE  CustomerNumber = '2222222222'
```

You can check this value with the following query:

```
SELECT  MovieFormat.Name
FROM    Inventory.MovieFormat as MovieFormat
          JOIN Rentals.Customer
              ON MovieFormat.MovieFormatId = Customer.DefaultMovieFormatId
WHERE   Customer.CustomerNumber = '2222222222'
```

This returns the following result:

```
Name
--------------------
Playstation Portable
```

Once this "fad" disappears and the rental store stops renting these movies, the store deletes `PlaystationPortable` as a possible `MovieFormat`:

```
DELETE FROM Inventory.MovieFormat
WHERE  Name = 'Playstation Portable'
```

Re-executing the `SELECT`, you can see the value has reverted to the default value:

```
Name
--------------------
DVD
```

Note Just like SET NULL, I won't demonstrate the UPDATE SET DEFAULT capability, as it's of limited use, for the same reasons as stated in the previous section.

Cross-Database Relationships

The primary limitation on constraint-based foreign keys is that the tables participating in the relationship cannot span different databases. When this situation occurs, these relationship types need to be implemented via triggers.

It's generally a bad idea to design databases with cross-database relationships. A database should be considered a unit of related tables that are always kept in sync. When designing solutions that extend over different databases or even servers, carefully consider how spreading around references to data that isn't within the scope of database will affect your solution. You need to understand that SQL Server cannot guarantee the existence of the value, because SQL Server uses databases as a restore point, and another user could restore a database with improper values, even an empty database, and the cross-database RI would be invalidated. Of course, as is almost always the case with anything that isn't "best-practice material," there are times when cross-database relationships are unavoidable, and I'll demonstrate building triggers to support this need in the next chapter.

Large-Value Datatype Columns

In SQL Server 2005, dealing with large datatypes has changed quite a bit. By using the max specifier on varchar, nvarchar, and varbinary types, you can now store way more data than was possible in previous versions while still being able to deal with the data using "normal" methods.

As with all datatype questions, only use the varchar(max) types when they're required, and you should always use the smallest types possible. The larger the datatype, the more possible data, and the more trouble the row can be to optimize. In cases where you know you need large data, or in the case where you sometimes need greater than 8,000 bytes in a column, the max specifier is a fantastic thing.

Previously, using image and text datatypes, dealing with data that was greater than 8,000 characters (or 4,000 for Unicode types) was done in a different way than data that was less than or equal to 8,000 characters long. Now, you can deal with all character and binary data in the same way, regardless of size. There are two concerns:

- There's no datatype conversion from the normal character types to the large-value types.

- Because of the possible large sizes of data, a special clause is added to the UPDATE statement.

The first issue is pretty simple, but it can be a bit confusing at times. For example, concatenate '12345' + '67890'. You've taken two varchar(5) values, and the result is varchar(10). But if you concatenate two varchar(8000) values, you don't get a varchar(16000) value, nor do you get a varchar(max) value. The values get truncated to a varchar(8000) value. This isn't always intuitively obvious. For example, consider the following code:

```
SELECT   len(
            cast(replicate('a',8000) as varchar(8000))
            + cast(replicate('a',8000) as varchar(8000))
         )
```

It returns 8,000. If you change one of the varchar(8000) values to varchar(max) then the result will be 16,000:

```
SELECT   len(
            cast(replicate('a',8000) as varchar(max))
            + cast(replicate('a',8000) as varchar(8000))
         )
```

Second, because the size of these values can be so huge, it wouldn't be favorable to always pass around these values just like you do with smaller values. Because the maximum size is 2GB, imagine having to update this value. It would be pretty nasty, because the client would need to get the whole value, make its changes, and then send the value. Most client machines don't have 2GB of physical RAM, so paging would occur and the whole thing would crawl and probably crash. Not good. So you can do what are referred to as *chunked* updates. This is done using the .WRITE clause in the UPDATE statement:

```
UPDATE TableName
SET    varcharMaxCol.WRITE('the value', <offset>, <expression>)
WHERE  . . .
```

I won't go over this in any more detail. Just understand that you might have to treat the data in these columns differently if you're going to have large quantities of data. In our model, I've used a varbinary(max) column in the Customer table to store the image of the customer for the records. Nothing more needs to be mentioned about this column.

Collation (Sort Order)

The collation sequence for SQL Server 2005 shows how data is sorted when needed, and how data is compared. SQL Server and Windows provide a tremendous number of collation types from which to choose.

It's a somewhat uncommon need for the average database to change the collation from the default, which usually is a case-insensitive collation. I've only used an alternative collation a few times for columns where case sensitivity was desired (one time was so that a client could force more four-character codes than a case-insensitive collation would allow!).

To see the current collation type for the server and database, you can execute the following commands:

```
SELECT serverproperty('collation')
SELECT databasepropertyex('MovieRental','collation')
```

On most systems installed in English-speaking countries, the default collation type is SQL_Latin1_General_CP1_CI_AS, where Latin1_General represents the normal Latin alphabet, CP1 refers to code page 1252 (the SQL Server default Latin 1 ANSI character set), and the last parts represent case insensitive and accent sensitive, respectively. You can find full coverage of all collation types in the SQL Server 2005 documentation.

To list all the sort orders installed in a given SQL Server instance, you can execute the following statement:

```
SELECT *
FROM ::fn_helpcollations()
```

On the computer on which I do testing, this query returned more than 1,000 rows, but usually you don't need to change from the default that the database administrator initially chooses. However, there are a few important reasons to specify a different collation:

- *Case sensitivity*: Depending on the application, you might need to have all your code and data treated as case sensitive. This would certainly be on a case-by-case basis. Note that this makes your code and object names case sensitive, too.

  Remember that case sensitivity causes searching difficulties. For example, when searching for all names starting with the letter "A," we have to search for all things starting with "A" or "a." We could use uppercase functions for columns or variables, but this defeats indexing, and is generally not a good idea.

- *Foreign character sorting*: The other reason is foreign characters. Using Unicode, you can use any character from any language in the world. However, few languages use the same A–Z character set that English-speaking countries use A possible use of a different collation type is in implementing columns for different languages. There's an example of this later in this section.

It's possible to set the collation at a server and database level as mentioned earlier, but you can also do so for a column, and even in the ORDER clause of a SELECT statement.

To set the collation sequence for a char, varchar, text, nchar, nvarchar, or ntext column when creating a table, you specify it using the COLLATE clause of the column definition, like so:

```
CREATE TABLE alt.OtherCollate
(
    OtherCollateId integer IDENTITY,
    Name nvarchar(30) NOT NULL,
    FrenchName nvarchar(30) COLLATE French_CI_AS_WS NULL,
    SpanishName nvarchar(30) COLLATE Modern_Spanish_CI_AS_WS NULL
)
```

Now, when you sort output by FrenchName, it's case insensitive, but arranges the rows according to the order of the French character set. The same applies with Spanish, regarding the SpanishName column.

In the next example, I'll briefly look at another cool use of the COLLATE keyword that can come in handy if you need to do case-sensitive searches on a column created as case insensitive. You can use this to affect the comparisons made in an expression. You do this by changing one or both the values on either side of the expression to a binary collation. Let's create a table, called collateTest:

```
CREATE TABLE alt.collateTest
(
    name    VARCHAR(20) COLLATE SQL_Latin1_General_CP1_CI_AS NOT NULL
)

INSERT INTO alt.collateTest(name)
VALUES ('BOB')
INSERT INTO alt.collateTest(name)
VALUES ('bob')
```

Note that for demonstration purposes, the COLLATE statement that I've included is the default for my server. This is likely to be your collation also if you have taken the default (I'll assume this collation for the rest of the book). Then execute the following against the database:

```
SELECT name
FROM alt.collateTest
WHERE name = 'BOB'
```

This returns both rows:

```
name
-------
bob
BOB
```

However, try changing the collation on the BOB literal, and executing it:

```
SELECT name
FROM    alt.collateTest
WHERE   name = 'BOB' COLLATE Latin1_General_BIN
```

You only get back the single row that matches BOB character for character:

```
name
-------
BOB
```

You should have noticed that you only cast the scalar value 'BOB' to a binary collation. Determining collation precedence can be a tricky matter, and it's one that won't be covered here (for more information, check SQL Server 2005 Books Online). In general, it's best to add the COLLATE function to both sides of the expression when performing such an operation to avoid any ambiguity.

In our case, instead of the collate on just the scalar value, it would be written this way:

```
SELECT name
FROM    alt.collateTest
WHERE name COLLATE Latin1_General_BIN = 'BOB' COLLATE Latin1_General_BIN
```

I won't delve any deeper into the subject of collation. In the SQL Server documentation, there's a large amount of information about collations, including the rules for collation precedence.

Computed Columns

Computed columns are a cool feature that was added in SQL Server 7.0 that allow us to make "virtual" columns from stored expressions to be output as part of SELECT statements without requiring a view to be created. They are perfect to implement "in-row denormalizations" without having to use "tricky" code.

The syntax is as follows:

```
<columnName> AS <computed definition> [PERSISTED]
```

A significant improvement in SQL Server 2005 is the ability to persist the data in the column automatically, so you don't have to do the calculation every time you fetch the row. As an example in our system, let's add a FullName column to the Personality table so you can avoid having to do the calculation every time:

```
ALTER TABLE Inventory.Personality
    ADD FullName as
            FirstName + ' ' + LastName + rtrim(' ' + NameUniqueifier)
```

Let's add a couple personalities with the same names (based on http://www.imdb.com, there are about 40 different John Smiths registered):

```
INSERT INTO Inventory.Personality (FirstName, LastName, NameUniqueifier)
VALUES ('John','Smith','I')
INSERT INTO Inventory.Personality (FirstName, LastName, NameUniqueifier)
VALUES ('John','Smith','II')
```

Then you can see the data by doing a SELECT:

```
SELECT *
FROM Inventory.Personality
```

This returns the following results:

PersonalityId	FirstName	LastName	NameUniqueifier	FullName
1	Cary	Grant		Cary Grant
2	Humphrey	Bogart		Humphrey Bogart
3	John	Smith	I	John Smith (I)
4	John	Smith	II	John Smith (II)

An example where computed columns came in handy in a database system I created was for building a grouping on the day, month, and year. In the following code, I have an example that's close to this. It groups on the second column to make the example easier to test.

```
CREATE TABLE alt.calcColumns
(
    dateColumn    datetime,
    dateSecond    AS datepart(second,dateColumn) PERSISTED -- calculated column
)
SET NOCOUNT ON
DECLARE @i int
SET @i = 1
WHILE (@i < 200)
BEGIN
    INSERT INTO alt.calcColumns (dateColumn) VALUES (getdate())
    WAITFOR DELAY '00:00:00.01' --or the query runs too fast
    SET @i = @i + 1
END

SELECT dateSecond, max(dateColumn) as dateColumn, count(*) AS countStar
FROM alt.calcColumns
GROUP BY dateSecond
ORDER BY dateSecond
```

This returns the following results (at least it did when I was writing this book; your mileage will vary a bit):

dateSecond	dateColumn	countStar
26	2005-03-26 20:45:26.990	24
27	2005-03-26 20:45:27.993	88
28	2005-03-26 20:45:28.873	87

An almost dangerous feature with calculated columns is that they're ignored when you're inserting data if you omit the insert-field list. SQL Server ignores any calculated columns and matches the fields up as if they don't exist. For example, create the following table:

```
CREATE TABLE alt.testCalc
(
    value varchar(10),
    valueCalc AS UPPER(value),
    value2 varchar(10)
)
```

Then create some new values without the list of columns to affect:

```
INSERT INTO designBook.testCalc
VALUES ('test','test2')
```

No error occurs. Execute the code:

```
SELECT *
FROM  alt.testCalc
```

You get back the following results:

value	valueCalc	value2
test	TEST	test2

■Caution Regardless of calculated columns, it's poor practice to code INSERT statements with no insert list. The insert should have been INSERT INTO designBook.testCalc (value, value2) VALUES ('test','test2').

Implementing Complex Datatypes

SQL Server's ability to implement complex datatypes has improved greatly. User-defined types have changed quite a bit from previous versions of SQL Server. Several features are going to be removed from a future version, so you should stop using them now. These features are as follows:

- sp_addtype: Added a user-defined type
- CREATE RULE: Created a rule that could be bound to columns
- sp_bindrule: Bound a rule to a column
- CREATE DEFAULT: Created a default that could be bound to columns
- sp_binddefault: Bound a default to a column

Also deprecated are any of the functions that are used to manage rules and default objects. However, there's far better support for UDTs now. UDTs are broken down into the following categories:

- *Datatype aliases*: Allow you to predefine a datatype based on the intrinsic types.

- *CLR-based datatypes*: Allow you to base a datatype on a CLR assembly. Allow for complex datatypes.

You create both types of UDTs using CREATE TYPE.

Datatype Aliases

You can use the datatype alias to specify a commonly used datatype configuration that's used in multiple places. The syntax is as follows:

```
CREATE TYPE <typeName>
        FROM <intrinsic type> --any type that can be used as a column of a table,
                              --with precision and scale or length, as required by
                              --the base type
        [NULL | NOT NULL]
```

When declaring a table, if nullability isn't specified, then NULL or NOT NULL will be based on this setting, not on the setting of ANSI_NULL_DFLT_ON (as discussed in an earlier section, "Nullability").

For example, let's create a type for an American Social Security number. We'll do this example using an alternate Person table in the alt schema, then we'll build the same thing in the CLR section and implement it in the People.Person table from the main example as follows:

```
CREATE TYPE SSN
        FROM char(11)
             NOT NULL
```

Then build the example table with it:

```
CREATE TABLE alt.Person
(
     PersonId      int NOT NULL,
     FirstName      varchar(30) NOT NULL,
     LastName       varchar(30) NOT NULL,
     SSN            SSN                       --no null specification to make a point
                                              --generally it is a better idea to
                                              --include a null spec.
)
```

Then create a new row:

```
INSERT Alt.Person
VALUES (1,'krusty','clown','234-43-3432')

SELECT PersonId, FirstName, LastName, SSN
FROM    Alt.Person
```

This returns the following result:

personId	firstName	lastName	SSN
1	krusty	clown	234-43-3432

Then, let's try to enter a row with a NULL SSN:

```
INSERT  Alt.Person
VALUES  (2,'moe','sizlack',NULL)
```

You get the following error:

```
Msg 515, Level 16, State 2, Line 1
Cannot insert the value NULL into column 'SSN', table 'tempdb. designBook.person';
column does not allow nulls. INSERT fails.
The statement has been terminated.
```

The biggest problem is that you cannot do anything with these aliases other than simply naming a type. For example, take the SSN type. It's char(11), so you cannot put a 12-character value in, sure. But what if the user had entered **234433432** instead of including the dashes? The datatype would have allowed it, but it isn't what's desired. The data will still have to be checked in other methods (such as CHECK constraints, which the next chapter covers).

Hence, datatype aliases aren't all that useful in practice, but they're available in cases where they make sense, such as if a tool expects a certain datatype name, other than one of the SQL Server ones. My advice is to shy away from them unless they make sense in your particular situation.

CLR-Based Datatypes

SQL Server 2005 introduces a new way to extend the type system by allowing DBAs and developers the ability to use .NET and the CLR to create user-defined datatypes. Chapter 10 discusses more details on all the database objects that you can create with the CLR integration, and how it works and performs.

Part of me simply wants to say "avoid them," as several quirks make these UDTs complex to use. For example, the CLR class they're based on has to be registered on any client that uses them. On the other hand, CLR-based UDTs allow for an interesting tool and can provide more flexibility than simply aliasing intrinsic datatypes. You can add properties and methods to the datatypes to extend their functionality, as well as include complex validation and manipulation logic for modifications and extensive formatting when returning values.

There are several rules to follow when creating your own UDTs with .NET. Your .NET class or structure must be serializable, support NULL values, allow for conversion to and from a string type, and follow the specific .NET "contract" for creating a UDT. Let's look at an example of creating a datatype for an American Social Security number again, this time as a CLR datatype coded in VB.NET. I want to give you the complete code required for a simple example. I won't go into the specifics of the code too much. For a deeper understanding of the code and all the details for coding CLR-based objects, consider the book *Pro SQL Server 2005 Assemblies* by Robin Dewson and Julian Skinner (Apress, 2005), or the books online.

To use CLR objects such as our UDT inside SQL Server, you must first enable the CLR for the server in the SQL Server 2005 Configuration Manager. By default, running code in .NET assemblies inside SQL Server is disabled. Note that the option to enable the CLR is a server-wide option and cannot be enabled per database. To enable the loading of .NET assemblies for the server, run the following commands:

```
EXEC sp_configure 'clr enabled', 1
go
RECONFIGURE
```

To finish the sample database that has been built throughout the chapter, I'm going to build a CLR datatype to implement an SSN type. You can use the following code to create a SocialSecurity datatype in VB.NET. (You can use any version of Visual Studio, even the command line if you aren't faint of heart, though the Professional Team System version comes with project templates to make building datatypes easier. There are resources on the Web to help you build CLR objects for SQL Server if you're using other versions.)

```vb
Imports System
Imports System.Data
Imports System.Data.SqlClient
Imports System.Data.SqlTypes
Imports System.Text.RegularExpressions


<Serializable()> _
<SqlUserDefinedType(Format.Native,IsByteOrdered:=True, IsFixedLength:=True)> _
' must be byte ordered to allow indexing. FixedLength because
' all SSNs are the same size
Public Structure udtSsn
    Implements INullable

    ' Private member
    Private m_Null As Boolean
    Private m_ssn As Integer

    Public Overrides Function ToString() As String
        ' format SSN for output
        Return Me.SSN.ToString("000-00-0000")
    End Function

    Private Property SSN() As Integer
        Get
            Return m_ssn
        End Get
        Set(ByVal value As Integer)
            m_ssn = value
        End Set
    End Property
```

```vb
    Public ReadOnly Property IsNull() As Boolean Implements INullable.IsNull
        Get
            Return m_Null
        End Get
    End Property

    Public Shared ReadOnly Property Null() As udtSsn
        Get
            Dim h As udtSsn = New udtSsn
            h.m_Null = True
            Return h
        End Get
    End Property

    Public Shared Function Parse(ByVal s As SqlString) As udtSsn
        If s.IsNull Then
            Return Null
        End If
        Dim u As udtSsn = New udtSsn
        If Regex.IsMatch(s.ToString(), _
        "^(?!000)([0-6]\d{2}|7([0-6]\d|7[012]))([ -]?)(?!00)\d\d\3(?!0000)\d{4}$", _
            RegexOptions.None) Then
            u.SSN = ConvertSSNToInt(s.ToString())
            Return u
        Else
            Throw New ArgumentException("SSN is not valid.")
        End If
    End Function

    Private Shared Function ConvertSSNToInt(ByVal ssn As String) As Integer
        Dim ssnNumbers As Integer
        Try
            ssnNumbers = Convert.ToInt32(ssn)
        Catch ex As Exception
            Dim ssnString As String = ""
            For i As Integer = 0 To ssn.Length - 1
                If "0123456789".IndexOf(ssn.Chars(i)) >= 0 Then
                    ssnString += ssn.Chars(i)
                End If
            Next
            ssnNumbers = Convert.ToInt32(ssnString)
        End Try
        Return ssnNumbers
    End Function
End Structure
```

After the UDT is coded, you must compile and deploy it to SQL Server. You can do this automatically using Visual Studio 2005 or manually using the .NET 2.0 SDK and T-SQL. To deploy our new UDT using Visual Studio 2005, I'll create a new project and select the SQL Server Project template from the database project type. Visual Studio then asks you to add a database reference. In the Solution Explorer, right-click your new project and select Add ➤ User-Defined Type. Name the file and click Add. Enter the code for the UDT and then select Build ➤ Deploy *Projectname*. This compiles the project, loads the assembly to the database specified when you added the database reference, and creates the UDT with the name you used for the structure in your code.

To create the UDT manually, you must first compile the UDT code using the appropriate compiler for your language: csc.exe for C# and vbc.exe for VB. Please see the .NET 2.0 SDK help for the command syntax. After compiling the code into a .NET DLL assembly, you deploy the code to SQL Server using the CREATE ASSEMBLY statement:

```
CREATE ASSEMBLY MyUDT from 'D:\Projects\udtSSN.dll' WITH PERMISSION_SET = SAFE
```

Once the assembly that contains your UDT is deployed to SQL Server, you must register the class in the assembly as a UDT type using the CREATE TYPE statement. Note that this is the same statement you use to create an alias datatype with a slightly different syntax.

In the following statement, SSN is the name of the type, MyUDT is the name of the assembly that was loaded with the CREATE ASSEMBLY statement, and SqlServerProject1.udtSsn is the namespace followed by the UDT structure name, as defined in the .NET code and project settings:

```
CREATE TYPE SSN
EXTERNAL NAME [MyUDT].[SqlServerProject1.udtSsn]
```

Now you can assign this new UDT just like you would any intrinsic SQL Server datatype such as int or datetime. It's even in the datatype dropdown when designing tables using SQL Server Management Studio.

There are some interesting things to note about the example. First, the class is tagged with the Serializable() attribute and a special SQL Server attribute for UDTs called SqlUserDefinedType(). These two attributes are required for CLR-based UDTs. The SqlUserDefinedType() attribute also requires a Format property. This property can either be Format.Native or Format.UserDefined.

Format.Native uses standard SQL Server binary serialization to store the data for the UDT column. IsByteOrdered defines that the values this datatype represents can be ordered, and it's sorted on the binary representation when the value is serialized. The good part is that you don't have to write any of the serialization yourself. The disadvantage is that it can only be used if all the public properties of the class are fixed-length and value-type datatypes. This includes a majority of .NET datatypes, such as numbers and dates. If your UDT uses reference types such as .NET strings, or you need more flexibility when serializing your data, you need to use the Format.UserDefined property and implement IBinarySerialize. Implementing IBinarySerialize requires writing your own Read and Write functions to serialize the UDT as binary data, a task that's beyond what we need to put in a section such as this.

An important optional parameter on the SqlUserDefined() attribute is the IsByteOrdered parameter. When this value is TRUE, this informs SQL Server that the stored data for columns that use this datatype is in binary order. The column can therefore be used in comparison operations, in ORDER BY and GROUP BY clauses, can be indexed, and can be used in primary and foreign key relationships. This means that the physical serialization of the value is sortable using the value. SQL Server can sort and compare the values *without* instantiating the CLR object.

There are two required conversion functions for UDTs: a Parse() function and a ToString() function. The Parse() function allows data to be inserted into a UDT column as a string, similar to the way you insert data into a column of type DateTime.

Let's add the new datatype to our Person table, which has already been established in this chapter:

```
/*
CREATE TABLE People.Person (
        PersonId             int NOT NULL IDENTITY(1,1)
          CONSTRAINT PKPerson PRIMARY KEY,
        FirstName            varchar(20) NOT NULL,
        MiddleName           varchar(20) NULL,
        LastName             varchar(20) NOT NULL,
        SocialSecurityNumber char(11) --will be redefined using CLR later
          CONSTRAINT AKPerson_SSN UNIQUE
)
*/
```

You'll change the datatype to the new type just created. Start out by adding it as a NULL type:

```
ALTER TABLE People.Person
    ADD SocialSecurityNumberCLR SSN NULL
```

Then update the new column to the existing values:

```
UPDATE People.Person
    SET SocialSecurityNumberCLR = SocialSecurityNumber
```

Then drop the column (and constraint) and rename the column to the original name:

```
ALTER TABLE People.Person
    DROP CONSTRAINT AKPerson_SSN
ALTER TABLE People.Person
    DROP COLUMN SocialSecurityNumber
EXEC sp_rename 'People.Person.SocialSecurityNumberCLR',
    'SocialSecurityNumber', 'COLUMN';
```

Put back the constraints:

```
ALTER TABLE People.Person
    ALTER COLUMN SocialSecurityNumber SSN NOT NULL
ALTER TABLE People.Person
    ADD CONSTRAINT AKPerson_SSN UNIQUE (SocialSecurityNumber)
```

Next, let's look at the data. If the type isn't registered on the client machine, simply using a type such as a normal SQL Server type will return the binary version of the data. To get the textual version, you can use the ToString() method:

```
SELECT SocialSecurityNumber, socialSecurityNumber.ToString() as CastedVersion
FROM  People.Person
```

This returns the following results:

```
SocialSecurityNumber  CastedVersion
--------------------  -----------
0x00869F6BC7          111-11-1111
0x008D3ED78E          222-22-2222
```

If you try to insert invalid data, the CLR object will throw an error that was coded in the Parse method, stating that the SSN isn't valid:

```
Msg 6522, Level 16, State 2, Line 2
A .NET Framework error occurred during execution of user defined routine or
aggregate 'SSN':
System.ArgumentException: SSN is not valid.
System.ArgumentException:
   at APress.udtSsn.Parse(SqlString s)
.
The statement has been terminated.
```

Note that there was the following validation logic in the Parse() function to verify that what's being entered is a valid SSN:

```
If Regex.IsMatch(s.ToString(), _
        "^(?!000)([0-6]\d{2}|7([0-6]\d|7[012]))([ -]?)(?!00)\d\d\3(?!0000)\d{4}$"
      , _
```

Here I chose to use the RegEx .NET class with a regular expression pattern for SSNs. It accepts the SSN as nine numbers, in the format 999-99-9999, or in the format 999 99 9999. It also checks against some published rules of SSNs, such as that the first three digits cannot be 000. (This pattern was found at http://www.regexlib.com/REDetails.aspx?regexp_id=535.) This is something that would certainly be more complex to do using only T-SQL code. It's a benefit of CLR UDTs over alias datatypes, and allows us to keep complex field-level validation close to the SQL Server engine.

Internally, I'll store the SSN as an Int32, but then format the output NNN-NN-NNNN by overriding the ToString() function:

```
Public Overrides Function ToString() As String
    ' format SSN for output
    Return Me.SSN.ToString("000-00-0000")
End Function
```

Note that the UDT assembly that's created must be registered in SQL Server, and must also be available in the client application to be functional. When accessing a column defined with the SSN datatype from a client application, you must have the UDT assembly registered on the client machine. You can then make use of any UDT properties or methods, and can serialize and deserialize the column as necessary.

■**Note** When SELECTing a UDT column using SQL Server Management Studio, Management Studio returns the byte representation of the UDT. To see the string representation of the UDT column, you must use the ToString() method of the UDT column.

Visual Studio

The preceding code for the Social Security CLR UDT can look a little bit daunting at first. When creating a CLR UDT, it's easiest to use a version of Visual Studio 2005 that includes the SQL Server project templates. A large portion of the code for the SSN UDT was created by the template inside the new SQL Server project type within Visual Studio 2005. The template provides a shell that handles most of the "rules" necessary for coding a CLR UDT, and example properties and methods that can be used as starting points for your own projects. Visual Studio also includes the ability to debug UDTs on the server, and automatically deploys the assembly and creates the UDT on the database specified when creating the UDT. I'll discuss more about creating CLR database objects using Visual Studio 2005 in Chapter 10.

Uses for CLR UDTs

CLR UDTs are best used to extend the SQL Server type system with additional scalar types or different ranges of data. Some examples include specialized datetime types for different countries, currency of various countries, a time- or date-only datatype, and unsigned integers. Here are some other potential uses of UDTs:

- *Geospatial datatypes*: Types such as points, or latitude and longitude, that have properties for each coordinate that can be set and retrieved independently. Methods could be included for things such as distance between points.

- *IP addresses*: Has properties for each of the four octets, and validates each IP address. It might also include a property for the class of IP address, such as whether it's a Class A, Class B, or Class C address. An interesting benefit of this datatype is that you could serialize it such that it would sort correctly, unlike what happens if you store an IP address as varchar or char datatypes.

- *A URL/URN/URI datatype*: It would include validation logic and perhaps some special serialization that allows for sorting by domain name.

- *A date or time datatype*: If you have to do a lot of operations using date-only or time-only values, instead of doing convoluted operations using datetime values, it could be best to implement your own type. You'd lose the intrinsic date functions, so that's a concern.

Although the possibilities are unlimited, I'd suggest that CLR UDTs only be considered for specialized circumstances that make the database design more robust and easy to work with. CLR UDTs are a nice addition to the DBA's and developer's toolkit, but they should be reserved for those times when adding a new scalar datatype solves a business problem.

Challenges with UDTs

With all the power of creating our own UDTs with .NET code, it might seem logical to want to create business objects inside of SQL Server as UDTs. After all, you can add properties and methods to your UDTs much the same way you would create an `Employee` business object. The ADO.NET code that's written to access the UDTs from SQL Server automatically marshals the binary data between client and server. Is there still a need for a middle tier that houses our custom business objects? Absolutely. Let's look at some of the drawbacks to using UDTs as business objects. It's more difficult to index individual properties of UDTs. For example, an employee business object might have a first name, last name, employee number, address, phone number, and so on. In a normalized table, each of these entities would have its own column. Any of these columns might have an index for optimized performance. It takes a lot more effort to persist a calculated column of a single property of a UDT to serve as an indexed column.

■Note It's possible to use the `ALTER ASSEMBLY` statement to update CLR UDTs without dropping them first. You can use this feature to update UDTs with fixes in the code. If the public properties change at all, the existing columns using this UDT will either have to be updated, or some special versioning code in the UDT will have to be used and persisted in the serialized data so you know which version of the UDT was used for the data.

For both types of UDTs, once the type is bound and used by any columns, you cannot change the type. This can be a real problem when you're developing, if you don't do a good enough job designing your datatypes.

■Tip Complex datatypes of either type have limited uses. Only use them in cases where they're absolutely necessary and provide a great benefit.

Documentation

In your modeling, you've created descriptions, notes, and various pieces of data that will be extremely useful in helping the developer to understand the whys and wherefores of using the tables you've created. In previous versions of SQL Server, it was difficult to make any use of this data directly in the server. In SQL Server 2000, Microsoft introduced extended properties that allow you to store specific information about objects. This is great, because it allows you to extend the metadata of your tables in ways that can be used by your applications using simple SQL statements.

By creating these properties, you can build a repository of information that the application developers can use to do the following:

- Understand what the data in the columns is used for

- Store information to use in applications, such as the following:

    - Captions to show on a form when a column is displayed

    - Error messages to display when a constraint is violated

    - Formatting rules for displaying or entering data

To maintain extended properties, you're given the following functions and stored procedures:

- `sys.sp_addextendedproperty`: Used to add a new extended property.

- `sys.sp_dropextendedproperty`: Used to delete an existing extended property.

- `sys.sp_updateextendedproperty`: Used to modify an existing extended property.

- `fn_listextendedproperty`: A system-defined function that can be used to list extended properties.

- `sys.extendedproperties`: Can be used to list all extended properties in a database. Less friendly than `fn_listextendedproperty`.

Each (other than `sys.extendedproperties`) has the following parameters:

- `@name`: The name of the user-defined property.

- `@value`: What to set the value to when creating or modifying a property.

- `@level0type`: Top-level object type, often schema, especially for most objects that users will use (tables, procedures, and so on).

- `@level0name`: The name of the object of the type that's identified in the `@level0type` parameter.

- `@level1type`: The name of the type of object such as `Table`, `View`, and so on.

- `@level1name`: The name of the object of the type that's identified in the `@level1type` parameter.

- `@level2type`: The name of the type of object that's on the level 2 branch of the tree under the value in the `@level1Type` value. For example, if `@level1type` is `Table`, then `@level2type` might be `Column`, `Index`, `Constraint`, or `Trigger`.

- `@level2name`: The name of the object of the type that's identified in the `@level2type` parameter.

For example, let's go back to the `Inventory.Movie` table (and schema) created a while back:

```
/*
CREATE SCHEMA Inventory --tables pertaining to the videos to be rented

CREATE TABLE Inventory.Movie
(
        MovieId                 int NOT NULL,
        Name                    varchar(20) NOT NULL,
        ReleaseDate             datetime NULL,
        Description             varchar(200) NULL,
        GenreId                 int NOT NULL,
        MovieRatingId           int NOT NULL
)
*/
```

To document this table, let's add a property to the table and columns named Description (or whatever you want to name it). You execute the following script after creating the table:

```
--dbo.person table description
EXEC sp_addextendedproperty @name = 'Description',
   @value = 'tables pertaining to the videos to be rented',
   @level0type = 'Schema', @level0name = 'Inventory'

--dbo.person table description
EXEC sp_addextendedproperty @name = 'Description',
   @value = 'Defines movies that will be rentable in the store',
   @level0type = 'Schema', @level0name = 'Inventory',
   @level1type = 'Table', @level1name = 'Movie'

--dbo.person.personId description
EXEC sp_addextendedproperty @name = 'Description',
   @value = 'Surrogate key of a movie instance',
   @level0type = 'Schema', @level0name = 'Inventory',
   @level1type = 'Table', @level1name = 'Movie',
   @level2type = 'Column', @level2name = 'MovieId'

--dbo.person.firstName description
EXEC sp_addextendedproperty @name = 'Description',
   @value = 'The known name of the movie',
   @level0type = 'Schema', @level0name = 'Inventory',
   @level1type = 'Table', @level1name = 'Movie',
   @level2type = 'Column', @level2name = 'Name'

--dbo.person.lastName description
EXEC sp_addextendedproperty @name = 'Description',
   @value = 'The date the movie was originally released',
   @level0type = 'Schema', @level0name = 'Inventory',
   @level1type = 'Table', @level1name = 'Movie',
   @level2type = 'Column', @level2name = 'ReleaseDate'
```

. . . and so on.

Now, when you go into Management Studio, right-click your table and select Properties. Choose Extended Properties, and you see your description, as shown in Figure 5-39.

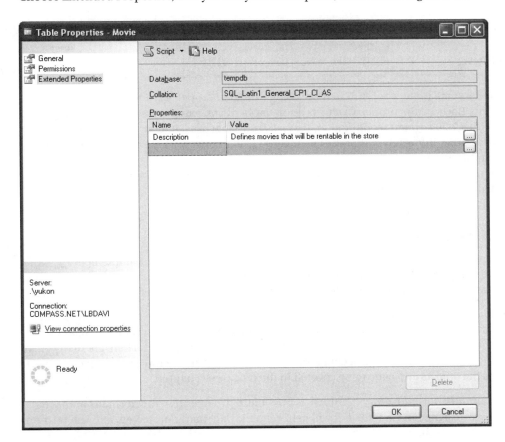

Figure 5-39. *Reward for hard work done. Descriptions in Management Studio.*

The fn_listExtendedProperty object is a system-defined function you can use to fetch the extended properties (the parameters are as discussed earlier—the name of the property, and then each level of the hierarchy):

```
SELECT objname, value
FROM   fn_listExtendedProperty ('Description',
                                 'Schema','Inventory',
                                 'Table','Movie',
                                 'Column',null)
```

This code returns the following results:

```
objname                value
-------------------    -----------------------------------------
MovieId                Surrogate key of a movie instance
Name                   The known name of the movie
ReleaseDate            The date the movie was originally released
```

There's some pretty cool stuff in there using extended properties, and not just for documentation. Because the property value is a `sql_variant`, you can put just about anything in there (with a 7,500-character limitation, that is). A possible use could be to store data entry masks and other information that the client could read in once and use to make the client experience more rich.

For more information, check the SQL Server 2005 Books Online section on "Using Extended Properties on Database Objects."

Best Practices

The following are a set of some of the most important best practices when implementing your database structures. Pay particular attention to the advice about UNIQUE constraints. Just having a surrogate key on a table is one of the worst mistakes made when implementing a database.

- *Make sure you've invested in proper database generation tools*: Do this after you know what the tool should be doing (not before). Implementing tables, columns, relationships, and so on is a tedious and painful task when done by hand. There are many great tools that double as logical data modeling tools and also generate these objects, as well as the objects and code to be covered in the next three chapters.

- *Maintain normalization*: As much as possible, try to maintain the normalizations that were designed in Chapter 4. It will help keep the data better protected, and will be more resilient to change.

- *Be careful when implementing subtypes*: Carefully consider if leaving subtypes as multiple tables makes more sense than rolling them up into a single table. The single-table solution always *seems* the easiest idea, but it can end up causing more trouble because you end up with tables that have complex logic to determine which fields are valuable in a given situation or not. Implementing subtypes makes UI coding more troublesome, because it isn't overly apparent which fields fit in which situation, whereas it's clear when the objects are subtyped.

- *Develop a real strategy for naming objects*: Keep the basics in mind:

  - Give all objects reasonably user-friendly names, such that it's obvious—at least to support personnel—what's being done.

  - Have either all plural or all singular names for tables. Consistency is the key.

  - Have all singular names for columns.

  - *I only use singular names for tables or columns.*

- *Develop template domains*: Reuse in every case where a similar datatype is needed. This cuts down on time spent implementing, and makes users of the data happy, because every time they see a column called `Description`, it's likely that it will have the same characteristics of other like columns.

- *Carefully choose the datatype and nullability for each column*: These are the first level of data protection to keep your data clean and pure. Also, improper datatypes can cause precision difficulties with numbers and even performance issues.

- *Make certain that every table has at least one `UNIQUE` constraint that doesn't include an artificial value*: It's a good idea to consider using an `IDENTITY` column as the primary key. However, if that is the only `UNIQUE` constraint on the table, then there can (and usually will) be duplication in the *real* columns of the table—a bad idea.

- *Be cautious with user-defined datatypes*:

  - Use CLR-based types only when needed to implement something special such as a complex datatype, such as a point `(x,y)`. Intrinsic types are faster and more standard to work with.

  - Generally avoid the use of datatype aliases. They're generally more trouble than they're worth.

- *Implement foreign keys using foreign key constraints*: They're fast, and no matter what kind of gaffes a client makes, the relationship between tables cannot be gotten wrong if a foreign key constraint is in place.

- *Document and script everything*: Using extended properties to document your objects can be extremely valuable. Most of all, when you create objects in the database, keep scripts of the T-SQL code for later use when moving to the QA and Production environments.

Summary

This has been a long chapter covering a large amount of ground. Understanding how to build tables, and how they're implemented, is the backbone of every database designer's knowledge.

I've taken our logical model and examined each entity to determine how feasible it is to implement. Then I dealt specifically with subtypes, as they can be problematic. In some cases, consider possible deviations from the strict normalization rules in extreme cases (though fight this as much as possible).

After getting satisfied that a model was ready to implement, I took a deep look at SQL Server tables, walking through limits on tables and the `CREATE TABLE` and `ALTER TABLE` syntax for adding constraints and modifying columns. General guidelines were given for naming tables, columns, indexes, and foreign key constraints. The key to good naming is consistency, and if the naming standards I suggested here seem too ugly, messy, or just plain weird to you, choose your own. Consistency is the most important thing for any naming convention. This is something I learn every day when I work with people who are so set in their ways that a value such as `'X-100'` means more to them than the full description that says exactly what the code means, which rarely bears any resemblance to the code. But it's what they're used to, and have been since the days when a code could only be five characters.

The two most important sections of this chapter were on choosing datatypes and implementing unique keys. We completed this process by discussing the process of choosing primary keys and at least one natural key per table. In the next chapter, we'll finish the task of implementing the base OLTP system by implementing the rest of the business rules required to keep the data in our database as clean as possible.

■ ■ ■

Protecting the Integrity of Your Data

When nothing seems to help, I go and look at a stonecutter hammering away at his rock perhaps a hundred times without as much as a crack showing in it. Yet at the hundred and first blow it will split in two, and I know it was not that blow that did it, but all that had gone before.

—Jacob August Riis

At the heart of a great database implementation is the ability to maintain that database in a state whereby the data within always conforms to your original design specifications. Perhaps in an ideal world, the database designers would be able to control all data input carefully, but in reality the database is designed and then turned over to the programmers and users to "go crazy and do their thing." The one thing that's generally true is that users will exploit any weakness in your design almost immediately. No matter how many times I've forgotten to apply a UNIQUE constraint, it's amazing to me how quickly the subsequent data duplications occurred. Ultimately, user perception is governed by the reliability and integrity of the data users retrieve from your database. If they detect data anomalies in their data sets (usually in skewed reported values), their faith in the whole application will plummet.

The foundations of strong data integrity lie in well-defined and normalized sets of tables, correctly defined relationships (PKs, FKs) and precise data type specifications—all of which I covered in previous chapters. In this chapter, we add the final layer of protection, in the form of the constraints and logic that control and validate data input and manipulation. With this in place, we hope we'll protect our database from "bad" data, no matter what the end users get up to. To this end, I'll discuss the following topics:

- *Use of* CHECK *constraints*: Constraints form an integral part of your table definitions. They're fast, declarative in nature, and require little coding. I covered NULL, DEFAULT, PRIMARY KEY, and FOREIGN KEY constraints in Chapter 5. The last constraint to cover is the CHECK constraint, which you can use to limit the values that can be entered into a single column or across all columns in a row.

- *Programmatic data protection in the database*: These are code modules, stored in the database, that can be used to control, validate, and monitor user actions on the data. Specifically, we can use the following:

  - *Triggers*: Units of code associated with a specific table (or tables). A trigger "fires" automatically whenever certain defined events occur on the table that it protects. Triggers are extremely flexible and can affect multiple columns, multiple rows, multiple tables, and even multiple databases.

  - *Stored procedures*: Units of code that are part of the database but aren't directly associated with a specific table. Certain data manipulation logic can be placed in a stored procedure and then, for example, you can grant users access to the procedure rather than the underlying table(s).

- *Programmatic data protection outside the RDBMS*: Sometimes data manipulation has to conform to complex business rules that are simply better implemented outside the database in, for example, a 3GL language such as C# or Visual Basic. Further, the issuing of user warnings ("Are you sure you wish to delete this row?") is most often implemented in user code, outside the database.

Best Practices

Applications come and applications go, but the data must always be protected.

Up to this point in the book, I don't consider the design principles I've covered to be open to much debate. There are levels of compliance, of course, but in general they're good guiding principles that should be followed as closely as possible.

At this point, however, opinions and strategies might diverge. Many people feel they achieve optimum flexibility by placing most data protection and validation logic outside the database. In this way, they avoid use of database-specific code (such as T-SQL) as far as possible. Others take a much more database-centric approach, placing as much of the data logic as possible right in the database, as close to the data as possible. Others (maybe most) adopt an approach that's "somewhere in between." Therefore, when I talk of "best practices," you have to consider them in the context of my overall stance on this issue: that is to adopt, as far as possible, a database-centric approach where the database is responsible for protecting its integrity (regardless of what validations occur outside the database).

I like to have the data validation and protection logic as close as possible to the data it guards, as this has the advantage that you only *have* to write this logic once. It's all stored in the same place, and it takes forethought to bypass.

It's important to remember that many different clients may access your data. I tend to group them into four broad classifications:

- Users using custom front-end tools

- Users using generic data manipulation tools, such as Microsoft Access

- Routines that import data from external sources

- Raw queries executed by data administrators to fix problems caused by user error

Each of these poses different issues for your integrity scheme. What's more important, each of these scenarios (with the possible exception of the second) forms part of nearly every database system developed. To best handle each scenario, the data must be safeguarded, using mechanisms that work without the responsibility of the user.

If you decide to implement your data logic in the client rather than the database, then you have to make sure that you implement it—and implement it *correctly*—in every one of those clients. If you update the logic, you have to update it in multiple locations. If a client is "retired" and a new one introduced, then the logic must be replicated in that new client. You're much more susceptible to coding errors if you have to write the code in more than one place. Having your data protected in a single location helps to prevent programmers from forgetting to enforce a rule in one situation, even if they remember *everywhere* else.

With that in mind, the following are my recommended best practices for implementing data protection and validation logic. Throughout the reminder of the chapter, I'll describe each methodology outlined, as follows:

- *Use* CHECK *constraints as often as possible to manage single row requirements*: CHECK constraints are fast and easy to apply.

- *Use triggers to perform data validations that* CHECK *constraints cannot handle*: The work of some trigger functionality may be moved off into middle-tier objects, though triggers do have performance benefits. Use triggers when the following types of validations need to be made:

  - *Cross-database referential integrity (RI)*: Just basic RI, but SQL Server doesn't manage declarative constraints across database boundaries.

  - *Intra-table, inter-row constraints*: For example, when you need to see that the sum of a column value over multiple rows is less than some value (possibly in another table).

  - *Inter-table constraints*: For example, if a value in one table relies on the value in another. This might also be written as a functions-based CHECK constraint.

  - *Introducing desired side effects to your queries*: For example, cascading inserts, maintaining denormalized data, and so on.

- *Make sure that triggers are able to handle multirow operations*: Although most modifications are in terms of a single row, if a user enters data in more than one row there's a possibility of invalid data being entered.

- *Consider using stored procedures to encapsulate SQL used to enforce additional rules*: When several SQL statements are involved in data modification, use stored procedures to batch statements together, usually using a transaction (covered in Chapter 9 in more detail).

- *Use client code appropriately*: When constraints and triggers won't cover a need, then you cannot implicitly trust that the data in the table will meet the requirements. This is because you can't get around triggers and constraints unless you make a conscious effort by dropping or disabling them.

In moving down this list, the solutions become less desirable (from an ease of use and maintenance point of view), yet each one has specific benefits that are appropriate in certain situations, so you need to understand them all.

Note In this chapter, I'll present various examples that aren't tied to previous chapters. I'll be building these objects in a new sample database I'll create called `ProtectionChapter`. You can use whatever database you wish. Also, some of the standalone examples use a different format for the example code. I did this to drive home the point that any standard is fine.

Constraints

Constraints are SQL Server devices that are used to enforce data integrity automatically on a single column or row. You should use constraints as extensively as possible to protect your data, as they're simple, declarative, and have minimal overhead.

One of the greatest things about constraints is that the query optimizer can use them to optimize queries. For example, say you place a constraint on a column that requires that all values for that column must fall between 5 and 10. If a query is executed that asks for all rows with a value of greater than 100 for that column, the optimizer will know without even looking at the data that no rows meet the criteria.

SQL Server has five different kinds of constraints:

- NULL: Though NULL constraints aren't technically constraints, they behave as constraints.

- PRIMARY KEY *and* UNIQUE *constraints*: Used to make sure that your keys contain only unique combinations of values.

- FOREIGN KEY: Used to make sure that any migrated keys have only valid values that match the keys that they reference.

- DEFAULT: Used to set an acceptable default value for a column when the user doesn't provide one. (Some people don't count defaults as constraints, as they don't constrain updates.)

- CHECK: Used to limit the values that can be entered into a single column or an entire row.

Having previously considered the first four of these in Chapter 5, I'll now focus attention on the final one, the CHECK constraint. You use CHECK constraints to disallow improper data from being entered into columns of a table. CHECK constraints are executed after DEFAULT constraints (so you cannot specify a default value that would contradict a CHECK constraint) and INSTEAD OF triggers (which I'll cover later in this chapter). CHECK constraints cannot affect the values being inserted or deleted, but are used to verify the validity of the supplied values.

There are two flavors of CHECK constraint: column and table. Column constraints reference a single column, and are only used when the individual column is referenced in a modification. CHECK constraints are considered table constraints when more than one column is referenced in the criteria. Fortunately, you don't have to worry about declaring a constraint as either a column constraint or table constraint. When SQL Server compiles the constraint, it verifies whether it needs to check more than one column and applies the appropriate constraint.

We'll be looking at building CHECK constraints using two methods:

- Simple expressions

- Expressions using user-defined functions

The two methods are similar, but you can build more complex constraints using functions, though the code in a function can be more complex and difficult to manage. In this section, we'll take a look at some examples of constraints built using each of these methods, then we'll take a look at a scheme for dealing with errors from constraints. First though, let's build the simple schema that will form the basis of the examples in this section.

Example Schema

All the examples in this section on creating CHECK constraints use the sample tables shown in Figure 6-1.

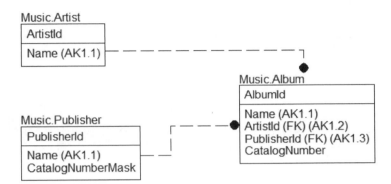

Figure 6-1. *The example schema*

To create and populate the tables, execute the following code:

```
CREATE SCHEMA Music
GO
CREATE TABLE Music.Artist
(
    ArtistId int NOT NULL,
    Name varchar(60) NOT NULL,

    CONSTRAINT PKNameArtist PRIMARY KEY CLUSTERED (ArtistId),
    CONSTRAINT AKNameArtist_Name UNIQUE NONCLUSTERED (Name)
)
CREATE TABLE Music.Publisher
(
        PublisherId             int primary key,
        Name                    varchar(20),
        CatalogNumberMask varchar(100)
        CONSTRAINT DfltNamePublisher_CatalogNumberMask default ('%'),
        CONSTRAINT AKNamePublisher_Name UNIQUE NONCLUSTERED (Name),
)
```

```
CREATE TABLE Music.Album
(
    AlbumId int NOT NULL,
    Name varchar(60) NOT NULL,
    ArtistId int NOT NULL,
    CatalogNumber varchar(20) NOT NULL,
    PublisherId int NOT null --not requiring this information

    CONSTRAINT PKAlbum PRIMARY KEY CLUSTERED(AlbumId),
    CONSTRAINT AKAlbum_Name UNIQUE NONCLUSTERED (Name),
    CONSTRAINT FKMusic_Artist$records$Music_Album
            FOREIGN KEY (ArtistId) REFERENCES Music.Artist(ArtistId),
    CONSTRAINT FKMusic_Publisher$published$Music_Album
            FOREIGN KEY (PublisherId) REFERENCES Music.Publisher(PublisherId)
)
```

Then seed the data with the following:

```
INSERT  INTO Music.Publisher (PublisherId, Name, CatalogNumberMask)
VALUES (1,'Capitol','[0-9][0-9][0-9]-[0-9][0-9][0-9a-z][0-9a-z][0-9a-z]-[0-9][0-9]')
INSERT  INTO Music.Publisher (PublisherId, Name, CatalogNumberMask)
VALUES (2,'MCA', '[a-z][a-z][0-9][0-9][0-9][0-9][0-9]')
GO


INSERT  INTO Music.Artist(ArtistId, Name)
VALUES (1, 'The Beatles')
INSERT  INTO Music.Artist(ArtistId, Name)
VALUES (2, 'The Who')
GO


INSERT INTO Music.Album (AlbumId, Name, ArtistId, PublisherId, CatalogNumber)
VALUES (1, 'The White Album',1,1,'433-43ASD-33')
INSERT INTO Music.Album (AlbumId, Name, ArtistId, PublisherId, CatalogNumber)
VALUES (2, 'Revolver',1,1,'111-11111-11')
INSERT INTO Music.Album (AlbumId, Name, ArtistId, PublisherId, CatalogNumber)
VALUES (3, 'Quadrophenia',2,2,'CD12345')
```

Basic Syntax

The basic syntax of the ALTER TABLE statement that concerns CHECK constraints is as follows:

```
ALTER TABLE <tableName> [WITH CHECK | WITH NOCHECK]
    ADD [CONSTRAINT <constraintName>]
    CHECK <BooleanExpression>
```

Most of this is exactly the same as presented in the previous chapter when I built DEFAULT constraints. However, two particular parts of this declaration need to be discussed:

- `<BooleanExpression>`

- `[WITH CHECK | WITH NOCHECK]`

Note also that you can include CHECK constraint declarations in the CREATE TABLE statements, just like you can for DEFAULT and FOREIGN KEY constraints.

\<BooleanExpression\>

The `<BooleanExpression>` component is similar to the WHERE clause of a typical SELECT statement, with no subqueries allowed. It may access system and user-defined functions, and use the name or names of any columns in the table. However, it cannot access any other table, nor can it access any row other than the current row being modified (except through a function, as we'll discuss in the next section). If multiple rows are modified, each row is checked against this expression individually.

The interesting thing about this expression is that unlike a WHERE clause, the condition is checked for falseness rather than truth. Without going completely into a discussion of NULL (a trip worth taking on your own), it's important to understand that CHECK constraints fail only on rows that are explicitly False. If the result of a comparison is UNKNOWN because of a NULL comparison, then the row will succeed.

This might be a bit confusing. For example, consider if the Boolean expression is value <> 'fred'. If value was NULL, then this would be accepted, because NULL <> 'fred' is UNKNOWN. If value is 'fred', it would fail because 'fred' <> 'fred' is False. You can look for NULL values by explicitly checking for them using IS NULL or IS NOT NULL.

For example, if you wanted to implement a rule that no artist with a name that includes the word "Duran" in it is allowed, you could code the following:

```
ALTER TABLE Music.Artist WITH CHECK
    ADD CONSTRAINT chkArtist$Name$NoDuranNames
            CHECK (Name not like '%Duran%')
```

Then test by trying to insert a new row with an offending value:

```
INSERT INTO Music.Artist(ArtistId, Name)
VALUES (3, 'Duran Duran')
```

This returns the following result:

```
Msg 547, Level 16, State 0, Line 1
The INSERT statement conflicted with the CHECK constraint
"chkArtist$Name$noDuranNames". The conflict occurred in database
"ProtectionChapter", table "Music.Artist", column 'Name'.
The statement has been terminated.
```

Thereby keeping my music collection safe from at least one band from the eighties.

[WITH CHECK | WITH NOCHECK]

When you create a CHECK constraint, the WITH CHECK setting (it's the default setting) gives you the opportunity to decide whether or not to check the existing data in the table.

Let's add a row for another musician that I don't want in my table:

```
INSERT INTO Music.Artist(ArtistId, Name)
VALUES (3, 'Madonna')
```

You might specify the constraint using WITH NOCHECK because you now want to allow this new constraint, but there's data in the table that conflicts (usually more difficult to clean up):

```
ALTER TABLE Music.Artist WITH NOCHECK
   ADD CONSTRAINT chkArtist$Name$noMadonnaNames
          CHECK (Name not like '%Madonna%')
```

The statement is added to the table definition, though the NOCHECK means that the bad value is retained in the table. However, any time a modification statement references the column, the CHECK constraint is fired. The next time you try to set the value of the table to the same bad value, an error occurs. In the following statement, I simply set every row of the table to the same name it has stored in it:

```
UPDATE Music.Artist
SET Name = Name
```

This gives you the following error message:

```
Msg 547, Level 16, State 0, Line 1
The UPDATE statement conflicted with the CHECK constraint
"chkArtist$Name$noMadonnaNames". The conflict occurred in database
"ProtectionChapter", table "Music.Artist", column 'Name'.
The statement has been terminated.
```

"What?" most users would exclaim. If the value was in the table, shouldn't it already be good? The user (in this isolated case) is correct. This kind of thing will confuse the heck out of your users, and cost you in support, unless the data in question is *never* used. But if it's never used, then just delete it, or include a time range for the values. CHECK Name not like %Madonna% OR rowCreationDate < '1/1/2005' is a reasonable compromise.

Using NOCHECK is a bad thing to do, in my opinion. If the constraint is built WITH CHECK, the optimizer could possibly make use of this fact when building plans if the constraint didn't use any functions, and just used simple comparisons such as less than, greater than, and so on. For example, say you have a constraint that says that a value must be lower than 10. If in a query you look for all values 11 and greater, the optimizer can use this fact and immediately return 0 rows, rather than having to scan the table to see if any value matches.

If a constraint is built with WITH CHECK, it's considered trusted, as the optimizer can trust that all values conform to the CHECK constraint. You can determine if a constraint is trusted by using the INFORMATION_SCHEMA and the object_property function:

```
SELECT CHECK_CLAUSE,
       objectproperty(object_id(CONSTRAINT_SCHEMA + '.' +
                            CONSTRAINT_NAME),'CnstIsNotTrusted') AS NotTrusted
FROM INFORMATION_SCHEMA.CHECK_CONSTRAINTS
WHERE CONSTRAINT_SCHEMA = 'Music'
  And CONSTRAINT_NAME = 'chkArtist$Name$noMadonnaNames'
```

This returns the following results (with some minor formatting of course):

```
CHECK_CLAUSE                        NotTrusted
----------------------------------- ----------------------
(NOT [Name] like '%Madonna%')       1
```

Make sure that the system trusts all your CHECK constraints so that the optimizer can use the information when building plans.

▮Caution Adding constraints with NOCHECK to save time hits upon one of the odd realities of dealing with very large systems. They take forever to modify, so often you'll feel like you need to cut corners to get it done fast. The problem is that the shortcut on design or implementation often costs way more in later maintenance costs, or even worse, in the user experience. If at all possible, it's best to try to get everything set up how you want it in production.

Simple Expressions

By far, most CHECK constraints are simple expressions that just test some characteristic of a value in a column or columns. These constraints don't reference any data other than the single column.
   As a few examples, consider the following:

- *Empty strings*: Prevent users from inserting a space character to avoid any real input into a column—CHECK (LEN(ColumnName) > 0).

- *Date range checks*: Make sure that a reasonable date is entered. For example:

  - Movie rental return date (as we had in the previous chapter) should be greater than one day—CHECK (ReturnDate > dateadd(day,1,RentalDate)).

  - Date of some event that's supposed to have occurred already in the past—CHECK (EventDate <= GETDATE()).

- *Value reasonableness*: Make sure some value, typically a number of some sort, is reasonable for the situation. For example:

  - *Values must be non-negative integers*: This is common, because there are often columns where negative values don't make sense (hours worked, miles driven, and so on)—CHECK (MilesDriven >= 0).

  - *Royalty rate for an author that's less than or equal to 30 percent*: If this rate ever could be greater, then it isn't a CHECK constraint. So if 15 percent is the typical rate, the UI might warn that it isn't normal, but if 30 percent is the absolute ceiling, it would be a good CHECK constraint—CHECK (RoyaltyRate <= .3).

CHECK constraints of this variety are always a good idea when you have situations where there are data conditions that *must* always be true. These CHECK constraints are generally extremely fast, and won't negatively affect performance except in extreme situations.

As an example, I'll just show the code for the first, empty string check, because simple CHECK constraints are easy to code once you have the syntax. A common CHECK constraint that I add to many string type columns (varchar, char, and so on) prevents blank data from being entered. This is because most of the time if a value is required, it isn't desired that the value for a column be blank, unless it's allowed to have no value for the column (as opposed to UNKNOWN for a NULL value).

For example, in the Album table, a Name column doesn't allow NULLs. The user has to enter something, but what about a single space character?

```
INSERT INTO Music.Album ( AlbumId, Name, ArtistId, PublisherId, CatalogNumber )
VALUES ( 4, '', 1, 1,'dummy value' )
```

If you allowed this in your database, you'd certainly end up with a blank row, because there would likely be one occasion for which a user would enter a row prematurely after having failed to input his name. The second time a space is entered instead of a name:

```
INSERT INTO Music.Album ( AlbumId, Name, ArtistId, PublisherId, CatalogNumber )
VALUES ( 5, '', 1, 1,'dummy value' )
```

an error would be returned:

```
Msg 2627, Level 14, State 1, Line 1
Violation of UNIQUE KEY constraint 'AKAlbum_Name'. Cannot insert duplicate
key in object 'Music.Album'.
The statement has been terminated.
```

Alternatively, you might have a nonunique, constraint-bound column, such as a description or notes column, where you might have many blank entries. You might add the following constraint to prevent this from ever happening again (after deleting the two blank rows). It works by trimming the value in Name, eliminating any space characters, and checking the length:

```
DELETE FROM Music.Album
WHERE  Name = ''
ALTER TABLE Music.Album WITH CHECK
    ADD CONSTRAINT chkAlbum$Name$noEmptyString
          CHECK (LEN(RTRIM(Name)) > 0)
```

The CHECK expression here uses the LEN function on a RTRIMed column to ensure that if there are no characters other than space characters, then a zero-length string is returned (or a NULL if your table allowed it). Of course, you know that you already entered a value that will clash with your constraint, so you get the following error message:

```
Msg 547, Level 16, State 0, Line 1
The ALTER TABLE statement conflicted with the CHECK constraint
'chkAlbum$Name$noEmptyString'. The conflict occurred in database 'tempdb',
 table 'Music.Album'.
```

This should signal the user interface to provide a warning so that the user can add data for the column (all too often nonsensical data, but it's impossible to decide if data that's entered makes sense without using more processing power than it's worth). What's generally the case is that the user interface will then (or before) prevent such data from being created via the UI, but the CHECK constraint prevents other processes from putting in invalid data as well.

Constraints Based on Functions

Far less typical, but in many ways more useful, can be to build CHECK constraints on conditions that use user-defined functions (UDFs). For the most part, CHECK constraints usually consist of the simple task of checking a stable format or value of a single column, and for these tasks a standard CHECK constraint using the simple <BooleanExpression> is perfectly adequate.

However, a CHECK constraint need not be so simple. A UDF can be complex, and might touch several tables in the server. For what reasons might we build a UDF and use a CHECK constraint? There are a couple reasons:

- Complex scalar validations; for example, in a situation where a regular expression would be easier to use than a LIKE comparison

- Validations that access other tables

Calling a UDF to do a simple scalar CHECK constraint incurs overhead. It's best to try to express your Boolean expression without a UDF unless it's entirely necessary to do so. In the following examples, I'll employ UDFs to provide generic range-checking functionality and powerful rule checking, which can implement complex rules that would prove difficult to code using a simple Boolean expression.

You can implement the UDFs in either T-SQL or in VB.NET (or in C#, or any .NET language that lets you exploit the new capability of SQL Server 2005 to write CLR-based objects in the database). In many cases, if you aren't doing any kind of table access in the code of the function, the CLR will perform much better than the T-SQL.

I'm going to build an example that implements an entry mask that varies based on the parent of a row. Consider that it's desirable to validate that catalog numbers for albums are of the proper format. However, different publishers have different catalog number masks for their clients' albums.

Note that the mask column, Publisher.CatalogNumberMask, is considerably larger (five times larger in fact) than the actual CatalogNumber column, because some of the possible masks use multiple characters to indicate a single character. You should also note that it's a varchar, because using char variables as LIKE masks can be problematic due to the space padding at the end of such columns.

To do this, I build a T-SQL function that accesses this column to check that the value matches the mask, as shown (note that we'd likely build this constraint using T-SQL rather than by using the CLR, as it accesses a table in the body of the function):

```
CREATE FUNCTION Music.Publisher$CatalogNumberValidate
(
    @CatalogNumber char(12),
    @PublisherId int --now based on the Artist ID
)
```

```
RETURNS bit
AS
BEGIN
   DECLARE @LogicalValue bit, @CatalogNumberMask varchar(100)

   SELECT @LogicalValue = CASE WHEN @CatalogNumber LIKE CatalogNumberMask
                               THEN 1
                          ELSE 0   END
   FROM   Music.Publisher
   WHERE  PublisherId = @PublisherId

   RETURN @LogicalValue
END
```

When I loaded the data in the start of this section, I preloaded the data with valid values for the CatalogNumber and the CatalogNumberMask columns:

```
SELECT Album.CatalogNumber, Publisher.CatalogNumberMask
FROM   Music.Album as Album
          JOIN Music.Publisher as Publisher
              ON Album.PublisherId = Publisher.PublisherId
```

This returns the following results:

CatalogNumber	CatalogNumberMask
433-43ASD-33	[0-9][0-9][0-9]-[0-9][0-9][0-9a-z][0-9a-z][0-9a-z]-[0-9][0-9]
111-11111-11	[0-9][0-9][0-9]-[0-9][0-9][0-9a-z][0-9a-z][0-9a-z]-[0-9][0-9]
CD12345	[a-z][a-z][0-9][0-9][0-9][0-9][0-9]

Now you can add the constraint to the table, as shown here:

```
ALTER TABLE Music.Album
   WITH CHECK ADD CONSTRAINT
      chkAlbum$CatalogNumber$CatalogNumberValidate
      CHECK (Music.Publisher$CatalogNumbervalidate(CatalogNumber,PublisherId) = 1)
```

If the constraint gives you errors because of invalid data existing in the table (in real development, this often occurs with test data from trying out the UI that someone is building), you can use a query like the following to find them:

```
--to find where your data is not ready for the constraint,
--you run the following query
SELECT Album.Name, Album.CatalogNumber, Publisher.CatalogNumberMask
FROM Music.Album AS Album
        JOIN Music.Publisher AS Publisher
          on Publisher.PublisherId = Album.PublisherId
WHERE Music.Publisher$CatalogNumbervalidate
                      (Album.CatalogNumber,Album.PublisherId) <> 1
```

Now, let's add a new row with an invalid value:

```
INSERT  Music.Album(AlbumId, Name, ArtistId, PublisherId, CatalogNumber)
VALUES  (4,'who''s next',2,2,'1')
```

This causes the error, because the catalog number of '1' doesn't match the mask:

```
Msg 547, Level 16, State 0, Line 2
The INSERT statement conflicted with the CHECK constraint
"chkAlbum$CatalogNumber$CatalogNumberValidate". The conflict occurred
in database "ProtectionChapter", table "Music.Album".
The statement has been terminated.
```

Now we change the number to something that matches our constraint:

```
INSERT  Music.Album(AlbumId, Name, ArtistId, CatalogNumber, PublisherId)
VALUES  (4,'who''s next',2,'AC12345',2)

SELECT * from Music.Album
```

This returns the following results:

AlbumId	Name	ArtistId	CatalogNumber	PublisherId
1	the white album	1	433-43ASD-33	1
2	revolver	1	111-11111-11	1
3	quadrophenia	2	CD12345	2
4	who's next	2	AC12345	2

Using this kind of approach, you can build any single-row validation code for your tables, though there's a drawback to this coding method. As described previously, each UDF will fire once for each row and each column that was modified in the update, and making checks over and over again might lead to degradation in performance.

Alternatively, you could create a trigger that checks for the existence of any rows returned by a query, based on the query used earlier to find improper data in the table:

```
SELECT *
FROM    Music.Album AS Album
          JOIN Music.Publisher AS Publisher
              on Publisher.PublisherId = Album.PublisherId
WHERE   Music.Publisher$CatalogNumbervalidate
              (Album.CatalogNumber,Album.PublisherId) <> 1
```

There's one drawback to this type of constraint. As it stands right now, the Album table is protected from invalid values being entered into the CatalogNumber column, but it doesn't say anything about what happens if a user changes the CatalogEntryMask on the Publisher table. If this is a concern, then you'd need to add a CHECK constraint to the Publisher table that validates changes to the mask against any existing data.

Tip A likely problem with this design is that it isn't normalized to the Fourth Normal Form. Publishers do usually have a mask that's valid at a point in time (or you can just set the mask to '%'), but everything changes. If the publishers lengthen the size of their catalog numbers, or change to a new format, what happens to the older data? For a functioning system, it would likely be valuable to have a release-date column and catalog number mask that was valid for a given range of dates. Otherwise, the enterprising user would create publishers such as 'MCA 1989-1990', 'MCA 1991-1994', and so on, and mess up your database. It's harder to design and implement (and way messier for an example on using CHECK constraints), but something to keep in mind nevertheless.

Handling Errors Caused by Constraints

Admit it. You were reading that last section and you were thinking, "What the heck do I do with those error messages? I certainly don't want to show *that* to a user, if for no other reason other than it will generate a helpdesk call every time it occurs." Handling errors is one of the more annoying parts of using constraints in SQL Server.

Whenever a statement fails a constraint requirement, SQL Server provides you with an ugly message, and no real method for displaying a clean message automatically. Luckily, SQL Server 2005 has vastly improved error-handling capabilities in T-SQL. In this chapter, we'll look at some strategies for dealing with these errors in our code.

In this section, I'll briefly detail a way to take the ugly messages you get from a constraint error message, much like the error from the previous statement:

```
Msg 547, Level 16, State 0, Line 1
The INSERT statement conflicted with the CHECK constraint
'chkAlbum$CatalogNumber$CatalogNumberValidate'. The conflict occurred in
database 'tempdb', table 'Music.Album'.
The statement has been terminated.
```

I'll show you how to map this to an error message that at least makes some level of sense. First, the parts of the error message are as follows:

- *Error number*—Msg 547: The error number that's passed back to the calling program. In some cases, this error number is significant; however, in most cases it's enough to say that the error number is nonzero.

- *Level*—Level 16: A severity level for the message. 0 through 18 are generally considered to be user messages, with 16 being the default. Levels 19–25 are severe errors that cause the connection to be severed (with a message written to the log), and typically involve data corruption issues.

- *State*—State 0: A value from 0–127 that represents the state of the process when the error was raised. This value is rarely used by any process.

- *Line*—Line 1: The line in the batch or object where the error is occurring. However, this value is useful for debugging purposes.

- *Error description*: A text explanation of the error that has occurred.

Unhandled, this is the exact error that will be sent to the client. Using the new TRY-CATCH error handling, we can build a simple error handler and a scheme for mapping constraints to error messages. Part of the reason we name constraints is to determine what the intent was in creating the constraint in the first place. In the following code, we'll implement a very rudimentary error-mapping scheme by parsing the text of the name of the constraint from the message, and then we'll look this value up in a mapping table. It isn't a "perfect" scheme, but it does the trick when using constraints as the only data protection for a situation.

First, let's create a mapping table where we put the name of the constraint that we've defined, and a message that explains what the constraint means:

```
--note, we use dbo here because the ErrorLog will be used by all schemas
CREATE TABLE dbo.ErrorMap
(
    ConstraintName sysname primary key,
    Message          varchar(2000)
)
go
INSERT dbo.ErrorMap(constraintName, message)
VALUES ('chkAlbum$CatalogNumber$CatalogNumberValidate',
        'The catalog number does not match the format set up by the Publisher')
```

Then we create a procedure to do the actual mapping, by taking the values that can be retrieved from the ERROR_%() procedures that are accessible in a CATCH block and using them to look up the value in the ErrorMap table:

```
CREATE PROCEDURE dbo.ErrorMap$MapError
(
    @ErrorNumber  int = NULL,
    @ErrorMessage nvarchar(2000) = NULL,
    @ErrorSeverity INT= NULL,
    @ErrorState INT = NULL
) AS
  BEGIN
    --use values in ERROR_ functions unless the user passes in values
    SET @ErrorNumber = Coalesce(@ErrorNumber, ERROR_NUMBER())
    SET @ErrorMessage = Coalesce(@ErrorMessage, ERROR_MESSAGE())
    SET @ErrorSeverity = Coalesce(@ErrorSeverity, ERROR_SEVERITY())
    SET @ErrorState = Coalesce(@ErrorState,ERROR_STATE())

    DECLARE @originalMessage nvarchar(2000)
    SET @originalMessage = ERROR_MESSAGE()
```

```
        IF @ErrorNumber = 547
          BEGIN
              SET @ErrorMessage =
                                (SELECT message
                                 FROM    dbo.ErrorMap
                                 WHERE   constraintName =
                   --this substring pulls the constraint name from the message
                   substring( @ErrorMessage,CHARINDEX('constraint "',@ErrorMessage) + 12,
                                charindex('"',substring(@ErrorMessage,
                                CHARINDEX('constraint "',@ErrorMessage) + 12,2000))-1)
                                )       END
        ELSE
             SET @ErrorMessage = @ErrorMessage

        SET @ErrorState = CASE when @ErrorState = 0 THEN 1 ELSE @ErrorState END

        --if the error was not found, get the original message
        SET @ErrorMessage = isNull(@ErrorMessage, @originalMessage)
        RAISERROR (@ErrorMessage, @ErrorSeverity,@ErrorState )
      END
```

Now, see what happens when we enter an invalid value for an album catalog number:

```
BEGIN TRY
    INSERT  Music.Album(AlbumId, Name, ArtistId, CatalogNumber, PublisherId)
    VALUES  (5,'who are you',2,'badnumber',2)
END TRY
BEGIN CATCH
    EXEC dbo.ErrorMap$MapError
END CATCH
```

The error message is as follows:

```
Msg 50000, Level 16, State 1, Procedure ErrorMap$mapError, Line 24
The catalog number does not match the format set up by the Publisher
```

instead of the following:

```
Msg 547, Level 16, State 0, Line 1
The INSERT statement conflicted with the CHECK constraint
'chkAlbum$CatalogNumber$CatalogNumberValidate'. The conflict occurred in
database 'tempdb', table 'Music.Album'.
The statement has been terminated.
```

This is far more pleasing, even if it was a bit of a workout getting to this new message. This isn't a programming book, so we won't go any deeper into programming error handling right now (we'll cover it a bit more in the next section on triggers).

■Note For more information on how error handling has changed in SQL Server 2005, consider the book *Pro SQL Server 2005* by Thomas Rizzo et al. (Apress, 2005). It has an overview of all changes in SQL Server 2005 from previous versions.

Programmatic Data Protection

There are quite a few types of data protection that we cannot (or should not) put into SQL Server 2005 constraints and table structures. There are a few reasons for this:

- You need to access other rows that you're inserting.
- The rules aren't *always* enforced.
- The rules need to access tables in different databases (or even not on the SQL Server, possibly even in the OS file structures).

For the remainder of this chapter, we'll look at examples of data validations that could not be reasonably implemented using simple constraints. To implement these, you have three different mechanisms at your disposal; namely triggers, stored procedures, or client code that runs outside the database. Let's start by examining use of DML triggers.

■Note SQL Server 2005 includes a new type of trigger called Data Definition Language (DDL) triggers. These are more of a DBA or security tool, which Chapter 7 covers. They can also be coded in T-SQL or the CLR languages.

DML Triggers

Triggers are a type of stored procedure attached to a table or view, and are executed automatically when the contents of a table are changed. You can use them to enforce almost any business rule, and they're especially important for dealing with situations that are too complex for a CHECK constraint to handle. As a simple case, consider a situation in which you want to ensure that an update of a value is performed on both the tables where that value occurs. You can write a trigger that disallows the update unless it occurs in both tables.

Use triggers when you need to do the following:

- Perform cross-database referential integrity
- Check inter-row rules, where just looking at the current row isn't enough for the constraints
- Check inter-table constraints, when rules require access to data in a different table
- Introduce desired side effects to your data-modification queries

The main advantage that triggers have over constraints is the ability to access other tables seamlessly, and to operate on multiple rows at once. In a trigger, you can run almost every T-SQL command, except for the following ones:

- ALTER DATABASE
- CREATE DATABASE
- DROP DATABASE
- RESTORE LOG

- RECONFIGURE
- RESTORE DATABASE
- LOAD LOG
- LOAD DATABASE

Also, you cannot use the following commands on the table that the trigger protects:

- CREATE INDEX
- ALTER INDEX
- DROP INDEX
- DBCC REINDEX

- ALTER PARTITION FUNCTION
- DROP TABLE
- ALTER TABLE

Note You can't use ALTER TABLE to add or modify columns, switch partitions, and add or drop primary key columns.

Truthfully, it isn't good design to change the schema of *any* table in a trigger, much less the one that caused the trigger, so these aren't overly restrictive requirements at all.

Types of DML Triggers

There are two different types of triggers:

- AFTER: These triggers fire after the DML statement (INSERT/UPDATE/DELETE) has affected the table. AFTER triggers are usually used for handling rules that won't fit into the mold of a constraint; for example, rules that require data to be stored, such as a logging mechanism. You may have an unlimited number of AFTER triggers that fire on INSERT, UPDATE, and DELETE, or any combination of them.

- INSTEAD OF: This means that the trigger operates instead of the command (INSERT, UPDATE, or DELETE) affecting the table or view. In this way, you can do whatever you want with the data, either doing exactly what was requested by the user, or doing something completely different (you can even just ignore the operation altogether). You can have a maximum of one INSTEAD OF INSERT, UPDATE, and DELETE trigger of each type per table. However, you can combine all three into one and have a single trigger that fires for all three operations.

Coding DML Triggers

Let's briefly review some of the most important aspects of trigger coding:

- *Accessing modified rows*: When coding triggers, you can access the data that has been changed by accessing two special tables: inserted and updated. The deleted table contains rows that have been deleted for a DELETE statement execution, and the original version for an UPDATE statement. The inserted table contains new rows for an INSERT, and the new version of a row for an UPDATE.

- *Determining modified columns*: For performance reasons, you usually don't want to validate data that's in a column that isn't affected by a DML statement. You can tell which columns were a part of the INSERT or UPDATE statement by using the UPDATE(<columnName>) function to check the column you're interested in. (You can use the function COLUMNS_UPDATED(columnBitmask) to check the columns by their position in the table. 1+2+4 = 7 would mean the first three columns were updated, but it's bad practice to address columns in a table positionally.)

- *Error handling and triggers*: Handling errors that occur in a trigger is somewhat different than in any other T-SQL code. I'll demonstrate the differences and implement an error handler for T-SQL triggers in the upcoming sections.

- *Nesting triggers*: Take care when building AFTER triggers that modify tables (the same table or other tables) because these updates could in turn cause other triggers to fire. INSTEAD OF triggers always cause other triggers to fire. There are two important settings to be concerned with:

  - *Database option*—ALTER DATABASE–RECURSIVE_TRIGGERS: When set to ON, when an AFTER trigger modifies the data in the same table, the triggers for that table execute again. This setting is usually set to OFF. Because it's common practice to modify the same table in the trigger, it's assumed that any modifications done in a trigger will meet all business rules for the same table.

  - *Server option*—sp_serveroption–nested triggers: When this setting is set to 1, it indicates that if you modify a different table, that table's trigger will be fired. This setting is usually set to 1, because it allows for data validations to occur in the other tables without coding every business rule again.

- *Having multiple AFTER triggers for the same action*: It's possible to have many different triggers on a table. This is a blessing and a curse. It gives us the ability to add triggers to third-party systems without touching their triggers. However, often the order of triggers can be important, especially when you have to deal with validating data that another trigger might modify. You do get some minor control over the order in which triggers fire. Using the sp_settriggerorder system stored procedure, you can choose the first and the last trigger to fire. Usually this is all you need, as there are places where you want to set the first trigger (often the third-party trigger) and the last trigger (such as a trigger to implement an audit trail, as we do in a later section).

- *Writing multirow validations*: Because triggers fire once for a multirow operation, statements within triggers have to be coded with multiple rows in mind. This can be confusing, because unlike what seems to be natural, trigger code for validations typically needs to look for rows that don't meet your criteria, instead of those that do. Unless you want to force users into entering one row at a time, you have to code your triggers in a way that recognizes that more than one row in the table might be being modified. In the next example, I've built a trigger with two similar validations, and while both work for single rows, only one catches multirow failures.

- *Performance*: When few rows are dealt with in a trigger, they are extremely fast, but as the number of modified rows increases, triggers can become tremendous performance drains. This is largely due to the fact that the inserted and deleted tables aren't "real" tables. Because they don't have indexes, and because the optimizer cannot guess how many rows will be modified each time, the plans chosen for the queries can be fairly optimistic about the number of rows in inserted and deleted tables. Because OLTP systems usually deal with small numbers of rows at a time, there's rarely a major performance hit because of using triggers.

It's worth considering further the implications of multiple row validations, in particular. If you insert a thousand rows, the INSERTED table will have a thousand rows. The DELETED table will remain empty on an insert. When you delete rows, the deleted table is filled, and the inserted table remains empty. For an UPDATE, both tables are filled with the rows in the updated table that had been modified as they appeared before and after the update.

Because multiple rows can be affected, writing validations must take this into consideration. For example, the following typical approach wouldn't be a good idea:

```
SELECT @column1 = column1 FROM INSERTED
IF @column1 < 0
    BEGIN
        --handle the error
```

This is wrong because only a single row would be checked—in this case, the last row that the SELECT statement came to (there's no order, but @column1 would be set to every value in the inserted table). Instead, the proper way to code this would be as follows:

```
If EXISTS (SELECT  *
           FROM    INSERTED
           WHERE   column1 < 0)
    BEGIN
            --handle the error
```

This does work because each row in the inserted table is checked against the criteria. If any rows do match the criteria, the EXISTS Boolean expression returns True, and the error block is started.

You'll see this more in the example triggers. However, you need to make a conscious effort as you start to code triggers to consider what the effect of modifying more than one row would be on your code, because you certainly don't want to miss an invalid value because of coding like the first wrong example.

If you need a full reference on the many details of triggers, refer to SQL Server Books Online. In the following section, we'll look at the different types of triggers, the basics of coding them, and using them to handle the common tasks for which we use triggers. Luckily, for the most part triggers are straightforward, and the basic settings will work just fine.

T-SQL AFTER Triggers

It's important to consider that whatever you're doing with AFTER triggers depends on pre-existing data in your table passing all constraint requirements. For instance, it wouldn't be proper to insert rows in a child table (thereby causing its entire trigger/constraint chain to fire) when the parent's data hasn't been validated. Equally, you wouldn't want to check the status of all the rows in your table until you've completed all your changes to them; the same could be said for cascading delete operations. The five examples that follow are but a small subset of all the possible uses for triggers, but they're representative of the common usages of AFTER triggers.

Before the examples, however, I need to set up the basic structure of the triggers. Each of the examples fits into a trigger (of any type), which is of the following format:

```
CREATE TRIGGER <schema>.<tablename>$<actions>[<purpose>]
ON <schema>.<tablename>
AFTER <comma delimited actions> AS
BEGIN

    DECLARE @rowsAffected int,     --stores the number of rows affected
            @msg varchar(2000)     --used to hold the error message

    SET @rowsAffected = @@rowcount

    --no need to continue on if no rows affected
    IF @rowsAffected = 0 return

    SET NOCOUNT ON --to avoid the rowcount messages
    SET ROWCOUNT 0 --in case the client has modified the rowcount

    BEGIN TRY
            --[validation blocks]
            --[modification blocks]
    END TRY
    BEGIN CATCH
            IF @@trancount > 0
                ROLLBACK TRANSACTION

            --or this will get rolled back
            EXECUTE dbo.ErrorLog$insert

            DECLARE @ERROR_MESSAGE nvarchar(4000)
            SET @ERROR_MESSAGE = ERROR_MESSAGE()
            RAISERROR (@ERROR_MESSAGE,16,1)

    END CATCH
END
```

You'll generally write your triggers so that when the first error occurs, you'll raise an error, and roll back the transaction to halt any further commands. The [validation blocks] section contains the validation logic that will be executed after the DML has been performed on the table. It might look something like this:

```
IF EXISTS (<some condition, commonly using inserted and/or deleted tables>)
    BEGIN
        IF @rowsAffected = 1 --custom error message for single row
            SELECT @msg = '<reason>' + inserted.value
            FROM   inserted -and/or deleted, depending on action
        ELSE
            SELECT @msg = '<more generic reason>'

        --in the TRY . . . CATCH block, this will redirect to the CATCH
        RAISERROR (@msg, 16, 1)
    END
```

The [modification blocks] section contains DML statements to modify the contents of tables. Thanks to the TRY-CATCH block, the code in the [modification block] needn't contain any code other than an INSERT, UPDATE, or DELETE statement. Any errors raised because of the DML (such as from a constraint or another trigger) will be caught and sent to a TRY-CATCH block. In the CATCH block, we use a procedure called dbo.ErrorLog$insert.

The dbo.ErrorLog$insert procedure is used to log the errors that occur in a table, to give you a history of errors that have occurred. The DML for the table and the code for the procedure is as follows:

```
--note, we use dbo here because the ErrorLog will be used by all schemas
CREATE TABLE dbo.ErrorLog(
        ERROR_NUMBER int NOT NULL,
        ERROR_LOCATION sysname NOT NULL,
        ERROR_MESSAGE varchar(4000),
        ERROR_DATE datetime NULL
                    CONSTRAINT dfltErrorLog_error_date  DEFAULT (getdate()),
        ERROR_USER sysname NOT NULL
                    CONSTRAINT dfltErrorLog_error_user_name DEFAULT (user_name())
)
GO
CREATE PROCEDURE dbo.ErrorLog$insert
(
        @ERROR_NUMBER int = NULL,
        @ERROR_LOCATION sysname = NULL,
        @ERROR_MESSAGE varchar(4000) = NULL
) as
 BEGIN
    BEGIN TRY
            INSERT INTO dbo.ErrorLog(ERROR_NUMBER, ERROR_LOCATION, ERROR_MESSAGE)
            SELECT isnull(@ERROR_NUMBER,ERROR_NUMBER()),
```

```
            isnull(@ERROR_LOCATION,ERROR_MESSAGE()),
            isnull(@ERROR_MESSAGE,ERROR_MESSAGE())
    END TRY
    BEGIN CATCH
        INSERT INTO dbo.ErrorLog(ERROR_NUMBER, ERROR_LOCATION, ERROR_MESSAGE)
        VALUES (-100, 'dbo.ErrorLog$insert',
                        'An invalid call was made to the error log procedure')
    END CATCH
END
```

This basic error logging procedure can make it much easier to understand what has gone wrong when a user has an error. Expand your own system to meet your organization's needs, but having an audit trail will prove invaluable when you find out that certain types of errors have been going on for weeks and your users "assumed" you knew about it!

Tip To log errors to the Windows Event Log (which isn't affected by transactions), you can use the xp_logevent extended stored procedure in the error handler. Using this method can be handy if you have deeply nested errors, in which all the dbo.ErrorLog rows get rolled back due to external transactions.

Common Uses for T-SQL AFTER Triggers

In this section, you'll look at how you use triggers to solve problems that are similar to most of the typical uses for AFTER triggers. I'll cover the following topics:

- Range checks on multiple rows

- Cascading inserts

- Child-to-parent cascades

- Relationships that span databases and servers

- Maintaining an audit trail

Range Checks on Multiple Rows

The first type of check we'll look at is the range check, in which we want to make sure that a column is within some specific range of values. You can do range checks using a CHECK constraint to validate the data in a single row (for example that column > 10) quite easily, but you can't use them to validate conditions based on aggregates of multiple rows (sum(column) > 10). You can't do this kind of validation using a CHECK constraint, even if you use UDFs, because CHECK constraints cannot see the newly inserted rows.

If you need to check that a row or set of rows doesn't violate a given condition, such as a maximum sum, you need to use a trigger. As an example, I'll look at a simple accounting system. As users deposit and withdraw money from an account, you need to make sure that the balance never dips below zero. All transactions for a given account have to be considered.

First, we create a schema for the accounting groups:

```
CREATE SCHEMA Accounting
```

Then we create a table for an Account, and then one to contain the activity for the Account:

```
CREATE TABLE Accounting.Account
(
        AccountNumber          char(10) constraint PKAccount primary key
        --would have other columns
)

CREATE TABLE Accounting.AccountActivity
(
        AccountNumber                  char(10)
            constraint Accounting_Account$has$Accounting_AccountActivity
                       foreign key references Accounting.Account(AccountNumber),
        --this might be a value that each ATM/Teller generates
        TransactionNumber      char(20),
        Date                           datetime,
        TransactionAmount      money,
        constraint PKAccountActivity
                       primary key (AccountNumber, TransactionNumber)
)
```

Now we add a trigger to the Accounting.AccountActivity table that checks to make sure that when you sum together the transaction amounts for an Account that the sum is greater than 0:

```
CREATE TRIGGER Accounting.AccountActivity$insertTrigger
ON Accounting.AccountActivity
AFTER INSERT,UPDATE AS
BEGIN
-----------------------------------------------------------------------------
-- Purpose : Trigger on the <action> that fires for any <action> DML
-----------------------------------------------------------------------------
   DECLARE @rowsAffected int,    --stores the number of rows affected
           @msg varchar(2000)    --used to hold the error message

   SET @rowsAffected = @@rowcount

   --no need to continue on if no rows affected
   IF @rowsAffected = 0 return

   SET NOCOUNT ON
   SET ROWCOUNT 0 --in case the client has modified the rowcount

   BEGIN TRY
```

```
        --disallow Transactions that would put balance into negatives
        IF EXISTS ( SELECT AccountNumber
                    FROM Accounting.AccountActivity as AccountActivity
                    WHERE EXISTS (SELECT *
                                  FROM   inserted
                                  WHERE  inserted.AccountNumber =
                                     AccountActivity.AccountNumber)
                    GROUP BY AccountNumber
                    HAVING sum(TransactionAmount) < 0)
          BEGIN
            IF @rowsAffected = 1
                SELECT @msg = 'Account: ' + AccountNumber +
                    ' TransactionNumber:' +
                    cast(TransactionNumber as varchar(36)) +
                    ' for amount: ' + cast(TransactionAmount as varchar(10))+
                    ' cannot be processed as it will cause a negative balance'
                FROM   inserted
            ELSE
              SELECT @msg = 'One of the rows caused a negative balance'
            RAISERROR (@msg, 16, 1)
          END
        END TRY
        BEGIN CATCH
                IF @@trancount > 0
                    ROLLBACK TRANSACTION

                --or this will not get rolled back
                EXECUTE dbo.ErrorLog$insert

                DECLARE @ERROR_MESSAGE varchar(4000)
                SET @ERROR_MESSAGE = ERROR_MESSAGE()
                RAISERROR (@ERROR_MESSAGE,16,1)

        END CATCH
END
```

VIEWING TRIGGER EVENTS

To see the events for which a trigger fires, you can use the following query:

```
SELECT sys.trigger_events.type_desc
FROM sys.trigger_events
        JOIN sys.triggers
                ON sys.triggers.object_id = sys.trigger_events.object_id
WHERE sys.triggers.name = 'AccountActivity$insertTrigger'
```

This returns INSERT and UPDATE in two rows.

The key to using this type of trigger is to look for the existence of rows in the base table, not the rows in the inserted table, because the concern is how the inserted rows affect the overall status for an Account. Take this query, which we'll use to determine if there are rows that fail the criteria:

```
SELECT AccountNumber
FROM Accounting.AccountActivity as AccountActivity
WHERE EXISTS (SELECT *
              FROM    inserted
              WHERE   inserted.AccountNumber = AccountActivity.AccountNumber)
GROUP BY AccountNumber
HAVING sum(TransactionAmount) < 0
```

The key here is that we could remove the bold part of the query, and it would check all rows in the table. The WHERE clause simply makes sure that the only rows we consider are for accounts that have new data inserted. This way, we don't end up checking all rows that we know our query hasn't touched. To see it in action, use this code:

```
--create some set up test data
INSERT into Accounting.Account(AccountNumber)
VALUES ('1111111111')
INSERT  into Accounting.AccountActivity(AccountNumber, TransactionNumber,
                                              Date, TransactionAmount)
VALUES ('1111111111','A0000000000000000001','20050712',100)
INSERT  into Accounting.AccountActivity(AccountNumber, TransactionNumber,
                                              Date, TransactionAmount)
VALUES ('1111111111','A0000000000000000002','20050713',100)
```

Now, let's see what happens when we violate this rule:

```
INSERT  into Accounting.AccountActivity(AccountNumber, TransactionNumber,
                                              Date, TransactionAmount)
VALUES ('1111111111','A0000000000000000003','20050713',-300)
```

Here's the result:

```
Msg 50000, Level 16, State 1, Procedure AccountActivity$insertTrigger, Line 47
Account: 1111111111 TransactionNumber:A0000000000000000002 for amount: -300.00
cannot be processed as it will cause a negative balance

Msg 3609, Level 16, State 1, Line 1
The transaction ended in the trigger. The batch has been aborted.
```

The first error message is the custom error message that we coded in the case where a single row was modified. The second is a message that SQL Server raises, starting in SQL Server 2005, when the batch is halted for a transaction rollback. Now, let's make sure that the trigger works when we have greater than one row in the INSERT statement:

```
--create new Account
INSERT  into Accounting.Account(AccountNumber)
VALUES ('2222222222')

--Now, this data will violate the constraint for the new Account:
INSERT  into Accounting.AccountActivity(AccountNumber, TransactionNumber,
                                        Date, TransactionAmount)
SELECT '1111111111','A0000000000000000004','20050714',100
UNION
SELECT '2222222222','A0000000000000000005','20050715',100
UNION
SELECT '2222222222','A0000000000000000006','20050715',100
UNION
SELECT '2222222222','A0000000000000000007','20050715',-201
```

This causes the following error:

```
Msg 50000, Level 16, State 1, Procedure AccountActivity$insertTrigger, Line 51
One of the rows in the operation caused a negative balance
Msg 3609, Level 16, State 1, Line 6
The transaction ended in the trigger. The batch has been aborted.
```

The multirow error message is much less informative, though you could expand it to include information about a row (or all the rows) that caused the violation. Usually a simple message is sufficient to deal with, because generally if multiple rows are being modified in a single statement, it's a batch process, and the complexity of building error messages is way more than it's worth. Processes would likely be established on how to deal with certain errors being returned.

Tip In the error message, note that the first error states it's from line 51. This is line 51 of the trigger where the error message was raised. This can be valuable information when debugging triggers. Note also that because the ROLLBACK command was used in the trigger, the batch was terminated, this being on line 6 of the batch you're in.

Cascading Inserts

A cascading insert refers to the situation whereby, after a row is inserted into a table, one or more other new rows are automatically inserted into other tables. This is frequently done when you need to initialize a row in another table, quite often a status of some sort.

For this example, we're going to build a small system to store URLs for a website-linking system. During low usage periods, the URLs are connected to, so that they can be verified (hopefully limiting broken links on web pages).

To implement this, I'll use the set of tables in Figure 6-2.

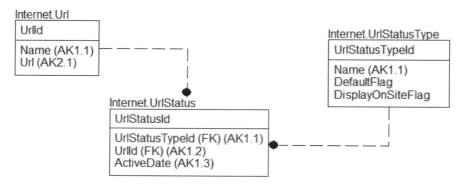

Figure 6-2. *Storing URLs for a website-linking system*

```
CREATE SCHEMA Internet
go
CREATE TABLE Internet.Url
(
    UrlId int not null identity(1,1) constraint PKUrl primary key,
    Name  varchar(60) not null constraint AKUrl_Name UNIQUE,
    Url   varchar(200) not null constraint AKUrl_Url UNIQUE
)

--Not a user manageable table, so not using identity key (as discussed in
--Chapter 5 when I discussed choosing keys) in this one table.  Others are
--using identity-based keys in this example
CREATE TABLE Internet.UrlStatusType
(
        UrlStatusTypeId  int not null constraint PKUrlStatusType PRIMARY KEY,
        Name varchar(20) NOT NULL CONSTRAINT AKUrlStatusType UNIQUE,
        DefaultFlag bit NOT NULL,
        DisplayOnSiteFlag bit NOT NULL
)

CREATE TABLE Internet.UrlStatus
(
        UrlStatusId int not null identity(1,1) CONSTRAINT PKUrlStatus PRIMARY KEY,
        UrlStatusTypeId int NOT NULL
          CONSTRAINT Internet_UrlStatusType$defines_status_type_of$Internet_UrlStatus
                    REFERENCES Internet.UrlStatusType(UrlStatusTypeId),
        UrlId int NOT NULL
           CONSTRAINT internet_Url$has_status_history_in$internet_UrlStatus
                    REFERENCES Internet.Url(UrlId),
        ActiveDate         datetime,
        CONSTRAINT AKUrlStatus_statusUrlDate
                    UNIQUE (UrlStatusTypeId, UrlId, ActiveDate)
)
```

```
--set up status types
INSERT  Internet.UrlStatusType (UrlStatusTypeId, Name,
                                DefaultFlag, DisplayOnSiteFlag)
SELECT 1, 'Unverified',1,0
UNION
SELECT 2, 'Verified',0,1
UNION
SELECT 3, 'Unable to locate',0,0
```

The Url table holds URLs to different sites on the Web. When someone enters a URL, we initialize the status to Unverified. A process should be in place in which the site is checked often to make sure nothing has changed (particularly the unverified ones!).

You begin by building a trigger that inserts a row into the UrlStatus table, on an insert that creates a new row with the UrlId and the default UrlStatusType based on DefaultFlag having the value of 1.

```
CREATE TRIGGER Internet.Url$afterInsert
ON Internet.Url
AFTER INSERT AS
BEGIN

    DECLARE @rowsAffected int,    --stores the number of rows affected
            @msg varchar(2000)    --used to hold the error message

    SET @rowsAffected = @@rowcount

    --no need to continue on if no rows affected
    IF @rowsAffected = 0 return

    SET NOCOUNT ON --to avoid the rowcount messages
    SET ROWCOUNT 0 --in case the client has modified the rowcount

    BEGIN TRY
            --[validation blocks]
            --[modification blocks]

            --add a record to the UrlStatus table to tell it that the new record
            --should start out as the default status
            INSERT INTO Internet.UrlStatus (UrlId, UrlStatusTypeId, ActiveDate)
            SELECT INSERTED.UrlId, UrlStatusType.UrlStatusTypeId,
                    current_timestamp
            FROM INSERTED
                    CROSS JOIN (SELECT UrlStatusTypeId
                                FROM   UrlStatusType
                                WHERE  DefaultFlag = 1) as UrlStatusType
                                            --use cross join with a WHERE clause
                                            --as this is not technically a join
                                            --between INSERTED and UrlType
    END TRY
```

```
     BEGIN CATCH
             IF @@trancount > 0
                 ROLLBACK TRANSACTION

             --or this will not get rolled back
             EXECUTE dbo.ErrorLog$insert

             DECLARE @ERROR_MESSAGE varchar(4000)
             SET @ERROR_MESSAGE = ERROR_MESSAGE()
             RAISERROR (@ERROR_MESSAGE,16,1)

     END CATCH
END
```

The idea here is that for every row in the inserted table, we'll get the single row from the UrlStatusType table that has DefaultFlag equal to 1. So let's try it out:

```
INSERT  into Internet.Url(Name, Url)
VALUES ('More info can be found here','http://spaces.msn.com/members/drsql')

SELECT * FROM Internet.Url
SELECT * FROM Internet.UrlStatus
```

This returns the following results:

UrlId	Name	Url
1	More info can be found here	http://spaces.msn.com/members/drsql

UrlStatusId	UrlStatusTypeId	UrlId	activeDate
1	1	1	2005-07-13

■**Tip** It's easier if users can't modify tables such as the UrlStatusType table, so there cannot be a case where there's no status set as the default (or too many rows). If there was no default status, then the URL would never get used, because the processes wouldn't see it. You could also create a trigger to check to see if more than one row is set to default, but the trigger still doesn't protect you against there being zero rows that are set to default.

Cascading from Child to Parent

All the cascade operations that you can do with constraints (CASCADE or SET NULL) are strictly from parent to child. Sometimes you want to go the other way around and delete the parents of a row when you delete the child. Typically you do this when the child is what you're interested in, and the parent is simply maintained as an attribute of the child. Usually you only want to delete the parent if all children are deleted.

A common (though nondatabase) application of this sort of operation is DLLs registered on a computer. When the last program that refers to the object is uninstalled, the DLL is unregistered and deleted (with a warning message, of course).

In our example, we have a small model of my game collection. I have several game systems, and quite a few games. Often, I have the same game on multiple platforms, so I want to track this fact, especially if I want to go and trade a game that I have on multiple platforms for something else. So we have a table for the GamePlatform (the system) and another for the game. This is a many-to-many relationship, so we have an associative entity called GameInstance. Each of these tables has a delete-cascade relationship, so all instances are removed. What about the games, though? If all GameInstance rows are removed for a given game, then we want to delete the game from the database. The tables are shown in Figure 6-3.

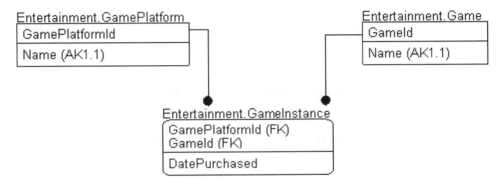

Figure 6-3. *The game tables*

```
--start a schema for entertainment-related tables
CREATE SCHEMA Entertainment
go
CREATE TABLE Entertainment.GamePlatform
(
    GamePlatformId int CONSTRAINT PKGamePlatform PRIMARY KEY,
    Name  varchar(20) CONSTRAINT AKGamePlatform_Name UNIQUE
)
CREATE TABLE Entertainment.Game
(
    GameId  int CONSTRAINT PKGame PRIMARY KEY,
    Name     varchar(20) CONSTRAINT AKGame_Name UNIQUE
    --more details that are common to all platforms
)

--associative entity with cascade relationships back to Game and GamePlatform
CREATE TABLE Entertainment.GameInstance
(
    GamePlatformId int,
    GameId int,
    DatePurchased smalldatetime,
```

```
        CONSTRAINT PKGameInstance PRIMARY KEY (GamePlatformId, GameId),
        CONSTRAINT Entertainment_Game$is_owned_on_platform_by$Entertainment_GameInstance
          FOREIGN KEY (GameId)REFERENCES Entertainment.Game(GameId) ON DELETE CASCADE,
          CONSTRAINT Entertainment_GamePlatform$is_linked_to$Entertainment_GameInstance
          FOREIGN KEY (GamePlatformId)
              REFERENCES Entertainment.GamePlatform(GamePlatformId)
                  ON DELETE CASCADE
)
```

Then I insert a sampling of data:

```
INSERT  into Entertainment.Game (GameId, Name)
VALUES (1,'Super Mario Bros')
INSERT  into Entertainment.Game (GameId, Name)
VALUES (2,'Legend Of Zelda')

INSERT  into Entertainment.GamePlatform(GamePlatformId, Name)
VALUES (1,'Nintendo 64')
INSERT  into Entertainment.GamePlatform(GamePlatformId, Name)
VALUES (2,'GameCube')

INSERT  into Entertainment.GameInstance(GamePlatformId, GameId, DatePurchased)
VALUES (1,1,'20000204')
INSERT  into Entertainment.GameInstance(GamePlatformId, GameId, DatePurchased)
VALUES (1,2,'20030510')
INSERT  into Entertainment.GameInstance(GamePlatformId, GameId, DatePurchased)
VALUES (2,2,'20030404')

--the full outer joins ensure that all rows are returned from all sets, leaving
--nulls where data is missing
SELECT  GamePlatform.Name as Platform, Game.Name as Game, GameInstance.DatePurchased
FROM    Entertainment.Game as Game
            FULL OUTER JOIN Entertainment.GameInstance as GameInstance
                on Game.GameId = GameInstance.GameId
            FULL OUTER JOIN Entertainment.GamePlatform
                on GamePlatform.GamePlatformId = GameInstance.GamePlatformId
```

As you can see, I have two games for Nintendo 64, and only a single one for GameCube.

Platform	Game	DatePurchased
Nintendo 64	Super Mario Bros	2000-02-04 00:00:00
Nintendo 64	Legend Of Zelda	2003-05-10 00:00:00
GameCube	Legend Of Zelda	2003-04-04 00:00:00

So we create a trigger on the table to do the "reverse" cascade operation. Nontemplate code is bolded:

```
CREATE TRIGGER Entertainment.GameInstance$delete
ON Entertainment.GameInstance
FOR delete AS
BEGIN

    DECLARE @rowsAffected int,     --stores the number of rows affected
            @msg varchar(2000)     --used to hold the error message

    SET @rowsAffected = @@rowcount

    --no need to continue on if no rows affected
    IF @rowsAffected = 0 return

    SET NOCOUNT ON --to avoid the rowcount messages
    SET ROWCOUNT 0 --in case the client has modified the rowcount

    BEGIN TRY
            --[validation blocks]

            --[modification blocks]
            --delete all Games
            DELETE Game        --where the GameInstance was delete
            WHERE  GameId in (SELECT deleted.GameId
                              FROM    deleted     --and there are no GameInstances left
                              WHERE   not exists (SELECT  *
                                                  FROM    GameInstance
                                                  WHERE   GameInstance.GameId =
                                                                   deleted.GameId))
    END TRY
    BEGIN CATCH
            IF @@trancount > 0
                ROLLBACK TRANSACTION

            --or this will not get rolled back
            EXECUTE dbo.ErrorLog$insert

            DECLARE @ERROR_MESSAGE varchar(4000)
            SET @ERROR_MESSAGE = ERROR_MESSAGE()
            RAISERROR (@ERROR_MESSAGE,16,1)

    END CATCH
END
```

It's as straightforward as that. Just delete the games, and let the error handler cover the rest. Delete the row for the GameCube:

```
DELETE  Entertainment.GamePlatform
WHERE   GamePlatformId = 1
go
SELECT  GamePlatform.Name as platform, Game.Name as Game, GameInstance.DatePurchased
FROM    Entertainment.Game as Game
            FULL OUTER JOIN Entertainment.GameInstance as GameInstance
                on Game.GameId = GameInstance.GameId
            FULL OUTER JOIN Entertainment.GamePlatform
                on GamePlatform.GamePlatformId = GameInstance.GamePlatformId
```

You can see that now we only have a single row in the Game table:

platform	Game	DatePurchased
GameCube	Legend Of Zelda	2003-04-04 00:00:00

Relationships That Span Databases and Servers

Prior to constraints, all relationships were enforced by triggers. Now, only special cases need to be coded using triggers. A common example is when you have relationships between tables that are on different databases. I have used this sort of thing when I had a common demographics database that many different systems used.

To implement a relationship using triggers, you need several triggers:

- Parent:

  - UPDATE: Make sure that you cannot change the primary key to something that doesn't match the child rows.

  - DELETE: Prevent deleting rows that have associated parent rows.

- Child:

  - INSERT: Check to make sure the key exists in the parent table.

  - UPDATE: Check to make sure the "possibly" changed key exists in the parent table.

Instead of coding full triggers for this example, I'm going to present a few templates to use to build these triggers. For these snippets of code, I refer to the tables as parent and child, with no schema or database named. Replacing the bits that are inside these greater than and less than symbols with appropriate code and tablenames that include the database and schema gives you the desired result, when plugged into the trigger templates we've been using throughout this chapter.

Parent Update

Note that you can omit the parent update step if using surrogate keys based on identity property columns, because they aren't editable.

```
IF update(<parent_key_columns>)
   BEGIN
        IF EXISTS ( SELECT  *
                    FROM    deleted
                                JOIN <child>
                                    on <child>.<parent_key> = deleted.<parent_key>
                   )
        BEGIN
           IF @rowsAffected = 1
                  SELECT @msg = 'one row message' + inserted.somedata
                  FROM   inserted
                ELSE
                  SELECT @msg = 'multi-row message'
              RAISERROR (@msg, 16, 1)
        END
   END
```

Parent Delete

Here's the code to prevent deleting rows that have associated parent rows:

```
if exists ( SELECT   *
            FROM     deleted
                         JOIN <child>
                             ON <child>.<parent_key> = deleted.<parent_key>
          )
   BEGIN
       IF @rowsAffected = 1
           SELECT @msg = 'one row message' + inserted.somedata
           FROM   inserted
       ELSE
           SELECT @msg = 'multi-row message'
       RAISERROR (@msg, 16, 1)
    END
  END
```

Child Insert and Child Update

Now, let's look at triggers on child tables:

```
--@numrows is part of the standard template
DECLARE @nullcnt int,
        @validcnt int

IF update(<parent_key>)
  BEGIN
     --omit this check if nulls are not allowed
     SELECT  @nullcnt = count(*)
     FROM    inserted
     WHERE   inserted.<parent_key> is null
```

```
          --does not include null values
          SELECT  @validcnt = count(*)
          FROM    inserted
                    JOIN <parent> as Parent
                         ON  inserted.<parent_key> = Parent.<parent_key>

      if @validcnt + @nullcnt != @numrows
        BEGIN
            IF @rowsAffected = 1
              SELECT @msg = 'The inserted <parent_key_name>: '
                              + cast(parent_key as varchar(10))
                              + ' is not valid in the parent table.'
                FROM    INSERTED
            ELSE
                SELECT @msg = 'Invalid <parent key> in the inserted rows.'
              RAISERROR (@msg, 16, 1)
        END
  END
```

Using basic blocks of code such as these, you can validate most any foreign key relationship using triggers. For example, say you have a table in your PhoneData database called Logs.Call, with a primary key of CallId. In the CRM database, you have a Contacts.Journal table that stores contacts made to a person. To implement the child update and insert a trigger, just fill in the blanks. (I've bolded the parts of the code where I've replaced the tags with the text specific to this trigger.)

```
CREATE TRIGGER Contacts.Journal$afterInsert
ON Contacts.Journal
AFTER INSERT, UPDATE AS
BEGIN

    DECLARE @rowsAffected int,    --stores the number of rows affected
            @msg varchar(2000)    --used to hold the error message

    SET @rowsAffected = @@rowcount

    --no need to continue on if no rows affected
    IF @rowsAffected = 0 return

    SET NOCOUNT ON --to avoid the rowcount messages
    SET ROWCOUNT 0 --in case the client has modified the rowcount

    BEGIN TRY
        --[validation blocks]
        --@numrows is part of the standard template
        DECLARE @nullcnt int,
                @validcnt int
```

```
        IF update(CallId)
         BEGIN
            --omit this check if nulls are not allowed (left in here for an example)
            SELECT  @nullcnt = count(*)
            FROM    inserted
            WHERE   inserted.CallId is null

            --does not include null values
            SELECT  @validcnt = count(*)
            FROM    inserted
                        JOIN PhoneData.Logs.Call as Parent
                            ON  inserted.CallId = Parent.CallId

           if @validcnt + @nullcnt <> @numrows
             BEGIN
                IF @rowsAffected = 1
                    SELECT @msg = 'The inserted CallId: '
                                    + cast(CallId as varchar(10))
                                    + ' is not valid in the'
                                    + ' PhoneData.Logs.Call table.'
                        FROM    INSERTED
                    ELSE
                        SELECT @msg = 'Invalid CallId in the inserted rows.'
                    RAISERROR (@msg, 16, 1)
            END
         END
         --[modification blocks]

    END TRY
    BEGIN CATCH
            IF @@trancount > 0
                ROLLBACK TRANSACTION

            --or this will not get rolled back
            EXECUTE dbo.ErrorLog$insert

            DECLARE @ERROR_MESSAGE varchar(4000)
            SET @ERROR_MESSAGE = ERROR_MESSAGE()
            RAISERROR (@ERROR_MESSAGE,16,1)

    END CATCH
END
```

Maintaining an Audit Trail

A common task that's implemented using triggers is the audit trail or audit log. You use it to record previous versions of rows or columns so you can determine who changed a given row. Often an audit trail is simply for documentation purposes, so we can go back to other users and ask why they made a change.

The audit trail can be straightforward to implement using triggers. In our example, we'll build an employee table, and audit any change to the table. I'll keep it simple and have a copy of the table that has a few extra columns for the date and time of the change, plus the user who made the change, and what the change was.

We implement an employee table (using names with underscores just to add variety), and then a replica to store changes into:

```
CREATE SCHEMA hr
go
CREATE TABLE hr.employee
(
    employee_id char(6) CONSTRAINT PKemployee PRIMARY KEY,
    first_name  varchar(20),
    last_name   varchar(20),
    salary      money
)
CREATE TABLE hr.employee_auditTrail
(
    employee_id             char(6),
    date_changed            datetime not null --default so we don't have to code for it
            CONSTRAINT DfltHr_employee_date_changed DEFAULT (current_timestamp),
    first_name              varchar(20),
    last_name               varchar(20),
    salary                  money,
    --the following are the added columns to the original structure of hr.employee
    action                  char(6)
            CONSTRAINT ChkHr_employee_action --we don't log inserts, only changes
                                CHECK(action in ('delete','update')),
    changed_by_user_name sysname
            CONSTRAINT DfltHr_employee_changed_by_user_name
                                DEFAULT (suser_sname()),
    CONSTRAINT PKemployee_auditTrail PRIMARY KEY (employee_id, date_changed)
)
```

Now we create a trigger with code to determine if it's an UPDATE or a DELETE, based on how many rows are in the inserted table:

```
CREATE TRIGGER hr.employee$insertAndDeleteAuditTrail
ON hr.employee
AFTER UPDATE, DELETE AS
BEGIN

    DECLARE @rowsAffected int,    --stores the number of rows affected
            @msg varchar(2000)    --used to hold the error message
```

```
    SET @rowsAffected = @@rowcount

--no need to continue on if no rows affected
IF @rowsAffected = 0 return

SET NOCOUNT ON --to avoid the rowcount messages
SET ROWCOUNT 0 --in case the client has modified the rowcount
BEGIN TRY
        --[validation blocks]
        --[modification blocks]
        --since we are only doing update and delete, we just
        --need to see if there are any rows
        --inserted to determine what action is being done.
        DECLARE @action char(6)
        SET @action = case when (SELECT count(*) from inserted) > 0
                        then 'update' else 'delete' end

        --since the deleted table contains all changes, we just insert all
        --of the rows in the deleted table and we are done.
        INSERT employee_auditTrail (employee_id, first_name, last_name,
                                salary, action)
        SELECT employee_id, first_name, last_name, salary, @action
        FROM    deleted

END TRY
BEGIN CATCH
        IF @@trancount > 0
            ROLLBACK TRANSACTION

        --or this will not get rolled back
        EXECUTE dbo.ErrorLog$insert

        DECLARE @ERROR_MESSAGE varchar(4000)
        SET @ERROR_MESSAGE = ERROR_MESSAGE()
        RAISERROR (@ERROR_MESSAGE,16,1)

    END CATCH
END
```

We create some data:

```
INSERT hr.employee (employee_id, first_name, last_name, salary)
VALUES (1, 'joe','schmo',10000)
```

Now, much unlike the real world in which we live, the person gets a raise immediately (though a salary of 11,000 American dollars is still not exactly an invitation to dance any sort of jig!):

```
UPDATE hr.employee
SET salary = salary * 1.10 --ten percent raise!
WHERE employee_id = 1
SELECT *
FROM   hr.employee
```

This returns the data with the new values:

employee_id	first_name	last_name	salary
1	joe	schmo	11000.00

Check the audit trail table:

```
SELECT *
FROM   hr.employee_auditTrail
```

You can see that the previous values for the row are stored here:

employee_id	first_name	last_name	salary	action
1	joe	schmo	10000.00	update

date_changed	changed_by_user_name
2005-05-01 13:58:11.847	DOMAIN\DRSQL

This is a cheap and effective auditing system for many smaller systems. If you have a lot of columns, it can be better to check and see which columns have changed, and implement a table that has tablename, columnname, and previous value columns, but often this simple strategy works quite well when the volume is low and the number of tables to audit isn't large. Keeping only recent history in the audit trail table helps as well.

INSTEAD OF Triggers

As alluded to in the beginning of this fairly long section of the book, INSTEAD OF triggers happen before the DML action, rather than after it. In fact, when you have an INSTEAD OF trigger on a table, it's the first thing that's done when you INSERT, UPDATE, or DELETE from a table. These triggers are named INSTEAD OF because they fire *instead of* the native action the user executed. Inside the trigger, you need to perform the action that the user performed. One thing that makes these triggers useful is that you can use them on views to make noneditable views editable. Doing this, you encapsulate calls to all the affected tables in the trigger, much like you would a stored procedure, except now this view has all the properties of a physical table, hiding the actual implementation from users.

One of the more obvious limitations of INSTEAD OF triggers is that you can only have one for each action (INSERT, UPDATE, and DELETE) on the table, or you can combine them just like you can for AFTER triggers. We'll use the same trigger template that we used for the T-SQL AFTER triggers, with only slight modifications (**bolded** for your reading pleasure):

```
CREATE TRIGGER <schema>.<tablename>$InsteadOf<actions>[<purpose>]
ON <schema>.<tablename>
INSTEAD OF <comma delimited actions> AS
BEGIN

    DECLARE @rowsAffected int,      --stores the number of rows affected
            @msg varchar(2000)      --used to hold the error message

    SET @rowsAffected = @@rowcount

    --no need to continue on if no rows affected
    IF @rowsAffected = 0 return

    SET NOCOUNT ON --to avoid the rowcount messages
    SET ROWCOUNT 0 --in case the client has modified the rowcount

    BEGIN TRY
            --[validation blocks]
            --[modification blocks]
            --<perform action>
    END TRY
    BEGIN CATCH
                IF @@trancount > 0
                    ROLLBACK TRANSACTION

                --or this will not get rolled back
                EXECUTE dbo.ErrorLog$insert

                DECLARE @ERROR_MESSAGE nvarchar(4000)
                SET @ERROR_MESSAGE = ERROR_MESSAGE()
                RAISERROR (@ERROR_MESSAGE,16,1)

    END CATCH
END
```

Initially, the most annoying part of the INSTEAD OF trigger is that you have to perform the operation yourself. It's obvious why this is, but it can be problematic if you need to add one to a table that has an INSTEAD OF trigger delivered by a third party (though it is pretty rare). This is the purpose of the <perform action> addition. Technically we could call the <perform action> addition optional, because in one of our examples we'll demonstrate how to use INSTEAD OF triggers to prevent a DML operation from occurring altogether.

INSTEAD OF triggers are most often used to set or modify values in your statements automatically before they're validated by constraints or AFTER triggers. It's generally a best practice not to use INSTEAD OF triggers to do validations, and only to use them to shape the way the data is seen by the time it's stored in the DBMS. There's one slight alteration to this. We can use

INSTEAD OF triggers to prevalidate data such that it's never subject to constraints or AFTER triggers. We'll see an example of this later in the chapter, as well.

I'll demonstrate four ways you can use INSTEAD OF triggers:

- Automatically maintained columns

- Formatting user input

- Redirecting invalid data to an exception table

- Forcing no action to be performed on a table, even by someone who technically has proper rights

Automatically Maintaining Columns

An INSTEAD OF trigger is an ideal way to handle "implementation-only" columns—those that aren't strictly part of the data model, but that are there to track database usage. Good examples of this are columns to indicate when a row was created, and by whom, as shown in Figure 6-4. In the following example code, we'll use an INSTEAD OF trigger to capture the time and user who originally created the row.

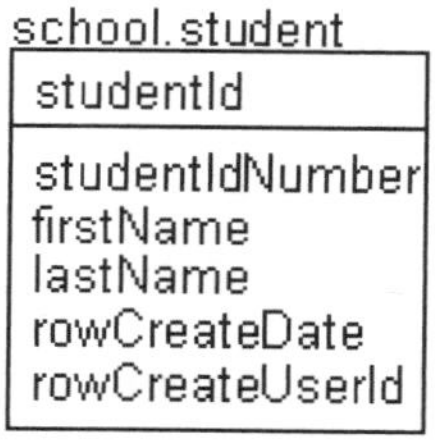

Figure 6-4. *A table that tracks database usage*

```
CREATE SCHEMA school
Go
CREATE TABLE school.student
(
       studentId       int identity not null CONSTRAINT PKschool_student PRIMARY KEY,
       studentIdNumber char(8) not null
            CONSTRAINT AKschool_student_studentIdNumber UNIQUE,
       firstName       varchar(20) not null,
       lastName        varchar(20) not null,
--Note that we add these columns to the implementation model, not to the logical
--model. These columns do not actually refer to the student being modeled, they are
--required simply to help with programming and tracking.
       rowCreateDate   datetime not null
            CONSTRAINT dfltSchool_student_rowCreateDate
                              DEFAULT (current_timestamp),
       rowCreateUser   sysname not null
            CONSTRAINT dfltSchool_student_rowCreateUser DEFAULT (current_user)
)
```

Note that we include default values so the consumer of this table doesn't need to include the columns in INSERT or UPDATE statements. Next we code the trigger to set these values automatically for us:

```
CREATE TRIGGER school.student$insteadOfInsert
ON school.student
INSTEAD OF INSERT AS
BEGIN

    DECLARE @rowsAffected int,     --stores the number of rows affected
            @msg varchar(2000)     --used to hold the error message


    SET @rowsAffected = @@rowcount

    --no need to continue on if no rows affected
    IF @rowsAffected = 0 return

    SET ROWCOUNT 0 --in case the client has modified the rowcount
    SET NOCOUNT ON --to avoid the rowcount messages

    BEGIN TRY
            --[validation blocks]
            --[modification blocks]
            --<perform action>
            INSERT INTO school.student(studentIdNumber, firstName, lastName,
                                    rowCreateDate, rowCreateUser)
            SELECT studentIdNumber, firstName, lastName,
                                    current_timestamp, suser_sname()
            FROM  inserted    --no matter what the user put in the inserted row
    END TRY           --when the row was created, these values will be inserted
    BEGIN CATCH
            IF @@trancount > 0
                ROLLBACK TRANSACTION

            --or this will not get rolled back
            EXECUTE dbo.ErrorLog$insert

            DECLARE @ERROR_MESSAGE nvarchar(4000)
            SET @ERROR_MESSAGE = ERROR_MESSAGE()
            RAISERROR (@ERROR_MESSAGE,16,1)

    END CATCH
END
```

Next, we try inserting some data:

```
INSERT  into school.student(studentIdNumber, firstName, lastName)
VALUES ( '0000001','Leroy', 'Brown' )
```

■Tip If we were to run SELECT scope_identity(), it would return NULL (because the actual insert was out of scope). Instead of scope_identity(), use the alternate key instead, in this case the studentIdNumber that equals '0000001'. You might also want to forgo using an IDENTITY value for a surrogate key in the case where another suitable candidate key can be found for that table. We have this situation later, when we look at updating views and subclasses. In that case, I choose to use a plain integer for the key.

Next, we can look at the values:

```
SELECT * FROM school.student
```

You can see that the rowCreateDate and rowCreateUser have been set automatically:

studentId	studentIdNumber	firstName	lastName
1	0000001	Leroy	Brown

rowCreateDate	rowCreateUser
2005-05-07 23:29:27.230	DOMAIN\username

This, you say, would have been the result without us adding the trigger, right? Yes, but what if the newbie programmer didn't realize that the default would take care of this for you, and just put whatever value into the INSERT for the rowCreateDate and rowCreateUser?

```
INSERT  school.student(studentIdNumber, firstName, lastName, rowCreateDate,
                       rowCreateUser)
VALUES ( '000002','Green', 'Jeans','99990101','some user' )
```

Without the trigger, horrible dates would be inserted, but because we have the INSTEAD OF trigger, the correct creation information is stored as follows:

studentId	studentIdNumber	firstName	lastName
1	0000001	Leroy	Brown
2	0000002	Green	Jeans

rowCreateDate	rowCreateUser
2005-05-07 23:29:27.230	DOMAIN\username
2005-05-07 23:30:25.243	DOMAIN\username

It put the actual date when I was working on the book, rather than allowing the data that was entered by the client. This is especially useful when you have users working in multiple time zones, because allowing the client to send the creation information would then require each client to translate the time to some time zone, possibly using Coordinated Universal Time (UTC).

From here, it's pretty easy to see that we could also add an UPDATE INSTEAD OF trigger that would fire on every UPDATE to keep up with the last user to modify the values in the table. Some people prefer to use columns like this, instead of using a column of the type rowversion. I generally end up having both pieces of information in most implemented tables, as I prefer the rowversion mechanism for optimistic locking. However, knowing the last user to modify the row and when that person modified it are often handy pieces of information.

Formatting User Input

Consider the columns firstName and lastName. (I took care to enter the data with a proper case, such that it looks good.) What if the users who were entering this were heads-down, paid-by-the-keystroke kinds of users? Would we want them to go back and futz around with "joHnson" and make sure that it was formatted "Johnson"? Or what about data received from services that still use mainframes, in which lower case letters are still considered a work of the underlord? We don't want to have to make anyone (even an intern) go in and reformat the data by hand.

A good place for this kind of operation is a trigger, often using a function to handle the formatting. Here I'll present them both in their basic state, generally capitalizing the first letter of each word. (This way, we can handle names that have two parts, such as "Von Smith," or other more reasonable names that are found in reality.) I'll build a schema to contain my functions for utility purposes, and build the function in it. The crux of the function is that I'm simply capitalizing the first character of every letter after a space. The function needs to be updated to handle special cases, such as "McDonald." I'm adding a schema that I'll put in all my databases that I build to hold generic functions that don't pertain specifically to any other.

I'll present two solutions to the function to do the formatting, one in T-SQL, the other in CLR. The CLR is preferred, but the T-SQL example is just in case you don't have access to the tools to build CLR functions. After this, I'll add this formatting code to the trigger from the previous section.

T-SQL Version

The first version of this code uses T-SQL. The syntax hasn't changed since SQL Server 2000, though Microsoft did get a bit more lenient on what you're allowed to call from a function, such as CURRENT_TIMESTAMP—the standard version of GETDATE()—which was one of the most requested changes to functions in SQL Server 2000.

```
CREATE SCHEMA Functions
Go

--tsql version
CREATE FUNCTION Functions.TitleCase
(
    @inputString varchar(2000)
)
RETURNS varchar(2000) AS
BEGIN
    -- set the whole string to lower
    SET @inputString = LOWER(@inputstring)
    -- then use stuff to replace the first character
```

```
    SET @inputString =
    --STUFF in the uppercased character in to the next character,
    --replacing the lowercased letter
    STUFF(@inputString,1,1,UPPER(SUBSTRING(@inputString,1,1)))

    --@i is for the loop counter, initialized to 2
    DECLARE @i int
    SET @i = 1

    --loop from the second character to the end of the string
    WHILE @i < LEN(@inputString)
    BEGIN
        --if the character is a space
        IF SUBSTRING(@inputString,@i,1) = ' '
        BEGIN
            --STUFF in the uppercased character into the next character
            SET @inputString = STUFF(@inputString,@i +
            1,1,UPPER(SUBSTRING(@inputString,@i + 1,1)))
        END
        --increment the loop counter
        SET @i = @i + 1
    END
    RETURN @inputString
END
```

CLR Version

This next code is the CLR version, which is likely the best way to go for a pure string manipulation function (assuming that you're allowed to use CLR functions on your server, as some DBAs might be hesitant to allow the CLR to be used at all). What makes using the CLR nice is that it uses functionality built into .NET to format strings with little effort.

```
--Contains only the bare necessities. You will want to use some of the framework
--items to set object properties.
Imports System
Imports System.Data
Imports System.Data.Sql
Imports System.Data.SqlTypes
Imports System.Reflection
Imports Microsoft.SqlServer.Server

Public Class UserDefinedFunctions

    <SqlFunction(IsDeterministic:=True, DataAccess:=DataAccessKind.None,
                                        Name:="TitleCase", IsPrecise:=True)> _
    Public Shared Function ProperCase(ByVal inputString As SqlString) As SqlString
```

```
        Return New SqlString(System.Threading.Thread.CurrentThread.CurrentCulture. _
                TextInfo.ToTitleCase(inputString.ToString().ToLower()))

    End Function

End Class
```

Compile and then declare (or let VS.NET do the deployment for you):

```
CREATE ASSEMBLY TitleCaseUDF_demo
AUTHORIZATION dbo  --this is a user, not a schema
FROM '<directory>\TitleCaseUDF_demo.DLL'
WITH PERMISSION_SET = SAFE
go

CREATE FUNCTION Functions.TitleCase(@inputString nvarchar(4000))
RETURNS nvarchar(4000) WITH EXECUTE AS CALLER
AS
EXTERNAL NAME TitleCaseUDF_demo.TitleCaseUDF_demo.UserDefinedFunctions.TitleCase
```

The Example Trigger

Now we can alter our trigger from the last section, which was used to set the rowCreateDate
rowCreate user for the school.student table. This time you'll modify the trigger to title-case
the name of the student. The changes are in **bold**:

```
ALTER TRIGGER school.student$insteadOfInsert
ON school.student
INSTEAD OF INSERT AS
BEGIN

    DECLARE @rowsAffected int,    --stores the number of rows affected
            @msg varchar(2000)    --used to hold the error message

    SET @rowsAffected = @@rowcount

    --no need to continue on if no rows affected
    IF @rowsAffected = 0 return

    SET ROWCOUNT 0 --in case the client has modified the rowcount
    SET NOCOUNT ON --to avoid the rowcount messages

    BEGIN TRY
            --[validation blocks]
            --[modification blocks]
            --<perform action>
            INSERT INTO school.student(studentIdNumber, firstName, lastName,
                                        rowCreateDate, rowCreateUser)
```

```
            SELECT studentIdNumber, Functions.titleCase(firstName),
                            Functions.TitleCase(lastName),
                                current_timestamp, suser_sname()
        FROM  inserted   --no matter what the user put in the inserted row
    END TRY              --when the row was created, these values will be inserted
    BEGIN CATCH

            IF @@trancount > 0
                ROLLBACK TRANSACTION

            --or this will not get rolled back
            EXECUTE dbo.ErrorLog$insert

            DECLARE @ERROR_MESSAGE nvarchar(4000)
            SET @ERROR_MESSAGE = ERROR_MESSAGE()
            RAISERROR (@ERROR_MESSAGE,16,1)


      END CATCH
END
```

Then insert a new row with funky formatted data:

```
INSERT school.student(studentIdNumber, firstName, lastName)
VALUES ( '0000007','CaPtain', 'von kaNGAroo')

SELECT *
FROM school.student
```

Now you see that this data has been formatted:

studentId	studentIdNumber	firstName	lastName
1	0000001	Leroy	Brown
2	0000002	Green	Jeans
3	0000003	Captain	Von Kangaroo

rowCreateDate	rowCreateUser
2005-05-07 23:9:27.230	DOMAIN\username
2005-05-07 23:30:25.243	DOMAIN\username
2005-05-08 15:31:07.887	DOMAIN\username

I'll leave it to you to modify this trigger for the UPDATE version, as there are few differences, other than updating the row rather than INSERTing it.

Redirecting Invalid Data to an Exception Table

On some occasions, instead of returning an error when an invalid value is set for a column, you simply want to ignore it, and log that an error had occurred. Generally this wouldn't be used for bulk-loading data, but some examples of why to do this might be as follows:

- *Heads-down key entry*: In many shops where customer feedback or payments are received by the hundreds or thousands, there are people who open the mail, read it, and key in what's on the page. These people become incredibly skilled in rapid entry, and generally make few mistakes. The mistakes they do make don't raise an error on their screen; rather, it falls to other people—exception handlers—to fix. You could use an INSTEAD OF trigger to redirect the wrong data to an exception table to be handled later.

- *Values that are read in from devices*: An example of this is on an assembly line, where a reading is taken but is so far out of range it couldn't be true, due to malfunction of a device, or just a human moving a sensor. Too many exception rows would require a look at the equipment, but only a few might be normal and acceptable.

For our example, I'll design a table to take weather readings from a single thermometer. Sometimes this thermometer sends back bad values that are impossible. We need to be able to put in readings, sometimes many at a time, as the device can cache results for some time if there is signal loss, but tosses off the unlikely rows.

We build the following table, initially using a constraint to implement the simple sanity check. In the analysis of the data, we might find anomalies, but in this process all we're going to do is look for the "impossible" cases:

```
CREATE SCHEMA Measurements
go
CREATE TABLE Measurements.WeatherReading
(
    WeatherReadingId int identity
            CONSTRAINT PKWeatherReading PRIMARY KEY,
    Date            datetime
                        CONSTRAINT AKWeatherReading_Date UNIQUE,
    Temperature     float CONSTRAINT chkNews_WeatherReading_Temperature
                                CHECK(Temperature between -80 and 120)
)
```

Then we go to load the data, simulating what we might do when importing the data all at once:

```
INSERT  into Measurements.WeatherReading (Date, Temperature)
SELECT '20050101 0:00',88.00
UNION ALL
SELECT '20050101 0:01',88.22
UNION ALL
SELECT '20050101 0:02',6000.32
UNION ALL
SELECT '20050101 0:03',89.22
UNION ALL
SELECT '20050101 0:04',90.01
```

As we know with CHECK constraints, this isn't going to fly:

```
Msg 547, Level 16, State 0, Line 5
The INSERT statement conflicted with the CHECK constraint
"chkNews_WeatherReading_Temperature". The conflict occurred in database
"ProtectionChapter", table "WeatherReading", column 'Temperature'.
The statement has been terminated.
```

Select all the data in the table, and you'll see that this data never gets entered. Does this mean we have to go through every row individually? Yes, in the current scheme, but if you've been following along, you know we're going to write an INSTEAD OF trigger to do this for us. Note that we won't check for duplicated data. For this, we do want a big, grand error message to slap the users' wrist, letting them know they're doing something wrong. In this case, we aren't looking at a *wrong* operation, just data that doesn't match reality.

First we add a table to hold the exceptions to the Temperature rule:

```
CREATE TABLE Measurements.WeatherReading_exception
(
    WeatherReadingId int identity
                CONSTRAINT PKWeatherReading_exception PRIMARY KEY,
    Date            datetime,
    Temperature     float
)
```

Then we create the trigger:

```
CREATE TRIGGER Measurements.WeatherReading$InsteadOfInsert
ON Measurements.WeatherReading
INSTEAD OF INSERT AS
BEGIN

    DECLARE @rowsAffected int,     --stores the number of rows affected
            @msg varchar(2000)     --used to hold the error message

    SET @rowsAffected = @@rowcount

    --no need to continue on if no rows affected
    IF @rowsAffected = 0 return

    SET NOCOUNT ON --to avoid the rowcount messages
    SET ROWCOUNT 0 --in case the client has modified the rowcount

    BEGIN TRY
            --[validation blocks]
            --BAD data
            INSERT Measurements.WeatherReading_exception (Date, Temperature)
            SELECT Date, Temperature
            FROM   inserted
            WHERE  NOT(Temperature between -80 and 120)
```

```
        --[modification blocks]
        --<perform action>
         --GOOD data
        INSERT Measurements.WeatherReading (Date, Temperature)
        SELECT Date, Temperature
        FROM    inserted
        WHERE   (Temperature between -80 and 120)
    END TRY
    BEGIN CATCH
            IF @@trancount > 0
                ROLLBACK TRANSACTION

            --or this will not get rolled back
            EXECUTE dbo.ErrorLog$insert

            DECLARE @ERROR_MESSAGE nvarchar(4000)
            SET @ERROR_MESSAGE = ERROR_MESSAGE()
            RAISERROR (@ERROR_MESSAGE,16,1)

      END CATCH
END
```

Now we try to insert the rows with the bad data still in there:

```
INSERT  into Measurements.WeatherReading (Date, Temperature)
SELECT '20050101 0:00',88.00
UNION ALL
SELECT '20050101 0:01',88.22
UNION ALL
SELECT '20050101 0:02',6000.32
UNION ALL
SELECT '20050101 0:03',89.22
UNION ALL
SELECT '20050101 0:04',90.01
go

SELECT *
FROM Measurements.WeatherReading
```

The good data is in the following output:

WeatherReading	Date	Temperature
6	2005-01-01 00:00:00.000	88
7	2005-01-01 00:01:00.000	88.22
8	2005-01-01 00:03:00.000	89.22
9	2005-01-01 00:04:00.000	90.01

The nonconformant (if you want to impress someone, otherwise "bad") data can be seen by viewing the data in the exception table:

```
SELECT *
FROM   Measurements.WeatherReading_exception
```

This returns the following result:

WeatherReadingId	Date	Temperature
1	2005-01-01 00:02:00.000	6000.32

Now, it might be possible to go back and work on the exceptions, perhaps extrapolating the value it should have been, based on the previous and the next measurements taken:

```
(88.22 + 89.22) /2 = 88.72?
```

Forcing No Action to Be Performed on a Table

Our final INSTEAD OF trigger example deals with what's almost a security issue. Often users have *too* much access, and this includes administrators who generally use sysadmin privileges to look for problems with systems. Some tables we simply don't ever want to be modified. We might implement triggers to keep any user—even a system administrator—from changing the data. We'll again look at something along these lines when we get to Chapter 7, because we can implement row-level security using this method as well.

In this example, we're going to implement a table to hold the version of the database. It's a single-row "table" that behaves more like a global variable. It's here to tell the application which version of the schema to expect, so it can tell the user to upgrade or lose functionality:

```
CREATE SCHEMA System
go
CREATE TABLE System.Version
(
    DatabaseVersion varchar(10)
)
INSERT  into System.Version (DatabaseVersion)
VALUES ('1.0.12')
```

Our application always looks to this value to see what objects it expects to be there when it uses them. We clearly don't want this value to get modified, even if someone has db_owner rights in the database. So we might apply an INSTEAD OF trigger:

```
CREATE TRIGGER System.Version$InsteadOfInsertUpdateDelete
ON System.Version
INSTEAD OF INSERT, UPDATE, DELETE AS
BEGIN

    DECLARE @rowsAffected int,     --stores the number of rows affected
            @msg varchar(2000)     --used to hold the error message
```

```
    SET @rowsAffected = @@rowcount

    --no need to complain if no rows affected
    IF @rowsAffected = 0 return

    --No error handling necessary, just the message.  We just don't do the action.
    RAISERROR
        ('The System.Version table may not be modified in production',
          16,1)
END
```

Attempts to delete the value

```
delete system.version
```

result in the following:

```
Msg 50000, Level 16, State 1, Procedure version$InsteadOfInsertUpdateDelete, Line 15
The system.version table may not be modified in production
```

The users, if they had permissions, would then have to take the conscious step of running the following code:

```
ALTER TABLE system.version
    DISABLE TRIGGER version$InsteadOfInsertUpdateDelete
```

This code enables the trigger to "close the gate," keeping the data safely in the table, even from accidental changes.

Handing Errors from Triggers

The last thing to consider about triggers is how you need to deal with the error handling done in the trigger templates. One of the drawbacks to using triggers is that the state of the database after a trigger error is different from when you have a constraint error. SQL Server 2005 complicates this even more, though in a good way.

In previous versions of SQL Server, doing error handling for triggers was easy. Error in trigger, everything stops in its tracks. Now this has changed. We need to consider two situations when we do a ROLLBACK in a trigger, using an error handler such as we have in this chapter:

- *You aren't using a* TRY-CATCH *block*: This situation is simple. The batch stops processing in its tracks. SQL Server handles cleanup for any transaction you were in.

- *You* are *using a* TRY-CATCH *block*: This situation can be a bit tricky.

Take a TRY-CATCH block, such as this one:

```
BEGIN TRY
        <DML STATEMENT>
END TRY
BEGIN CATCH
        <handle it>
END CATCH
```

If the T-SQL trigger rolls back and an error is raised, when you get to the `<handle it>` block, you won't be in a transaction. For CLR triggers, you're in charge of whether the connection ends or not. When a `CHECK` constraint causes the error, or executes a simple `RAISERROR`, then you'll be in a transaction. Generically, here's the `CATCH` block that I use (making use of the objects we've already been using in the triggers):

```
BEGIN CATCH
        IF @@trancount > 0
            ROLLBACK TRANSACTION

        --or this will not get rolled back
        EXECUTE dbo.ErrorLog$insert

        DECLARE @ERROR_MESSAGE nvarchar(4000)
        SET @ERROR_MESSAGE = ERROR_MESSAGE()
        RAISERROR (@ERROR_MESSAGE,16,1)

    END CATCH
```

In almost every case, I rollback any transaction, log the error, then re-raise the error message. This solution covers any situation in the most straightforward manner, which works in most every case. I will talk more about error handling and triggers in Chapter 9 when I cover transactions.

Stored Procedures

The rules I've discussed in the sections on datatypes, constraints, and triggers are rules that I feel strongly should be applied to any database that's implemented in SQL Server (or any RDBMS, really). Even if the UI or middle tier duplicates some of the work, it's still valuable to have these rules implemented as close to the data as possible, so that no matter what tool is used to put data into the table, the table is still protected from bad data.

The rules in this section (and the next on client code) aren't those kinds of rules, in that there's no reasonable way to implement them using triggers or constraints, as they generally are hard to code and can require a user to do something. The reason is that these rules are optional rules that a user can opt out of for various reasons, or they might require human intervention.

From a data-integrity standpoint, it can almost be stated that these rules don't matter. The static rules that have already been implemented have placed a hedge of protection around the data in the tables, such that data that isn't "reasonable" cannot be stored. However, the rules that we've put on there aren't open to debate, and will be the rules unless a major change is made to the structures (hopefully based on requirements).

On the other hand, rules that will be implemented in stored procedures (T-SQL or CLR) are looser, and should generally not be considered when writing other code. What do I mean by this? Consider a column named `salary` that has been declared as `INT NOT NULL` with a `CHECK` constraint (`salary between 10000 and 30000`). When writing queries, you won't need to be concerned that a value might be `NULL`, or if you were summing 1,000 values, you don't have to worry about arithmetic overflow of the `integer` datatype, because `30000 * 1000 = 30,000,000`, far short of the approximately two billion maximum value for an integer.

However, if the rule was that salary should be between 10000 and 30000, and it was declared as NULL, then things aren't quite so straightforward. All comparisons with this column would require you to consider NULL comparisons, and there easily could be negative values.

Optional rules can be categorized as rules that are meant to be broken. The best litmus test for such a rule is to see whether the user is able to bypass it. A rule containing the word "should" is a good example. Most checking programs give you the option of entering a category for a transaction, but they don't force it. They only open a dialog saying, "Are you sure you want to be careless and not enter a category? A good person would."

Say we have the tables shown in Figure 6-5.

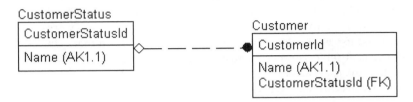

Figure 6-5. *A customer status table links to the customer details*

"When a new customer is created, the user should assign a status." "Should" cannot be Booleanized. Every rule we implement in the database must say "will." In this case, we might need to determine what "should" means. We generally have two options:

- Make the CustomerStatusId in the Customer table nullable and hence optional, thereby allowing the user to create a new Customer without supplying a status. To follow the rule "should," the front end would then likely open a dialog box asking the user, "Are you sure you don't want to assign a status to the customer?"

- Alternatively, you could rephrase the business rule as, "The user could enter an invalid status." This would mean that the database could allow any value for the CustomerStatusId, and indeed lets the client application handle the validation by checking the value to see if it's correct. The client application then sends a dialog box stating the following: "Are you sure you don't want to assign a status to this customer?" Worse still: "You have entered an invalid CustomerStatusId; you should enter a valid one." You would then have to drop the database validations in case the user says, "Nah, let me enter the invalid value."

The point is that SQL Server code doesn't converse with the user in an interactive manner. The hard-and-fast trigger and constraint validations still depend largely on the process of submitting a request and waiting to see if it completes successfully. Often you need a more interactive method of communication, in which you can influence events after the request has been submitted, and before the result becomes complete. When rules are coded in stored procedures, there can be no points in the code where you code MessageBox("Are you sure?"). Instead, you have to provide parameters or multiple procedures that enforce rules as if they were not optional. It's up to the client interface to use such rules as it needs.

In the following examples, you'll look at situations concerning rules that you can't realistically implement via triggers and constraints. Admittedly, where there's a will there's a way. It's possible, using temporary tables as messaging mechanisms, to "pass" values to a trigger or constraint. In this manner, you can optionally override functionality. However, triggers and constraints aren't generally considered suitable places to implement optional business rules.

A common example of this is an optional cascading delete. Cascading deletes are a great resource, but as we covered back in Chapter 5, you should use them with care. As discussed, they automatically remove child rows that are dependent on the content of the deleted parent row. However, when tables are just associated to one another (for example Customer–Invoice), and not a part of the entity (Invoice–Invoice Line Item), you probably don't want to delete all associated data when you delete a row in an associated table. Most likely, in the case of a customer and invoices, you wouldn't want to delete the customer if he or she had made purchases, but if you want to delete a Customer and all references, a cascade operation would be ideal.

However, this wouldn't be ideal in the case of a bank account. Let's say that you have the tables in Figure 6-6 (Xaction means transaction, because "transaction" is a reserved word).

In this case, it makes sense to cascade deletions of AccountOption rows automatically if you delete a row from the Account table. However, if an account has entries in the Xaction table, you need to ensure that the users are aware of these, and thus warn them if a cascading delete is requested. This increases complexity, because you won't be able to delete an account, as well as its properties and transactions, in a single statement.

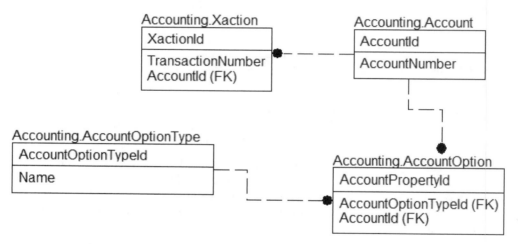

Figure 6-6. *A banking model*

Instead of a single statement, you have to execute the following steps:

- Run a SELECT statement for each child table that you optionally want to cascade-delete to, so you can show the user what exists.

- If the user accepts, execute a DELETE statement for each child table that has rows related to your primary table, and in the same atomic operation, delete the row you're interested in.

This code could be built into a single stored procedure that checks for the children, and if they exist, returns a result set of rows for the user to see what needs to be deleted. It also includes a parameter to allow the user to ignore the existence of rows, and go ahead and delete them. The following code shows you an example of how you might handle this situation (note that for clarity I've removed transactions and error handling):

```
CREATE PROCEDURE Accounting.Account$delete
(
    @AccountId int,
    @RemoveChildTransactionsFl bit = 0
) as

-- if they asked to delete them, just delete them
IF @RemoveChildTransactionsFl = 1
   DELETE Xaction --transaction
   WHERE  AccountId = @AccountId
ELSE --check for existence
  BEGIN
     IF EXISTS (SELECT *
                FROM   Xaction
                WHERE  AccountId = @AccountId)
       BEGIN
          RAISERROR ('Child transactions exist that must be deleted before the
                     account can be deleted.',16,1)
          RETURN -100
       END
  END
```

Now the user could try to execute the stored procedure with the flag equal to 0, and if any children existed, the user would get a notification. If not, the account would be deleted, and presumably the properties would be removed as well, via a cascading relationship.

For these sorts of procedures, you can use either T-SQL or CLR-based functions with the same success. However, in either case it's important to remember that there's no way to solicit answers to questions between server and client except when a batch begins to run. Ideally, when stored procedures are written to handle business-rule needs, they're written such that there's a way to make one call to the server to handle as many operations as possible, using transactions (which are covered in Chapter 9) to make sure that commands that need to succeed as one don't do part of the job they were sent to do, but not others.

Programmatic Data Protection Outside the RDBMS

For quite a while, there has been a groundswell of support to move much of the business-rule implementation and data-protection code out of SQL Server and into a middle-tier set of interface objects. In this way, the database, client and business rules exist in three units that can be implemented independently. Thus, business rules that you may well have thought about implementing via constraints and triggers get moved out of this "data" layer and into client-based code, such as a .NET object and stored procedures.

Such a multitier design also attempts to make the users' lives easier, because users edit data using custom front-end tools using the same objects that the middle-tier services maintain, and protect data that passes through them. Doing the majority of coding in a functional language protects the programmer from having to write and maintain all the required SQL code. Not only that, but these services can also directly handle any errors that occur and present the user with meaningful error messages. Because application users primarily edit rows one at a time, rather than a large number of rows, this works great.

The other point is that, in most enterprise applications (for instance, situations with hundreds of thousands of users on a website), the database is usually considered as the "system bottleneck." Though it's possible to distribute the load on multiple servers, in many cases it can be easier to spread the load across many application servers and use the database as a data storage device.

However, almost any data protection mechanism that's enforced without the use of constraints or triggers will almost inevitably prove problematic. Let's consider the list of possible users that I introduced at the beginning of the chapter, namely the following:

- *Users using custom front-end tools*: When users all use the custom front-end tools that are developed for the interface, there's no problem with employing the middle tier. In fact, it can have some great benefits, because as discussed, the object methods used to enforce the rules can be tuned for maximum performance. Unfortunately, it's hard to force all users to use the same tools.

- *Users using generic data manipulation tools such as Microsoft Access*: Let's consider a case in which a user needs to modify a set of "live" data, but only needs it for a week or a weekend, and there's no time to write a full-blown application. You won't be able to let the user directly access the data because it's in a raw unprotected state. Hence, you either have to code a relevant business rule into the Access database, or deny the user and make him or her wait until an application is created. This type of thing is relatively rare, and you can usually stop this kind of activity with strict policies against such data access.

- *Data import routines that acquire data from external sources*: Almost every system of any magnitude includes some import facilities to take data in a raw format from external systems, maybe from another part of your company or another company altogether, and place this data in a table on the database server. This can be in as simple a form as a user application to import a spreadsheet, or as complex as an interface between all the schools in a state and the respective state's Department of Education. The tools range from user applications, SQL Server Integration Services (SSIS), or even BCP (a bulk copy program that comes with SQL Server). When the middle tier owns all the business rules and data-integrity checks, you either have to go in through the middle tier one row at a time, or extract all the business rules and recode checks into your import routines.

- *Raw queries executed by data administrators to fix problems caused by user error*: Almost anybody with administration experience has had to remove a few rows from a database that users have erroneously created but cannot easily remove, and in so doing might have mistakenly deleted the wrong rows (for example, active account rows rather than inactive ones). In this situation, if you had business rules built into a trigger that allowed the deletion of inactive accounts only, an error message would have been returned to the user warning that active accounts couldn't be deleted. Obviously, you cannot protect against a bad action, such as systematically deleting every row in a table, but when a fully featured database is implemented and the data protected using constraints and triggers, it's next to impossible to make even small mistakes in data integrity.

I very much desire the possibilities offered by the multitier architecture. However, the load of business-rule and data-integrity–rule implementation should be "shared" between the middle tier and database server as appropriate. In this version of SQL Server, Microsoft is blurring this sort of tiering of data access with CLR objects. Things can be coded in the CLR almost exactly the same way in SQL Server as out of it. Hence, the CLR tier of code could be shifted from the client, to a middle tier, to the database server using the same language. Theoretically, this is a great idea, but it bears repeating that we must be careful that we aren't misusing technology and avoiding the tool that's most appropriate for data-access queries: T-SQL. I discuss when to use the CLR versus T-SQL in Chapter 10.

Two specific types of such rules that are far better implemented in the database are as follows:

- *Any rule that can be covered by a datatype,* NULL, *foreign key, or* CHECK *constraint*: This is because, when building additional external interfaces, this kind of check will generally make up quite a bit of the coding effort. Furthermore, base data integrity should be guaranteed at the lowest level possible, which allows as many programs as possible to code to the database. As a final point, the optimizer uses these constraints to make queries run faster.

- *Rules that require inter-table validations*: For example, whenever you save a value, you must check to see if a value exists in a different table. You have to access the additional table automatically to make certain that the state that was expected still exists. In some cases, the middle tier tries to cache the data on the database to use in validation, but there's no way to spread this cached data to multiple servers in a manner that ensures that the value you're entering has proper data integrity.

Rules that certainly should never be implemented in the database are *mutable rules*: rules that can and do change over time. Although the majority of rules in a system might be hard and fast rules at any given time, many rules change over time. For example:

- Today we give a customer a 20 percent discount, tomorrow a 10 percent discount.

- The maximum age that we offer this discount to is 35; next week we'll change it to 30.

- Send out the red toy with the meal, until the red toys run out; then send out the blue.

Mutable rules differ a great deal from optional rules, because these rules are hard and fast at a given point in time. The problem is that tomorrow the rule changes based on the changing realities of business. Much like optional rules, the RDBMS tables, and queries on those tables, cannot make any assumptions about data in the tables based on these ever-changing requirements.

Probably the worst of these are rules that seem *very* obvious. Take the following:

- All customers must pay a 10 percent deposit at the time of rental.

- Before the product is shipped, payment must be processed.

- Customer Y requires quality level X for his product and won't accept anything less.

Sounds perfect, right? Wrong.

- Well, all customers except Bob. We always let him pay 5 percent, though we'd prefer it if he would pay full price. Don't let him know about the discount.

- Customer Z is in a big need, so we accepted a PO from him this time instead of requiring payment up front.

- Customer Y has a big order, so for this week, quality level X * .85 will be fine.

All, except? This time? Sometimes different? Aughhh! These things should have come up in design, but often don't. This is what I often refer to as "rules based on how a person feels."[1] These rules make it tricky for SQL programmers because we tend to think in terms of the business, not the semantic model on which we've based the tables. If a payment is optional, all SQL must assume that there's a possibility that there will be no payment row, so an OUTER JOIN might have to be used instead of an INNER JOIN in queries to the Payment table if the query isn't centered on payments.

Mutable rules such as this certainly may have data stored for them, such as the current discount percentage, toy style, and minimum quality level, but this data is often as transitory as the rules. Rules in the database generally should center around the core data that's stored for later analysis, as it pertains to all instances of a particular activity. Non–data-tier code is best for this type of operation because it can be changed much more easily. The database's job is to maintain data integrity over the long run in a relatively unchanging manner.

More Best Practices

The main best practice is to use the right tool for the job. There are many tools in (and around) SQL to use to protect the data. Picking the right tool for a given situation is essential. For example, every column in every table could be defined as nvarchar(max). There are few pieces of data that you couldn't represent; for example, numbers and binary values. Using CHECK constraints, you could then constrain the values to look like almost any data type. It sounds silly, perhaps, but it is possible. But you know better after reading this and the previous chapter, right?

When choosing your method of protecting data, it's best to apply the following types of objects, in this order:

- *Defaults*: Though you might not think defaults can be considered data-protection resources, you should know that you can use them to set columns automatically where the purpose of the column might not be apparent to the user (and the database adds a suitable value for the column).

- CHECK *constraints*: These are important in ensuring that your data is within specifications. You can use almost any scalar functions (user-defined or system), as long as you end up with a single logical expression.

---

1. Kind of like when you were a kid and Dad had football to watch, he didn't care about your chores, but when he wasn't happy, out came the white glove on the basement floor (just me?).

- *Triggers*: Used to enforce rules that are too complex for CHECK constraints. Triggers allow you to build pieces of code that fire automatically on any INSERT, UPDATE, and DELETE operation that's executed against a single table.

- *User code*: Important for enforcing rules that are optional, or frequently changing. The major difference between user code and the previous three methods is that the other three are automatic and cannot (accidentally) be overridden. On the other hand, using stored procedures or .NET objects isn't required. A simple UPDATE statement can be executed from Management Studio, which violates rules enforced in a stored procedure.

Don't be afraid to enforce rules in more than one location, either. Although having rules as close to the data storage as possible is essential to trusting the integrity of the data when you use the data, there's no reason why the user needs to suffer through a poor user interface with a bunch of simple textboxes with no validation. If the tables are designed and implemented properly, you *could* do it this way, but the user should get a nice rich interface as well.

Summary

Now you've finished the task of developing the data storage for your databases. If you've planned out your data storage, the only bad data that can get into your system has nothing to do with the design (if a user wants to type the name "John" as "Jahn" or even "Bill," there's nothing that can be done in the database server to prevent it). As architects and programmers, it isn't possible to stop users from putting the names of pieces of equipment in a table named Employee. There's no semantic checking built in, and it would be impossible to do so without tremendous work and tremendous computing power. Only education can take care of this. Of course, it helps if you've given the users tables to store all their data, but still, users will be users.

In the last chapter, you built the physical storage for the data by creating the tables. In this chapter, you took the next step and completed your scheme to safeguard it. During this process, you looked at the resources that SQL Server gives you to protect your data from having invalid values.

Once you've built and implemented a set of appropriate data-safeguarding resources, you can then trust that the data in your database has been validated. You should never need to revalidate keys or values in your data once it's stored in your database, but it's a good idea to do random sampling so you know that no integrity gaps have slipped by you, especially during the testing process.

The Continuing Story of the Book So Far

Wow, you're awesome to have made it this far, unless you're still flipping around for the pictures of models, or possibly you're wondering why there is only one Dilbert cartoon in this book. (That's because I could only afford the one; thanks for asking. Maybe if you buy ten copies and give them to ten people and insist they purchase ten copies . . .)

If you're at this point in the process, you should celebrate, because essentially you're done with the implementation of the database (assuming you did your homework throughout the process and don't have to go back and make major changes).

Let's recap:

- In the first part of the book, we defined data needs and formed a logical model.

- This logical model was taken and fitted for implementation in the RDBMS as follows:

  - We added columns to assist in using the data.

  - We chose datatypes to match up with our data needs.

  - We implemented keys by which to identify our data.

  - We added foreign keys to make sure that relationship data always has proper matches, so our joins don't give us spurious results.

  - We added default constraints to make data entry easier.

  - We used CHECK constraints to make sure that the data in each row meets basic row-level criteria.

  - We added triggers to do the heavy lifting for validations across rows, tables, databases, or even servers.

- Finally, we briefly discussed how nondatabase code is used to make sure that our data meets the ever-changing rule set that dynamic businesses often require.

One word of caution: I know this database design stuff can get pretty compelling, but if your spouse is yelling at you to put down the darn book and come talk to her in the bedroom, put the book, down my friend. It will still be there tomorrow, and your spouse may not.

I'm about to switch gears one more time (consider this little section the clutch), and start putting the finishing touches on the system, such as the following:

- Securing access to the data

- Working with the physical model, and looking at the optimum ways to work with SQL Server data (the "optimization" part of the book title), including table structures and indexing

- Discussing how to maximize the number of users who can concurrently access the system, particularly working with the same data all at once

- Talking a bit about the finer points of structuring SQL code to access the data

- Finally, priming you on some of the things you should think about if you're going to be using your same design on multiple database server platforms

---

■**Note** You might have noticed that I didn't write any triggers using the CLR. I see great use in coding UDFs in the CLR for use in T-SQL triggers, but there are no great use cases, as of the writing of this book, for CLR triggers. Over the lifetime of the product, this might change, perhaps based on changes in a service pack release of SQL Server 2005. Check the Source Code area of the Apress website (http://www.apress.com) for updated information about each of the service packs as they come out, or my blog at http://spaces.msn.com/members/drsql.

Securing Access to the Data

We use our best efforts to ensure the security of personal information . . . Unfortunately, no electronic communication over the Internet can be guaranteed to be 100% secure.

—Dilbert.com privacy policy

[W]e intend to take reasonable and appropriate steps to protect the Personal Information that you share with us from unauthorized access or disclosure.

—Sun.com privacy policy

We use a variety of security technologies and procedures to help protect your personal information from unauthorized access, use, or disclosure.

—Microsoft.com privacy policy

Privacy policies: they're *everywhere*, and if your company does business with anyone, it likely has one too. As the preceding quotes emphasize, securing your data can involve implementation of numerous technologies and techniques, especially if your data is connected in some way to the Internet (the last frontier), where numerous threats are posed. For too many organizations, security is like Dorothy and the red shoes: she already had the power, she just didn't know she did. Luckily, most average users aren't adventurous, or they'd find that they probably have incredible power to see more than they probably need to.

Note the term "average user" for whom the system in question was built, be it an employee or a customer. It's beyond the scope of this chapter to consider measures for protecting data from superusers with high-privilege accounts (db_owner or higher), such as DBAs or programming staff. Further, because our focus is on the database, I'll avoid any in-depth discussion of exactly how data access applications will use the security, such as whether or not to use trusted connections (Windows Authentication) or SQL Server Standard security.

This chapter focuses on database-level security, so it doesn't cover many security precautions that are implemented outside the database (such as firewalls). It also assumes that certain measures have been put in place to protect your system from malicious hackers. For example, I assume the following:

- Strong passwords have been applied to all accounts—certainly all known system accounts (such as sa, if you haven't changed the name). *Certainly there are no blank passwords for accounts!*

- SQL Server isn't just sitting unguarded on the Web, with no firewall and no logging of failed login attempts.

- The guest user has probably been removed from all databases.

- You've guarded against SQL injection accounts by avoiding query strings whereby a user could simply inject 'SELECT * FROM sys.sql_logins' and get a list of all your logins in a textbox in your application. (Chapter 10 covers SQL injection, where I contrast ad hoc SQL with stored procedures.)

- You've secured access to your application passwords and put them where only the necessary people can see them (such as the DBA, and application programmers who use them in their code), and have encrypted the password into application code modules when using application logins.

- You've made certain that few people have file-level access to the server where the data is stored, and probably more importantly, where the backups are stored. If one malicious user has access to your backup file or tape, then that person has access to your data, and you can't stop him or her from accessing the data (even encryption isn't 100 percent secure if the hacker has unlimited time).

Note To make SQL Server 2005 as secure as possible "out of the box," many features are disabled by default, and have to be enabled explicitly before you can use them. For example, remote connections, Database Mail, HTTP connectivity, CLR programming, and others are all "off by default." You can enable these features using the Surface Area Configuration tool found in the Configuration Tools menu in the SQL Server 2005 Program menu.

Because this is a database design and optimization book, this chapter focuses squarely on security from the *database* perspective. We'll consider the security features that we might need to design into our physical schema, to control and monitor what data can be accessed by certain users, what data can be seen, and so on. I'll cover some of the common SQL Server security techniques you can use to protect your data from unauthorized viewing and access, including the following:

- *Controlling data access*: I demonstrate how to do this using permissions, and by giving users access to coded objects rather than the underlying database tables.

- *Obfuscating sensitive data (such as credit card details)*: You can use encryption to do this, so that if a user does somehow gain "rogue" access to the database, this data remains protected.

- *Monitoring and auditing user actions*: You can watch users, so you can go back after the fact and identify any improper usage.

■**Note** You can place the code in this chapter in any database. I include a `CREATE DATABASE`
`SecurityChapter` statement in the downloadable code for this book (in the Source Code area of
the Apress website at `http://www.apress.com`). I also include a script to clean up the many users
that will be created. I suggest that you not execute the scripts from this chapter on a production server,
because you'll be creating many system-level logins, which might make the DBA mad (unless you're the
DBA, and then you'd simply be mad at me).

I should also note that not everyone will use many, if any, of the guidelines in this chapter
in their security implementations. Often it's left to the application layer to do the security,
showing or hiding functionality from the user. This is a common approach, but it can leave
gaps in security, especially when you have to give users ad hoc access to the database, or you
have multiple user interfaces that have to implement different methods of security. My advice
is to make use of the permissions in the database server as much as possible. However, having
the application layer control security isn't a tremendous hole in the security, as long as the
passwords used are seriously complex and well guarded. Later in the chapter, the "Application
Roles" section presents an approach to this sort of security. This approach can be useful for
implementing database-server permissions without having to lose the identity of the user.

Controlling Data Access

The major goal of security inside a database is to restrict user access to the data you wish to
allow users to see. This section examines access control techniques in SQL Server 2005,
including the following:

- *Principals and securables*: How to use simple permissions-based security to control
  access to certain data, either at the table level or the column level.

- *Permissions overview*: This section gives an overview of how permissions work for a
  database.

- *Using coded objects*: Use these to present users with only the data to which they have
  access, in stored procedures, functions, and views.

Principals and Securables

The SQL Server 2005 security model relies on the concepts of *principals* and *securables*. Principals are those objects that may be granted permission to access particular database objects,
while securables are those objects to which access can be controlled.

Principals can represent a *specific user*, a *role* that may be adopted by multiple users, or
an *application*. SQL Server divides principals into three classes:

- *Windows principals*: These represent Windows user accounts or groups, authenticated using Windows security.

- *SQL Server principals*: These are server-level logins or groups that are authenticated using SQL Server security.

- *Database principals*: These include database users, groups, and roles, as well as application roles.

In this chapter, I'll focus on what you can do to secure the database. I won't cover how the user gets access to the database via some Windows or SQL Server principal in any depth, other than to create test logins to support the examples. SQL Server 2005 gives you a rich set of ways for a user to connect, including using certificates to connect with.

On the other hand, the important aspects relevant to database design are pretty straight-forward. Database principals are users who are members of roles. You can map database principals to server principals, so when setting up security on a database server, most security is applied to database roles. For most normal, non-DBA, non-programmer–type users, at a system level the only thing granted to a user is access to databases.

Inside the database, database roles (groups of users and other roles) and users are granted rights to use database objects. Best practice is to set up roles to grant rights to, putting database users in the roles. I talk more about roles and users in the "Permissions" section.

■**Caution** Most of the examples in this book grant rights to users, only to keep the examples reasonable to follow. Use roles for almost every right you grant in the database, except where it makes sense for exceptions (for example, if you want to give rights to one user only).

Securables are the database objects to which you can control access and to which you can grant principals permissions. SQL Server 2005 distinguishes between three scopes at which different objects can be secured:

- *Server scope*: Server-scoped securables include logins, HTTP endpoints, event notifications, and databases. These are objects that exist at the server level, outside of any individual database, and to which access is controlled on a server-wide basis.

- *Database scope*: Securables with database scope are objects such as users, roles, and CLR assemblies, which exist inside a particular database, but not within a schema.

- *Schema scope*: This group includes those objects that reside within a schema in a database, such as tables, views, and stored procedures. A SQL Server 2005 schema corresponds roughly to the owner of a set of objects (such as dbo) in SQL Server 2000.

In this chapter, I'll focus on objects at the database and schema scope, focusing more on schema scope objects, because this is generally what you need to know in terms of data protection.

Database Security Overview

Permissions are the rights, granted (or denied) to a principal, to access a securable. I'll cover the basics of database permissions for a foundation of best practices. Taken to the full extreme, SQL Server 2005 has a far richer security setup, especially at the server level, but 80 percent of security is down to securing tables and procedures, and this is what's specifically interesting from a database-design standpoint. As discussed, at the database level there's one primary principal, and this is the user.

I'll cover the following topics, which revolve around giving users permissions to use securables:

- *User impersonation*: This allows one user to impersonate another user temporarily. User impersonation is used often in testing security, but can also be used in an object to give a user enhanced security for the life of the procedures.

- *Grantable permissions*: This section covers the different sorts of database permissions, and how to grant and revoke permission on securables.

- *Roles and schemas*: You'll learn how to use roles and schemas to grant rights efficiently to database securables.

These three topics will give you most of the information you need to know about setting up your database-level security.

Impersonation

To demonstrate security in a reasonable manner on a single SQL Server connection, I need to introduce a new SQL Server 2005 feature. In 2000 and earlier, if the dbo wanted to impersonate another user, he used SETUSER. For our examples, SETUSER would have been sufficient, but SETUSER was never a good tool to use in your production code. 2005 introduces the concept of impersonation, a tool that I believe will one day eliminate having DBAs logging in as a database owner and even as the system administrator. You achieve impersonation using the EXECUTE AS statement. You can impersonate any server login or a database user principal, and you get all rights that user has (and consequently lose the rights you previously had). You can go back to the previous security context by executing REVERT.

As an example, I'll look at a way that you can have a user impersonating a member of the server-system sysadmin role. This is how I'll be setting up my users once servers are upgraded to SQL Server 2005. Using impersonation in such a way takes some getting used to, but it certainly makes it easier to have full sysadmin power only when it's needed. As said previously, there are lots of server privileges, so you can mete out rights that are needed on a day-to-day basis. As an example (and this is the kind of example that I'll have throughout this chapter), we first create a login that we never expect to be logged into directly. I use a standard login, but you could map it to a certificate, a key, a Windows user (like a failsafe user who has a password stored "just in case"), or whatever. Standard logins make it much easier to learn tools because they're self contained. Then we add the login to the sysadmin role. You probably also want to use a name that isn't so obviously associated with system administration. If a hacker got hold of the name somehow, the name 'itchy' wouldn't so obviously be able to do serious damage to your database server.

■Caution You might not want to execute this code on your server. It isn't included in the code downloads, either.

```
USE Master --the following command must be executed in the context of
             --master database
GO
CREATE LOGIN system_admin WITH PASSWORD = 'tooHardToEnterAndNoOneKnowsIt'
EXEC sp_addsrvrolemember 'system_admin','sysadmin'
```

■Tip There have been many changes in syntax when it comes to creating and managing users. Instead of using the system stored procedures sp_addlogin and sp_adduser (which will be likely be removed in the next version of SQL Server after 2005), there are the more standard commands CREATE LOGIN and CREATE USER, as well as ALTER counterparts. For more information, check SQL Server 2005 Books Online.

Then we create a regular login (again standard, but whenever possible a normal user's login should use integrated security), and give rights to impersonate the system_admin user:

```
CREATE LOGIN louis with PASSWORD = 'reasonable', DEFAULT_DATABASE=tempdb
GRANT IMPERSONATE ON LOGIN:: system_admin TO louis;
```

■Tip Defaulting the database to the tempdb for system administrator–type users is useful because it requires a conscious effort to go to a user database and start building objects, or even dropping them. However, any work done in tempdb is deleted when the server is stopped.

We login as the user, louis, and try to run the following code:

```
USE AdventureWorks
```

The following error is raised:

```
Msg 916, Level 14, State 1, Line 1
The server principal "louis" is not able to access the database "AdventureWorks"
under the current security context.
```

Now, we change security context to the system_admin user:

```
EXECUTE AS LOGIN = 'system_admin'
```

We now have control of the server!

```
USE    AdventureWorks
SELECT user
```

This returns the following result:

```
--------------------
dbo
```

Then we execute the following code:

```
REVERT --go back to previous context
```

We see the following result:

```
Msg 15447, Level 16, State 1, Line 1
The current security context cannot be reverted. Please switch to the original
database where 'Execute As' was called and try it again.
```

We started in tempdb, so we use the following code:

```
USE tempdb

REVERT
SELECT user
```

This returns the following result:

```
----------------
guest
```

Impersonation gives you a lot of control over what a user can do, and allows you to situationally play one role or another, such as creating a new database. We'll use impersonation a lot to change user context to demonstrate security concepts.

■**Note** The user here is guest, which is a user I recommended that you drop in every database. You cannot drop the guest user in the tempdb or master database, because users must have access to the tempdb to do any work. Executing DROP USER guest in these databases returns an error: "Cannot disable access to the guest user in master or tempdb."

Using impersonation, you can execute your code as a member of the sysadmin server or db_owner database role, and then test your code as a typical user without opening multiple connections (and making the sample code considerably easier to follow).

Permissions

Using SQL Server security, we can easily build a security plan that prevents unwanted usage of our objects by any user. We can control rights to almost every object type, and in SQL Server 2005 we can secure a tremendous number of object types. For our purposes, we're going to be looking at data-oriented security specifically, limited to the objects and the actions we can give or take away access to (see Table 7-1).

Table 7-1. *Database Objects and Permissions*

Object Type	Permission Type
Tables and views	SELECT, INSERT, UPDATE, DELETE, REFERENCES
Columns (view and table)	SELECT, INSERT, UPDATE, DELETE
Functions	EXECUTE (scalar) SELECT (table valued)
Stored procedures	EXECUTE

Most of these are straightforward, and probably are familiar if you've done any SQL Server administration, although perhaps REFERENCES isn't familiar. This is for the situation in which tables are owned by schemas that are then owned by different principals. If you wanted to apply a foreign key between the tables, you'd be required to give the child table REFERENCES permissions.

You can then grant or deny usage of these objects to the roles that have been created. You certainly don't want to have to grant access to each user individually, as you might have a multitude of users in your databases. SQL Server provides you with the concept of a *role* (previously known as *groups* in SQL Server 6.x and earlier) to which you can grant rights, and then you can associate each role with relevant users.

SQL Server uses three different commands to give or take away rights from each of your roles:

- GRANT: Gives the privilege to use an object.

- DENY: Denies access to an object, regardless of whether the user has been granted the privilege from any other role.

- REVOKE: Used to remove any GRANT or DENY permissions statements that have been applied to an object. Behaves like a delete of an applied permission.

Typically, you'll simply give permissions to a role to perform tasks that are specific to the role. You should only use the DENY command as an "extreme" type of command, as no matter how many other times the user has been granted privileges to an object, the user won't have access to it while there's one DENY.

As an example, consider that you have an Invoice table. If you wanted to remove access to this table from user Steve because of a job change, you'd execute a REVOKE. If Steve was in another group that had rights to the Invoice table, he could still access it. If you used DENY, Steve would lose rights to the object completely, even if another manager GRANTed rights.

Once you've built all your objects—including tables, stored procedures, views, and so on—you can grant rights to them. For stored procedures, views, and functions, as long as the schema is the same, you don't have to grant rights to the underlying objects that are used in these objects.

For example, to give a privilege on a table or stored procedure to a user, the command would be as follows:

```
GRANT <privilege> ON <object> to <userName>
```

Next, if you want to remove the privilege you have two choices. You can either REVOKE the permission, which just deletes the granted permission, or you can DENY the permission. Execute the following:

```
REVOKE <privilege> ON <object> to <userName>
```

I haven't covered role membership yet (it's covered later in the chapter), but if the user was a member of a role that had access to this object, the user would still have access. However, execute the following code:

```
DENY <privilege> ON <object> to <userName>
```

Because of the DENY command, the users will not be able to access the object, regardless of any right granted to them. To remove the DENY, you again use the REVOKE command. This will all become clearer when I cover roles later in the chapter, but in my experience, DENY isn't a typical thing to use on a principal's privilege set. It's punitive in nature, and is confusing to the average user. More commonly, users are given rights and not denied access.

To see the user's rights in the database, you can use the sys.database_permissions catalog view. For example, use the following code to see all the rights that have been granted in the database:

```
SELECT  object_name(major_id), permission_name, state_desc,
        user_name(grantee_principal_id) as Grantee
FROM    sys.database_permissions
WHERE   objectproperty(major_id,'isTable') = 1
  AND   objectproperty(major_id,'isMsShipped') = 0
```

For more information on the security catalog views, check Books Online.

Controlling Access to Objects

One of the worst things that can happen in an organization is for a user to see data out of context and start a worry- or gossip-fest. Creating roles and associating users with them is a fairly easy task and is usually worth the effort. Once you've set up the security for a database using sufficiently high-level object groupings (as low level as need be, of course), management can be relatively straightforward. What I mean by high-level groupings will become clearer as the chapter progresses.

Your goal is to allow the users to perform whatever tasks they need to, but to prohibit any other tasks, and not to let them see any data that they shouldn't. You can control access at several levels. At a high level, you might wish to grant (or deny) a principal access to all invoices—in which case you might control access at the level of a table. At a more granular level, you might wish to control access to certain columns or rows within that table. In a more functional approach, you might only give rights to use stored procedures to access data. All these approaches are commonly used in the exact same database in some way, shape, or form.

In this section, I'll cover table and column security as it's done using the built-in vanilla security, before moving on to the more complex strategies I'll outline during the rest of the book.

■**Note** In this chapter, you'll be creating a lot of logins that are based on the Standard security type. In general, it's best to create your logins using Windows Authentication mode, but in an example space, it's far too difficult to pull off, because we would need to create local or domain groups and logins. Database security is not significantly affected by using either the Standard or Windows Authentication mode. You may substitute any Windows Authentication login in lieu of the standard users if your server doesn't allow standard authentication.

Table Security

As already mentioned, for tables at an object level, you can grant a principal rights to INSERT, UPDATE, DELETE, or SELECT data from a table. This is the most basic form of security when dealing with data. The goal when using table-based security is to keep users looking at, or modifying, the entire set of data, rather than specific rows. We'll progress to the specific security types as we move through the chapter.

■**Note** As mentioned in the introduction to this section, all objects should be owned by the same user for most normal databases (not to be confused with the owner from the previous versions of SQL Server), so we won't deal with the REFERENCES permission type.

As an example of table security, you'll create a new table, and I'll demonstrate, through the use of a new user, what the user can and cannot do.

```
--start with a new schema for this test
CREATE SCHEMA TestPerms
GO

CREATE TABLE TestPerms.TableExample
(
    TableExampleId int identity(1,1)
                CONSTRAINT PKTableExample PRIMARY KEY,
    Value   varchar(10)
)
```

Then create a new user, not associating it with a login. You won't need a login for any of the examples, as you'll use impersonation to pretend to be the user without logging in.

```
CREATE USER Tony WITHOUT LOGIN
```

You change to impersonate user Tony and try to create a new row:

```
EXECUTE AS USER = 'Tony'
INSERT INTO TestPerms.TableExample(Value)
VALUES ('a row')
```

Well, as you would expect, here's the result:

```
Msg 229, Level 14, State 5, Line 2
INSERT permission denied on object 'TableExample', database 'SecurityChapter',
schema 'TestPerms'.
```

You then go back to being the dbo using the REVERT command, give the user rights, then go back to being Tony and try to insert again:

```
REVERT
GRANT INSERT on TestPerms.TableExample to Tony

EXECUTE AS USER = 'Tony'
INSERT INTO TestPerms.TableExample(Value)
VALUES ('a row')
```

No errors here. Now, because Tony just created the row, the user should be able to select the row, right?

```
SELECT TableExampleId, value
FROM    TestPerms.TableExample
```

No, the user only had rights to INSERT data, not to view it:

```
Msg 229, Level 14, State 5, Line 1
SELECT permission denied on object 'tableExample', database 'SecurityChapter',
schema 'TestPerms'.
```

Now, you can give the user Tony rights to SELECT data from the table using the following GRANT statement:

```
REVERT
GRANT SELECT on TestPerms.TableExample to Tony
```

The SELECT statement does return data. At a table level, you can do this for the four DML statements: INSERT, UPDATE, DELETE, and SELECT.

Column-Level Security

For the most part, it's enough simply to limit a user's access to data at a table or view level, but as the next two major sections will discuss, sometimes the security needs to be more granular. Sometimes you need to restrict users to using merely part of a table. In this section, I'll look at the security syntax that SQL Server provides at a basic level to grant rights at a column level. Later in the chapter, I'll present other methods that use views or stored procedures.

For our example, we'll create a couple database users:

```
CREATE USER Employee WITHOUT LOGIN
CREATE USER Manager WITHOUT LOGIN
```

Then we'll create a table to use for our column-level security examples for a Product table. This Product table has the company's products, including the current price and the cost to produce this product:

```
CREATE SCHEMA Products
go
CREATE TABLE Products.Product
(
    ProductId    int identity CONSTRAINT PKProduct PRIMARY KEY,
    ProductCode varchar(10) CONSTRAINT AKProduct_ProductCode UNIQUE,
    Description varchar(20),
    UnitPrice    decimal(10,4),
    ActualCost  decimal(10,4)
)
INSERT INTO Products.Product(ProductCode, Description, UnitPrice, ActualCost)
VALUES ('widget12','widget number 12',10.50,8.50)
INSERT INTO Products.Product(ProductCode, Description, UnitPrice, ActualCost)
VALUES ('snurf98','Snurfulator',99.99,2.50)
```

Now, we want our employees (as a reminder, there should be an employee role, but it's just a cleaner example to use two users) to be able to see all the products, but we don't want them to see what the product costs to manufacture. The syntax is the same as the GRANT on a table, but we include in parentheses the columns, comma delimited, to which the user is being denied access. In the next code block, we grant SELECT rights to both users but take away these rights on the ActualCost column:

```
GRANT SELECT on Products.Product to employee,manager
DENY SELECT on Products.Product (ActualCost) to employee
```

To test our security, we impersonate the manager:

```
EXECUTE AS USER = 'manager'
SELECT  *
FROM    Products.Product
```

This returns all columns with no errors:

ProductId	ProductCode	Description	UnitPrice	ActualCost
1	widget12	widget number 12	10.5000	8.5000
3	snurf98	Snurfulator	99.9900	2.5000

Tip I know some of you are probably thinking that it's bad practice to use SELECT * in a query. It's true that using SELECT * in your permanent code is a bad idea, but generally speaking, when writing ad hoc queries most users use the * shorthand for all columns.

The manager worked fine; what about the employee?

```
REVERT --revert back to SA level user
GO
EXECUTE AS USER = 'employee'
GO
SELECT *
FROM    Products.Product
```

This returns the following result:

```
Msg 230, Level 14, State 1, Line 1
SELECT permission denied on column 'ActualCost' of object 'Product',
database 'SecurityChapter', schema 'Products'.
```

"Why did I get this error?" the user first asks, then (and this is harder to explain): "How do I correct it?"

You might try to explain to the user, "Well, just list out all the columns, without the columns you cannot see, like this":

```
SELECT ProductId, ProductCode, Description, UnitPrice
FROM    Products.Product
```

This returns the following results for user employee:

```
ProductId   ProductCode Description       UnitPrice
----------- ----------- ---------------- ----------------
1           widget12    widget number 12 10.5000
3           snurf98     Snurfulator      99.9900
```

The answer, although technically correct, isn't even vaguely what the user wants to hear. "So every time I want to build an ad hoc query on the Product table (which has 50 columns instead of the 5 I've generously mocked up for your learning ease) I have to type out all the columns?"

This is why, for the most part, column-level security is rarely used as a primary security mechanism, because of how it's implemented. You don't want users getting error messages when they try to run a query on a table. You might add column-level security to the table "just in case," but for the most part, use coded objects such as stored procedures or views to control access to certain columns. I'll discuss these solutions in the next section.

One last tidbit about column security syntax. That is, once you've used the DENY option on a column, you cannot REVOKE the DENY to restore rights. You must use the GRANT option:

```
DENY SELECT on Products.Product (ActualCost) to Employee
```

Roles and Schemas

Core to the process of granting rights is who to grant rights to. I've introduced the database user, commonly referred to as just "user." The user is the lowest level of security principal in the database, and can be mapped to logins, certificates, asymmetrical keys, or even not mapped to a login at all.

In this section, I'll cover some of the ways the following two objects are used in conjunction with users at a database level, to make the process of granting permissions to use objects easier to manage:

- *Roles*: Sometimes referred to as *groups*, these are groupings of users and other roles that can be granted rights.

- *Schemas*: We've discussed and used schemas throughout the past two chapters; now we discuss how they can be used to secure objects.

Roles

Roles are groups of users and other roles that allow you to grant object access to multiple users at once. Every user in a database is a member of at least the public role, but may be a member of multiple roles. In fact, roles may be members of other roles. I'll discuss two types of roles:

- *Standard database roles*: Roles that are used to group Windows users together to grant rights as a group, rather than individually

- *Application roles*: Roles that are used to give an application specific rights, rather than to a group or individual user

Each of these types of roles are used to give rights to objects in a more convenient manner than granting them directly to an individual user.

Standard Database Roles

A standard database role is a named group of users that allows you to grant rights to a group of users, rather than to each user individually. Take, for example, any typical human-resources system that has employee information such as name, address, position, manager, pay grade, and so on. We'll likely need several roles, such as the following:

- HRManagers: Can do any task in the system.

- HRWorkers: Can maintain any attribute in the system, but approval rows are required to modify salary information.

- Managers: All managers in the company would be in this role, but they can only see the information for their own workers, using further techniques I'll present in the section "Implementing Configurable Row-Level Security with Views" later in this chapter.

- Employees: Can only see their own information, and can only modify their own personal address information.

And so on, to cover all the common groups that are needed for a particular situation. Setting up a tight security system isn't an easy task, and takes some thought and hard work to get it done right. Enabling the UI to use the security system is even more of a challenge, which I won't take up here.

Each of the roles would then be granted access to all the resources that they need. A member of the Managers role would likely also be a member of the Employees role. Then, as stated, the managers could see the information for their employees, and also for themselves.

Users can be members of multiple roles, and roles can be members of other roles. Permissions are additive, so if a user is a member of three roles, the user has an effective set of permissions that's the union of all permissions of the groups. For example:

- Managers: Can view the Employees table

- Employees: Can view the Product table

- HRWorkers: Can see employment history

If the Managers role was a member of the Employees role, a member of the Managers role could also do activities that were enabled by either role. If a user was a member of the HRWorkers group and the Employees role, then the user could see employment history and the Product table (it might seem logical that users could see the Employees table, but this hasn't been explicitly set in our tiny example).

As shorthand to giving users permissions, I should note that each database has a special set of built-in roles:

- db_owner: Users associated with this role can perform any activity in the database.

- db_accessadmin: Users associated with this role can add or remove users from the database.

- db_backupoperator: Users associated with this role are allowed to back up the database.

- db_datareader: Users associated with this role are allowed to read any data in any table.

- db_datawriter: Users associated with this role are allowed to write any data in any table.

- db_ddladmin: Users associated with this role are allowed to add, modify, or drop any objects in the database (in other words, execute any DDL statements).

- db_denydatareader: Users associated with this role are denied the ability to see any data in the database, though they may still see the data through stored procedures.

- db_denydatawriter: Much like the db_denydatareader role, users associated with this role are denied the ability to modify any data in the database, though they still may modify data through stored procedures.

- db_securityadmin: Users associated with this role can modify and change permissions and roles in the database.

In addition to these fixed roles, your own database roles give rights to database objects. New to SQL Server 2005, you can also grant database-level rights such as ALTER, ALTER ANY USER, DELETE (from any table), CREATE ROLE, and so on. (There are also new server-level rights too, but I won't cover this topic because it's more of a DBA task.) Using these new right types, you can control rights to database management and data usage at a high level, as well as the lower levels I've already discussed.

Programmatically, you can determine some basic information about a user's security information in the database:

- IS_MEMBER ('<role>'): Tells you if the current user is the member of a given role. Useful for building security-based views.

- USER: Tells you the current user's name.

- HAS_PERMS_BY_NAME: Lets you interrogate the security system to see what rights a user has. This function has a complex public interface, but it's powerful and useful.

You can use these functions in applications and T-SQL code to determine at runtime what the user can do. For example, if you wanted only HRManager members to execute a procedure, you could check:

```
SELECT is_member('HRManager')
```

A return value of 1 means the user is a member, 0 means not a member of the role. A procedure might start out like the following:

```
if (SELECT is_member('HRManager')) = 0
        SELECT 'get out!'
```

This prevents even the database owner from executing the procedure, though this user can get the code for the procedure and execute the procedure if he or she is malicious enough (the last section of this chapter covers some security precautions to handle bad DBA types, though this is generally a hard task). Also, if there isn't an HRManager role, is_member will return NULL, which won't return anything. If this is a consideration, be certain and code for it.

As an example, take the HR system we were just discussing. If we wanted to remove access to the salaryHistory table just from the Employees role, we wouldn't deny access to the Employees role, because managers are employees also, and would need to have rights to the salaryHistory table. To deal with this sort of change, we might have to revoke rights to the Employees role, and then give rights to the other groups, rather than deny rights to a group that has lots of members.

For example, consider that you have three users in the database:

```
CREATE USER Frank WITHOUT LOGIN
CREATE USER Julie WITHOUT LOGIN
CREATE USER Paul WITHOUT LOGIN
```

Julie and Paul are members of the HRWorkers role:

```
CREATE ROLE HRWorkers

EXECUTE sp_addrolemember 'HRWorkers','Julie'
EXECUTE sp_addrolemember 'HRWorkers','Paul'
```

Next you have a Payroll schema, and in this is (at the least) an EmployeeSalary table:

```
CREATE SCHEMA Payroll

CREATE TABLE Payroll.EmployeeSalary
(
    EmployeeId  int,
    SalaryAmount decimal(12,2)

)
```

```
GRANT SELECT ON Payroll.EmployeeSalary to HRWorkers
```

Next, test the users:

```
EXECUTE AS USER = 'Frank'
```

```
SELECT *
FROM   Payroll.EmployeeSalary
```

This returns the following error, because Frank isn't a member of this group:

```
Msg 229, Level 14, State 5, Line 1
SELECT permission denied on object 'EmployeeSalary', database 'SecurityChapter',
schema 'Payroll'.
```

However, change over to Julie:

```
REVERT
EXECUTE AS USER = 'Julie'
```

```
SELECT *
FROM   Payroll.EmployeeSalary
```

She can view the data of tables in the Payroll schema because she's a member of the role that was granted EXECUTE permissions to the table:

```
EmployeeId   SalaryAmount
-----------  ----------------------------------------
```

Roles are always the best way to apply security in a database. Instead of giving individual users specific rights, develop roles that match job positions. Not that granting rights to an individual is not necessarily bad. To keep this section reasonable, I won't extend the example to include multiple roles, but a user can be a member of many roles, and the user gets the cumulative effect of the chosen rights. So if there was an HRManagers role, and Julie was a member of this group as well as the HRWorkers role, the rights of the two groups would effectively be UNIONed. This would be the user's rights.

There's one notable exception. As mentioned earlier in the chapter, one DENY prevents another's GRANTs from applying. Say Paul had his rights to the EmployeeSalary table denied:

```
REVERT
DENY SELECT ON payroll.employeeSalary TO Paul
```

Say he tried to select from the table:

```
EXECUTE AS USER = 'Paul'
SELECT *
FROM   payroll.employeeSalary
```

He would be denied:

```
Msg 229, Level 14, State 5, Line 1
SELECT permission denied on object 'EmployeeSalary',
database 'SecurityChapter', schema 'Payroll'.
```

This is true even though he was granted rights via the HRWorkers group. This is why DENY is generally not used much. Rarely will you punish users via rights. You might apply a DENY to a sensitive table or procedure to be certain it wasn't used, but only in limited cases.

■**Note** For most examples in this chapter, I'll apply rights to users to keep examples as simple as possible.

If you want to know from which tables the user can SELECT, you can use a query such as the following:

```
--note, this query only returns rows for tables where the user has SOME rights
SELECT  table_schema + '.' + table_name as tableName,
        has_perms_by_name(table_schema + '.' + table_name, 'object', 'SELECT')
                                                              as allowSelect
FROM    information_schema.tables
```

Application Roles

People commonly like to set up applications using a single login, and manage security in the application. This can be a fine way to implement security, but it requires you to re-create all the login stuff, when you could use simple Windows Authentication to check whether a user can execute an application. Application roles let you use the Active Directory to manage who a person is and if that person has rights to the application, and simply let the application perform the finer points of security.

To be honest, this can be a nice mix, because the hardest part of implementing security isn't restricting a person's ability to do an activity, it's nicely letting them know by hiding actions they cannot do. I've shown you a few of the security catalog views already, and there are more in Books Online. Using them, you can query the database to see what a user can do to help facilitate this process. However, it isn't a trivial task, and is often considered too much trouble, especially for home-grown apps built for smaller organizations.

An application role is almost analogous to using EXECUTE AS to set rights to another user, but instead of a user, it's clearer in its use that the user is an application. You change to the context of the application role using sp_setapprole. You grant the application role permissions just like any other role, by using the GRANT statement.

As an example of using an application role, you'll create both a user named Bob and an application role, and give them totally different rights. The TestPerms schema was created earlier, so if you didn't create it before, go ahead and create it.

```
CREATE TABLE TestPerms.BobCan
(
    BobCanId int identity(1,1) CONSTRAINT PKBobCan PRIMARY KEY,
    Value varchar(10)
)
CREATE TABLE TestPerms.AppCan
(
    AppCanId int identity(1,1) CONSTRAINT PKAppCan PRIMARY KEY,
    Value varchar(10)
)
```

Now create the new login and give it rights to the database:

```
CREATE USER Bob WITHOUT LOGIN
```

Next, give Bob SELECT rights to his table, and the application SELECT rights to its table:

```
GRANT SELECT on TestPerms.BobCan to Bob
GO
CREATE APPLICATION ROLE AppCan_application with password = '39292ljasll23'
GO
GRANT SELECT on TestPerms.AppCan to AppCan_application
```

You probably note that one of the drawbacks to using an application role is that it requires a password. This password is passed around in clear text to the application, so make sure that first, the password is complex, and second, that you encrypt any connections that might be using these when there's a threat of impropriety. Look up Secure Sockets Layer (SSL) in Books Online for more information on encrypting connections. Then, set the user you're working as to Bob:

```
EXECUTE AS USER = 'Bob'
```

Now, select from the BobCan table:

```
SELECT * FROM TestPerms.BobCan
```

It works with no error:

```
BobCanId      Value
------------- -----------
```

However, try selecting from the AppCan table:

```
SELECT * FROM TestPerms.AppCan
```

The following error is returned:

```
Msg 229, Level 14, State 5, Line 1
SELECT permission denied on object 'AppCan', database 'SecurityChapter',
schema 'TestPerms'.
```

This isn't surprising, because Bob has no permissions on the AppCan table. Next, still logged in as Bob, use the sp_setapprole procedure to change the security context of the user to the application role, and the security is reversed:

```
EXECUTE sp_setapprole 'AppCan_application', '39292ljasll23'
go
SELECT * FROM TestPerms.BobCan
```

This returns the following error:

```
Msg 229, Level 14, State 5, Line 1
SELECT permission denied on object 'BobCan', database 'SecurityChapter',
schema 'TestPerms'.
```

That's because you're now in context of the application role, and the application role doesn't have rights to the table. Finally, the application role can read from the AppCan table:

```
SELECT * from TestPerms.AppCan
```

This doesn't return an error:

```
AppCanId     Value
------------ -----------
```

When you're in the application role context, you look to the database as if you're the application, not your user, as evidenced by the following code:

```
SELECT user as userName, suser_sname() as login
```

This returns the following result:

```
userName                login
----------------------- ----------------------
AppCan_application      DOMAIN\USER
```

The login returns whatever login name you're logged in as, without regards to the impersonation you're doing, because the user is database level and the login is server level. Once you've executed sp_setapprole, the security stays as this role until you disconnect from the SQL server, or you execute sp_unsetapprole. However, sp_unsetapprole doesn't work nearly as elegantly as REVERT. For example:

```
--Note that this must be executed as a single batch because of the variable
--for the cookie
DECLARE @cookie varbinary(8000);
EXECUTE sp_setapprole 'AppCan_application', '39292ljasll23'
          , @fCreateCookie = true, @cookie = @cookie OUTPUT

SELECT @cookie as cookie
SELECT USER as beforeUnsetApprole
```

```
EXEC sp_unsetapprole @cookie

SELECT USER as afterUnsetApprole

REVERT --done with this user
```

This returns the following results:

```
cookie
--------------------------------------------------------------------------
0x224265207375726520746F206472696E6B20796F7572204F76616C74696E652E20220000

beforeUnsetApprole
--------------------------------
AppCan_application

afterUnsetApprole
--------------------------------
dbo
```

The cookie is an interesting value, much larger than a GUID—it was declared as varbinary(8000) in Books Online, so I used that as well. It does change for each execution of the batch.

Schemas

Schemas were introduced and used heavily in the past two chapters, and up to this point, they've been used merely as a grouping mechanism. I used them in the "Setting up Schemas" section of Chapter 5 to group that chapter's example tables together, and you listed the schemas in the AdventureWorks sample database if you installed it. (I'd suggest you install it on any development box. Although it isn't perfect, AdventureWorks contains some workable data for example code, much like the Northwind database did for SQL Server 2000.)

Security is where schemas can pay off. A user owns a schema, and a user can also own multiple schemas. For most any database that you'll develop for a system, the best practice is to let all schemas be owned by the dbo system user. You might remember from previous versions that the dbo owned all objects, and this hasn't changed. What has changed is that instead of the reasonably useless dbo. prefix being attached to all objects, you can nicely group together objects of a common higher purpose, and then (because this is a security chapter) grant rights to users at a schema level, rather than at an individual object level.

For our database-design purposes, assign rights for users to use the following:

- Tables (and columns)

- Views

- Synonyms

- Functions

- Procedures

You can grant rights to other types of objects, including user-defined aggregates, queues, and XML schema collections, but I won't cover them here. As an example, in the AdventureWorks database, there's a HumanResources schema. Use the following query of the sys.objects catalog view (which reflects schema-scoped objects):

```
USE AdventureWorks
GO
SELECT  type_desc, count(*)
FROM    sys.objects
WHERE   schema_name(schema_id) = 'HumanResources'
  AND   type_desc in ('SQL_STORED_PROCEDURE','CLR_STORED_PROCEDURE',
                      'SQL_SCALAR_FUNCTION','CLR_SCALAR_FUNCTION',
                      'CLR_TABLE_VALUED_FUNCTION','SYNONYM',
                      'SQL_INLINE_TABLE_VALUED_FUNCTION',
                      'SQL_TABLE_VALUED_FUNCTION','USER_TABLE','VIEW')
GROUP BY type_desc
GO
USE SecurityChapter --or your own db if you are not using mine
```

This query shows how many of each object can be found in the HumanResources schema:

```
type_desc
------------------------------------------------------------ -----------
SQL_STORED_PROCEDURE                                         3
USER_TABLE                                                   7
VIEW                                                         6
```

Although I'll introduce permissions in the next section, I should note here that to grant permissions to a schema to a role or user, you use :: between SCHEMA and the schema name. To give the users full usage rights to all these, you can use the following command:

```
GRANT EXECUTE, SELECT, INSERT, UPDATE, DELETE on SCHEMA::<schemaname> to <username>
```

In the example, user Tom now has complete access to SELECT from tables, views, and table-valued user-defined functions, and EXECUTE rights to all procedures, scalar functions, and so on. By using schemas and roles liberally, the complexity of granting rights to users on database objects can be vastly simpler than in previous versions of SQL Server. That's because, instead of having to make sure rights are granted to 10 or even 100 stored procedures to support your application's Customer section, you need just a single line of code:

```
GRANT EXECUTE on SCHEMA::Customer to CustomerSupport
```

Bam! Every user in the CustomerSupport role now has access to the stored procedures in this schema. Be prudent by not going so far down this path that you forget any special cases, but certainly this is a good technique for many cases.

Controlling Object Access Via Coded Objects

Just using the database-level security in SQL Server allows us to give a user rights to access only certain objects, but as we've seen, the database-level security doesn't work in an altogether user-friendly manner, nor does it give us a great amount of specific control. We can control access to the entire table, or at the most restrict access at a column level.

In this chapter, we get down to the business of taking complete control over database access by using the following types of objects:

- *Stored procedures and scalar functions*: You can give users an API to the database, which only presents them with actions that can be secured at the object level.

- *Views and table-valued functions*: In cases where the tools being used can't use stored procedures, you can still use views to present an interface to the data that appears to the user as a normal table would. In terms of security, views and table-valued functions can be used for partitioning data vertically by hiding columns or even horizontally by providing row-level security.

These objects let you take control of the data in ways that not only give you security over the data from a visibility or modifiability standpoint, but let you control everything the user can do. No, modifiability is probably not technically a word, but it will be if you just start using it.

One term that I need to introduce is *ownership chaining*. Just because a user can use a stored procedure or function doesn't necessarily mean that he or she has to have rights to every object to which the stored procedure refers. As long as the owner or the object owns all the schemas for all the objects that are referenced, the ownership chain isn't broken, and any user granted rights to use the object can see any referenced data. If you break the ownership chain and reference data in a schema not owned by the same user, the user will require rights granted directly to the object, instead of the object being created. This concept of the ownership chain is at the heart of why controlling object access via coded objects is so nice.

Stored Procedures and Scalar Functions

Security in stored procedures and functions is always at the object level. This is nice because we can give the user rights to do many things without the user knowing how it's done. Also, the user needn't have the ability to do any of the actions without the stored procedures.

In some companies, stored procedures are used as the primary security mechanism, by requiring that all access to the server be done without executing a single "raw" DML statement against the tables. By building code that encapsulates all functionality, you then can apply permissions to the stored procedures to restrict what the user can do.

Beyond the performance benefits of restricting the number of distinct possible queries that you have to tune, this allows you to have *situational control* on access to a table. This means that you might have two different procedures that functionally do exactly the same operation, but giving a user rights to one procedure doesn't imply that he or she has rights to the other.

For example, if you have a column, and you want to force the user to be able only to bump the value by one, this is easily done by building a procedure to do only this without the users of the procedure having to guess what they need to do. Also, if one user has special powers or needs, and can add any amount to the value instead of just one, you can easily build two procedures. Of course, this could get out of hand if taken to the nth degree, and maintenance could become a nightmare with hundreds of procedures. This is rarely necessary, and you could simply use the methods discussed earlier to check if a user is a member of a group for a given range of parameter values.

```
IF NOT(is_member('groupName'))
    IF @parameter NOT BETWEEN 1 and 10
        RAISERROR ('Only members of ''groupName'' can...
```

You could also create a procedure that called the other procedure with only limited parameter values. What's nice is that stored procedures become a sort of API to the database, which gives you granular control over security, and from which the user is isolated.

So, if a screen is built using one procedure, the user might be able to do an action, such as deleting a row from a specific table, but not when the screen uses a different procedure. What makes this even nicer is that with decent naming of your objects, you can give end users or managers rights to dole out security based on actions they want their employees to have, without needing the IT staff to handle it.

The first step is to create a new login and user for the demonstration:

```
CREATE USER procUser WITHOUT LOGIN
```

Then (as dbo), create a new schema and table:

```
CREATE SCHEMA procTest
CREATE TABLE procTest.misc
(
    Value varchar(20),
    Value2 varchar(20)
)
GO
INSERT INTO procTest.misc
VALUES ('somevalue','secret')
INSERT INTO procTest.misc
VALUES ('anothervalue','secret')
```

Next, create a new procedure to return the values from the value column in the table, not the value2 column:

```
CREATE PROCEDURE procTest.misc$select
AS
    SELECT Value
    FROM    procTest.misc
GO
GRANT EXECUTE on procTest.misc$select to procUser
```

Then change context to the procUser user and try to SELECT from the table:

```
EXECUTE AS USER = 'procUser'
GO
SELECT Value, Value2
FROM    procTest.misc
```

You get the following error message, because the user hasn't been given rights to access this table:

```
Msg 229, Level 14, State 5, Line 1
SELECT permission denied on object 'misc', database 'SecurityChapter',
schema 'procTest'.
```

However, execute the following procedure:

```
EXECUTE procTest.misc$select
```

The user does have access to execute the procedure, so you get the results expected:

```
Value
-------------------
somevalue
anothervalue
```

For most database architects, this is the best way to architect a database solution. It leaves a manageable surface area, gives you a lot of control over what SQL is executed in the database, and lets you control data security nicely.

You can see what kinds of access a user has to stored procedures by executing the following statement (this is an alternate method to the sys.database_permissions catalog view used earlier):

```
SELECT  routine_schema + '.' + routine_name as procedureName,
        has_perms_by_name(routine_schema + '.' + routine_name, 'object', 'EXECUTE')
                                                        as allowExecute

FROM    information_schema.routines
WHERE   routine_type = 'PROCEDURE'

REVERT
```

If you were only using stored procedures to access the data, this query could be executed by the application programmer to know everything the user can do in the database.

Crossing Database Lines

So far, all the code and issues we've discussed have been concerned with everything owned by a single owner in a single database. When our code and/or relationships must go outside the database limits, the complexity is greatly increased. This is because in SQL Server architecture, databases have generally been thought of as independent containers of data (more on the architecture of SQL Server databases in the next chapter). However, often you need to share data from one database to another, often for some object that's located in a third-party system your company has purchased.

This can be a real problem for the following reasons:

- Foreign key constraints cannot be used to handle referential integrity needs.

- Backups must be coordinated. You lose some of the protection from a single database-backup scenario. This is because when, heaven forbid, a database restore is needed, it isn't possible to make certain that the data in the two databases is in sync.

Although accessing data in outside databases causes difficulties, sometimes it's unavoidable. A typical example might be tying an off-the-shelf system into a home-grown system. Accessing data in a different database but on the same server is similar to the normal (same database, same server) situation.

Beyond the coding and maintenance aspects, which aren't trivial, one of the most important things to deal with is security. As mentioned in the first paragraph of this section, databases are generally considered independent in the security theme of how SQL Server works. This causes issues when you need to include data outside the database, because users are scoped to a database. That's why userA in database1 is never the same as userA in database2, even if they're mapped to the same login.

The ownership chain inside the boundaries of a database is relatively simple. If the owner of the object refers only to other objects he owns, then the chain isn't broken. Any user to whom he grants rights can use the object. However, when leaving the confines of a single database, things get murky. Even if a database is owned by the exact same system login, the ownership chain is broken when an object references data outside the database. So, not only does the object creator need to have access to the objects outside the database, the caller needs rights also.

There are three reasonable ways to handle this:

- Using cross-database chaining

- Impersonation

- Certificate-based trusts

I'll briefly explain and demonstrate each type of solution.

Using Cross-Database Chaining

The cross-database chaining solution is to tell the database to recognize that indeed the owners of database1 and database2 are the same. Then, if you as system admistrator want to allow users to use your objects seamlessly across databases, then it's fine. However, a few steps and requirements need to be met:

- Each database that participates in the chaining relationship must be owned by the same system login.

- The DB_CHAINING database option (set using ALTER DATABASE) must be set to ON for each database involved in the relationship. It's OFF by default.

- The database where the object uses external resources must have the TRUSTWORTHY database option set to ON; it's OFF by default. (Again, set this using ALTER DATABASE.)

- The users who use the objects need to have a user in the database where the external resources reside.

■**Caution** It's important to understand the implications of doing this. You're effectively opening up the external database resources completely to the users in the database who are members of the db_owner database role, even if they have no rights in the external database. Because of the last two criteria, this isn't a bad thing to do for most corporate situations where you simply have to retrieve data from another database. However, opening access to the external database resources can be especially bad for shared database systems, as this can be used to get access to the data in a chaining-enabled database. All that needs to be known is the username and login name of a user in the other database.

Note that if you need to turn chaining on or off for *all* databases, you can use this code:

```
EXEC sp_configure 'Cross DB Ownership Chaining', '1';
RECONFIGURE
--'1' turns it on, '0' turns it off. '0' is default
```

As an example, consider the following scenario. We'll create two databases with a table in each database, and then a procedure. First, we create the new database, and add a simple table. We won't add any rows or keys, as this isn't important to our demo. Note that we have to create a login for this demo, as the user must be based on the same login in both databases:

```
CREATE DATABASE externalDb
GO
USE externalDb
GO
                                    --smurf theme song :)
CREATE LOGIN smurf WITH PASSWORD = 'La la, la la la la, la, la la la la'
CREATE USER smurf FROM LOGIN smurf
CREATE TABLE dbo.table1 ( value int )
```

Next, we create a local database, the one where we'll be executing our queries. We add the login we created as a new user, and again create a table:

```
CREATE DATABASE localDb
GO
USE localDb
GO
CREATE USER smurf FROM LOGIN smurf
```

We then set the chaining and trustworthy attributes for the localDb, and chaining for the externalDb:

```
ALTER DATABASE localDb
   SET DB_CHAINING ON
ALTER DATABASE localDb
   SET TRUSTWORTHY ON

ALTER DATABASE externalDb
   SET DB_CHAINING ON
```

Making these settings requires sysadmin rights. We can see the metadata for these databases using the sys.databases catalog view:

```
SELECT cast(name as varchar(10)) as name,
       cast(suser_sname(owner_sid) as varchar(10)) as owner,
       is_trustworthy_on, is_db_chaining_on
FROM   sys.databases where name in ('localdb','externaldb')
```

This returns the following results:

name	owner	is_trustworthy_on	is_db_chaining_on
externalDb	DOMAIN\Username	0	1
localDb	DOMAIN\Username	1	1

Next, we create a simple procedure, selecting data from both databases, the objects being owned by the same owner. We then give rights to our new user:

```
CREATE PROCEDURE dbo.externalDb$testCrossDatabase
AS
SELECT Value
FROM   externalDb.dbo.table1
GO
GRANT execute on dbo.externalDb$testCrossDatabase to smurf
```

Now try it out.

```
EXECUTE AS USER = 'smurf'
go
EXECUTE dbo.externalDb$testCrossDatabase
REVERT
```

This returns the following result, because this user doesn't have rights to the table, and the ownership chain is broken because of changing ownership chains:

```
Value
-----------
```

Impersonation

An alternative to using the DB_CHAINING setting is to use impersonation. As long as the database is set as TRUSTWORTHY, you can rewrite the procedure as follows:

```
CREATE PROCEDURE dbo.externalDb$testCrossDatabase_Impersonation
WITH EXECUTE AS SELF --as procedure creator
AS
SELECT Value
FROM    externalDb.dbo.table1
GO
GRANT execute on dbo.externalDb$testCrossDatabase_impersonation to smurf
```

If the login of the owner of the dbo schema (in this case my login, because I created both databases) has access to the other database, then you can impersonate the dbo in this manner. In fact, you can access the external resources seamlessly. This is probably the simplest method of handling cross-database chaining for most corporate needs. However, impersonation should raise a big flag if you're working on a database server that's shared among many different companies.

Because it requires sysadmin privileges to set TRUSTWORTHY on, using impersonation isn't a tremendous hole, but note that the members of the sysadmin role aren't required to understand the implications if one of their users calls up and asks for TRUSTWORTHY to be turned on for them.

If TRUSTWORTHY is set to OFF, you'll receive the following error:

```
Msg 916, Level 14, State 1,
Procedure externalDb$testCrossDatabase_Impersonation, Line 4
The server principal "COMPASS.NET\lbdavi" is not able to access the database
"externalDb" under the current security context.
```

Using a Certificate-Based User

The final thing I'll demonstrate is using a single certificate installed in both databases. We'll use it to sign the stored procedure and map a user to this certificate in the target database. This is a straightforward technique, and is the best way to do cross-database security chaining when the system isn't a dedicated corporate resource. It takes a bit of setup, but it isn't overwhelmingly difficult. What makes using a certificate nice is that you don't need to open the hole left in the system's security by setting the database to TRUSTWORTHY. This is because the user who will be executing the procedure is a user in the database, just as if the target login or user was given rights in the externalDB. Because the certificate matches, SQL Server knows that this cross-database access is acceptable.

First turn off the TRUSTWORTHY setting:

```
REVERT
GO
USE localDb
GO
ALTER DATABASE localDb
    SET TRUSTWORTHY OFF
```

Then create another procedure and give the user smurf rights to execute it, just like the others (which won't work now because TRUSTWORTHY is turned off):

```
CREATE PROCEDURE dbo.externalDb$testCrossDatabase_Certificate
AS
SELECT Value
FROM   externalDb.dbo.table1
GO
GRANT EXECUTE on dbo.externalDb$testCrossDatabase_Certificate to smurf
```

Then create a certificate:

```
CREATE CERTIFICATE procedureExecution ENCRYPTION BY PASSWORD = 'Cert Password'
 WITH SUBJECT =  'Used to sign procedure:externalDb$testCrossDatabase_Certificate'
```

Then add this certificate as a signature on the procedure:

```
ADD SIGNATURE TO dbo.externalDb$testCrossDatabase_Certificate
BY CERTIFICATE procedureExecution WITH PASSWORD = 'Cert Password'
```

Finally, make an OS file out of the certificate, so a certificate object can be created in the externalDb based on the same certificate (choose a directory that works best for you):

```
BACKUP CERTIFICATE procedureExecution TO FILE = 'c:\temp\procedureExecution.cer'
```

This completes the setup of the localDb. Next, you have to apply the certificate to the externalDb:

```
USE externalDb
GO
CREATE CERTIFICATE procedureExecution FROM FILE = 'c:\temp\procedureExecution.cer'
```

Next, map the certificate to a user, and give this user rights to the table1 that the user in the other database is trying to access:

```
CREATE USER procCertificate FOR CERTIFICATE procedureExecution
GO
GRANT SELECT on dbo.table1 TO procCertificate
```

Now you're good to go. Change back to the localDb and execute the procedure:

```
USE localDb
GO
EXECUTE AS LOGIN = 'smurf'
EXECUTE dbo.externalDb$testCrossDatabase_Certificate
```

This isn't as simple as the other possiblities, but it's more secure, for certain. I didn't cover any of the intricacies of using certificates. However, now you have a safe way of crossing database boundaries that doesn't require giving the user direct object access, and doesn't open up a hole in your security. Hence, you could use this solution on any server in any situation. Make sure to secure/destroy the certificate file once you've used it, so no other user can use it to gain access to your system. Then we can clean up the databases used for the example.

```
REVERT
GO
USE MASTER
GO
DROP DATABASE externalDb
DROP DATABASE localDb
GO
USE SecurityChapter
```

Changing Execution Context

I already talked about the EXECUTE AS statement, and it has some great applications, but the WITH EXECUTE clause on a procedure declaration can give you some incredible flexibility to give the executor of a procedure greater powers that might not have been possible. Instead of changing context before doing an operation, you can change context while executing stored procedures, functions, and DML triggers (plus queues for service brokers, but I won't be covering that topic).

By adding the following code, we can change the security context of the procedure to this principal when the execution begins:

```
CREATE PROCEDURE <schemaName>.<procedureName>
WITH EXECUTE AS <'loginName' | caller | self | owner>
```

The different options for who to execute as are as follows:

- 'userName': A valid username in the database

- caller: The default, it's in the context of the user who called the procedure

- self: It's in the context of the user who created the procedure

- owner: It's executed in the context of the owner of the module or schema

Note that using EXECUTE AS doesn't affect the ownership chaining of the call. The security of the statements in the object is still based on the security of the schema owner. Only when the ownership chain is broken will the ownership chaining come into play. The following statements go along with the EXECUTE AS clause:

- EXECUTE AS CALLER: You can execute this in your code to go back to the default, where access is as user.

- REVERT: This reverts the security back to the security specified in the WITH EXECUTE AS clause.

As an example (and this does get messy), we'll build a situation where one schema owner has a table, and the next schema owner has a table and a procedure that the schema owner wants to use to access the first user's table. Finally, we have an average user who wants to do his or her job by executing the stored procedure.

First, we create a few users and give them rights to create objects in the database. The three users are named as follows:

- schemaOwner: This user owns the primary schema where one of the objects resides.

- procedureOwner: This user owns the owner of an object, and a stored procedure.

- aveSchlub: This is the average user who finally wants to use procedureOwner's stored procedure.

```
USE SecurityChapter
GO
--this will be the owner of the primary schema
CREATE USER schemaOwner WITHOUT LOGIN
GRANT CREATE SCHEMA to schemaOwner
GRANT CREATE TABLE to schemaOwner

--this will be the procedure creator
CREATE USER procedureOwner WITHOUT LOGIN
GRANT CREATE SCHEMA to procedureOwner
GRANT CREATE PROCEDURE to procedureOwner
GRANT CREATE TABLE to procedureOwner
GO

--this will be the average user who needs to access data
CREATE USER aveSchlub WITHOUT LOGIN
```

Then we change to the context of the main object owner, create a new schema, and then a table with some rows:

```
EXECUTE AS USER = 'schemaOwner'
GO
CREATE SCHEMA schemaOwnersSchema
GO
CREATE TABLE schemaOwnersSchema.Person
(
    PersonId    int constraint PKtestAccess_Person primary key,
    FirstName   varchar(20),
    LastName    varchar(20)
)
Go
INSERT INTO schemaOwnersSchema.Person
VALUES (1, 'Paul','McCartney')
INSERT INTO schemaOwnersSchema.Person
VALUES (2, 'Pete','Townshend')
```

Next, this user gives SELECT permissions to the procedureOwner user:

```
GRANT SELECT on schemaOwnersSchema.Person to procedureOwner
```

Then we set context to the secondary user to create the procedure:

```
REVERT --we can step back on the stack of principals, but we can't change directly
        --to procedureOwner. Here I step back to the db_owner user you have
        --used throughout the chapter
GO
EXECUTE AS USER = 'procedureOwner'
```

Then we create a schema and another table:

```
CREATE SCHEMA procedureOwnerSchema
GO

CREATE TABLE procedureOwnerSchema.otherPerson
(
    personId     int constraint PKtestAccess_person primary key,
    FirstName    varchar(20),
    LastName     varchar(20)
)
go
INSERT INTO procedureOwnerSchema.otherPerson
VALUES (1, 'Rocky','Racoon')
INSERT INTO procedureOwnerSchema.otherPerson
VALUES (2, 'Sally','Simpson')
```

Then we create two procedures as the secondary users, one for the WITH EXECUTE AS as CALLER, which is the default, then SELF, which puts it in the context of the creator, in this case procedureOwner:

```
CREATE PROCEDURE  procedureOwnerSchema.person$asCaller
WITH EXECUTE AS CALLER --this is the default
AS
SELECT  personId, FirstName, LastName
FROM    procedureOwnerSchema.otherPerson --<-- ownership same as proc

SELECT  personId, FirstName, LastName
FROM    schemaOwnersSchema.person   --<-- breaks ownership chain
GO

CREATE PROCEDURE procedureOwnerSchema.person$asSelf
WITH EXECUTE AS SELF --now this runs in context of procedureOwner,
                     --since it created it
AS
SELECT  personId, FirstName, LastName
FROM    procedureOwnerSchema.otherPerson --<-- ownership same as proc

SELECT  personId, FirstName, LastName
FROM    schemaOwnersSchema.person   --<-- breaks ownership chain
```

Next we grant rights on the proc to the aveSchlub user:

```
GRANT EXECUTE ON procedureOwnerSchema.person$asCaller to aveSchlub
GRANT EXECUTE ON procedureOwnerSchema.person$asSelf to aveSchlub
```

Then we change to the context of the aveSchlub:

```
REVERT
GO
EXECUTE AS USER = 'aveSchlub'
```

We then execute the procedure:

```
--this proc is in context of the caller, in this case, aveSchlub
execute procedureOwnerSchema.person$asCaller
```

This gives us the following output, because the ownership chain is fine for the procedureOwnerSchema object, but not for the schemaOwnerSchema:

personId	FirstName	LastName
1	Rocky	Racoon
2	Sally	Simpson

```
Msg 229, Level 14, State 5, Procedure person$asCaller, Line 4
SELECT permission denied on object 'person', database 'SecurityChapter',
schema 'schemaOwnerSchema'.
```

Next we execute the asSelf variant:

```
--procedureOwner, so it works
execute procedureOwnerSchema.person$asSelf
```

This returns two result sets:

personId	FirstName	LastName
1	Rocky	Racoon
2	Sally	Simpson

personId	FirstName	LastName
1	Paul	McCartney
2	Pete	Townshend

What makes this different is that when the ownership chain is broken, the security context we're in is the secondaryUser, not the context of the caller, aveSchlub. This is a cool feature, as we can now give a user temporary rights that won't even be apparent to him or her, and won't require granting any permissions.

However, EXECUTE AS isn't a feature that should be overused, as it could be all too easy just to build your procs in the context of the dbo and forget about doing decent security altogether.

One nice side effect of this is that we could use EXECUTE AS instead of chaining, by setting the EXECUTE AS to a user who can access a different database directly, so the system user may have rights to the database, but the executing user cannot.

One thing that you can do with this is to give a user super-rights temporarily in a database. For example, consider the following procedure:

```
REVERT
GO
CREATE PROCEDURE dbo.testDboRights
AS
 BEGIN
    CREATE TABLE dbo.test
    (
        testId int
    )
 END
```

This procedure isn't executable by any user other than one that has rights in the database. Say we have the following user:

```
CREATE USER leroy WITHOUT LOGIN
```

We give him rights (presuming Leroy is a male name) to execute the procedure:

```
GRANT EXECUTE on dbo.testDboRights to leroy
```

Then we execute the procedure:

```
EXECUTE AS USER = 'leroy'
EXECUTE dbo.testDboRights
```

The result would be predictably bad, because leroy isn't a member of the db_owner's role.

```
Msg 262, Level 14, State 1, Procedure testDboRights, Line 5
CREATE TABLE permission denied in database 'SecurityChapter'.
```

If we alter the procedure with EXECUTE AS 'dbo', the result is that the table is created, if there isn't already a table with that name:

```
REVERT
GO
CREATE PROCEDURE dbo.testDboRights
WITH EXECUTE AS dbo
AS
 BEGIN
    CREATE TABLE dbo.test
    (
        testId int
    )
 END
```

For more detailed information about EXECUTE AS, check the "Extending Database Impersonation by Using EXECUTE AS" topic in Books Online.

■**Tip** As discussed previously in this chapter, to use external resources using impersonation, you need to set TRUSTWORTHY to ON using the ALTER DATABASE command.

In Chapter 10, a rather large section discusses the value of ad hoc SQL versus stored procedures, and we make use of the EXECUTE AS functionality to provide security when it comes to executing dynamic SQL in stored procedures. This is a great new feature that will bring stored procedure development—including stored procedures that are CLR-based—to new heights because dynamic SQL-based stored procedures were a security issue in earlier versions of SQL Server.

Different Server (Distributed Queries)

I want to make brief mention of distributed queries, and introduce the functions that can be used to establish a relationship between two SQL Servers, or a SQL Server and an OLE DB or ODBC data source. You can use two methods:

- *Linked servers*: You can build a connection between two servers by registering a "server" name that you then access via a four-part name (<linkedServerName>.<database>.➡ <owner>.<table>), or through the OPENQUERY interface. The linked server name is the name you specify using sp_addlinkedserver. This could be a SQL Server, or anything that can connected to via OLE DB.

- *Ad hoc connections*: Using the OPENROWSET or OPENDATASOURCE interfaces, you can return a table of data from any OLE DB source.

In either case, the security chain will be broken when crossing SQL Server instance connections, and certainly when using any data source that isn't SQL Server–based. Whether or not this is a problem is based on the connection properties and/or connection string used to create the linked server or ad hoc connection. Using linked servers, you could be in the context of the Windows login, or the SQL Server Standard login, or even a single login that everyone uses to "cross over" to the other server.

As I mentioned briefly in the previous section, one use for EXECUTE AS could be to deal with the case where you're working with distributed databases. One user might be delegated to have rights to access the distributed server, and then you execute the procedure as this user to give access to the linked server objects.

Views and Table-Valued Functions

In this section, I'll talk about using views and table-valued functions to encapsulate the views of the data in ways that leave the data in table-like structures. This then allows for more straightforward usage, especially when you don't have the ability to use stored procedures, or when you want to do something behind the scenes every time a user uses a table.

I'll look at the following:

- *General usage*: Basic use of triggers to implement security
- *Configurable row-level security*: You can use views to implement security at the row level, and this can be extended to provide user-manageable security

General Usage

We'll use two properties of views to build a more secure database. The first is assigning privileges to a user such that he can use a view, though not the underlying tables. For example, let's go back to the Products.Product table used earlier in this chapter. As a reminder, execute this statement (after executing REVERT, if you haven't already, from the previous example):

```
SELECT *
FROM    Products.Product
```

The following data is returned:

ProductId	ProductCode	Description	UnitPrice	ActualCost
1	widget12	widget number 12	10.5000	8.5000
2	snurf98	Snurfulator	99.9900	2.5000

We could construct a view on this:

```
CREATE VIEW Products.allProducts
AS
SELECT ProductId,ProductCode, Description, UnitPrice, ActualCost
FROM    Products.Product
```

Selecting data from either the table or the view returns the same data. However, they're two separate structures to which we can separately assign access privileges, and deal with separately. If we need to tweak the table, we might not have to modify the view. Usually the view won't include the exact same columns and rows as the base table.

What makes views useful as a security mechanism is the ability to partition a table structure, by limiting the rows or columns visible to the user. First, we'll look at using views to implement *column-level security*, which is also known as *projection* or *vertical partitioning* of the data, as we'll be dividing the view's columns. For example, consider that the users in a warehouseUsers role need only to see a list of products, not how much they cost, and certainly not how much they cost to produce. We might create a view like the following to partition the columns accordingly:

```
CREATE VIEW Products.WarehouseProducts
AS
SELECT ProductId,ProductCode, Description
FROM    Products.Product
```

By the same token, we can use table-valued functions in much the same way, though we can do more using them. For example, we might code the following function to list all products that are less than some price:

```
CREATE FUNCTION Products.ProductsLessThanPrice
(
    @UnitPrice   decimal(10,4)
)
RETURNS table
AS
    RETURN ( SELECT ProductId, ProductCode, Description, UnitPrice
             FROM    Products.Product
             WHERE   UnitPrice <= @UnitPrice)
```

This can be executed like the following:

```
SELECT * FROM Products.ProductsLessThanPrice(20)
```

This returns the following result:

```
ProductId    ProductCode Description            UnitPrice
-----------  ----------- --------------------   ----------------------------------------
1            widget12    widget number 12       10.5000
```

> ■**Tip** One of the most painful downfalls of using views for security is that we cannot "overload" the name of the object with several different objects. One might see products as having ProductId, ProductCode, and Description, although a different user might see the Product row with all columns. Hence, we have to come up with "coy" names for our views, such as allProducts, ProductSimple, and so on, which can be kind of annoying.

Now, using the same GRANT syntax as in the "Table Security" section, you can give a user rights to use the view for SELECT, INSERT, UPDATE, or DELETE. If the view is a view of multiple tables, the view might not support modifications or deletions, but you can implement INSTEAD OF triggers (as discussed in the previous chapter) to allow these operations on a view to do nearly anything you need.

What makes this grand is that if you aren't able to use stored procedures, due to some technical or political reason, you can do most of the things that you need to do using triggers, and the client programmers needn't know that they exist. The only concern here is that if you change any data that the client might have cached, you might have to work this out so the data and cached copies aren't significantly out of sync.

Implementing Configurable Row-Level Security with Views

I've covered vertical partitioning, which is pretty easy. Row-level security, or *horizontally partitioning* data, isn't quite so elegant, especially if you can't use stored procedures. Using stored procedures, you could have a procedure that fixes certain operations, such as modifying active customers, or just certain products of a specific type, and so on.

The same could be true of views, and you could implement views that included all of a given type of product, and another view for a different type, and yet another for other types. This scheme can work, but it isn't altogether flexible, and it's unnatural for a UI to call different objects to do ostensibly the same operation, just with a slightly different filter of data. It makes the objects tightly coupled with the data in the table. For some fixed domain tables that never change, this isn't a problem. But for many situations, users don't want to have to go back to the programming staff and ask for an implementation for which they have to jump through hoops, because the change will cost money for planning, programming, testing, and such.

In this section, I'll demonstrate a way to implement runtime configurable row-level security, using views. Views let us cut the table in sections that include all the columns, but not all the rows, based on some criteria. To our example table, we're going to add a productType column that we'll use to partition on:

```
ALTER TABLE Products.Product
    ADD ProductType varchar(20) NULL
GO
UPDATE Products.Product
SET    ProductType = 'widget'
WHERE  ProductCode = 'widget12'
GO
UPDATE Products.Product
SET    ProductType = 'snurf'
WHERE  ProductCode = 'snurf98'
```

Looking at the data in the table, we see the following results:

ProductId	ProductCode	Description	UnitPrice	ActualCost	ProductType
1	widget12	widget number 12	10.5000	8.5000	widget
2	snurf98	Snurfulator	99.9900	2.5000	snurf

As discussed, the simplest version of row-level security is just building views to partition the data. For example, suppose we want to share the widgets only with a certain group in a company, mapped to a role. We can build the following view:

```
CREATE VIEW Products.WidgetProducts
AS
SELECT ProductId, ProductCode, Description, UnitPrice, ActualCost
FROM    Products.Product
WHERE   ProductType = 'widget'
WITH CHECK OPTION
```

Now, we can select data from this table and never know that other products exist:

```
SELECT *
FROM    Products.WidgetProducts
```

This returns the following result:

ProductId	ProductCode	Description	UnitPrice	ActualCost
1	widget12	widget number 12	10.5000	8.5000

■**Note** We can grant INSERT, UPDATE, and DELETE rights to the user to modify the view as well, because it's based on one table and we set the WITH CHECK OPTION. This option ensures that the rows after modification remain visible through the view after the change, or in this case, that the user couldn't change the ProductType if it were in the SELECT list. The only rows a user of this view would be able to modify would be the ones WHERE ProductType = 'widget'. Using INSTEAD OF triggers as discussed in Chapter 6, we can code almost any security we want to for modifications on our views. For simple views the CHECK OPTION might work fine; otherwise use triggers or stored procedures as needed.

This view can then have permissions granted to let only certain people use it. This is a decent technique when you have an easily described set, or possibly few types to work with, but can become a maintenance headache.

A better method is to vary the security by security group and some grouping of the data. In our next step, ramping up row-level security, we build the following view to let users only see snurfs if they're members of the snurfViewer role, using the is_member function:

```
CREATE VIEW Products.ProductsSelective
AS
SELECT ProductId, ProductCode, Description, UnitPrice, ActualCost
FROM    Products.Product
WHERE   ProductType <> 'snurf'
   or   (is_member('snurfViewer') = 1)
   or   (is_member('db_owner') = 1) --can't add db_owner to a role
WITH CHECK OPTION
GO
GRANT SELECT ON Products.ProductsSelective to public
```

Then we create a principal named Chrissy and the snurfViewer role. Note that we don't add this user to the group yet; we'll do that later in the example:

```
CREATE USER chrissy WITHOUT LOGIN
CREATE ROLE snurfViewer
```

Then we change security context to chrissy and select from the view:

```
EXECUTE AS USER = 'chrissy'
SELECT * from Products.ProductsSelective
```

This returns the one row to which she has access:

ProductId	ProductCode	Description	UnitPrice	ActualCost	ProductType
1	widget12	widget number 12	10.5000	8.5000	widget

Next, we add Chrissy to the `snurfViewer` group, go back to context as this user, and run the statement again:

```
REVERT
execute sp_addrolemember 'snurfViewer', 'chrissy'

EXECUTE AS USER = 'chrissy'
SELECT * from Products.ProductsSelective
```

Now we see all the rows:

ProductId	ProductCode	Description	UnitPrice	ActualCost	ProductType
1	widget12	widget number 12	10.5000	8.5000	widget
2	snurf98	Snurfulator	99.9900	2.5000	snurf

This is even better, but still rigid, and requires foreknowledge of the data during the design phase. Instead, we'll create a table that maps database role principals with different types of products. Now this gives us total control. We create the following solution:

```
REVERT
GO
CREATE TABLE Products.ProductSecurity
(
    ProductsSecurityId int identity(1,1)
                CONSTRAINT PKProducts_ProductsSecurity PRIMARY KEY,
    ProductType varchar(20), --at this point you probably will create a
                        --ProductType domain table, but this keeps the example
                        --more simple
    DatabaseRole    sysname,
            CONSTRAINT AKProducts_ProductsSecurity_typeRoleMapping
                    UNIQUE (ProductType, DatabaseRole)
)
```

Then we insert a row that will be used to give everyone with database rights the ability to see widget-type products:

```
INSERT INTO Products.ProductSecurity(ProductType, DatabaseRole)
VALUES ('widget','public')
```

Then we alter the `ProductsSelective` view to show only rows to which the user has rights, based on row security:

```
ALTER VIEW Products.ProductsSelective
AS
SELECT Product.ProductId, Product.ProductCode, Product.Description,
       Product.UnitPrice, Product.ActualCost, Product.ProductType
FROM   Products.Product as Product
          JOIN Products.ProductSecurity as ProductSecurity
              on  (Product.ProductType = ProductSecurity.ProductType
                  and is_member(ProductSecurity.DatabaseRole) = 1)
                  or is_member('db_owner') = 1 --don't leave out the dbo!
```

This view joins the Product table to the ProductSecurity table, and checks the matching roles against the role membership of the principal. Now we test it:

```
EXECUTE AS USER = 'chrissy'
SELECT * FROM ProductsSelective
```

This returns the following result:

ProductId	ProductCode	Description	UnitPrice	ActualCost	ProductType
1	widget12	widget number 12	10.5000	8.5000	widget

Then we add the snurfViewer role to the ProductSecurity table and try again:

```
REVERT
INSERT INTO Products.ProductSecurity(ProductType, databaseRole)
VALUES ('snurf','snurfViewer')
go
EXECUTE AS USER = 'chrissy'
SELECT * FROM ProductsSelective
```

Now you see it returns all data:

ProductId	ProductCode	Description	UnitPrice	ActualCost	ProductType
1	widget12	widget number 12	10.5000	8.5000	widget
2	snurf98	Snurfulator	99.9900	2.5000	snurf

This causes a bit of overhead, but then again, all solutions for row-level security will. If you need it, you need it, and not much more can be said. The important aspect of this solution is that we can now use this view in a stored procedure, and regardless of who owns the stored procedure, we can restrict column usage in a generic manner that only uses SQL Server security.

■**Tip** You can take this type of thing to the nth degree and get really specific with the security. You can even selectively hide and show columns to the user (replacing values with NULLs, or 'securevalue', or something). What's better is that once you have set it up, it's a no-brainer to add a principal to a group, and bam, that person has everything he or she needs, without costly setup.

Obfuscating Data

It isn't always possible to keep users from accessing the data. We database-administrator types too often have unfettered access to entire production systems with way too much access. Even with the far-improved security granularity provided by SQL Server 2005, a few users will still have rights to run as a member of the sys_admin server role, giving them access to *all* data.

Also, technically, once a person has access to the backups of the system, he or she can technically, and with great ease, access any data in the database. If you can attach the database, the data is going to be viewable, in some fashion. If you're dealing with sensitive data—and who isn't these days—you need to be wary of how you deal with this data:

- Do you back the database up? Where are these backups?

- Do you send the backups to an offsite safe location? Who takes them there?

- Who has access to the servers where data is stored? Do you trust the fate of your company in their hands? Could these servers be hacked?

You have to do something with sensitive data to make sure that if the users get access, there's a far lesser chance that the data will be compromised. For this, you generally use some form of encryption, and in 2005 encryption is built in. The key to encryption is that you don't include all the information needed to decrypt the data in the same package. Otherwise, it's as bad as putting a sign on your new Mustang saying, "Please don't steal my car; I left the keys in it and a full tank of gas!"

You need to prepare the data by making it look "funny" and unusable without having an additional "key" with which to view it. SQL Server has a rich set of encryption features, featuring a key- and certificate-management system. You can use this system to encrypt data from each user, and from people who might get access to the data outside of the server.

In the following example, I'll use the simplest encryption that SQL Server 2005 gives you, using the encryptByPassPhrase. (You can also use keys, asymmetric keys, and certificates). The encryptByPassPhrase function lets you specify your key as a string value that SQL Server uses to "munge" the data, such that you must have this key to reconstitute the data.

As an example, we'll build an incredibly simple encryption scheme that you could use to secure a column in your database. First, as a quick demonstration of how the function works, consider the following:

```
SELECT encryptByPassPhrase('hi', 'Secure data')
```

'Secure data' is the value to be encrypted, and 'hi' is the passphrase that's required to get this value back later. Executing this statement returns the following result:

```
---------------------------------------------------------------------
0x010000004D2B87C6725612388F8BA4DA082495E8C836FF76F32BCB642B36476594B4F014
```

This is a clearly unreadable binary string, and even cooler, the value is different every time you execute it. To decrypt it, just use the following:

```
SELECT decryptByPassPhrase('hi',
        0x010000004D2B87C6725612388F8BA4DA082495E8C836FF76F32BCB642B36476594B4F014)
```

This returns the following result:

```
-----------------------
0x5365637572652064617461
```

This is the binary representation of our original string, which makes it easy to represent most any datatype. To use the value, you have to cast it back to the original varchar type:

```
SELECT cast(decryptByPassPhrase('hi',
        0x010000004D2B87C6725612388F8BA4DA082495E8C836FF76F32BCB642B36476594B4F014)
                                                            as varchar(30))
```

This returns the following result:

```
------------------------------
Secure data
```

Tip The data is different each time because the encryption scheme uses various nonencrypted data, such as the time value, to encrypt the data (this is generally known as the salt value of the encryption). You cannot infer the decryption of all values based on breaking a single value.

Let's take this to the next level. In this example, we'll encrypt a credit card number in the database, a common need in many databases. Such personal and financial information needs to be kept where it can only be used by the correct people or processes.

The first step is to create a database that no one has rights to, other than the owner of the database. This database should be as isolated as possible from any of the staff, because if the value is known, the encryption is easy pickings.

This database has a single table with the password for encrypting and decrypting data (which is credit cards, in our example):

```
CREATE DATABASE EncryptionMaster
go
USE EncryptionMaster
go
CREATE SCHEMA Security
CREATE TABLE Security.passphrase
(
    passphrase nvarchar(4000) --the max size of the passphrase
)
```

This is the passphrase that all encryption and decryption will use for our solution:

```
INSERT  into Security.passphrase
VALUES ('ljlOIUEojljljieo#*JlLjlIu*o7G8i&t87*&Yh[pOO') --the more unobvious the
                                                --better!
```

Then we create the application database to hold Customer rows, including our encrypted CreditCardNumber:

```
CREATE DATABASE CreditInfo
GO
ALTER DATABASE EncryptionMaster   -- we will be using impersonation to keep the
    SET TRUSTWORTHY ON            -- example simple, in practice I would
                                  -- probably use certificates
GO
USE CreditInfo
GO

CREATE SCHEMA Sales
GO
CREATE TABLE Sales.Customer
(
    CustomerId   char(10),
    FirstName    varchar(30),
    LastName     varchar(30),
    CreditCardLastFour char(4),
    CreditCardNumber varbinary(44)
)
```

Now, the key here is to build the procedure without enabling database security chaining on the server or enabling it on the encryptionMaster database. No user should have direct access to the passphrase table. We use the WITH EXECUTE AS setting we discussed earlier in this chapter. This allows us not to give the caller any rights to the encryption database, but the user can still get values out:

```
CREATE PROCEDURE Customer$insert
(
    @CustomerId   char(10),
    @FirstName    varchar(10),
    @LastName     varchar(10),
    @CreditCardNumber char(16)
)
WITH EXECUTE AS 'dbo'
as

INSERT INTO Sales.Customer (CustomerId,FirstName, LastName, CreditCardLastFour,
                            CreditCardNumber)
SELECT  @CustomerId, @FirstName,@LastName,substring(@CreditCardNumber,13,4),
        encryptByPassPhrase(pass.passPhrase, @CreditCardNumber)
FROM    encryptionMaster.Security.passphrase as pass
```

Now we can test the procedure using the following code:

```
EXEC Customer$insert 'cust1','Bob','jones','0000111122223333'
```

To view the data, we use a stored procedure:

```
CREATE PROCEDURE Sales.CustomerWithCreditCard
WITH EXECUTE AS 'dbo'
AS
 BEGIN
        SELECT  Customer.CustomerId, FirstName, LastName,
                CreditCardLastFour,
                cast(decryptByPassPhrase(pass.passPhrase,CreditCardNumber)
                        as char(16)) as CreditCardNumber
        FROM    Sales.Customer
                    CROSS JOIN encryptionMaster.Security.passphrase as pass
 END
```

Then we execute as:

```
EXEC Sales.CustomerWithCreditCard
```

This returns the row with decrypted values:

CustomerId	FirstName	LastName	CreditCardLastFour	CreditCardNumber
1	Bob	Jones	3333	0000111122223333

Now granting rights to this procedure and giving access to it gives the user rights to view credit card numbers, but not to see how they're encrypted or decrypted. Also note that the procedure would likely only be used by a computer process to send the credit card to the authorization authority.

Now, here's the most important part. *Don't back up the* encryptionMaster *database* to the same media as the CreditInfo database, because if someone gets both databases, it's child's play to steal your data. It's good policy to back up this database to a CD (or two), write down the key (it might take a day to enter, but that would be better than losing all your data), and store it in a cool dry place where no one can get access to it.

Now, say your backup tape is pocketed by an employee who's changing jobs from legit IT worker to a credit-card–number salesperson. The data is worthless, and all your press release need say is: "Company X regrets to say that some financial data tapes were stolen from our vaults. All data was encrypted; hence, there is little chance any usable data was acquired." And you, as DBA, will be worshipped!

Keeping an Eye on Users

Often a client won't care too much about security, so he or she doesn't want to limit what a user can do in the database. However, many times there's a hidden subtext: "I don't want to be restrictive, but how can we keep up with what users have done?"

An alternative to implementing a full-blown security system can be simply to watch what users do, in case they do something they shouldn't. To implement our "Big Brother" security scenario, I'll demonstrate three possible techniques:

- *Watching table history using triggers*: Keep up with a history of previous values for rows in a table.

- *DDL triggers*: Use these to log any DDL events, such as creating users, creating or modifying tables, and so on.

- *Using Profiler*: Profiler catches everything, so you can use it to watch user activity.

In some cases, these techniques are used to augment the security of a system; for example, to make sure system administrators keep out of certain parts of the system.

Watching Table History Using Triggers

As discussed in Chapter 6, about using triggers, you can run code whenever a user executes an INSERT, UPDATE, or DELETE DML statement on a table or view. We already constructed an auditing trigger in Chapter 6 in the section "DML Triggers" that audited change, and we'll create another one here. When finished, a history of the previous values for a column in a table will be maintained, in case some user changes the data improperly.

The scenario is that we have a slice of the Sales and Inventory sections of the database for products and invoices (see Figure 7-1).

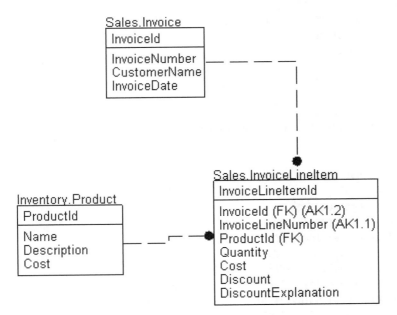

Figure 7-1. *Sample tables for Table History example*

On each invoice line item, there's a cost and a discount percentage. If the cost value doesn't match the current value in the Product table, and the discount percentage isn't zero, we want to log the difference. A report of differences will be built and sent to the manager to let the values be checked, to make sure everything is within reason.

First we build the tables, going back to the SecurityChapter database (or whatever database you're using):

```
USE SecurityChapter
GO
CREATE SCHEMA Sales
GO
CREATE SCHEMA Inventory
GO
CREATE TABLE Sales.invoice
(
    InvoiceId   int not null identity(1,1) CONSTRAINT PKInvoice PRIMARY KEY,
    InvoiceNumber char(10) not null
                    CONSTRAINT AKInvoice_InvoiceNumber UNIQUE,
    CustomerName varchar(60) not null , --should be normalized in real database
    InvoiceDate smalldatetime not null
)
CREATE TABLE Inventory.Product
(
    ProductId int identity(1,1) CONSTRAINT PKProduct PRIMARY KEY,
    name varchar(30) not null CONSTRAINT AKProduct_name UNIQUE,
    Description varchar(60) not null ,
    Cost numeric(12,4) not null
)
CREATE TABLE Sales.InvoiceLineItem
(
    InvoiceLineItemId int identity(1,1)
                    CONSTRAINT PKInvoiceLineItem PRIMARY KEY,
    InvoiceId int not null,
    ProductId int not null,
    Quantity numeric(6,2) not null,
    Cost numeric(12,4) not null,
    discount numeric(3,2) not null,
    discountExplanation varchar(200) not null,
    CONSTRAINT AKInvoiceLineItem_InvoiceAndProduct
            UNIQUE (InvoiceId, ProductId),
    CONSTRAINT FKSales_Invoice$listsSoldProductsIn$Sales_InvoiceLineItem
            FOREIGN KEY (InvoiceId) REFERENCES Sales.Invoice(InvoiceId),
    CONSTRAINT FKSales_Product$isSoldVia$Sales_InvoiceLineItem
            FOREIGN KEY (InvoiceId) REFERENCES Sales.Invoice(InvoiceId)
    --more constraints should be in place for full implementation
)
```

Now, we create another table to hold the audit of the line item of the invoice:

```
CREATE TABLE Sales.InvoiceLineItemDiscountAudit
(
    InvoiceId    int,
    InvoiceLineItemId int,
    AuditDate    datetime,
    CONSTRAINT PKInvoiceLineItemDiscountAudit
        PRIMARY KEY (InvoiceId, InvoiceLineItemId, AuditDate),
    SetByUserId sysname,
    Quantity numeric(6,2) not null,
    Cost numeric(12,4) not null,
    Discount numeric(3,2) not null,
    DiscountExplanation varchar(300) not null
)
```

Note that the primary key of the table includes the date and time of the change, because multiple changes can be made. Then we code a trigger, using the same trigger template as in the previous chapter:

```
CREATE TRIGGER Sales.InvoiceLineItem$insertAndUpdateAuditTrail
ON Sales.InvoiceLineItem
AFTER INSERT,UPDATE AS
BEGIN

    DECLARE @rowsAffected int,    --stores the number of rows affected
            @msg varchar(2000)    --used to hold the error message

    SET @rowsAffected = @@rowcount

    --no need to continue on if no rows affected
    IF @rowsAffected = 0 return

    SET NOCOUNT ON --to avoid the rowcount messages
    SET ROWCOUNT 0 --in case the client has modified the rowcount
    BEGIN TRY
        --[validation blocks]
        --[modification blocks]
        INSERT INTO Sales.InvoiceLineItemDiscountAudit (InvoiceId,
                    InvoiceLineItemId, AuditDate, SetByUserId, Quantity,
                    Cost, Discount, DiscountExplanation)
        SELECT inserted.InvoiceId, inserted.InvoiceLineItemId,
                current_timestamp, suser_sname(), inserted.Quantity,
                inserted.Cost, inserted.Discount,
                inserted.DiscountExplanation
```

```
            FROM    inserted
                        JOIN Inventory.Product as Product
                            ON inserted.ProductId = Product.ProductId
            --if the Discount is more than 0, or the cost supplied is less than the
            --current value
            WHERE   inserted.Discount > 0
                or   inserted.Cost < Product.Cost
                            -- if it was the same or greater, that is good!
    END TRY
    BEGIN CATCH
                IF @@trancount > 0
                        ROLLBACK TRANSACTION

                --or this will not get rolled back
                --EXECUTE dbo.errorLog$insert

                DECLARE @ERROR_MESSAGE varchar(8000)
                SET @ERROR_MESSAGE = ERROR_MESSAGE()
                RAISERROR (@ERROR_MESSAGE,16,1)

        END CATCH
END
```

We then test the code by creating a few products:

```
INSERT INTO Inventory.Product(name, Description,Cost)
VALUES ('Duck Picture','Picture on the wall in my hotelRoom',200.00)
INSERT INTO Inventory.Product(name, Description,Cost)
VALUES ('Cow Picture','Picture on the other wall in my hotelRoom',150.00)
```

Then we start an invoice:

```
INSERT INTO Sales.Invoice(InvoiceNumber, CustomerName, InvoiceDate)
VALUES ('IE00000001','The Hotel Picture Company','1/1/2005')
```

Then we add an InvoiceLineItem that's clean, same price, no discount:

```
INSERT INTO Sales.InvoiceLineItem(InvoiceId, ProductId, Quantity,
                                    Cost, Discount, DiscountExplanation)
SELECT  (SELECT InvoiceId FROM Sales.Invoice WHERE InvoiceNumber = 'IE00000001'),
        (SELECT ProductId FROM Inventory.Product WHERE name = 'Duck Picture'),
        1,200,0,''
```

We check our log:

```
SELECT * FROM Sales.InvoiceLineItemDiscountAudit
```

Nothing is returned on insert:

InvoiceId	InvoiceLineItemId	AuditDate	SetByUserId	Quantity

Cost	Discount	DiscountExplanation

Then we create a row with a discount percentage:

```
INSERT INTO Sales.InvoiceLineItem(InvoiceId, ProductId, Quantity,
                                  Cost, Discount, DiscountExplanation)
SELECT  (SELECT InvoiceId FROM Sales.Invoice WHERE InvoiceNumber = 'IE00000001'),
        (SELECT ProductId FROM Inventory.Product where name = 'Cow Picture'),
        1,150,.45,'Customer purchased two, so I gave 45% off'

SELECT * FROM Sales.InvoiceLineItemDiscountAudit
```

Now we see that a result has been logged:

InvoiceId	InvoiceLineItemId	AuditDate	SetByUserId	Quantity
1	4	2005-06-23 22:06:43.933	DOMAIN\USER	1.00

Cost	Discount	DiscountExplanation
150.0000	0.45	Customer purchased two, so I gave 45% off

Triggers make wonderful security devices for keeping an eye on what users do, because they can be completely transparent to the user *and* the programmer building a user interface. The only catch can be when an application layer isn't passing the security through to the application, but most of the time when this is true, you'll have already dealt with this using some method (such as just passing it around in the application).

DDL Triggers

DDL triggers supply a different sort of security. They let us protect and monitor changes to the server or database structure by firing when a user executes any DDL statement. The list of DDL statements you can monitor is quite long. (There are 9 for server-level events, such as creating and altering logins, and well more than 60 for the database, including creating and modifying tables, indexes, views, procedures, and so on. For a full list, check SQL Server 2005 Books Online in the "DDL Events for Use with DDL Triggers" topic.)

DDL triggers are of no value in protecting data per se, as they don't fire for DML operations. They are good for monitoring and preventing changes, even by users who have the rights to do so. For example, consider the all-too-frequent case where the manager of the IT group has system-administration powers on the database server (if this power wasn't granted, it would seem like a slight to the abilities of this manager). For the sake of argument, let's assume that this manager is just knowledgeable enough to point and click his way around the UI. However, once in a while, the click is to the wrong place and the manager clicks the OK button on the Delete Object table. Bam! Someone is going to spend an afternoon cleaning up a mess.

With a simple DDL trigger, we can prevent this from occurring by trapping for the event and stopping it. (Note also that DDL triggers are AFTER triggers, and specifying INSTEAD OF gives you an error.)

```
CREATE TRIGGER tr_server$allTableDDL_prevent --note, not a schema owned object
ON DATABASE
AFTER CREATE_TABLE, DROP_TABLE, ALTER_TABLE
AS
 BEGIN
    BEGIN TRY  --note the following line will not wrap
        RAISERROR ('The trigger: tr_server$allTableDDL_prevent must be disabled
                    before making any table modifications',16,1)
    END TRY
    --using the same old error handling
    BEGIN CATCH
            IF @@trancount > 0
                    ROLLBACK TRANSACTION

            --or this will not get rolled back
            --commented out, build from Chapter 6 if desired
            --EXECUTE dbo.errorLog$insert

            DECLARE @ERROR_MESSAGE varchar(8000)
            SET @ERROR_MESSAGE = ERROR_MESSAGE()
            RAISERROR (@ERROR_MESSAGE,16,1)

      END CATCH
END
```

Now we try to create a simple table:

```
CREATE TABLE dbo.test  --dbo for simplicity of example
(
    testId int identity CONSTRAINT PKtest PRIMARY KEY
)
```

We get the following error message:

```
Msg 50000, Level 16, State 1, Procedure tr_server$allTableDDL_prevent, Line 19
The trigger: tr_server$allTableDDL_prevent must be disabled before making any
table modifications
```

No harm, no foul. We do log the error message so we can see if this happens often, but we can do better, in that we can see the exact command that the user tries to execute. We drop this trigger:

```
--Note: Slight change in syntax to drop DDL trigger, requires clause indicating
--where the objects are
DROP TRIGGER tr_server$allTableDDL_prevent ON DATABASE
```

Now, we create a table to contain the history of changes to our table:

```
--first create a table to log to
CREATE TABLE dbo.TableChangeLog
(
    TableChangeLogId INT IDENTITY
        CONSTRAINT pkTableChangeLog PRIMARY KEY (TableChangeLogId),
    DateOfChange    datetime,
    UserName        sysname,
    Ddl             varchar(max)--so we can get as much of the batch as possible
)
```

And we build another trigger to fire when a user creates, alters, or drops a table:

```
--not a schema bound object
CREATE TRIGGER tr_server$allTableDDL
ON DATABASE
AFTER CREATE_TABLE, DROP_TABLE, ALTER_TABLE
AS
 BEGIN
    SET NOCOUNT ON --to avoid the rowcount messages
    SET ROWCOUNT 0 --in case the client has modified the rowcount

    BEGIN TRY

        --we get our data from the EVENT_INSTANCE XML stream
        INSERT INTO dbo.TableChangeLog (DateOfChange, userName, Ddl)
        SELECT getdate(), user,
EVENTDATA().value('(/EVENT_INSTANCE/TSQLCommand/CommandText)[1]','nvarchar(max)')

    END TRY
    --using the same old error handling
    BEGIN CATCH
            IF @@trancount > 0
                    ROLLBACK TRANSACTION

            --or this will not get rolled back
            EXECUTE dbo.errorLog$insert

            DECLARE @ERROR_MESSAGE varchar(8000)
            SET @ERROR_MESSAGE = ERROR_MESSAGE()
            RAISERROR (@ERROR_MESSAGE,16,1)

    END CATCH
END
```

Now we run this to create the dbo.test table:

```
CREATE TABLE dbo.test
(
    id int
)
GO
DROP TABLE dbo.test
```

We check out the TableChangeLog data to see what has changed:

```
SELECT * FROM dbo.TableChangeLog
```

This shows us our commands:

TableChangeLogId	DateOfChange	UserName	Ddl
1	2005-06-01 23:43:35.577	dbo	CREATE TABLE dbo.test (id int)
2	2005-06-01 23:43:35.647	dbo	DROP TABLE dbo.test

Now we can see what users have been up to in the database without them knowing. I've had this situation when using packages that require the user to create new tables, either to store lists, or sometimes the application will do it. With some work, we could filter out events that worked on the user tables, but not any permanent tables that resided in the same database.

■**Tip** It's usually best when building production-quality applications not to have users dropping and creating tables, even with a good set of schema structures with which to work. DDL triggers give us the power to see what kind of activity is occurring. You can also use DDL triggers to prevent unwanted DDL from occurring, as I demonstrated earlier in this section as well.

Logging with Profiler

The last line of defense is the "security camera" approach. Just watch the activity on your server and make sure it looks legit. This is probably the only approach that has a chance to work with malicious (or stupid) programmers and DBAs. I include DBAs in here because there's often no way to avoid giving a few of them system-administration powers. Hence, they might have access to parts of the data that they should never go to, unless there's a problem. They might stumble into data they shouldn't see, though as we discussed previously, we can use encryption to obfuscate this data. Unfortunately, even encryption won't stop a user with sys_admin rights.

Using Profiler, we can set up filters to look at certain events that we know shouldn't be happening, even when a DBA has access. For example, think back to our encryption example, where we stored the encryption password in the table. We could formulate a Profiler task to log only usage of this object. This log might be pretty small, especially if we filter out users who *should* be regularly accessing encrypted data. None of this is perfect, because any users who have admin rights to the Windows server and the database server could hide their activity with enough effort.

An expedient and fairly cheap way to set up the tracing is using a startup stored procedure and the sp_trace% procedures. The following procedure starts up a simple trace each time you start SQL Server. I use this script on my test box on my laptop to capture every change and every script I run on my 2005 server in case I have a crash. Or say I press the wrong button when the dialog "Do you want to save file: 'big_query_you_worked_on_for_five_hours.sql'?" comes up, and I hit "No" because I want to go home and start my night job. This procedure logs up to 10MB in each file, and it creates up to 20 files (incrementing the filenames as it goes up).

```
CREATE PROCEDURE dbo.Server$Watch
as

--note that we have to do some things because these procedures are very picky
--about datatypes.
declare @traceId int, @retval int,
        @stoptime datetime, @maxfilesize bigint, @filecount int
set @maxfilesize = 10 --MB
set @filecount = 20


--creates a trace, placing the file in the root of the server (clearly you should
--change this location to something that fits your own server standards other than
--the root of the c: drive)
exec @retval =  sp_trace_create @traceId = @traceId output,
                    @options = 2, --rollover to a different file
                                  --once max is reached
                    @tracefile = N'c:\trace.trc',
                    @maxfilesize = @maxfilesize,
                    @stoptime = @stoptime,
                    @filecount = 20


--this is because the fourth parameter must be a bit, and the literal 1 thinks it is
--an integer
declare @true bit
set @true = 1


--then we manually add events
exec sp_trace_setevent @traceID, 12, 1, @true --12 = sql:batchstarting 1=textdata
exec sp_trace_setevent @traceID, 12, 6, @true --12 = sql:batchstarting 6=NTUserName
exec sp_trace_setevent @traceID, 12, 7, @true --12 = sql:batchstarting
                                                        --7=NTDomainName
exec sp_trace_setevent @traceID, 12, 11, @true --12 = sql:batchstarting 11=LoginName
exec sp_trace_setevent @traceID, 12, 14, @true --12 = sql:batchstarting 14=StartTime
```

```
exec sp_trace_setevent @traceID, 13, 1, @true --13 = sql:batchending 1=textdata
exec sp_trace_setevent @traceID, 13, 6, @true --13 = sql:batchending 6=NTUserName
exec sp_trace_setevent @traceID, 13, 7, @true --13 = sql:batchending 7=NTDomainName
exec sp_trace_setevent @traceID, 13, 11, @true --13 = sql:batchending 11=LoginName
exec sp_trace_setevent @traceID, 13, 14, @true --13 = sql:batchending 14=StartTime

--and start the trace
exec sp_trace_setstatus @traceId = @traceId, @status = 1 --1 starts it

--this logs that we started the trace to the event viewer
declare @msg varchar(2000)
set @msg = 'logging under trace:' + cast(@traceId as varchar(10)) + ' started'
exec xp_logevent 60000, @msg, 'informational'
```

Now, you can set this procedure to execute every time the server starts by setting its procedure properties:

```
exec master..sp_procoption 'dbo.Server$Watch','startup','true'
```

You can view the trace data by opening the file it creates in Profiler, the latest being c:\trace.trc. (There will be others as the tool cycles through the generations you tell it to create. We set it to rotate at 20 in our procedure.) See Figure 7-2.

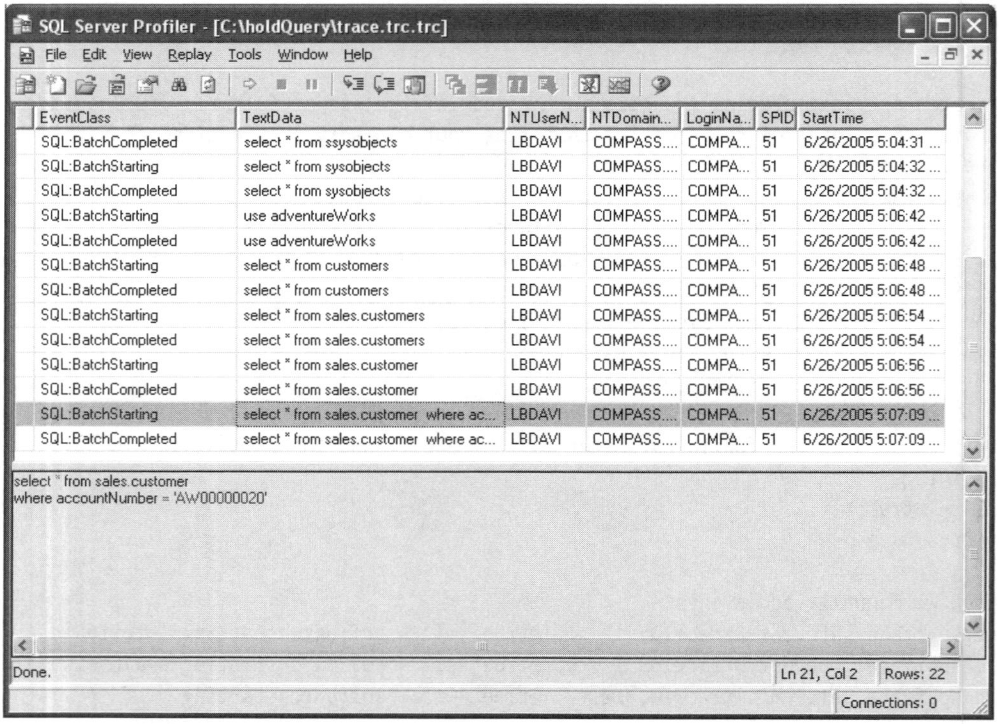

Figure 7-2. *Viewing a trace in Profiler*

This is an effective device to diagnose security issues *after* they occur, so don't think that this is the best form of security. However, sometimes it's the only kind of security we can get.

■**Tip** I keep it running on my test box in case I accidentally forget to save my code when I'm testing.

Best Practices

Security is always one of the most important tasks to consider when implementing a system. Storing data could be worse than not storing it, if it can be used for improper purposes.

- *Secure the server first*: Although this topic is outside the scope of this book, be certain that the server is secure. If a user can get access to your backup files and take them home, all the database security in the world won't help.

- *Grant rights to roles rather than users*: People come and people go, but the roles that they fulfill will be around for a long time. By defining common roles, you can make adding a new user easy (possibly to replace another user). Just make the users a member of the same role, rather than adding rights directly to the user.

- *Use schemas to simplify security*: Because you can grant rights at a schema level, you can grant rights to SELECT, INSERT, UPDATE, DELETE, and even EXECUTE everything within a schema. Even new objects that are added to the schema after the rights are granted are usable by the grantees.

- *Consider security using stored procedures*: Using stored procedures as the only way for a user to get access to the data presents the user with a nice interface to the data. If procedures are well named, you can also easily apply security to match up with the interfaces that use them.

- *Don't overuse the impersonation features*: EXECUTE AS is a blessing, and it opens up a world of possibilities. However, it can open up too much without careful consideration of its use. Add in a database with TRUSTWORTHY access set to on, and a procedure can be written to do anything on the server, which could be exploited as a big security hole by a programmer.

- *Encrypt sensitive data*: SQL Server has several means of encrypting data. Use it as much as necessary, but make sure not to store everything needed to decrypt the data with the encrypted data, in case someone gets hold of the data.

- *Use Profiler and DDL triggers to monitor system activity*: Sometimes it's advantageous to keep an eye on user activity, and these tools give you the ability to do this in an easy manner.

Summary

Security is a large topic, and understanding all the implications is way more than we covered in this chapter. I discussed some of the ways to secure your data inside a single SQL Server database. This isn't an easy subject, but it's far easier than dealing with securing the SQL Server. The reason for this is that usually in the database we're looking to protect ourselves from ordinary users. I have assumed that the server is secure and is keeping out hackers/users who shouldn't be on the server at all.

Ordinary users won't go to long lengths to hack your database because getting caught can cause loss of employment. Hence just setting up basic security is generally good enough. A good example of this kind of security in the real world is locker-room doors. Just putting a picture of a man or a woman on the door is enough to keep reasonable people of the opposite sex from going in the door. There's nothing to stop you from walking right in, other than good taste and the promise of future trouble. Usually when bad people break rules of this sort they don't go through obvious ways.

The same is true about most business users. They'll peruse data to which they have access, but if you put up even a paper barrier saying, "Do not enter," they won't. If they do, they won't go through the paper barrier, they'll go outside of it. This outside access is why the DBA and network engineers are there: to put locks on the outside doors and secure hallways and corridors that users shouldn't go into.

To provide this security, I discussed several topics for which we need to design security into our database usage:

- Permissions-based security using SQL Server 2005 DDL statements:

  - *Basics of SQL Server security*: How security works on SQL Server objects, including using principals of several types: users, roles, and application roles.

  - *Table security*: Keeping users out of tables they shouldn't be in.

  - *Column security*: Restricting access to only parts of tables.

- Using coded objects:

  - *Stored procedures and scalar functions*: Giving advanced usages to users without letting them know *how* they're doing it. Included in this section was how security works across database lines and server lines.

  - *Views and table-valued functions*: Used to break tables up in a simple manner, either row-wise or column-wise. The goal is to make security seamless, such that the users feel that only this database has the data to which they have rights.

- Obfuscating data is about making it too darn hard to access the data, by using encryption to make the data unreadable without a key.

- Watching users with something that's analogous to a store security camera:

  - *Using an audit trail*: Giving the user an audit of what goes on in given rows and columns in the database. This is the typical method when it comes to most data, as it's easy to give the users access to the lists of what has changed (and why, if the application asks for a reason with certain types of changes).

  - *DDL triggers*: Auditing users who have rights to create new objects in your databases or server, to make sure they aren't doing anything out of the ordinary.

  - *Logging with a profiler*: The most silent of devices, can be used to capture all moves made on the server.

The fact is, if you can build an outer shell of protective devices such as firewalls, proper domain security, and so on, building the inside security will be a snap. It will be the most tedious and time consuming part of database development, there's no question about that, and it will fall off the radar slightly faster than testing will in many projects. There's no way to combat the problem of schedule slippage, because it's a management issue, not a technical issue, but if planned for ahead of time, security isn't a difficult thing to put in the application.

CHAPTER 8

■■■

Table Structures and Indexing

To the optimist, the glass is half full. To the pessimist, the glass is half empty. To the engineer, the glass is twice as big as it needs to be.

—Unknown, http://www.boardofwisdom.com

I chose a quote about engineering to start out this chapter because we're moving from the data architecture and logical modeling phase of the book into the physical modeling part. Everything we've done so far has been centered on the idea that the data quality is the number one concern. Although this is still true, for the rest of the book let's assume that we've done our job in the logical and implementation phases and that the data quality is covered. Slow and right is better than fast and wrong (how would you like to get paid a week early, but only get half your money?), but the obvious goal of building a computer system is to do things fast *and* right.

A key element in query performance optimization is the judicious use of *indexes*. The goal of this chapter is to provide an understanding of the types of indexes that are available to you, how they work, and how to use them in an effective indexing strategy. However, this understanding relies on a sound knowledge of the physical data structures upon which we based these indexes—in other words, of how the data is structured in the physical SQL Server storage engine. In this chapter, I'll discuss the following topics:

- *Physical database structure overview*: An overview of how the database and tables are stored. This acts mainly as foundation material for subsequent indexing discussion, but the discussion also highlights the importance of choosing and sizing your datatypes carefully.

- *Indexing overview*: A survey of the different types of indexes and their structure. I'll demonstrate many of the index settings and how these might be useful when developing your strategy, to correct any performance problems identified during optimization testing.

- *Index usage scenarios*: I'll discuss a few cases of how to apply and use indexes.

Once you understand the physical data structures, you can optimize data storage and access without losing correctness. It's essential to the goals of database design and implementation that the physical model not affect the logical model. This is what Codd's eighth rule—the Physical Data Independence rule—is about. It states that the physical storage can be implemented in any manner as long as the users don't know about it. It also implies that if you change the physical storage, the users shouldn't be affected. Indexes should change the physical model, but not the implemented or logical models. All we want to do with the physical model is enhance performance, and understanding the way SQL Server stores data is an important step.

Physical Database Structure

In SQL Server, databases are physically structured as several layers of "containers" that allow you to move parts of the data around to different disk drives for optimum access. As discussed in Chapter 1, a database is a collection of related data. At the logical level, it contains tables that have columns that contain data. At the physical level, databases contain *files* of data, which can be grouped into *filegroups* and are stored on the disk. Each file contains a number of *extents*. An extent is a 64K allocation in a database file that's made up of eight individual contiguous 8K *pages*. Finally, the page is the basic unit of data storage in SQL Server databases. Everything that's stored in SQL Server is stored on pages of several types: data, index, and overflow. The following sections describe each of these "containers" in more detail so you understand the basics of how data is laid out on disk.

■**Note** Because of the extreme variety of hardware possibilities and needs, it's impossible in a book on design to go into serious depth about how and where to place all your files in physical storage. I'll leave this task to the DBA-oriented books. For detailed information about choosing and setting up your hardware, check out http://msdn.microsoft.com or http://www.sql-server-performance.com.

Files and Filegroups

Figure 8-1 provides a high-level depiction of the objects used to organize the files (I'm ignoring logs in this chapter because you don't have direct access to them).

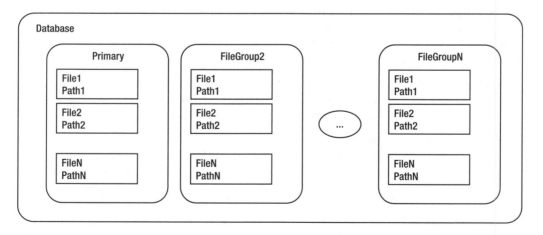

Figure 8-1. *Database storage organization*

At the top level we have the database. The database is comprised of one or more filegroups, which are a logical grouping of one or more files. We can place different filegroups on different disk drives (hopefully on a different disk drive controller) to distribute the I/O load evenly across the available hardware. It's possible to have multiple files in the filegroup, in which case

SQL Server allocates space across each file in the filegroup. For best performance, it's best to have no more files in a filegroup than you have physical CPUs (not including hyperthreading).

Note There's usually very little, if any, performance benefit to using multiple filegroups if they're all on the same physical drive, and in fact it can harm performance. The benefit of having multiple filegroups is getting data spread about to maximize I/O across different controllers. There can be some benefit to having multiple files in a filegroup on the same drive, but no more than available physical CPUs.

A filegroup contains one or more files, which are actual operating system files. Each database has at least one primary filegroup, whose files are called *primary files* (commonly suffixed as .mdf, although there's no requirement to give the files any particular names or extension). Each database can possibly have other secondary filegroups containing the secondary files (commonly suffixed as .ndf), which are in any other filegroups. Files may only be a part of a single filegroup. SQL Server proportionally fills files by allocating extents in each filegroup equally.

You control the placement of objects that store physical data pages at the filegroup level (code and metadata is always stored on the primary filegroup, along with all the system objects). Unless you specify otherwise in a CREATE TABLE statement, any new objects created are placed in the *default* filegroup, which is the primary filegroup unless another filegroup is specified. To place an object in a filegroup other than the default, you need to specify the name of the filegroup using the ON clause of the table- or index-creation statement. For example:

```
CREATE TABLE <tableName>
(...)  ON <fileGroupName>
```

This assigns the table to the filegroup, but not to any particular file. Where on the files the object is created is strictly out of your control. There also isn't syntax for moving an object from one filegroup to another. It must be dropped and re-created. Use this code to create indexes:

```
CREATE INDEX <indexName> ON <tableName> (<columnList>) ON <filegroup>
```

Use this type of command (or use ALTER TABLE) for constraints that create indexes (UNIQUE, PRIMARY KEY):

```
CREATE TABLE <tableName>
(
    ...
    <primaryKeyColumn> int CONSTRAINT PKTableName ON <fileGroup>
    ...
)
```

For the most part, having just one filegroup and one file is the best practice for many databases. As activity increases and you build better hardware with multiple CPUs and multiple drive channels, you might place indexes on their own filegroup, or even place files of the same filegroup across different controllers.

In the following example, I create a sample database with two filegroups, with the secondary filegroup having two files in it:

```
CREATE DATABASE demonstrateFilegroups ON
PRIMARY ( NAME = Primary1, FILENAME = 'c:\demonstrateFilegroups_primary.mdf',
         SIZE = 10MB),
FILEGROUP SECONDARY
         ( NAME = Secondary1,FILENAME = 'c:\demonstrateFilegroups_secondary1.ndf',
           SIZE = 10MB),
         ( NAME = Secondary2,FILENAME = 'c:\demonstrateFilegroups_secondary2.ndf',
           SIZE = 10MB)
LOG ON ( NAME = Log1,FILENAME = 'c:\demonstrateFilegroups_log.ldf', SIZE = 10MB)
```

You can define other file settings, such as minimum and maximum sizes, and growth. The values you assign depend on what hardware you have. For growth, you can set a FILEGROWTH parameter that allows you to grow the file by a certain size or percentage of the current size, and a MAXSIZE, so the file cannot just fill up existing disk space. For example, if you wanted the file to start at 1GB and grow in chunks of 100MB up to 2GB, you could specify the following:

```
CREATE DATABASE demonstrateFileGrowth ON
PRIMARY ( NAME = Primary1,FILENAME = 'c:\demonstrateFileGrowth_primary.mdf',
                         SIZE = 1GB, FILEGROWTH=100MB, MAXSIZE=2GB)
LOG ON ( NAME = Log1,FILENAME = 'c:\demonstrateFileGrowth_log.ldf', SIZE = 10MB)
```

The growth settings are fine for smaller systems, but it's usually better to make the files large enough so there's no need for them to grow. File growth can be slow and cause ugly bottlenecks when OLTP traffic is trying to use a file that's growing. When running on Windows XP or Windows Server 2003, you can improve things by using "instant" file allocation. Instead of initializing the files, the space on disk can simply be allocated and not written to immediately. To use this capability, the system account cannot be LocalSystem, and the user must have SE_MANAGE_VOLUME_NAME Windows permissions. Despite this, it's still better to have the space allocated beforehand.

You can query the sys.filegroups catalog view to view the files in the newly created database:

```
USE demonstrateFilegroups
GO
SELECT fg.name as file_group,
       df.name as file_logical_name,
       df.physical_name as physical_file_name
FROM   sys.filegroups fg
         JOIN sys.database_files df
           ON fg.data_space_id = df.data_space_id
```

This returns the following results:

file_group	file_logical_name	physical_file_name
PRIMARY	Primary1	c:\demonstrateFilegroups_primary.mdf
SECONDARY	Secondary1	c:\demonstrateFilegroups_secondary1.ndf
SECONDARY	Secondary2	c:\demonstrateFilegroups_secondary2.ndf

There's a lot more information in the catalog views referenced than just names, which I won't cover here.

■**Tip** An interesting feature of filegroups is that you can back them up and restore them individually. If you need to restore and back up a single table for any reason, placing it on its own filegroup can achieve this.

These databases won't be used anymore, so if you created them, just drop them if you desire:

```
DROP DATABASE demonstrateFileGroups
```

■**Note** The LOG file isn't part of a filegroup, so it isn't shown in the results.

Extents and Pages

As shown in Figure 8-2, files are further broken down into a number of *extents*, each consisting of eight separate 8K pages. It's in extents that space is allocated for tables, indexes, and so on. SQL Server only allocates space in a database to extents. You'll also notice that the size of files will be incremented only in 64K increments.

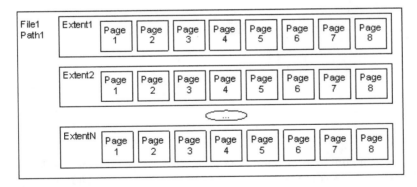

Figure 8-2. *Files and extents*

Each extent in turn has eight pages that hold one specific type of data each:

- *Data*: Table data.

- *Index*: Index data.

- *Overflow data*: Used when a row is greater than 8,060 bytes, or varchar(max), varbinary(max) values.

- *Allocation map*: Information about the allocation of extents.

- *Page free space*: Information about what different pages are allocated for.

- *Index allocation*: Information about extents used for table or index data.

- *Bulk changed map*: Extents modified by a bulk INSERT operation.

- *Differential changed map*: Extents that have changed since the last backup database command. This is used to support differential backups.

In larger databases, most every extent will contain just one type of page, but in smaller databases SQL Server can place any kind of page in the same extent. When all data is of the same type, it's known as a *uniform* extent. When pages are mixed, it's referred to as a *mixed* extent.

SQL Server places all table data in pages, with a header that contains metadata about the page (object ID of the owner, type of page, and so on), as well as the rows of data (which I'll cover later in this chapter). At the end of the page are the offset values that tell the relational engine where the rows start.

Figure 8-3 shows a typical data page from a table.

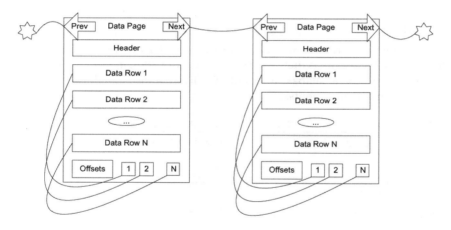

Figure 8-3. *Data pages*

The header of the page contains identification values such as the page number, the object ID of the object the data is for, and so on. The data rows hold the actual data, which I'll cover more in a moment. Finally, there's an allocation block that has the offsets to the row data.

Figure 8-3 showed that there are pointers from the next to the previous rows. These pointers are only used when pages are ordered, and their existence is completely dependent on the indexing of the table (I'll cover this in the next section on index structures).

Each data row on the data page is comprised of metadata, fixed length fields, and variable length fields, as shown in Figure 8-4.

Figure 8-4. *Data row*

The metadata describes the row, gives information about the variable length fields, and so on.

■**Note** I use the term *column* when discussing SQL objects, but when discussing the physical table implementation, *field* is the proper term. A field is a physical location within a record.

The maximum amount of data that can be placed on a single page (including overhead from variable fields) is 8,060 bytes. When a data row grows larger than this 8,060 bytes, the data in variable length columns can spill out onto an overflow page. A 16-byte pointer is left on the original page and points to the page where the overflow data is placed.

There are two reasons an overflow page is used:

1. The combined length of all data in a row grows beyond 8,060 bytes. In previous versions of SQL Server, this would cause an error. In SQL Server 2005, data goes on the overflow page automatically.

2. By setting the sp_tableoption setting on a table for large value types out of row to 1, all the (max) and XML datatype values are immediately stored out of row on an overflow page. If you set it to 0, then SQL Server places all data on the main row, as long as it fits into the 8,060 byte row.

For example, Figure 8-5 depicts the type of situation that might occur for a table that has the large value types out of row set to 1. Here, Data Row 1 has a pointer to a varbinary(max) column that spans two pages. The value of the same column for Data Row 2 only requires a single overflow page.

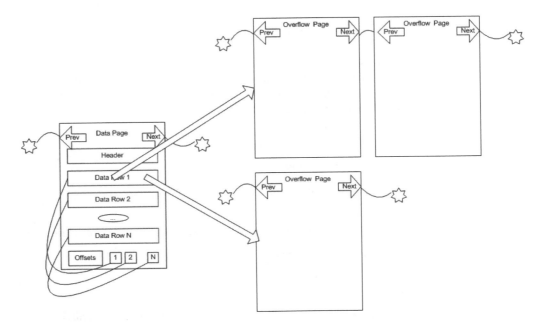

Figure 8-5. *Sample overflow pages*

The overflow pages are linked lists that can accommodate up to 2GB of storage in a single column. Generally speaking, it isn't a good idea to store 2GB in a single column (or even a row), but it's available if needed.

Understand that using these large values when they're placed off of the main page will be far more costly when you need these values than if they're all in the same data page. On the other hand, if you seldom use the data in your queries, placing them off the page can give you a much smaller footprint, requiring far less disk access. Imagine a table scan or columns that are on the overflow pages. Not only do you have to read extra pages, you have to be redirected to the overflow page for every row that's overflowed.

Be careful when allowing data to overflow the page. It's guaranteed to make your processing more costly, especially if you include the data that's stored on the overflow page in your queries (like if you use the dreaded SELECT * regularly in production code!). It's important to choose your datatypes correctly to minimize the size of the data row to include only frequently needed values. If you frequently need a large value, keep it in row, otherwise place it off row.

■**Tip** The need to access overflow pages is one of the main reasons to avoid using SELECT * FROM <tablename>—type queries in your production code. Too often you get data that you don't intend to use, and when that data is located off the main data page, performance could suffer needlessly.

Indexes Overview

Indexes allow the SQL Server engine to perform fast, targeted data retrieval rather than simply scanning though the entire table. A well-placed index can speed up data retrieval by orders of magnitude (though a scattershot approach to indexing tends to have the opposite effect).

Indexing your data effectively requires a sound knowledge of how that data will change over time, the sort of questions that will be asked of it, and the volume of data that you expect to be dealing with. Unfortunately, this is what makes this topic so challenging. To index effectively, you need knowledge of your hardware and your exact data usage patterns. Nothing in life is free, and the creation and maintenance of indexes can be costly. When deciding to (or not to) use an index to improve the performance of one query, you have to consider the effect on the overall performance of the system.

In the upcoming sections, I'll do the following:

- Introduce the basic structure of an index

- Discuss the two fundamental types of indexes and how their structure heavily affects the structure of the table

- Demonstrate basic index usage, introducing you to the basic syntax and usage of indexes

- Show you how to determine whether SQL Server is likely to use your index

Basic Index Structure

An index is an object that SQL Server can maintain to optimize access to the physical data in a table. You can build an index on one or more columns of a table. In essence, an index in SQL

Server works on the same principle as the index of a book. It organizes the data in a manner that's conducive to fast, efficient searching. It provides a means to jump quickly to a specific piece of data, rather than just starting on page 1 each time and scanning through until you find what you're looking for. Much like the index of a book, which is a separate entity from the content, so a database index is separate from the actual table.

For example, take a case of an Employee table that you generally search, based on people's surnames, for details. You might commonly execute queries such as the following:

```
SELECT LastName, ReviewDate FROM Employee WHERE LastName = 'Davidson'
```

In the absence of an index, SQL Server performs a full table scan (meaning it touches every row individually) on the Employee table, looking for rows that satisfy the query predicate. A full table scan generally won't cause you too many problems with small tables, but it can cause poor performance for large tables with many pages of data.

However, if you create an index on the LastName column, the index sorts the LastName rows in some logical fashion (probably in ascending alphabetical order) so that the database engine can move directly to rows where the last name is Davidson, and retrieve the required data quickly and efficiently.

Indexes are implemented using a *balanced tree* (B-tree) structure. The index is made up of index pages structured much like an index of a book or a phone book. Each index page contains the first value in a range, and a pointer to the next lower page in the index. The last level in the index is referred to as the *leaf page*, which contains the actual data values in the underlying column, or pointers to them.

■**Note** I'll discuss the leaf pages in later sections on clustered and nonclustered indexes.

Figure 8-6 shows an example of the type of B-tree that SQL Server uses for indexes. Each of the outer rectangles is an 8K index page, just as we discussed earlier. The three values—A, J, and P—are the *index keys* in this top-level page of the index. The index page has as many index keys as is possible. To decide which path to follow to reach the lower level of the index, we have to decide if the value requested is between two of the keys: A to I, J to P, or greater than P. For example, say the value we want to find in the index happens to be I. We go to the first page in the index. The database determines that I doesn't come after J, so follows the A pointer to the next index page. Here, it determines that I comes after C, so it follows the G pointer to the leaf page

Each of these pages is 8K in size. Depending on the size of the key (determined by summing the data lengths of the columns in the key, up to a maximum of 900 bytes), it's possible to have anywhere from 8 entries to over 1,000 on a single page. The more keys fit on a page, the greater the number of pages you can have on each level of the index. The more pages, the fewer numbers of steps from the top page of the index to reach the leaf.

B-tree indexes can be extremely efficient, because for an index that stores only 500 different values on a page—a reasonable number for an typical index of an integer—it has 500 pointers on the next level in the index, and the second level has 500 pages with 500 values each. That makes 250,000 different pointers on that level, and the next level has up to 250,000 * 500 = 125,000,000. That's 125,000,000 different values in just a three level index! Obviously, there's overhead to each index key, and this is a very rough calculation.

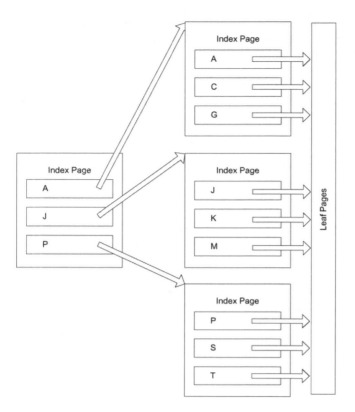

Figure 8-6. *Basic index structure*

Another term that's mentioned occasionally is how *balanced* the tree is. If the tree is perfectly balanced, every index page would have exactly the same number of keys on it. Once the index has lots of data moved around for insertions or deletions, the tree can be ragged, with one end having one level, and another many levels. This is why you have to do some basic maintenance on the indexes, which I'll cover a bit later (the command to use is ALTER TABLE).

Index Types

For the nonleaf pages of an index, everything is the same for all indexes. However, at the leaf node, the indexes get quite different—and the type of index used plays a large part in how the data in a table is physically organized.

There are two different types of indexes:

- *Clustered*: This type orders the physical table in the order of the index.

- *Nonclustered*: These are completely separate structures that simply speed access.

In the upcoming sections, I'll discuss how the different types of indexes affect the table structure, and which is best in which situation.

Clustered Indexes

A clustered index physically orders the pages of the data table. The leaf pages of the clustered indexes are the data pages of the table. Each of the data pages is then linked to the next page in a doubly linked list. The leaf pages of the clustered index are the actual data pages. In other words, the data rows in the table are sorted according to the columns used in the index. Tables with clustered indexes are referred to as *clustered tables*.

Figure 8-7 shows at a high level what a clustered index might look like.

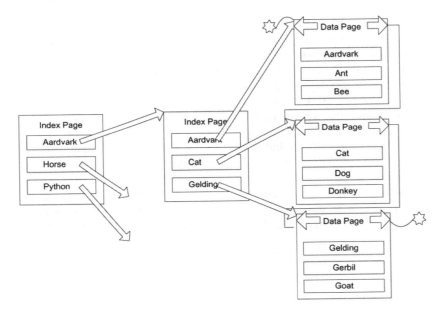

Figure 8-7. *Clustered index example*

You can only have a single clustered index on the table, because the table cannot be ordered in more than one direction. This organization saves having to go from the index structure to the data pages, making the clustered index one of the most important performance choices you can make for your data access plan.

A good real-world example of a clustered index would be a dictionary. You can think of each word in the dictionary as a row in a database. These rows are "clustered" on the word in the dictionary, just as the example was clustered on the name of the animal.

Why are the words in a dictionary sorted, rather than just having a separate index with the words not in order? I presume that at least part of the reason is to let the readers scan through words they don't know exactly how to spell, checking the definition to see if the word matches. SQL Server can do the same thing with indexes when you do a search for a partial value, plus some other column in the table. For example, back in Figure 8-7, if you were looking for a cat named George, you'd use the clustered index to find rows where animal = 'Cat', then scan the data pages for the matching pages for name = 'George'.

I must caution you that although it's true, physically speaking, that tables have order, logically speaking, tables have no order. This is a fundamental truth of relational programming: *you aren't required to get back data in the same order when you run the same query twice.* It's true that you do almost always get the same rows back in the same order, mostly because the optimizer is going to put together the same plan every time the same query is executed under the same conditions. However, load the server up with many requests, and the order of the data might change so SQL Server can best use its resources, regardless of the order of the data in the structures. SQL Server can choose to return data to us in any order that's fastest for it. If disk drives are busy in part of a table and it can fetch a different part, it will. If order matters, use ORDER BY clauses to make sure that data is returned as you want.

Nonclustered Indexes

If you don't have a clustered index, the table is referred to as a *heap*. One definition of a heap is, "a group of things placed or thrown one on differences top of the other." This is a great way to explain what happens in a table when you have no clustered index: SQL Server simply puts every new row on the end of the last page for the table.

It isn't usually a best practice to have tables without a clustered index in an OLTP system, but it's important to understand what a heap will look like if you don't include a clustered index. Nonclustered index structures are independent of the underlying table. Where clustered indexes were like dictionaries, with the index running throughout, nonclustered indexes are more like indexes in a textbook. The index is separate from the text, with pointers to a page to go to for the information.

In the same way, the leaf pages of a nonclustered index simply have pointers to the rows in the underlying table. For example, if the previous clustered index example was changed into a nonclustered index, our structure would change to something more like Figure 8-8.

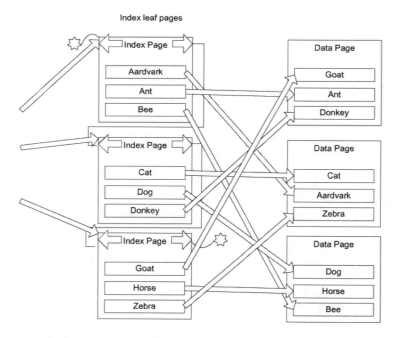

Figure 8-8. *Sample nonclustered index*

The leaf page of the nonclustered index contains a pointer to the data row containing the key value. The pointer from the clustered index to the data row is known as a *row locator*.

■Tip You can place nonclustered indexes on a different filegroup than the data pages to maximize the use of your disk subsystem in parallel. Note that the filegroup you place the indexes on should be on a different controller channel than the table, or there will likely be no gain. Also, this is more useful for systems with a need for high concurrency, but can be useful for either case (testing is the key, due to the complexities of each particular need).

The structure of the row locator depends on whether the table has a clustered index or not. In the next two sections, I'll show you the differences between nonclustered indexes on a heap, and those on a clustered table.

Nonclustered Indexes on Heap Tables

For the "heap" table, with no clustered index, the row locator is a pointer to the physical page on disk that contains the row. As an example, suppose that you have a table called animal, with a nonclustered index on the name column, represented in Figure 8-9.

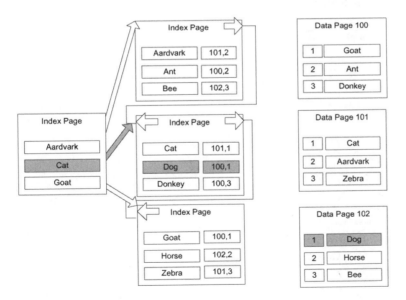

Figure 8-9. *Nonclustered index on a heap*

If you want to find 'Dog' in the index, first find the path through the index from the top-level page to the leaf page. Once you get to the leaf page, you get a pointer to the page that has a row with the value. This pointer consists of the page location and the record number on the page to find the row values (the pages are numbered from 0, and the offset is numbered from 1). The most important fact about this pointer is that it points directly to the row on the page that has the values you're looking for. The pointer for a table with a clustered index (a clustered table) is different, and is an important distinction to understand because it affects how well the different types of indexes perform.

When a row must be moved to a different physical location, the pointers in the index aren't changed. Instead, a pointer is left in the table, which points to the new page where the data is now. All existing indexes that have the old pointer simply go to the old page, then follow the new pointer on that page to the new location of the data. Data is rarely moved around within a heap, so this is seldom an issue, but if you're often adding data to a variable length column that's used as an index key, it's possible that a row may be moved to a different page. This adds another step to finding the data, and if the data is moved to a page on a different extent, another read to the database.

Nonclustered Indexes on Clustered Tables

When a clustered index exists on the table, the index key for the leaf node of any nonclustered index is no longer a pointer to a physical disk location. Instead, it's the key used in the clustered index, commonly referred to as the *clustering key*.

In Figure 8-10, the structure on the right side is the clustered index, and on the left is the nonclustered index. To find the value 'Dog' as you did back on Figure 8-9, you still start at the leaf node of the index and traverse to the leaf pages. This time you get the clustering key, rather than a pointer. You then would use the clustering key to traverse the clustered index to reach the data, as seen in Figure 8-10.

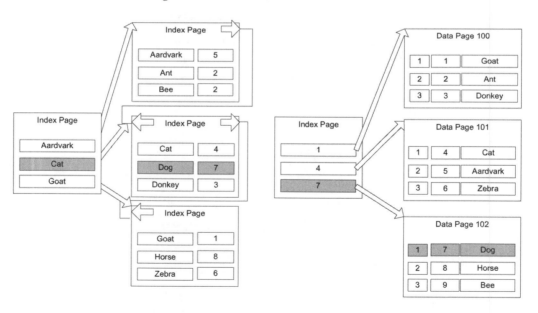

Figure 8-10. *Nonclustered index on a clustered table*

The overhead of this operation is minimal, and it's better than having direct pointers to the table, because only minimal reorganization is required for any modification of the clustered index or the clustering key. The people with better understanding of such things also tell us that when the size of the clustering key is adequately small, this method is faster than having pointers directly to the table.

This is certainly true when we talk about modification operations. Because the clustering key is the same irregardless of physical location, only the lowest level of the clustered index need know where the physical data is, and because all data is organized sequentially, this significantly lowers the overhead of modifying indexes. Of course, this is only true if the clustering key rarely changes, if ever. This is why the general suggestion is to make the clustering key a small non-changing value, such as an identity column (but the advice section is still a few pages away).

Basics of Index Creation

The basic syntax for creating an index is as follows:

```
CREATE [UNIQUE] INDEX [CLUSTERED | NONCLUSTERED] <indexName>
   ON <tableName> (<columnList>)
```

As you can see, you can specify either a clustered or nonclustered index, with nonclustered being the default type. Each type of index can be unique or nonunique. If you specify that your index must be unique, then it means that every row in the indexed column must have a different value—no duplicate entries are accepted.

The <columnList> is a comma-delimited list of columns in the table. Each column can be specified either in ascending (ASC) or descending (DESC) order for each column, with ascending being the default (unless you're strictly using the index for descending searches, ascending is generally fine). SQL Server can traverse the index in either direction for searches. For example, the following statement creates an index called XtableA_column1AndColumn2 on column1 and column2 of tableA, with ascending order for column1 and descending order for column2:

```
CREATE INDEX XtableA_column1AndColumn2 ON tableA (column1, column2 DESC)
```

Let's take a look at a full example. First, we need to create a base table. (Use whatever database you desire. I used tempdb on my test machine, and included the USE statement in the code download.)

```
CREATE SCHEMA produce
GO
CREATE TABLE produce.vegetable
(
    --PK constraint defaults to clustered
    vegetableId int CONSTRAINT PKvegetable PRIMARY KEY,
    name varchar(10)
                    CONSTRAINT AKvegetable_name UNIQUE,
    color varchar(10),
    consistency varchar(10)
)
```

Now we create two single-column nonclustered indexes on the color and consistency columns, respectively:

```
CREATE INDEX Xvegetable_color ON produce.vegetable(color)
CREATE INDEX Xvegetable_consistency ON produce.vegetable(consistency)
```

Then we create a unique composite index on the vegetableID and color columns. We make this index unique, not to guarantee uniqueness of the values in the columns, but because the values in vegetableId must be unique because it's part of the PRIMARY KEY constraint. Making this unique signals to the optimizer that the values in the index are unique. (Note that this index is probably not very useful, but is created to demonstrate a unique index that isn't a constraint.)

```
CREATE UNIQUE INDEX Xproduce_vegetable_vegetableId_color
        ON produce.vegetable(vegetableId, color)
```

Finally, we add some test data:

```
INSERT INTO produce.vegetable(vegetableId, name, color, consistency)
VALUES (1,'carrot','orange','crunchy')
INSERT INTO produce.vegetable(vegetableId, name, color, consistency)
VALUES (2,'broccoli','green','treelike')
INSERT INTO produce.vegetable(vegetableId, name, color, consistency)
VALUES (3,'mushroom','brown','squishy')
INSERT INTO produce.vegetable(vegetableId, name, color, consistency)
VALUES (4,'pea','green','squishy')
INSERT INTO produce.vegetable(vegetableId, name, color, consistency)
VALUES (5,'asparagus','green','crunchy')
INSERT INTO produce.vegetable(vegetableId, name, color, consistency)
VALUES (6,'sprouts','green','leafy')
INSERT INTO produce.vegetable(vegetableId, name, color, consistency)
VALUES (7,'lettuce','green','leafy')
```

To see the indexes on the table, we check the following query:

```
SELECT  name, type_desc
FROM    sys.indexes
WHERE   object_id('produce.vegetable') = object_id
```

This returns the following results:

name	type_desc
PKvegetable	CLUSTERED
AKvegetable_name	NONCLUSTERED
Xvegetable_color	NONCLUSTERED
Xvegetable_consistency	NONCLUSTERED
Xvegetable_vegetableId_color	NONCLUSTERED

One thing to note here is that PRIMARY KEY and UNIQUE constraints are implemented "behind the scenes" using indexes. The PK constraint is, by default, implemented using a clustered index and the UNIQUE constraint via a nonclustered index. As the primary key is generally chosen to be an optimally small value, it tends to make a nice clustering key. I'll discuss this further later in the chapter.

■**Note** Foreign key constraints aren't automatically implemented using an index, though an index on the migrated foreign key column(s) is often useful for performance reasons. I'll return to this topic later when I discuss foreign key indexes.

The remaining entries in the output show the three nonclustered indexes that we explicitly created. Before moving on, briefly note that to drop an index, use the following statement:

```
DROP INDEX produce.vegetable.Xvegetable_consistency
```

Basic Index Usage

In this section, I'll look at some of the basic usage patterns of different indexes, as well as how to see the use of the index within a query plan:

- *Clustered indexes*: I'll discuss the choices you need to make when choosing which columns in which to put the clustered index.

- *Nonclustered indexes*: After the clustered index is applied, you need to decide where to apply nonclustered indexes.

- *Unique indexes*: I'll look at why it's important to use unique indexes as frequently as possible.

All plans that I present were obtained using the SET SHOWPLAN ON statement. When you're doing this locally, it can be easier to use the graphical showplan from Management Studio. However, when you need to post the plan or include it in a document, use one of the SET SHOWPLAN_TEXT commands. You can read about this more in SQL Server Books Online.

For example, say you execute the following query:

```
SET SHOWPLAN_TEXT ON
GO
SELECT *
FROM    produce.vegetable
GO
SET SHOWPLAN_TEXT OFF
GO
```

Running these statements echoes the query as a single column result set of StmtText, and then returns another with the same column name that displays the plan:

```
|--Clustered Index Scan
            (OBJECT:([tempdb].[produce].[vegetable].[PKvegetable]))
```

Although this is the best way to communicate the plan in text, I'd suggest that you use the Management Studio tool to view estimated plans. By clicking the Query menu and choosing Display Estimated Execution Plan (Ctrl+L), you'll see the plan in a more interesting way, as shown in Figure 8-11.

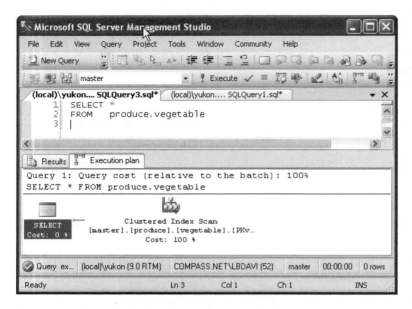

Figure 8-11. *Plan display in Management Studio*

Using Clustered Indexes

The column you use for the clustered index will become a part of every index for your table, so it has heavy implications for all indexes. Because of this, for a typical OLTP system you usually choose the primary key of the table, often implemented as a surrogate key. This is because these key sets are frequently accessed by queries involving JOIN clauses. It also keeps the clustered index small and efficient. Because of the way nonclustered indexes are implemented, nonclustered indexes require use of the clustered "key" for all their fetches.

Using the surrogate key as the clustering key is great, because not only is it a small key (most often the datatype is an integer that requires only 4 bytes), but because it's always a unique value. For clustered indexes that aren't unique, all values where there are duplicates have a 4-byte value added to each nonunique value in the index. If you have many duplicate values, this can harm the value of all your indexes. It also helps the optimizer that an index has only unique values, because it knows immediately that for an equality operator, either 1 or 0 values will match. Because the surrogate key is often used in joins, it's helpful to have smaller keys for the primary key.

The clustered index won't always be used for the surrogate key, or even the primary key. Other possible uses can fall under the following types:

- *Range queries*: Having all the data in order usually makes sense when there's data that you often need to get a range, such as from A to F.

- *Data that's always accessed sequentially*: Obviously, if the data needs to be accessed in a given order, having the data already sorted in that order will significantly improve performance.

- *Queries that return large result sets*: This point will make more sense once I cover nonclustered indexes, but for now, note that having the data on the leaf index page saves overhead.

The choice of how to pick the clustered index depends on a couple factors, such as how many other indexes will be derived from this index, how big the key for the index will be, and how often the value will change. When a clustered index value changes, every index on the table must also be touched and changed. This goes back to understanding the users of your data, and finally testing the heck out of the system to verify that your index choices don't hurt overall performance more than they help. Speeding up one query by using one clustering key could hurt all queries that use the nonclustered indexes, especially if you chose a large key for the clustered index.

Now let's look at an example of a clustered index in use. If you have a clustered index on a table, instead of Table Scan, you'll see a Clustered Index Scan in the plan:

```
SELECT *
FROM    produce.vegetable
```

The plan is for this query is as follows:

```
|--Clustered Index Scan
            (OBJECT:([tempdb].[produce].[vegetable].[PKvegetable]))
```

This is the same thing as a table scan, though there's an order to the scanning that can be useful to other query operators, such as a merge join, which joins two ordered sets. If you query on a value of the clustered index, the scan will change to a seek. Although a scan touches all the data pages, a clustered index seek uses the index structure to touch one page in each level of the index to find a single value on a single data page:

```
SELECT *
FROM    produce.vegetable
WHERE   vegetableId = 4
```

The plan for this query now does a seek:

```
|--Clustered Index Seek
        (OBJECT:([tempdb].[produce].[vegetable].[PKvegetable]),
            SEEK:([tempdb].[produce].[vegetable].[vegetableId]=
            CONVERT_IMPLICIT(int,[@1],0)) ORDERED FORWARD)
```

In this case, you're seeking in the clustered index based on the SEEK predicate of vegetableId = 1. Search for two rows:

```
SELECT *
FROM    produce.vegetable
WHERE   vegetableId in (1,4)
```

Pretty much the same plan is used, except for the seek criteria:

```
|--Clustered Index Seek
        (OBJECT:([tempdb].[produce].[vegetable].[PKvegetable]),
            SEEK:([tempdb].[produce].[vegetable].[vegetableId]=(1) OR
            [tempdb].[produce].[vegetable].[vegetableId]=(4)) ORDERED FORWARD)
```

This all looks pretty mundane, but it will become more clear how useful a clustered index seek is in the next section, "Using Nonclustered Indexes."

Tip You might have noticed the differences between this plan:

```
CONVERT_IMPLICIT(int,[@1],0)) ORDERED FORWARD)
```

and this one:

```
([tempdb].[produce].[vegetable].[vegetableId]=(1) OR
[tempdb].[produce].[vegetable].[vegetableId]=(4)
```

This is part of the parameterization feature of SQL Server. The first query was parameterized by the query optimizer such that other queries can use the same plan. The second one wasn't, because the WHERE clause was more complex. Parameterization of *ad hoc* SQL is a great feature that I'll cover in Chapter 10.

Using Nonclustered Indexes

Once you've chosen the clustered index, all other indexes will be nonclustered. These are the general-purpose indexes that are used to speed up queries, after all the UNIQUE constraints have been added. Generally speaking, don't immediately start adding indexes until after you've executed queries against your data.

I'll talk about nonclustered indexes in the following situations:

- General considerations

- Composite index considerations

- Nonclustered indexes with clustered tables

- Nonclustered indexes on heaps

General Considerations

We generally know that indexes are needed because queries are very slow. Most often this is apparent because either `|--Clustered Index Scan` or `|--Table Scan` shows up in your query plan, and most importantly, this operator is taking a large percentage of time of the query to execute. Simple, right? Essentially, this is true enough statement, but it's hard to make specific indexing changes before knowing about usage, because the usage pattern will greatly affect these decisions. For example:

- Is this query executed only once a day or once an hour? Once a minute?

- Is a background process inserting into this table rapidly? Or perhaps inserts are taking place during off hours?

Once you understand the usage patterns of a table, you have to consider how indexes help and hurt the different types of operations in different ways:

- SELECT: Indexes can only have a beneficial effect on SELECT queries.

- INSERT: An index can only hurt the process of inserting new data into the table. As data is created in the table, there's a chance that the index will have to be modified and reorganized to accommodate the new values.

- UPDATE: An update requires two or three steps: find the row(s) and change the row(s), or find the row(s), delete them, and reinsert them. During the phase of finding the row, the index is beneficial, such as for a SELECT. Whether or not it hurts during the second phase depends on several factors; for example:

  - Did the index key value change such that it needs to be moved around to different leaf nodes?

  - Will the new value fit on an existing page, or will it require a page split? (More on that later in this section.)

- DELETE: The delete requires two steps: to find the row and to remove it. Indexes are beneficial to find the row, but on deletion, you might have to do some reshuffling to accommodate the deleted values from the indexes.

You should also realize that for INSERT, UPDATE, or DELETE operations, if triggers on the table exist (or constraints exist that execute functions that reference tables), indexes will affect those operations in the same ways as in the list. For this reason, I'm going to shy away from any generic advice about what types of columns to index. In practice, there are just too many variables to consider.

You could probably boil performance tuning to a math equation if you had an advanced degree in math, but truthfully it would take longer than just testing in most cases (especially if you have a good performance-testing plan for your system). Even once you know the customer's answer to these questions, you should probably test your database code on your performance-testing platform. Performance testing can be tricky, but it doesn't usually take tremendous amounts of time to identify your hot spots and optimize them, and to do the inevitable tuning of queries in production.

In the next two subsections, I'll cover page splits, which occur when a page has reached its limit and new data needs to be added in the middle of the index keys on a page, and how to determine when an index is useful.

Page Splits

Index pages, which include all pages of the index—including the leaf nodes, which are the table data for clustered tables—are ordered by the values in the index key. As mentioned in the previous section, when inserting or updating rows, SQL Server might have to rearrange the rows on the pages of the table, which can be a particularly costly operation. Consider the following situation from our example, shown in Figure 8-12, assuming that only three values could fit on a page.

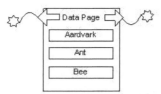

Figure 8-12. *Sample data page before page split*

Say we want to add a value of Bear onto the page. Because it won't fit on the page, the pages need to be reorganized. Pages are split into two, generally with 50 percent of the data on one page, and 50 percent on the other. (There are always more than three values on a real page!) Once split, and the value inserted, the pages would be changed to look like Figure 8-13.

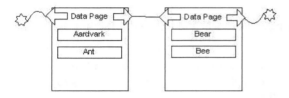

Figure 8-13. *Sample data page after page split*

This can be even worse if you tend to enlarge the values beyond the size of the index and cause lots of page splits. These are awfully costly operations and hurt performance, because data won't be located on successive physical pages. Page splits occur often, and are a part of adding data. It's important to understand the effect that they can have on your data and indexes as you tune performance on tables that have large numbers of inserts or updates.

■**Tip** When you create an index you can specify a FILL FACTOR, which specifies how full to fill each page in the index when it's created. During a page split, the data page is always split 50–50, and it is left half empty on each page (not half full!).

One great thing about using the clustered index on a monotonously increasing value is that page splits over the entire index are greatly decreased. The table grows only on one end of the index and does need to be rebuilt occasionally using ALTER INDEX REORGANIZE or ALTER INDEX REBUILD. You can decide which to do by using the criteria stated by SQL Server Books Online. By looking in the dynamic management view sys.dm_db_index_physical_stats, you can use REBUILD on indexes with greater than 30 percent fragmentation, and REORGANIZE otherwise.

Determining Index Usefulness

It might seem at this point that all you need to do is look at the plans of queries, look for the search arguments, put an index on the columns, and things will improve. There's a bit of truth to this, but indexes have to be useful to be used by a query. What if the index of this book had two entries:

General Topics Page 1

Determining Index Usefulness Page 417

This means that one page was classified such that the topic started on this page, and all other pages covered general topics. This would be useless to you, unless you needed to know about indexes. One thing is for sure: you could determine that the index was useless pretty quickly. Another thing we all do with the index of a book to see if it's useful is to take a value and look it up in the index. If what you're looking for is in there (or something close), you go to the page and check it out.

SQL Server determines whether or not to use your index in much the same way. It has two specific measurements that it uses to decide if an index is useful: the *density* of values (sometimes known as the *selectivity*), and a histogram of a sample of values in the table to check against.

You can see these in detail for indexes by using DBCC SHOW_STATISTICS. Our table is very small, so it doesn't need stats to decide which to use. Instead, we'll look at an index in the AdventureWorks database:

```
DBCC SHOW_STATISTICS('humanResources.employee', 'IX_Employee_ManagerID')
                                              WITH DENSITY_VECTOR
DBCC SHOW_STATISTICS('humanResources.employee', 'IX_Employee_ManagerID')
                                              WITH HISTOGRAM
```

This returns the following sets (truncated for space), the first of which tells us the size and density of the keys. The second shows the histogram of where the table was sampled to find representative values:

All density	Average Length	Columns
0.02083333	3.986207	ManagerID
0.003448276	7.986207	ManagerID, EmployeeID

RANGE_HI_KEY	RANGE_ROWS	EQ_ROWS	DISTINCT_RANGE_ROWS	AVG_RANGE_ROWS
3	0	7	0	1
6	0	8	0	1
7	0	6	0	1
12	0	1	0	1
...	...	...	...	...

218	0	2	0	1
263	0	2	0	1
268	0	10	0	1
273	0	3	0	1
274	0	11	0	1
284	0	3	0	1
288	0	1	0	1

I won't cover the DBCC SHOW_STATISTICS command in great detail, but there are a couple important things to understand. First, consider the density of each column set. The ManagerID column is the only column in the index, but note that it includes the density of the index column and the clustered index key as well (it's known as the clustering key, which I'll cover more later in this chapter).

All the density is calculated approximately by the 1/ number of distinct rows:

```
--managerId can be null, use isnull to deal with this
SELECT 1.0/ count(distinct isnull(managerId,0)),
                    count(distinct isnull(managerId,0))
FROM    humanResources.employee

SELECT 1.0/ count(*), count(*) --since employeeId, managerId are unique
FROM    humanResources.employee
```

The smaller the number, the better the index, and the more likely it will be easily chosen for use. There's no magic number, *per se*, but this value fits into the calculations of which way is best to execute the query. (The actual numbers returned from this query might vary slightly from the DBCC value, as a sampled number might be used for the distinct count.)

The second thing to understand in the DBCC SHOW_STATISTICS output is the histogram. Even if the density of the index isn't low, SQL Server can check a given value (or set of values) in the histogram to see how many rows will likely be returned. SQL Server keeps statistics about columns in a table as well as in indexes, so it can make informed decisions as to how to employ indexes or table columns. For example, consider the following rows from the histogram:

RANGE_HI_KEY	RANGE_ROWS	EQ_ROWS	DISTINCT_RANGE_ROWS	AVG_RANGE_ROWS
...				
21	0	22	0	1
30	5	5	1	5

In the second row, the row values tell us the following:

- RANGE_HI_KEY: The sampled ManagerId value was 30. (If there was a RANGE_LOW_KEY, it would be 21, from the previous row.)

- RANGE_ROWS: There were five rows where the value was between 21 and 30. These values aren't known. However, if a user used 23 as a search argument, the optimizer can now know that a maximum of five rows would be returned.

- EQ_ROWS: There were five rows where ManagerId = 30.

- DISTINCT_RANGE_ROWS: There was only one distinct value between 21 and 30, hence the maximum number of matching rows would either be five or zero. The optimizer could then use five as its estimate.

- AVG_RANGE_ROWS: This is the average number of duplicate values in the range.

One thing that having this histogram can do is allow a seemingly useless index to become valuable in some cases. For example, say you want to index a column with only two values. If the values are evenly distributed, the index would be useless. However, if there are only a few of a certain value, it could be useful (going back to the tempdb):

```
CREATE TABLE testIndex
(
    testIndex int identity(1,1) constraint PKtestIndex primary key,
    bitValue bit,
    filler char(2000) not null default (replicate('A',2000))
)
CREATE INDEX XtestIndex_bitValue on testIndex(bitValue)
GO

INSERT INTO testIndex(bitValue)
VALUES (0)
GO 20000 --runs current batch 20000 times in Management Studio.
INSERT INTO testIndex(bitValue)
VALUES (1)
GO 10 --puts 10 rows into table with value 1
```

You can guess that few rows will be returned if the only value desired is 1. Check the plan for bitValue = 0:

```
SELECT *
FROM    testIndex
WHERE   bitValue = 0
```

This shows a clustered index scan:

```
|--Clustered Index Scan(OBJECT:([tempdb].[dbo].[testIndex].[PKtestIndex]),
                  WHERE:([tempdb].[dbo].[testIndex].[bitValue]=(0)))
```

However, change the 0 to a 1 and the optimizer chooses an index seek:

```
|--Nested Loops(Inner Join,
             OUTER REFERENCES:([tempdb].[dbo].[testIndex].[testIndex]) OPTIMIZED)
       |--Index Seek(OBJECT:([tempdb].[dbo].[testIndex].[XtestIndex_bitValue]),
             SEEK:([tempdb].[dbo].[testIndex].[bitValue]=(1)) ORDERED FORWARD)
       |--Clustered Index Seek(OBJECT:([tempdb].[dbo].[testIndex].[PKtestIndex]),
             SEEK:([tempdb].[dbo].[testIndex].[testIndex]=
                  [tempdb].[dbo].[testIndex].[testIndex]) LOOKUP ORDERED FORWARD)
```

Note that this may look a bit odd, but this plan shows that the query processor will do the index seek to find the rows that match, and then a nested loop join to the clustered index to get the rest of the data for the row (because we chose to do SELECT *, getting the entire data).

You can see why in the histogram:

```
UPDATE STATISTICS dbo.testIndex
DBCC SHOW_STATISTICS('dbo.testIndex', 'XtestIndex_bitValue')
                                        WITH HISTOGRAM
```

This returns the following results:

RANGE_HI_KEY	RANGE_ROWS	EQ_ROWS	DISTINCT_RANGE_ROWS	AVG_RANGE_ROWS
0	0	19993.92	0	1
1	0	16.0809	0	1

The statistics gathered estimated that about 17 rows match (you can't round that number down) for bitValue = 1. That's because statistics gathering isn't an exact science—it uses a sampling mechanism rather than checking every value (your values might vary as well). Check out the TABLESAMPLE clause and you can use the same mechanisms to gather random samples of your data.

The optimizer knew that it would be advantageous to use the index when looking for bitValue = 1, because approximately 17 rows are returned when the index key with a value of 1 is desired, but 19,994 are returned for 0.

Indexing and Multiple Columns

So far, the indexes I've talked about were mostly on single columns, but it isn't all that often that you only need indexes on single columns. When multiple columns are included in the WHERE clause of a query on the same table, there are three possibilities:

- Covering indexes by including all columns that a query touches

- Having one composite index on all columns

- Having multiple indexes on separate columns

Covering Query Data with Indexes

When only retrieving data from a table, if an index exists that has all the data that's needed for a query, the base table needn't be touched. Back in Figure 8-10, there was a nonclustered index on the type of animal. If the name of the animal was the only data the query needed to touch, the data pages of the table wouldn't need to be accessed directly. The index *covers* all the data needed for the query, and is commonly referred to as a *covering* index. Covering indexes with index pages only is a nice feature, and even works with clustered indexes (though with clustered indexes, it scans the lowest index structure page, because scanning the leaf nodes of the clustered index is the same as a table scan).

SQL Server 2005 adds a new feature to the index-creation syntax to improve the ability to implement covering indexes. This is the INCLUDE (<columns>) clause of the CREATE INDEX statement. The included columns can be almost any datatype, even the (max)-type columns.

The only types that aren't allowed are text, ntext, and image datatypes, but you shouldn't use these types anyhow, as they're in the process of being deprecated.

Using the INCLUDE keyword gives you the ability to add columns to cover a query without including the columns in the index pages, causing overhead in the use of the index. Instead, the data is added only to the leaf pages of the index. It won't help in index seeking, but it does eliminate the need to go to the data pages to get the data.

Let's run the following query:

```
SELECT name, color
FROM produce.vegetable
WHERE color = 'orange'
```

The plan for this is a simple clustered index scan:

```
|--Clustered Index Scan
        (OBJECT:([tempdb].[produce].[vegetable].[PKvegetable]),
         WHERE:([tempdb].[produce].[vegetable].[color]='orange'))
```

Now, let's modify this index and include the name column:

```
DROP INDEX produce.vegetable.Xvegetable_color
CREATE INDEX Xvegetable_color ON produce.vegetable(color) INCLUDE (name)
```

Now the query goes back to scanning the index because it has all the data in the index:

```
|--Index Seek(OBJECT:([tempdb].[produce].[vegetable].[Xvegetable_color]),
SEEK:([tempdb].[produce].[vegetable].[color]=[@1]) ORDERED FORWARD)
```

This feature is way useful in a lot of situations. Too many poor indexes were created to solve situations just like this, to cover a query to avoid accessing the base table. Now, using INCLUDE, you get the benefits of a covering index without the overhead of bloating the nonleaf pages of the index with values that are useless from a row-accessing standpoint.

■Tip Be careful not to overuse covering indexes unless you can see a large benefit. The INCLUDE feature costs less to maintain than including the values in the index structure, but it doesn't make the index structure free to maintain. It requires more space in the database, and double the space is used for columns used in the INCLUDE statement.

Composite Indexes

When you include greater than one column in the WHERE clause of a query, it's referred to as a *composite index*. Composite indexes are usually the way to go to optimize common queries with only a few columns. As the number of columns grows, or the number of bytes in the keys grows, the effectiveness of the index is reduced. How large and how many columns isn't something that can be predicted without knowing the entire situation.

The order of the columns in the query is important. There are a couple important considerations:

- *Which column is most selective?* If one column includes unique or mostly unique values, this is possibly a good candidate for the first column. The key is that the first column is the one by which the index is sorted. Searching on the second column only is less valuable (though queries using only the second column can scan only the index leaf pages for values).

- *Which column is used most often without the other columns?* One composite index can be useful to several different queries, in lesser amounts.

For example, consider this query (noting that the index will always cover the query data needed):

```
SELECT color, consistency
FROM produce.vegetable
WHERE color = 'orange'
  and consistency = 'crunchy'
```

If the plan that was being produced by the optimizer was to do a table scan, then you might consider adding a composite index on color and consistency. This isn't a bad idea to consider, and composite indexes are great tools, but just how useful this index will be is completely dependent on how many rows will be returned by color = 'orange' and consistency = 'crunchy'.

Executing this query with existing indexes is optimized with the following plan:

```
|--Clustered Index Scan(OBJECT:([tempdb].[produce].[vegetable].[PKvegetable]),
           WHERE:([tempdb].[produce].[vegetable].[color]='orange' AND
           [tempdb].[produce].[vegetable].[consistency]='crunchy'))
```

It would seem likely that adding an index on color and consistency would be a good way to optimize the query, but first you should look at the data (consider future usage of the index too, but existing data is a good place to start):

```
color        consistency
----------   -----------
brown        squishy
green        crunchy
green        leafy
green        leafy
green        squishy
green        treelike
orange       crunchy
```

Consistency comprises more distinct values, so we add the following index:

```
CREATE INDEX xvegetable_consistencyAndColor
       ON produce.vegetable(consistency, color)
```

The plan changes to the following results (note that this index covers the query we're doing):

```
|--Index Seek(
        OBJECT:([tempdb].[produce].[vegetable].[xvegetable_consistencyAndColor]),
        SEEK:([tempdb].[produce].[vegetable].[consistency]=[@2] AND
        [tempdb].[produce].[vegetable].[color]=[@1]) ORDERED FORWARD)
```

If we only search for color, this index could be used to scan, rather than hit the physical table.

```
SELECT color
FROM   produce.vegetable
WHERE  color = 'green'
```

The plan for this query is as follows:

```
|--Index Scan(
        OBJECT:([tempdb].[produce].[vegetable].[xvegetable_consistencyAndColor]),
        WHERE:([tempdb].[produce].[vegetable].[color]=[@1]))
```

If this table had quite a few other columns, or large varchar columns, using this query plan with the composite index would likely be far faster than having to scan the table.

Multiple Indexes

Sometimes we might not have a single index on a table that meets the given situation. But we might have the case where we have two or more indexes that meet the need. When processing a query with multiple indexes, SQL Server uses the indexes as if they were tables, joins them together, and returns a set of rows. The more indexes used, the larger the cost, but using multiple indexes can be dramatically faster in some cases.

Multiple indexes aren't usually something to rely upon to optimize known queries. It's almost always better to support a known query with a single index. However, if you need to support *ad hoc* queries that cannot be foretold as a system designer, having several indexes including multiple situations might be the best idea. If you're building a read-only table, a decent starting strategy might be to index every column that might be used as a filter for a query.

My focus throughout this book has been on OLTP databases, and for that type of database, it isn't usual to use multiple indexes in a single query. However, it's possible that the need for using multiple indexes will arise if you have a table with several columns that you'll allow users to query against in any combination.

For example, consider that you want data from four columns in a table that contains telephone listings. You might create a table for holding phone numbers called phoneListing, with these columns: phoneListingId, firstName, lastName, zipCode, areaCode, exchange, and number (assuming US-style phone numbers).

You have a clustered primary key index on phoneListingId, nonclustered composite indexes on lastName and firstName, one on areaCode and exchange, and another on the zipCode. From these indexes, you can effectively perform a large variety of searches, though generally speaking none of these will be perfect standing alone.

For less typical names (such as Joe Shlabotnik, for example), a person can find this name without knowing the location. For other names, there are hundreds and thousands of other people with the same first and last name. I always thought I was the only schmuck with the name Louis Davidson, but there are others!

We could build a variety of indexes on these columns, such that SQL Server would only need a single index. However, these indexes would not only have a lot of columns in them, but you'd need several indexes. A composite index can be useful for searches on the second and third columns, but it requires a scan of the index, rather than a seek. Instead, for large sets, SQL Server can find the set of data that meets one index's criteria, and then join it to the set of rows that matches the other index's criteria.

This technique can be useful when dealing with large sets of data, especially when users are doing *ad hoc* querying, and you cannot anticipate what columns they'll need until runtime. Users have to realize that they need to specify as few columns as possible, because if the multiple indexes can cover a query such as the one in the last section, the indexes will be far more likely to be used.

As an example, we'll use the data already created, and add an index on the consistency column:

```
CREATE INDEX Xvegetable_consistency ON produce.vegetable(consistency)
--existing index repeated as a reminder
--CREATE INDEX Xvegetable_color ON produce.vegetable(color) INCLUDE (name)
```

We'll force the optimizer to use multiple indexes (because the sample table is far too small to require multiple indexes):

```
SELECT consistency, color
FROM   produce.vegetable with (index=Xvegetable_color,
                               index=Xvegetable_consistency)
WHERE  color = 'green'
 and   consistency = 'leafy'
```

This produces the following plan (I've only included the portion of the plan pertaining to the indexes):

```
|--Merge Join(Inner Join, MERGE:([tempdb].[produce].[vegetable].[vegetableId])
          =([tempdb].[produce].[vegetable].[vegetableId]),
          RESIDUAL:([tempdb].[produce].[vegetable].[vegetableId] =
          [tempdb].[produce].[vegetable].[vegetableId]))
     |--Index Seek(OBJECT:
          ([tempdb].[produce].[vegetable].[Xvegetable_color]),
           SEEK:([tempdb].[produce].[vegetable].[color]='green') ORDERED FORWARD)
     |--Index Seek(OBJECT:
          ([tempdb].[produce].[vegetable].[Xvegetable_consistency]),
           SEEK:([tempdb].[produce].[vegetable].[consistency]='leafy')
          ORDERED FORWARD)
```

Looking at a snippet of the plan for this query, you can see that there are two index seeks to find rows where `color = 'green'` and `consistency = 'leafy'`. These seeks would be fast on even a very large set, as long as the index was reasonably selective. Then a join is done between the sets using a merge join, because the sets are ordered by the clustered index (there's a clustered index on the table, so the clustering key is included in the index keys).

Nonclustered Indexes on a Heap

Although there are rarely compelling use cases for leaving a table as a heap structure in a production OLTP database, I do want at least to show you how this works. As an example of using a nonclustered index with a heap, we'll drop the primary key on our table and replace it with a nonclustered version of the `PRIMARY KEY` constraint:

```
ALTER TABLE produce.vegetable
    DROP CONSTRAINT PKvegetable

ALTER TABLE produce.vegetable
    ADD CONSTRAINT PKvegetable PRIMARY KEY NONCLUSTERED (vegetableID)
```

Now we look for a single value in the table:

```
SELECT *
FROM   produce.vegetable
WHERE  vegetableId = 4
```

We optimize this query with the following plan:

```
|--Nested Loops(Inner Join, OUTER REFERENCES:([Bmk1000]))
     |--Index Seek(OBJECT:([tempdb].[produce].[vegetable].[PKvegetable]),
          SEEK:([tempdb].[produce].[vegetable].[vegetableId]=
          CONVERT_IMPLICIT(int,[@1],0)) ORDERED FORWARD)
     |--RID Lookup(OBJECT:([tempdb].[produce].[vegetable]),
          SEEK:([Bmk1000]=[Bmk1000]) LOOKUP ORDERED FORWARD)
```

First we probe the index for the value, then we have to look up the row from the row ID in the index (the RID lookup operator). Say we look for more than one row:

```
SELECT *
FROM   produce.vegetable
WHERE  vegetableId in (1, 4)
```

This produces a plan that uses a table scan when only looking for two values:

```
|--Table Scan(OBJECT:([tempdb].[produce].[vegetable]),
     WHERE:([tempdb].[produce].[vegetable].[vegetableId]=(1) OR
     [tempdb].[produce].[vegetable].[vegetableId]=(4)))
```

SQL Server quickly resorts to a table scan in our small table, and does for many situations when a nonclustered index is used on a heap, because it can be expensive to do the row lookup on the table. As the number of values rises, the row lookup becomes costly, because each row has to be fetched from the base table, and the data may be on any page in the database.

Now we add back the constraint as clustered for our upcoming examples:

```
ALTER TABLE produce.vegetable
    DROP CONSTRAINT PKvegetable

ALTER TABLE produce.vegetable
    ADD CONSTRAINT PKvegetable PRIMARY KEY CLUSTERED (vegetableID)
```

Indexes on heaps are generally not as efficient as tables with clustered indexes, which the next section will cover. The most important thing I wanted to show in this section was the RID lookup operator.

Nonclustered Indexes with Clustered Tables

In the following example, I'll demonstrate how the nonclustered index appears in the plan on a clustered table. Consider the alternate key we've set up on the name of the vegetable. Look for a single value in this index:

```
SELECT  *
FROM    produce.vegetable
WHERE   name = 'asparagus'
```

This derives the following plan:

```
|--Nested Loops
   (Inner Join, OUTER REFERENCES:([tempdb].[produce].[vegetable].[vegetableId]))
     |--Index
        Seek(OBJECT:([tempdb].[produce].[vegetable].[AKvegetable_name]),
        SEEK:([tempdb].[produce].[vegetable].[name]=[@1]) ORDERED FORWARD)
     |--Clustered Index
        Seek(OBJECT:([tempdb].[produce].[vegetable].[PKvegetable]),
         SEEK:([tempdb].[produce].[vegetable].[vegetableId]=
        [tempdb].[produce].[vegetable].[vegetableId]) LOOKUP ORDERED FORWARD)
```

It uses an index seek to find the matching row, and a nested loop join to join to the clustered index to get the rest of the row. The optimizer chose to use the AKvegetable_name index, because as a unique index, a very small set was guaranteed to be returned. Hence the join to the clustered index won't be very costly.

On the other hand, take the index we placed on the color value. Try executing the following query from a nonselective value in our color column:

```
SELECT *
FROM    produce.vegetable
WHERE   color = 'orange'
```

The plan calls for a full table scan:

```
|--Clustered Index
        Scan(OBJECT:([tempdb].[produce].[vegetable].[PKvegetable]),
        WHERE:([tempdb].[produce].[vegetable].[color]='green'))
```

The same number of rows is returned, with the exact same amount of data. The difference is that the Xvegetable_color isn't selective at all, and with the small size of the produce.vegetable table, instead of checking the histogram for the index, the optimizer simply chose the index scan. (If you're unsure whether your table has this index any longer, execute sp_help 'produce.vegetable' to check.)

The optimizer can stop looking for better plans as soon as it comes up with one that it believes can run in as much or less time than looking for a more optimal plan.

Using Unique Indexes

An important index setting is UNIQUE. In the design of the tables, UNIQUE and PRIMARY KEY constraints were created to enforce keys. Behind the scenes, SQL Server employs unique indexes to enforce uniqueness over a column or group of columns. The reason that SQL Server uses them for this purpose is because, to determine if a value is unique, you have to look it up in the table. Because SQL Server uses indexes to speed access to the data, you have the perfect match.

Enforcing uniqueness is a business rule, and as I covered in Chapter 6, the rule of thumb is to use UNIQUE or PRIMARY constraints to enforce uniqueness on a set of columns. Now, as you're improving performance, use unique indexes when the data you're indexing allows it.

For example, say you're building an index that happens to include a column (or columns) that are already a part of another unique index. Another possibility might be if you're indexing a column that's naturally unique, such as a GUID. It's up to the designer to decide if this GUID is a key or not, and that depends completely on what it's used for. Using unique indexes lets the optimizer determine more easily the number of rows it has to deal with in an equality operation.

Also note that it's important for the performance of your systems that you use unique indexes whenever possible, as they enhance the SQL Server optimizer's chances of predicting how many rows will be returned from a query that uses the index. If the index is unique, the maximum number of rows that can be returned from a query that requires equality is one. This is common when working with joins.

Advanced Index Usage Scenarios

So far we've dealt with the mechanics of indexes, and basic situations where they're useful. Now we need to talk about a few special uses of indexes that deserve some pre-planning or understanding to use.

I'll discuss the following topics:

- Indexing foreign keys

- Indexing views to optimize denormalization

Foreign Key Indexes

Foreign key columns are a special case where often we need an index of some sort. This is because we build foreign keys so we can match up rows in one table to rows in another. For this, we have to take a value in one table and match it to another.

In an OLTP database that has proper constraints on alternate keys, it's often the case that we won't need to index foreign keys beyond what we're given with the unique indexes that are built as part of the structure of the database. This is probably why SQL Server 2005 doesn't implement unique indexes for us when creating a foreign key constraint.

However, it's important to make sure that any time you have a foreign key constraint declared, there's the potential for need of an index whenever you have a parent table and you want to see the children of the row. A special and important case where this type of access is essential is when you have to delete the parent row in any relationship, even one of a domain type.

Say you have five values in the parent table, and five billion in the child. For example, consider the case of a click log for a sales database, a snippet of which is shown in Figure 8-14.

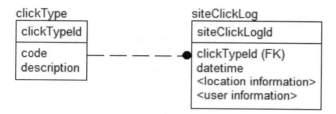

Figure 8-14. *Sample foreign key relationship*

Consider that you want to delete a clickType that someone added inadvertently. Creating the row took several milliseconds. Deleting it shouldn't take long at all, right? If you don't have an index on the foreign key in the siteClickLog table, it will take just over ten seconds longer than eternity will take (or just five seconds longer than the line to ride Splash Mountain at Disney World on a hot summer's day!). Because the value doesn't exist in the table, the query processor would need to touch and check the entire five billion rows for the value. However, if you have an index, deleting the row will take a short period of time indeed, because in the upper pages of the index you'll have all the unique values in the index, in this case five values. There will be a fairly substantial set of leaf pages for the index, because each row needs to be pointed to, but if there are only a few clickType rows, the top page of the index tree will have no more key values than there are rows in clickType. Hence, deciding if the row can be deleted takes no time at all.

This adds more decisions when building indexes. Is the cost of building and maintaining the index during creation of siteClickLog rows justified, or do you just bite the bullet and do deletes during off hours? Add a trigger such as the following (ignoring error handling in this example for brevity):

```
CREATE TRIGGER clickType$insteadOfDelete
ON clickType
INSTEAD OF DELETE
AS
    INSERT INTO clickType_deleteQueue (clickTypeId)
    SELECT clickTypeId
    FROM   inserted
```

Then you let your queries that return lists of clickType rows check this table when presenting rows to the users:

```
SELECT code, description, clickTypeId
FROM   clickType
WHERE  not exists (SELECT *
                   FROM   clickType_deleteQueue
                   WHERE  clickType.clickTypeId = clickType_deleteQueue.clickTypeId)
```

Now the users will never see the value, so it won't be an issue, and you can delete the row during the wee hours of the night without building the index.

Deciding when to build a foreign key index can be tricky, just like any index. I think that it's rarely an automatic decision to build any index that isn't built as part of a constraint, but I feel that using constraints liberally as needed is important, not only for data integrity, but for the built-in performance gains you'll get as part of the package.

Whether or not an index proves useful depends on the purpose of the foreign key. I'll mention specific types of foreign keys individually, each with their own signature usage:

- *Domain tables*: Used to implement a defined set of values and their descriptions

- *Ownership*: Used to implement a multivalued attribute of the parent

- *Many-to-many resolution*: Used to implement a many-to-many relationship physically

- *One-to-one relationships*: Cases where a parent may have only a single value in the related table

We'll look at examples of these types and discuss when it's appropriate to index them before the typical trial-and-error performance tuning, where the rule of thumb is to add indexes to make queries faster, while not slowing down other operations that create data.

In all cases, deleting the parent row requires a table scan of the child if there's no index on the child row. This is an important consideration if there are deletes.

Domain Tables

You use a domain table to enforce a domain using a table, rather than using a scalar value with a constraint. This is often done to enable a greater level of data about the domain value, such as a descriptive value. For example, consider the tables in Figure 8-15.

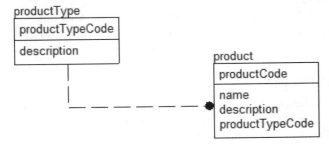

Figure 8-15. *Sample domain table relationship*

In this case, there are a small number of rows in the productType table. It's unlikely that an index on the product.productTypeCode column would be of any value in a join. That's because you'll generally be getting a productType row for every row you fetch from the product table.

What about the other direction, when you want to find all products of a single type? This can be useful if there aren't many products, but in general, with domain tables there aren't enough unique values to merit an index. The general advice is that tables of this sort don't need an index on the foreign key values, by default.

Ownership Relationships

You use an ownership relationship to implement multivalued attributes of an object. The main performance characteristic of this situation is that most of the time when the parent row is retrieved, the child rows are retrieved as well. It's less likely that you'll need to retrieve a child row and then look for the parent row.

For example, take the case of an invoice and its line items in Figure 8-16.

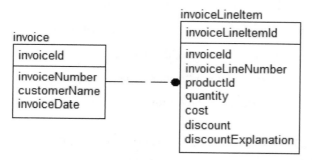

Figure 8-16. *Sample ownership relationship*

In this case, it's essential to have an index on the invoiceLineItem.invoiceId column. Most access to the invoiceLineItem table results from a user's need to get an invoice first. What also makes this an ideal situation for an index is that, generally speaking, this is a very selective index (unless you have large numbers of items and few sales).

Note that you should already have a UNIQUE constraint (and a unique index as a consequence of this) on the alternate key for the table, in this case invoiceId and invoiceLineNumber. As such, you might or might not want to have a index on just invoiceId. This is largely based on the size of your key values, and the usage of the data. If the other columns in the index are large and the foreign key is small, adding an index on just the foreign key column might be valuable. Your mileage will vary, but in general I stick with the UNIQUE constraint unless it turns out that it isn't useful for common queries.

Many-to-Many Resolution Table Relationships

When we have a many-to-many relationship, there certainly needs to be an index on the two migrated keys from the two parent tables. Think back to our previous examples of games owned on a given platform (diagram repeated in Figure 8-17).

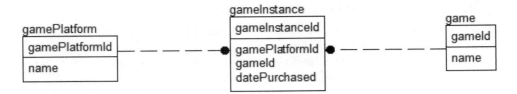

Figure 8-17. *Sample many-to-many relationship*

There's certainly a need for a composite UNIQUE constraint and index on the gamePlatformId and gameId columns, as well as the primary key on gameInstanceId. In some cases, you might want to add an index to individual columns if neither direction is dominant and you have a lot of data. Just as in all cases, testing is the key when adding most performance-based indexes.

Take this example. If we usually look up a game by name (which would be alternate key indexed) and then get the platforms for this game, an index only on gameInstance.gameId would be much more useful and two-thirds the size of the alternate key index (assuming a clustering key of gameInstanceId).

One-to-One Relationships

One-to-one relationships generally don't require some form of unique index on the key in the parent table as well as on the migrated key in the child table. For example, consider the subclass example of a bankAccount, shown in Figure 8-18.

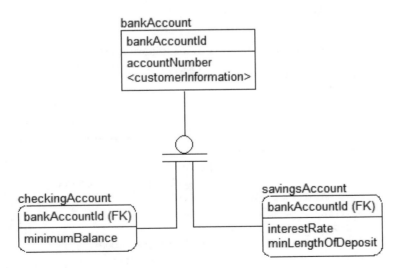

Figure 8-18. *Sample one-to-one relationship*

Because these are one-to-one relationships, and there are already indexes on the primary key of each table, no other indexes would need to be added for the relationship.

Using Indexed Views to Optimize Denormalizations

By indexing a view, we now have the ability to build triggerless summary data, which SQL Server automatically maintains in a way that makes a usually tricky operation as simple as writing a query. Instead of the view definition being used as in ordinary views, the optimizer can choose to use the index, which has the current values for the index pre-materialized.

Instead of building triggers and such to manage denormalized data, we can create a view that does this automatically. What makes creating an indexed view even more interesting is that when using the Enterprise Edition of SQL Server, the optimizer can use these indexed views even if the querier has no idea that the indexed view exists! (I'll demonstrate this later in the section.)

For example, going back to our `item` and `sale` tables, we could create the following view. Note that only schema-bound views can be indexed. This makes certain that the tables and structures that the index is created upon won't change underneath the view. Consider the following example on the `AdventureWorks` database:

```
CREATE VIEW Production.ProductAverageSales
WITH SCHEMABINDING
AS
SELECT  Product.productNumber,
        SUM(SalesOrderDetail.lineTotal) as totalSales,
        COUNT_BIG(*) as countSales
FROM    Production.Product as Product
            JOIN Sales.SalesOrderDetail as SalesOrderDetail
                ON product.ProductID=SalesOrderDetail.ProductID
GROUP  BY Product.productNumber
```

This would do the calculations at execution time. We run the following query:

```
SELECT  productNumber, totalSales, countSales
FROM    Production.ProductAverageSales
```

The plan looks like this:

```
---------------------------------------------------------------------
|--Hash Match(Inner Join, HASH:([SalesOrderDetail].[ProductID])=
                                    ([Product].[ProductID]))
    |--Hash Match(Aggregate, HASH:([SalesOrderDetail].[ProductID])
                    DEFINE:([Expr1004]=SUM([AdventureWorks].[Sales].
                    [SalesOrderDetail].[LineTotal] as
                    [SalesOrderDetail].[LineTotal]), [Expr1005]=COUNT(*)))
    |    |--Compute   Scalar(DEFINE:([SalesOrderDetail].[LineTotal]=
                    [AdventureWorks].[Sales].[SalesOrderDetail].[LineTotal] as
                    [SalesOrderDetail].[LineTotal]))
    |        |--Compute Scalar(DEFINE:([SalesOrderDetail].[LineTotal]=
                    isnull((CONVERT_IMPLICIT(numeric(19,4),
                    [AdventureWorks].[Sales].[SalesOrderDetail].[UnitPrice] as
                    [SalesOrderDetail].[UnitPrice],0)*
                    ((1.0)-CONVERT_IMPLICIT(numeric(19,4),[AdventureWorks].
```

```
                    [Sales].[SalesOrderDetail].[UnitPriceDiscount] as
                    [SalesOrderDetail].
                    [UnitPriceDiscount],0)))*CONVERT_IMPLICIT(numeric(5,0),
                    [AdventureWorks].[Sales].[SalesOrderDetail].[OrderQty] as
                    [SalesOrderDetail].[OrderQty],0),(0.000000))))
      |                  |--Clustered Index
                            Scan(OBJECT:([AdventureWorks].[Sales].[SalesOrderDetail].
                            [PK_SalesOrderDetail_SalesOrderID_SalesOrderDetailID]
                            AS [SalesOrderDetail]))
      |--Index Scan(OBJECT:([AdventureWorks].[Production].[Product].
                    [AK_Product_ProductNumber] AS [Product]))
```

This is a big plan for such a small query, for sure, and hard to follow, but it scans the SalesOrderDetail table, computes our scalar values, then does a hash match aggregate and a hash match join to join the two sets together. For further reading on the join types, consider the book *Inside SQL Server 2005 Query Processing and Optimization* by Kalen Delaney (Microsoft Press), due out in mid-2006.

This query executes pretty fast on my 1.8 GHz 1GB laptop, but there's a noticeable delay. Say this query wasn't fast enough, or it used too many resources to execute, or it was used extremely often. In this case, we might add an index on the view, such as this:

```
CREATE UNIQUE CLUSTERED INDEX XPKProductAverageSales on
                                Production.ProductAverageSales(productNumber)
```

SQL Server would then build the view and store it. Now our queries to the view will be *very* fast. However, although we've avoided all the coding issues involved with storing summary data, we have to keep our data up to date. Every time data changes in the underlying tables, the index on the view changes its data, so there's a performance hit due to maintaining the index for the view. Hence, indexing views means that performance is great for reading, but not necessarily for updating.

You can build indexed views in any edition of SQL Server, but in the Enterprise Edition, SQL Server automatically considers the view whenever you execute any query, even if you haven't specified the view. That's because an executed query has some of the same needs that the indexed view has already calculated and maintained. In other versions, you have to specify a table hint (NOEXPAND) when using the view in queries, to have the optimizer use the index rather than expanding the view text as part of the query.

Now, run the query again:

```
SELECT productNumber, totalSales, countSales
FROM   Production.ProductAverageSales
```

The plan looks like the following:

```
------------------------------------------------------------------------
  |--Clustered Index
          Scan(OBJECT:([AdventureWorks].[Production].
          [ProductAverageSales].[XPKProductAverageSales]))
```

Big deal; we obviously expected this result because we directly queried the view. On my test system, running the Developer Edition (which is functionally comparable to the Enterprise Edition), you get a great insight into how cool this feature is in the following query for getting the average sales per product:

```
SELECT Product.productNumber, sum(SalesOrderDetail.lineTotal) / COUNT(*)
FROM   Production.Product as Product
            JOIN Sales.SalesOrderDetail as SalesOrderDetail
                ON product.ProductID=SalesOrderDetail.ProductID
GROUP  BY Product.productNumber
```

We'd expect the plan for this query to be the same as the first query of the view was, because we haven't referenced anything other than the base tables, right? I already told you the answer, so here's the plan:

```
|--Compute
    Scalar(DEFINE:([Expr1006]=[AdventureWorks].[Production].ProductAverageSales].
    [totalSales]/CONVERT_IMPLICIT(numeric(10,0),[Expr1005],0)))
    |--Compute Scalar(DEFINE:([Expr1005]=
            CONVERT_IMPLICIT(int,[AdventureWorks].[Production].
            [ProductAverageSales].[averageTotal],0)))
        |--Clustered Index
                Scan(OBJECT:([AdventureWorks].[Production].
                [ProductAverageSales].[XPKProductAverageSales]))
```

There are two scalar computes—one for the division, one to convert the `bigint` from the `COUNT_BIG(*)` to an integer—and the other to scan through the indexed view's clustered index. The ability to use the optimizations from an indexed view indirectly is a cool feature that allows you to build in some guesses as to what *ad hoc* users will be doing with the data, and giving them performance they didn't even ask for.

There are some pretty heavy caveats, though. The restrictions on what can be used in a view, prior to it being indexed, are fairly tight. The most important things that cannot be done are as follows:

- Use the `SELECT *` syntax—columns must be explicitly named
- Use `UNION`, `EXCEPT`, or `INTERSECT` in the view
- Use any subqueries
- Use any outer joins or recursively join back to the same table
- Specify `TOP` in the `SELECT` clause
- Use `DISTINCT`
- Include a `SUM()` function if it references more than one column
- Use `COUNT(*)`, though `COUNT_BIG(*)` is allowed
- Use almost any aggregate function against a nullable expression

- Reference any other views

- Reference any nondeterministic functions

- Reference data outside the database

- Reference tables owned by a different owner

And this isn't all. You must meet several pages of requirements, documented in SQL Server Books Online in the section "Creating Indexed Views," but these are the most significant ones that you need to consider before using indexed views.

Although this might all seem pretty restrictive, there are good reasons for all these rules. Maintaining the indexed view is analogous to writing our own denormalized data maintenance functions. Simply put, the more complex the query to build the denormalized data, the greater the complexity in maintaining it. Adding one row to the base table might cause the view to need to recalculate, touching thousands of rows.

Indexed views are particularly useful when you have a view that's costly to run, but the data on which it's based doesn't change a tremendous amount. As an example, consider a decision-support system where you load data once a day. There's overhead either maintaining the index, or possibly just rebuilding it, but if you can build the index during off hours, you can omit the cost of redoing joins and calculations for every view usage.

Tip With all the caveats, indexed views can prove useless for some circumstances. An alternative method is to materialize the results of the data by inserting the data into a permanent table. For example, for our sample query we'd create a table with three columns (`productNumber`, `totalSales`, and `countSales`), then we'd do an `INSERT INTO ProductAverageSales SELECT. . .` We'd put the results of the query in this table. Any query works here, not just one that meets the strict guidelines. It doesn't help out *ad hoc* users who don't directly query the data in the table, but it certainly improves performance of queries that directly access the data.

Best Practices

Indexing is a complex subject, and we've only scratched the surface. The following best practices are what I use as a rule of thumb when creating a new database solution. Note that I assume that you've applied UNIQUE constraints in all places where they make logical sense. These constraints most likely should be there, even if they slow down your application (there are exceptions, but if a set of values needs to be unique, it needs to be unique). From there, it's all a big tradeoff. The first rule is the most important.

- *There are few reasons to add indexes to tables without testing*: Add nonconstraint indexes to your tables only as needed to enhance performance. In many cases it will turn out that no index is needed to achieve decent performance. A caveat can be foreign key indexes.

- *Carefully consider foreign key indexes*: If child rows are selected because of a parent row (including on a foreign key checking for children on a delete operation), then an index on the columns in a foreign key is generally a good idea.

- *Keep indexes as thin as possible*: Only index the columns that are selective enough in the main part of the index. Use the INCLUDE clause on the CREATE INDEX statement if you want to include columns only to cover the data used by a query.

- *Consider several thin indexes rather than one monolithic index*: SQL Server can use multiple indexes in a query efficiently. This can be a good tool to support *ad hoc* access where the users can choose between multiple situations.

- *Be careful of the cost of adding an index*: When you insert, update, or delete rows from a table with an index, there's a definite cost to maintaining the index. New data added might require page splits, and inserts, updates, and deletes can cause a reshuffling of the index pages.

- UNIQUE *constraints are used to enforce uniqueness, not unique indexes*: Unique indexes are used to enhance performance by telling the optimizer that an index will only return one row in equality comparisons. Users shouldn't get error messages from a unique *index* violation.

Summary

Indexing, like the entire gamut of performance tuning topics, is hard to cover with any specificity on a written page. I've given you some information about the mechanics of tables and indexes, and a few best practices, but to be realistic, it's never going to be enough without you working with a realistic, active working test system.

Tuning with indexes requires a lot of basic knowledge applied on a large scale. Joins use indexes or not based on many factors, and the indexes available to a query affect the join operators chosen. The best teacher for this is the school of "having to wait for a five-hour query to process." Most people, when starting out, start on small systems and code any way they want, slap indexes on everything, and it works great. SQL Server covers a multitude of such sins, particularly on a low-concurrency, low-usage system. As your system grows and requires more and more resources, it becomes more and more difficult to do performance tuning haphazardly.

The steps I generally suggest for indexing are straightforward:

- Apply all the UNIQUE constraints that can possibly be added without annoying the users by enforcing uniqueness that they don't care about.

- Index all foreign key constraints where the parent table is likely to be the driving force behind fetching rows in the child (such as invoice ➤ line item).

- Start performance testing, running load tests to see how things perform.

- Identify queries that are slow, and consider the following:

  - Adding indexes.

  - Eliminating clustered index row lookups by covering queries, possibly using the new INCLUDE keyword on indexes.

- Materializing query results, either by indexed view or by putting results into permanent table.

- Working on data location strategies with filegroups.

Do this last step over and over, adding indexes and removing indexes, moving data around to different disk channels, and so on until you arrive at the happy medium. Every added index is more overhead, but it can greatly improve performance of reads. Only you can decide if your system does more reads or writes, and even more important, which delay bothers you most. If queries take 10 seconds, but users only need results within 20, who cares? But if a query takes 500 milliseconds, and you have a machine that you feel could be working at 100 milliseconds per operation, then you might be tempted to optimize for that performance at all costs. Once you optimize this query, ten others might be affected negatively. Be very aware that performance tuning is a balancing act, and most every performance gain is also going to hurt some other performance. Luckily it is not a one-to-one match, performance gain to loss. An optimization that saves you 1,000 ms per query may cost you 10 ms in another. Of course, don't forget frequency. Saving 30 minutes of nightly processing probably isn't worth making your online queries run one second longer each—not if these queries are run 10,000 times a day. (That's 2.7 hours of lost work a day!).

Indexes are an important step to building high-performance systems, and highly concurrent ones with many users executing simultaneously. In the next chapter, I'll look at some of the other concerns for concurrency. Having moderate- to high-level server-class hardware with fast RAID arrays and multiple channels to the disk storage, you can spread the data out over multiple filegroups, as I discussed in the basic table structure section earlier. However, if you only have one hard disk on your server, or a single array of disks, you won't get much, if any, benefit out of moving your data around on the disk.

CHAPTER 9
■ ■ ■

Coding for Concurrency

Multitasking: Screwing everything up simultaneously.

—Anonymous

Concurrency is all about multitasking, or having more than one thing done at the same time, particularly when serving multiple users. The key here is that when multiple users are accessing the same resources, each user expects to see a consistent view of the data, and certainly not to have other users stomping on his or her results.

In this chapter, I'll discuss some of the concepts and issues surrounding concurrency in SQL Server applications:

- *Query optimization basics*: The basics of how queries get optimized and then executed by the query engine.

- *OS and hardware issues*: I'll briefly discuss various issues that are out of the control of SQL code.

- *Transactions*: I'll give an overview of how transactions work and how to code them in T-SQL code.

- *SQL Server concurrency controls*: In this section, I'll explain locks and isolation levels.

- *Coding for concurrency*: I'll discuss methods of coding data access to protect from users simultaneously making changes to data and placing data into less-than-adequate situations. You'll also learn how to deal with users stepping on one another, and how to maximize concurrency.

I'll talk about many of the kinds of things SQL Server does to make it fast and safe to have multiple users doing the same sorts of tasks with the same resources, and how you can optimize your code to make it easier for this to happen.

What Is Concurrency?

Concurrency can be boiled down to the following statement:

Maximize the amount of work that can be done by all users at the same time, and most importantly, make all users feel like they're important.

Because of the need to balance the amount of work with the user's perception of the amount of work being done, there are going to be the following tradeoffs:

- *Amount of concurrency*: How many users can (or need to) be served at the same time

- *Overhead*: How complex the algorithms are to maintain concurrency

- *Accuracy*: How correct results must be

- *Performance*: How fast each process finishes

- *Cost*: How much you're willing to spend on hardware and programming time

As you can probably guess, if all the users of a database system never shared the same resources, life in database-system–design land would be far simpler. However, in building database solutions, there's always more to it. If no one ever shared resources, multitasking servers would be unnecessary. All files could be places on a user's local computer, and that would be enough. Servers are set up to give access to large amounts of data by many people. For example, a common scenario involves a sales and shipping database. You might have 50 salespersons in a call center trying to sell the last 25 closeout items that are in stock. It isn't desirable to promise the last physical item accidentally to multiple customers. That's because two users might happen to read that it was available at the same time, and then are both allowed to place an order for it. In this case, stopping the first order wouldn't be necessary, but once stock is depleted, any further order should be disallowed, or one of these customers would end up placing an order that can never be fulfilled.

Most programmers write code to check that this sort of thing doesn't happen. Code is generally written that does something along these lines:

- Check to make sure that there's adequate stock

- Create a shipping row

Simple enough, but what if one person checks to see if the product is available at the same time as another, and more orders are placed than you have adequate stock for? Is this acceptable? If you've ever ordered a product that you were promised in two days, and then you find out your items are on backorder for a month, you know the answer to this question: "No, it isn't!"

The problems presented by concurrency aren't the same as those for *parallelism*, which is having the same thing done by multiple resources. In writing SQL Server code, parallelism is done automatically, as tasks can be split among resources. When I refer to concurrency, I generally mean having multiple *different* operations happening at the same time by different connections to SQL Server.

Tip In SQL Server 2005, there's a new way to execute multiple batches of SQL code from the same connection simultaneously, known as Multiple Active Result Sets (MARS). It allows interleaved execution of several statements, such as `SELECT`, `FETCH`, `RECEIVE READTEXT`, or `BULK INSERT`.

MARS is principally a client technology, and must be enabled by connection, but it can change some of the ways that SQL Server handles concurrency. I'll note the places where MARS affects the fundamentals of concurrency.

Query Optimization Basics

SQL Server is a batch-oriented system. A batch of commands is sent to the server, then the client waits for messages and tabular data sets to be returned. Nothing should be done in an interactive manner at all. Each batch executes sequentially, one statement at a time (even in MARS, each batch is sequentially executed, though you can execute multiple batches on the same connection). SQL Server can spawn multiple threads to perform a single operation, but each operation gets executed one at a time.

To optimize the query, SQL Server takes the text of the query and parses it. The query is then compiled down to a series of *operators*. Operators are essentially black-box modules that have inputs (usually one or two) and a single output. For every query, many operators are used to handle I/O, messaging, and algorithms. We, as database programmers, generally deal with the algorithm type of operator most of all, as I/O and messaging are pretty much internal.

To understand this, it's best to look at the execution plan of a query. It isn't the first time we've done this, as we looked at many plans to show index usage in Chapter 8. Take the following query in the AdventureWorks database:

```
SELECT  productModel.name as productModel,
        product.name as productName
FROM    production.product as product
        JOIN production.productModel as productModel
            ON productModel.productModelId = product.productModelId
WHERE   product.name like '%glove%'
```

SQL Server's optimizer breaks this down into several operations. You can see a graphical representation of this by selecting the Query ➤ Display Estimated Execution Plan menu item in SQL Server Management Studio, with this code in the edit window. The graphic in Figure 9-1 is displayed (or something close, as optimization can be more than just the query and database objects, depending on hardware).

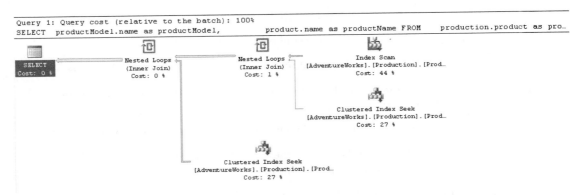

Figure 9-1. *Sample graphical query plan*

Each of the items in Figure 9-1 is a query operator. Hovering over any of the operators brings up a dialog like the one in Figure 9-2.

The numbers represent costs and size, and are generally good for comparisons to the other values for nodes. (Look up SHOWPLAN—and _ALL, _TEXT, and _XML derivatives—in Books

Online for alternative ways to view the plan, and for more detailed explanations of each of these values.) In general, the goal is to reduce all these values as much as possible.

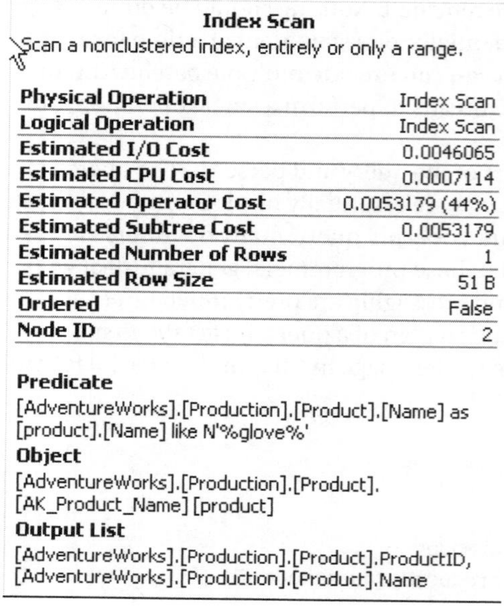

Index Scan
Scan a nonclustered index, entirely or only a range.

Physical Operation	Index Scan
Logical Operation	Index Scan
Estimated I/O Cost	0.0046065
Estimated CPU Cost	0.0007114
Estimated Operator Cost	0.0053179 (44%)
Estimated Subtree Cost	0.0053179
Estimated Number of Rows	1
Estimated Row Size	51 B
Ordered	False
Node ID	2

Predicate
[AdventureWorks].[Production].[Product].[Name] as [product].[Name] like N'%glove%'
Object
[AdventureWorks].[Production].[Product].
[AK_Product_Name] [product]
Output List
[AdventureWorks].[Production].[Product].ProductID,
[AdventureWorks].[Production].[Product].Name

Figure 9-2. *Sample query plan operator detail*

Plans are executed right to left, and there's always a single operator on the left that's the final output or result. SQL Server can take any of these operations and spread them across multiple processors, but you have little control over this happening (other than limiting the maximum degree of parallelism).

There are operators for all sorts of things; for example:

- *Scans*: Scanning a data set, such as index leaf nodes or tables.

- *Seeks*: Seeking into an index structure using the B-tree structures to find items.

- *Joins*: Taking two sets of data and forming one set, based on connecting rows one to the other on some criteria.

- *Computing values*: Evaluating functions or expressions to return a scalar value for a column.

- *Output*: Sending tabular data sets to the client, or DML operations such as INSERT, UPDATE, and DELETE. There's always one output from each query.

Each of these types of operators can have many different types of actions. You can see from the preceding plan that data of some form flows from one operator to the next, leading to the final output. What all this means is that each of these operators must be executed in some order, because (using the logical ordering imposed by the graphical plan) every single operator on the right side needs be executed before the one directly on its left.

Because code isn't executed while time stands still, this brings up questions that I'll try to answer in the rest of this chapter, such as the following (considering our small query plan):

- What effect will there be if a query modifies rows that have already been used by a query in a different batch?

- What if the other query creates new rows that would have been important to the other batch's query? What if the other query deletes others?

- Most importantly, can one query corrupt another's results?

You must consider a few more questions as well. Just how important is concurrency to you, and how much are you willing to pay in performance? The whole topic of concurrency is a big set of tradeoffs between performance, consistency, and the number of simultaneous users.

OS and Hardware Issues

SQL Server is designed to run on a variety of hardware types that's almost staggering. The same code runs on a low-end PC, and on a clustered array of servers that would rival many supercomputers. There's even the SQL Server 2005 Mobile Edition running on devices with the Windows Mobile OS and the Tablet PC OS. (In its current version, it doesn't support stored procedures.) Every machine running a version of SQL Server, from Express to the Enterprise Edition, can have a vastly different concurrency profile. In this section, I'll briefly touch upon some of the issues governing concurrency that our T-SQL code needn't be concerned with.

SQL Server and the OS balance all the different requests and needs for multiple users. It's beyond the scope of this book to delve too deeply into the details, but it's important to mention that concurrency is heavily tied to hardware architecture. For example, consider the following subsystems:

- *Processor*: The heart of the system is the CPU. It controls the other subsystems, as well as does any calculations needed. If you have too few processors, excessive time can be wasted switching between requests.

- *Disk subsystem*: This is usually the biggest I/O issue to be dealt with. A slow disk subsystem is the downfall of many systems, particularly because doing it right can be quite expensive. Each drive can only read one sector at a time, so to do concurrent disk access, it's necessary to have multiple disk drives, and even multiple controllers or channels to disk drive arrays. Especially important is the choice between RAID systems, which take multiple disks and configure them for performance and redundancy:

    - *0*: Striping across all disks with no redundancy, performance only.

    - *1*: Mirroring between two disks, redundancy only.

    - *5*: Striping with distributed parity; excellent for reading, but can be slow for writing.

    - *0+1*: Mirrored stripes. Two RAID 1 arrays, mirrored. Great for performance, but not tremendously redundant.

    - *1+0 (also known as 10)*: Striped mirrors. Some number of RAID 0 mirrored arrays, then striped across the mirrors. Usually the best balance of performance and redundancy.

- *Network interface*: Bandwidth to the users is critical, but is usually less of a problem than disk access. However, it's important to attempt to limit the number of round trips between the server and the client. This is highly dependent on whether the client is connecting over a dialup connection or a gigabit Ethernet (or even multiple network interface cards). Turning on SET NOCOUNT in all stored procedures and triggers is a good first step, because otherwise a message is sent to the client for each query executed, requiring bandwidth (and processing) to deal with them.

- *Memory*: One of the cheapest commodities is memory. SQL Server 2005 can use a tremendous amount of memory (whatever your hardware can support for the Standard and Enterprise Editions).

Each of these subsystems needs to be in balance to work properly. You could have 100 CPUs and 128GB of RAM and your system would be slow. You could have a slow disk subsystem and tons of RAM, and your system could still be slow. The goal is to maximize all these subsystems—the faster the better—but it's useless to have super-fast CPUs with a super-slow disk subsystem. Ideally, as your load increases, disk, CPU, and memory usage would increase proportionally, though this is a heck of a hard thing to do. The bottom line is that the number of CPUs, disk channels and disk drives, network cards, and the amount of RAM you have all affect concurrency.

Monitoring hardware and OS performance issues is a job primarily for perfmon. Watching counters for CPU, memory, SQL Server, and so on lets you see the balance between all the different subsystems. In the end, poor hardware configuration can kill you just as quickly as can poor SQL Server implementation.

For the rest of this chapter, I'm going to ignore these types of issues, and leave them to others with a deeper hardware focus, such as the MSDN website (http://msdn.microsoft.com) or http://www.sql-server-performance.com. I'll be focusing on software-coding–related issues pertaining to how to code better SQL to manage concurrency between SQL Server processes.

Transactions

Transactions are used to keep the data that's written to and read from tables consistent throughout a batch, as required. A transaction is a mechanism whereby one or more statements are guaranteed either to be completed or to fail totally.

Whenever data is modified in the database, the changes are not only written to the physical tables, but a log of every change is written to the transaction log. You have to be cognizant that every modification operation is logged when considering how large to make your transaction log. It also needs to be on a very fast disk-drive subsystem.

How long the log is stored is based on the recovery model under which your database is operating. There are three models:

- *Simple*: The log is maintained only until the operation is executed and a checkpoint is executed (done by SQL Server automatically or manually).

- *Full*: It's maintained until you explicitly clear out the log.

- *Bulk-logged*: Keeps a log much like the Full model, but doesn't log some operations, such as SELECT INTO, bulk loads, index creations, or text operations.

Even in Simple model, you must be careful about log space, because if large numbers of changes are made in a single transaction, the log rows must be stored at least until all transactions are committed and a checkpoint takes place. This is just a taste of transaction log management; for a fuller explanation, please see SQL Server 2005 Books Online.

The purpose of transactions is to provide a mechanism to allow multiple processes access to the same data simultaneously, while ensuring that logical operations are either carried out entirely or not at all. To explain the purpose of transactions, there's a common acronym: ACID. It stands for the following:

- *Atomicity*: Every operation within a transaction is treated as a singular operation; either all its data modifications are performed, or none of them is performed.

- *Consistency*: Once the transaction is completed, the system must be left in a consistent state. This means that all the constraints on the data that are part of the RDBMS definition must be honored.

- *Isolation*: This means that the operations within a transaction must be suitably isolated from other transactions. In other words, no other transactions should see data in the intermediate state, within the transaction, until it's finalized. This is done by using locks (for details on locks, refer to the section "SQL Server Concurrency Controls," later in this chapter).

- *Durability*: Once a transaction is completed, all changes must be persisted as requested. The modifications should persist even in the event of a system failure.

Transactions are used in two different ways. First, every statement that's executed in SQL Server is run within the control of a transaction. This includes INSERT, UPDATE, DELETE, and even SELECT statements. For modification statements such as INSERT, UPDATE, and DELETE, locks are placed and all system changes are recorded in the transaction log. If any operation fails, or if the user asks for an operation to be undone, SQL Server uses the transaction log to undo the operations already performed.

Second, the programmer can use transactions to batch together commands. This section is specifically about defining and demonstrating this syntax.

The key for using transactions is that when writing statements to modify data using one or more SQL statements, you need to make use of transactions to ensure that data is written safely and securely. A typical problem with procedures and operations in T-SQL code is to underuse transactions, so that when unexpected errors (such as security problems, constraint failures, and so on) occur in code, orphaned or inconsistent data is the result.

Transaction Syntax

The syntax for transactions is pretty simple. I'll cover four variants of the transaction syntax in this section:

- *Basic transactions*: The syntax of how to start and complete a transaction

- *Nested transactions*: How transactions are affected when one is started when another is already executing

- *Savepoints*: Used to selectively cancel part of a transaction

- *Distributed transactions*: Using transactions to control saving data on multiple SQL Servers

These sections will give you the foundation needed to move ahead and start building proper code, ensuring that each modification is done properly, even when multiple SQL statements are necessary to form a single-user operation.

Basic Transactions

In their basic form, three commands are required: BEGIN TRANSACTION (to start the transaction), COMMIT TRANSACTION (to save the data), and ROLLBACK TRANSACTION (to undo the changes that were made). It's as simple as that.

For example, consider the case of building a stored procedure to modify two tables. Call these tables table1 and table2. You'll modify table1, check the error status, and then modify table2 (these aren't real tables, just examples):

```
BEGIN TRY
   BEGIN TRANSACTION
   UPDATE table1
   SET    value = 'value'

   UPDATE table2
   SET value = 'value'
   COMMIT TRANSACTION
END TRY
BEGIN CATCH
  ROLLBACK TRANSACTION
  RAISERROR ('An error occurred',16,1)
END CATCH
```

Now, in case some unforeseen error occurs while updating either table1 or table2, you won't get into the case where the update of table1 happens and not the update of table2. It's also imperative not to forget to close the transaction (either commit it, or roll it back), because in this situation the open transaction can cause lots of issues. For example, if the transaction stays open and other operations get executed within that transaction, you might end up losing all work done on that connection.

There's an additional setting for simple transactions that I'll introduce for completeness, known as *named transactions*. You can extend the functionality of transactions by adding a transaction name, as shown:

```
BEGIN TRANSACTION <tranName> or <@tranvariable>
```

This is a confusing extension to the BEGIN TRANSACTION statement. It names the transaction to make sure you rollback to it. For example:

```
BEGIN TRANSACTION one
ROLLBACK TRANSACTION one
```

Only the first transaction mark is registered in the log, so the following code returns an error:

```
BEGIN TRANSACTION one
BEGIN TRANSACTION two
ROLLBACK TRANSACTION two
```

The error message is as follows:

```
Server: Msg 6401, Level 16, State 1, Line 3
Cannot roll back two. No transaction or savepoint of that name was found.
```

Even worse, after this error has occurred, the transaction is still left open. For this reason, it's seldom a good practice to use named transactions in your code. A place where named transactions are used is with the WITH MARK setting. This allows marking the transaction log, which can be used when restoring a transaction log instead of a date and time. The mark is only registered if data is modified within the transaction. A good example of its use might be to build a process that marks the transaction log every day before some daily batch process, especially one where the database is in single-user mode. The log is marked, then you run the process, and if there are any troubles, the database log can be restored to just before the mark in the log, no matter when the process was executed. Using the AdventureWorks database, I'll demonstrate this capability. You can do the same, but be careful to do this somewhere where you know you have a proper backup (just in case something goes wrong).

We first set up the scenario by putting the AdventureWorks database in Full recovery model.

■**Tip** You can see the current setting using the following code:

```
SELECT  recovery_model_desc
FROM    sys.databases
WHERE   name = 'AdventureWorks'
```

```
USE Master
GO

ALTER DATABASE AdventureWorks
    SET RECOVERY FULL
```

Next, we create a couple backup devices to hold the backups we're going to do:

```
EXEC sp_addumpdevice 'disk', 'TestAdventureWorks', 'C:\Temp\AdventureWorks.bak'
EXEC sp_addumpdevice 'disk',
                     'TestAdventureWorksLog', 'C:\Temp\AdventureWorksLog.bak'
```

Next, we back up the database to the dump device we created:

```
BACKUP DATABASE AdventureWorks TO TestAdventureWorks
```

Now we change to the AdventureWorks database and delete some data from a table:

```
USE AdventureWorks
GO
SELECT count(*)
FROM    SALES.StoreContact
```

```
BEGIN TRANSACTION Test WITH MARK 'Test'
DELETE Sales.StoreContact
COMMIT TRANSACTION
```

This returns 753. Now back up the transaction log to the other backup device:

```
BACKUP LOG AdventureWorks  to TestAdventureWorksLog
```

Now we can restore the database using the RESTORE DATABASE command. (The NORECOVERY setting keeps the database in a state ready to add transaction logs.) We apply the log with RESTORE LOG. For the example, we'll only restore just up to before the mark that was placed, not the entire log:

```
USE Master
GO
RESTORE DATABASE AdventureWorks FROM TestAdventureWorks WITH REPLACE, NORECOVERY

RESTORE LOG AdventureWorks FROM TestAdventureWorksLog WITH STOPBEFOREMARK = 'Test'
```

If you wanted to include the actions within the mark, you could use STOPATMARK instead of STOPBEFOREMARK.

Nesting Transactions

Transactions can be nested. Note that you have to execute the same number of COMMIT TRANSACTION commands as the number of BEGIN TRANSACTION commands that have been executed. To tell how many BEGIN TRANSACTION commands have been executed, without being committed, you can use the @@TRANCOUNT global variable. When it's equal to one, then one BEGIN TRANSACTION has been executed, if it's equal to two then two, and so on. When @@TRANCOUNT equals zero, you aren't within a transaction context.

There doesn't seem to be any functional limit to the number of transactions that can be nested, short of memory and processor limitations. I've tested ten million nest levels on my test machine, and although it took fifty seconds on my 1.8-GHz laptop with 512MB of RAM, it's clearly more than most any process should ever need.

As an example, execute the following:

```
SELECT @@TRANCOUNT AS zeroDeep
BEGIN TRANSACTION
SELECT @@TRANCOUNT AS oneDeep
```

It returns the following results:

```
zeroDeep
-----------
0

oneDeep
-----------
1
```

Then, nest another transaction and check @@TRANCOUNT to see whether it has incremented. Afterwards, commit that transaction and check @@TRANCOUNT again:

```
BEGIN TRANSACTION
SELECT @@TRANCOUNT AS twoDeep
COMMIT TRANSACTION --commits very last transaction started with BEGIN TRANSACTION
SELECT @@TRANCOUNT AS oneDeep
```

This returns the following results:

```
twoDeep
-----------
2

oneDeep
-----------
1
```

Finally, close the final transaction:

```
COMMIT TRANSACTION
SELECT @@TRANCOUNT AS zeroDeep
```

It returns the following result:

```
zeroDeep
-----------
0
```

One additional "feature" of transactions is that it only takes one ROLLBACK TRANSACTION command to rollback as many transactions as you have nested. So, if you've nested 100 transactions (that would be fun to debug, eh?), and you issue one rollback transaction, all transactions are rolled back. For example:

```
BEGIN TRANSACTION
BEGIN TRANSACTION
BEGIN TRANSACTION
BEGIN TRANSACTION
BEGIN TRANSACTION
BEGIN TRANSACTION
BEGIN TRANSACTION
SELECT @@trancount as InTran
ROLLBACK TRANSACTION
SELECT @@trancount as OutTran
```

This returns the following results:

```
InTran
-----------
7

OutTran
-----------
0
```

This is by far the trickiest part of using transactions in your code. It's a bad idea to just issue a ROLLBACK TRANSACTION command without being cognizant of what will occur once you do—especially the command's influence on the following code. If code is written expecting it to be within a transaction and it isn't, your data can get corrupted.

In the preceding example, if an UPDATE statement had been executed immediately after the ROLLBACK command, it wouldn't be executed within an explicit transaction. Also, if a COMMIT TRANSACTION is executed immediately after the ROLLBACK command, the following error will occur:

```
Server: Msg 3902, Level 16, State 1, Line 12
The COMMIT TRANSACTION request has no corresponding BEGIN TRANSACTION.
```

■**Note** Transactions are nested in syntax only. They aren't implemented as such in the database engine. There's only ever one engine-level transaction open at a time (hence the reason that a single ROLLBACK TRANSACTION is all that's required to rollback multiple transactions).

Savepoints

In the last section, I explained that all open transactions are rolled back using a ROLLBACK TRANSACTION call. This isn't always desirable, so a tool is available to rollback only certain parts of a transaction. Unfortunately, it requires forethought and a special syntax. *Savepoints* are used to provide "selective" rollback.

For this, from within a transaction, issue the following statement:

```
SAVE TRANSACTION <savePointName> --savepoint names must follow the same rules for
                                 --identifiers as other objects
```

For example, use the following code in whatever database you desire. In the source code, I'll place it in the tempdb:

```
CREATE SCHEMA arts
CREATE TABLE arts.performer
(
    performerId int identity,
    name varchar(100)
)
```

```
GO
BEGIN TRANSACTION
INSERT INTO arts.performer(name) VALUES ('Elvis Costello')

SAVE TRANSACTION savePoint

INSERT INTO arts.performer(name) VALUES ('Air Supply')

--don't insert Air Supply, yuck! ...
ROLLBACK TRANSACTION savePoint

COMMIT TRANSACTION

SELECT *
FROM arts.performer
```

The output of this listing is as follows:

```
performerId   name
-----------   ---------------
1             Elvis Costello
```

In the code, there were two INSERT statements within our transaction, but in the output there's only one row. Obviously, the row that was rolled back to the savepoint wasn't persisted.

Note that you don't commit a savepoint; SQL Server simply places a mark in the transaction log to tell itself where to rollback to if the user asks for a rollback to the savepoint. The rest of the operations in the overall transaction aren't affected. Savepoints don't affect the value of @@trancount, nor do they release any locks that might have been held by the operations that are rolled back, until all nested transactions have been committed or rolled back.

Savepoints give the power to effect changes on only part of the operations transaction, giving you more control over what to do if you're deep in a large number of operations.

I'll mention savepoints later in this chapter when writing stored procedures, as they allow the rolling back of all the actions of a single stored procedure without affecting the transaction state of the stored procedure caller (which isn't required).

You can't use savepoints in a couple situations:

- When using MARS and you're executing more than one batch at a time

- When the transaction is enlisted into a distributed transaction (the next section discusses this)

Distributed Transactions

It would be wrong not to brush up at least on the subject of distributed transactions. Occasionally, you might need to update data on a different server, from the one on which your code resides. The Microsoft Distributed Transaction Coordinator service (MS DTC) gives us this ability.

If the server is running the MS DTC service, you can use the `BEGIN DISTRIBUTED TRANSACTION` command to start a transaction that covers the data residing on your server, as well as the remote server. If the server configuration `'remote proc trans'` is set to 1, then any transaction that touches a linked server will start a distributed transaction (check `sys.configurations` for the current setting, and set the value using `sp_configure`). Note also that savepoints aren't supported for distributed transactions.

The following code is just pseudocode and won't run as is, but this is representative of the code needed to do a distributed transaction:

```
BEGIN TRY
    BEGIN DISTRIBUTED TRANSACTION

    --remote server is a server set up as a linked server

    UPDATE remoteServer.dbName.schemaName.tableName
    SET value = 'new value'
    WHERE keyColumn = 'value'

    --local server
    UPDATE dbName.schemaName.tableName
    SET value = 'new value'
    WHERE keyColumn = 'value'

    COMMIT TRANSACTION
END TRY
BEGIN CATCH
    ROLLBACK TRANSACTION
    DECLARE @ERRORMessage varchar(2000)
    SET @ERRORMessage = ERROR_MESSAGE()
    RAISERROR (@ERRORMessage,16,1)
END CATCH
```

HOW MARS AFFECTS TRANSACTIONS

There's a slight wrinkle in how multiple statements can behave when using OLE DB or ODBC native client drivers to retrieve rows in 2005. When executing batches under MARS, there can be a couple scenarios:

- *Connections set to autocommit:* Each executed batch is within its own transaction, so there are multiple transaction contexts on a single connection.

- *Connections set to manual commit:* All executed batches are part of one transaction.

When MARS is enabled for a connection, any batch or stored procedure that starts a transaction (either implicitly in any statement or by executing `BEGIN TRANSACTION`) must commit the transaction or it will be rolled back. These transactions are new to SQL Server 2005, and are referred to as *batch-scoped transactions*.

The distributed transaction syntax also covers the local transaction. Setting the configuration option `REMOTE PROC TRANS` automatically upgrades a `BEGIN TRANSACTION` command to a `BEGIN DISTRIBUTED TRANSACTION` command. This is useful if you frequently use distributed transactions. Without this setting, the remote command is executed, but it won't be a part of the current transaction.

Explicit vs. Implicit Transactions

Before finishing the discussion of transactions, there's one last thing that needs to be covered for the sake of completeness. I've alluded to the fact that every statement is executed in a transaction. This is an important point that must be understood when writing code. Internally, SQL Server starts a transaction every time a SQL statement is started. Even if a transaction isn't started explicitly with a `COMMIT TRANSACTION` statement, SQL Server automatically starts a new transaction whenever a statement starts, and commits or rolls it back depending on whether or not any errors occur. This is known as an *autocommit* transaction, when the SQL Server engine commits the transaction it starts for each statement-level transaction.

SQL Server gives us a setting to change this behavior of automatically committing the transaction: `SET IMPLICIT_TRANSACTIONS`. When this setting is turned on and the execution context isn't already within an explicitly declared transaction using `BEGIN TRANSACTION`, a `BEGIN TRANSACTION` is automatically (logically) executed when any of the following commands are executed: `ALTER TABLE`, `FETCH`, `REVOKE`, `CREATE`, `GRANT`, `SELECT`, `DELETE`, `INSERT`, `TRUNCATE TABLE`, `DROP`, `OPEN`, or `UPDATE`. Additionally, a `COMMIT TRANSACTION` or `ROLLBACK TRANSACTION` command has to be executed to end the transaction. Otherwise, once the connection terminates, all data is lost (and until the transaction terminates, locks that have been accumulated are held, other users are blocked, and pandemonium might occur).

`SET IMPLICIT_TRANSACTIONS` isn't a typical setting used by SQL Server programmers, but is worth mentioning, because if you set the setting of `ANSI_DEFAULTS ON`, `IMPLICIT_TRANSACTIONS` will be enabled.

I've mentioned that every `SELECT` statement is executed within a transaction, but this deserves a bit more explanation. The entire process of rows being considered for output, then transporting them from the server to the client—all this is inside a transaction. The `SELECT` statement isn't finished until the entire result set is exhausted (or the client cancels the fetching of rows), so the transaction doesn't end either. This is an important point that will come back up in the "Isolation Levels" section, as I discuss how this transaction can seriously affect concurrency based on how isolated you need your queries to be.

Compiled SQL Server Code

Now that I've discussed the basics of transactions, it's important to understand some of the slight differences involved in using them within compiled code. It's almost the same, but there are some subtle differences. You can't use transactions in user-defined functions (you can't change system state in a function, so they aren't necessary anyhow), but you can use them in stored procedures and triggers. You need to understand a few things about their use.

Stored Procedures

Stored procedures, simply being compiled batches of code, use transactions as previously discussed, with one caveat. The transaction nesting level cannot be affected during the execution of a procedure. In other words, you must commit as many transactions as you begin in a stored procedure.

Although you can rollback any transaction, you shouldn't roll it back unless the @@TRANCOUNT was zero when the procedure started. However, it's better not to execute a ROLLBACK TRANSACTION command at all in a stored procedure, so there's no chance of rolling back to a transaction count that's different from when the procedure started. This protects you from the situation where the procedure is executed in another transaction. Rather, it's generally best to start a transaction, then follow it by a savepoint. Later, if the changes made in the procedure need to be backed out, simply rollback to the savepoint, and commit the transaction. It's then up to the stored procedure to signal to any caller that it has failed, and to do whatever it wants with the transaction.

As an example, let's build the following simple procedure that does nothing but execute a BEGIN TRANSACTION and a ROLLBACK TRANSACTION:

```
CREATE PROCEDURE tranTest
AS
BEGIN
  SELECT @@TRANCOUNT AS trancount

  BEGIN TRANSACTION
  ROLLBACK TRANSACTION
END
```

Executing this procedure outside a transaction is fine and returns a single row with a 0 value. However, say you execute it as follows:

```
BEGIN TRANSACTION
EXECUTE tranTest
COMMIT TRANSACTION
```

The procedure returns the following results:

```
Server: Msg 266, Level 16, State 2, Procedure tranTest, Line 5
Transaction count after EXECUTE indicates that a COMMIT or ROLLBACK TRANSACTION
statement is missing. Previous count = 1, current count = 0.

Server: Msg 3902, Level 16, State 1, Line 3
The COMMIT TRANSACTION request has no corresponding BEGIN TRANSACTION.
```

The errors occur because the transaction depth has changed, while rolling back the transaction inside the procedure.

Finally, say you recode the procedure as follows:

```
ALTER PROCEDURE tranTest
AS
BEGIN
  DECLARE @savepoint nvarchar(128)
  --gives us a unique savepoint name, trim it to 125 characters if the
  --user named the procedure really really large, to allow for nestlevel
  SET @savepoint = cast(object_name(@@procid) AS nvarchar(125)) +
                       cast(@@nestlevel AS nvarchar(3))

  BEGIN TRANSACTION
  SAVE TRANSACTION @savepoint
    --do something here
  ROLLBACK TRANSACTION @savepoint
  COMMIT TRANSACTION
END
```

Now you can execute it from within any number of transactions, and it will never fail. You can call procedures from other procedures (even recursively from the same procedure) or external programs. It's important to take these precautions to make sure that the code is safe under any calling circumstances.

■**Caution** As mentioned in the "Savepoints" section, you can't use savepoints with distributed transactions or when sending multiple batches over a MARS-enabled connection. To make the most out of MARS, you might not be able to use this strategy. It might simply be prudent to execute modification procedures one at a time, anyhow.

Naming savepoints is important. As savepoints aren't scoped to a procedure, you must ensure that they're always unique. I tend to use the procedure name (retrieved here by using the object_name function called for the @@procId, but you could just enter it textually) and the current transaction nesting level. This guarantees that I can never have the same savepoint active, even if calling the same procedure recursively. It would be also possible to use @@nestLevel, as it would always be unique in the calling chain for a given connection.

Let's look briefly at how to code this into procedures using proper error handling:

```
ALTER PROCEDURE tranTest
AS
BEGIN
  DECLARE @savepoint nvarchar(128)
  --gives us a unique savepoint name, trim it to 125
  --characters if the user named it really large
  SET @savepoint = cast(object_name(@@procid) AS nvarchar(125)) +
                       cast(@@nestlevel AS nvarchar(3))
```

```
BEGIN TRY
  BEGIN TRANSACTION
  SAVE TRANSACTION @savepoint

  --do something here
  RAISERROR ('ouch',16,1)

  COMMIT TRANSACTION
END TRY
BEGIN CATCH
  --if the transaction has not been rolled back elsewhere (like a trigger)
  --back out gracefully
  IF xact_state() = -1 --the transaction is doomed
    rollback transaction
  ELSE IF xact_state() = 1 --the error did not cause a rollback,
    BEGIN
      ROLLBACK TRANSACTION @savepoint
      COMMIT TRANSACTION
    END
  IF @@TRANCOUNT > 0
    BEGIN
      ROLLBACK TRANSACTION @savepoint
      COMMIT TRANSACTION
    END

  DECLARE @ERRORmessage varchar(2000)
  SET @ERRORmessage = ERROR_MESSAGE()
  RAISERROR (@ERRORmessage,16,1)
  RETURN -100
END CATCH
END
```

In the CATCH block, instead of rolling back the transaction, I simply rolled back the savepoint. An error is returned for the caller to deal with. You could also eliminate the RAISERROR altogether if the error wasn't critical, and let whatever process gets this back interrogate the return value, if it cared what the return value was. You can place any form of error handling in the CATCH block, as long as you don't rollback the entire transaction. If this procedure called another procedure that used the same error handling, it would rollback its part of the transaction. It would then raise an error, which in turn would cause the CATCH block to be called, and rollback the savepoint and commit the transaction (which at that point wouldn't contain any changes at all). You might ask, why go through this exercise if you're just going to rollback the transaction anyhow? The key is that each level of the calling structure can decide what to do with its part of the transaction.

As an example of how this works, consider the following schema and table (create it in any database you desire, likely tempdb, as this sample is isolated to this section):

```
CREATE SCHEMA menu
CREATE TABLE menu.foodItem
(
    foodItemId int not null identity(1,1)
        CONSTRAINT PKmenu_foodItem PRIMARY KEY,
    name varchar(30) not null
        CONSTRAINT AKmenu_foodItem_name UNIQUE,
    description varchar(60) not null,
        CONSTRAINT CHKmenu_foodItem_name CHECK (name <> ''),
        CONSTRAINT CHKmenu_foodItem_description CHECK (description <> '')
)
```

Now create a procedure to do the insert:

```
CREATE PROCEDURE menu.foodItem$insert
(
    @name       varchar(30),
    @description varchar(60),
    @newFoodItemId int = null output --we will send back the new id here
)
AS
BEGIN
  SET NOCOUNT ON
  DECLARE @savepoint nvarchar(128)

  --gives us a unique savepoint name
  SET @savepoint = cast(object_name(@@procid) AS nvarchar(125)) +
                   cast(@@nestlevel AS nvarchar(3))

  BEGIN TRY
    BEGIN TRANSACTION
    SAVE TRANSACTION @savepoint

    INSERT INTO menu.foodItem(name, description)
    VALUES (@name, @description)

    SET @newFoodItemId = scope_identity() --if you use an instead of trigger
                                          --you will have to use name to do the
                                          --identity "grab"
    COMMIT TRANSACTION
  END TRY
  BEGIN CATCH
    --if the transaction has not been rolled back elsewhere (like a trigger)
    --back out gracefully
    IF xact_state() = -1 --the transaction is doomed
      ROLLBACK TRANSACTION
    ELSE IF xact_state() = 1 --the error did not cause a rollback,
```

```
          BEGIN
            ROLLBACK TRANSACTION @savepoint
            COMMIT TRANSACTION
          END
      IF @@TRANCOUNT > 0
        BEGIN
            ROLLBACK TRANSACTION @savepoint
            COMMIT TRANSACTION
        END

      --uncomment to use the error log procedure created back in chapter 6
      --EXECUTE dbo.errorLog$insert

      DECLARE @ERROR_MESSAGE varchar(8000)
      SET @ERROR_MESSAGE = ERROR_MESSAGE()
      RAISERROR (@ERROR_MESSAGE,16,1)
      RETURN -100
   END CATCH
END
```

Now try out the code:

```
DECLARE @foodItemId int, @retval int
EXECUTE @retval = menu.foodItem$insert  @name ='Burger',
                                        @description = 'Mmmm Burger',
                                        @newFoodItemId = @foodItemId output
SELECT  @retval as returnValue
IF @retval >= 0
    SELECT  foodItemId, name, description
    FROM    menu.foodItem
    WHERE   foodItemId = @foodItemId
```

No error, so the row we created is returned:

foodItemId	name	description
1	Burger	Mmmm Burger

Now try out the code with an error:

```
DECLARE @foodItemId int, @retval int
EXECUTE @retval = menu.foodItem$insert  @name ='Big Burger',
                                        @description = '',
                                        @newFoodItemId = @foodItemId output
SELECT  @retval as returnValue
IF @retval >= 0
    SELECT  foodItemId, name, description
    FROM    menu.foodItem
    WHERE   foodItemId = @foodItemId
```

Because the description is blank, an error is returned:

```
Msg 50000, Level 16, State 1, Procedure foodItem$insert, Line 36
The INSERT statement conflicted with the CHECK constraint
"CHKmenu_foodItem_description". The conflict occurred in database "tempdb",
table "foodItem", column 'description'.

returnValue
-----------
-100
```

Triggers

Just as in stored procedures, you can start transactions, set savepoints, and rollback to a savepoint. However, if you execute a ROLLBACK TRANSACTION statement in a trigger, two things can occur:

- Outside a TRY-CATCH block, the entire batch of SQL statements is canceled.

- Inside a TRY-CATCH block, the batch isn't canceled, but the transaction count is back to zero.

Back in Chapter 6, we discussed and implemented triggers that consistently used rollbacks when any error occurred. If not using TRY-CATCH blocks, this approach is generally exactly what's desired, but when using TRY-CATCH blocks, it can make things more tricky. To handle this, in the CATCH block of stored procedures I've included this code:

```
--if the transaction has not been rolled back elsewhere (like a trigger)
--back out gracefully
IF xact_state() = -1 --the transaction is doomed
   ROLLBACK TRANSACTION
ELSE IF xact_state() = 1 --the error did not cause a rollback,
   BEGIN
      ROLLBACK TRANSACTION @savepoint
      COMMIT TRANSACTION
   END
IF @@TRANCOUNT > 0
   BEGIN
      ROLLBACK TRANSACTION @savepoint
      COMMIT TRANSACTION
   END
```

This is an effective, if perhaps limited method of working with errors from triggers that works in most any situation. Removing all ROLLBACK TRANSACTION commands from triggers dooms the transaction, which is just as much trouble as the rollback. The key is to understand how this might affect the code that you're working with, and to make sure that errors are handled in an understandable way. More than anything, test all types of errors in your system (trigger, constraint, and so on).

■**Caution** If a trigger causes a rollback to occur, there's a chance that you might receive a 266 error message—"Transaction count after EXECUTE indicates that a COMMIT or ROLLBACK"—if you execute this code within a transaction and outside a TRY-CATCH block. This won't be the first error message, and isn't harmful, but processing will continue, so you need to understand this situation.

SQL Server Concurrency Controls

In the previous section, I introduced transactions, but the real goal of this chapter is to demonstrate how multiple users can be manipulating and modifying the exact same data, making sure that all users get consistent usage of the data.

To understand the basics of the Isolation part of the ACID properties discussed earlier, this section will introduce a couple important concepts that are essential to building concurrent applications:

- *Locks*: These are holds put by SQL Server on objects that are being used by users.

- *Isolation levels*: These are settings used to control the length of time for which SQL Server holds onto the locks.

These two important topics come into play over and over when trying to optimize a server.

Locks

Locks are tokens laid down by the SQL Server processes to "stake their claim" to the different resources available, so as to prevent one process from stomping on another and causing inconsistencies. They are a lot like the "Diver Down" markers that deep sea divers place on top of the water when working below the water. They do this to alert other divers, pleasure boaters, fishermen, and so on, that they're below. Every SQL Server process applies a lock to almost anything it does, to try to make sure that no other users can affect the operation that SQL Server is doing, and vice versa.

Consider the scenario in Figure 9-3, in which you have two concurrent users. Each of them executes some SQL statements, but in the end the final value is going to be the wrong value, and the additional 500 will be lost. Why? Because each user fetched a reality from the database that was correct at the time, and then acted upon it as if it would always be true. This is called a *lost update*, and this is exactly why locks are required.

Locks act as a message to other processes that a resource is being used, kind of like a railroad crossing sign. When the bar crosses the road, it acts as a lock to tell you not to drive across the tracks because the train is using the resource. This lock can be ignored (as can SQL Server locks), but it's generally not advisable to do so. (Ignoring locks isn't usually as messy as ignoring a train-crossing signal, but what if the lock that was ignored pertained to the oncoming train? The crossing-gate operator could open the gate too soon, and *wham*!)

Locks are made up of two things: the type of lock and the mode of the lock. These elements include what's being locked, and just how locked it is, respectively. If you've been around for a few versions of SQL Server, you probably know that since SQL Server 7.0, SQL Server uses row-level locks. That is, a user locking some resource in SQL Server does it on rows, rather than on pages of data, or even on complete tables.

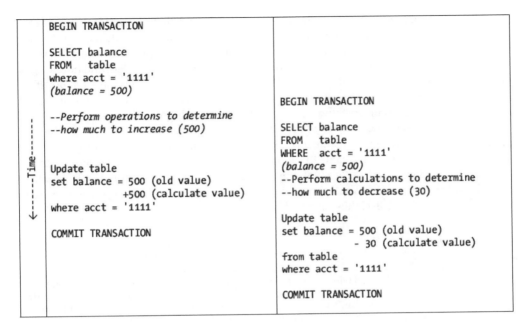

```
BEGIN TRANSACTION

SELECT balance
FROM    table
where acct = '1111'
(balance = 500)                          BEGIN TRANSACTION

--Perform operations to determine        SELECT balance
--how much to increase (500)             FROM    table
                                         WHERE   acct = '1111'
                                         (balance = 500)
                                         --Perform calculations to determine
                                         --how much to decrease (30)
Update table
set balance = 500 (old value)            Update table
            +500 (calculate value)       set balance = 500 (old value)
where acct = '1111'                                  - 30 (calculate value)
                                         from table
COMMIT TRANSACTION                       where acct = '1111'

                                         COMMIT TRANSACTION
```

Time → (vertical label on left)

Figure 9-3. *Lost update illustration*

However, thinking that SQL Server only locks at the page level is misleading, as SQL Server can use six different types of locks to lock varying portions of the database, with the row being the finest type of lock, all the way up to a full database lock. The types of locks in Table 9-1 are supported.

Table 9-1. *Lock Types*

Type of Lock	Granularity
Row or row identifier (RID)	A single row in a table
Key or key range	A single value or range of values (for example, to lock rows with values from A-M, even if no rows currently exist)
Page	An 8K index or data page
Extent	A group of eight 8K pages (64K), generally only used when allocating new space to the database
Table	An entire table, including all rows and indexes
Database	The entire database

■**Tip** In terms of locks, database object locks are all you have much knowledge of or control over in SQL Server, so this is all I'll cover. However, you should be aware that many more locks are in play, as SQL Server manages its hardware and internal needs as you are execute queries. Hardware locks are referred to as *latches*, and you'll occasionally see them referenced in Books Online, though little is explained about them.

At the point of request, SQL Server determines approximately how many of the database resources (a table, a row, a key, a key range, and so on) are needed to satisfy the request. This is calculated on the basis of several factors, the specifics of which are unpublished. Some of these factors include the cost of acquiring the lock, the amount of resources needed, and how long the locks will be held. The next major section, "Isolation Levels," will discuss these factors. It's also possible for the query processor to upgrade the lock from a more granular lock to a less specific type if the query is unexpectedly taking up large quantities of resources.

For example, if a large percentage of the rows in a table are locked with row locks, the query processor might switch to a table lock to finish out the process. Or, if you're adding large numbers of rows into a clustered table in sequential order, you might use a page lock on the new pages that are being added. Although the type of lock defines the amount of the database to lock, the second part of the lock is the mode. It refers to how strict the lock is when dealing with other locks. Table 9-2 lists these available modes.

Table 9-2. *Lock Modes*

Mode	Description
Shared	Generally used when users are looking at the data but not editing. It's called *shared* because multiple processes can have a shared lock on the same resource, allowing read-only access to the resource. However, sharing resources prevents other processes from modifying the resource.
Exclusive	As the name implies, this gives exclusive access to a resource. Only one process may have an active exclusive lock on a resource.
Update	Used to inform other processes that you're planning to modify the data, but aren't quite ready to do so. Other connections may also issue shared locks while still preparing to do the modification, but not update or exclusive. Update locks are used to prevent deadlocks (I'll cover them later in this section) by marking rows that a statement will possibly update, rather than upgrading from shared directly to an exclusive lock.
Intent	Communicates to other objects that it might be necessary to take one of the previously listed modes. You might see these as intent shared, intent exclusive, or shared with intent exclusive.
Schema	Used to lock the structure of an object when it's in use. That's so you cannot alter a table when a user is reading data from it.

Each of these modes, coupled with the granularity, describes a locking situation. For example, an exclusive table lock would mean that no other user can access any data in the table. An update table lock would say that other users could look at the data in the table, but any statement that might modify data in the table would have to wait until after this process has been completed.

The next concept to discuss is lock compatibility. Each lock mode may be compatible or not with the other lock mode on the same resource. If the types are compatible, then two or more users may lock the same resource. Incompatible lock types would require the second user(s) simply to wait until the incompatible lock(s) have been released.

Table 9-3 shows which types are compatible with which others.

Table 9-3. *Lock Compatibility Modes*

Mode	IS	S	U	IX	SIX	X
Intent shared (IS)	•	•	•	•	•	
Shared (S)	•	•	•			
Update (U)	•	•				
Intent exclusive (IX)	•			•		
Shared with intent exclusive (SIX)	•					
Exclusive (X)	•					

Although locks are great for data consistency, as far as concurrency is considered, locked rows stink. Whenever a resource is locked in a way that another process cannot use it to complete its processing, concurrency is lowered, as the process must wait for the other to complete before it can continue. This is generally referred to as *blocking*: one process is blocking another from doing something, so the blocked process must wait its turn, no matter how long it takes.

Simply put, locks allow consistent views of the data by only letting a single process modify a single row of data at a time, while allowing multiple viewers. Locks are a necessary part of SQL Server architecture, as is blocking to honor those locks when needed, to make sure one user doesn't trample on the other's data, ending up with invalid data in some cases.

In the next section, I'll discuss isolation levels, which determine how long locks are held. Executing SELECT * FROM sys.dm_os_waiting_tasks gives you a list of all processes that tells you if any users are blocking, and which user is doing the blocking. Executing SELECT * FROM sys.dm_tran_locks lets you see locks that are being held. SQL Server Management Studio has a decent Activity Monitor, accessible via the Object Explorer in the Management folder.

It's possible to force SQL Server to use a different type of lock than it might ordinarily choose, by using *table hints* on your queries. For individual tables in a FROM clause, you can set the type of lock to be used for the single query like so:

```
FROM    table1 [WITH] (<tableHintList>)
            JOIN table2 [WITH] (<tableHintList>)
```

Note that these hints work on all query types. In the case of locking, you can use quite a few. A partial list of the more useful hints follows:

- PageLock: Forces the optimizer to choose page locks for the given table.

- NoLock: Leaves no locks, and honors no locks for the given table.

- RowLock: Forces row-level locks to be used for the table.

- Tablock: Goes directly to table locks, rather than row or even page locks. This can speed some operations, but seriously lowers write concurrency.

- TablockX: Same as Tablock, but it always uses exclusive locks (whether it would have normally done so or not). Forces single threaded use of the table, other than NoLock access (or SNAPSHOT isolation level access, which I'll discuss in the section "Isolation Levels").

- XLock: Uses exclusive locks.

- UpdLock: Uses update locks.

Note that SQL Server can override your hints if necessary. For example, take the case where a query sets the table hint of NoLock, but then rows are modified in the table in the execution of the query. No shared locks are taken or honored, but exclusive locks are taken and held on the table for the rows that are modified, though not on rows that are only read (this is true even for resources that are read as part of a trigger).

One term that's frequently bandied about is *deadlocks*. A deadlock is a circumstance where two processes are trying to use the same objects, but neither will ever be able to complete because it's blocked by the other connection. For example, consider two processes (Processes 1 and 2), and two resources (Resources A and B). The following steps lead to a deadlock:

- Process 1 takes a lock on Resource A, and at the same time Process 2 takes a lock on Resource B.

- Process 1 tries to get access to Resource B. As it's locked by Process 2, Process 1 goes into a wait state.

- Process 2 tries to get access to Resource A. Because it's locked by Process 1, Process 2 goes into a wait state.

At this point, there's no way to resolve this issue without ending one of the processes. SQL Server arbitrarily kills one of the processes (unless one of the processes has voluntarily raised the likelihood of being the killed process by using SET DEADLOCK_PRIORITY LOW, and the other process has not). SQL Server raises error 1205 to the client to tell the client that the process was stopped:

```
Server: Msg 1205, Level 13, State 1, Line 4
Transaction (Process ID 55) was deadlocked on lock resources with another process
 and has been chosen as the deadlock victim. Rerun the transaction.
```

At this point, you could resubmit the request, as long as the call was coded such that any data access was treated as an atomic operation. This all assumes that a transaction was used for multiple data modifications, and the program can tell what was rolled back.

■**Tip** Proper deadlock handling requires that you build your applications in such a way that you can easily tell how much of an operation succeeded or failed. This is done by proper use of transactions. A good practice is to send one transaction per batch from a client application. Keep in mind the engine views nested transactions as one transaction, so what I mean here is to start and complete a high-level transaction per batch.

Deadlocks can be hard to diagnose, as you can deadlock on many things, even hardware access. A common trick to try to alleviate frequent deadlocks between pieces of code is to order object access in the same order, if possible. This makes it more likely that locks taken are taken in the same order. Note that I said "alleviate *frequent* deadlocks." Most often, the best thing to do is handle deadlocks in your code by resubmitting the last transaction executed (too many applications just raise the deadlock as an error that users don't understand).

Using SQL Server Profiler, you can add the DeadLock Graph event class to see deadlock events, which helps diagnose them. For more information about Profiler, check SQL Server Books Online.

■Note There's also a Bulk Update mode that I didn't mention, which you use to lock the table when inserting data in bulk into the table and applying the TABLOCK hint. It's analogous to an exclusive table lock for concurrency issues.

Isolation Levels

In the previous section on locks, I made this statement: "Every SQL Server process applies a lock to almost anything it does, to try to make sure that no other users can affect the operation that SQL Server is doing." Why did I say "try to make sure"? Locks are placed to make sure that while SQL Server is using the resource, the resource is protected. The *isolation level* is the setting that tells SQL Server how long to hold these locks, or even whether or not to take them.

The safest method to provide consistency in operations would be to take an exclusive lock on the entire database, do your operations, and then release the lock. Then the next user does the same thing. Although this was relatively common in early file-based systems, it isn't a reasonable alternative when you need to support 20,000 concurrent users (or even just a few people who won't take "just wait" for an answer), no matter how beefy your hardware platform may be.

To improve concurrency, locks are held for the minimum time necessary to provide a reasonable amount of data consistency. (If the word "reasonable" concerns you, read on, because SQL Server defaults don't provide perfect coverage.) Isolation levels control how long locks are held, and there are five distinct levels. From inside a transaction, locks can be held for a variable amount of time to protect the data that's being worked with. For example, consider the following hypothetical code snippet:

```
BEGIN TRANSACTION
SAVE TRANSACTION savePoint

IF EXISTS ( SELECT * FROM tableA WHERE tableAId = 'value' )
BEGIN
  UPDATE tableB
  SET status = 'UPDATED'
  WHERE tableAId = 'value'

  IF @@error <> 0
  BEGIN
    RAISERROR ('Error updating tableB',16,1)
    ROLLBACK TRANSACTION savePoint
  END
END

COMMIT TRANSACTION
```

First, check to see if a value exists in `tableA`, then if it does, update a value in `tableB`. On first glance, this seems safe—if a record exists when checked for in `tableA`, it will exist once the execution gets to the `tableB` update. However, how well this works is based solely on how long the locks are held on the `SELECT` from `tableA`. Although the row might exist when the `IF EXISTS` block executed, what if a table lock exists on `tableB` when you try to execute the update of `tableB`, and the process gets blocked waiting for the lock to be cleared? During this period of time waiting for the table lock on `tableB` to be cleared, the key row that previously existed could have been deleted from `tableA`, if the lock isn't maintained on the row in `tableA` until the transaction is completed.

What's interesting is that under the default isolation level in which SQL Server connections operate, no lock would have been kept on `tableA`, leaving a potential hole in your data integrity.

Deeply ingrained in the concepts of isolation levels are the concepts of *repeatable reads* and *phantom rows*. Consider that you execute a statement such as the following:

```
SELECT * FROM table
```

The following rows are returned:

```
ColumnName
----------
row1
row2
```

For this `SELECT` statement to claim to support repeatable reads within a transaction, you must be able to execute it multiple times and get back *at least the same results*. This means that no other user could change the data that had been retrieved in the operation. Other users are allowed to create new rows, so you might get back the following results:

```
ColumnName
----------
row1
row2
row3
```

Note that the term "repeatable read" can seem confusing, because the exact results of the read weren't repeatable, but that's how it's defined. The value `row3` is considered a phantom row.

The following bulleted list contains the isolation levels to adjust how long locks are held to prevent phantom rows and nonrepeatable reads:

- `READ UNCOMMITTED`: Doesn't honor or take locks, unless data is modified.

- `READ COMMITTED`: Takes and honors locks, but releases read locks after data is retrieved.

- `REPEATABLE READ`: Holds locks to prevent users from changing data.

- `SERIALIZABLE`: Like `REPEATABLE READ`, but adds locks on ranges of data to make sure no new data is added.

- `SNAPSHOT`: New for SQL Server 2005, this allows the user to look at data as it was when the transaction started.

The syntax for setting the isolation level is as follows:

```
SET TRANSACTION ISOLATION LEVEL <level>
```

<level> is any of the five preceding settings. The default isolation level is READ COMMITTED, and is a good balance between concurrency and integrity. It does bear mentioning that READ COMMITTED isn't always the proper setting. Quite often when only reading data, the SNAPSHOT isolation level gives the best results.

Referring to the previous example code block—checking that a value exists in one table, then modifying another—keep in mind that the types of tables that tableA and tableB represent will greatly affect the isolation level. For example, if implementing a medical sales system that allows the user to ship a critical product to a customer, you'd perform the following types of checks (in pseudocode):

```
BEGIN TRANSACTION
IF (product in inventory) > (amount requested)
BEGIN
   Decrement inventory
   Save Bill of Lading
END
COMMIT TRANSACTION
```

I'd probably suggest using the SERIALIZABLE isolation level, because you wouldn't want to decrement inventory twice accidentally because a process checked inventory, then some other process simultaneously checked it also. What might happen would be to have multiple users blocked on the step to decrement inventory, after the check to see if the decrementing was valid. SERIALIZABLE is often the best isolation level for critical sections of your code, but be sure to keep these sections short lived, or you'll have lots more blocking than you desire. Why? Because maximum locks are being held, and other users who might need to do a table scan as part of a query might have to wait, even if they don't need the data in the table.

Keep in mind that locks aren't just held for operations that you directly execute. They're held for any constraints that fire to check existence in other tables, and any code executed in trigger code. The isolation level in effect also controls how long these locks are held.

When considering solutions, you must keep in mind locking and isolation levels. As more and more critical solutions are being built upon SQL Server, it's imperative to make absolutely sure to protect data at a level that's commensurate with the value of the data. If you are building procedures to support a system on a space shuttle or a life support system, this becomes more important than it would be in the case of a sales system, or even a pediatrician's schedule. In the next major section, "Coding for Integrity and Concurrency," I'll look at coding schemes aimed at improving the concurrency of your stored procedure programs.

In the next subsections, I'll briefly discuss the different isolation levels and demonstrate how they work using the following table. (Again, build these in any database of your choice. I'll create them in tempdb.)

```
CREATE TABLE dbo.testIsolationLevel
(
    testIsolationLevelId int identity(1,1)
                CONSTRAINT PKtestIsolationLevel PRIMARY KEY,
    value varchar(10)
)
```

```
INSERT dbo.testIsolationLevel(value)
VALUES ('Value1')
INSERT dbo.testIsolationLevel(value)
VALUES ('Value2')
```

■**Tip** Just as for locking modes, there are table query hints to apply an isolation level only to a given table in a query, rather than an entire query. These hints are READUNCOMMITTED, READCOMMITTED, REPEATABLEREAD, and SERIALIZABLE, and they behave as their corresponding isolation levels do, only with respect to a single table.

READ UNCOMMITTED

Ignore all locks, and don't issue locks. Queries can see any data that has been saved to the table, regardless of whether or not it's part of a transaction that hasn't been committed (hence the name). However, READ UNCOMMITTED still leaves exclusive locks if you do modify data, to keep other users from changing data that you haven't committed.

For the most part, READ UNCOMMITTED is a good tool for developers to use to check the progress of operations, and to look at production systems when SNAPSHOT isn't available. For example, say you execute the following code on one connection:

```
--CONNECTION A
SET TRANSACTION ISOLATION LEVEL READ COMMITTED --this is the default
BEGIN TRANSACTION
INSERT INTO dbo.testIsolationLevel(value)
VALUES('Value3')
```

Then execute on a second connection:

```
--CONNECTION B
SET TRANSACTION ISOLATION LEVEL READ UNCOMMITTED
SELECT *
FROM dbo.testIsolationLevel
```

This returns the following results:

```
testIsolationLevelId value
-------------------- ----------
1                    Value1
2                    Value2
3                    Value3
```

This is valuable, especially when you're in the middle of a long-running process. That's because you won't block the process that's running, but you can see the data being modified. Finally, commit the transaction you started earlier:

```
--CONNECTION A

COMMIT TRANSACTION
```

■**Note** This isolation level was often used in earlier versions of SQL Server for reporting on active OLTP databases. For future usage, consider the SNAPSHOT isolation level in your OLTP database applications as a replacement for READ UNCOMMITTED. It doesn't allow dirty reads, but it does give the other concurrency benefits of READ UNCOMMITTED.

READ COMMITTED

READ COMMITTED, the default isolation level, doesn't allow you to see uncommitted data. All shared and update locks are released as soon as the process is finished using the resource. Exclusive locks are held until the end of the transaction. Data modifications are usually executed under this isolation level. However, understand that this isolation level isn't perfect, as there isn't protection for repeatable reads or phantom rows. This means that as the length of the transaction increases, there's a growing possibility that some data that was read during the first operations within a transaction might have been changed or deleted by the end of the transaction. It happens only rarely when transactions are kept short, so it's an acceptable risk.

For example:

```
--CONNECTION A

SET TRANSACTION ISOLATION LEVEL READ COMMITTED

BEGIN TRANSACTION
SELECT * FROM dbo.testIsolationLevel
```

You see all the rows in the table from the previous section (though the testIsolationLevelId might be different if you had errors when you built your code). Then on the second connection, delete a row:

```
--CONNECTION B

DELETE FROM dbo.testIsolationLevel
WHERE testIsolationLevelId = 1
```

Finally, go back to the other connection and execute, still within the transaction:

```
--CONNECTION A
SELECT *
FROM dbo.testIsolationLevel
COMMIT TRANSACTION
```

This returns the following results:

```
testIsolationLevelId  value
--------------------  ----------
2                     Value2
3                     Value3
```

The key to the success of using READ COMMITTED isolation is simple probability. The chances of two users stepping on each other's processes within milliseconds is pretty unlikely, not to mention the unlikelihood that one user will do the exact thing that would cause inconsistency. However, the longer your transactions, and the higher the concurrent number of users on the system, the more likely that this will produce anomalies. In 12 years of working with SQL Server, I've never seen any kinds of issues other than when I've forced them to occur. However, I'd use one of the following two isolation levels if I needed to implement critical parts of a system, or a life-critical system.

For example, consider the issues involved in implementing a system to track drugs given to a patient in a hospital. For a system such as this, you'd never want to give a user too much medicine accidentally, because when you started a process to set up a schedule via a batch system, a nurse was administering the dosage off schedule. Although this situation is unlikely, as you will see in the next few sections, an adjustment in isolation level would prevent it from occurring at all.

REPEATABLE READ

The REPEATABLE READ isolation level includes protection from data being deleted from under your operation. Shared locks are now held during the entire transaction, to prevent other users from modifying the data that has been read. You would be most likely to use this isolation level if your concern is the absolute guarantee of existence of some data when you finish your operation.

As an example on one connection, execute the following statement:

```
--CONNECTION A

SET TRANSACTION ISOLATION LEVEL REPEATABLE READ

BEGIN TRANSACTION
SELECT * FROM dbo.testIsolationLevel
```

Then, on a different connection, run the following:

```
--CONNECTION B

INSERT INTO dbo.testIsolationLevel(value)
VALUES ('Value4')
```

This executes, but try executing the following code:

```
DELETE FROM dbo.testIsolationLevel
WHERE value = 'Value3'
```

You go into a blocked state, because CONNECTION B has an exclusive lock on that particular value. Back on the other connection, run the following code:

```
--CONNECTION A

SELECT * FROM dbo.testIsolationLevel
COMMIT TRANSACTION
```

Your other connection completes.

SERIALIZABLE

SERIALIZABLE takes everything from REPEATABLE READ, and adds in phantom-row protection. SQL Server does this by not only taking locks on existing data that it has read, but now taking key locks on any ranges of data that *could possibly* match any SQL statement executed. This is the most restrictive isolation level, and is the best in any case where data integrity is absolutely necessary. It can cause lots of blocking; for example, try executing the following code:

```
SELECT *
FROM dbo.testIsolationLevel
```

No other user will be able to modify the table until all rows have been returned and the transaction (implicit or explicit) is completed. If multiple users are viewing data in the table under any of the previously mentioned isolation levels, it can be difficult to get any modifications done. If you're going to use SERIALIZABLE, you need to be careful with your code that it only uses the minimum number of rows needed, especially if you are not using SNAPSHOT isolation level for read processes, as covered in the next section.

SNAPSHOT

SNAPSHOT isolation is a cool new feature in SQL Server 2005. It lets you read the data as it was when the transaction started, regardless of any changes. It's a special case, because although it doesn't allow for phantom rows, nonrepeatable reads, or dirty reads from any queries within the transaction, it doesn't represent the current state of the data. You might check a value in a table at the beginning of the transaction and it's in the physical table, but later you requery the table. Although the value exists in your virtual table, it needn't exist in the physical table any longer (in fact, the physical table needn't exist either!). This provides that the results of your query will reflect a consistent state of the database at some time, which is generally very desirable.

What makes SNAPSHOT particularly useful is that it doesn't use locks in the normal way, as it looks at the data as it was at the start of the transaction. Modifying data under this isolation level has its share of problems, which I'll demonstrate later in this section. However, I don't want to scare you off, as this isolation level can become a major part of a highly concurrent design strategy (particularly useful for reads in an optimistic locking strategy, which the last sections of this chapter cover).

The largest downside is performance. This history data is written not only to the log, but the data that will be used to support other users that are in a SNAPSHOT isolation level transaction is written to the tempdb. Hence, you have to make sure that your tempdb is up to the challenge, especially if you're supporting large numbers of concurrent users. The good news is that if set up correctly, data readers will no longer block data writers. So when the vice president of the company decides to write a 20-table join query in the middle of the busiest part of the day, all other users won't get stuck behind him with software locks. The bad news is that eventually his query might take up all the resources and cause a major system slowdown that way. (Hey, if it was too easy, they wouldn't need DBAs. If you're like me, I wouldn't survive in a nontechnical field.)

To use (and demonstrate) SNAPSHOT isolation level, you have to alter the database you're working with (you can even do this to tempdb):

```
ALTER DATABASE tempDb
SET ALLOW_SNAPSHOT_ISOLATION ON
```

Now the SNAPSHOT isolation level is available for queries.

■**Caution** SNAPSHOT isolation level uses copies of changed data placed into the tempdb. Because of this, you should make sure that your tempdb is set up optimally. For more on setting up hardware, consider checking out the website http://www.sql-server-performance.com.

Let's look at an example. On the first connection, start a transaction and select from the testIsolationLevel table:

```
--CONNECTION A

SET TRANSACTION ISOLATION LEVEL SNAPSHOT
BEGIN TRANSACTION
SELECT * from dbo.testIsolationLevel
```

This returns the following results:

```
testIsolationLevelId value
-------------------- ----------
2                    Value2
4                    Value4
```

On a second connection, run the following:

```
--CONNECTION B

SET TRANSACTION ISOLATION LEVEL READ COMMITTED
INSERT INTO dbo.testIsolationLevel(value)
VALUES ('Value5')
```

This executes with no waiting. Going back to the other connection, reexecuting the SELECT returns the same set as before. Now, still on the second connection, run the following code:

```
--CONNECTION B

DELETE FROM dbo.testIsolationLevel
WHERE   value = 'Value4'
```

This doesn't have to wait either. Going back to the other connection again, nothing has changed. So what about modifying data in SNAPSHOT isolation level? If no one else has modified the row, you can make any change:

```
--CONNECTION A

UPDATE  dbo.testIsolationLevel
SET     value = 'Value2-mod'
WHERE   testIsolationLevelId = 2
```

This runs, but going back to the B connection, if you try to select this row, it will be blocked, and the connection is forced to wait. Commit the transaction in CONNECTION A and you'll see rows such as these:

```
--CONNECTION A
COMMIT TRANSACTION
SELECT * from dbo.testIsolationLevel
```

This returns the current contents of the table:

```
testIsolationLevelId value
-------------------- ----------
2                    Value2-mod
6                    Value5
```

The troubling bit with modifying data under the SNAPSHOT isolation level is what happens when one user modifies a row that another user has also modified, and committed the transaction for it. To see this, in CONNECTION A run the following, simulating a user fetching some data into the cache:

```
--CONNECTION A
SET TRANSACTION ISOLATION LEVEL SNAPSHOT
BEGIN TRANSACTION

--touch the data
SELECT * FROM dbo.testIsolationLevel
```

Then a second user changes the value:

```
--CONNECTION B
SET TRANSACTION ISOLATION LEVEL READ COMMITTED --any will do

UPDATE dbo.testIsolationLevel
SET    value = 'Value5-mod2'
WHERE  testIsolationLevelId = 6 --might be different in yours
```

Then the user on CONNECTION A tries to update the row also:

```
--CONNECTION B
UPDATE dbo.testIsolationLevel
SET    value = 'Value5-mod'
WHERE testIsolationLevelId = 6 --might be different in yours
```

As this row has been deleted by a different connection, the following error message rears its ugly head:

```
Msg 3960, Level 16, State 2, Line 1
Snapshot isolation transaction aborted due to update conflict. You cannot use
snapshot isolation to access table 'dbo.testIsolationLevel' directly or indirectly
in database 'tempdb' to update, delete, or insert the row that has been modified
or deleted by another transaction. Retry the transaction or change the isolation
level for the update/delete statement.
```

As such, it's my recommendation that almost all retrieval-only operations can execute under the SNAPSHOT isolation level, and the procedures that do data modifications execute under the READ COMMITTED isolation level. As long as data is only read, the connection will see the state of the database as it was when the data was first read.

■**Caution** If you do data validations under SNAPSHOT isolation level, such as in a trigger or constraint, the data might already be invalid in the live database, especially if the transaction runs long. This is far worse than REPEATABLE READ, where the data is always valid when the check is done, but might be changed after the violation.

Another interesting setting can make using snapshots a better idea. The database setting READ_COMMITTED_SNAPSHOT changes the isolation level of READ COMMITTED to behave like SNAPSHOT isolation level on a *statement* level:

```
--must be no active connections other than the connection executing
--this ALTER command
ALTER DATABASE <databasename>
    SET READ_COMMITTED_SNAPSHOT ON
```

By doing this, every *statement* is now in SNAPSHOT isolation level by default. Note that I said "statement" and not "transaction." In SNAPSHOT isolation level, once you start a transaction, you get a consistent view of the database *as it was* when the transaction started until you close it. READ_COMMITTED_SNAPSHOT gives you a consistent view of the database for a single statement. For example, imagine you're at the midpoint of the following pseudo-batch:

```
BEGIN TRANSACTION
SELECT column FROM table1
--midpoint
SELECT column FROM table1
COMMIT TRANSACTION
```

If you're in SNAPSHOT isolation level, table1 could change completely—even get dropped— and you wouldn't be able to tell when you execute the second SELECT statement. You're given a consistent view of the database for reading. With the READ_COMMITTED_SNAPSHOT database setting turned on, and in a READ COMMITTED transaction, your view of table1 would be consistent with how it looked when you started reading, but when you started the second pass through the table, it might not match the data the first time you read through. This behavior is similar to plain READ COMMITTED, except that you cannot get phantoms and nonrepeatable reads while retrieving rows produced by the individual statement (other users can delete and add rows while you scan through the table, but you won't be affected by the changes), and SQL Server doesn't need to take locks or block other users.

This can be better than just using READ COMMITTED, though it does suffer from the same issues with data consistency as did plain READ COMMITTED, and maybe just a bit worse. You should remember that in the previous section on READ COMMITTED, I noted that because SQL Server releases locks immediately after reading the data, another user could come behind you and change data that you just finished using to do some validation. This same thing is true for READ_COMMITTED_SNAPSHOT, but the window of time can be slightly longer because it reads only history as it passes through different tables. This amount of time is generally insignificant and usually isn't worried about, but it *can* be important based on the type of system you're creating. For places where you might need more safety, consider using the higher isolation levels, such as REPEATABLE READ or SERIALIZABLE.

SNAPSHOT isolation level and the READ_COMMITTED_SNAPSHOT settings are majorly important upgrades to SQL Server's concurrency feature set. They cut down on blocking and the need to use the dirty reads to look at active OLTP data for small reports and for read-only queries to cache data for user-interface processes.

Coding for Integrity and Concurrency

When building database systems, you must consider that multiple users will be attempting to modify your data, at the same time. So far in this chapter, I've talked at length about the different mechanisms, such as transactions, varying isolation levels, and so on, for protecting your data. Now I'll present some of the different coding mechanisms to keep your users from stepping on one another.

The general progression of events for most applications is the same: fetch some data for a user or a process to look at, operate on this data, make changes to the data, or make some decision based on the retrieved values. Once the users have performed their operations, they'll either commit their changes to the database, or possibly save data to a different table based on their decision.

Our coding decisions generally surround how to deal with the lag time while the users have the data cached on their client. For example, what happens if a different user wants the data, and wants to make a change to the same data?

For this situation, you can use a couple common schemes while coding your database application:

- *Pessimistic locking*: Assume it's likely that users will try to modify the same data, so single-thread access to important resources.

- *Optimistic locking*: Assume it's unlikely that users will try to modify the exact same row at the same time another user wants to. Only verify that the cached data is valid when the user wants to change the data.

Using one or parts of both these schemes, it's usually possible to protect data in a multi-user system at an acceptable level of integrity and concurrency.

Pessimistic Locking

A pessimistic locking scheme is restrictive. Generally, the idea is straightforward: begin a transaction, most likely a serializable one; fetch the data; manipulate the data; modify the data; and finally commit the transaction. The goal is to serialize or single-thread all access to the resource in which the process is interested, making sure that no other user can modify or even view the data being worked on.

The main concern is blocking all access to given resources. This sounds easy and reasonable, but the main issue is that any query to a locked resource has to wait for the user to complete access. Even if the parts of the resource won't be involved in the answer to a query, if a locked resource *might* be involved, there's a possibility that unnecessary blocking will occur.

For example, say one user has a single row locked in a table. The next user executes a different query that requires a table scan on the same table. Even if the results of this query needn't use the locked row, the second user will be blocked until the other connection has completed, as SQL Server won't know if the next user needs the row until it's unlocked.

■**Note** You might be thinking that SQL Server could simply check to see if the locked resource would be needed. However, this cannot be known, because once a row is locked with a noncompatible lock, all other users must assume that the values might change. Hence, you're forced to wait until the lock is dropped.

Any users who need data that this next user has locked also have to wait, and soon a chain of users is waiting on one particular user.

Except for one thing—time—all this might even be reasonable. If the lock only lasted milliseconds (or possibly seconds), this would be fine. Small applications based on file managers have implemented concurrency this way for years. However, what if the user decides to take a break (a common issue with smaller systems)? All other users have to wait until this user finishes his or her access to the data, and if this user has modified one piece of data (possibly with complex triggers), and still has more to go, access might be blocked to most of the system data because a user was forgetful and didn't press the Save button.

It's possible to relieve some of the long-term stress on the system by reducing the time locks can be held for, such as setting time limits on how long the user can keep the data before rolling back the transaction. However, either way, it's necessary to block access to large quantities of data for a more-than-reasonable period of time. That's because you'd need to lock any domain tables that the users will rely on to choose values for their table, so that users change no related table values or any related data that other users might need.

Implementing pessimistic locks isn't all that easy, as you have to go out of your way to force locks on data that keep other users from even viewing the data. One method is to lock data using exclusive lock hints, coupled with the SERIALIZABLE isolation level, when you fetch data and maintain the connection to the server as you modify the data. This is messy, and will likely cause lots of undesired locks if you aren't extremely careful how you write queries to minimize locking.

SQL Server does have a built-in method you can use to implement a form of pessimistic locking: SQL Server *application locks*. These locks, just like other locks, must be taken inside a transaction (otherwise you'll get a nasty error message). The commands that you have to work with application locks are as follows:

- sp_getAppLock: Places a lock on an application resource. The programmer names application resources, and they can be named with any string value. In the string, you could name single values, or even a range. Enforcement is totally up to the client.

- sp_releaseAppLock: Releases locks taken inside a transaction.

- APPLOCK_MODE: Used to check the mode of the application lock.

- APPLOCK_TEST: Used to see if you could take an application lock before starting the lock and getting blocked.

As an example, we'll run the following code. We'll implement this on a resource named 'invoiceId=1', which represents an invoice that we'll lock. We'll set it as an exclusive lock so no other user can touch it. In one connection, we run the following code:

```
--CONNECTION A

BEGIN TRANSACTION
    DECLARE @result int
    EXEC @result = sp_getapplock @Resource = 'invoiceId=1', @LockMode = 'Exclusive'
    SELECT @result
```

This returns 0, stating that the lock was taken successfully. Now, if another user tries to execute the same code to take the same lock, their process has to wait until the user has finished with the resource 'invoiceId=1':

```
--CONNECTION B

BEGIN TRANSACTION
    DECLARE @result int
    EXEC @result = sp_getapplock @Resource = 'invoiceId=1', @LockMode = 'Exclusive'
    PRINT @result
```

This transaction has to wait. Let's cancel the connection, and then execute the following code using the APPLOCK_TEST function to see if we can take the lock (allowing the application to check before taking the lock):

```
--CONNECTION B

BEGIN TRANSACTION
SELECT  APPLOCK_TEST('public','invoiceId=1','Exclusive','Transaction')
                                                    as CanTakeLock

ROLLBACK TRANSACTION
```

This returns 0, meaning we cannot take this lock currently. APPLOCKs can be a great resource for building locks that don't fit into the mold of SQL Server locks, and could be used by a user interface to lock access to a given screen in an application. The key is that every application must implement the locking mechanism, and every application must honor the locks taken.

Tip You can use application locks to implement more than just pessimistic locks using different lock modes other than exclusive, but exclusive is what you'd use to implement a pessimistic locking mechanism. For more information about application locks, SQL Server 2005 Books Online gives some good examples and a full reference to using application locks.

Optimistic Locking

The opposite of pessimistic locking is optimistic locking. Here, the premise is simply to assume that the likelihood of users stepping on one another is limited (it really is!). Instead of locking resources, locks are only taken during actual data-modification activities, because most of the time users just look around, and even if the data they're looking at is slightly out of date, it won't hurt anything (this is where the SNAPSHOT isolation level is perfect).

This is true of almost all applications, including banking ones. Consider the ATM machine, where you go to withdraw money. It only allows you to withdraw as much money as it believes you have, but if your spouse has withdrawn money somewhere else simultaneously, and the result is that you happen to take out more money than you have, the bank doesn't mind, and the system simply penalizes you with "you don't have any money left" fees, so you have even less money. Now, not only is your bank account drained, when you do happen to deposit some money, the bank takes an extra share.

The idea behind optimistic locking is that, in all cases, only lock the data at the point where the user modifies the data. Data is protected in the server using constraints, triggers, and so on. Choose the best isolation level depending upon how important perfection is. That's because, as noted in the section "Isolation Levels," the default of READ UNCOMMITTED is flawed, because for some amount of time (hopefully milliseconds), it leaves open the possibility that one user can change data on which your transaction is dependent. For the most part, it's considered appropriate to use the default, as it greatly enhances concurrency, and the probability of someone modifying data that your transaction is reliant on is close to the chances of being hit by lightning on ten sunny days in a row. It could happen, but it's a slim chance.

Thinking back to the normal progression of events when a user works in an application, the user fetches data, modifies data, and finally commits data to the database. There can easily be a long interval between fetching the data and committing the changes to the database. In fact, it's also possible that other users could have also fetched and modified the data during the same period of time. Because of this, you need to implement some method to make sure that the data that the client originally fetched matches the data that's stored in the database. Otherwise, the new changes could trample important changes made by another user.

So, instead of locking the data by using SQL Server locks, simply employ one of the following schemes to leave data unlocked after it has been fetched to the client. Later, after the user makes desired changes and goes back to update the data, one of the following schemes is employed:

- *Unchecked*: Just let it happen. If two users modify the same row in the database, then the last user wins. It's not the best idea, as the first user might have had something important to say, and this method rejects the first user's changes. I won't cover this any further because it's straightforward. (This is all too often the most commonly employed scheme.)

- *Row-based*: Protect your data at the row level, by checking to see if the rows being modified are the same as in the table. If not, refresh the data from the table, showing the user what was changed. When optimistic locking is implemented, this is by far the most common method used.

- *Logical unit of work*: A logical unit of work is used to group a parent record with all its child data to allow a single optimistic lock to cover multiple tables. For example, you'd group an invoice and the line items for that invoice. Treat modifications to the line items the same way as a modification to the invoice, for locking purposes.

Although it isn't typically a good idea to ignore the problem of users overwriting one another altogether, if the application is small then it isn't a real issue whatsoever. On the other hand, the best plan is optimally a mixture of the row-based solution for most tables, and a logical unit of work for major groups of tables that make up some common object. If you remember back to Chapter 6, the reasons for using a logical-unit-of-work solution mirror the reasons to use cascading operations between two tables. If multiple tables compose a larger entity, such as an invoice and line items, then it might make sense to implement this method. However, any situation that can use a row-based solution is fine. It's completely based upon what you desire, as the architect.

Before discussing the details of how to modify our data, let's briefly discuss details of the isolation level for retrieving and modifying data. I mentioned earlier that using the SNAPSHOT isolation level gives us "lock-free" operations that won't block other users. This makes it perfect for optimistic locking situations, because we expect that no two users will want to modify the same rows, but they often want might look at the same rows. For this reason, I suggest using the following:

- SNAPSHOT *isolation level*: Use for all retrieval operations where no data is going to be modified; for example, when you want to fetch a row or set of rows to possibly modify. This includes reporting, editors (especially when you're going to use ADO disconnected recordsets), and so on.

- READ COMMITTED: Use for update operations, as it's the best balance of safe operations and performance.

- *Higher isolation levels*: Use as needed when the situation merits.

An important point about optimistic locking is that it isn't enforced by the database, and must be coded into every query that's executed against the tables. If the user has a row with an older optimistic lock value, SQL Server won't deny access to the data. It's all up to the programmers to follow the rules that the database architect lays down.

In the following sections, I'll cover row-based locking and the logical unit of work. The unchecked method ignores the concern that two people might modify the same row twice, so there's no coding (or thinking!) required.

Row-Based Locking

You must implement a row-based scheme to check on a row-by-row basis whether or not the data that the user has retrieved is still the same as the one that's in the database. The order of events now is fetch data, modify data, check to see that the row (or rows) of data are still the same as they were, and then commit the changes.

There are three common methods to implement row-based optimistic locking:

- *Check all columns in the table*: If you cannot modify the table structure, which the next two methods require, you can check to make sure that all the data you had fetched is still the same, and then modify the data. This method is the most difficult, because any procedure you write must contain parameters for the previous values of the data, which isn't a good idea. Checking all columns is useful when building bound data-grid types of applications, where there are direct updates to tables, especially if not all tables can follow the rather strict rules of the next two methods.

- *Add a date and time column to the table*: Set the datetime value when the table is inserted and subsequently updated. Every procedure for modifying or deleting data from the table needs a column for the previous value of the timestamp. Every update to the table is required to modify the value in the table to set the updateDatetime column. Generally, it's best to use a trigger for keeping the datetime column up to date, and often it's nice to include a column to tell which user last modified the data (you need someone to blame!). Later in this section, I'll demonstrate a simple INSTEAD OF trigger to support this approach.

- *Use a* rowversion *column*: In the previous method, you used a manually controlled value to manage the optimistic lock value. This method uses column with a rowversion datatype. The rowversion datatype automatically gets a new value for every command used to modify a given row in a table.

The next two sections cover adding the optimistic lock columns to your tables, and then using them in your code.

Adding Optimistic Lock Columns

In this section, we'll add an optimistic lock column to a table to support either adding the datetime column or the rowversion column. The first method mentioned, checking all columns, needs no table modifications.

As an example, let's create a new simple table, in this case hr.person (again, use any database you like). Here's the structure:

```
CREATE SCHEMA hr
CREATE TABLE hr.person
(
    personId int IDENTITY(1,1) CONSTRAINT PKperson primary key,
    firstName varchar(60) NOT NULL,
    middleName varchar(60) NOT NULL,
    lastName varchar(60) NOT NULL,
```

```
    dateOfBirth datetime NOT NULL,
    rowLastModifyDate datetime NOT NULL
        CONSTRAINT DFLTperson_rowLastModifyDate default getdate(),
    rowModifiedByUserIdentifier nvarchar(128) NOT NULL
        CONSTRAINT DFLTperson_rowModifiedByUserIdentifier default suser_sname()
```

)

Note the two columns for our optimistic lock, named rowLastModifyDate and rowModifiedByUserIdentifier. I'll use these to hold the last date and time of modification, and the SQL Server's login principal name of the principal that changed the row. There are a couple ways to implement this:

- *Let the manipulation layer manage the value like any other column*: This is often what client programmers like to do, and it's acceptable, as long as you're using trusted computers to manage the timestamps. I feel it's inadvisable to allow workstations to set such values, as it can cause confusing results. For example, say your application displays a message stating that another user has made changes, and the time the changes were made is in the future, based on the client's computer. Then the user checks out his or her PC clock, and it's set perfectly.

- *Using SQL Server code*: For the most part, triggers are implemented to fire on any modification to data.

As an example of using SQL Server code, I'll implement an INSTEAD OF trigger on the update of the hr.person table (note that the errorLog$insert procedure was created back in Chapter 6, and has been commented out for this demonstration):

```
CREATE TRIGGER hr.person$InsteadOfUpdate
ON hr.person
INSTEAD OF UPDATE AS
BEGIN

    DECLARE @rowsAffected int,     --stores the number of rows affected
            @msg varchar(2000)     --used to hold the error message

    SET @rowsAffected = @@rowcount

    --no need to continue on if no rows affected
    IF @rowsAffected = 0 return

    SET NOCOUNT ON --to avoid the rowcount messages
    SET ROWCOUNT 0 --in case the client has modified the rowcount

    BEGIN TRY
            --[validation blocks]
            --[modification blocks]
            --remember to update ALL columns when building instead of triggers
            UPDATE hr.person
```

```
        SET     firstName = inserted.firstName,
                middleName = inserted.middleName,
                lastName = inserted.lastName,
                dateOfBirth = inserted.dateOfBirth,
                rowLastModifyDate = default, --tells SQL Server to set the value to
                rowModifiedByUserIdentifier = default --the value in the default
        FROM    hr.person                            --constraint
                    JOIN inserted
                            ON hr.person.personId = inserted.personId
    END TRY
    BEGIN CATCH
            IF @@trancount > 0
                ROLLBACK TRANSACTION

            --EXECUTE dbo.errorLog$insert

            DECLARE @ERROR_MESSAGE varchar(8000)
            SET @ERROR_MESSAGE = ERROR_MESSAGE()
            RAISERROR (@ERROR_MESSAGE,16,1)

    END CATCH
END
```

Then insert a row into the table:

```
INSERT INTO hr.person (firstName, middleName, lastName, dateOfBirth)
VALUES ('Leroy','T','Brown','19391212')

SELECT *
FROM    hr.person
```

Now you can see that the data has been created:

personId	firstName	middleName	lastName	dateOfBirth
1	Leroy	T	Brown	1939-12-12 00:00:00.000

rowLastModifyDate	rowModifiedByUserIdentifier
2005-07-30 01:26:10.780	<username>

Now update the row:

```
UPDATE hr.person
SET     middleName = 'Tee'
WHERE   personId = 1

SELECT rowLastModifyDate
FROM    hr.person
```

You should see that the update date has changed. In my case, it was pretty doggone late:

```
rowLastModifyDate
----------------------
2005-07-30 01:28:28.397
```

If you want to set the value on insert, or implement `rowCreatedByDate` or `userIdentifier` columns, the code would be similar. Because this has been implemented in an `INSTEAD OF` trigger, the user or even the programmer cannot overwrite the values, even if they include it in the column list of an `INSERT`.

As previously mentioned, the other method that requires table modification is to use a `rowversion` column. In my opinion, this is the best way to go, and I almost always use a `rowversion`. I usually have the row modification columns on there as well, for the user's benefit. I find that the modification columns take on other uses and have a tendency to migrate to the control of the application developer, and `rowversion` columns never do. Plus, even if the triggers don't make it on the table for one reason or another, the `rowversion` column continues to work. Sometimes you may be prohibited from using `INSTEAD OF` insert triggers for some reason (recently I couldn't use them in a project I worked on because they invalidate the `identity` functions).

Tip You might know this as the `timestamp` datatype, which is what it has been named since the early days of SQL Server. In the ANSI standard, a `timestamp` column is a date and time value. `rowversion` is a much better name for the datatype.

Let's add a `rowversion` column to our table to demonstrate using it as an optimistic lock:

```
ALTER TABLE hr.person
   ADD rowversion rowversion
GO
SELECT personId, rowversion
FROM   hr.person
```

You can see now that the `rowversion` has been added and magically updated:

```
personId    rowversion
----------- ------------------
1           0x00000000000007D1
```

Now, when the row gets updated, the `rowversion` is modified:

```
UPDATE  hr.person
SET     firstName = 'Leroy'
WHERE   personId = 1
```

Then, looking at the output, you can see that the value of the `rowversion` has changed:

```
SELECT personId, rowversion
FROM   hr.person
```

This returns the following result:

```
personId    rowversion
----------- ------------------
1           0x00000000000007D2
```

■**Caution** You aren't guaranteed anything when it comes to `rowversion` values, other than that they'll be unique in a database. Don't use the value for any reason other than to tell when a row has changed.

Coding for Row-Level Optimistic Locking

Next, include the checking code in your stored procedure. Using the `hr.person` table previously created, the following code snippets will demonstrate each of the methods (note that I'll only use the optimistic locking columns germane to each example, and not include the others).

Check all the cached values for the columns:

```
UPDATE  hr.person
SET     firstName = 'Fred'
WHERE   personId = 1  --include the key
  and   firstName = 'Leroy'
  and   middleName = 'Tee'
  and   lastName = 'Brown'
  and   dateOfBirth = '19391212'
```

Note that it's a good practice to check your rowcount after an update with an optimistic lock to see how many rows have changed. If it is 0, you could check to see if the row exists with that primary key:

```
IF EXISTS ( SELECT *
            FROM   hr.person
            WHERE  personId = 1)
  --raise an error, or return an error
```

Use a date column:

```
UPDATE  hr.person
SET     firstName = 'Fred'
WHERE   personId = 1  --include the key
  and   rowLastModifyDate = '2005-07-30 00:28:28.397'
```

Use a `rowversion` column:

```
UPDATE  hr.person
SET     firstName = 'Fred'
WHERE   personId = 1
  and   rowversion = 0x00000000000007D3
```

Which is better performance-wise? Either of these performs just as well as the other, because in all cases you're using the primary key to do your update. There's a bit less overhead with the last two columns because you don't have to pass as much data into the statement, but the difference is negligible.

Deletions use the same WHERE clause, because if another user has modified the row, it's probably a good idea to see if that user's changes make the row still valuable.

If you want to delete the row, you'd use the same WHERE clause:

```
DELETE FROM hr.person
WHERE   rowversion = 0x00000000000007D3
```

I typically prefer using a rowversion column, because it requires the least amount of work to always work perfectly. On the other hand, many client programmers prefer to have the manipulation layer of the application set a datetime value.

Logical Unit of Work

Although row-based optimistic locks are helpful, they do have a slight downfall. In many cases, several tables together make one "object." A good example is an invoice and line items. The idea behind a logical unit of work is that instead of having a row-based lock on the invoice and all the line items, you might only implement one on the invoice, and use the same value for the line items. This does require that the user always fetch not only the invoice line items, but at least the invoice's timestamp into the client's cache when dealing with the invoice line items. Assuming you're using a rowversion column, I'd just use the same kind of logic as previously used on the hr.person table. In this example, we'll build the procedure to do the modifications.

When the user wants to insert, update, or delete line items for the invoice, the procedure requires the @objectVersion parameter, and checks the value against the invoice, prior to update. Consider that there are two tables, minimally defined as follows:

```
CREATE SCHEMA invoicing
go
--leaving off who invoice is for
CREATE TABLE invoicing.invoice
(
    invoiceId int IDENTITY(1,1),
    number varchar(20) NOT NULL,
    objectVersion rowversion not null,
    constraint PKinvoicing_invoice primary key (invoiceId)
)
--also forgetting what product that the line item is for
CREATE TABLE invoicing.invoiceLineItem
```

```
(
    invoiceLineItemId int NOT NULL,
    invoiceId int NULL,
    itemcCount int NOT NULL,
    cost int NOT NULL,
     constraint PKinvoicing_invoiceLineItem primary key (invoiceLineItemId),
     constraint FKinvoicing_invoiceLineItem$references$invoicing_invoice
          foreign key (invoiceId) references invoicing.invoice(invoiceId)
)
```

For our delete procedure for the invoice line item, the parameters would have the key of the invoice and the line item, plus the rowversion value:

```
CREATE PROCEDURE invoiceLineItem$del
(
    @invoiceId int, --we pass this because the client should have it
                    --with the invoiceLineItem row
    @invoiceLineItemId int,
    @objectVersion rowversion
) as
  BEGIN
    DECLARE @savepoint nvarchar(128)
    --gives us a unique savepoint name, trim it to 125
    --characters if the user named it really large
    SET @savepoint = cast(object_name(@@procid) AS nvarchar(125)) +
                    cast(@@nestlevel AS nvarchar(3))

    BEGIN TRY
        BEGIN TRANSACTION
        SAVE TRANSACTION @savepoint

        UPDATE  invoice
        SET     number = number
        WHERE   invoiceId = @invoiceId
          And   objectVersion = @objectVersion

        DELETE  invoiceLineItem
        FROM    invoiceLineItem
        WHERE   invoiceLineItemId = @invoiceLineItemId

        COMMIT TRANSACTION

    END TRY
    BEGIN CATCH
            IF xact_state() = -1 --transaction is doomed
                 rollback transaction
            ELSE IF xact_state() = 1 --the error did not cause
                                     --a rollback,
```

```
        BEGIN
            ROLLBACK TRANSACTION savePointName
            COMMIT TRANSACTION
        END

    --or this will get rolled back
    --EXECUTE dbo.errorLog$insert

    DECLARE @ERROR_MESSAGE varchar(8000)
    SET @ERROR_MESSAGE = ERROR_MESSAGE()
    RAISERROR (@ERROR_MESSAGE,16,1)

    END CATCH
END
```

Instead of checking the rowversion on an invoiceLineItem row, we check the rowversion (in the objectVersion column) on the invoice table. Additionally, we must update the rowversion value on the invoice table when we make our change, so we update the invoice row, simply setting a single column to the same value. There's a bit more overhead when working this way, but it's normal to update multiple rows at a time from the client. You'd probably want to architect your solution with multiple procedures, one to update and check the optimistic lock, and then others to do the insert, update, and delete operations.

Best Practices

The number one issue when it comes to concurrency is data quality. Maintaining consistent data is why you go through the work of building a database in the first place. Generally speaking, if the only way to get consistent results was to have every call single threaded, it would be worth it. Of course, we don't have to do that except in rare situations, and SQL Server gives us tools to make it happen with the isolation levels. Use them as needed. It's the data that matters:

- *Use transactions as liberally as needed*: It's important to protect your data, 100 percent of the time. Each time data is modified, it isn't a bad practice to enclose the operation in a transaction. This gives you a chance to check status, number of rows modified, and so on, and if necessary, rollback the modification.

- *Keep transactions as short as possible*: The smaller the transaction, the less chance there is of it holding locks. Try not to declare variables, create temporary tables, and so on inside a transaction unless it's necessary. Make sure that all table access within transactions is required to be executed as an atomic operation.

- *Recognize the difference between hardware limitations and SQL Server concurrency issues*: If the hardware is maxed out (excessive disk queuing, 90-percent–plus CPU usage, and so on), consider adding more hardware. However, if you're single-threading calls through your database due to locking issues, you could add 20 processors and a terabyte of RAM and still see little improvement.

- *Fetch all rows from a query as fast as possible*: Depending on the isolation level and editability of the rows being returned, locks held can interfere with other users' ability to modify or even read rows.

- *Make sure that all queries use reasonable execution plans*: The better all queries execute, the faster the queries will execute, and it follows that more code can be executed.

- *Use some form of optimistic locking mechanism*: Do optimistic locking, preferably using a `rowversion` column, as it requires the smallest amount of coding, and is managed entirely by SQL Server. The only code that's required when programming is to validate the value in the `rowversion` column.

- *Consider using some form of the* SNAPSHOT *isolation level:* Either code all your optimistic-locked retrieval operations with SET SNAPSHOT ISOLATION LEVEL, or change the database setting for READ_COMMITTED_SNAPSHOT to ON. This alters how the READ COMMITTED isolation level reads snapshot information at the statement level. Be careful to test existing applications if you're going to make this change, because these settings do alter how SQL Server works, and might negatively alter how your programs work. I suggest using full SNAPSHOT isolation level for read-only operations anyhow, if it's reasonable for you to do so.

Summary

Concurrency is an important topic, and also a difficult one. It sounds easy: keep the amount of time a user needs to be in the database to a minimum; have adequate resources on your machine.

The fact is, concurrency is a juggling act for SQL Server, Windows, the disk system, the CPUs, and so on. If you have reasonable hardware for your situation, use the SNAPSHOT isolation level for retrieval and READ COMMITTED for other calls, and you should have no trouble with large-scale blocking on your server. This sounds perfect, but the greater the number of users, the more difficult a time you'll have making things perform the way you want. Concurrency is one of the fun jobs for a DBA, because it's truly a science that has a good deal of artsy qualities. You can predict only so much about how your user will use the system, and then experience comes in to tune queries, tune hardware, and tweak settings until you have it right.

I discussed some of the basics of how SQL Server implements controls to support concurrent programming, such that many users can be supported using the same data with locks and transactions. Then I covered isolation levels, which allow you to tweak the kinds of locks taken and how long they're held on a resource. The most important part of the chapter was the part on optimistic locking. As the trend for implementing systems is to use cached data sets, modify that set, and then flush it back, you must make sure that other users haven't made changes to the data while it's cached.

■ ■ ■

Code-Level Architectural Decisions

It is only about things that do not interest one that one can give a really unbiased opinion, which is no doubt the reason why an unbiased opinion is always absolutely valueless.

—Oscar Wilde

Having designed and implemented the database, devised effective security and indexing strategies, and so on, the next step in the process for most projects is to decide on the data-access strategy, and how best to implement and distribute data-centric business logic. This chapter will discuss, at a reasonably high level, the following topics: data-access strategies and choosing between CLR and T-SQL.

Regarding the first, I'll discuss the philosophy of where to code transactional logic. The second topic is new to SQL Server 2005. It's almost a given that at some point, you'll build a stored procedure, a function, or a trigger. With the new CLR objects, there's yet another decision to make, concerning how to implement an object. I'll go over all the types of objects, and look at some of the pros and cons of this exciting new addition to our toolkit.

Data-Access Strategies

Regardless of whether your application is a traditional client-server or a multitier web application, data must be stored in and retrieved from tables. Therefore, most of the advice presented in this chapter will be relevant regardless of the type of application you're building.

In this section, I'll tackle the question of how to code the data-access part of the system. There's a common split between two particular approaches:

- *Using* ad hoc *SQL*: Formulating queries in the application's presentation and manipulation layer (typically functional code stored in objects, such as .NET or Java, and run on a server or a client machine).

- *Using stored procedures*: Creating an interface between the presentation/manipulation layer and the data layer of the application. Note that views and functions, as well as procedures, also form part of this data-access interface. You can use all three of these object types.

The following sections will analyze some of the pros and cons of each approach, in terms of flexibility, security, performance, and so on. Along the way, I'll offer some personal opinions on optimal architecture, and give advice on how best to implement both types of access. Bear in mind that a lot of this is just my personal opinion.

Choosing between *ad hoc* SQL and stored procedures is a polarizing topic, and is the cause of many a programmer-versus-DBA 15-round cage match, where neither side comes out a winner. It's likely that some of you will disagree with my advice, which is fine. Others, regardless, might simply tend to adopt their own "tried and true" method of data access that worked in previous applications.

I must be open, in that my experience is different from yours, and often it's different from that of other people, whose opinions I look to for advice about architecture. I wish there were an easy, straightforward answer for all situations, but it's impossible to be that rigid, even when working for a small company where you're the only architect. Everyone who has any experience building data-oriented systems will likely have some strong opinions on what's right, but as a consultant I have to be flexible and ready to work with anything, even situations that I might find abhorrent. The funny thing is that if you're open to change, you'll notice the good parts of a situation you once felt was horrible, and you can incorporate those parts into your own projects.

Ad Hoc SQL

Ad hoc SQL is sometimes referred to as "straight SQL," and generally refers to the formulation of SELECT, INSERT, UPDATE, and DELETE statements (as well as any others) in the client. These statements are then sent to SQL Server either individually or in batches of multiple statements.

The distinction of using *ad hoc* SQL to precompile objects is that these statements are syntax checked, compiled, then a plan is generated at runtime. (SQL Server may use a cached plan from a previous execution, however.) This is the way that most tools tend to converse with SQL Server, and is, for example, how SQL Server Management Studio works. There's no question that users will perform some *ad hoc* queries against your system, especially when you simply want to write a query and execute it just once. However, the more pertinent question is: should you be using *ad hoc* SQL when building a permanent interface to an OLTP system's data?

■**Note** This topic doesn't include *ad hoc* SQL executed from stored procedures (commonly called dynamic SQL), which I'll discuss in the section "Stored Procedures."

Advantages

Using uncompiled *ad hoc* SQL has some advantages over building compiled stored procedures:

- *Flexibility and control*: Queries are built at runtime, without having to know every possible query that might be executed.

- *Better performance in some situations*: As queries can be formed at runtime, you can retrieve only necessary data for SELECT queries, or modify data that's changed for UPDATE operations.

Flexibility and Control

Unlike stored procedures, which are prebuilt and then stored in the SQL Server system tables, *ad hoc* SQL is formed at the time it's needed: at runtime. Hence, it doesn't suffer from some of the inflexible requirements of stored procedures. For example, say you want to build a user interface to a list of customers. You can add several columns to the SELECT clause, based on the tables listed in the FROM clause. It's simple to build a list of columns into the user interface that the user can use to customize his or her own list. Then the program can issue the list request with only the columns in the SELECT list that are requested by the user. Because some columns might be large and contain quite a bit of data, it's better only to send back a few columns instead of a bunch of columns the user doesn't care about.

For instance, consider that you have the following table to document contacts to prospective customers (it's barebones for this example). In each query, you might return the primary key, but show or not show it to the user based on whether the primary key is implemented as a surrogate or natural key (it isn't important to our example either way). You can create this table in any database you like. (In the sample code, I've created a database named architectureChapter):

```
CREATE SCHEMA sales
GO
CREATE TABLE sales.contact
(
    contactId    int CONSTRAINT PKsales_contact PRIMARY KEY,
    firstName    varchar(30),
    lastName     varchar(30),
    companyName varchar(100),
    contactNotes  varchar(max),
    personalNotes varchar(max),
    CONSTRAINT AKsales_contact UNIQUE (firstName, lastName, companyName)
)
```

One user might want to see the person's name and the company, plus the end of the contactNotes, in his or her view of the data:

```
SELECT  contactId, firstName, lastName, companyName,
        right(contactNotes,500) as notesEnd
FROM    sales.contact
```

Another user might want to see less:

```
SELECT contactId, firstName, lastName, companyName
FROM sales.contact
```

Allowing the user to choose the columns for output can be useful. Consider how the file-listing dialog works in Windows, as shown in Figure 10-1.

Figure 10-1. *The Windows file-listing dialog*

You can see as many or as few of the attributes of a file in the list as you like, based on some metadata you set on the directory. This is a useful method of letting the users choose what they want to see. Let's take this one step further. Consider that the contact table is then related to a table that tells us if a contact has purchased something:

```
CREATE TABLE sales.purchase
(
    purchaseId int CONSTRAINT PKsales_purchase PRIMARY KEY,
    amount      numeric(10,2),
    purchaseDate datetime,
    contactId   int
        CONSTRAINT FKsales_contact$hasPurchasesIn$sales_purchase
            REFERENCES sales.contact(contactId)
)
```

Now consider that you want to calculate the sales totals and dates for the contact, and add these columns to the allowed pool of choices. By tailoring the output when transmitting the results of the query back to the user, you can save bandwidth, CPU, and disk I/O. As I've stressed, values such as this should usually be calculated rather than stored, especially when working on an OLTP system.

In this case, consider the following two possibilities. If the user asks for a sales summary column, then the client will send the whole query:

```
SELECT  contact.contactId, contact.firstName, contact.lastName,
                sales.yearToDateSales, sales.lastSaleDate
FROM   sales.contact as contact
        LEFT OUTER JOIN
```

```
        (SELECT  contactId,
                 SUM(amount) AS yearToDateSales,
                 MAX(purchaseDate) AS lastSaleDate
         FROM    sales.purchase
         WHERE   purchaseDate >= --the first day of the current year
                              cast(datepart(year,getdate()) as char(4)) + '0101'
         GROUP   by contactId) AS sales
         ON contact.contactId = sales.contactId
WHERE    contact.lastName like 'Johns%'
```

If the user doesn't ask for a sales summary column, the client will send only the bolded query:

```
SELECT  contact.contactId, contact.firstName, contact.lastName
                --,sales.yearToDateSales, sales.lastSaleDate
FROM    sales.contact as contact
--            LEFT OUTER JOIN
--                (SELECT  contactId,
--                         SUM(amount) AS yearToDateSales,
--                         MAX(purchaseDate) AS lastSaleDate
--                 FROM    sales.purchase
--                 WHERE   purchaseDate >= --the first day of the current year
--                                      cast(datepart(year,getdate()) as char(4)) + '0101'
--                 GROUP   by contactId) AS sales
--                 ON contact.contactId = sales.contactId
WHERE    contact.lastName like 'Johns%'
```

In this way, you have the flexibility to execute only the code that's needed. You can achieve the same kind of thing with INSERT and UPDATE statements.

■**Note** Conversely, it's hard to vary the columns, and especially the INSERT and UPDATE lists, in your stored procedure code.

In the same vein, when using *ad hoc* calls, it's trivial (from a SQL standpoint) to build UPDATE statements that include only the columns that have *changed* in the set lists, rather than updating all columns, as can be necessary for a stored procedure. For example, take the customer columns from earlier: customerId, name, and number. You could just update all columns:

```
UPDATE sales.contact
SET    firstName = 'First Name',
       lastName = 'Last Name',
       companyName = 'Company Name',
       contactNotes = 'Notes about the contact',
       personalNotes = 'Notes about the person'
WHERE contactId = 1
```

But what if only the firstName column changed? What if the company column is part of an index, and it has data validations that take three seconds to execute? How do you deal with varchar(max) columns (or other long types)? Should the application pass the entire value back and forth each time, or should it do some sort of complex procedure logic to do a chunked write using the .WRITE option on the UPDATE statement? Using straight SQL, to update the firstName column only, you can simply execute the following code:

```
UPDATE sales.contact
SET    firstName = 'First Name'
WHERE  contactId = 1
```

Some of this can be done with dynamic SQL calls built into the stored procedure, but it's far easier to know if data changed right at the source where the data is being edited, rather than having to check the data beforehand. For example, you could have every textbox and combo box implement a "data changed" property, and only perform a column update when the original value doesn't match the value currently displayed.

One place where using *ad hoc* SQL can produce more reasonable code is in the area of optional parameters. Say in your query to the sales.contact table your UI allowed you to filter on either firstName, lastName, or both. For example, take the following code to filter on both firstName and lastName:

```
SELECT firstName, lastName, companyName
FROM   sales.contact
WHERE  firstName like 'firstNameValue%'
  AND  lastName like 'lastNamevalue%'
```

What if the user only needed to filter by last name? Sending the '%' wildcard for firstName can cause code to perform less than adequately, especially when the query is parameterized. (I'll cover query parameterization in the next section, "Performance.")

Using *ad hoc* SQL, you can simply change to code to the following:

```
SELECT firstName, lastName, companyName
FROM   sales.contact
WHERE  lastName like 'lastNamevalue%'
```

This doesn't require any difficult coding. Just remove one of the criteria from the WHERE clause, and the optimizer needn't consider the other. What if you want to OR the criteria instead? Simply build the query with OR instead of AND. This kind of flexibility is one of the biggest positives to using *ad hoc* SQL calls.

For a stored procedure, you might need to write code such as the following:

```
IF @firstNameValue <> '%'
      SELECT firstName, lastName, companyName
      FROM   sales.contact
      WHERE  firstName like @firstNameValue
        AND  lastName like @lastNameValue
ELSE
      SELECT firstName, lastName, companyName
      FROM   sales.contact
      WHERE  lastName like @lastNameValue
```

A better way to do this with stored procedures is to create two stored procedures, one with the first query, and another with the second query. You'd change this to the following code:

```
IF @firstNameValue <> '%'
        EXECUTE sales.contact$get @firstNameValue, @lastNameValue
ELSE
        EXECUTE sales.contact$getLastOnly @firstNameValue, @lastNameValue
```

You can do some of this kind of *ad hoc* SQL writing using dynamic SQL in stored procedures. However, you might have to do a good bit of these sorts of IF blocks to arrive at which parameters aren't applicable in various datatypes. Because you know which parameters are applicable, due to knowing what the user filled in, it can be far easier to handle this situation using *ad hoc* SQL.

Performance

Performance gains from using straight SQL calls are centered around performance topics, as in the previous section. Because you can omit parts of queries that don't make sense in some cases, it's easier to avoid executing unnecessary code.

The age-old reason that people used stored procedures was that the query processor cached their plans. Every time you executed a procedure, you didn't have to decide the best way to execute the query. In SQL Server 7.0, cached plans were extended to include *ad hoc* SQL. However, the standard for what can be cached is pretty strict. For two calls to the server to use the same plan, the statements that are sent must be identical, except possibly for the scalar values in search arguments. Identical means identical; add a comment, change the case, or even add a space character, and the plan is blown. SQL Server can build query plans that have parameters, which allow plan reuse by subsequent calls. However, overall, stored procedures are better when it comes to using cached plans for performance.

For example, consider the following two queries (using AdventureWorks tables for this example, as that database has a nice amount of data to work with):

```
SELECT address.AddressLine1, address.AddressLine2,
        address.City, state.StateProvinceCode, address.PostalCode
FROM    Person.Address as address
            join Person.StateProvince as state
                on address.stateProvinceId = state.stateProvinceId
WHERE   address.AddressLine1 = '1, rue Pierre-Demoulin'
```

Also consider this query:

```
SELECT address.AddressLine1, address.AddressLine2,
        address.City, state.StateProvinceCode, address.PostalCode
FROM    Person.Address AS address
            join Person.StateProvince AS state
                on address.stateProvinceId = state.stateProvinceId
WHERE   address.AddressLine1 = '1, rue Pierre-Demoulin'
```

These queries can't share plans because the AS in the first query is lowercase, but in the second it's uppercase. This isn't a big problem, because when you use this from an application you probably won't be reformatting the query too often. Whenever this exact query is sent again, the query processor reuses the plan. However, let's say these two queries did match up perfectly. How often do you send the same query to the server with the same values? SQL Server can parameterize certain types of queries, so you can vary the literal values and use the same plans.

By default, the optimizer doesn't parameterize most queries, and caches most plans as straight text, unless the query is simple. For example, it can only reference a single table (check for "Forced Parameterization" in Books Online for the complete details). When the query meets the strict requirements, it changes each literal it finds in the query string into a parameter. The next time the query is executed with different literal values, the same plan can be used. For example, take this simpler form of the previous query:

```
SELECT address.AddressLine1, address.AddressLine2
FROM   Person.Address AS address
WHERE  address.AddressLine1 = '1, rue Pierre-Demoulin'
```

The plan (from setting showplan_text on) is as follows:

```
|--Index Seek(OBJECT:([AdventureWorks].[Person].[Address].
    [IX_Address_AddressLine1_AddressLine2_City_StateProvinceID_PostalCode]
                                                          AS [address]),
    SEEK:([address].[AddressLine1]=CONVERT_IMPLICIT(nvarchar(4000),[@1],0))
                                                          ORDERED FORWARD)
```

The value of '1,%' has been changed to @1 (which is in **bold** in the plan), and the value is filled in from the literal at execute time. However, try executing this query:

```
SELECT address.AddressLine1, address.AddressLine2,
       address.City, state.StateProvinceCode, address.PostalCode
FROM   Person.Address AS address
       join Person.StateProvince AS state
            on address.stateProvinceId = state.stateProvinceId
WHERE  address.AddressLine1 ='1, rue Pierre-Demoulin'
```

The plan won't recognize the literal and parameterize it:

```
|--Nested Loops(Inner Join, OUTER REFERENCES:([address].[StateProvinceID]))
     |--Index Seek(OBJECT:([AdventureWorks].[Person].[Address].
         [IX_Address_AddressLine1_AddressLine2_City_StateProvinceID_PostalCode]
         AS [address]),
         SEEK:([address].[AddressLine1]=N'1, rue Pierre-Demoulin')
                                                     ORDERED FORWARD)
     |--Clustered Index Seek(OBJECT:([AdventureWorks].[Person].[StateProvince].
             [PK_StateProvince_StateProvinceID] AS [state]),
                    SEEK:([state].[StateProvinceID]=
                    [AdventureWorks].[Person].[Address].[StateProvinceID]
                         as [address].[StateProvinceID]) ORDERED FORWARD)
```

Note that the literal (which is bolded in this plan) from the query is still in the plan, rather than a parameter. Both plans are cached, but the first one can be used regardless of the literal value included in the WHERE clause. In the second, the plan won't be reused unless the value '1,%' is passed in.

If you want the optimizer to be more liberal in parameterizing queries, you can use the ALTER DATABASE command to force the optimizer to parameterize:

```
ALTER DATABASE AdventureWorks
    SET PARAMETERIZATION FORCED
```

Recheck the plan of the query with the join. It now has replaced the N'1,%' with CONVERT_IMPLICIT(nvarchar(4000),[@0],0). Now the query processor can reuse this plan no matter what the value for the literal is. This can be a costly operation in comparison to normal, text-only plans, so every system shouldn't use this setting. As always when discussing performance-related system settings, test, test, test your system with real test scenarios to see which is better, and don't just guess that a nondefault setting will be better. Generally speaking, using the defaults for most settings is the right way to go for SQL Server optimization.

Performance can certainly be less of a worry than you might have thought when using *ad hoc* calls to the SQL Server in your applications. Also, because you can mold queries as desired, you can gain even better performance in some cases.

Not every query will be parameterized when forced parameterization is enabled. For example, change the equality to a LIKE condition:

```
SELECT address.AddressLine1, address.AddressLine2,
        address.City, state.StateProvinceCode, address.PostalCode
FROM   Person.Address AS address
        JOIN Person.StateProvince as state
            ON address.stateProvinceId = state.stateProvinceId
WHERE  address.AddressLine1 like '1, rue Pierre-Demoulin'
```

The plan contains the literal, rather than the parameter. This is because it cannot parameterize the second and third arguments of the LIKE operator (the arguments are arg1 LIKE arg2 [ESCAPE arg3]). If you change the query to end with WHERE '1, rue Pierre-Demoulin' like address.AddressLine1, it would be parameterized, but that construct is rarely useful.

Pitfalls

I'm glad you didn't stop reading at the end of the previous section, because although I have covered the good points of using *ad hoc* SQL, there are significant downfalls as well:

- Low cohesion, high coupling

- Batches of statements

- Performance tuning

- Security

I'll discuss each of these in the following sections.

Low Cohesion, High Coupling

The number-one pitfall is what you learned is bad in Programming 101: strive for high cohesion, low coupling. Cohesion means that the different parts of the system work together to form a meaningful unit. This is a good thing, as you don't want to include lots of irrelevant code in the system, or be all over the place. On the other hand, *coupling* refers to how connected the different parts of a system are to one another. It's considered bad when a change in one part of a system breaks other parts of a system. (If you aren't too familiar with these terms, I suggest you go to http://www.wikipedia.org and search for these terms. You should build all the code you create with these concepts in mind.)

When issuing T-SQL statements directly from the application, the structures in the database are tied directly to the client interface. This sounds perfectly normal and acceptable at the beginning of a project, but it means that any change in database structure might require a change in the user interface. This makes making small changes to the system just as costly as large ones, because a full testing cycle is required.

For example, consider that you've created an employee table and you're storing the employee's spouse, as shown in Figure 10-2.

Figure 10-2. *An employee table*

Now some new regulation appears that you have to include the ability to have greater than one spouse, which requires a new table, as shown in Figure 10-3.

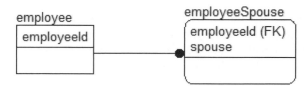

Figure 10-3. *Adding the ability to have more than one spouse*

The user interface must immediately be morphed to deal with this case, or at the least you need to add some code to abstract this new way of storing data. In a scenario such as this, where the condition is quite rare (certainly most everyone will have zero or one spouse), a likely solution would be simply to encapsulate the one spouse into the employee table via a view, and then support some sort of otherSpouse functionality that would be used if the employee had more than one spouse. Then the original UI would continue to work, but a new form would be built for the case where count(spouse) > 1.

Batches of Greater Than One Statement

When you have only individual statements, it's easy to manage *ad hoc* SQL, for the most part. Some queries can get mighty complicated and difficult, but generally speaking all this works great when you have a single, fairly simple statement. However, as complexity rises in a single statement, things get more tough. What about the case where you have 20 rows to insert, update, and/or delete at one time, and in a transaction?

Two different things usually occur in this case. The first way to deal with this situation is to start a transaction using functional code. For the most part, as discussed in Chapter 9, the best practice was stated as never to let transactions span batches, and you should minimize starting transactions using an ADO.NET object (or something like it). This isn't a hard and fast rule, as it's usually fine to do this with a middle-tier object that requires no user interaction. However, if something occurs during the execution of the object, you can still leave open connections to the server.

The second way to deal with this is to build a batching mechanism for batching SQL calls. Implementing the first method is self explanatory, but the second is to build a code-wrapping mechanism, such as the following:

```
BEGIN TRY
BEGIN TRANSACTION

    <-- statements go in here

COMMIT TRANSACTION
END TRY
BEGIN CATCH
    ROLLBACK TRANSACTION
    RAISERROR ('<describe what happened>',16,1)
END CATCH
```

If you want to send a new invoice and line items, use the following code:

```
BEGIN TRY
BEGIN TRANSACTION

        INSERT invoice (columns) values (values)

        INSERT invoiceLineItem (columns) values (values)
        INSERT invoiceLineItem (columns) values (values)
        INSERT invoiceLineItem (columns) values (values)

COMMIT TRANSACTION
END TRY
BEGIN CATCH
    ROLLBACK TRANSACTION
  --or this will not get rolled back
    EXECUTE dbo.errorLog$insert --from back in chapter 6
    RAISERROR ('Invoice creation did not succeed',16,1)
END CATCH
```

Now executing multiple statements in a transaction is done solely on the server, and no matter what the client does, the transaction either completes or not. There's no chance that you'll end up with a transaction swinging in the wind, ready to block the next user who needs to access the locked row (even in a table scan for unrelated items!).

Starting the transaction outside of the server is likely easier, but building this sort of batching interface is always the preferred way to go. First, it's better for concurrency, because only one batch needs to be executed instead of many little ones. Second, the execution of this batch won't have to wait on communications back and forth from the server before sending the next command. It's all there, and happens in the single batch of statements.

Security Issues

The problem with security and *ad hoc* T-SQL is that you have to give the user direct access to the tables, or possibly views, in some way, shape, or fashion. Many folks avoid this by just giving the application complete rights (and its own login) and manage security at the application level. This works, and having a user use his Windows Security login (which most users do remember) avoids having his other passwords written on a sticky note attached to his monitor, embossed in bold letters: **PAYROLL SYSTEM ID: FRED, PASSWORD: FREDSWIFESNAME**. It also avoids having to hard-code passwords for application logins. If you try to use *ad hoc* SQL alone, without using an application login, you'll have to grant the users rights to the base tables. Hence, say users connect to the server using Management Studio, open a table, and start editing it. If they could edit the row with the UI, then they can do it here, and without any UI protection for business rules.

Another issue is your query being hacked by a SQL injection attack. Unless you program your *ad hoc* SQL cleverly, a user can inject something such as the following:

```
' + char(13) + char(10) + 'SHUTDOWN WITH NOWAIT' + '--'
```

Or the user could use something similar, possibly using a semicolon (the T-SQL command delimiter), and cause damage to your server. In this case, just shut it down if the user has rights, but clearly you can see far greater attack possibilities. Preventing this kind of attack is a user interface issue, but there are methods of preventing this sort of problem out there. I'll discuss more about injection attacks and how to avoid them in the "Stored Procedures" section. When using *ad hoc* SQL, you must be careful to avoid these types of issues for *every* call.

The other issues security-wise are performance related. SQL Server must evaluate security for every object as it's used, rather than once at the object level for stored procedures (if the owner of the procedure owns all objects, that is.) This isn't generally a big issue, but as your need for greater concurrency increases, everything becomes an issue!

Performance Tuning

Performance tuning is far more difficult when having to deal with *ad hoc* requests, for a few reasons:

- *Unknown queries*: The application can be programmed to send any query it wants, in any way. Unless perfect testing is done, slow or dangerous scenarios can slip through.

- *Cannot change queries without recompile*: Hence, if you want to add a tip to a query to use an index, a rebuild and redeploy is required. For stored procedures, you'd simply modify the query without the client knowing.

These reasons seem small, but often they're the real killers for tuning. This is especially true when you get a third-party application, and its developers have implemented a dumb query that you could easily change, but it isn't possible to do so (not that this regularly happens; no, not at all).

Stored Procedures

Stored procedures are compiled batches of SQL code that can be parameterized for complex cases. The structure is as follows:

```
CREATE PROCEDURE <procedureName>
[(
        @parameter1  <datatype> [ = <defaultvalue> [OUTPUT]]
        @parameter2  <datatype> [ = <defaultvalue> [OUTPUT]]
        ...
        @parameterN  <datatype> [ = <defaultvalue> [OUTPUT]]
)]
AS
<T-SQL statements> | <CLR Assembly reference>
```

There isn't much more to it. You can put any statements that could have been sent as *ad hoc* calls to the server into a stored procedure and call them as a unit. You can return an integer value from the procedure by using the RETURN statement, or return any datatype by declaring the parameter as an output parameter [other than text or image, though you should be using (max) datatypes instead]. After the AS, you can execute any T-SQL commands you need to, using the parameters like variables. (You can also declare an object that's part of a CLR assembly, which I'll cover in some detail in the last half of the chapter.)

Here's an example of a basic procedure to retrieve rows from a table (continuing to use the AdventureWorks tables for these examples):

```
CREATE PROCEDURE person.address$select
(
    @addressLine1 nvarchar(120) = '%',
    @city         nvarchar(60) = '%',
    @state        nchar(3) = '___', --special because it is a char column
    @postalCode   nvarchar(8) = '%'
) AS
--simple procedure to execute a single query
SELECT address.AddressLine1, address.AddressLine2,
        address.City, state.StateProvinceCode, address.PostalCode
FROM   Person.Address as address
        join Person.StateProvince as state
            on address.stateProvinceId = state.stateProvinceId
WHERE  address.AddressLine1 like @addressLine1
  AND  address.City like @city
  AND  state.StateProvinceCode like @state
  AND  address.PostalCode like @postalCode
```

Now instead of having the client programs formulate a query by knowing the table structures, the client can simply issue a command, knowing a procedure name and the parameters. Clients can choose from four possible criteria to choose the addresses they want. For example, they'd use this if they want to find people in London:

```
person.address$select @city = 'London'
```

Or they could use the other parameters:

```
person.address$select @postalCode = '373%', @addressLine1 = '%mulberry street%'
```

The client doesn't know whether the database or the code is well built, or even if it's horribly designed. Originally our state value might have been a part of the address table, but changed to its own table when we realized that it was necessary to store more information about a state than a simple code. The same might be true for the city, the postalCode, and so on. Often the tasks the client needs to do won't change based on the database structures, so why should the client need to know the database structures?

For much greater detail about how to write stored procedures and good T-SQL, consider the book *Inside Microsoft SQL Server 2005: T-SQL Programming* by Itzik Ben-Gan et al. (Microsoft Press, 2006), or search for "stored procedures" in Books Online. In this section, I'll look at some of the characteristics of using stored procedures as our *only* interface between client and data. I'll discuss the following topics:

- *Encapsulation*: Limits client knowledge of the database structure by providing a simple interface for known operations

- *Dynamic procedures*: Gives the best of both worlds, allowing for *ad hoc*–style code without giving *ad hoc* access to the database

- *Security*: Provides a well-formed interface for known operations that allows you to apply security only to this interface, and disallow other access to the database

- *Performance*: Allows for efficient parameterization of any query, as well as tweaks to the performance of any query, without changes to the client interface

- *Pitfalls*: Drawbacks associated with the stored-procedure–access architecture

Encapsulation

To me, encapsulation is the primary reason for using stored procedures, and it's the leading reason behind all the other topics that I'll discuss. When talking about encapsulation, the idea is to hide the working details from processes that have no need to know about the details. Encapsulation is a large part of the desired "low coupling" of our code that I discussed in the pitfalls of *ad hoc* access. When we coded the person.address$select procedure, it's unimportant to the client how the procedure was coded. We could have built it based on a view and selected from it, or the procedure could call 16 different stored procedures to improve performance for different parameter combinations. We could even have used the dreaded cursor version that you find in some production systems:

```
--pseudocode:
CREATE PROCEDURE person.address$select
...
Declare cursor for (select all rows from the address table)
Fetch first row
While not end of cursor (@@fetch_status)
 Begin
        Check columns for a match to parameters
        If match, put into temp table
        Fetch next row
 End
SELECT * from temp table
```

This would be horrible, horrible code to be sure. I didn't give real code so it wouldn't be confused for a positive, and imitated (and somebody would, though not you!). However, it certainly could be built to return correct data, and possibly could even be fast enough for smaller data sets. Even better, when the client executes the following code, they get the *same* result:

```
person.address$select @city = 'london'
```

What makes this great is that you can rewrite the guts of the procedure without any concern for breaking any client code. This means that anything can change, including table structures, column names, and coding method (cursor, join, and so on), and no client code need change. You'll see this even more clearly in the next section, "Dynamic SQL," as I'll re-create this procedure in a different way.

Dynamic Procedures

You can dynamically create and execute code in a stored procedure, just like you can from the front end. Often, this is necessary when it's just too hard to get a good answer using the rigid requirements of precompiled stored procedures. For example, say you need a procedure that needs a lot of optional parameters. It can be easier to let the compilation be done at execution time, especially if the procedure isn't used all that often.

Some of the problems of straight *ad hoc* SQL pertain here as well. You must always make sure that no input users can enter can allow them to return their own results, allowing them to poke around your system without anyone knowing. A common way to avoid this sort of thing is always to check the parameter values and immediately double up the single quotes so that the caller can't inject the old ' + SHUTDOWN WITH NOWAIT + ', or any other far more malicious code.

Also, make sure that any parameters that don't need quotes (such as numbers) are placed into the correct datatype. If you use a string value for a number, you can insert things such as 'novalue' and check for it in your code, but another user could put in the injection attack value and be in like Flint. For example, take the sample procedure from earlier, and turn it into a dynamically created statement in a stored procedure:

```
ALTER PROCEDURE person.address$select
(
    @addressLine1 nvarchar(120) = '%',
    @city         nvarchar(60) = '%',
    @state        nchar(3) = '___',
    @postalCode   nvarchar(50) = '%'
) AS
BEGIN
    DECLARE @query varchar(max)
    SET @query =
                'SELECT address.AddressLine1, address.AddressLine2,
                        address.City, state.StateProvinceCode, address.PostalCode
                FROM    Person.Address as address
                        join Person.StateProvince as state
                                on address.stateProvinceId = state.stateProvinceId
                WHERE   address.City like ''' + @city + '''
                    AND state.StateProvinceCode like ''' + @state + '''
                    AND address.PostalCode like ''' + @postalCode + '''
                    --this param is last because it is largest to make the example
                    --easier as this column is very large
                    AND address.AddressLine1 like ''' + @addressLine1 + ''''

    SELECT @query --just for testing purposes
    EXECUTE (@query)
END
```

There are two problems with this procedure. The first is that you don't get the full benefit, because in the final query you can end up with useless parameters used as search arguments that make using indexes more difficult. I'll fix that in the next version of the procedure, but the most important problem is the injection attack. For example, let's assume that the user that's running the application has dbo powers, or rights to sysusers. The user executes the following statement:

```
EXECUTE person.address$select
                        @addressLine1 = '~''select name from sysusers--'
```

This returns two result sets. No rows are returned because no address lines happen to be equal to '~', but the other result set is the list of users in the database. Not good. The way to correct this is to use the quotename() function to make sure that all varchar values are quoted in such a way that no matter what a user sends to the parameter, it cannot cause a problem. Change the procedure to the following:

```
ALTER PROCEDURE person.address$select
(
    @addressLine1 nvarchar(120) = '%',
    @city         nvarchar(60) = '%',
    @state        nchar(3) = '___',
    @postalCode   nvarchar(50) = '%'
) AS
```

```
BEGIN
    DECLARE @query varchar(max)
    SET @query =
                'SELECT address.AddressLine1, address.AddressLine2,
                        address.City, state.StateProvinceCode, address.PostalCode
                 FROM   Person.Address as address
                        join Person.StateProvince as state
                             on address.stateProvinceId = state.stateProvinceId
                 WHERE  1=1'
    IF @city <> '%'
        SET @query = @query + ' AND address.City like ' + quotename(@city,'''')
    IF @state <> '___'
        SET @query = @query + ' AND state.StateProvinceCode like ' +
                                                    quotename(@state,'''')

    IF @postalCode <> '%'
        SET @query = @query + ' AND address.City like ' + quotename(@city,'''')
    IF @addressLine1 <> '%'
        SET @query = @query + ' AND address.addressLine1 like ' +
                                        quotename(@addressLine1,'''')

    SELECT  @query
    EXECUTE (@query)
END
```

Now you might get a much better plan, especially if there are several useful indexes on the table. That's because SQL Server can make the determination of what indexes to use at runtime, rather than using a stored plan. You also don't have to worry about injection attacks, because it's impossible to put something into any parameter that will be anything other than a search argument, and that will execute any code other than what you expect.

I should also note that in previous versions of SQL Server, using dynamic SQL procedures would break the security chain, and you'd have to grant a lot of extra rights to objects just used in a stored procedure. This little fact was enough to make using dynamic SQL not a best practice for SQL Server 2000 and earlier versions. However, in SQL Server 2005 you no longer have to grant these extra rights, as I'll explain in the next section.

Security

The second most important reason for using stored-procedure access is security (as previously discussed in Chapter 7). You can grant access to just the stored procedure, instead of giving users the rights to all the different resources used by the stored procedure. Granting users rights to all the objects in the database gives them the ability to open Management Studio and do the same things (and more) that the application allows them to do. This is rarely the desired effect, as an untrained user let loose on base tables can wreak havoc on the data. I should note that if the database is properly designed, users can't violate business rules, but they can circumvent business rules in the middle tier, and can execute poorly formed queries that chew up important resources.

Now you have a far clearer surface area on which to manage security, rather than tables. Should a user be able to delete a contact? Possibly. It's easier for an end user to decide if a user can execute deletePersonalContact (meaning a contact that the user owned), certainly.

Making this choice easy would be based on how well you name your procedures. I use a naming convention of `<tablename | subject area>$<action>`. For example, to delete a contact, the procedure might be `contact$delete`, if users were allowed to delete any contact. Naming of objects is completely a personal choice.

A lot of architects simply avoid this issue altogether by letting objects connect to the database as a single user, and let the application handle security. That is fine (though not as good as the user being the one logged in), and the security implications of this are the same for stored procedures or *ad hoc* usage. It will still be clearer what you can or cannot apply security to when using stored procedures.

An exciting improvement in SQL Server 2005 is the `EXECUTE AS` clause on the procedure declaration. In previous versions of SQL Server, if a different user owned any object in the procedure (or function, view, or trigger), the caller of the procedure had to have explicit rights to the resource. This was particularly annoying when having to do some small dynamic SQL operation in a procedure, as discussed in the previous section.

The `EXECUTE AS` clause gives the programmer of the procedure the ability to build procedures where the procedure caller has the same rights in the procedure code as the owner of the procedure—or if permissions have been granted, the same rights as any user or login in the system.

For example, consider that you need to do a dynamic SQL call to a table (in reality it ought to be more complex). First, create a test user:

```
CREATE LOGIN fred with password = 'freddy'
CREATE USER  fred from login fred
```

Next, create a simple stored procedure:

```
CREATE PROCEDURE testChaining
AS
EXECUTE ('SELECT * FROM sales.contact')
GO
GRANT EXECUTE ON testChaining TO fred
```

Now execute the procedure (changing your security context to be this user):

```
EXECUTE AS user = 'fred'
EXECUTE testChaining
REVERT
```

You're greeted with the following error:

```
Msg 229, Level 14, State 5, Line 1
SELECT permission denied on object 'Contact', database 'AdventureWorks',
        schema 'Sales'.
```

You could grant rights to the user directly to the object, but this gives users more usage than just from this procedure, which is probably not desirable. Now change the procedure to `EXECUTE AS SELF`:

```
ALTER PROCEDURE testChaining
WITH EXECUTE AS SELF
AS
EXECUTE ('SELECT * FROM sales.contact')
```

You get back data. You use SELF to set the context the same as the principal creating the procedure. OWNER is usually the same as SELF, and you can only specify a singleton user in the database (it mustn't be a group).

Tip The value of SUSER_SNAME(), which is typically used for logging user actions, won't be usable if you use WITH EXECUTE AS in procedures. That's because after the EXECUTE AS, this function returns the login of the user that you've changed security context to. Use ORIGINAL_LOGIN() instead.

Warning: the EXECUTE AS clause can easily be abused. Consider the following query:

```
CREATE PROCEDURE dbo.doAnything
(
    @query nvarchar(4000)
)
WITH EXECUTE AS OWNER
AS
EXECUTE (@query)
```

This procedure gives the person that has access to execute it full access to the database. Bear in mind that *any* query can be executed, which could easily be used to execute improper code on the database.

Tip Although I am not suggesting that you should avoid EXECUTE AS completely, it must be noted that in the wrong hands it can be harmful to security.

Performance

There are a couple reasons why stored procedures are great for performance:

- Parameterization of complex plans is controlled by you at design time rather than controlled by the optimizer at compile time.
- You can performance-tune your queries without making invasive program changes.

Parameterization of Complex Plans

Stored procedures, unlike *ad hoc* SQL, always have parameterized plans for maximum reuse of the plans. This lets you avoid the cost of recompilation, as well as the advanced costs of looking for parameters in the code. Any literals are always literal, and any variable is always a parameter.

This can lead to some performance issues as well, as occasionally the plan for a stored procedure that gets picked by the optimizer might not be as good of a plan as might be picked for an *ad hoc* procedure. A good example of that is when you use a partitioned view. In the plan, it isn't possible to decide which table to use at plan-creation time, so the query processor might have to touch all tables, rather than just the appropriate table based on the constraints.

The interesting thing here is that although you can save the plan of a single query with *ad hoc* calls, with procedures you can save the plan for a large number of statements. With all the join types, possible tables, indexes, view text expansions, and so on, optimizing a query is a nontrivial task that might take quite a few milliseconds. Now, admittedly, when building a single-user application, you might say, "Who cares?" However, as user counts go up, the amount of time begins to add up. With stored procedures, this only has to be done once. (Or perhaps a bit more frequently. SQL Server can create multiple copies of the plan if the procedure is heavily used.)

Of course, stored procedure parameterization isn't always a perfect thing. When you pass values to your stored procedure, SQL Server uses *parameter sniffing* to take the set of parameters and plug them into the queries being used to build the plan. This is fine and dandy, except when you have a situation where you have some values that will work nicely for a query, but others that work pitifully. Much like I talked about in Chapter 8 on indexing, two different values that are being searched for can end up creating two different plans. Often, this is where you might pass in a value that tells the query that there are no values, and SQL Server uses that value to build the plan. When you pass in a real value, it takes far too long to execute. Using `WITH RECOMPILE` avoids the problems of parameter sniffing, but it then means you have to wait for the plan to be created for each execute, which can be costly. It's possible to branch the code out to allow for both cases, but this can get costly if you have a couple different scenarios to deal with.

This brings me to the next point: tuning procedures without changing the procedure's public interface.

Fine-Tuning Without Program Changes

Even if you didn't have the performance capabilities of parameterization for stored procedures (say every query was forced to do dynamic SQL), the ability to fine-tune the queries in the stored procedure without making *any* changes to the client code is of incredible value. Of course, this is the value of encapsulation, but again, fine-tuning is such an important thing.

Often a third-party system is purchased that doesn't use stored procedures. If you're a support person for this type of application, you know that there's little you can do, other than to add an index here and there.

"But," you're probably thinking, "shouldn't the third party have planned for all possible cases?" Sure they should, because the performance characteristics of a system with 10 rows is identical to one with 100,000. Plus, a system running on a 1-processor laptop with its slow disk subsystem behaves exactly like a RAID 10 system with 20 high-speed 32GB drives, right?

The answer is no (duh). In general, the performance characteristics of database systems vary wildly based on hardware and data sizing issues. By using stored procedures, it's possible to tweak how queries are written, as needed. For example, I've had many queries that ran great with 10,000 rows, but when the needs grew to millions of rows, the queries ran for hours. Rewriting my procedure using temporary tables gave me performance that was several orders of magnitude better. And I have had the converse be true, where I have removed temp tables and consolidated queries into a single statement. The user of the procedures did not even know.

Pitfalls

So far, everything has been all sunshine and lollipops for using stored procedures, but this isn't always true. There are several pitfalls to discuss:

- The initial effort to create procedures can be prohibitive.

- It isn't always easy to implement optional parameters in searches in an optimum manner.

- It's more difficult to affect only certain columns in an operation.

One pitfall that I won't cover too much in this chapter is cross-platform coding. If you're going to build a data layer that needs to be portable to different platforms such as Oracle or MySQL, this need for cross-platform coding can complicate your effort (though it can still be worth it in some cases). Chapter 11 covers the differences and similarities between the SQL dialects and the procedure methodologies of each different platform.

Initial Effort

Of all the pros and cons of stored procedures, initial effort is most often the straw that breaks the camel's proverbial back. For every time I've failed to get stored-procedure access established as the method of access, this is the reason given. There are lots of tools out there that can map a database to objects or screens to reduce development time. The problem is that they suffer from some or all of the issues discussed in the *ad hoc* SQL pitfalls.

It's an indefensible stance that writing lots of stored procedures takes less time up front—quite often it takes quite a bit more time for initial development. Writing stored procedures is definitely an extra step in the process of getting an application up and running.

An extra step takes extra time, and extra time means extra money. You see where this is going, because people like activities where they see results, not infrastructure. When a charismatic programmer comes in and promises results, it can be hard to back up claims that stored procedures are certainly the best way to go. The best defense is knowing the pros and cons, and especially understanding the application development infrastructure you'll be dealing with.

Optional Parameters in Searches

I already mentioned something similar to optional parameters earlier, in the section "Stored Procedures," when we created our stored procedures using LIKE parameters with character strings. But what about integer values? Or numeric ones? You can use NULL values by doing something along the lines of the following code:

```
WHERE  (integerColumn = @integerColumn or @integerColumn is null)
   AND (numericColumn = @numericColumn or @numericColumn is null)
   AND (characterColumn like @characterColumn)
```

Generally speaking, it's possible to come up with some scheme along these lines to implement optional parameters alongside the rigid needs of procedures in stored procedures. If it isn't possible, then you can always use dynamic SQL for these types of queries, with optional parameters. One thing that can help this process is to add the WITH RECOMPILE clause to the stored-procedure declaration. This tells the procedure to create a new plan for every execution of the procedure.

Although I try to avoid dynamic SQL because of the complexity, if the set you need to do this search on is large, dynamic SQL can be the best way to deal with the situation. Using dynamically built stored procedures is the same speed or only slightly slower than using *ad hoc* access from the client, so the benefits from encapsulation still exist.

Affecting Only Certain Columns in an Operation

When you're coding stored procedures without dynamic SQL, the code you'll write is usually pretty rigid. If you want to write a stored procedure to modify a row in the table created earlier in the chapter—sales.contact—you'd write something along the lines of this skeleton procedure (back in the architectureChapter database):

```
CREATE PROCEDURE sales.contact$update
(
    @contactId    int,
    @firstName    varchar(30),
    @lastName     varchar(30),
    @companyName varchar(100),
    @contactNotes  varchar(max),
    @personalNotes varchar(max)
)
AS
BEGIN TRY
        UPDATE   sales.contact
        SET      firstName = @firstName,
                 lastName = @lastName,
                 companyName = @companyName,
                 contactNotes = @contactNotes,
                 personalNotes = @personalNotes
         WHERE   contactId = @contactId
 END TRY
BEGIN CATCH
        EXECUTE dbo.errorLog$insert --from back in chapter 6
        RAISERROR ('Error creating new sales.contact',16,1)
END CATCH
```

This is fine most of the time, because it usually isn't a big performance concern just to pass all values. This problem isn't something you can easily change in the stored procedure, because even with dynamic SQL, the procedure has no knowledge of what has changed in the client. It would be silly to spend the time looking this up.

Generally speaking, in this case I use this sort of procedure as is. If any of the columns require a large amount of costly validations, I might add an INSTEAD OF trigger to conditionally do the update on the column in question if the inserted and deleted columns don't match. In this case, let's assume that it isn't desired to update the contactNotes or personalNotes unless they've changed:

```
CREATE TRIGGER sales.contact$insteadOfUpdate
ON sales.contact
INSTEAD OF UPDATE
AS
BEGIN
    DECLARE @rowsAffected int,      --stores the number of rows affected
            @msg varchar(2000)      --used to hold the error message

    SET @rowsAffected = @@rowcount

    --no need to continue on if no rows affected
    IF @rowsAffected = 0 return

    SET NOCOUNT ON --to avoid the rowcount messages
    SET ROWCOUNT 0 --in case the client has modified the rowcount

    BEGIN TRY
          --[validation blocks]
          --[modification blocks]
          --<perform action>
          UPDATE contact
          SET     firstName = inserted.firstName,
                  lastName = inserted.lastName,
                  companyName = inserted.companyName
          FROM    sales.contact as contact
                      JOIN inserted
                          on inserted.contactId = contact.contactId


          UPDATE contact
          SET     personalNotes = inserted.personalNotes
          FROM    sales.contact as contact
                      JOIN inserted
                          ON inserted.contactId = contact.contactId
          --this correlated subquery checks for rows that have changed
          WHERE   EXISTS (SELECT *
                          FROM    deleted
                          WHERE   deleted.contactId = inserted.contactId
                            AND   deleted.personalNotes <> inserted.personalNotes
                                  or (deleted.personalNotes is null and
                                                  inserted.personalNotes is not null)
                                  or (deleted.personalNotes is not null and
                                                  inserted.personalNotes is null))
```

```
            UPDATE contact
            SET    contactNotes = inserted.contactNotes
            FROM   sales.contact as contact
                      JOIN inserted
                          ON inserted.contactId = contact.contactId
            --this correlated subquery checks for rows that have changed
            WHERE  EXISTS (SELECT *
                              FROM   deleted
                              WHERE  deleted.contactId = inserted.contactId
                                 AND deleted.contactNotes <> inserted.contactNotes
                                     or (deleted.contactNotes is null and
                                                     inserted.contactNotes is not null)
                                     or (deleted.contactNotes is not null and
                                                     inserted.contactNotes is null))
    END TRY
    BEGIN CATCH
            IF @@trancount > 0
                    ROLLBACK TRANSACTION

            EXECUTE dbo.errorLog$insert

            DECLARE @ERROR_MESSAGE varchar(8000)
            SET @ERROR_MESSAGE = ERROR_MESSAGE()
            RAISERROR (@ERROR_MESSAGE,16,1)

        END CATCH
END
```

This is a lot of code, but it's simple. This is one of the rare uses of INSTEAD OF triggers, but it's pretty simple to follow. Just update the simple columns and not the "high cost" columns. Keep in mind that I used varchar(max) columns in the example, and they can be small or large. If these are pretty small—in general, 2,000 to 10,000 characters—this strategy might work fine. However, when (max) columns of any type get large, you need to switch to using the UPDATE with the .WRITE method of modifying these values.

Opinions

Let's recap the pros and cons of the different approaches. The pros of using *ad hoc* SQL are as follows:

- It gives a great deal of flexibility over the code, as the code can be generated right at runtime, based on metadata, or even the user's desires. The modification statement can only update column values that have changed.

- It can give adequate or even improved performance by only caching and parameterizing obviously matching queries. It also can be much easier to tailor queries in which you have wildly varying parameter and join needs.

- The other major benefit is that it's just easy. If the programmer can write a SQL statement, there's less overhead learning about how to write stored procedures.

The cons are as follows:

- Your client code and database structures are tightly coupled, and when any little thing changes (column name for example) in the database, it's often required to make a change to the client code, requiring greater costs in deploying changes.

- Tying multiple statements together can be cumbersome, especially when transactions are required.

- Performance-tuning database calls can be much harder to do, because modifying a statement, even to add a query hint, requires a recompile.

For stored-procedure access, the pros are as follows:

- The encapsulation of database code reduces what the user interface needs to know about the implemented database structures. If they need to change, often you can change the structures and tweak a procedure, and the client needn't know.

- You can easily manage security at the procedure level, with no need whatsoever to grant rights to base tables. This way, users don't have to have rights to modify any physical tables.

- You have the ability to do dynamic SQL in your procedures. In SQL Server 2005, you finally can do this without the need to grant rights to objects using EXECUTE AS.

- Performance is improved, due to the parameterizing of all plans (unless otherwise specified).

- Performance tuning is made far simpler, due to the ability to tune a procedure without the client knowing the difference.

The cons for stored-procedure access are as follows:

- The rigid code of precompiled stored procedures can make coding them difficult (though you can use dynamic SQL to optimize certain parts of the code as needed).

- You can't effectively vary the columns affected by any T-SQL statement.

- There's a larger initial effort required to create the procedures.

With no outside influence other than this list of pros and cons, and experience, I can state without hesitation that stored procedures are the way to go, if for no other reason other than the encapsulation angle. By separating the database code from the client code, you get an effective separation of T-SQL code from user interface code. I'm not suggesting that *all* code that works on data should be in stored procedures. This is often one of the sticking points between the two different opinions on how to do things. More or less, what's called for is to build stored procedures whenever you need to make T-SQL calls. Several types of code act on data that shouldn't be in stored procedures or T-SQL:

- *Mutable business logic and rules*: T-SQL is a rigid language that can be difficult to work with. Even writing CLR SQL Server objects (covered in the next major section of this chapter) is unwieldy in comparison to building an adequate business layer in your application.

- *Formatting data*: When you want to present a value in some format, it's best to leave this to the presentation layer or user interface of the application. You should use SQL Server primarily to do set-based operations using basic DML, and have as little of the T-SQL control of flow language as possible.

The main drawback in earlier versions of SQL Server to using procedures has been eliminated, as it's now possible to use dynamic SQL calls when needed without having to grant a lot of rights to base objects, opening up security holes and complicating security greatly. By carefully using the EXECUTE AS clause, you can change the security context of the executor of a procedure when the ownership chain is broken. So, in any places where a dynamic call is needed, you can make a dynamic call, and it will look to the user exactly as a normal precompiled stored procedure would.

I don't want to sound as if any system based on *ad hoc* SQL is permanently flawed and just a piece of garbage. Many systems have been built on letting the UI handle all the code, especially when tools are built that need to run on multiple platforms. (Chapter 11 covers multiplatform considerations.) This kind of access is exactly what SQL-based servers were originally designed for, so it isn't going to hurt anything. At worst, you're simply not using one of the advanced features that SQL Server gives you in stored procedures.

The one thing that often tips the scales to using *ad hoc* access is time. The initial effort required to build stored procedures is going to be increased over just using *ad hoc* SQL. In fact, for every system I've been involved with where our access plan was to use *ad hoc* SQL, the primary factor was time. "It takes too long to build the procedures," or "It takes too long to develop code to access the stored procedures." "The tool we are using doesn't support stored procedures." All this inevitably swings to the statement that "the DBA is being too rigid, why do we want to . . ."

These responses are a large part of why this section of the chapter needed to be written. It's never good to state that the *ad hoc* SQL is just plain wrong, because that's clearly not true. The issue is which is better, and stored procedures clearly tip the scale, at least until outside forces and developer talents are brought in. However, developer talents using functional programming languages can come in handy building CLR procedures, which the next section will cover.

Choosing Between T-SQL and CLR

In the last section, I approached the topic of stored procedures versus *ad hoc* access, but in SQL Server 2005, there's another option to consider. Now, Microsoft provides a choice in how to program objects by using the enhanced programming architecture of the CLR for SQL Server objects. By hosting the .NET Common Language Runtime (CLR) inside SQL Server 2005, developers and DBAs can develop SQL Server objects using any .NET-compatible language, such as C# or Visual Basic. This opens up an entire new world of possibilities for programming SQL Server objects, and makes the integration of the CLR one of the most powerful new development features of SQL Server.

Of the people I've talked to, this is probably the most feared new feature. One reason is that it's a new thing that isn't fully understood, but it's also feared because the programmers who use the CLR languages aren't generally accustomed to writing set-based code. Objects written in the CLR need to follow many of the same principals as T-SQL.

This is going to be the problem when CLR programmers start writing SQL Server code using C# or VB. If you don't understand T-SQL objects, you might overlook them, and code some uncomfortable objects using the CLR. On the other hand, the same will be said of those of us who have made our living coding T-SQL objects. Some things are done better in the CLR, and some things are better in T-SQL.

In this section, I'll look at the differences between CLR objects and T-SQL objects that you can use directly in the database, exactly the same way as one another (meaning, whatever technology being used is invisible to the client). Because CLR objects are totally new to SQL Server 2005, I'll spend a bit more time introducing how they can be used, versus what has been done with T-SQL objects.

The most important thing is to identify the useful bits and the bits you might want to leave alone until a later version of SQL Server. This fairly large section is going to introduce the new CLR functionality and give you examples of the different objects. Most importantly, I'll discuss when it makes sense to use the CLR and when to stick with T-SQL.

In this latter half of the chapter, I'll cover the following topics:

- *Good reasons to use .NET*: I'll give a list of applications where the .NET objects come in handy and are useful.

- *Hosting the CLR*: I'll discuss how to enable hosting the CLR.

- *Using the .NET CLR for SQL Server objects*: I'll offer examples and discussions on each of the types of objects that can be created in the CLR.

- *Guidelines and opinions*: I'll give you tips on deciding when to use the CLR or T-SQL.

Good Reasons to Use .NET

Many world-class and mission-critical corporate applications have been created using T-SQL and SQL Server, so why integrate SQL Server with the .NET CLR? Integrating the CLR provides a host of benefits to developers and DBAs that wasn't possible or wasn't easy with SQL Server 2000 and earlier. Although Microsoft chose to host the CLR inside SQL Server 2005 for many reasons, the following represent some of the most important motivations:

- *Rich language support*: .NET integration allows developers and DBAs to use any .NET-compatible language for coding SQL Server objects. This includes such popular languages as C# and VB.NET.

- *Complex procedural logic and computations*: T-SQL is great at set-based logic, but .NET languages are superior for procedural code. .NET languages have enhanced looping constructs that are more flexible and perform better than does T-SQL. You can more easily factor .NET code into functions, and it has much better error handling than T-SQL. T-SQL has some computational commands, but .NET has a much larger selection of computational commands. Most important for complex code, .NET ultimately compiles into native code while T-SQL is an interpreted language. This can result in huge performance wins for .NET code.

- *String manipulation, complex statistical calculations, custom encryption, and so on*: As discussed earlier, heavy computational requirements such as string manipulation, complex statistical calculations, and custom encryption algorithms that don't use the native SQL Server 2005 encryption fare better with .NET than with T-SQL in terms of both performance and flexibility.

- *.NET Framework classes*: The .NET Framework provides a wealth of functionality within its many classes, including classes for data access, file access, registry access, network functions, XML, string manipulation, diagnostics, regular expressions, arrays, and encryption.

- *Leverage existing skills*: Developers familiar with .NET can be productive immediately coding SQL Server objects. This includes familiarity with languages such as C# and VB.NET, as well as being familiar with the .NET Framework. Microsoft has made the server-side data-access model in ADO.NET similar to the client-side model, using many of the same classes to ease the transition. This is a double-edged sword, as it's necessary to determine where using .NET inside SQL Server provides an advantage over using T-SQL. This is something I'll consider throughout this section.

- *"Easier" and "safer" substitute for extended stored procedures*: You can write extended stored procedures in C++ to provide additional functionality to SQL Server. This ability necessitates an experienced developer fluent in C++ and able to handle the risk of writing code that can crash the SQL Server engine. Stored procedures written in .NET that extend SQL Server's functionality can operate in a managed environment, which eliminates the risk of code crashing SQL Server, and also allows developers to pick the .NET language with which they're most comfortable.

- *New SQL Server objects and functionality*: If you want to create user-defined aggregates or user-defined types (UDTs) that extend the SQL Server type system, .NET is your only choice. You can't create these objects with T-SQL. There's also some new functionality only available to .NET code that allows for streaming table-valued functions. I'll cover streaming table-valued functions later in this chapter in the "User-Defined Functions" section.

- *Integration with Visual Studio 2005*: Visual Studio 2005 is the premier development environment from Microsoft for developing .NET code. This environment has many productivity enhancements for developers. The Professional version and higher also include a new SQL Server project, with code templates for developing SQL Server objects with .NET. These templates significantly ease the development of .NET SQL Server objects. Visual Studio .NET also makes it easier to debug and deploy .NET SQL Server objects.

Hosting the CLR

Hosting the .NET CLR in SQL Server is a huge advance in SQL Server programmability. To use the CLR inside SQL Server, you must first enable it for the server. By default, running code in .NET assemblies inside SQL Server is disabled. Note that the option to enable the CLR is a server-wide option, and cannot be enabled per database. To enable the loading of .NET assemblies for the server, run the following commands:

```
EXEC sp_configure 'show advanced options', 1
GO
RECONFIGURE
GO
EXEC sp_configure 'clr enabled', 1
GO
EXEC sp_configure 'show advanced options', 0
GO
RECONFIGURE
```

■**Note** To disable the CLR functionality inside SQL Server, execute the same code as earlier, but with the `'clr enabled'` option set to 0. Even if the CLR is disabled, you can still load assemblies and catalog the SQL Server objects—such as functions and stored procedures—that are represented by the .NET assemblies. You get an error when you try to run the objects. Also note that as soon as you try to load an assembly, even with `'clr enabled'` set to 0, and even if the assembly doesn't exist, the CLR loads into memory and takes up more than 20MB of SQL Server's memory pool.

To host a .NET assembly inside SQL Server, you must follow several steps (see Figure 10-4).

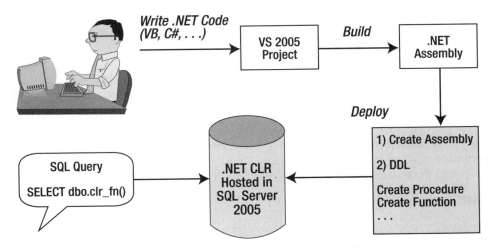

Figure 10-4. *Building and deploying a .NET assembly in SQL Server 2005*

First, a developer writes .NET code using a .NET language such as C# or VB. The developer then builds the .NET code into a .NET assembly for deploying to SQL Server. You use the CREATE ASSEMBLY command to load the assembly into a SQL Server database and verify that SQL Server can host the assembly. For example, to register an assembly in a file named UDFGetToken.dll, you could execute the following code:

```
CREATE ASSEMBLY UDFGetToken
FROM 'c:\ProDatabaseDesignSqlClr\VB\UDFGetToken\bin\UDFGetToken.dll'
```

Once the assembly resides in a database, execute DDL to register the appropriate assembly entry points for use by other SQL Server commands. These DDL statements create SQL Server objects that are assigned to specific code in the assembly. For example, you could use the following DDL code to register a SQL Server function called GetToken that has been created in .NET:

```
CREATE FUNCTION dbo.GetToken(@s nvarchar(4000),
            @delim nvarchar(10), @tokennum tinyint)
RETURNS nvarchar(4000)
AS EXTERNAL NAME
[UDFGetToken].[Apress.ProSqlServerDatabaseDesign.UserDefinedFunctions].GetToken
```

> **Note** The first time an assembly is loaded into SQL Server, or when code in a .NET assembly is called, SQL Server loads the CLR into its process space (if it's not already loaded), and it remains loaded until SQL Server is shut down.

When loading a .NET assembly into a SQL Server database, the DBA chooses between three security permission sets or "buckets" in which to put the assembly, based on the code requirements. These buckets are as follows:

- SAFE: Managed code and local SQL Server data access (default)

- EXTERNAL_ACCESS: SAFE plus access to external resources via managed APIs such as files, registry, and so on

- UNSAFE: Can call unmanaged code and unverifiable code

There's another step to load assemblies with EXTERNAL_ACCESS or UNSAFE permissions. You must mark the database as TRUSTWORTHY using the following command:

```
ALTER DATABASE architectureChapterTest SET TRUSTWORTHY ON
```

Or you must create a strong-named assembly and sign the assembly with an asymmetric key or certificate that has a corresponding login with the appropriate permission (EXTERNAL ACCESS ASSEMBLY or UNSAFE ASSEMBLY):

```
USE master
GO
CREATE ASYMMETRIC KEY CopyFileKey FROM EXECUTABLE FILE =
      'C:\ProDatabaseDesignSqlClr\SPCopyFile\bin\SPCopyFile.dll'
CREATE LOGIN CopyFileLogin FROM ASYMMETRIC KEY CopyFileKey
GRANT EXTERNAL ACCESS ASSEMBLY TO CopyFileLogin
```

> **Tip** This process is much like the process used in Chapter 7 to provide cross-database security.

Using the .NET CLR for SQL Server Objects

Though it used to be the sole domain of T-SQL, developers and DBAs can now create SQL Server objects using any supported .NET language. Table 10-1 lists the various objects created by T-SQL and .NET. Note that the CLR integration and .NET allow us to create two additional SQL Server objects that we didn't have in previous versions of SQL Server.

Table 10-1. *SQL Server Objects in T-SQL and .NET*

Object	T-SQL	.NET
Stored procedures	X	X
User-defined functions	X	X
Triggers	X	X
User-defined aggregates		X
User-defined types		X

Versions of Visual Studio 2005 Professional and higher contain a new SQL Server project that has default code templates for creating each of the SQL Server objects listed in Table 10-1. Using these templates makes it easier for developers to use the proper method-declaration syntax for SQL Server routines (procedures, functions, and triggers) and structure-declaration syntax for aggregates and UDTs. The code templates also include new SQL Server–specific attributes to create the SQL Server objects for use automatically, when the assembly is deployed to SQL Server using the automatic deploy feature within Visual Studio 2005 Professional and higher. These custom attributes include `SqlProcedure`, `SqlFunction`, and `SqlTrigger`.

When deploying SQL Server objects created in .NET, the binary assembly is loaded directly into the `sys.assembly_files` table in the specified database. You can also load the source code and debug symbol files into the same table for debugging and trouble-shooting. Once the assembly exists in SQL Server, DDL is executed to register the entry points in the .NET assembly as typical SQL Server objects. The DDL includes the commands `CREATE PROCEDURE/FUNCTION/TRIGGER/AGGREGATE/TYPE`. This DDL is automatically executed when a SQL Server project assembly is deployed via Visual Studio 2005. Once the .NET entry points are registered, the .NET objects are called just like T-SQL objects. For example, you can call a function from a query or stored procedure, and you can call a stored procedure from a client application or a T-SQL batch.

Let's look at some real-world examples of programming SQL Server objects using .NET and the CLR. I'll cover the following objects:

- User-defined functions
- Stored procedures
- User-defined types
- User-defined aggregates
- Triggers

User-Defined Functions

User-defined functions are the "sweet spot" of coding SQL Server objects with .NET. Let's start with an example of a function that tokenizes a string. To see the benefit that .NET can provide, let's compare a T-SQL version and a .NET version of the function. First, the T-SQL version:

```
CREATE FUNCTION dbo.fn_get_token
(
 @string VARCHAR(8000),
 @delimiter VARCHAR(10),
 @tokennum TINYINT
)
RETURNS VARCHAR(8000)
AS
BEGIN
  DECLARE @startpos SMALLINT
  DECLARE @endpos SMALLINT
  DECLARE @tokencount TINYINT
  DECLARE @return VARCHAR(8000)
  DECLARE @delimlength TINYINT

  SET @delimlength = LEN(@delimiter)
  SET @tokencount = 1
  SET @startpos = 1

  WHILE @tokencount <= @tokennum
  BEGIN
    IF @tokencount < @tokennum
    BEGIN
      SET @startpos = CHARINDEX(@delimiter, @string, @startpos)
      IF @startpos > 0
        SET @startpos = @startpos + @delimlength
      ELSE
        BREAK
    END
    ELSE
    BEGIN
      SET @endpos = CHARINDEX(@delimiter, @string, @startpos)
      IF @endpos = 0
        SET @endpos = LEN(@string) + 1
    END
    SET @tokencount = @tokencount + 1
  END

  IF @startpos = 0
    SET @return = null
  ELSE
    SET @return = LTRIM(RTRIM(SUBSTRING(@string, @startpos, @endpos - @startpos)))

  RETURN(@return)
END
```

Here's a comparable version written in VB:

```vb
Imports System
Imports System.Data
Imports System.Data.Sql
Imports System.Data.SqlTypes
Imports Microsoft.SqlServer.Server

Partial Public Class UserDefinedFunctions
    <Microsoft.SqlServer.Server.SqlFunction(DataAccess:=DataAccessKind.None, _
                Name:="GetToken", IsDeterministic:=True, IsPrecise:=True)> _
    Public Shared Function GetToken(ByVal s As SqlString, _
                    ByVal delimiter As SqlString, _
                    ByVal tokenNumber As SqlByte) As SqlString
    If s.IsNull() Then
        Return SqlString.Null
    End If
    'split string into array at each delimiter
    Dim tokens() As String = Strings.Split(s.ToString(), delimiter.ToString(), _
                                    -1, CompareMethod.Text)

        ' return string at array position specified by parameter
        If tokenNumber > 0 AndAlso tokens.Length >= tokenNumber.Value Then
        Return tokens(tokenNumber.Value - 1).Trim()
    Else
        Return SqlString.Null
    End If
    End Function
End Class
```

Not only is the code for the .NET version simpler to write and debug, it performs significantly faster than the T-SQL version. In an informal test I ran, calling each function against a column in a SELECT query showed more than 100 times the performance benefit using the .NET user-defined function over the T-SQL version.

Let's now look at an example of a streaming table-value function. Our example returns a list of files and the attributes of a specified folder of the file system. This requires using a combination of xp_cmdshell and some parsing logic in SQL Server 7/2000. The VB version follows:

```vb
Imports System
Imports System.Data
Imports System.Data.Sql
Imports System.Data.SqlTypes
Imports Microsoft.SqlServer.Server
Imports System.Collections
Imports System.IO
```

```vb
Partial Public Class UserDefinedFunctions
    <Microsoft.SqlServer.Server.SqlFunction(DataAccess:=DataAccessKind.None, _
        Name:="GetFilesInFolder", FillRowMethodName:="FillRow", TableDefinition:= _
        "FileName nvarchar(255), FileSize int, FileDate datetime")> _
    Public Shared Function GetFilesInFolder(ByVal path As SqlString, _
                                    ByVal pattern As SqlString) As IEnumerable
        Return CType(New FileList(path.ToString(), pattern.ToString()), IEnumerable)
    End Function

    ' this is the function pointed to by FillRowMethodName parameter
    ' of SqlFunction attribute
    ' parameters must include the IEnumerable object returned by
    ' function above (GetFilesInFolder)
    ' followed by each column returned from the function
    Public Shared Sub FillRow(ByVal obj As Object, ByRef FileName As SqlString, _
                                    ByRef FileSize As SqlInt32, _
                                    ByRef FileDate As SqlDateTime)

        Dim fi As FileInfo = CType(obj, FileInfo)
        FileName = New SqlString(fi.Name)
        FileSize = New SqlInt32(Convert.ToInt32(fi.Length))
        FileDate = New SqlDateTime(fi.CreationTime)
    End Sub
End Class

' IEnumerable object that will be returned
' to SQL Server as a relational table
' Note that FillRowMethodName provides access to the "columns"
Partial Public Class FileList
    Implements IEnumerable

    Dim m_path As String
    Dim m_pattern As String

    Public Function GetEnumerator() As IEnumerator _
                    Implements IEnumerable.GetEnumerator
        Return New FileListEnumerator(m_path, m_pattern)
    End Function

    Public Sub New(ByVal path As String, ByVal pattern As String)
        m_path = path
        m_pattern = pattern
    End Sub

    Partial Private Class FileListEnumerator
        Implements IEnumerator
```

```vb
        Dim m_files As String() ' holds list of files in folder
        Dim m_fileInfo As FileInfo() ' includes file information for list of files
        Dim m_fileNumber As Integer = -1


        ' constructor that includes folder path and any file search pattern
        Public Sub New(ByVal path As String, ByVal pattern As String)
            Try
                ' try to get top level files in specified folder using
                ' pattern if supplied
                m_files = Directory.GetFiles(path, pattern,
SearchOption.TopDirectoryOnly)
            Catch
                m_files = Nothing
            End Try
        End Sub


        ' must be implemented according to IEnumerator interface -- returns current
        ' file information for current array number we are on while SQL Server is
        ' looping through collection
        Public ReadOnly Property Current() As Object _
                    Implements System.Collections.IEnumerator.Current
        Get
            Return New FileInfo(m_files(m_fileNumber))
        End Get
        End Property


        ' must be implemented according to IEnumerator interface -- moves to next
        ' array number of files
        Public Function MoveNext() As Boolean Implements _
                        System.Collections.IEnumerator.MoveNext
        m_fileNumber += 1
        If m_files Is Nothing OrElse m_fileNumber > m_files.Length - 1 Then
            Return False
        Else
            Return True
        End If
        End Function


        ' must be implemented according to IEnumerator interface -- resets
        ' array number
        Public Sub Reset() Implements System.Collections.IEnumerator.Reset
        m_fileNumber = -1
        End Sub
    End Class


End Class
```

Because the object is accessing the file system, you must load the assembly where this function lives into SQL Server with the permission set of EXTERNAL_ACCESS. You can mark the project in Visual Studio 2005 Professional and higher with a permission level of External, and you can use Visual Studio to deploy the assembly with the correct permission set. Alternatively, you can manually control the permission set when you execute the CREATE ASSEMBLY statement:

```
CREATE ASSEMBLY TVFFileList
FROM 'c:\ProDatabaseDesignSqlClr\TVFFileList\VB\bin\TVFFileList.dll'
WITH PERMISSION_ SET = EXTERNAL_ACCESS
```

Please see the description earlier in the "Hosting the CLR" section about the requirements for loading EXTERNAL_ACCESS and UNSAFE assemblies.

This code isn't trivial, but it provides a large benefit. For arbitrary data outside a relational database such as the file system, registry, an RSS feed, or perhaps a web service, it's possible to stream even large amounts of data in an efficient manner as a typical rowset that the query processor can use. Note this approach doesn't have to load the entire set of data in memory before returning each row of data as the result of the function.

Stored Procedures

As a replacement for extended stored procedures, .NET stored procedures provide a safe and relatively easy means to extend the functionality of SQL Server 2005. Examples of extended stored procedures that can be used to extend SQL Server include xp_sendmail, xp_cmdshell, and xp_regread. Traditionally, extended stored procedures required using a language such as C++, and ran in-process with the sqlservr.exe process. .NET stored procedures have the same capabilities as traditional extended stored procedures, but they're easier to code and run in the safer environment of managed code. You can assign the special security permissions discussed earlier in this chapter to each .NET assembly, and they provide an additional layer of ensuring the safety of the code. Another means of extending SQL Server was using the extended stored procedures beginning with sp_OA%. These used OLE automation to call COM objects that could be used to do things that T-SQL was unable to accomplish on its own. .NET is an admirable replacement for the sp_OA% procedures and COM objects, as you can now use the .NET Framework classes to perform the same functionality as COM objects can.

Let's see an example of a stored procedure written in VB that copies a file, given a source and destination locations:

```
Imports System
Imports System.Data
Imports System.Data.Sql
Imports System.Data.SqlTypes
Imports Microsoft.SqlServer.Server
Imports System.IO

Partial Public Class StoredProcedures
    <Microsoft.SqlServer.Server.SqlProcedure(Name:="CopyFile")> _
    Public Shared Sub CopyFile(ByVal sourceFile As SqlString, _
            ByVal destinationFile As SqlString, ByVal overwrite As SqlBoolean)
        ' check if source file exists
```

```
    If File.Exists(sourceFile.ToString()) Then
        ' if destination file exists, try to delete it if overwrite
        ' flag is set to true
        If File.Exists(destinationFile.ToString()) Then
            If overwrite = True Then
                File.Delete(destinationFile.ToString())
            Else
                Throw New ArgumentException("Destination file already exists.")
            End If
        End If
        ' Use .NET class to copy file
        Try
            File.Copy(sourceFile.ToString(), destinationFile.ToString())
        Catch ex As Exception
            Throw New Exception("Could not copy file. " & ex.Message)
        End Try
    Else
        Throw New ArgumentException("Source file does not exist.")
    End If
End Sub
End Class
```

■ Note This stored procedure must be part of an assembly that's loaded with the EXTERNAL_ACCESS permission set. See the description earlier in the "Hosting the CLR" section on the steps to do this.

Extending SQL Server with stored procedures that perform tasks other than accessing data is relatively easy and safe to code with .NET. However, most stored procedures are used to access data. When does it make sense to use .NET to code stored procedures that access data? Let's first take a look at example T-SQL and .NET stored procedures that get a count of orders for a specified customer using the Northwind database. Here's the T-SQL version:

```
CREATE PROCEDURE dbo.sales$orderCount
(@CustID INT)
AS
SET NOCOUNT ON
SELECT COUNT(*) FROM Sales.SalesOrderHeader WHERE CustomerID = @CustID
RETURN
```

Here's the same stored procedure written using VB:

```
Imports System
Imports System.Data
Imports System.Data.Sql
Imports System.Data.SqlTypes
Imports Microsoft.SqlServer.Server
Imports System.Data.SqlClient
```

```
Partial Public Class StoredProcedures
    <Microsoft.SqlServer.Server.SqlProcedure(Name:="sales$orderCount")> _
    Public Shared Sub GetSalesOrderCount(ByVal customerId As SqlInt32)
        Dim sql As String = "SELECT COUNT(*) FROM Sales.SalesOrderHeader " _
                            & "WHERE CustomerID = @CustId"
        ' context connection=true for connection string indicates
        ' we will be accessing
        ' data from instance of SQL Server that code is running from
        Using cn As New SqlConnection("context connection=true")
            Using cmd As New SqlCommand(sql, cn)
                Dim prmCustId As SqlParameter = cmd.Parameters.Add _
                            (New SqlParameter("@CustId", SqlDbType.Int, 4))
                prmCustId.Value = customerId.Value
                cn.Open()
                ' SqlContext is context that code is running in on SQL Server.
                ' Pipe is a class used to send data to client
                SqlContext.Pipe.ExecuteAndSend(cmd)
                cn.Close()
            End Using
        End Using
    End Sub
End Class


-- register the .NET stored procedure with SQL Server
CREATE PROCEDURE dbo.sales$orderCount(@CustId int)
AS EXTERNAL NAME [SPDataAccess].[Apress.ProDatabaseDesignSqlClr.StoredProcedures].
    GetSalesOrderCount --line formatted for the book
```

We're using in-process ADO.NET to access SQL Server data, as denoted by the connection string context connection=true. This is an efficient means of getting data within .NET stored procedures and functions where the data resides on the same SQL Server 2005 instance as the stored procedure or function. In the preceding .NET example, I used the SqlConnection, SqlCommand, and SqlParameter classes, similarly to how you'd typically use them when writing client-side ADO.NET. The only two differences in the preceding code when running in the CLR on SQL Server is the connection string used to denote that the object is accessing data in-process with SQL Server, and the use of the SqlContext and SqlPipe server-side classes to send data back to the client from SQL Server.

When comparing the two versions of the stored procedure, it's easy to see that the T-SQL version is more compact, and easier to debug and maintain. You also don't have to make the transition into and out of the CLR for the T-SQL version. For stored procedures such as this, it makes sense to choose T-SQL. Are there valid reasons for choosing .NET to code stored procedures when accessing SQL Server data? Consider using .NET and the SqlDataReader class if you *must* iterate through a set of data and perform some logic on it. It can be faster than using cursors. That said, it's best to start with T-SQL for your stored procedures that access SQL Server data. If performance of the stored procedure becomes a factor, and there's lots of procedural and computational logic within the stored procedure, it might be worth experimenting by rewriting the stored procedure using .NET. Do this to determine if the procedural and computational logic benefits of .NET make a large-enough performance impact to convert the procedure.

This brings up an interesting topic. It might also be worth considering moving the procedural and computational logic away from the database to the middle tier, and using the stored procedure(s) primarily for data-access routines.

User-Defined Types

.NET user-defined types are an interesting addition to SQL Server 2005. They give us the ability to extend the SQL Server type system. You need to decide exactly where it makes sense to do this. You should consider .NET UDTs only for primitive types such as points and dates, not for traditional object-oriented classes, such as an employee or an order class. Another factor to consider when deciding to employ .NET UDTs is how the client will access them. Part of the power of .NET UDTs is the ability to have the same type defined on the client as it is on the server. This will only occur if the client is a .NET client. If the client isn't a .NET client, the access to the UDT will be through the type methods that return and accept strings. Let's look at an example that was included in earlier betas of SQL Server 2005, but later pulled—a date-only type:

```vb
Imports System
Imports System.Data
Imports System.Data.Sql
Imports System.Data.SqlTypes
Imports Microsoft.SqlServer.Server

<Serializable()> _
<Microsoft.SqlServer.Server.SqlUserDefinedType(Format.Native, _
        IsByteOrdered:=True, IsFixedLength:=True, Name:="Date")> _
    Public Structure DateUDT
    Implements INullable

    ' Private members
    Private m_Null As Boolean
    Private m_year As Integer
    Private m_month As Integer
    Private m_day As Integer

    ' overloaded constructor accepting datetime
    Public Sub New(ByVal sqlDate As SqlDateTime)
        Dim dt As DateTime = CType(sqlDate, DateTime)
        Me.Year = dt.Year
        Me.Month = dt.Month
        Me.Day = dt.Day
    End Sub

    ' overloaded constructor accepting year, month, and day as integers
    Public Sub New(ByVal year As SqlInt32, ByVal month As SqlInt32, _
                ByVal day As SqlInt32)
        Me.Year = CType(year, Integer)
        Me.Month = CType(month, Integer)
        Me.Day = CType(day, Integer)
    End Sub
```

```vb
' overload ToString function
Public Overrides Function ToString() As String
    If Me.IsNull Then
        Return "NULL"
    End If
    Return Me.DateOnly.ToShortDateString()
End Function

' Implement INullable.IsNull
Public ReadOnly Property IsNull() As Boolean Implements INullable.IsNull
    Get
        Return m_Null
    End Get
End Property

' return our UDT as Null value
Public Shared ReadOnly Property Null() As DateUDT
    Get
        Dim h As DateUDT = New DateUDT
        h.m_Null = True
        Return h
    End Get
End Property

' accept a string and parse into our UDT
Public Shared Function Parse(ByVal s As SqlString) As DateUDT
    If s.IsNull Then
        Return Null
    End If
    Return New DateUDT(DateTime.Parse(s.ToString))
End Function

' private property to return date only
Private ReadOnly Property DateOnly() As Date
    Get
        Return DateSerial(Me.Year, Me.Month, Me.Day)
    End Get
End Property

' year property
Public Property Year() As Integer
    Get
        Return m_year
    End Get

    Set(ByVal value As Integer)
        m_year = value
    End Set
End Property
```

```
' month property
Public Property Month() As Integer
    Get
        Return m_month
    End Get

    Set(ByVal value As Integer)
        m_month = value
    End Set
End Property

' day property
Public Property Day() As Integer
    Get
        Return m_day
    End Get

    Set(ByVal value As Integer)
        m_day = value
    End Set
End Property

' sets and returns current date only
Public Shared Function Today() As DateUDT
    Return New DateUDT(DateTime.Now())
End Function

' method to pass in a datetime value from SQL Server
Public Shared Function FromSqlDate(ByVal sqlDate As SqlDateTime) As DateUDT
    Return New DateUDT(CType(sqlDate, DateTime))
End Function

' formats the date with the specified format
Public Function FormatDate(ByVal format As SqlString) As SqlString
    If Me.IsNull Then
        Return "NULL"
    End If
    Return New SqlString(Me.DateOnly.ToString(format.ToString()))
End Function

End Structure
```

To use this UDT, register the assembly with SQL Server, and issue the CREATE TYPE statement to make the new CLR UDT available to the list of types for the specified database:

```
CREATE TYPE Date
EXTERNAL NAME [UDTDate].[Apress.ProSqlServerDatabaseDesign.DateUDT]
```

After you add the type to the database, you can use it just like the intrinsic datatypes, such as int or nvarchar. What's different about .NET UDTs is that they can have properties and methods, and you can load and use the datatype in a .NET client application. You can use T-SQL to declare the UDT like any other datatype, then access its properties or methods:

```
DECLARE @today Date
SET @today = CAST('20052305' AS Date)
SET @today = CAST(CAST(getdate() AS varchar) AS Date)
SET @today = Date::FromSqlDate(getdate())
SET @today = '20050523'
SET @today = Date::Today()
SET @today.Year = 2005
SET @today.Month = 5
SET @today.Day = 23


SELECT @today.ToString()
SELECT Date::Today().ToString()
SELECT Date::FromSqlDate(getdate()).Year
SELECT @today.FormatDate('MMMM dd, yyyy')
SELECT @today.Year
CREATE TABLE dbo.testDate (dt Date)
INSERT INTO dbo.TestDate (dt) VALUES ('20050523')
SELECT dt, dt.ToString(), dt.FormatDate('MMMM yyyy'), dt.Month FROM dbo.testDate
```

The @today variable value is assigned five different ways: casting a string representation as the Date type; casting the result of the getdate() function after converting it to a VARCHAR; setting it to a string representation of a date; using the static function Today() that was coded as part of our udtDate type; and setting the individual properties of Year, Month, and Day. Note that when SELECTing the Date variable or the Date column by itself, it returns the binary representation of the data. To return the string representation, you must use the ToString() method. You can also use any other user-defined methods, such as the FormatDate method, as shown in the preceding code.

To access the methods or properties of the UDT in a client application, the type must be available in an assembly on the client.

ADO.NET has been enhanced to accommodate the new .NET UDTs when accessing UDT columns in SQL Server. You can access UDT parameters in ADO.NET, similarly to how intrinsic SQL Server datatypes are accessed:

```
Imports Apress.ProSqlServerDatabaseDesign
Imports System.Data.SqlClient


Module Module1
    Sub Main()
        Using cn as New SqlConnection _
                ("server=.;trusted_connection=yes;database=architectureChapter")
            Dim cmd as New SqlCommand _
                ("INSERT INTO dbo.testDate (dt) VALUES (@dt)", cn)
```

```
            Dim prm As SqlParameter = _
                    cmd.Parameters.Add(New SqlParameter("@dt", SqlDbType.Udt))
            prm.UdtTypeName = "TestDate.dbo.Date"
            prm.Value = New DateUDT(2006, 2, 5)
            cn.Open
            cmd.ExecuteNonQuery()
            cn.Close
        End Using
    End Sub
End Module
```

You specify the type to use by setting the SqlParamter.UdtTypeName to the appropriate type as registered in the database. Note that you still must have the UDT type available to the client, or the code will fail.

Extending the SQL Server type system using UDTs is certainly an interesting technology and one that has its uses, but it comes with a price. To update the code for a UDT, you must change all columns in any table of the database that are of the specific UDT datatype to a different datatype (most likely an NVARCHAR or VARCHAR), and you must drop the UDT using the DROP TYPE statement. After the new UDT has been loaded and the type created, the columns of any table that referenced the UDT must be changed back to the UDT.

To access the properties and methods of a UDT on the client, and take full advantage of the new datatype, each client must have a copy of the UDT available in an assembly accessible by the client. If the .NET code for a UDT is updated on SQL Server, the UDT class that's registered on each client that makes use of the UDT should stay in sync with the server version to avoid any data problems.

User-Defined Aggregates

User-defined aggregates are entirely new in SQL Server 2005. SQL Server already includes some common aggregate functions such as SUM, COUNT, and AVG. There might be a time when your particular business has a special type of aggregate it needs, or you need a complex statistical aggregate not supplied out of the box by SQL Server. One aggregate that I've always wanted is one that concatenates a list of strings in a column separated by a comma, such as the List() aggregate in Sybase. For example, suppose you wanted to list all the products ordered, separated by a comma in a single column for each order in the AdventureWorks database. To do this prior to SQL Server 2005, you could write a function that concatenated the column using a cursor, or use a T-SQL trick to concatenate the column into a variable. Here's an example using T-SQL and the AdventureWorks database:

```
CREATE FUNCTION dbo.products$byOrderTsql(@OrderId int)
RETURNS nvarchar(4000)
AS
BEGIN
    DECLARE @products nvarchar(4000)
    SET @products= NULL
    SELECT @products = ISNULL(@products + ', ', '') + p.Name
    FROM
        Sales.SalesOrderDetail sod
        JOIN Production.Product p ON sod.ProductID = p.ProductID
```

```
    WHERE
        sod.SalesOrderID = @OrderId
    ORDER BY
        p.Name

    RETURN @products
END

SELECT
    sod.SalesOrderID
  , dbo. products$byOrderTsql (sod.SalesOrderID)
FROM
  Sales.SalesOrderDetail sod
WHERE
  sod.SalesOrderID BETWEEN 50000 AND 51800
```

This avoids using cursors with the dangerous variable-concatenation trick, which makes our function faster, a valid way to get the job done with SQL Server 7 or SQL Server 2000.

■**Note** I say that this trick is occasionally dangerous, because it isn't documented and can give spurious results if using a complex ORDER BY clause.

With SQL Server 2005 and user-defined aggregates, a new option is more generic and potentially much faster:

```
Imports System
Imports System.Data
Imports System.Data.Sql
Imports System.Data.SqlTypes
Imports Microsoft.SqlServer.Server
Imports System.Text

<Serializable()> _
<Microsoft.SqlServer.Server.SqlUserDefinedAggregate(Format.UserDefined, _
                                    Name:="List", MaxByteSize:=8000)> _
Public Structure List : Implements IBinarySerialize
    Private m_sb As StringBuilder

    ' Called when aggregate is initialized by SQL Server
    Public Sub Init()
        m_sb = New StringBuilder()
    End Sub
```

```
' returns string representation of List aggregate
Public Overrides Function ToString() As String
    Return m_sb.ToString()
End Function

' Called once for each row being aggregated -- can be null
Public Sub Accumulate(ByVal value As SqlString)
    ' concatenate strings and separate by a comma
    If m_sb.Length > 0 Then
        m_sb.Append(", ")
    End If
    m_sb.Append(value.ToString())
End Sub

' merge 2 List aggregates together -- used during parallelism
Public Sub Merge(ByVal value As List)
    Accumulate(New SqlString(value.ToString()))
End Sub

' called when aggregate is finished -- return aggregated value
Public Function Terminate() As SqlString
    Return (New SqlString(m_sb.ToString()))
End Function

' implement IBinarySerialize.Read since we used Format.UserDefined
Public Sub Read(ByVal r As System.IO.BinaryReader) _
                        Implements IBinarySerialize.Read
    m_sb = New StringBuilder(r.ReadString())
End Sub

' implement IBinarySerialize.Write since we used Format.UserDefined
Public Sub Write(ByVal w As System.IO.BinaryWriter) _
                        Implements IBinarySerialize.Write
    w.Write(m_sb.ToString())
End Sub
End Structure
```

To use this user-defined aggregate, you must register the aggregate using the CREATE AGGREGATE statement. You can then call it like any other built-in aggregate in SQL Server, with the exception that it needs to be prefixed with the owner of the user-defined aggregate:

```
CREATE AGGREGATE dbo.List(@value nvarchar(1000))
RETURNS nvarchar(4000)
EXTERNAL NAME [UDAggList]. [Apress.ProSqlServerDatabaseDesign.List]

SELECT
    sod.SalesOrderID
, dbo.List(p.Name)
```

```
FROM
   Sales.SalesOrderDetail sod
   JOIN Production.Product p ON sod.ProductID = p.ProductID
WHERE
   sod.SalesOrderID BETWEEN 50000 AND 51800
GROUP BY
   sod.SalesOrderID
```

In my informal testing, running this code using our custom aggregate gives us a performance boost over the T-SQL version (it's 275 times faster) for the 10,000-plus rows that are returned in each. Admittedly, this isn't the fairest test, as the T-SQL version is executing a query for each order to combine the products, while the .NET version is simply aggregating over the products returned from the single query. However, it does demonstrate the new power that's available with the .NET integration, and how it can be leveraged. Versions of Visual Studio 2005 Professional and higher provide a SQL Server project, and a template that includes the stub for the functions that must be included as part of the contract for coding a .NET user-defined aggregate. For each aggregate, you must implement the Init, Accumulate, Merge, and Terminate functions. Besides the obvious performance benefit, there's also the flexibility benefit of being able to use this aggregate with any column of any table. That's unlike the T-SQL version, where it was required to hard-code which column and table was being used.

Triggers

Triggers are probably my least favorite of the new SQLCLR objects. The CLR objects have all the functionality you'd need to make use of triggers, such as control of the current transaction, and knowing which event caused the trigger to fire, but I suspect that the majority of triggers will continue to access data and be best suited for T-SQL. Even in situations where you'd need to use some complex functions, such as regular expression functions or string manipulation, you'd write a .NET scalar user-defined function and call the function from a T-SQL trigger. For example, if there was a need to validate a Social Security number inside of a trigger, I'd first consider writing a user-defined function that validated the SSN, and then call it from a standard T-SQL trigger:

```
Imports System
Imports System.Data
Imports System.Data.Sql
Imports System.Data.SqlTypes
Imports Microsoft.SqlServer.Server
Imports System.Text.RegularExpressions

Partial Public Class UserDefinedFunctions
    <Microsoft.SqlServer.Server.SqlFunction(DataAccess:=DataAccessKind.None, _
            IsDeterministic:=True, IsPrecise:=True, Name:="IsValidSsn")> _
    Public Shared Function IsValidSsn(ByVal ssn As SqlString) As SqlBoolean
        ' use RegEx matching to validate SSN -- returns true if valid, false if not
        Return New SqlBoolean(Regex.IsMatch(ssn.ToString(), _
        "^(?!000)([0-6]\d{2}|7([0-6]\d|7[012]))([ -]?)(?!00)\d\d\3(?!0000)\d{4}$", _
            RegexOptions.None))
    End Function
End Class
```

```
CREATE FUNCTION dbo.IsValidSsn(@ssn nvarchar(1))
RETURNS bit
AS EXTERNAL NAME
[UDFSsn].[Apress.ProSqlServerDatabaseDesign.UserDefinedFunctions].IsValidSsn

CREATE TRIGGER tiu_testTriggerTSQL ON dbo dbo.testTriggerTSQL
FOR INSERT, UPDATE AS
IF UPDATE(ssn)
  IF EXISTS(SELECT 1 FROM inserted WHERE dbo.IsValidSsn(ssn) = 0)
  BEGIN
    ROLLBACK TRAN
    RAISERROR('Invalid social security number', -1, 16)
  END
```

.NET triggers can show a benefit when there's a need to loop through rows and process them one at a time, or when there's complex procedural logic that would be difficult to implement using T-SQL. Using a SqlDataReader with .NET code on SQL Server is the fastest way to loop through rows on SQL Server, outperforming T-SQL cursors. Procedural logic can be easier to code and maintain, and is potentially faster using .NET instead of T-SQL. However, you should probably consider T-SQL first for any triggers that you might write with .NET. Keep .NET triggers in your bag of tricks, should the need arise.

Code Location

I've discussed how we can best use the new SQLCLR objects to help the design and performance of our database applications. Another architecture issue that needs discussing is exactly where to locate our code. One of the design goals of integrating the CLR with SQL Server is the ability to write .NET code easily that can run on both the database server and the middle-tier servers without much change. This gives us the benefit of not having to choose where the code resides until later in the development cycle, and to move the code without significant effort even after our application is deployed. Our code can start out in the middle tier, and we can then port it relatively easily to SQL Server, or vice versa. I think it still makes sense to keep most of the complex business logic in the middle tier, and free up SQL Server to do its job with the data.

If there's complex logic that requires significant data access and frequent roundtrips to the database, it's possible that moving the code to SQL Server could be beneficial. Running the code close to the database removes any network latency, and should improve performance. The tradeoff with moving business logic to SQL Server is the use of resources on SQL Server. There are no definitive rules on when the code should be moved to SQL Server. You should handle it on a case-by-case basis, when the benefit of improved performance exceeds the cost of extra resources on SQL Server. In this case, the design of the CLR integration makes it easy to test the code in each location and determine what's best for the application.

Keep in mind that your database might be one of many databases running on the same SQL Server. Although your code might run great on the database server, the extra resources taken up by business logic on the data tier could eventually tax SQL Server and cause performance issues for other applications. It's easier to scale out an application with additional web servers and application servers than it is to add SQL Servers. It's recommended to try to keep the database code on the database server and the business logic on the middle tier, which is often a web server.

Guidelines and Opinions

The inclusion of the CLR inside SQL Server offers an excellent enabling technology that brings with it power, flexibility, and design choices. There's a concern among DBAs that the CLR is unnecessary and will be misused by developers. Although any technology has the possibility of misuse, you shouldn't dismiss the SQLCLR without consideration as to where it can be leveraged as an effective tool to improve your database designs.

Scalar and table-valued functions written in a .NET language seem to be a great first place to look for improved designs. The SQLCLR as a replacement for extended stored procedures makes sense if you need the functionality to run on the database server. UDTs and user-defined aggregates are two new ways to extend SQL Server. UDTs are an interesting new feature of SQL Server. However, I'd suggest some careful thought before implementing UDTs, as they come with some maintenance and versioning issues.

User-defined aggregates can be a little difficult to write, but if your database design calls for a special aggregate that can be written, downloaded, or purchased, it could help improve your design and performance. You should carefully weigh the benefit of using .NET over using T-SQL to write stored procedures and triggers that access data. T-SQL isn't going away, and is the preferred language for set-based code.

There's a benefit to using .NET to code data access on SQL Server, because you can migrate it relatively easily between SQL Server and the middle tier. However, I think it makes sense to start with a T-SQL implementation for set-based code, and make use of any new features of the T-SQL language in SQL Server 2005 before writing a .NET version. Integrating the CLR with SQL Server gives you some additional tools to design great database applications.

Guidelines for Choosing T-SQL

T-SQL isn't going away with SQL Server 2005. On the contrary, it's being enhanced, along with the addition of the CLR. Much of the same code that you write today with T-SQL in SQL Server 7 or 2000 is still best done the same way with SQL Server 2005. If your routines primarily access data, I would first consider using T-SQL.

The exception to this guideline of using T-SQL for SQL Server routines that access data is if the routine contains a significant amount of conditional logic, looping constructs, and/or complex procedural code that isn't suited to set-based programming. What's a significant amount? You must review that on a case-by-case basis. If there are performance gains, or the routine is much easier to code and maintain when using .NET, it's worth considering a .NET approach instead of T-SQL. T-SQL is the best tool for set-based logic, and should be your first consideration if your routine calls for set-based functionality. I suggest avoiding rewriting your T-SQL routines in .NET unless there's a definite benefit. Otherwise, the code can be a little less efficient, and is arguably more difficult to maintain.

Keep in mind that T-SQL has been enhanced with such features as recursive queries, the ability to PIVOT data, new TRY-CATCH syntax for improved error handling, and other features you can now take advantage of. If there are new T-SQL features you can use to make code faster, easier to write, and/or easier to maintain, you should consider this approach before trying to write the equivalent functionality in .NET. A good practice is to continue writing your data-access routines using T-SQL until you see a significant advantage in doing otherwise.

If you choose to use triggers in your database architecture, they're almost the exclusive domain of T-SQL. There's no magic guideline for a good scenario where .NET triggers are a good use of the technology. For any complex validation that might be done in a trigger, it's probably better to use a .NET scalar function and call it from within a T-SQL trigger. Perhaps if there's significant procedural logic in a trigger, .NET would be a better choice than T-SQL. However, be careful when using complex triggers, and triggers in general, as discussed in Chapter 6.

Guidelines for Choosing .NET

The integration of .NET is an enabling technology. It's not best suited for all occasions, but it has some advantages over T-SQL that merit consideration. As we've discussed, .NET compiles to native code, and is better suited to complex logic and CPU-intensive code than T-SQL. One of the best scenarios for the CLR approach to code is writing scalar functions that don't need to access data. Typically, these will perform an order of magnitude faster than their T-SQL counterparts. .NET user-defined functions can take advantage of the rich support of the .NET Framework, which includes optimized classes for functions such as string manipulation, regular expressions, and math functions. In addition to .NET scalar functions, streaming table-valued functions is another great use of .NET. This allows you to expose arbitrary data structures—such as the file system or registry—as rowsets, and allows the query processor to understand the data.

Another excellent use for .NET is as a safe and relatively easy alternative to coding extended stored procedures. .NET provides access to a host of classes in the .NET Framework, and is a much safer environment than using C++, as I discussed earlier in this chapter. "Regular" stored procedures that access data are most often written with T-SQL. The exception discussed in the preceding section is when the stored procedure contains a lot of procedural code and moves a lot of data around close to the server.

The next two scenarios where .NET can be useful are user-defined aggregates and .NET-based UDTs. You can only write user-defined aggregates with .NET. They allow a developer to perform any aggregate such as SUM or COUNT that SQL Server doesn't already do. Complex statistical aggregations would be a good example. I've already discussed .NET UDTs. These have a definite benefit when used to extend the type system with additional primitives such as point, SSN, and date (without time) types. As I discussed in Chapter 5, you shouldn't use .NET UDTs to define business objects in the database.

Best Practices

The first half of the chapter discussed the two primary methods of architecting a SQL Server application, either by using stored procedures as the primary interface, or by using *ad hoc* calls built outside the server. Either is acceptable, but in my opinion the best way to go is to use stored procedures as much as possible. There are a few reasons:

- As precompiled batches of SQL statements that are known at design and implementation time, you get a great interface to the database that encapsulates the details of the database from the caller.

- They can be a performance boost, primarily because tuning is on a known set of queries, and not just on any query that the programmer might have written that slips by untested (not even maliciously; it could just be a bit of functionality that only gets used "occasionally").

- They allow you to define a consistent interface for security that lets you give users access to a table in one situation but not in another. Plus, if procedures are consistently named, giving access to database resources is far easier.

However, not every system is written using stored procedures. *Ad hoc* access can serve to build a fine system as well. You certainly can build a flexible architecture, but it can also lead to hard-to-maintain code that ends up with the client tools being tightly coupled with the database structures.

I wish I could give you definitive best practices, but there are so many possibilities, and either method has pros and cons. This topic will continue to be hotly contested, and rightly so. In the last few releases of SQL Server, Microsoft continues to improve the use of *ad hoc* SQL, but it's still considered a best practice to use stored procedures if you can. I realize that in a large percentage of systems that are created, stored procedures are only used when there's a compelling reason to do so.

Whether or not you decide to use stored-procedure access or use *ad hoc* calls instead, you'll probably want to code some objects for use in the database. New to SQL Server 2005, there's another interesting decision to make regarding what language and technology to use when building several of these database objects. The best practices for the CLR usage are a bit more clear cut:

- *User-defined functions*: When there's no data access, the CLR is almost always a better way to build user-defined functions. When data access is required, it will be dependent on the types of operations being done in the function, but most data access functions would be best at least done initially in T-SQL.

- *Stored procedures*: For typical data-oriented stored procedures, T-SQL is usually the best course of action. On the other hand, when using the CLR, it's far easier and much safer to create replacements for extended stored procedures (procedures typically named xp_) that do more than simply touch data.

- *User-defined types*: For the most part, the advice here is to avoid them, unless you have a compelling reason to use them. For example, you might need complex datatypes that have operations defined between them (such as calculating the distance between two points) that can be encapsulated into the type. The client needs the datatype installed to get a natural interface; otherwise the clunky .NET-like methods need to be used (they aren't SQL-like).

- *User-defined aggregates*: You can only create these types of objects using .NET. User-defined aggregates allow for some interesting capabilities for operating on groups of data, like the example of a string aggregation.

- *Triggers*: There seems to be little reason to use triggers built into a CLR language. Triggers are about data manipulation. Even with DDL triggers, the primary goal is usually to insert data into a table to make note of a situation.

Summary

In this chapter full of opinions, what's clear is that SQL Server 2005 has increased the number of options for writing code that accesses data. I've covered two topics that you need to consider when architecting your relational database applications using SQL Server. The structure of the database is (reasonably) easy enough. Follow the principles set out by normalization to ensure that you have limited, if any, redundancy of data and limited anomalies when you modify or create data. On the other hand, once you have the database architected from an internal standpoint, you have to write code to access this data, and this is where you have a couple choices.

The case for using stored procedures is compelling (at least to many SQL architects), but it isn't a definite. Many programmers use *ad hoc* T-SQL calls to access SQL Server, and this isn't ever likely to change completely. This topic is frequently debated in newsgroups, with little budge from either side. I strongly suggest stored procedures for the reasons laid out in this chapter, but I do concede that it isn't the only way.

I then introduced the new CLR features, and presented examples and opinions about how and when to use them. I dare say that some of the opinions concerning the CLR in this chapter might shift a little over time (especially as service packs begin to arrive), but for the most part, the CLR is going to be most valuable as a tool to supercharge parts of queries, especially in places where T-SQL was poor because it was interpreted at runtime, rather than compiled. Usually this isn't a problem, because decent T-SQL usually has few functional statements, and all the real work is done in set-based SQL statements.

On the other hand, at times in T-SQL you'd need to loop through a set, iterate over the characters in a string, or something along these lines, where it would seemingly take forever to do a single operation. Add onto this putting a function that did some heavy computing into a SELECT or WHERE clause, and life got worse. Proper application of a CLR user-defined function speeds up many slow-running queries where the user-defined functions based on T-SQL were ill-advised at best. The CLR can add performance benefits and additional functionality to your database solutions when used with care.

The primary thing to take from this chapter is that lots of tools are provided to access the data in your databases. Use them wisely, and your results will be excellent. Use them poorly, and your results will be poor. Hopefully our advice will be of value to you, but as you were warned at the start of the chapter, a good amount of this chapter was opinion.

CHAPTER 11

■■■

Database Interoperability

Designing databases for interoperability imposes a whole new set of requirements on the database designer over and above those imposed for needs of efficiency, availability, or scalability. This chapter describes a number of issues you should consider when designing a database to be interoperable between multiple database platforms. The idea behind interoperability is to design a database from the start that requires little or no redesigning to work on another database platform. I'll discuss interoperability from the perspective of a user who's designing a SQL Server database that is portable to other database platforms.

Step One: Datatypes

The first step in designing a database with interoperability in mind is to start from the ground up. Thus, whenever you design tables or procedural code that requires datatypes, you should use datatypes that are easily transferable among the major database platforms.

It's important to remember that database platforms can support similarly named datatypes, but their implementation could vary. Please consult Table 11-1 for specific requirements of each platform's datatypes.

Table 11-1. *Datatype Compatibility Chart*

All Datatypes on All Database Platforms	DB2	MySQL	Oracle	MSSQL	For Interoperability Use
bfile			X		image
bigint	X	X		X	bigint
binary				X	image
binary_float			X		varbinary
binary_double			X		varbinary
bit		X		X	bit
blob	X	X	X		image
bool, boolean		X			bit, char(1)
char, character	X	X	X	X	
char for bit data	X				char(1)
clob	X		X		text, varchar(max)
cursor				X	None

continued

Table 11-1. *Continued*

All Datatypes on All Database Platforms	DB2	MySQL	Oracle	MSSQL	For Interoperability Use
datalink	X				varchar
date	X	X	X		datetime
datetime		X		X	
dbclob	X				text
dlob			X		text
dec, decimal	X	X	X	X	
double, double precision	X	X	X	X	
enum		X			varchar
float	X	X	X	X	
graphic	X				image
image				X	
int, integer	X	X	X	X	
interval day to second			X		varchar
interval year to month			X		varchar
long			X		text, varchar(max)
long varchar	X				text, varchar(max)
longblob		X			image
long raw			X		image
long vargraphic	X				image
longtext		X			text, varchar(max)
mediumtext		X			varchar
mediumblob		X			image
money				X	float
national character varying, national char varying, nchar varying, nvarchar	X	X	X		
nchar, national char, national character			X	X	
nclob			X		ntext
ntext, national text				X	nclob
nvarchar2(n)			X		varchar
number	X	X	X	X	
raw			X		image
real	X	X	X	X	

All Datatypes on All Database Platforms	DB2	MySQL	Oracle	MSSQL	For Interoperability Use
rowid			X		`int with identity`
rowversion				X	None
set		X			varchar
smalldatetime				X	datetime
smallint	X	X	X	X	
smallmoney				X	None
sql_variant				X	None
table				X	None
text		X		X	clob
time	X				datetime
timestamp	X		X	X	datetime
tinyint				X	int
uniqueidentifier				X	varchar
urowid			X		uniqueidentifier
varbinary				X	binary
varchar, char varying, character varying	X	X	X	X	
varchar2			X		varchar
varchar for bit data	X				varbinary
vargraphic	X				image
XML			X		dlob, clob

This table shows you the various datatypes supported by the database platforms discussed in this chapter. Using the chart, you can see the datatypes supported by Microsoft SQL Server. If you need to convert Microsoft SQL Server T-SQL or SQL code to one of the other platforms, use the datatype referenced in the column headed by "For Interoperability Use." Similarly, use the value in this same column when you wish to convert a datatype from one of the other platforms over to SQL Server. Note that when this column is empty, all database platforms support the datatype on the row of the table.

Step Two: Identifier Rules

When you want to create new objects within a SQL Server database (or any database for that matter), you must abide by the identifier rules for that platform. Identifiers are commonly used to name the columns of a table or variables in procedural code, such as a user-defined function or a stored procedure. It's important to learn the ins and outs of identifiers. Table 11-2 contrasts the identifier rules for SQL Server 2005 as compared to several other popular database platforms.

Table 11-2. *Platform-Specific Rules for Regular Object Identifiers (Excludes Quoted Identifiers)*

Characteristic	Platform	Specification
Identifier size	DB2	128 characters, depending on the object
	MySQL	64 characters
	Oracle	30 bytes (number of characters depends on the character set); database names are limited to 8 bytes
	SQL Server	128 characters (temp tables are limited to 116 characters); old versions of SQL Server that use the DB-LIB limit result set column names to 30 characters
Identifier may contain	DB2	Any number, uppercase character, digit, or the underscore character
	MySQL	Any number, character, or symbol
	Oracle	Any number, character, and the underscore (_), pound (#), and dollar ($) symbols
	SQL Server	Any number, character, and the underscore (_), at sign (@), pound (#), and dollar ($) symbols
Identifier must begin with	DB2	A letter
	MySQL	A letter or number (but cannot be composed entirely of numbers)
	Oracle	A letter
	SQL Server	A letter (in the Unicode Standard 3.2), underscore (_), at sign (@), or pound (#)
Identifier cannot contain	DB2	Spaces or special characters
	MySQL	Period (.), slash (/), or ASCII(0) and ASCII(255); quote (') and double-quote (") are only allowed in quoted identifiers
	Oracle	Spaces, double-quotes ("), or special characters
	SQL Server	Spaces or special characters
Allows quoted identifiers	DB2	Yes
	MySQL	Yes
	Oracle	Yes
	SQL Server	Yes
Quoted identifier symbol	DB2	Double-quote (")
	MySQL	Quote (') or double-quote (") in ANSI compatibility mode
	Oracle	Double-quote (")
	SQL Server	Double-quote (") or brackets ([ ]); brackets are preferred

Characteristic	Platform	Specification
Identifier may be reserved	DB2	Yes
	MySQL	No, unless as a quoted identifier
	Oracle	No, unless as a quoted identifier
	SQL Server	No, unless as a quoted identifier
Schema addressing	DB2	Schema.object
	MySQL	Database.object
	Oracle	Schema.object
	SQL Server	Server.database.schema.object
Identifier must be unique	DB2	Yes
	MySQL	Yes
	Oracle	Yes
	SQL Server	Yes
Other rules	DB2	None
	MySQL	May not contain numbers only
	Oracle	Database links are limited to 128 bytes and may not be quoted identifiers
	SQL Server	None

You can break, or at least bend, many of the rules described in Table 11-2 through the use of quoted identifiers. Quoted identifiers are object names encapsulated within a special delimiter, usually double quotes. SQL Server 2000 and SQL Server 2005 also commonly use brackets ([ ]) as delimiters. You can use quoted identifiers to put normally illegal characters into an object name or to bestow an object name that's normally illegal, such as a reserved word. All the platforms discussed in this chapter support quoted identifiers. Once you have declared an object as a quoted identifier, you should always reference it using its quoted identifier name.

Tip Follow these three rules of thumb when naming objects and choosing identifiers. First, avoid any kind of reserved word in identifiers. Second, avoid specific national characters in identifiers. Finally, avoid key words in identifiers; that is, words that might become reserved words in a future release of the product.

Step Three: Basic SQL Statements

In this section, I'll describe the best way to create interoperable versions of the standard SQL statements: DELETE, INSERT, SELECT, and UPDATE. Note that a full discussion of the syntax and usage of each command is beyond the scope of this chapter. Instead, I focus on the interoperability challenges between SQL Server and other database platforms.

■**Note** Italic syntax shown in the following tables isn't interoperable between database platforms.

Thus, I'll describe the most interoperable syntax to create each database object, and follow that up with important notes and details about variations on each database platform. The assumption is that you might want to move code both *from* SQL Server and *to* SQL Server, so I explain both scenarios.

To learn the full syntax and usage of any of these statements, please refer to SQL Server Books Online.

The DELETE Statement

The DELETE statement erases records from a specified table or tables. The only 100 percent safe and interoperable form of the DELETE statement follows this syntax:

```
DELETE FROM table_name
[WHERE search_condition]
```

Using this syntax, the FROM table_name clause identifies the table where one or more rows will be deleted. The table_name assumes the current schema if one isn't specified. You can alternately specify a view name, as long as the view is built on a single table. The WHERE search_condition clause defines the search criteria for the DELETE statement, using one or more search conditions to ensure that only the target rows are deleted. Any legal WHERE clause is acceptable in the statement. Typically, these criteria are evaluated against each row of the table before the deletion occurs.

Table 11-3 compares the DELETE statement syntax on several major platforms. Note that the syntax displayed in italics is platform specific and cannot interoperate on other database platforms.

Table 11-3. *Comparison of DELETE Statement Syntax*

Database Platform	Syntax

SQL Server	DELETE *[TOP number [PERCENT]]* [FROM] table_name
	  [[AS] alias]
	[FROM table_source [,...]]
	[[{INNER | CROSS | [{LEFT | RIGHT | FULL] OUTER}]
	  JOIN joined_table ON condition][,...]
	[WHERE search_condition |
	  WHERE CURRENT OF *[GLOBAL]* cursor_name]
	[OPTION (query_hint[,...n])]

DB2	DELETE FROM { table_name | ONLY (table_name) } *[AS alias]* [WHERE {search_conditions | CURRENT OF cursor_name}] *[WITH { RR | RS | CS | UR }]*
MySQL	DELETE *[LOW_PRIORITY] [QUICK]* [table_name[.*] [,...]] {FROM *table_name[.*]* [,...] | *[USING table_name[.*] [,...]] }* [WHERE search_condition] *[ORDER BY clause]* *[LIMIT nbr_of_rows]*

Database Platform	Syntax
Oracle	`DELETE [FROM]` ` {table_name	ONLY (table_name)} [alias]` ` [{PARTITION (partition_name) |` ` SUBPARTITION (subpartition_name)}] |` ` (subquery [WITH {READ ONLY |` ` CHECH OPTION [CONSTRAINT constraint_name]}]) |` ` TABLE (collection_expression) [(+)]}` ` [WHERE search_condition]` ` [RETURNING expression [,...] INTO variable [,...]]`

SQL Server

Most significantly, SQL Server also allows a second FROM clause to allow JOIN constructs, as shown in the syntax in Table 11-3. The following clauses aren't transportable to other database platforms:

```
TOP number [PERCENT]
FROM table_source [,...]  (second FROM clause)
[{INNER | CROSS | [{LEFT | RIGHT | FULL] OUTER}]
JOIN joined_table ON condition [,...]
WHERE CURRENT OF [GLOBAL] cursor_name
OPTION (query_hint[,...n])
```

For example, the following interoperable DELETE statement uses a rather complex subquery to erase all the sales records of computer books:

```
DELETE sales
WHERE title_id IN
    (SELECT title_id
    FROM titles
    WHERE type = 'computer')
```

However, SQL Server allows a more elegant construction using a FROM clause and a JOIN clause, which isn't transportable to other database platforms:

```
DELETE s
FROM sales AS s
INNER JOIN titles AS t ON s.title_id = t.title_id
    AND type = 'computer'
```

The second DELETE clause would be illegal on any other database platform.

DB2

DB2 supports the basic DELETE statement, with the addition of transaction isolation control. Note that DB2 does support SQL Server's WHERE CURRENT OF subclause, though it doesn't support the GLOBAL keyword. Clauses that are legal on DB2 but aren't legal on SQL Server include the following:

```
ONLY (table_name)
WITH {RR | RS | CS | UR}
```

The ONLY (table_name) clause restricts cascading deletes in any subtables of the target table or view. There's no correlating clause on SQL Server, though triggers perform the same function.

The WITH {RR | RS | CS | UR} clause controls the transaction isolation level for the DELETE statement. When using this clause, RR means repeatable read (SERIALIZABLE on SQL Server), RS means read stability (READ COMMITTED on SQL Server), CS means cursor stability (SNAPSHOT on SQL Server), and UR means uncommitted read (READ UNCOMMITTED on SQL Server). You can simulate this functionality in SQL Server DELETE statements by using the OPTION clause to control locking behavior manually, or by using the SET TRANSACTION ISOLATION LEVEL command.

MySQL

MySQL allows a number of extensions to the basic DELETE statement, but doesn't support several clauses allowed on SQL Server, such as the WHERE CURRENT OF clause. The following clauses are legal on MySQL, but illegal on SQL Server:

```
USING table_name[.*] [,...]
[ORDER BY clause]
[LIMIT nbr_of_rows]
```

As you can see in the syntax, MySQL also supports a FROM clause for building more effective JOIN constructs. The USING table_name[.*] [,...] clause substitutes the table or tables before the FROM clause and those after the FROM clause.

The ORDER BY clause specifies the order in which rows will be deleted. This is useful only in conjunction with LIMIT. The LIMIT nbr_of_row clause places an arbitrary cap on the number of records deleted before control is passed back to the client. You can simulate this behavior on SQL Server by using a DELETE statement with a SELECT TOP statement as a WHERE clause condition.

MySQL allows deletion from more than one table at a time. For example, the following two DELETE statements are functionally equivalent:

```
DELETE sales FROM clients, sales
WHERE clients.clientid = sales.clientid
  AND sales.salesdate BETWEEN '20040101' AND '20071231'

DELETE FROM sales USING clients, sales
WHERE clients.clientid = sales.clientid
  AND sales.salesdate BETWEEN '20040101' AND '20071231'
```

MySQL does a lot of things behind the scenes to speed up processing. For example, when MySQL is in AUTOCOMMIT mode, it even substitutes a TRUNCATE statement for a DELETE statement without a WHERE clause, because TRUNCATE is faster. The speed of a MySQL delete operation is directly related to the number of indexes on the table and the available index cache. You can speed up delete operations by executing the command against tables with few or no indexes, or by increasing the size of the index cache.

Oracle

When moving between SQL Server and Oracle, it's best to stick with the basic DELETE statement. Oracle allows lots of unique behavior in its implementation of the DELETE statement, such as deleting from materialized views, nested subqueries, and partitioned views and tables, as follows:

```
ONLY (table_name)
PARTITION (partition_name)
SUBPARTITION (subpartition_name)
Subquery [WITH {READ ONLY | CHECK OPTION [CONSTRAINT constraint_name]}]
TABLE (collection_expression) [ (+) ]
RETURNING expression [,...] INTO variable [,...]
```

Oracle has a lot of unique clauses, such as the clause (subquery [WITH {READ ONLY | CHECK OPTION [CONSTRAINT constraint_name] }]), which specifies that the target for deletion is a nested subquery, not a table, view, or other database object. In addition to a standard subquery (without an ORDER BY clause), the parameters of this clause are the WITH READ ONLY subclause, which specifies that the subquery cannot be updated. In addition, the WITH CHECK OPTION subclause tells Oracle to abort any changes to the deleted table that wouldn't appear in the result set of the subquery. The CONSTRAINT constraint_name subclause tells Oracle to restrict changes further based upon a specific constraint identified by constraint_name. You can simulate this behavior on SQL Server using T-SQL procedural code.

You can apply the delete operation to a table-like expression using the TABLE (collection_expression) [(+)] clause, and to a specific partition or subpartition using PARTITION partition_name and SUBPARTITION subpartition_name, respectively. You can query and manipulate specific partitions by using the $PARTITION range function. $PARTITION returns an integer that designates the partition number that you want to query or manipulate. For example, use the following code to select all the rows that are in partition 2 of the Sales_History table, which uses the Xact_range_Fcn partition function based upon the Sales_Date column:

```
SELECT * FROM Production.Sales_History
WHERE $PARTITION.Xact_Range_Fcn(Sales_Date) = 2 ;
```

The RETURNING expression retrieves the rows affected by the command, where DELETE normally only shows the number of rows deleted. The INTO variable clause specifies the variables into which the values are stored that are returned as a result of the RETURNING clause. There must be a corresponding variable for every expression in the RETURNING clause.

The INSERT Statement

The INSERT statement inserts one or more rows into a table or view. The basic and most interoperable form of the statement follows this syntax:

```
INSERT INTO {table_name | view_name} [(column1 [,...] )]
{VALUES (value1 [,...]) | SELECT statement }
```

The clause INSERT INTO table_name (col1, col2, col3) specifies the name of the table (in this case, table_name) and the specific columns within the table that will receive the inserted values (in this case, col1, col2, and col3). You may alternately choose the VALUES (value1, value2, value3) clause, or issue a SELECT statement with the same number and datatype of columns as specified in the column list.

Table 11-4 compares the INSERT statement syntax on several major platforms. Note that the syntax displayed in italics is platform specific and cannot interoperate on other database platforms.

Table 11-4. *Comparison of INSERT Statement Syntax*

Database Platform	Syntax

SQL Server	```INSERT [INTO] table_name [(column1 [,...])```
	 ```{[DEFAULT] VALUES |```
	 ``` VALUES (variable1 [,...]) |```
	 ``` SELECT_statement |```
	 ``` EXEC[UTE] proc_name```
	 ``` { [[@param =] value {[OUTPUT]} [,...]] }```

DB2	```INSERT INTO table_name [(column1 [,...])]``` ```{VALUES	VALUES (value1 [,...])	SELECT_statement }``` ```[WITH { RR	RS	CS	UR }]```

MySQL	```INSERT [LOW_PRIORITY	DELAYED] [IGNORE]```
		 ```[INTO] [[database_name.]owner.] table_name [(column1 [,...])]```
		 ``{VALUES (value1 [,...])
			SELECT_statement	```
				 ``` SET column1=value1, column2=value2 [,...]}```

Oracle	```standard INSERT statement```
	 ``INSERT [INTO] {table_name [[SUB]PARTITION (prtn_name)]
		``
		 `` (subquery) [WITH {READ ONLY
			CHECK OPTION```
			 `` [CONSTRAINT constr_name] }]
				``
				 ``` TABLE (collection) [(+)] } [alias]```
				 ``` [(column1 [,...])]```
				 ```{VALUES (value1[,...])```
				 `` [RETURNING expression1 [,...] INTO variable1 [,...]]
					``
					 ``subquery [WITH {READ ONLY
						``
						 ``` CHECK OPTION [CONSTRAINT constr_name]} }```
						
						 ```conditional INSERT statement```
						 ``INSERT {[ALL
							FIRST]} WHEN condition```
							 ``` THEN standard_insert_statement```
							 ```ELSE standard_insert_statement```

SQL Server

SQL Server supports one unique extension to the basic INSERT statement that isn't interoperable: the ability to insert the results from stored procedures and extended procedures directly into the target table. The following clauses aren't transportable to other database platforms:

```
EXEC[UTE] proc_name { [[@param =] value {[OUTPUT]} [,...] ] }
```

The clause EXEC[UTE] proc_name { [[@param =] value {[OUTPUT]} [,...]] } tells SQL Server to execute a dynamic T-SQL statement or a routine—such as stored procedure, a remote procedure call (RPC), or an extended stored procedure—and insert the result set into a local table. proc_name is the name of the stored procedure you wish to execute, and @param is the parameter(s) of the routine (the @ sign is required). You can also assign a value to the parameters, and optionally designate the parameter as an OUTPUT parameter. The columns returned by the result set must match the datatype of the columns in the target table.

DB2

DB2 supports the basic form of INSERT, with the exception of some added syntax for transaction isolation settings:

```
WITH {RR | RS | CS | UR}
```

As with the DELETE statement, the WITH   {RR | RS | CS | UR} clause controls transaction isolation level. When using this clause, RR means repeatable read, RS means read stability, CS means cursor stability, and UR means uncommitted read. You can duplicate this behavior on SQL Server by adding hints or by using the SET TRANSACTION ISOLATION LEVEL statement.

DB2 strictly enforces rules, such as that values inserted must be compatible with the column datatype. Other circumstances that might force a DB2 INSERT statement to fail include integer and string values exceeding the storage capability of the target column, inserted values not passing CHECK or UNIQUE constraints, and values inserted into a foreign key column not existing in a corresponding primary key elsewhere in the database.

MySQL

MySQL supports several INSERT syntax options that aren't interoperable:

```
LOW_PRIORITY | DELAYED
IGNORE
SET column1 = value1 [,...]
```

Most of MySQL's specialized features engender MySQL's reputation for quick response times to the end user using the LOW_PRIORITY and DELAYED clauses. LOW_PRIORITY defers the execution of the insert operation until no other clients are reading from the table, possibly resulting in a long wait. (You shouldn't use this option on MyISAM tables.) The DELAYED clause enables the client to continue working, even when the insert operation hasn't completed on MySQL.

The IGNORE operation tells MySQL not to insert duplicate values. If MySQL encounters duplicate records and this clause isn't used, the INSERT will fail. The SET column = value clause is an alternative syntax that allows you to specify values for target columns by name.

MySQL behaves quirkily when it comes to datatype mismatches and oversized inserts on CHAR, VARCHAR, TEXT, BLOB, and numeric columns. MySQL trims any portion of a value that has a size or datatype mismatch. Thus, inserting '19.66 Y' into a decimal datatype column inserts '19.66' and trims '...Y' from the value. If you attempt to insert a numeric value into a column that's beyond the range of the column, MySQL will trim the value. Inserting an illegal time or date value in a column results in a zero value for the target column. Inserting the ten-character string into a CHAR(5) column inserts just the first five characters of the string into the column.

Oracle

Oracle's implementation of the INSERT statement allows inserts into many tables simultaneously, conditional inserts, and data insertion into a given table, view, partition, subpartition, or object table:

```
PARTITION (partition_name)
SUBPARTITION (subpartition_name)
Subquery [WITH {READ ONLY | CHECK OPTION [CONSTRAINT constraint_name]}]
TABLE (collection_expression) [ (+) ]
RETURNING expression [,...] INTO variable [,...]
INSERT {[ALL | FIRST]} WHEN...
```

Oracle has a lot of unique clauses for this statement, such as the PARTITION (partition_name) clause and SUBPARTITION (subpartition_name) clause, which identify a specific partition or subpartition of a table where the insert operation should occur.

The (Subquery [WITH {READ ONLY | CHECK OPTION [CONSTRAINT constraint_name]}]) clause specifies that the target for record insertion is a nested subquery, not a table, view, or other database object. Subqueries in the VALUES clause are interoperable with SQL Server, but not with the WITH subclause.

In addition to a standard subquery (without an ORDER BY clause), the parameters of this clause are the WITH READ ONLY subclause, which specifies that the subquery cannot be updated. In addition, the WITH CHECK OPTION subclause tells Oracle to abort any changes to the table concerned that wouldn't appear in the result set of the subquery. The CONSTRAINT constraint_name subclause tells Oracle to restrict changes further based upon a specific constraint identified by constraint_name.

You can apply the insert operation to a table-like expression using the TABLE (collection_expression) [(+)] clause. You should remove this clause when you move the code to SQL Server, because there's no corollary on SQL Server.

The RETURNING expression retrieves the rows affected by the command, where INSERT normally only shows the number of rows deleted. The INTO variable clause specifies the variables into which the values returned as a result of the RETURNING clause are stored. There must be a corresponding variable for every expression in the RETURNING clause.

The conditional and/or multitable INSERT is another of Oracle's unique capabilities. Oracle can use the optional ALL keyword to perform an insert operation on many tables simultaneously. Although this command is beyond the scope of this book, the syntax of the INSERT statement is included so that you can recognize it should you ever see it and need to translate it to SQL Server. You can simulate this behavior on SQL Server only via T-SQL procedural code.

The SELECT Statement

The SELECT statement retrieves rows, columns, and derived values from one or many tables of a database. The basic and most interoperable form of the statement follows this syntax:

```
SELECT [{ALL | DISTINCT}] select_item [[AS] alias] [,...]
FROM {table_name  [[AS] alias] | view_name [[AS] alias]} [,...]
[ [ {INNER | FULL | LEFT [OUTER] | RIGHT [OUTER]} ] JOIN join_condition ]
[WHERE [NOT] search_condition] [ {AND | OR } [ NOT] search_condition [...] ]
[GROUP BY group_by_columns  [HAVING search_condition] ]
[ORDER BY {order_expression [ASC | DESC]} [,...] ]
```

Table 11-5 compares the SELECT statement syntax on several major platforms. Note that the syntax displayed in italics is platform specific and cannot interoperate on other database platforms.

Table 11-5. *Comparison of SELECT Statement Syntax*

Database Platform	Syntax

SQL Server	SELECT {[ALL | DISTINCT] | *[TOP number [PERCENT]*
	    [WITH TIES]]} select_item [AS alias]
	[INTO new_table_name]
	[FROM {[rowset_function | table1 [,...]} [AS alias]]
	*[[join type]*JOIN table2 {[ON *join_condition*]]
	[WHERE search_condition]
	[GROUP BY {grouping_column [,...]| ALL}] [WITH { CUBE |
	    ROLLUP }]
	[HAVING search_condition]
	[ORDER BY order_by_expression [ASC | DESC]]
	[COMPUTE {aggregation (expression)} [,...]
	    [BY expression [,...]]]
	[FOR {BROWSE | XML { RAW | AUTO | EXPLICIT}
	    [, XMLDATA][, ELEMENTS][, BINARY base64]]
	[OPTION (<hint> [,...])]

DB2	SELECT { [ALL | DISTINCT] } select_item [AS alias] [,...]
	[INTO host_variable [,...]]
	FROM *[ONLY | OUTER]* {*table_name* | *view_name* |
	    TABLE ({*function_name*
	    subquery}) [AS alias] [,...] }
	[[join type] JOIN table2]
	[WHERE search_condition] [{AND | OR | NOT} search_condition
	    [,...]]
	[GROUP BY group_by_expression [HAVING search_condition]]
	[ORDER BY order_expression [ASC | DESC]]
	[FETCH FIRST {n} {ROW | ROWS} ONLY]

MySQL	INSERT *[LOW_PRIORITY | DELAYED] [IGNORE]* [INTO] [[database_name.]owner.] table_name [(column1 [,...])] {VALUES (value1 [,...]) | SELECT_statement | SET column1=value1, column2=value2 [,...]}

Oracle	standard INSERT statement
	INSERT [INTO] {table_name [[SUB]PARTITION (prtn_name)] |
	    (subquery) [WITH {READ ONLY | CHECK OPTION
	    [CONSTRAINT constr_name] }] |
	    TABLE (collection) [(+)] } [alias]
	    [(column1 [,...])]
	{VALUES (value1[,...]) *[RETURNING expression1 [,...]*
	    INTO variable1 [,...]] |
	    SELECT_statement *[WITH {READ ONLY |*
	    CHECK OPTION [CONSTRAINT constr_name]} }
	
	conditional INSERT statement
	INSERT {[ALL | FIRST]} WHEN condition
	    THEN standard_insert_statement
	ELSE standard_insert_statement

SQL Server

SQL Server supports most of the basic elements of the ANSI SELECT statement, including all the various join types. SQL Server offers several variations on the SELECT statement, including optimizer hints, the INTO clause, the TOP clause, GROUP BY variations, COMPUTE, and WITH OPTIONS.

When writing interoperable SELECT statements on SQL Server, avoid the following clauses:

```
[TOP number [PERCENT] [WITH TIES]]
[INTO new_table_name ]
[WITH { CUBE | ROLLUP } ]
[COMPUTE {aggregation (expression)} [,...]    [BY expression [,...] ] ]
[FOR {BROWSE | XML { RAW | AUTO | EXPLICIT}[, XMLDATA][, ELEMENTS]
   [, BINARY base64] ]
[OPTION ( <hint> [,...]) ]
```

When moving SELECT statements from SQL Server with these clauses to other database platforms, you'll often have to build elaborate statements or even programs in the native procedural language to implement a workaround. There are no silver bullets for substituting specific interoperable code for each of the different clauses that are unique to SQL Server.

The one exception to this rule is that most database platforms support hints of a similar nature, though the command itself is likely to be different.

DB2

DB2 supports all the typical clauses of the basic SELECT statement. DB2 also supports a subclause of the GROUP BY clause not supported by SQL Server, called concatenated GROUPING SETS. Plus, DB2 supplements the most common clauses with its own variation of the SELECT INTO clause and a FETCH FIRST clause. Clauses on DB2 that aren't interoperable with SQL Server include the following:

```
 INTO host_variable [,...]
FROM [ONLY | OUTER] {table_name | view_name | TABLE ( {function_name |
   subquery} ) }
FETCH FIRST {n} {ROW | ROWS} ONLY
```

The INTO host_variable clause assigns the values returned by the query to the host variable(s). The ONLY and OUTER keywords are optional components of the FROM clause. The TABLE ({function_name | subquery}) clause specifies that the query will return a function result set or the results of a fully declared subquery. The FETCH FIRST {n} {ROW | ROWS} ONLY clause sets a maximum number of rows that the query will retrieve.

DB2 supports four possible join types: INNER, LEFT OUTER, RIGHT OUTER, and FULL OUTER.

MySQL

MySQL's implementation of SELECT includes a few unique clauses, such as the INTO clause, the LIMIT clause, and the PROCEDURE clause, among others. The following MySQL clauses aren't interoperable with SQL Server:

```
[STRAIGHT_JOIN][ {SQL_SMALL_RESULT | SQL_BIG_RESULT} ][SQL_BUFFER_RESULT]
   [HIGH_PRIORITY]
INTO {OUTFILE | DUMPFILE} 'file_name' options
```

```
FROM table_name [{ USE INDEX (index1 [,...]) | IGNORE INDEX (index1 [,...]) } ]
    [LIMIT [[offset_position,] number_of_rows] ]
    [PROCEDURE procedure_name (param [,...] ) ]
{FOR UPDATE | LOCK IN SHARE MODE}
```

You can couple many performance options with a MySQL SELECT statement, similar to hints on SQL Server. The STRAIGHT_JOIN clause forces the optimizer to join tables in the exact order they appear in the FROM clause. The SQL_SMALL_RESULT clause and SQL_BIG_RESULT clause tell the query optimizer to expect a small or large result set, respectively, on a query containing a GROUP BY clause or a DISTINCT clause. As a result of the hint, MySQL builds a temporary work table either in memory (quickly, using SQL_SMALL_RESULT) or on disk (less quickly, using SQL_BIG_RESULT). The SQL_BUFFER_RESULT clause forces the result set into a temporary table so that MySQL can free table locks earlier and speed the result set to the client. Finally, the HIGH_PRIORITY gives the query a higher priority than other statements that modify data within the table. You should use this only for special, high-speed queries.

The FROM ... USE INDEX | IGNORE INDEX clause tells MySQL that the query should use only the named index, or without using one or more indexes, respectively.

The INTO {OUTFILE | DUMPFILE} 'file_name' clause writes the result set of the query to a host file named file_name using the OUTPUT option. The DUMPFILE variation writes a single continuous stream of data to a specified host file. The dumpfile contains no column terminations, line terminations, or escape characters, and is best suited for Binary Large Objects (BLOBs). In addition, there are a couple optional parameters with the INTO clause. The LIMIT subclause constrains the number of rows returned by the query, starting at the record numbered offset_position and returning number_of_rows. You have to provide at least one integer value, which is the number of records to return, and a starting record of zero is assumed. Alternately, you can use the PROCEDURE procedure_name (param [,...]) names with an external C or C++ procedure that processes the data in the result set.

The final optional clause allows the choice of FOR UPDATE or LOCK IN SHARE MODE. The FOR UPDATE clause specifies a write lock on the rows returned by the query on an InnoDB table or Berkeley Database (BDB) table. The LOCK IN SHARE clause specifies read locks on the rows returned by the query so that other users may see the rows, but may not modify them.

MySQL supports the following additional types of JOIN syntax: CROSS JOIN, STRAIGHT_JOIN, and NATURAL JOIN.

MySQL implements something like a SELECT statement called the HANDLER statement. The HANDLER statement is a high-speed SELECT statement, and should be converted to a SELECT statement when moving queries to SQL Server from MySQL.

Oracle

Oracle allows a large number of extensions to the SELECT statement. The following code lists clauses that are specific to Oracle:

```
WITH query_name AS (subquery) [,...]
INTO {variable [,...] | record}
FROM {[ONLY] ... [@database_link] [AS [OF] {SCN | TIMESTAMP} expression] |
    subquery [WITH {READ ONLY | CHECK OPTION [CONSTRAINT constraint_name]}] |
        [[VERSIONS BETWEEN {SCN | TIMESTAMP}
            {exp | MINVALUE AND {exp | MAXVALUE}] AS OF {SCN | TIMESTAMP} expression] |
```

```
    TABLE (nested_table_column) [(+)]
        {[PARTITION (partition_name) | SUBPARTITION (subpartition_name)]}
        [SAMPLE [BLOCK] [sample_percentage] [SEED (seed_value)]}
JOIN ... [PARTITION BY expression [,...] ]
[START WITH value] CONNECT BY [PRIOR] condition
ORDER [SIBLINGS] BY order_expression ... {[NULLS FIRST | NULLS LAST]}
FOR UPDATE [OF [schema.][table.]column] [,...] {[NOWAIT | WAIT (integer)]}
```

The WITH query_name AS (subquery) references a common table expression, which is essentially a named subquery that can be referenced frequently. The INTO clause retrieves a result set into a set of PL/SQL variables or a PL/SQL record.

The FROM clause in Oracle has a variety of options. The ONLY keyword applies to a hierarchical view where you want to retrieve records only from the named view. (Oracle supports hierarchies of tables and views where each higher-level object in the hierarchy contains all the records of objects lower in the hierarchy.) The @database_link clause references a remote Oracle database instance. The AS [OF] {SCN | TIMESTAMP} expression clause implements a flashback query that applies system change numbers (SCNs) to each record that existed at the time of the SCN or TIMESTAMP. Because SQL Server doesn't support flashback queries, you'll have to take an alternative strategy to reproduce this capability on SQL Server. The same applies to the VERSIONS BETWEEN subclause. The VERSIONS BETWEEN subclause defines a flashback query clause to retrieve the changes made to data from a table, view, or materialized view over time.

The TABLE clause is necessary when querying a hierarchically declared nested table. The PARTITION and SUBPARTITION restricts a query to the specified partition or a partition of the table. In essence, rows are retrieved only from the named partition, not the entire table. The SAMPLE clause tells Oracle to select records at random using a random sampling of rows, either as a percentage of rows or blocks, within the result set instead of the whole table. The JOIN clause allows a PARTITION subclause.

The WHERE ... [[START WITH value] CONNECT BY [PRIOR] condition] clause allows control of hierarchical queries across multiple tables in the hierarchy. When translating hierarchical queries from Oracle to SQL Server, you'll most likely have to account for this by doing the following:

- Using a different database design on the SQL Server database

- Using T-SQL procedural code

- Using Common Table Expressions (CTE) on SQL Server

Oracle has a couple variations of the ORDER BY clause that aren't interoperable with SQL Server. The SIBLINGS subclause is used for hierarchical queries. The NULL FIRST and NULL LAST subclauses specify that the records containing NULLs should appear either first or last, respectively.

The FOR UPDATE clause exclusively locks the records of the result set so that other users cannot lock or update them until the transaction is completed. The NOWAIT and WAIT keywords return control immediately if a lock already exists, or wait integer seconds before returning control, respectively.

Oracle Database 10g features a powerful new feature, called MODEL, which enables spreadsheet-like result sets from a SELECT statement. The MODEL clause is a syntactically complex clause. You can reproduce many of its features using SQL Server 2005's PIVOT and UNPIVOT clauses. MODEL, unlike PIVOT, allows you to insert or update values back into the base table.

Note It's well known that cursors on SQL Server can have a profound impact on performance. However, this caveat doesn't apply to Oracle. The reason that cursors don't slow down Oracle's performance is that all SELECT statements execute an implicit cursor behind the scenes. Thus, Oracle SELECT statements and cursors are virtually the same thing. SQL Server, on the other hand, uses different engine operations to execute queries and cursors, thus resulting in a possible performance hit with cursors.

The UPDATE Statement

The UPDATE statement alters values within existing records of a table. The most interoperable syntax for the UPDATE statement follows:

```
UPDATE {table_name | view_name}
SET column_name = { DEFAULT | NULL | scalar_expression} [,...] }
WHERE {search_condition | CURRENT OF cursor_name}
```

Table 11-6 compares the UPDATE statement syntax on several major platforms. Note that the syntax displayed in italics is platform specific and cannot interoperate on other database platforms.

Table 11-6. *Comparison of UPDATE Statement Syntax*

Database Platform	Syntax

SQL Server	UPDATE {table_name | view_name | rowset}
	[WITH (hint1, hint2 [,...])]
	SET {column_name = {DEFAULT | NULL | scalar_expression }
	   | variable_name = scalar_expression
	   | variable_name = column_name = scalar_expression }
	[,...]
	[FROM {table1 | view1 | nested_table1 | rowset1} [,...]]
	[AS alias]
	[JOIN {table2 [,...]}]
	WHERE {conditions | CURRENT OF [GLOBAL] cursor_name}
	[OPTION (hint1, hint2 [,...])]

DB2	UPDATE *[ONLY]* ({table_name | view_name}) AS alias SET { {column_name = { DEFAULT | NULL | expression } [,...]} | subquery statement } [WHERE {search_conditions | CURRENT OF cursor_name}] *[WITH { RR | RS | CS | UR }]*
MySQL	UPDATE *[LOW PRIORITY]* *[IGNORE]* table_name SET column_name = {scalar_expression} [,...] WHERE search_conditions *[ORDER BY column_name1 [{ASC | DESC}] [,...]]* *[LIMIT integer]*

continued

Table 11-6. *Continued*

Database Platform	Syntax

Oracle	UPDATE *[hint] [ONLY]*
	  { [schema.]{view_name | materialized_view_name | table_name}
	    [@database_link] [alias]
	    {[PARTITION (partition_name)] |
	     [SUBPARTITION (subpartition_name)]}
	    | subquery *[WITH {[READ ONLY] [[CHECK OPTION*
	     [CONSTRAINT constraint_name]]
	    | *[TABLE (collection_expression_name) [(+)]]* }
	  SET {column_name *[,...]* = {expression *[,...]* | subquery} |
	    VALUE [(alias)] = { value | (subquery)} *[,...]*
	  WHERE { search_conditions | CURRENT OF cursor_name}
	  RETURNING expression [,...] INTO variable [,...]

SQL Server

SQL Server supports a couple unique clauses within the UPDATE statement, such as the WITH clause, query hints using the OPTION clause, and a secondary FROM clause:

```
WITH (hint1, hint2 [,...])
FROM {table1 | view1 | nested_table1 | rowset1} [,...] [JOIN {table2 [,...]}]
OPTION (hint1, hint2 [,...])
```

To achieve interoperability with other database platforms, you should remove these clauses from your UPDATE statement.

DB2

DB2 supports the basic UPDATE statement, with the addition of transaction isolation control. Clauses that are legal on DB2 but aren't legal on SQL Server include the following:

```
ONLY (table_name)
WITH {RR | RS | CS | UR}
```

The ONLY (table_name) clause prevents cascading the updated records to any subtables of the target table or view. There's no correlating clause on SQL Server, though triggers perform the same function.

The WITH {RR | RS | CS | UR} clause controls transaction isolation level for the UPDATE statement. When using this clause, RR means repeatable read, RS means read stability, CS means cursor stability, and UR means uncommitted read. You can simulate this functionality in SQL Server UPDATE statements by using the OPTION clause to control locking behavior manually, or by using the SET TRANSACTION ISOLATION LEVEL command.

MySQL

MySQL allows a number of extensions over the basic DELETE statement, but doesn't support several clauses allowed on SQL Server, such as the WHERE CURRENT OF clause. The following clauses are legal on MySQL, but illegal on SQL Server:

```
LOW_PRIORITY
IGNORE
ORDER BY clause [LIMIT nbr_of_rows]
```

MySQL allows you to declare transaction priority compared to other transactions using the LOW_PRIORITY and IGNORE clauses. The LOW_PRIORITY clause tells MySQL to perform the update operation only when no other users have a lock on the table. The IGNORE clause tells MySQL to ignore any duplicate key errors generated by constraint violations. You can simulate this behavior using SQL Server hints.

The ORDER BY clause specifies the order that rows will be updated. This is useful only in conjunction with LIMIT. The LIMIT nbr_of_rows clause places an arbitrary cap on the number of records updated before control is passed back to the client. You can simulate this behavior on SQL Server by using an UPDATE statement with a SELECT TOP statement as a WHERE clause condition.

The following example limits the UPDATE to the first ten records encountered in the inventory table according to inventory_id. Also, the values of wholesale_price and retail_price are updated:

```
UPDATE inventory
SET wholesale_price = price * .85,
    retail_price = price + 1
ORDER BY inventory_id
LIMIT 10;
```

Oracle

When moving between Oracle and SQL Server, it's best to stick with the basic UPDATE statement. Oracle allows lots of unique behavior in its implementation of the UPDATE statement, such as deleting from materialized views, nested subqueries, and partitioned views and tables, as follows:

```
ONLY (table_name)
PARTITION (partition_name)
SUBPARTITION (subpartition_name)
Subquery [WITH {READ ONLY | CHECK OPTION [CONSTRAINT constraint_name]}]
TABLE (collection_expression) [ (+) ]
RETURNING expression [,...] INTO variable [,...]
```

Oracle has a lot of unique clauses, such as the clause (Subquery [WITH {READ ONLY | CHECK OPTION [CONSTRAINT constraint_name] }]   ), which specifies that the record to be updated is a result set of a nested subquery, not a table, view, or other database object. In addition to a standard subquery (without an ORDER BY clause), the parameters of this clause are the WITH READ ONLY subclause, which specifies that the subquery cannot be updated. In addition, the WITH CHECK OPTION subclause tells Oracle to abort any changes to the updated table that wouldn't appear in the result set of the subquery. The CONSTRAINT constraint_name subclause tells Oracle to restrict changes further, based upon a specific constraint identified by constraint_name. You can simulate this behavior on SQL Server using T-SQL procedural code.

You can apply the update operation to a table-like expression using the TABLE (collection_expression) [(+)] clause, and to a specific partition or subpartition using the PARTITION partition_name and SUBPARTITION subpartition_name clauses, respectively.

Specific partitions may be affected using the UPDATE statement by including the $PARTITION function to tell SQL Server 2005 which partition to update.

The RETURNING expression retrieves the rows affected by the command, where UPDATE normally only shows the number of rows deleted. The INTO variable clause specifies the variables into which the values returned as a result of the RETURNING clause are stored. There must be a corresponding variable for every expression in the RETURNING clause.

Step Four: Creating Database Objects

In this section, I describe the process of creating interoperable database objects. However, unlike the previous section, I don't detail the exact syntax of every database platform–specific variation. When it comes to database objects such as tables, views, and stored procedures, the differences between databases are manifold and complex. Consequently, I'll describe the most interoperable syntax to create each database object, and follow that up with important notes and details about variations on the various database platforms.

Creating Tables

Manipulating tables is a common activity for database administrators and database programmers. The amount of variation in the CREATE TABLE statement among the various database platforms is quite extreme. The greatest area of variation is in the ways that database platforms implement tables physically on the file system. This variation is because the ANSI SQL standards are abstracted, and don't include any definition for physical implementation of tables. (In fact, because indexes are a means of simply speeding the physical execution of queries against tables, indexes aren't part of the ANSI SQL standard either, believe it or not!) This section details how to create and modify tables.

When writing an interoperable CREATE TABLE statement, use the following syntax:

```
CREATE [TEMPORARY] TABLE table_name
   (column_name data_type attributes [,...] ) |
   [CONSTRAINT constraint_type [constraint_name]
      [constraint_column [,...] ]  [,...] ]
```

The basic CREATE TABLE command describes whether the table is temporary or not, using the keyword TEMPORARY. Next, a comma-delimited series of column definitions follow: the name of the column followed by its datatype—such as INT or VARCHAR(10)—and one or more special attributes.

The two special attributes that are most interoperable are nullability (that is, NULL and NOT NULL), and assigning a DEFAULT value (using the syntax DEFAULT expression, where the expression is an acceptable value for the datatype).

Finally, you may append one or more CONSTRAINT clauses to the CREATE TABLE statement. You use constraints to create PRIMARY KEY and FOREIGN KEY constraints, UNIQUE constraints, CHECK constraints, and to insert DEFAULT values. The constraints are as follows:

- PRIMARY KEY: Declares one or more columns whose values uniquely identify each record in the table

- FOREIGN KEY: Defines one or more columns in the table as referencing columns to a UNIQUE or PRIMARY KEY in another table

- UNIQUE: Declares that the values in one column, or the combination of values in more than one column, must be unique

- CHECK: Compares values inserted into the column that match specific conditions that you define

- DEFAULT: Declares that if no value is provided for the column, then the DEFAULT value will be inserted into the field

The following example shows how to create a table called partners on any major database platform:

```
CREATE TABLE partners
    (prtn_id CHAR(4) NOT NULL,
    prtn_name VARCHAR(40),
    prtn_address1 VARCHAR(40),
    prtn_address2 VARCHAR(40),
    city VARCHAR(20),
    state CHAR(2),
    zip CHAR(5) NOT NULL,
    phone CHAR(12),
    sales_rep INT,
CONSTRAINT pk_prtn_id  PRIMARY KEY (prtn_id),
CONSTRAINT fk_emp_id   FOREIGN KEY (sales_rep)
    REFERENCES employee(emp_id),
CONSTRAINT unq_zip      UNIQUE (zip) );
```

SQL Server

As mentioned earlier, the greatest area of variation among the database platforms is in the physical implementation of a given table. Therefore, avoid the following clauses in the SQL Server implementation of the CREATE TABLE statement when trying to build a statement usable on multiple database platforms:

```
IDENTITY
NOT FOR REPLICATION
ROWGUIDCOL
CLUSTERED | NONCLUSTERED
WITH FILLFACTOR = n
ON filegroup
TEXTIMAGE ON filegroup
```

Although many other platforms support a clause for CLUSTERED or NONCLUSTERED tables, they often mean something quite different from what Microsoft means with its SQL Server tables. In a sense, the term *clustered* means a table that's physically organized according to an index, while the term *nonclustered* means the table is organized as a heap (that is, data is written physically as it arrives, but in no specific order other than the time that it was created).

DB2

IBM's flagship database supports a variety of additions and extensions compared to SQL Server. You should avoid or translate the following clauses of DB2's implementation of the CREATE TABLE statement when interoperating with SQL Server:

```
OF type
AS subquery
FOR tablename PROPAGE IMMEDIATE
ORGANIZE BY DIMENSIONS
DATA CAPTURE
VALUE COMPRESSION
WITH RESTRICT ON DROP
NOT LOGGED INITIALLY
REPLICATED
OPTIONS
```

You can use the additional clauses described in Table 11-7 on SQL Server when translated to their SQL Server corollary clause.

Table 11-7. *DB2 CREATE TABLE Clauses That Translate to SQL Server Clauses*

DB2 Clause	SQL Server Clause
CREATE TABLE ... LIKE	SELECT...INTO
ORGANIZE BY (column_name)	CONSTRAINT PRIMARY KEY CLUSTERED (column_name)
IN tablespace	ON filegroup
INDEX IN tablespace	ON filegroup
LONG IN tablespace	ON filegroup

Notice that DB2 allows you to organize a table by a specific column, which is essentially the same as SQL Server's clustered index. However, be careful to read the vendor's documentation, because you cannot assume that a DB2 column-organized table will have every behavior of a SQL Server clustered index.

You should also be aware that DB2 supports a variety of hierarchical table structures and object-oriented table structures. Also note that DB2 doesn't support the TEMPORARY keyword.

MySQL

MySQL is somewhat different from the other database platforms due to its open-source origins. In fact, you can plug several different types of transaction-processing engines into MySQL, which in turn can have a dramatic impact on the type and functionality of tables available to you. For example, only the BDB and InnoDB transaction-processing engines support fully atomic transactions. If you use other types of tables, you won't be able to execute COMMIT and ROLLBACK statements against transactions operating against the tables in question.

When working on MySQL, avoid the following CREATE TABLE clauses to ensure the highest level of interoperability:

```
IF NOT EXISTS
TYPE = {ISAM | MYISAM | MERGE | MRG_MYISAM}
AVG_ROW_LENGTH = int
COMMENT = 'string'
MAX_ROWS = int
MIN_ROWS = int
PACK_KEYS = {0 | 1}
ROW_FORMAT = {default | dynamic | static | compressed}
RAID_TYPE
RAID_CHUNKS
RAID_CHUNKSIZE
INSERT_METHOD
IGNORE subquery
REPLACE subquery
```

Many of these clauses are only supported by a single specific MySQL table type. For example, all the RAID_xxx clauses are only supported by MyISAM tables.

SQL Server can closely reproduce a number of MySQL clauses in the CREATE TABLE statement, as shown in Table 11-8.

Table 11-8. *MySQL CREATE TABLE Clauses That Translate to SQL Server Clauses*

DB2 Clause	SQL Server Clause
CREATE TABLE ... LIKE	SELECT...INTO
TYPE = HEAP	PRIMARY KEY NONCLUSTERED
TYPE = {BDB	InnoDB}	<no clause needed>
AUTO_INCREMENT = int	IDENTITY(seed)
DATA DIRECTORY = path (MyISAM table type only)	ON filegroup
INDEX DIRECTORY = path (MyISAM table type only)	ON filegroup
GLOBAL TEMPORARY	TEMPORARY

When translating a SQL Server table to MySQL, be sure to use either the BDB table type or InnoDB table type, depending on which transaction-processing engine is installed with your version of MySQL.

Oracle

Oracle has the most elaborate set of syntax for its CREATE TABLE statement. If you were to compare the vendor documentation of the CREATE TABLE statement, you would find that SQL Server has a little more than 50 pages of documentation, but Oracle has more than 150 pages!

Naturally, any such discussion of the Oracle implementation here will be rather high level and cursory. However, a few patterns in the Oracle implementation of the CREATE TABLE statement bear mentioning. First, Oracle allows an enormous amount of control over the way in which a table is physically implemented on disk. For example, you can define all the physical storage characteristics not only of tables, but also of every type of Large Object (LOB) column, redo logs, and archive logs. You can also do this recursively for each of these structures inside the table.

Oracle also supports several types of tables that aren't supported by SQL Server, including XMLTYPE, object-oriented tables, flashback tables, and more.

When working with Oracle, avoid the following CREATE TABLE clauses to ensure the highest level of interoperability:

```
AS objectype [[NOT] SUBSTITUTABLE AT ALL LEVELS]
    <and subordinate clauses>
OF XMLTYPE
    <and subordinate clauses>
ON COMMIT
NO LOGGING
GROUP loggroup
CLUSTER (columnname [,...])
ORGANIZATION EXTERNAL
{ENABLE | DISABLE} ROW MOVEMENT
PARALLEL | NOPARALLEL
NOSORT
COMPRESS | NOCOMPRESS
{ENABLE | DISABLE} [NO]VALIDATE
```

Note that both OBJECT and XMLTYPE tables in Oracle have a number of associated subordinate clauses that apply only to this type of table. Because SQL Server doesn't have an analogous type of table, you should avoid these top-level clauses and all subclauses associated with them.

You can closely reproduce a number of Oracle clauses in the CREATE TABLE statement using SQL Server clauses, as shown in Table 11-9.

Table 11-9. *Oracle CREATE TABLE Clauses That Translate to SQL Server Clauses*

DB2 Clause	SQL Server Clause
ORGANIZATION INDEX	PRIMARY KEY NONCLUSTERED
ORGANIZATION HEAP	<no clause needed>
PCTFREE	FILLFACTOR
TABLESPACE tablespace_name	ON filegroup
USING INDEX create_index_statement	CONSTRAINT PRIMARY KEY CLUSTERED

Note that although the ORGANIZATION INDEX clause is somewhat like a CLUSTERED INDEX, the syntax is different. Refer to the Oracle documentation for more information about index-organized tables.

Oracle supports the keywords GLOBAL and TEMPORARY.

Creating Indexes

Indexes are contracts that speed query processing by providing (usually) a B-tree of pointers to record locations within a table. Whenever a query has a search argument, such as a WHERE clause, against an indexed column, the query-processing engine can search the much smaller index rather than the entire table, and thereby accelerate query processing. Indexes, as useful as they are, aren't part of the ANSI SQL standard. That's because the ANSI standard doesn't concern itself with questions of physical implementation, and because indexes process directly against the physical layer.

However, there's an "industry-standard" CREATE INDEX clause that's highly interoperable across the database platforms:

```
CREATE [UNIQUE] INDEX index_name ON table_name (column_name [, ...])
```

The CREATE INDEX statement first gives a name to the index, then specifies the table and column(s) to which the index applies, in a comma-delimited list. You may alternately declare that the index is UNIQUE, thus preventing the index columns from ever containing a duplicate value. Any insert operation or update operation that attempts to put a duplicate value into a UNIQUE indexed column will fail.

SQL Server

When creating a SQL Server index that's interoperable with other database platforms, avoid the following clauses:

```
[NON]CLUSTERED
DESC
WITH option
ON filegroup
```

You should avoid all keywords of the WITH option clause.

DB2

When writing CREATE INDEX statements on DB2 that you wish to carry over to SQL Server 2005, avoid the following clauses:

```
SPECIFICATION ONLY
[DIS]ALLOW REVERSE SCANS
COLLECT [SAMPLED [DETAILED] STATISTICS
EXTEND USING ...
INCLUDE (columnname [,...])
MINPCTUSED int
```

You may substitute the DB2 clause CLUSTER for SQL Server's CLUSTERED, and DB2's PCTFREE for SQL Server's WITH FILLFACTOR.

MySQL

MySQL has two distinctive variations on the standard CREATE INDEX statement. First, you may issue the CREATE FULLTEXT INDEX statement to build a full-text search catalog on a BLOB column. Second, when declaring a column or columns to be indexes, you may also declare a length (in parenthesis) of the column to index. Thus, you might only want to index, say, the first 100 characters of a column that's VARCHAR(300).

Oracle

Oracle allows you to create indexes on tables, partitioned tables, clusters, index-organized tables, scalar objects of a typed table or cluster, and nested tables. You can specify the physical attributes of an Oracle index, just as you can an Oracle table. You can also specify whether the creation of the index should be parallelized or not. Plus, you can choose from a few types of indexes, including the normal B-tree indexes, partial indexes, function-based indexes, domain indexes, and BITMAP indexes.

Avoid the following Oracle variations of the CREATE INDEX statement for greatest interoperability:

```
CREATE BITMAP INDEX
INDEX TYPE IS index-type
[NO]PARALLEL
CLUSTER
[NO]LOGGING
[NO]COMPRESS
[NO]SORT
REVERSE
ONLINE
```

You can partition Oracle tables.

■**Note** Although Oracle has a CLUSTER clause in this statement, it isn't the same thing as a SQL Server clustered index.

You can use the PCTFREE clause to simulate SQL Server's FILLFACTOR and PAD_INDEX clauses.

Creating Views

A *view* is a virtual table that's created from the result set of a predefined query, and is rendered to the user at the time it's queried. In some cases, you can use views not only to retrieve a database, but also insert, update, and delete data from the base tables of the view. The most interoperable form of the CREATE VIEW statement is as follows:

```
CREATE VIEW view_name {[(column [,...])] |
AS
subquery [WITH [CASCADED | LOCAL] CHECK OPTION]
```

SQL Server doesn't support the subquery WITH clause, but this syntax exists on the other major database platforms, and is fairly common. Therefore, you should at least know what this clause means when writing interoperable SQL code or translating from or to SQL Server. The WITH CASCADED CHECK OPTION clause and the WITH LOCAL CHECK OPTION clause tell the DBMS how to behave with nested views. When using the former option, both the main view and any other views it's built upon are checked when an insert, update, or delete operation occurs against the main view. When using the latter option, only the main view is checked against insert, update, and delete operations—even if the main view is built upon other views.

SQL Server

SQL Server allows you to create a basic view with a few extra options. The only statement to avoid when crafting an interoperable `CREATE VIEW` statement on SQL Server is the `WITH` option. No other platform supports the view encryption, schemabinding, or view_metadata options.

SQL Server's implementation of the `WITH CHECK OPTION` is essentially the same as the standard `WITH LOCAL CHECK OPTION`.

DB2

DB2 allows the creation of hierarchical and object-oriented views. You should generally avoid these for greatest interoperability, along with the following other clauses:

```
OF type MODE DB2SQL
REF IS
UNDER parent_view INHERIT SELECT PRIVILEGES
WITH common_table_expression
```

DB2 doesn't support materialized views (also known as indexed views on SQL Server).

MySQL

MySQL added support for the ANSI standard `CREATE VIEW` statement in version 5.0. Avoid using MySQL's subclause `ALGORITHM = {UNDEFINED | MERGE | TEMPTABLE}`. Note that MySQL doesn't allow views against temporary tables, while SQL Server does.

Oracle

Oracle supports a rich variety of clauses to the `CREATE VIEW` statement. Avoid the following clauses when building an interoperable form of the statement:

```
[NO] FORCE
OF type ...
OF XMLTYPE ...
```

The `FORCE` clause forces the creation of the view regardless of errors, such as missing base tables in the view definition. In this regard, the `FORCE` clause is somewhat like deferred name resolution in SQL Server.

Also note that Oracle supports the standard `WITH CHECK OPTION` clause with some optional subclauses, but its functionality is essentially the same as the standard `WITH LOCAL CHECK OPTION` clause.

Oracle allows you to create a materialized view using the `CREATE MATERIALIZED VIEW` statement. This is essentially the same as SQL Server's indexed view. Refer to the vendor documentation for details about creating a materialized view.

Creating Triggers

All database platforms covered in this chapter support a certain lowest common denominator for the `CREATE TRIGGER` statement, as follows:

```
CREATE TRIGGER trigger_name
{BEFORE | AFTER} {DELETE | INSERT | UPDATE }
ON table_name
[FOR EACH {ROW | STATEMENT} ]
BEGIN
    statements
END
```

Using this generic syntax, you can set a trigger to fire before the actual delete, insert, or update operation, or afterwards (though not both) on a given table. The most interoperable triggers specify a trigger time of either BEFORE or AFTER, meaning that the trigger should fire and process its code either before the data manipulation operation takes place or after it takes place.

You may optionally specify whether the trigger logic should fire for each row of a transaction, if the transaction spans many records, or if it should fire for each statement in the transaction, firing only once for a statement that might span many records. Finally, a BEGIN...END block encases the logic that will substitute for the actual DELETE, INSERT, or UPDATE statement.

Also note that triggers, according to the ANSI SQL standard, have programmatic access to two important pseudotables: OLD and NEW. The OLD pseudotable contains all the data or records before the data manipulation operation that fired the trigger occurs. Conversely, the NEW pseudotable contains all the data or records after the data manipulation operation fired against the table. These pseudotables have the exact same schema of the base table that the trigger is operating against. Thus, you can use these pseudotables to see what the data is before and after the trigger fires, to manipulate the data conditionally as you see fit.

SQL Server

SQL Server supports the syntax for the interoperable CREATE TRIGGER statement with some minor variations. SQL Server triggers always operate in FOR EACH STATEMENT mode. First, SQL Server allows you to create a single time, but multiple events trigger in a single statement. Thus, the following code is possible:

```
CREATE TRIGGER my_trigger ON my_table
AFTER DELETE, INSERT, UPDATE
AS  BEGIN
    statements
END
```

■**Note** SQL Server uses the keyword FOR instead of BEFORE.

On the other hand, you should avoid the following clauses altogether when writing an interoperable CREATE TRIGGER statement on SQL Server:

```
INSTEAD OF
WITH ENCRYPTION
WITH APPEND
NOT FOR REPLICATION
IF UPDATE...
```

SQL Server supports an additional trigger activation event called INSTEAD OF. Rather than firing before or after the data-manipulation operation that invoked the trigger, INSTEAD OF triggers completely substitute their processing for that of the invoking data-manipulation operation.

SQL Server allows you to create many triggers for a given time and event for a single table or view. Thus, you could have three FOR UPDATE triggers and two AFTER DELETE triggers. You may only have one INSTEAD OF trigger per DML operation per table. You can set the first and last trigger to fire using the sp_settriggerorder system stored procedure. Otherwise, the order in which the triggers fire is undefined.

As the odd man out, SQL Server refers to the trigger pseudotables as DELETED and INSERTED, rather than OLD and NEW.

SQL Server 2005 also supports DDL trigger events on actions such as GRANT or CREATE. This is a useful addition for users who might want to build a trigger-based auditing system for their application that encompasses not only data manipulation activities but also database administration activities.

DB2

DB2 supports the syntax of the interoperable CREATE TRIGGER statement, but you should avoid the MODE DB2SQL and WHEN conditions clauses. DB2 defaults to calling the two pseudotables OLD and NEW, but it allows you to rename the OLD and NEW pseudotables using the following optional syntax:

```
REFERENCING
[OLD[_TABLE] [AS] old_table_name ]
[NEW[_TABLE] [AS] new_table_name]
DEFAULTS NULL
```

Note that DB2 also supports an INSTEAD OF trigger type like SQL Server, and that DB2 uses the clause NO CASCADE BEFORE instead of simply BEFORE.

DB2 allows you to create many triggers on a given table. The triggers will be fired in the order that they're created.

Also note that DB2 doesn't remove a trigger when the table it's based on is deleted. You must manually follow a DROP TABLE statement with a DROP TRIGGER statement (or vice versa) to destroy the trigger.

MySQL

MySQL supports the interoperable version of the CREATE TRIGGER statement with the exception that it only supports the FOR EACH ROW clause and not the FOR EACH STATEMENT clause. MySQL calls the two trigger pseudotables OLD and NEW, as does the standard.

MySQL currently allows only one trigger of each time and action (for example, a BEFORE INSERT trigger or an AFTER UPDATE trigger) on a given table.

Oracle

Oracle supports the interoperable form of the CREATE TRIGGER statement with the added trigger time of INSTEAD OF, as does SQL Server. Oracle also calls the trigger pseudotables OLD and NEW, though you can rename them using the following syntax:

```
REFERENCING [OLD [AS] old_table_name] [NEW [AS] new_table_name]
```

When building an interoperable CREATE TRIGGER statement on Oracle, avoid the [OR] clause, the PARENT clause, and the WHEN condition clause.

Oracle allows a number of object events to fire whenever Oracle encounters a specific keyword such as DROP, GRANT, or TRUNCATE. You can easily translate these into SQL Server 2005 using DDL triggers. You'll have to do some fancy programming via a stored procedure if you want to translate this behavior to SQL Server 2000 or earlier.

Creating Procedures and Functions

Most of the database platforms in this chapter support the ability to create stored procedures and user-defined functions. Because the ANSI SQL standard only approached the issue of procedural extensions in the 2003 standards, each of the database platforms has had to address issues of providing adequate procedural language capability at various points in their history by creating their own widely divergent SQL dialects.

■**Note** The ANSI standard calls both procedures and user-defined functions *routines*. Other types of procedural code such as types and methods are also grouped into the wide term of "routines."

SQL Server (and its forebear Sybase) uses the T-SQL dialect. SQL Server 2005 now also allows .NET languages such as C# to be compiled into stored procedures via the CLR interface. Oracle uses the venerable and powerful PL/SQL dialect, as well as Java. DB2 allows third-generation languages, such as C and Fortran, plus the SQL and ANSI 2003 SQL/PL extension statements. MySQL allows only SQL stored procedures and user-defined functions.

■**Note** SQL Server allows stored procedures to pass out result sets, such as the result from an entire SELECT statement. Most other database platforms, most notably Oracle, don't allow stored procedures to do this. Instead, you must design your stored procedures to dump any important result sets to temporary holding tables where you can later pull out and process those result sets according to the needs of your application.

A full description of each of these SQL dialects is far beyond the scope of this chapter. However, all the platforms in this chapter support a rudimentary syntax for the CREATE PROCEDURE and CREATE FUNCTION statement.

For CREATE PROCEDURE, use the following code:

```
CREATE PROCEDURE routine_name
   ( [{[IN | OUT | INOUT]} [parameter_name] data type [,...] ])
BEGIN
   routine_body
END
```

For CREATE FUNCTION, use the following code:

```
CREATE FUNCTION routine_name ([parameter[,...]])
   ( [{[IN | OUT | INOUT]} [parameter_name] data type [,...] ])
   RETURNS scalar_value
BEGIN
   routine_body
END
```

The parameter_name uniquely identifies one or more parameters for the routine. The parameter can carry a value IN to the routine, OUT from the routine, or both into and out of (INOUT) the routine. Functions must pass out a single scalar value, though stored procedures may pass out other sorts of values.

The routine_body should contain only SQL statements or procedure calls for maximum interoperability. If the routine_body contains any sort of code for a local SQL dialect, you can expect to have a good deal of work ahead in translating the procedural code.

Note that only SQL Server supports options such as ENCRYPTION and SCHEMABINDING.

Best Practices

A constant theme of this chapter is: *the closer you can stick to the ANSI standard the more interoperable you will be*. This is just a rule of thumb, because SQL Server isn't totally compliant with the ANSI standards itself, but it's a strong rule. Here are some other broader best practices that, while not strictly expansions of the ANSI standard best practice rule, are at least corollaries:

- When using datatypes, be sure to stick to the ANSI standard datatypes. In particular, when designing for interoperability, avoid the following datatypes: CURSOR, IMAGE, SQL_VARIANT, TABLE, VARCHAR(max), and TEXT. DATETIME is problematic because the SQL Server implementation is so different from the ANSI standard and the implementation of the datatype.

- Avoid quoted, bracketed, or otherwise delimited identifiers.

- When working with DELETE, INSERT, SELECT, and UPDATE statements, avoid hints, non-ANSI function calls, the WITH clause, and the ANSI ONLY clause.

- Don't use the second FROM clause to implement JOINS in the SQL Server DELETE and UPDATE statements.

- Avoid the SQL Server INSERT...EXECUTE statement.

- Remember that the SQL Server SELECT statement has many clauses that aren't interoperable, including the INTO clause, CUBE and ROLLUP clause, COMPUTE clause, and the FOR XML clauses.

- Avoid PARTITIONs in your database schema unless you only plan to interoperate with SQL Server and Oracle.

- Remember that clustered indexes on SQL Server are different from a "clustered" index on other platforms.

- Recognize that database routines (procedures, functions, and so on) are predicated on the database platform's SQL dialect (T-SQL for SQL Server, PL/SQL for Oracle, and so forth). Do not plan to build interoperable database routines. They almost always require a rather extended migration effort.

With these best practices alone, you'll be cranking out SQL code and SQL Server databases that are far more interoperable than before, and require little work to make fully interoperable.

Summary

Looking back over this chapter, you can see that there are a number of issues when writing code that's interoperable between SQL Server and the other major database platforms. Whether you want to move code from SQL Server 2005 or to SQL Server 2005 from another database platform, you'll likely have to change some of the code so that it can run properly. There are a number of areas where you have to be careful, from naming identifiers and choosing datatypes to writing transportable SELECT and CREATE TABLE statements. This chapter helped ease all those requirements by informing you how SQL Server implements each statement, and comparing that to how the other database platforms accomplish the same thing. Thus, you're able to write much more interoperable and transportable code from the start.

■■■

Codd's 12 Rules for an RDBMS

Although most of us think that any database that supports SQL is automatically considered a relational database, this isn't always the case—at least not completely. In Chapter 1, I discussed the basics and foundations of relational theory, but no discussion on this subject would be complete without looking at the rules that were formulated in 1985 in a two-part article published by *Computerworld* magazine ("Is Your DBMS Really Relational?" and "Does Your DBMS Run By the Rules?" by E. F. Codd, *Computerworld*, October 14 and October 21, 1985). Many websites also outline these rules. These rules go beyond relational theory and define a more specific set of criteria that need to be met in an RDBMS, if it's to be truly relational.

It might seem like old news, but the same criteria are still used today to measure how relational a database is. These rules are frequently brought up in conversations when discussing how well a particular database server is implemented. I present the rules, along with brief comments as to whether SQL Server 2005 meets each of them, or otherwise. Relational theory has come a long way since these rules were first published, and "serious" theorists have enhanced and refined relational theory tremendously since then, as you'd expect. A good place for more serious learning is the website `http://www.dbdebunk.com`, run by C. J. Date and Fabian Pascal, or any of their books. If you want to see the debates on theory, the newsgroup `comp.databases.theory` is a truly interesting place. Of course, as the cover of this book states, my goal is practicality, based on theory, so I won't delve too deeply into theory here at all. I present these 12 rules simply to set a basis for what a relational database is and what it should be.

All these rules are based upon what's sometimes referred to as the *foundation principle*, which states that for any system to be called a relational database management system, the relational capabilities must be able to manage it completely.

For the rest of this appendix, I'll treat SQL Server 2005 specifically as a relational database engine, not in any of the other configurations in which it might be used, such as a plain data store, a document storage device, or whatever other way you might use SQL Server as a storage engine.

Rule 1: The Information Rule

All information in the relational database is represented in exactly one and only one way—by values in tables.

This rule is an informal definition of a relational database, and indicates that every piece of data that we permanently store in a database is located in a table.

In general, SQL Server fulfills this rule, as we cannot store any information in anything other than a table. We can't use the variables in this code to persist any data, and therefore they're scoped to a single batch.

Rule 2: Guaranteed Access Rule

Each and every datum (atomic value) is guaranteed to be logically accessible by resorting to a combination of table name, primary key value, and column name.

This rule stresses the importance of primary keys for locating data in the database. The table name locates the correct table, the column name finds the correct column, and the primary key value finds the row containing an individual data item of interest. In other words, each (atomic) piece of data is accessible by the combination of table name, primary key value, and column name. This rule exactly specifies how we access data in SQL Server. In a table, we can search for the primary key value (which is guaranteed to be unique, based on relational theory), and once we have the row, the data is accessed via the column name. We can also access data by any of the columns in the table, though we aren't always guaranteed to receive a single row back.

Rule 3: Systematic Treatment of NULL Values

NULL *values (distinct from empty character string or a string of blank characters and distinct from zero or any other number) are supported in the fully relational RDBMS for representing missing information in a systematic way, independent of data type.*

This rule requires that the RDBMS support a distinct NULL placeholder, regardless of data type. NULLs are distinct from an empty character string or any other number, and are always to be considered as an unknown value.

NULLs must propagate through mathematic operations as well as string operations. NULL + <anything> = NULL, the logic being that NULL means "unknown." If you add something known to something unknown, you still don't know what you have, so it's still unknown.

There are a few settings in SQL Server that can customize how NULLs are treated. Most of these settings exist because of some poor practices that were allowed in early versions of SQL Server:

- ANSI_NULLS: Determines how NULL comparisons are handled. When OFF, then NULL = NULL is True for the comparison, and when ON (the default), NULL = NULL returns UNKNOWN.

- CONCAT_NULL_YIELDS_NULL: When the CONCAT_NULL_YIELDS_NULL setting is set ON, NULLs are treated properly, such that NULL + 'String Value' = NULL. If the CONCAT_NULL_YIELDS_NULL setting is OFF, which is allowed for backward compatibility with SQL Server, NULLs are treated in a nonstandard way such that NULL + 'String Value' = 'String Value'.

Rule 4: Dynamic On-Line Catalog Based on the Relational Model

The database description is represented at the logical level in the same way as ordinary data, so authorized users can apply the same relational language to its interrogation as they apply to regular data.

This rule requires that a relational database be self-describing. In other words, the database must contain certain system tables whose columns describe the structure of the database itself, or alternatively, the database description is contained in user-accessible tables.

This rule is becoming more of a reality in each new version of SQL Server, as with the implementation of the INFORMATION_SCHEMA system views. The INFORMATION_SCHEMA is a schema that has a set of views to look at much of the metadata for the tables, relationships, constraints, and even the code in the database.

Anything else you need to know can most likely be viewed in the system views (in the SYS schema). They're the new system views that replace the system tables we've used since the beginning of SQL Server time. These views are far easier to read and use, and most all the data is self explanatory, rather than requiring bitwise operations on some columns to find the value. For more information on the topic of new system views, consider the book *Pro SQL Server 2005* by Thomas Rizzo et al. (Apress, 2005).

Rule 5: Comprehensive Data Sublanguage Rule

A relational system may support several languages and various modes of terminal use. However, there must be at least one language whose statements are expressible, per some well-defined syntax, as character strings and whose ability to support all of the following is comprehensible:
  a. data definition
  b. view definition
  c. data manipulation (interactive and by program)
  d. integrity constraints
  e. authorization
  f. transaction boundaries (begin, commit, and rollback).

This rule mandates the existence of a relational database language, such as SQL, to manipulate data. SQL isn't specifically required. The language must be able to support all the central functions of a DBMS: creating a database, retrieving and entering data, implementing database security, and so on. Transact-SQL (T-SQL) fulfils this function for SQL Server, and carries out all the data definition and manipulation tasks required to access data.

SQL is a nonprocedural language, in that you don't specify "how" things happen, or even where. You simply ask a question of the relational server and it does the work.

Rule 6: View Updating Rule

All views that are theoretically updateable are also updateable by the system.

This rule deals with views, which are virtual tables used to give various users of a database different views of its structure. It's one of the most challenging rules to implement in practice, and no commercial product fully satisfies it today.

A view is theoretically updateable as long as it's made up of columns that directly correspond to real table columns. In SQL Server, views are updateable as long as you don't update more than a single table in the statement; neither can you update a derived or constant field. SQL Server 2000 also implements INSTEAD OF triggers that you can apply to a view (see Chapter 6). Hence, this rule can be technically fulfilled using INSTEAD OF triggers, but in what can be a less-than-straightforward manner. You need to take care when considering how to apply updates, especially if the view contains a GROUP BY clause and possibly aggregates.

Rule 7: High-Level Insert, Update, and Delete

The capability of handling a base relation or a derived relation as a single operand applies not only to the retrieval of data but also to the insertion, update, and deletion of data.

This rule stresses the set-oriented nature of a relational database. It requires that rows be treated as sets in insert, delete, and update operations. The rule is designed to prohibit implementations that only support row-at-a-time, navigational modification of the database. The SQL language covers this via the INSERT, UPDATE, and DELETE statements.

Even the CLR doesn't allow you to access the physical files where the data is stored, but BCP does kind of go around this. As always, you have to be extra careful when you use the low-level tools that can modify the data without going through the typical SQL syntax, as it can ignore the rules you have set up, introducing inconsistencies into your data.

Rule 8: Physical Data Independence

Application programs and terminal activities remain logically unimpaired whenever any changes are made in either storage representation or access methods.

Applications must still work using the same syntax, even when changes are made to the way in which the database internally implements data storage and access methods. This rule implies that the way the data is stored physically must be independent of the logical manner in which it's accessed. This is saying that users shouldn't be concerned about how the data is stored or how it's accessed. In fact, users of the data need only be able to get the basic definition of the data they need.

Other things that shouldn't affect the user's view of the data are as follows:

- *Adding indexes*: Indexes determine how the data is stored, yet the user, through SQL, will never know that indexes are being used.

- *Modifications to the storage engine*: From time to time, Microsoft has to modify how SQL Server operates (especially in major version upgrades). However, SQL statements must appear to access the data in exactly the same manner as they did in any previous version, only (we hope) faster.

Microsoft has put a lot of work into this area, as SQL Server has a separate relational engine and storage engine, and OLE DB is used to pass data between the two. Further reading on this topic is available in SQL Server 2005 Books Online in the "Database Engine Components" topic, or in *Inside Microsoft SQL Server 2005: The Storage Engine* by Kalen Delaney (Microsoft Press, 2006).

Rule 9: Logical Data Independence

> *Application programs and terminal activities remain logically unimpaired when information preserving changes of any kind that theoretically permit unimpairment are made to the base tables.*

Along with rule 8, this rule insulates the user or application program from the low-level implementation of the database. Together, they specify that specific access or storage techniques used by the RDBMS—and even changes to the structure of the tables in the database—shouldn't affect the user's ability to work with the data.

In this way, if we add a column to a table, and if tables are split in a manner that doesn't add or subtract columns, then the application programs that call the database should be unimpaired.

For example, say we have the table in Figure A-1.

Figure A-1. *Small sample table*

Then, say we vertically break it up into two tables (see Figure A-2).

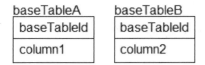

Figure A-2. *Small sample table split into two tables*

We then could create this view:

```
CREATE VIEW baseTable
AS
SELECT baseTableId, column1, column2
FROM   baseTableA
         JOIN baseTableB
             ON baseTableA.baseTableId = baseTableB.baseTableId
```

The user should be unaffected. If we were to implement INSTEAD OF triggers on the view that had the same number of columns with the same names, we could seamlessly meet the need to manage the view in the exact manner the table was managed. Note that the handling of identity columns can be tricky in views, as they require data to be entered, even when the data won't be used. See Chapter 6 for more details on creating INSTEAD OF triggers.

Of course, we cannot always make this rule work if columns or tables are removed from the system, but we can make the rule work if columns and data are simply added.

■**Tip** Always access data from the RDBMS by name, and not by position or by using the SELECT * wild-card. The order of columns shouldn't make a difference to the application.

Rule 10: Integrity Independence

Integrity constraints specific to a particular relational database must be definable in the relational data sublanguage and storable in the catalog, not in the application programs.

The database must support a minimum of the following two integrity constraints:

- *Entity integrity*: No component of a primary key is allowed to have a NULL value.

- *Referential integrity*: For each distinct non-NULL foreign key value in a relational database, there must exist a matching primary key value from the same domain.

This rule says that the database language should support integrity constraints that restrict the data that can be entered into the database, and the database modifications that can be made. In other words, the RDBMS must internally support the definition and enforcement of entity integrity (primary keys) and referential integrity (foreign keys).

It requires that the database be able to implement constraints to protect the data from invalid values, and that careful database design is needed to ensure that referential integrity is achieved. SQL Server 2005 does a great job of providing the tools to make this rule a reality. We can protect our data from invalid values for most any possible case using constraints and triggers. Most of Chapter 6 was spent covering the methods that we can use in SQL Server to implement integrity independence.

Rule 11: Distribution Independence

The data manipulation sublanguage of a relational DBMS must enable application programs and terminal activities to remain logically unimpaired whether and whenever data are physically centralized or distributed.

This rule says that the database language must be able to manipulate data located on other computer systems. In essence, we should be able to split the data on the RDBMS out onto multiple physical systems without the user realizing it. SQL Server 2005 supports distributed transactions among SQL Server sources, as well as other types of sources using the Microsoft Distributed Transaction Services.

Another distribution-independence possibility is a group of database servers working together more or less as one. Database servers working together like this are considered to be *federated*. With SQL Server 2005, the notion of federated database servers seamlessly sharing the load is a reality. More reading on this subject can be found in the SQL Server 2005 Books Online in the "Federated Database Servers" topic.

Rule 12: Non-Subversion Rule

If a relational system has or supports a low-level (single-record-at-a-time) language, that low-level language cannot be used to subvert or bypass the integrity rules or constraints expressed in the higher-level (multiple-records-at-a-time) relational language.

This rule requires that alternate methods of accessing the data are not able to bypass integrity constraints, which means that users can't violate the rules of the database in any way. For most SQL Server 2005 applications, this rule is followed, as there are no methods of getting to the raw data and changing values other than by the methods prescribed by the database. However, SQL Server 2005 violates this rule in two places:

- *Bulk copy*: By default, you can use the bulk copy routines to insert data into the table directly, and around the database server validations.

- *Disabling constraints and triggers*: There's syntax to disable constraints and triggers, thereby subverting this rule.

It's always good practice to make sure you use these two features carefully. They leave gaping holes in the integrity of your data, because they allow any values to be inserted in any column. Because you're expecting the data to be protected by the constraint you've applied, data value errors might occur in the programs that use the data, without revalidating it first.

Summary

Codd's 12 rules for relational databases can be used to explain much about how SQL Server operates today. These rules were a major step forward in determining whether a database vendor could call his system "relational," and presented stiff implementation challenges for database developers. Fifteen years on, even the implementation of the most complex of these rules is becoming achievable, though SQL Server (and other RDBMSes) still fall short of achieving all their objectives.

APPENDIX B

■■■

Datatype Reference

Choosing proper datatypes to match the domain to satisfy logical modeling is an important task. One datatype might be more efficient than another of a similar type. For example, you can store integer data in an integer datatype, a numeric datatype, a floating point datatype, a character type, or even a binary column, but these datatypes certainly aren't alike in implementation or performance.

In this appendix, I'll introduce you to all the intrinsic datatypes that Microsoft provides and discuss the situations where they're best used. Following is a list of the datatypes we'll look at. I'll discuss when to use them, and in some cases why not to use them.

- *Precise numeric data*: Stores data with no loss of precision due to storage.

    - bit: Stores either 1, 0, or NULL. Used for Boolean-type columns.

    - tinyint: Non-negative values between 0 and 255.

    - smallint: Integers between -32,768 and 32,767.

    - int: Integers between 2,147,483,648 and 2,147,483,647 (-2^{31} to $2^{31} - 1$).

    - bigint: Integers between 9,223,372,036,854,775,808 and 9,223,372,036,854,775,807 (that is, -2^{63} to $2^{63} - 1$).

    - decimal: Values between $-10^{38} + 1$ through $10^{38} - 1$.

    - money: Values from -922,337,203,685,477.5808 through 922,337,203,685,477.5807.

    - smallmoney: Values from -214,748.3648 through +214,748.3647.

- *Approximate numeric data*: Stores approximations of numbers. Provides for a large range of values.

    - float (N): Values in the range from -1.79E + 308 through to 1.79E + 308.

    - real: Values in the range from -3.40E + 38 through to 3.40E + 38. real is a synonym for a float(24) datatype.

- *Date and time*: Stores date values, including time of day.

    - smalldatetime: Dates from January 1, 1900 through June 6, 2079.

    - datetime: Dates from January 1, 1753 to December 31, 9999.

- *Character (or string) data*: Used to store textual data, such as names, notes, and so on.

  - char: Fixed-length character data up to 8,000 characters long.

  - varchar: Variable-length character data up to 8,000 characters long.

  - varchar(max): Large variable-length character data, max length of $2^{31} - 1$ (2,147,483,647) bytes or 2GB.

  - text: Large text values, max length of $2^{31} - 1$ (2,147,483,647) bytes or 2GB. *[Note that this datatype is outdated and should be phased out for the* varchar(max) *datatype.]*

  - nchar, nvarchar, ntext: Unicode equivalents of char, varchar, and text.

- *Binary data*: Data stored in bytes, rather than as human-readable values; for example, files or images.

  - binary: Fixed-length binary data up to 8,000 bytes long.

  - varbinary: Variable-length binary data up to 8,000 bytes long.

  - varbinary(max): Large binary data, max length of $2^{31} - 1$ (2,147,483,647) bytes or 2GB.

  - image: Large binary data, max length of $2^{31} - 1$ (2,147,483,647) bytes or 2GB. *[Note that this datatype is outdated and should be phased out for the* varbinary(max) *datatype.]*

- *Other datatypes*: Six datatypes don't fit into any other group nicely.

  - timestamp *(or* rowversion*)*: Used for optimistic locking.

  - uniqueidentifier: Stores a globally unique identifier (GUID) value.

  - cursor: Datatype used to store a cursor reference in a variable.

  - table: Used to hold a reference to a local temporary table.

  - XML: Used to store and manipulate XML values.

  - sql_variant: Stores most any datatype.

Although we'll look at all these datatypes, this doesn't mean that you'll have any need for all of them. Choosing a datatype needs to be a specific task to meet the needs of the client with the proper datatype. We could just store everything in unlimited-length character strings (this was how some systems worked in the old days), but this is clearly not optimal. From the list, we'll choose the best datatype, and if we cannot find one good enough, we can use the CLR and implement our own (I cover this in Chapter 5). The proper datatype choice is the first step in making sure the proper data is stored for a column.

Precise Numeric Data

You can store numerical data in many base datatypes. Here you'll learn to deal with two different types of numeric data: precise and approximate. The differences are important and must be well understood by any architect who's building a system that stores readings, measurements, or other numeric data.

Precise values have no error in the way they're stored, from integer to floating point values, because they have a fixed number of digits before and after the decimal point (or radix). It might seem odd to make this distinction, but as I'll discuss in the next major section, some datatypes are considered approximate that don't always store exactly what you expect them to. However, they aren't as bad as they sound, and are useful for scientific applications, and places where the range of values varies greatly.

The precise numeric values include the `bit`, `int`, `bigint`, `smallint`, `tinyint`, `decimal`, and money datatypes (`money` and `smallmoney`). I'll break these down again into two additional subsections: whole numbers and fractional numbers. This is done so we can isolate some of the discussion down to the values that allow fractional parts to be stored, because quite a few mathematical "quirks" need to be understood surrounding using those datatypes. I'll mention a few of these quirks, most importantly with the money datatypes. However, when you do any math with computers, you must be careful how rounding is achieved and how this affects your results.

Integer Numbers

Whole numbers are, for the most part, integers stored using base-2 values. You can do bitwise operations on them, though generally it's frowned upon in SQL (think back to Chapter 4 in the First Normal Form sections, if you don't remember why). Math performed with integers is generally fast because the CPU can perform it directly using registers. I'll cover five integer sizes: `bit`, `tinyint`, `smallint`, `int`, and `bigint`.

bit

Domain: 0, 1, or `NULL`.

Storage: A `bit` column requires 1 byte of storage per eight instances in a table. Hence, having eight `bit` columns will cause your table to be no larger than if your table had only a single `bit` column.

Discussion:

You use `bit` values as a kind of imitation Boolean value. A `bit` isn't a Boolean value, in that it has values 0 and 1, not `True` and `False`. This is a minor distinction, but one that needs to be made. You cannot execute code such as this:

```
IF (bitValue) DO SOMETHING
```

A better term than a "Boolean" is a "flag." A value of 1 means the flag has been set (such as a value that tells us that a customer does want e-mail promotions). Many programmers like to use character values `'yes'` or `'no'` for this, as this can be easier for viewing, but can be harder to program with using built-in programming methods. In fact, the use of the `bit` datatype as a Boolean value has occurred primarily because many programming languages usually use 0 for `False` and nonzero for `True` (some use 1 or –1 explicitly).

You can index a `bit` column, but usually it isn't of any value only to index it. Having only two distinct values in an index (technically three with `NULL`) makes for a poor index (see Chapter 8 for more information about indexes). Clearly, a `bit` value most often should be indexed in conjunction with other columns.

■**Tip** There's always a ton of discussion on the newsgroups about using the bit datatype. It isn't a standard datatype, but in my opinion it's no different in usage than an integer that has been constrained to the values 0, 1, or NULL.

It's often asked why we don't have a Boolean datatype. This is due largely to the idea that datatypes need to support NULL in RDBMSes, and a Boolean datatype would have to support UNKNOWN and NULL, resulting in four valued logic tables that are difficult to contemplate (without taking a long nap) and hard to deal with. So we have what we have, and it works well enough.

---

tinyint

Domain: Non-negative whole numbers from 0 through 255.

Storage: 1 byte.

Discussion:

tinyints are very small integer values. Using a single byte for storage, if the values you'll be dealing with are guaranteed always to be in this range, a tinyint is perfect. A great use for this is for the primary key of a domain table that can be guaranteed to have only a couple values. The tinyint datatype is especially useful in a data warehouse to keep the surrogate keys small. However, you have to make sure that there will never be more than 256 values, so unless the need for performance is incredibly great (such as if the key will migrate to tables with billions and billions of rows), it's best to use a larger datatype.

smallint

Domain: Whole numbers from -32,768 through to 32,767 (or -2^{15} through $2^{15} - 1$).

Storage: 2 bytes.

Discussion:

If you can be guaranteed to need only values in this range, the smallint can be a useful type. It requires 2 bytes of storage.

Just as before with tinyint, it's often a bad idea to use a smallint for a primary key. Uniformity (just using int) makes your database code more consistent. This might seem like a small point, but in most average systems it's much easier to code when you automatically know what the datatype is.

One use of a smallint that crops up from time to time is as a Boolean. This is because, in earlier versions of Visual Basic, 0 equals False and -1 equals True (technically, VB would treat any nonzero value as True, but it used -1 as a False). Storing data in this manner is not only a tremendous waste of space—2 bytes versus potentially 1/8th of a byte for a bit, or even a single byte for a char(1)—'Y' or 'N'. It's also confusing to all the other SQL Server programmers. ODBC and OLE DB drivers do this translation for you, but even if they didn't, it's worth the time to write a method or a function in VB to translate True to a value of 1.

int

Domain: Whole numbers from -2,147,483,648 to 2,147,483,647 (that is, -2^{31} to $2^{31} - 1$).

Storage: 4 bytes.

Discussion:

The integer (int) datatype is used to store signed (+ or -) whole number data. The integer datatype is frequently employed as a primary key for tables, as it's small (it requires 4 bytes of storage) and efficient to store and retrieve.

The only real downfall of the int datatype is that it doesn't include an unsigned version, which could store non-negative values from 0 to 4,294,967,296 (2^{32}). As most primary key values start out at 1, this would give you more than two billion extra values for a primary key value. This might seem unnecessary, but systems that have billions of rows are becoming more and more common.

An application where the storage of the int column plays an important part is the storage of IP addresses as integers. An IP address is simply a 32-bit integer broken down into four octets. For example, if you had an IP address of 234.23.45.123, you would take (234 * 23) + (23 * 22) + (45 * 21) + (123 * 20). This value fits nicely into an unsigned 32-bit integer, but not into a signed one. However, the 64-bit integer (bigint, which is covered in the next item) in SQL Server covers the current IP address standard nicely, but requires twice as much storage. Of course, bigint will fall down in the same manner when we get to IPv6 (the forthcoming Internet addressing protocol), because it uses a full 64-bit unsigned integer.

bigint

Domain: Whole numbers from -9,223,372,036,854,775,808 to 9,223,372,036,854,775,807 (that is, -2^{63} to $2^{63} - 1$).

Storage: 8 bytes.

Discussion:

One of the main reasons to use the 64-bit datatype is as a primary key for tables where you'll have more than two billion rows, or if the situation directly dictates it, such as the IP address situation I previously discussed.

Decimal Values

The decimal datatype is precise, in that whatever value you store, you can always retrieve it from the table. However, when you must store fractional values in precise datatypes, you pay a performance and storage cost in the way they're stored and dealt with. The reason for this is that you have to perform math with the precise decimal values using SQL Server engine code. On the other hand, math with IEEE floating point values (the float and real datatypes) can use the floating point unit (FPU), which is part of the core processor in all modern computers. This isn't to say that the decimal type is slow, *per se*, but if you're dealing with data that doesn't require the perfect precision of the decimal type, use the float datatype. I'll discuss the float and real datatypes more in the next major section, "Approximate Numeric Data."

decimal (or Numeric)

Domain: All numeric data (including fractional parts) between $-10^{38} + 1$ through $10^{38} - 1$.

Storage: Based on precision (the number of significant digits). 1–9 digits, 5 bytes; 10–19 digits, 9 bytes; 20–28 digits, 13 bytes; and 29–38 digits require 17 bytes.

Discussion:

The decimal datatype is a precise datatype because it's stored in a manner that's like character data (as if the data only had 12 characters, 0 to 9 and the minus and decimal point symbols). The way it's stored prevents the kind of imprecision you'll see with the float and real datatypes a bit later. However, decimal does incur an additional cost in getting and doing math on the values, because there's no hardware to do the mathematics.

To specify a decimal number, you need to define the precision and the scale:

- *Precision* is the total number of significant digits in the number. For example, the number 10 would need a precision of 2, and 43.00000004 would need a precision of 10. The precision may be as small as 1 or as large as 38.

- *Scale* is the possible number of significant digits to the right of the decimal point. Reusing the previous example, 10 would have a scale of 0, and 43.00000004 would need 8.

Numeric datatypes are bound by this precision and scale to define how large the data is. For example, take the following declaration of a numeric variable:

```
DECLARE @testvar decimal(3,1)
```

This allows you to enter any numeric values greater than -99.94 and less than 99.94. Entering 99.949999 works but entering 99.95 doesn't, because it's rounded up to 100.0, which can't be displayed by decimal(3,1). Take the following, for example:

```
SELECT @testvar = -10.155555555
SELECT @testvar
```

This returns the following result:

```
-----------
-10.2
```

This rounding behavior is both a blessing and a curse. You must be careful when butting up to the edge of the datatype's allowable values. Note that a setting—SET NUMERIC_ROUNDABORT ON—causes an error to be generated when a loss of precision would occur from an implicit data conversion. That's kind of like what happens when you try to put too many characters into a character value.

Take the following code:

```
SET NUMERIC_ROUNDABORT ON
DECLARE @testvar decimal(3,1)
SELECT @testvar = -10.155555555
```

This causes the following error:

```
Msg 8115, Level 16, State 7, Line 5
Arithmetic overflow error converting numeric to data type numeric.
```

SET NUMERIC_ROUNDABORT can be quite dangerous to use, and might throw off applications using SQL Server if set to ON. However, if you need to prevent implicit round-off due to system constraints, it's there.

As far as usage is concerned, you should generally use the decimal datatype as sparingly as possible, and I don't mean this negatively. There's nothing wrong with the type at all, but it does take that little bit more processing than integers or real data, and hence there's a performance hit. You should use it when you have specific values that you wish to store where you can't accept any loss of precision. Again, I'll deal with the topic of loss of precision in more detail in the section "Approximate Numeric Data."

Monetary Values

The money datatypes can be used for storing monetary amounts. There are two different types: money and smallmoney.

money

Domain: -922,337,203,685,477.5808 to 922,337,203,685,477.5807.

Storage: 8 bytes.

smallmoney

Domain: -214,748.3648 to 214,748.3647.

Storage: 4 bytes.

Discussion:

The money datatypes are generally considered a poor choice of datatype, even for storing monetary values, because they have a few inconsistencies that can cause a good deal of confusion. First off, you can specify units, such as $ or £, but the units are of no real value:

```
CREATE TABLE dbo.testMoney
(
    moneyValue money
)
go

INSERT INTO dbo.testMoney
VALUES ($100)
INSERT INTO dbo.testMoney
VALUES (100)
INSERT INTO dbo.testMoney
VALUES (£100)
GO
SELECT  * FROM dbo.testMoney
```

This returns the following results:

```
moneyValue
--------------------
100.00
100.00
100.00
```

The second problem is that the money datatypes have well-known rounding issues with math:

```
DECLARE @money1 money, @money2 money

SET    @money1 = 1.00
SET    @money2 = 800.00
SELECT cast(@money1/@money2 as money)
```

This returns the following result:

```
--------------------
0.0012
```

However, try the following code:

```
DECLARE @decimal1 decimal(19,4), @decimal2 decimal(19,4)
SET    @decimal1 = 1.00
SET    @decimal2 = 800.00
SELECT  cast(@decimal1/@decimal2 as decimal(19,4))
```

It returns the following result:

```
------------------------------------
0.0013
```

Why? Because money only uses four decimal places for intermediate results, where decimal uses a much larger precision:

```
SELECT    @money1/@money2
SELECT    @decimal1/@decimal2
```

This code returns the following results:

```
--------------------
0.0012
```

```
----------------------------------------
0.0012500000000000000
```

Hence the roundoff issues. The common consensus among database architects is to avoid the money datatype and use a numeric type instead, due to the following reasons:

- It gives the answers to math problems in the natural manner that's expected.

- It has no built-in units to confuse matters.

Even in the previous version of SQL Server, the following statement was included in the Monetary Data section: "If a greater number of decimal places are required, use the decimal datatype instead." Using a decimal type instead gives you the precision needed. To replicate the range for money, use DECIMAL(19,4), or for smallmoney, use DECIMAL (10,4). However, you needn't use such large values if you don't need them. Otherwise, if you happen to be calculating the national debt or my yearly gadget allowance, you might need to use a larger value.

Approximate Numeric Data

Approximate numeric values contain a decimal point, are stored in a format that's fast to manipulate. They are called floating point because they have a fixed number of significant digits, but the placement of the decimal point "floats," allowing for really small numbers or really large numbers. Approximate numeric values have some important advantages, as you'll see later in this appendix.

"Approximate" is such a negative term, but it's technically the proper term. It refers to the real and float datatypes, which are IEEE 75454 standard single- and double-precision floating point values. The number is stored as a 32-bit or 64-bit value, with four parts:

- *Sign*: Determines if this is a positive or negative value.

- *Exponent*: The exponent in base 2 of the mantissa.

- *Mantissa*: Stores the actual number that's multiplied by the exponent.

- *Bias*: Determines whether or not the exponent is positive or negative.

A complete description of how these datatypes are formed is beyond the scope of this book, but may be obtained from the IEEE body at http://www.ieee.org.

float [(N)]

Domain: -1.79E + 308 through to 1.79E + 308. The float datatype allows you to specify a certain number of bits to use in the mantissa, from 1 to 53. You specify this number of bits with the value in N. The default is 53.

Storage: See Table B-1.

Table B-1. *Floating Point Precision and Storage Requirements*

N (Number of Mantissa Bits for Float)	Precision	Storage Size
1–24	7	4 bytes
25–53	15	8 bytes

At this point, SQL Server rounds all values of N up to either 24 or 53. This is the reason that the storage and precision are the same for each of the values.

Note There's another approximate datatype named real. It's a synonym for a float(24) datatype. It can store values in the range from -3.40E + 38 through to 3.40E + 38.

Discussion:

Using these datatypes, you can represent most values from -1.79E + 308 to 1.79E + 308 with a maximum of 15 significant digits. This isn't as many significant digits as the numeric datatypes can deal with, but the range is enormous, and is plenty for almost any scientific application. These datatypes have a *much* larger range of values than any other datatype. This is because the decimal point isn't fixed in the representation. In numeric types, you always have a pattern such as NNNNNNN.DDDD for numbers. You can't store more digits than this to the left or right of the decimal point. However, with float values, you can have values that fit the following patterns (and much larger):

- 0.DDDDDDDDDDDDDDDD

- NNNNN.DDDDDDDDDD

- 0.00000000000000000000000000000DDDDDDDDDDDDDDDD

- NNNNNNNNNNNNNNNN00000000000000000000

So you have the ability to store tiny numbers, or large ones. This is important for scientific applications where you need to store and do math on an extreme range of values. The float datatypes are well suited for this usage.

Date and Time Data

There are two datatypes for working with date and time values: datetime and smalldatetime. Both have a time element and a date element, and you cannot separate them. Not having a simple date or time datatype can be a real bother at times, because often we want to store just the time of an event, or just the date of the event. For date-only values, it's simple: we just ignore the time by making sure that the time value is exactly midnight, and it works OK. Time values can be more of an issue. Although we can set the date to some arbitrary date and just use the time value, the date value then looks funny when viewed without formatting. We often build our own datatype for these values. I'll discuss this in this section as well.

smalldatetime

Domain: Date and time data values between January 1, 1900 and June 6, 2079.

Storage: 4 bytes (two 2-byte integers, one for the day offset from January 1, 1900, the other for the number of minutes past midnight).

Accuracy: One minute.

Discussion:

The smalldatetime datatype is accurate to one minute. It requires 4 bytes of storage. smalldatetime values are the best choice when you need to store just the date, and possibly the time, of some event where accuracy of a minute isn't a problem.

datetime

Domain: Date and time data values between January 1, 1753 and December 31, 9999.

Storage: 8 bytes (two 4-byte integers, one for the day offset from January 1, 1753 and the other for the number of 3.33 millisecond periods past midnight).

Accuracy: 3.33 milliseconds.

Discussion:

Using 8 bytes, datetime does require a sizable chunk of memory unless you need this range or precision. There are few cases where you need this kind of precision. A primary example of where you do need this kind of precision is a timestamp column (not to be confused with the timestamp datatype, which I'll discuss in a later section), used to denote exactly when an operation takes place. This isn't uncommon if you need to get timing information, such as the time taken between two activities in seconds, or if you want to use the datetime value in a concurrency control mechanism.

When working with datetime values in text, using a standard format is always best. There are many different formats used around the world for dates, most confusingly MMDDYYYY and DDMMYYYY (is 01022004 or 02012004 the same day, or a different day?). Although SQL Server uses the locale information on your server to decide how to interpret your date input, using one of the following formats ensures that SQL Server doesn't mistake the input regardless of where the value is entered.

Generally speaking, it's best to use the stay with 'YYYY-MM-DD' for representing dates as text, and append 'HH:MM:SS.LLL' (L is milliseconds) when representing datetime values as literals. For example:

```
select cast ('2006-01-01' as smalldatetime) as dateOnly
select cast('2006-01-01 14:23:00.003' as datetime) as withTime
```

You might also see values that are close to this format, such as the following:

```
select cast ('20060101' as smalldatetime) as dateOnly
select cast('2006-01-01T14:23:00.120' as datetime) as withTime
```

These are acceptable variations as well. For more information, check SQL Server 2005 Books Online under "dates" in the index.

Using User-Defined Datatypes to Manipulate Dates and Times

Employing the datetime datatypes when you only need the date part, or just the time, at times can be a pain. Take the following code sample. You want to find every row where the date is equal to July 12, 2001. Try coding this in the obvious manner (this example uses the AdventureWorks database):

```
SELECT *
FROM HumanResources.employee
WHERE birthDate = '1966-03-14'
```

You get a match for every employee where birthDate exactly matches '1967-07-12 00:00:00.000'. However, what if the date is stored with time values '1967-07-12 10:05:23.300', as it might be by design (that is, she was born at that exact time), or by error (that is, a date control might send the current time by default if you forget to clear it)? In this case, you can get stuck with having to write queries such as the following to answer the question of who was born on July 12, 1967. To do this, you'd need to rewrite your query like so:

```
SELECT *
FROM   HumanResources.employee
WHERE  birthDate >= '1966-03-14 0:00:00.000'
  AND  birthDate < '1966-03-15 0:00:00.000'
```

Note that you don't use BETWEEN for this operation. If you do, the WHERE clause would have to state the following:

```
WHERE birthDate BETWEEN '1967-07-12 0:00:00.00'
AND '1967-07-12 23:59:59.997'
```

It would do so, first to exclude any July 13 dates, then to avoid any round-off with the `datetime` datatype. As it's accurate to 0.00333 of a second, when a value of `datetime` evaluates `'July 12, 1967 23:59:59.999'`, it would round off to `'July 13, 1967 0:00:00.00'`. If you need to look for people who were born on July 12, without the year, then you have to use the date manipulation functions, in this case the `DATEPART` function.

This isn't only troublesome and cumbersome, it also can be inefficient. In the case where you don't need the date or the time parts of the `datetime` datatype, it might best suit you to create your own representation of a date datatype. For example, let's take a typical need for storing the time when something occurs, without the date. There are two possibilities for dealing with this situation: using multiple columns or using a single column. Both are much better than simply using the `datetime` datatype, but each has its own set of inherent problems.

When using multiple columns, use one simply for year, month, hour, minute, second, and whatever fractions of a second you might need. The problem here is that this isn't easy to query. You need at least three columns to query for a given time, and you need to index all the columns involved in the query to get good performance on large tables. Storage will be better, as you can fit all the different parts into `tinyint` columns. If you want to look at what has happened during the tenth hour of the day over a week, then you could use this method.

An offshoot of this possibility is to add computed columns to break out the parts of the date, and by persisting them get the value of a real column without having to maintain it (avoiding normalization issues):

```
--note, no key on table just for quick demo purposes,
--please wear all protective gear in designed databases

--in tempdb
USE tempdb
GO

CREATE TABLE date
(
        dateValue    datetime,
        year         as (datepart(yy, dateValue)) persisted,
        month        as (datepart(m, dateValue)) persisted
)
go

INSERT INTO date(dateValue)
VALUES ('2005-04-12')
SELECT * FROM date
```

This returns the following result:

dateValue	year	month
2005-04-12 00:00:00.000	2005	4

You could even index these values if you needed access to the individual parts of the date for otherwise costly queries.

You can also use a single column that holds the number of seconds (or parts of seconds between midnight and the current time). However, this method suffers from an inability to do a reasonable query for all values that occur during, say, the tenth hour. Also, if you specified the number of seconds, this would be every value between 36,000 and 39,600. However, using a single column is ideal if you're using these dates in some sort of internal procedure with which human users wouldn't need to interact.

As another example, you could simply store your date value in an integer and then use a user-defined function to convert the integer value into an intrinsic datetime variable, to use in date calculations or simply to show to a client:

```
CREATE FUNCTION intDateType$convertToDatetime
(
    @dateTime    int
)
RETURNS datetime
AS
BEGIN
    RETURN ( dateadd(second,@datetime,'1990-01-01'))
END
```

To test your new function, you could start with looking at the second day of the year, by converting date one to a datetime variable:

```
SELECT dbo.intDateType$convertToDatetime(485531247) as convertedValue
```

This returns the following result:

```
convertedValue
-----------------------
2005-05-21 13:47:27.000
```

By defining your own standards for dates for a particular situation, you can fit the needs to your own situation. I tend to avoid doing this for the most part, but in some cases it can be a handy trick if you need to deal with nonstandard time usage.

Character Strings

Most data that's stored in SQL Server uses character datatypes. In fact, usually far too much data is stored in character datatypes. Frequently, character columns are used to hold non-character data, such as numbers and dates. Although this might not be technically wrong, it isn't ideal. For starters, storing a number with 8 digits in a character string requires at least 8 bytes, but as an integer it requires 4 bytes. Searching on integers is far easier because 1 always precedes 2, whereas 11 comes before 2 in character strings. Additionally, integers are stored in a format that can be manipulated using intrinsic processor functions, as opposed to having SQL Server–specific functions deal with the data.

char(length)

Domain: ASCII characters, up to 8,000 characters long.

Storage: 1 byte * length.

Discussion:

The char datatype is used for fixed-length character data. You must choose the size of the data that you wish to store. Every value will be stored with exactly the same number of characters, up to a maximum of 8,000 bytes. Storage is exactly the number of bytes as per the column definition, regardless of actual data stored; any remaining space to the right of the last character of the data is padded with spaces.

You can see the possible characters by executing the following query:

```
SELECT number, CHAR(number)
FROM   dbo.sequence
WHERE  number >=0 and number <= 255
```

Tip The sequence table is a common table that every database should have. It's a table of integers that can be used for many utility purposes. I've included the code to generate one such table in the code downloads (in the Source Code area of the Apress website at http://www.apress.com).

The maximum limit for a char is 8,000 bytes, but if you ever get within a mile of this limit for a fixed-width character value, you're likely making a big design mistake. Not necessarily, but it's rare to have massive character strings of exactly the same length. You should only employ the char datatype in cases where you're guaranteed to have exactly the same number of characters in every row.

The char datatype is most often used for codes and identifiers such as customer numbers, or invoice numbers where the number includes alpha characters as well as integer data. An example is the vehicle identification number (VIN), which is stamped on most every vehicle produced around the world. Note that this is a composite attribute, as you can determine many things about the automobile from its VIN.

Another example where a char column is usually found is in Social Security numbers (SSNs), which always have nine characters and two dashes embedded.

Note The setting ANSI_PADDING determines exactly how padding is handled. If this setting is ON, the table is as I've described; if not, data will be stored as I'll discuss in the "varchar" section that follows. It's best practice to leave this ANSI setting ON.

---

varchar(length)

Domain: ASCII characters, up to 8,000 characters long.

Storage: 1 byte * length + 2 bytes (for overhead).

Discussion:

For the varchar datatype, you choose the maximum length of the data you wish to store, up to 8,000 bytes. The varchar datatype is far more useful than the char, as the data doesn't have to be of the same length, and SQL Server doesn't pad out excess memory with spaces. There's some reasonably minor overhead in storing variable-length data. First, it costs an additional 2 bytes per column. Second, it's a bit more difficult to get to the data, as it isn't always in the same location of the physical record.

Use the varchar datatype when your character data varies in length. The good thing about varchar columns is that, no matter how long you make the maximum, the space used by the column is based on the actual size of the characters being stored plus the few extra bytes that specify how long the data is.

You'll generally want to choose a maximum limit for your datatype that's a reasonable value, large enough to handle most situations, but not too large as to be impractical to deal with in your applications and reports. For example, take people's first names. These obviously require the varchar type, but how long should you allow the data to be? First names tend to be a maximum of 15 characters long, though you might want to specify 20 or 30 characters for the unlikely exception.

The most prevalent storage type for non-key values that you'll use is varchar data, because generally speaking, the size of the data is one of the most important factors in performance tuning. The smaller the amount of data, the less has to be read and written. This means less disk access, which is one of the two most important bottlenecks we have to deal with (networking speed is the other).

varchar(max)

Domain: ASCII characters, up to $2^{31} - 1$ characters (that is a maximum of 2GB worth of text!)

Storage: There are a couple possibilities for storage based on the setting of the table option 'large value types out of row':

- OFF =: If the data for all the columns fits in a single row, the data is stored in the row with the same storage costs for non-max varchar values. Once the data is too big to fit in a single row, data can be placed on more than one row.

- ON =: You store varchar(max) values using 16-byte pointers to separate pages outside of the table. Use this setting if the varchar(max) data will only seldom be used in queries.

Discussion:

The `varchar(max)` datatype is possibly the greatest thing since someone said, "Chocolate and peanut butter—I wonder if they might go together?" Too long have we struggled with the painful `text` datatype and all its quirks. You can deal with `varchar(max)` values using mostly the same functions and methods that you do with normal `varchar` values. There's a minor difference, though. As the size of your `varchar(max)` column grows towards the upper boundary, it's likely true that you aren't going to want to be sending the entire value back and forth over the network most of the time. I know that on my 100MB LAN, sending 2GB is no instantaneous operation, for sure.

There are a couple things to look at, which I'll just touch on here:

- The `UPDATE` statement has been enhanced with a `.WRITE()` clause to write chunks of data to the `(max)` datatypes. This is also true of `varbinary(max)`.

- Unlike `text` and `image` values, `(max)` datatypes are accessible in `AFTER` triggers.

One word of warning when your code mixes normal `varchar` and `varchar(max)` values in the same statement. For example, write a statement such as the following:

```
DECLARE @value varchar(max)
SET @value = replicate('X',8000) + replicate('X',8000)
SELECT len(@value)
```

This returns the following result:

```
--------------------
8000
```

The reason is that the type of the `REPLICATE` function is `varchar`, when replicating normal `char` values. Adding two `varchar` values together doesn't result in a `varchar(max)` value. However, most of the functions return `varchar(max)` values when working with `varchar(max)` values:

```
DECLARE @value varchar(max)
SET @value = replicate(cast('X' as varchar(max)),16000)
SELECT len(@value)
```

This returns the following result:

```
--------------------
16000
```

text

Don't use the text datatype for any reason in new designs. It very well may not exist in the next version of SQL Server. Replace with varchar(max) in any location you can. See SQL Server Books Online for more information, or if you need to manipulate existing text column data.

Unicode Character Strings: nchar, nvarchar, nvarchar(max), ntext

Domain: ASCII characters, up to $2^{15} - 1$ characters (2GB of storage).

Storage: Same as other character datatypes, though every character takes 2 bytes rather than 1.

Discussion:

So far, the character datatypes we've been discussing have been for storing typical ASCII data. In SQL Server 7.0 (and NT 4.0), Microsoft implemented a new standard character format called Unicode. This specifies a 16-bit character format that can store characters beyond just the Latin character set. In ASCII—a 7-bit character system (with the 8 bits for Latin extensions)—you were limited to 256 distinct characters. This was fine for most English-speaking people, but was insufficient for other languages. Asian languages have a character for each different syllable and are nonalphabetic; Middle Eastern languages use several different symbols for the same letter according to its position in the word. A standard was created for a 16-bit character system, allowing you to have 65,536 distinct characters.

For these datatypes, you have the nchar, nvarchar, nvarchar(max), and ntext datatypes. They are exactly the same as the similarly named types (without the "n") that I've already described, except for one thing: Unicode uses double the number of bytes to store the information, so it takes twice the space, thus cutting by half the number of characters that can be stored.

One quick tip: if you want to specify a Unicode value in a string, you append an N to the front of the string, like so:

```
SELECT N'Unicode Value'
```

■**Tip** You should migrate away from ntext as a datatype just as you should for the text datatype.

Binary Data

Binary data allows you to store a string of bytes. It's useful for storing just about anything, especially data from a client that might or might not fit into a character or numeric datatype. In SQL Server 2005, binary columns have become even more useful, as you can use them when storing encrypted data. In Chapter 7, I took a look at the encryption capabilities of SQL Server 2005.

One of the restrictions of binary datatypes is that they don't support bitwise operators, which would allow you to do some powerful bitmask storage by being able to compare two binary columns to see not only if they differ, but how they differ. The whole idea of the binary datatypes is that they store strings of bits. The bitwise operators can operate on integers, which are physically stored as bits. The reason for this inconsistency is fairly clear from the point of view of the internal query processor. The bitwise operations are operations that are handled in the processor, whereas the binary datatypes are SQL Server specific.

Binary literal values are specified as 0xB1B2B3 . . . BN. 0x tells us that it's a hexadecimal value. B1 specifies the first single byte in hexadecimal.

binary(length)

Domain: Fixed-length binary data with a maximum length of 8,000 bytes.

Storage: Number of bytes the value is defined for.

Discussion:

Use of binary columns is fairly limited. You can use them to store any binary values that aren't dealt with by SQL Server. Data stored in binary is simply a string of bytes:

```
declare @value binary(10)
set @value = cast('helloworld' as binary(10))
select @value
```

This returns the following result:

```
----------------------
0x68656C6C6F776F726C64
```

Now you can reverse the process:

```
select cast(0x68656C6C6F776F726C64 as varchar(10))
```

This returns the following result:

```
----------
helloworld
```

Note that casting the value HELLOWORLD gives us a different value:

```
----------------------
0x48454C4C4F574F524C44
```

This fact that these two binary values are different, even for textual data that would be considered equivalent on a case insensitive collation, has been one use for the binary datatype: case sensitive searches. It's far more efficient to use the COLLATE keyword and use a different collation if you want to do a case-insensitive comparison on text data.

varbinary(length)

Domain: Variable-length binary data with a maximum length of 8,000 bytes.

Storage: Number of bytes the value is defined for, plus 2 bytes for variable-length overhead.

Discussion:

Usage is the same as binary, except the number of bytes is variable.

varbinary(max)

Domain: Binary data, up to $2^{31} - 1$ bytes (up to 2GB for storage).

Storage: There are a couple possibilities for storage based on the setting of the table option 'large value types out of row':

- OFF =: If the data for all the columns fits in a single row, the data is stored in the row with the same storage costs for non-max varchar values. Once the data is too big to fit in a single row, data can be placed on greater than one row.

- ON =: You store varbinary(max) values using 16-byte pointers to separate pages outside the table. Use this setting if the varchar(max) data will only seldom be used in queries.

Discussion:

The varbinary(max) datatype provides the same kinds of benefits for large binary values as the varchar(max) did. Pretty much, you can deal with varbinary(max) values using the same functions and the same methods as you do with the normal varbinary values.

What's cool is that you can store text, JPEG and GIF images, even Word documents and Excel spreadsheet data. On the other hand, it can be much slower and more programming work to use SQL Server as a storage mechanism for file data, mostly because it's slow to retrieve really large values from the database when compared to the file system.

When you need to store binary file data in the database (such as images), it's generally easier to store the name of a file on shared access. The accessing program simply uses the filename to go to external storage to fetch the file. File systems are built for storing and serving up files, so you use them for their strengths. However, if you require the integrity that storing the file in the database gives you, the varbinary(max) datatype allows you to store the image with the other data and be protected from change by an external program without the database knowing. (I discuss this concept of choosing where to store image data in Chapter 5.)

image

Just like the text datatype, the image datatype has always been a real bother and is being depre-cated in this version of SQL Server. Don't use the image datatype in new designs if at all possible. It very well may not exist in the next version of SQL Server. Replace with varchar(max) in any location you can. See SQL Server Books Online for more information, or if you have existing image column data that you need to manipulate.

Other Datatypes

The following datatypes are somewhat less frequently employed in OLTP systems, but are still useful:

- rowversion (timestamp)
- uniqueidentifier
- cursor
- table
- XML
- sql_variant

rowversion (a.k.a. timestamp)

The rowversion datatype is a database-wide unique number. When you have a rowversion col-umn in a table, the value of the rowversion column changes for each modification to each row. The value in the rowversion column is guaranteed to be unique across all tables in the datatype. It's also known as a timestamp value, but it doesn't have any time implications—it's merely a unique value to tell you that your row has changed.

Tip In the SQL standards, a timestamp is the same as a datetime, so if you're used to the timestamp datatype, it's now suggested to use rowversion.

The rowversion column of a table (you may only have one) is usually used as the data for an optimistic locking mechanism. I'll discuss this further later in this appendix when I talk about physical-only columns.

The rowversion datatype is a mixed blessing. It's stored as an 8-byte varbinary value. Binary values aren't always easy to deal with, and depend on which mechanism you're using to access your data.

As an example of how the rowversion datatype works, consider the following batch:

```
SET nocount on
CREATE TABLE testRowversion
(
   value    varchar(20) NOT NULL,
   auto_rv   rowversion NOT NULL
)

INSERT INTO testRowversion (value) values ('Insert')

SELECT value, auto_rv FROM testRowversion
UPDATE testRowversion
SET value = 'First Update'

SELECT value, auto_rv from testRowversion
UPDATE testRowversion
SET value = 'Last Update'

SELECT value, auto_rv FROM testRowversion
```

This returns the following results:

value	auto_rv
Insert	0x0000000000000089

value	auto_rv
First Update	0x000000000000008A

value	auto_rv
Last Update	0x000000000000008B

You didn't touch the auto_rv variable, and yet it incremented itself twice. However, you can't bank on the order of the rowversion variable being sequential, as updates of other tables will change this. It's also in your best interest not to assume that the number is an incrementing value in your code. How rowversions are implemented is a detail that will likely change in the future. If a better method of building database-wide unique values comes along that's even a hair faster, Microsoft will likely use it.

You can create variables of the rowversion type for holding rowversion values, and you can retrieve the last used rowversion via the @@dbts configuration function. Rowversion columns are used in Chapter 9, when I demonstrate optimistic locking.

uniqueidentifier

GUIDs are fast becoming a mainstay of Microsoft computing. The name says it all—these identifiers are globally unique. According to the way that GUIDs are formed, there's a tremendously remote chance that there will ever be any duplication in their values. They're generated by a formula that includes the current date and time, a unique number from the CPU clock, and some other "magic numbers."

In your databases, the uniqueidentifier has an important purpose. For example, you might need to have a unique key that's guaranteed to be unique across databases and servers:

```
DECLARE @guidVar uniqueidentifier
SET @guidVar = newid()

SELECT @guidVar as guidVar
```

returns

```
guidVar
---------------------------------------------------------------
6C7119D5-D48F-475C-8B60-50D0C41B6EBF
```

GUIDs are stored as 16-byte binary values. Note that a GUID isn't exactly a straight 16-byte binary value. You may not put just any binary value into a uniqueidentifier column, as the value must meet the criteria for the generation of a GUID, which aren't well documented, for obvious reasons. (For more information, a good resource is http://en.wikipedia.org/wiki/Guid.)

If you need to create a uniqueidentifier column that's auto-generating, you can set a property in the CREATE TABLE statement (or ALTER TABLE for that matter). It's the rowguidcol property, and it's used like so:

```
CREATE TABLE guidPrimaryKey
(
    guidPrimaryKeyId uniqueidentifier NOT NULL rowguidcol DEFAULT newId(),
    value varchar(10)
)
```

I've introduced a couple new things here: rowguidcol and default values. Suffice it to say that, if you don't provide a value for a column in an insert operation, the default operation will provide it. In this case, you use the newId() function to get a new uniqueidentifier. Execute the following INSERT statement:

```
INSERT INTO guidPrimaryKey(value)
VALUES ('Test')
```

Then run the following command to view the data entered:

```
SELECT *
FROM guidPrimaryKey
```

This returns the following result (though of course your key value will be different):

guidPrimaryKeyId	value
8A57C8CD-7407-47C5-AC2F-E6A884C7B646	Test

The rowguidcol property of a column built with the uniqueidentifier notifies the system that this is just like an identity column value for the table—a unique pointer to a row in a table. Note that neither the identity nor the rowguidcol properties guarantee uniqueness. To provide such a guarantee, you have to implement your tables using UNIQUE constraints.

It would seem that the uniqueidentifier would be a better way of implementing primary keys, because when they're created, they're unique across all databases, servers, and platforms. However, there are two main reasons why you won't use uniqueidentifier columns to implement all your primary keys:

- *Storage requirements*: As they're 16 bytes in size, they're considerably more bloated than a typical integer column.

- *Typeability*: As there are 36 characters in the textual version of the GUID, it's hard to type the value of the GUID into a query, and it isn't easy to enter.

If you're using the GUID values for the primary key of a table and you're clustering on this value, you can use another function to generate the values: newSequentialId(). You can only use this function in a default constraint. It's used to guarantee that the next GUID chosen will be greater than the previous value:

```
DROP TABLE guidPrimaryKey
go
CREATE TABLE guidPrimaryKey
(
    guidPrimaryKeyId uniqueidentifier NOT NULL
                     rowguidcol DEFAULT newSequentialId(),
    value varchar(10)
)
GO
INSERT INTO guidPrimaryKey(value)
SELECT 'Test'
UNION ALL
SELECT 'Test1'
UNION ALL
SELECT 'Test2'
GO

SELECT *
FROM guidPrimaryKey
```

This returns something like the following:

```
guidPrimaryKeyId                     value
------------------------------------ ----------
AA52457C-339B-DA11-9A3C-001422E6CCC3 Test
AB52457C-339B-DA11-9A3C-001422E6CCC3 Test1
AC52457C-339B-DA11-9A3C-001422E6CCC3 Test2
```

Now, using a GUID for a primary key is just as good as using an identity column for building a surrogate key, particularly one with a clustered index. That's because all new values will be added to the end of the index rather than randomly thoughout the index (Chapter 8 covers indexes). This is true at least in terms of the way the rows are added to the index. Columns of the uniqueidentifier type will still be four times as large as an integer column, hence requiring four times the storage space.

cursor

A cursor is a mechanism that allows row-wise operations instead of using the normal set-wise way. You use the cursor datatype to hold a reference to a SQL Server T-SQL cursor. You may not use a cursor datatype as a column in a table. Its only use is in T-SQL code to hold a reference to a cursor.

table

The table datatype has a few things in common with the cursor datatype, but holds a reference to a result set. The name of the datatype is a pretty bad choice, as it will make functional programmers think that they can store a pointer to a table. It's actually used to store a result set as a temporary table. In fact, the table is exactly like a temporary table in implementation. However, you don't get any kind of statistics on the table, nor are you able to index the table datatype, other than to apply PRIMARY KEY and UNIQUE constraints in the table declaration.

Unlike local temporary tables (those declared with # preceding the name), table datatype variables won't cause recompiles in stored procedures that use them, because they don't have any statistics to change the plan anyway. Use them only for modestly small sets of data (hundreds of rows, not thousands, generally), such as when all the data in the table can fit on a single data page.

The following is an example of the syntax needed to employ the table variable type:

```
DECLARE @tableVar TABLE
(
    id int IDENTITY PRIMARY KEY,
    value varchar(100)
)
INSERT INTO @tableVar (value)
VALUES ('This is a cool test')

SELECT id, value
FROM @tableVar
```

This returns the following result:

```
id          value
----  -----------------------------------
1           This is a cool test
```

As with the cursor datatype, you may not use the table datatype as a column in a table, and it may only be used in T-SQL code to hold a set of data. One of the primary purposes for the table datatype is for returning a table from a user-defined function, as in the following example:

```
CREATE FUNCTION table$testFunction
(
    @returnValue varchar(100)

)
RETURNS @tableVar table
(
    value varchar(100)
)
AS
BEGIN
   INSERT INTO @tableVar (value)
   VALUES (@returnValue)

   RETURN
END
```

Once created, you can use the table datatype returned by the function using typical SELECT syntax:

```
SELECT *
FROM dbo.table$testFunction('testValue')
```

This returns the following result:

```
value
-------------
testValue
```

One interesting thing about the table datatype is that it isn't subject to transactions. For example:

```
DECLARE @tableVar TABLE
(
   id int IDENTITY,
   value varchar(100)
)
BEGIN TRANSACTION
   INSERT INTO @tableVar (value)
   VALUES ('This will still be there')
ROLLBACK TRANSACTION

SELECT id, value
FROM @tableVar
```

This returns the following result:

```
id          value
----------- ---------------------------------------
1           This will still be there
```

For this reason, these tables are useful for logging errors, because the data is still available after the ROLLBACK TRANSACTION.

XML

The XML datatype is a cool new addition to SQL Server, giving us the ability to store XML documents in a column in a table, with searching and indexing capabilities, just to mention a few things. Although in previous versions of SQL Server, you could have used the text datatype— or varchar(max) in SQL Server 2005—to store XML, to SQL Server it was just a big blob of text. The XML datatype gives you a much richer set of functionality. You can have checked values, defaults, and even validate the XML against a schema. XQuery (for querying XML data) is implemented, as well as special XML DML statements for inserting, deleting, and "replacing value of" (not update) XML data. It's quite a rich set of functionality for dealing with XML.

Throughout the book, I've steered away from XML, for the reason that it isn't relational data, and therefore is outside what the topic of this book is about. The XML datatype can have great usage; for example, storing and searching through XML documents. How about document searches, such as searching for Visio documents stored in XML format? You could search for a specific element on one of the models, or you could use SELECT to search all the documents in a single operation, instead of opening them one at a time. The most important thing, in my opinion, is that you use the XML datatype only when the relational solution won't suffice, and not as a replacement for design. It would be too easy for a lazy implementer to start an XML column on every table just to hold "stuff that was forgotten." XML should be used to supplement proper design, not circumvent it.

The topic of XML documents is a book unto itself. For extensive coverage of XML in SQL Server, consider the book *Microsoft SQL Server 2005 XML* by Michael Rys (Sams), due out in mid 2006.

sql_variant Data

The catch-all datatype, the sql_variant type allows you to store almost any datatype that I've discussed. This allows you to create a column or variable where you don't know exactly what kind of data will be stored. The sql_variant datatype allows you to store values of various SQL Server–supported datatypes—except for varchar(max), varbinary(max), xml, text, ntext, rowversion/timestamp, and sql_variant.

■Note While the `rowversion` datatype cannot be stored directly in a `sql_variant`, the data of a `rowversion` can be stored in a `binary(8)`, which can be stored in a `sql_variant`. Also, it might seem strange that you can't store a variant in a variant, but this is just saying that the `sql_variant` datatype doesn't exist as such—SQL Server chooses the best type of storage in which to store the value you give to it.

The `sql_variant` datatype allows you to create user-definable "property bag"–type tables that help you avoid having long tables with many columns that might or might not be filled in. Take the `entityProperty` table in the following example.

In this example, you have N columns with N datatypes that are all nullable, to let the user store any one or more of the values. The best case is that the `propertyValue` columns have actual explicit names, though often "user-defined" properties are implemented in tables such as this. This type of table is generally known as a *sparse table*. The problem with this example is that, if the user comes up with a new property, you might be forced to modify the table, the UI, and any programs that refer to the columns in the table.

Then, by adding a column to the `entityProperty` table, each of the properties that you implemented in the previous example would now be added as an instance in the `entityProp-ertyType` table, and the value would be stored in the `propertyValue` column. Whatever type of data that's needed for the property could be stored as a `sql_variant`.

You could extend the `entityPropertyType` table to include many other properties without the user having to carry out major changes to the database. Also, if you implement your reporting solution in such a way that your new reports know about any changes, you won't have to recode for any new properties. As an example, consider the two tables in Figure B-1.

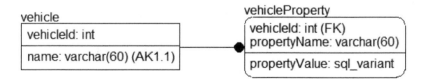

Figure B-1. *Sample property table*

Create the `vehicle` table, and add a couple rows:

```
CREATE TABLE vehicle
(
    vehicleId    int constraint PKvehicle Primary Key,
    name         varchar(60) constraint AKvehicle UNIQUE
)
INSERT INTO vehicle
SELECT 1, 'Main Car'
UNION ALL
SELECT 2, 'Backup Truck'
```

Then create the property table:

```
CREATE TABLE vehicleProperty
(
vehicleId int,
propertyName varchar(30),
propertyValue sql_variant,
constraint PKproperty primary key (vehicleId, propertyName),
constraint property$suppliespropertyvaluesfor$vehicle
            foreign key (vehicleId) references vehicle (vehicleId)
)
```

Then insert data. I put the data into two INSERT statements because one of the values is a numeric value:

```
INSERT INTO vehicleProperty
SELECT 1,'main driver','Joe'
UNION ALL
SELECT 1, 'interior color','beige'
UNION ALL
SELECT 2,'trailer hitch style','small'
UNION ALL
SELECT 2,'interior color','tan'

INSERT INTO vehicleProperty
SELECT 2,'tow capacity (lbs)',2000
```

Looking at the data, you see that all the values are stored vertically:

```
SELECT *
FROM vehicleProperty
```

This returns the following results:

vehicleId	propertyName	propertyValue
1	interior color	beige
1	main driver	Joe
2	interior color	tan
2	tow capacity (lbs)	2000
2	trailer hitch style	small

You can use the PIVOT keyword in a SELECT statement to rotate the data to a normal, horizontal orientation:

```
SELECT  vehicleName, vehicleId, [main driver], [interior color],
        [trailer hitch style], [tow capacity (lbs)]
FROM
(SELECT vehicle.name as vehicleName, vehicleProperty.vehicleId,
        vehicleProperty.propertyName, vehicleProperty.propertyValue
 FROM vehicle
      join vehicleProperty
          on vehicle.vehicleId = vehicleProperty.vehicleId) as properties
PIVOT
(
max (propertyValue)
FOR PropertyName IN
( [main driver], [interior color], [trailer hitch style], [tow capacity (lbs)])
) AS pvt
ORDER BY VehicleName;
```

This returns the following results:

vehicleName	main driver	interior color	trailerHitchStyle	tow capacity (lbs)
Backup Truck	NULL	tan	small	2000
Main Car	Joe	beige	NULL	NULL

I won't go into the exact details of the PIVOT statement. For more details, consider the book *Pro SQL Server 2005* by Thomas Rizzo et al. (Apress, 2005).

I've used this method on occasion when the attributes of some entity couldn't be determined at design time. The prime example was of a system that stored the details from Internet equipment. They had hundreds of attributes, and each device was a little bit different. It was clunky to work with, but all the data got stored. In general, use this form of table design only as a last resort.

The Disadvantages of Storing Variant Data

It isn't easy to manipulate the data once it has been stored in a sql_variant column. I'll leave it to the reader to read the information fully in the parts of SQL Server Books Online that deal with variant data. The issues to consider are as follows:

- *Assigning data from a* sql_variant *column to a stronger typed datatype*: You have to be careful, as the rules for casting a variable from one datatype to another are difficult, and might cause errors if the data can't be cast. For example, you can't cast a varchar(10) value 'Not a Date' to a datetime datatype. Such problems become an issue when you start to retrieve the variant data out of the sql_variant datatype and try to manipulate it.

- NULL sql_variant *values are considered to have no datatype*: Hence, you'll have to deal with sql_variant NULLs differently from other datatypes.

- *Comparisons of* variants *to other datatypes could cause difficult-to-catch programmatic errors, because of the* sql_variant *value instance's datatype*: The compiler will know if you try to run a statement that compares two incompatible datatypes, such as @intVar = @varcharVar. However, if the two variables in question were defined as sql_variants, and the datatypes don't match, then the values won't match due to the datatype incompatibilities.

A function discovers the datatype of a value stored in a variant column:

```
DECLARE @varcharVariant sql_variant
SET @varcharVariant = '1234567890'
SELECT @varcharVariant AS varcharVariant,
    SQL_VARIANT_PROPERTY(@varcharVariant,'BaseType') as baseType,
    SQL_VARIANT_PROPERTY(@varcharVariant,'MaxLength') as maxLength,
    SQL_VARIANT_PROPERTY(@varcharVariant,'Collation') as collation
```

The preceding statement returns the following result:

VarcharVariant	baseType	maxLength	collation
1234567890	varchar	10	SQL_Latin1_General_CP1_CI_AS

For numeric data, you can also find the precision and scale:

```
DECLARE @numericVariant sql_variant
SET @numericVariant = 123456.789
SELECT @numericVariant AS numericVariant,
    SQL_VARIANT_PROPERTY(@numericVariant,'BaseType') as baseType,
    SQL_VARIANT_PROPERTY(@numericVariant,'Precision') as precision,
    SQL_VARIANT_PROPERTY(@numericVariant,'Scale') as scale
```

This returns the following result:

numericVariant	baseType	precision	scale
123456.789	numeric	9	3

Summary

There are two large changes in 2005 versus earlier versions of SQL Server: The image and text datatypes have been replaced by varbinary(max) and varchar(max), respectively.

You could use a sql_variant datatype for every column, which initially could sound like the easiest way to go, but that would cause far more problems. SQL Server 2005 gives you a large variety of specific datatypes from which to choose. It's essential to know them and choose the best possible datatype for each column. Using the right datatype can make a big difference in performance and ease of programming.

Index

Find it faster at http://superindex.apress.com/

Find it faster at http://superindex.apress.com/

Find it faster at http://superindex.apress.com/

Find it faster at http://superindex.apress.com/

Find it faster at http://superindex.apress.com/

Find it faster at http://superindex.apress.com/

Find It faster at http://superindex.apress.com/

Find it faster at http://superindex.apress.com/

Find it faster at http://superindex.apress.com/

Find it faster at http://superindex.apress.com/

Find It Faster at http://superindex.apress.com

Find it faster at http://superindex.apress.com/